THE UNITED STATES ARMY

THE UNITED STATES ARMY

A CHRONOLOGY, 1775 TO THE PRESENT

JOHN C. FREDRIKSEN

ABC-CLIO

Santa Barbara, California • Denver, Colorado • Oxford, England

Copyright © 2010 by ABC-CLIO, LLC

Library of Congress Cataloging-in-Publication Data is available at www.loc.gov

ISBN: 978-1-59884-344-6
EISBN: 978-1-59884-345-3

14 13 12 11 10   1 2 3 4 5

This book is also available on the World Wide Web as an eBook.
Visit www.abc-clio.com for details.

ABC-CLIO, LLC
130 Cremona Drive, P.O. Box 1911
Santa Barbara, California 93116-1911

This book is printed on acid-free paper ∞
Manufactured in the United States of America

Contents

Introduction

THE U.S. ARMY today evokes imagery of high-tech soldiers striding across the globe, accompanied by huge tanks and sleek helicopter gunships, all demonstrative of the world's sole remaining superpower. However, the origins of this formidable force completely belie its imposing mien, for military establishments cannot escape the political culture that occasions their rise. In 1775 the nascent nation was struggling against Great Britain, a military superpower of its day, and the Continental army raised to oppose them took some extremely hard knocks in the course of independence. They improved in performance with experience, and by war's end they approximated the professional soldiery of Europe.

The new United States government distrusted standing forces, though, so the Continental army was disbanded, save for a handful of companies. The new concept of citizen soldiery dominated military thinking for nearly a century and placed greater emphasis on episodic militias and volunteers. Despite an Indian war in the Old Northwest, 1790–1794, and events in Europe that placed the Americans on a second collision course with England, the U.S. Army remained neglected and decidedly second place to more state levies. The folly of this practice was painfully underscored in the War of 1812–1815, when the lessons of the Revolutionary War had to be painfully relearned, but thereafter those regular forces retained in the peacetime establishment were abetted by growing professionalism and an influx of graduates from the U.S. Military Academy.

This invigorated army, fleshed out by volunteer forces, performed superbly in the war with Mexico, 1846–1848, but it remained a small, scattered force up through the cusp of civil war in 1861. Manpower then rose in excess of 50,000 men, but it remained totally dwarfed by the volunteer forces employed, which numbered close to one million men. The military was drastically demobilized again and dispatched to battle Indians along the plains for many years before war with Spain in 1898 again led to its enlargement. Numbers again rose, principally through volunteers, and both volunteers and regulars fought well in combat, though they remained hard-pressed to secure and garrison America's new empire.

The onset of world war in 1914 again found the United States unprepared militarily but, by virtue of its sizable population and burgeoning industrial base, the U.S. Army expanded to over one million men by 1918, and provided a decisive manpower advantage to the Allies. The ensuing cutbacks of peace and the Great Depression resulted in other severe contractions, and by 1941 the military establishment was again unprepared for its greatest challenge, World War II. Once again, the U.S. Army could draw from a large manpower pool and a very advanced technological base, which enabled it to expand to 11 million rank and file, its largest size ever.

The U.S. Army bore a large measure of fighting and gained its share of victory in this far-flung conflict, and, in contrast to the periods following earlier wars, the nation was saddled by global commitments after 1945, necessitating the retention of sizable forces and a peacetime draft. The ensuing Cold War confrontations in Korea and Vietnam included their share of triumphs for the U.S. Army, but victory itself proved elusive in Asia, and the conflicts were unpopular for reasons transcending military considerations. After 1975 the Army reverted back to its original volunteer format, although now abetted by greater emphasis on the latest and most modern military technologies to offset relatively small numbers. Its major engagements since then, the Gulf War in 1991, Afghanistan in 2001, and Iraq in 2003, clearly demonstrate that the concept of volunteer citizen soldiery has lost none of its potency on the battlefield, even if the nature of America's enemies have dramatically changed. The

U.S. Army continues to meets its national and global obligations in the war on terror, and it can rightfully be judged one of the great military forces in human history.

This chronology is an attempt to capture the great canvass of U.S. Army history in a relatively modest space. To that end, all the important battles and personages are mentioned to contextualize them to military affairs at the time when they unfolded. However, great care is also taken to mention notable draft laws, military texts, schools, weapons systems, and occasional political developments that affected military affairs. Overall, this book should impart on lay readers the scope and sweep of Army history, whereas a more detailed bibliography of all the latest scholarship can refer them to greater details. The book also affords prospective researchers a workable time frame, or stepping off point, from which they can pursue events and individuals that interest them. The author would like to thank editors Padraic Carlin and Andrew McCormick for their support and advice in compiling what I hope will be a useful and relevant addition to any library shelf, public, or personal.

—*John C. Fredriksen*

1775

FEBRUARY 20   The war clouds are gathering with Great Britain. At Concord, Massachusetts, the Second Provincial Congress reconvenes and enacts positive steps for enhancing colonial defense, including establishment of a military commissary, recruitment of Stockbridge Indians, rules for military governance, and appealing for reinforcements and supplies from nearby colonies.

FEBRUARY 26   Governor General Thomas Gage orders that a cache of colonial supplies and cannon stored at Salem, Massachusetts, be seized by force by the 64th Foot under Colonel Alexander Leslie. Leslie lands at Marblehead, Massachusetts, and marches inland, but his path is blocked by irate civilians and militia, who refuse him passage over the drawbridge. Leslie is preparing to fire on his antagonists when Colonel Timothy Pickering arranges for the British to cross and examine the building in question, then depart. The British perform their task, then sail back to Boston. The entire affair is derided by colonials as "Leslie's Retreat," and it emboldens them to confront Imperial authority.

APRIL   The Provisional Army is created in Massachusetts by the extralegal Provincial Congress. This 30,000-man force comprises detachments from all six New England states, and it employs British cannon seized from various forts. Concord, New Hampshire, is selected as the major entrepot, and detachments begin drifting in from New Hampshire, Connecticut, and Rhode Island.

APRIL 18   Governor General Thomas Gage orders the colonial cache of arms and supplies at Concord, Massachusetts, seized.

That night, a column of 700 light troops, grenadiers, and Royal Marines under Lieutenant Colonel Francis Smith and Major John Pitcairn is ferried across the Charles River and begins marching overland toward Concord. The colonists, however, are alert for such a move, and riders Paul Revere and William Dawes are dispatched to warn the militia. Both riders are caught en route and detained by the British, however, so it falls upon Dr. Samuel Prescott to deliver the actual warning.

APRIL 19   The War for Independence begins in the picturesque village of Concord, Massachusetts, when 700 British troops under Lieutenant Colonel Francis Smith confront a small party of Minutemen under Captain Thomas Parker. Major John Pitcairn warns the rebels to disperse, and they are in the act of doing so when a musket inexplicably discharges. The startled British troops fire into the milling militia, killing three and wounding eight. As the day progresses, large numbers of Americans gather in nearby woods and snipe at the British column as it retires back to Boston, killing 72 and wounding 201.

APRIL 20–30   In Cambridge, Massachusetts, General Artemas Ward takes charge of the 13,000-man Provincial Army gathering there, assisted by Generals William Heath and John Thomas. They slowly envelop Boston from the land side, commencing a long siege.

APRIL 28   At Castleton, Vermont, Colonel Ethan Allen and a group of the Green Mountain Boys gather and begin debating how to seize British stores and munitions kept at Fort Ticonderoga, New York.

MAY 3 In Cambridge, Massachusetts, Connecticut officer Benedict Arnold prevails upon the Committee of Safety to assemble a force and preemptively capture Fort Ticonderoga, New York, for the valuable cache of cannon and supplies stored there. Arnold is consequently commissioned a colonel in the Massachusetts militia and receives 400 men for the expedition, which promises to net 50 cannon and 20 brass pieces for the Patriot cause.

MAY 8 Colonel Ethan Allen departs Castleton, Vermont, with 100 of his Green Mountain Boys and makes for the cannon and stores held at Fort Ticonderoga, New York. En route he encounters Benedict Arnold pursuing the same objective, so the two headstrong leaders grudgingly agree to coordinate their efforts.

MAY 9–10 Colonels Benedict Arnold and Ethan Allen cross Lake Champlain under cover of a rainstorm and surprise the garrison at Fort Ticonderoga, New York. When British officer Lieutenant Jocelyn Feltham, 26th Foot, demands to know by what authority the Americans enter His Majesty's fort, Allen bellows, "Come on out of there, you British sons of whores, or I'll smoke you out!" The garrison capitulates without resistance, and so concludes America's first offensive operation of the war.

MAY 15–16 A committee of the Second Continental Congress, to which Virginia delegate George Washington belongs, begins debating plans for the defense of New York City. Another Virginia delegate, Henry Lee, also advocates creating a new "Congressional Army."

Washington, George (1732–1799)

George Washington was born in Westmoreland County, Virginia, on February 22, 1732, part of the minor landed gentry. In 1753 he commenced his military career by gaining a militia commission and precipitated the bloody French and Indian War by building Fort Necessity on land claimed by France. Washington subsequently accompanied the ill-fated expedition of English general Edward Braddock and survived the crushing defeat at Monongahela on July 9, 1755. Afterward, Washington married wealthy Martha Custis and entered colonial politics. He opposed Great Britain's tax policies and sided with the Patriots when the Revolutionary War commenced in 1775. Washington, by dint of his commanding persona, was chosen to head the new Continental Army, and he successfully forced the British to evacuate Boston, Massachusetts. However, in the fall of 1776, he was roundly defeated near New York City and conducted a mid-winter retreat to escape. Washington then suddenly turned and attacked in New Jersey, defeating the British and their Hessian allies at Trenton and Princeton in December 1776 and February 1777, respectively. Thereafter, while Washington continued losing battles, his men invariably improved in their battlefield performances. The impasse continued until the summer of 1781, when Washington, assisted by his French ally, the Comte de Rochambeau, led a lightning march from New York that trapped General Charles Cornwallis at Yorktown, Virginia, forcing him to surrender on October 19, 1781. With independence won, Washington advocated discarding the Articles of Confederation in favor of the more centralized Constitution. This became a reality in 1789, and Washington became the nation's first president and commander in chief. He guided the shaky new republic with a firm hand, appointed General Anthony Wayne to defeat the Northwest Indians of Ohio in 1794, and surmounted another military crisis when farmers in western Pennsylvania rebelled rather than pay taxes on whiskey. Washington died at Mount Vernon, Virginia, on December 14, 1799, a capable military leader hailed as the "father of his country."

MAY 17–18 At Skeensboro, New York, Colonel Benedict Arnold boards a captured schooner and sails to Saint Johns, Quebec, where he seizes the garrison and several small vessels. Hastening back to Ticonderoga, Arnold encounters Colonel Ethan Allen and 60 Green Mountain Boys heading north to the same locale, despite warnings not to do so. Allen nonetheless approaches Fort Saint John's, finds it reoccupied by 200 British soldiers, and is quickly driven off.

JUNE 10 At the Second Continental Congress in Philadelphia, Massachusetts delegate John Adams lends support to creation of a Continental Army to expedite the coming and inevitable showdown with Great Britain.

JUNE 14 In a significant move, the first United States army is born when the Continental Congress votes to raise 10 companies of riflemen. These troops constitute the nucleus of what emerges as the Continental Army, and a committee, including George Washington and Philip J. Schuyler, is tasked with formulating regulations to govern it. Congress also votes to take control of colonial forces gathered outside Boston, upon the urging of the Provincial Congress in Massachusetts.

JUNE 15 In Philadelphia, Massachusetts delegate John Adams, wishing to cement Virginia to the revolutionary cause, nominates George Washington to serve as "General & Commander in Chief of American forces." The imposing, austere Washington inspires confidence and is one of few senior leaders with actual military experience. Congress also authorizes creation of four major generals and five brigadiers to lead the rapidly forming Continental Army. Although it could not have been known at the time, Washington's appointment proves to be one of the most fortuitous decisions of world history.

JUNE 16 Outside Boston, Massachusetts, Colonel Richard Gridley's engineers begin constructing fortifications on Breed's Hill, overlooking Boston harbor. A large redoubt arises on the hilltop before the British garrison can react, and it is garrisoned by 1,200 men under Colonel William Prescott and General Israel Putnam.

In Philadelphia, George Washington accepts the nomination as commander in chief, but he declines a salary and asks only for a stipend to cover expenses. He is joined by Charles Lee, Israel Putnam, Philip J. Schuyler, and Artemas Ward, who are also commissioned as major generals. Congress brooks no delay in formalizing the new Continental Army by establishing unit types and strengths, and it authorizes appointments of a chief engineer, adjutant general, paymaster, commissary general, and quartermaster.

JUNE 17 A momentous day unfolds in Boston harbor as Governor General Thomas Gage, determined to cow the rebels with a show of British strength, orders General William Howe to drive them from their works on Breeds Hill, usually mistaken as Bunker Hill. Howe, commanding 2,250 well-trained regulars, performs bravely as ordered, but he is blasted back twice by the concentrated musketry of Colonel William Prescott's 2,000 militia. The American works are not abandoned until the militia runs out of ammunition during a third charge, and falls back in good order to the mainland. For a loss of 140 killed and 271 wounded, Prescott inflicts 226 dead and 828 injured—nearly one-half of Howe's force. The British score a pyrrhic victory at best.

On June 17, 1775, Colonel William Prescott and his troops repulsed two assaults by the larger British force under Major General William Howe. Though a lack of ammunition during the third attack cost the rebel forces the fight, the heavy British casualties sustained at the Battle of Bunker Hill reinforced the American determination to win independence from Britain. (Library of Congress)

JUNE 20–30 In Philadelphia, General George Washington is ordered north by the Continental Congress to assume command of American forces gathered outside Boston. He also conducts the firstknown American military review by parading several city militia companies.

JUNE 21 In Providence, Rhode Island, Nathanael Greene, an obscure bookseller with a pronounced limp, becomes a brigadier general of militia.

JUNE 25 General Philip J. Schuyler is appointed commander of the Northern Department in New York by the Continental Congress. He also enjoys discretionary authority to invade Canada to bring that region into the American fold.

JUNE 30 The Continental Congress approves 69 Articles of War, drawn mostly from existing British regulations, to govern, discipline, and administer the Continental Army. Unlike brutal British practices, most punishments are restricted to 39 lashes, and the death penalty is reserved for only the most serious crimes. Consistent with the mores of the day, all rank and file are encouraged to attend church to enforce good behavior and proper morality.

JULY 3 General George Washington arrives at Cambridge, Massachusetts, and replaces a resentful Artemas Ward as commander of the Continental Army. His first priority is keeping the 14,000-man force trained and fed, and he tries to impose a greater military and logistical order by dividing the army into three wings under Generals Artemas Ward, Israel Putnam, and Charles Lee. Washington also orders the fortifications surrounding Boston to be extended between Dorchester and the Mystic

River to completely bottle up the British. Still, the greatest challenge confronting Washington is enlistments expiring by year's end.

JULY 4 At Cambridge, Massachusetts, General George Washington issues General Order No. 1, declaring that all the troops are completely subordinated to the Continental Congress. However, some local officers resign rather than submit to other than state authority.

JULY 10 At Cambridge, Massachusetts, General and Adjutant General Horatio Gates issues orders forbidding free African Americans from serving with the Continental Army.

JULY 18 In New York, General Philip J. Schuyler arrives at Fort Ticonderoga only to discover it weakly manned and garrisoned by raw troops.

JULY 24 General Philip J. Schuyler dispatches a small reconnaissance party under Major John Brown from Fort Ticonderoga into Canada. Once there, Brown is to gather intelligence about British forces in Montreal and ascertain attitudes of the inhabitants.

JULY 25 Captain Michael Doudel of York, Pennsylvania, arrives at Cambridge, Massachusetts, with the first company of Continental riflemen. In time, American riflemen become renowned for superb marksmanship and unstinting insubordination.

AUGUST 3 At Cambridge, Massachusetts, General George Washington convenes a war council to address the deteriorating state of American supplies, especially gunpowder. Because these are improperly stored under damp conditions and spoil rapidly, the council appeals to the states for fresh supplies.

AUGUST 14 Back at Fort Ticonderoga, Major John Brown completes a major reconnaissance mission into Canada and reports back to General Philip J. Schuyler. He feels that the inhabitants are overwhelmingly neutral toward the Revolution, and states that the strategic post of Saint Johns is only lightly garrisoned. This information encourages Schuyler to launch an invasion immediately.

AUGUST 28 With General Philip J. Schuyler incapacitated by illness, Brigadier General Richard Montgomery leads 1,200 men from Fort Ticonderoga, New York, on a fateful campaign into Canada. The men embark at Ile aux Noir and begin rowing north.

SEPTEMBER 5 Colonel Benedict Arnold of Connecticut sails from Newburyport, Massachusetts, with 1,054 men and makes for the Kennebec River. Once ashore, he intends to march on Quebec by an overland route through the Maine wilderness. However, this ambitious foray is undertaken with the barest minimum of supplies and inadequate knowledge of the terrain to be crossed. Nor has the Continental Congress been advised beforehand. Ultimately, Arnold's trek lasts 45 days and covers 350 miles—twice what was anticipated.

SEPTEMBER 10 In Cambridge, Massachusetts, disgruntled riflemen in the camp outside Boston mutiny at Prospect Hill after one of their number is arrested. General George Washington immediately orders a battalion of 500 men to surround the rebels and march them back to camp. Consequently, thirty-three men are court-martialed and fined for disobedience.

SEPTEMBER 18 In Canada, General Richard Montgomery severs British communications along the Richelieu

River while besieging Saint Johns, Canada. Meanwhile, Major John Brown and 135 Americans also ambush a British supply train approaching from Fort Chambly.

SEPTEMBER 23   Colonel Benedict Arnold's Quebec expedition departs Gardiner, Maine, and advances through the wilderness in three divisions, separated by one-day intervals.

SEPTEMBER 25   Outside St. Johns, Canada, General Richard Montgomery dispatches Colonel Ethan Allen to recruit Canadian volunteers at Chambly. While returning Allen encounters the force of Major John Brown, and they decide to launch a two-pronged assault against Montreal with only 200 men. Governor General Guy Carleton detects the weakness of Allen's force and counterattacks attacks with superior force, capturing him and 40 men. Allen thus becomes the first significant American captive of the war, and he is transported to England where he is detained under harsh conditions.

OCTOBER 6   Colonel Benedict Arnold's hard-slogging expedition reaches Norridgewock Falls on the Kennebec River. His men are forced to portage (carry) their vessels and equipment overland for several miles.

OCTOBER 8   A Council of General Officers enforces its racial prejudices by declaring that no African American, either free or slave, can enlist in the Continental Army. Over time, acute manpower shortages force this policy to change.

OCTOBER 18   The town of Chambly, Quebec, falls to an American naval unit, assisted by Canadian dissenters, and 88 prisoners from the 7th Foot and several tons of gunpowder fall into American hands. Victory here also cuts British supply lines to strategic Saint Johns, then closely besieged by General Richard Montgomery.

OCTOBER 23   In Philadelphia, the Second Continental Congress formally outlaws African Americans from serving in the Continental Army.

OCTOBER 25   Near Dead River, Maine, Colonel Benedict Arnold's Quebec expedition struggles to traverse a flooded countryside in freezing weather. Arnold also loses the service of Colonel Roger Enos and his 300 men when they vote to return home.

OCTOBER 28   General Benedict Arnold's Quebec expedition, surmounting incredible hardship and constant desertion, reaches the Atlantic and St. Lawrence watersheds. His men are reduced to eating dogs and shoe leather, but the doughty general determines to press on ahead.

NOVEMBER 2   The British post of St. Johns, Canada, surrenders to General Richard Montgomery after a siege of 55 days. The advance to Montreal is now cleared, but taking St. Johns consumes two months of good weather; all subsequent operations against Quebec will be in the dead of winter.

NOVEMBER 4–8   To prevent the Continental Army from dissolving en masse due to expiring enlistments, General George Washington convinces Congress to extend the period of military service to one year. Congress further refines the Continental Army, decreeing that it will consist of 26 infantry regiments of eight companies each, with a prescribed military uniform of a brown coat. The various regiments are denoted by collar and cuff colors.

NOVEMBER 5 In Canada, General Richard Montgomery hurriedly departs St. Johns and presses onward for Montreal, Quebec, before the weather worsens.

NOVEMBER 9 The 350-mile long Canadian expedition of Colonel Benedict Arnold concludes, once he reaches the St. Lawrence River opposite Quebec City. Of the 1,100 men in his original command, he is reduced by death and desertion to 675 survivors.

NOVEMBER 12 Taking his cue from Congress, General George Washington, as commander in chief of the Continental Army, prohibits recruiting officers from enlisting African Americans.

NOVEMBER 13 In Canada, General Richard Montgomery advances upon Montreal and obtains its surrender. Concurrently, Colonel Benedict Arnold's Canadian expedition prepares to cross the St. Lawrence River and assemble outside Quebec City to cow its garrison into submission.

NOVEMBER 15 Colonel Benedict Arnold finally crosses the St. Lawrence River, assembles on the Plains of Abraham where General James Wolfe stood in 1759, and tries to bluff the 1,200-man garrison under Lieutenant Colonel Allan MacLean into surrendering. MacLean refuses, and Arnold concludes he needs several cannon and a minimum of 2,000 men to capture the city.

NOVEMBER 17 In Boston, Colonel Henry Knox succeeds Colonel Richard Gridley as commander of the new Continental Regiment of Artillery. Significantly, Knox is urgently dispatched to Fort Ticonderoga, New York, to retrieve the captured British ordnance stored there.

DECEMBER 1 At Montreal, General Richard Montgomery departs with 330 men and sails down the St. Lawrence River to Quebec. Once there he intends to join forces with Colonel Benedict Arnold's depleted force at Point aux Trembles to commence siege operations. The Americans are under an acute timetable as expiring enlistments, the onset of winter, and endemic supply shortages all militate against them.

DECEMBER 5 Colonel Henry Knox arrives at Fort Ticonderoga and hurriedly prepares to move an entire artillery train overland in the dead of winter, an unprecedented feat.

DECEMBER 7 In Philadelphia, the Continental Congress promotes Brigadier General Richard Montgomery to major general, although he never lives to accept the promotion.

DECEMBER 8 Colonel Henry Knox departs Fort Ticonderoga, New York, and begins a perilous, midwinter transit back to Boston; his artillery train consists of 40 sleds drawn by 80 oxen. This much ordnance has never before been relocated under such arduous conditions.

DECEMBER 9 Virginia governor John Murray, Lord Dunmore, commanding a British force of 600 Loyalists and 200 regulars, confronts Colonel William Woodford's 300 American riflemen at Great Bridge on the Elizabeth River. Dunmore impatiently orders Captain Samuel Leslie's grenadier company to storm the bridge head on, and the British rush up only to receive sudden and accurate fire from concealed troops. A second charge is also defeated with a loss of 13 dead and 49 wounded to only one American injured. Woodford then suddenly sorties across the bridge, but the British escape under cover of darkness and march for Norfolk.

DECEMBER 31   Outside Quebec, Canada, General Richard Montgomery and Colonel Benedict Arnold launch a desperate attack on the 1,800-man garrison of General Guy Carleton. Covered by a howling blizzard, Montgomery personally leads the charge, but is killed by enemy fire; he is also the first American general to die in combat. Arnold's 600-man column enjoys better success and overruns several enemy positions, but Arnold is wounded and succeeded in command by Major Daniel Morgan, who is ultimately surrounded and forced to surrender. The Americans sustain 30 dead, 42 injured, and 425 captured to a British tally of only five killed and 13 wounded; Arnold had no recourse but to gather up his survivors and establish a loose siege of the city for the remainder of the winter.

In light of chronic manpower shortages, General George Washington reverses official policy and allows recruiting officers to sign up any free African Americans willing to serve in the Continental Army. This expedient will flesh out the dwindling manpower pool as enlistments expire, but Washington still opposes using slaves as soldiers.

1776

JANUARY 1   General George Washington unfurls a new flag with 13 alternating red and white stripes at Cambridge, Massachusetts. He also reorganizes the Continental Army into three divisions and six brigades, the whole consisting of 27 Continental regiments and various state militia formations. However, enlistment terms are authorized to remain at one year.

JANUARY 4   The remains of General Richard Montgomery are uncovered by British forces at Quebec, and he is subsequently interred with full military honors. His body reposes there until 1818, when it is reinterred at St. Paul's Church, New York.

JANUARY 6   In Boston, General William Howe dispatches General Henry Clinton on an amphibious expedition from Boston to Cape Fear, North Carolina, to assist Loyalist forces under Governor Josiah Martin. There Clinton is joined by a squadron sailing from Ireland under Commodore Sir Peter Parker and General Charles Cornwallis. British authorities hope their combined presence will spark a Loyalist resurgence throughout the countryside.

JANUARY 10   In Philadelphia, Congress finally promotes hard-charging Benedict Arnold to brigadier general, although the issues of rank and seniority dog him throughout his distinguished military career.

JANUARY 16   In Philadelphia, Congress finally reverses itself and allows the enlistment of African American freemen into the Continental Army. This is less for altruistic reasons than to stop the hemorrhaging of troop strength from expiring enlistments.

JANUARY 24   At Cambridge, Massachusetts, Colonel Henry Knox successfully transports 44 cannon and 16 mortars from Fort Ticonderoga, New York, having traversed 300 miles of wilderness in the dead of winter. Moreover, his arrival decisively tips the military equation at Boston in favor of the Americans.

FEBRUARY 16 Outside Boston, General George Washington suggests a large-scale attack across the frozen bay to keep his men from withering away due to prolonged inactivity. However, he defers to his officers when they suggest seizing strategic Dorchester Heights for the purpose of planting Colonel Henry Knox's newly arrived cannon. This move will force British general William Howe to either come out and fight Washington's 16,000 men in the open—or abandon the city.

FEBRUARY 27 A force of 1,900 Americans under Colonels James Moore, Alexander Lillington, John Ashe, and Richard Caswell confronts 1,500 Loyalist Highlanders under Captain Alexander Macleod at Moore's Creek Bridge, North Carolina. Macleod storms the bridge in full view of the defenders, only to discover that the planks have been removed. His attack flounders. Macleod is killed along with 30 soldiers, and 850 British prisoners are taken. The Americans suffer one dead and one injured in this three-minute affair.

More importantly, the victory thwarts British intentions of using nearby Wilmington as a base of operations.

MARCH 4 Outside Boston, General John Thomas and engineer Colonel Richard Gridley are ordered to take 2,000 men on a nighttime foray to seize Dorchester Heights at night. They are concealed by an intense artillery bombardment, which also masks the noise of their digging. At daybreak, the British behold a complete line of breastworks and artillery emplacements that have literally sprung up overnight. General William Howe is urged by Admiral Molyneux Shuldham to either eliminate the threat to his fleet or evacuate the town. Howe prepares 2,200 men to storm Castle William, but, when thwarted by boisterous weather, he begins preparations to abandon Boston.

MARCH 17 The 11-month siege of Boston concludes as General William Howe embarks 9,000 troops and 1,000 Loyalists onboard 125 ships. He also conclude a gentleman's agreement with General George

The British evacuate Boston on March 17, 1776, after George Washington and his troops threatened to bombard Howe's forces from Dorchester Heights. (Library of Congress)

Washington not to burn the town as long as his withdrawal is not interfered with. Washington, meanwhile, anticipates that Howe intends to switch his attention toward New York City and begins ordering men and matériel shifted to that theater.

APRIL 13   General George Washington and his entourage arrive in New York City to and prepare its defenses. Washington is apprehensive that if the city falls to the British, they can divide New England from the remainder of the colonies.

MAY 6   Off Quebec City, an armada arrives bearing reinforcements for General Guy Carleton, bringing British strength up to 13,000 men. Suitably augmented, Carleton then launches a 900-man probe of the American encampment outside the city, which completely routs a 250-man detachment under General John Thomas. The governor-general, however, forsakes pursuit in favor of offloading the balance of soldiers from the fleet, and Thomas escapes.

MAY 24   In Philadelphia, General George Washington arrives for high-level strategic discussions with the Continental Congress. Like the general, Congress is particularly apprehensive over what might happen, should the British capture New York City.

MAY 26   In a quick strike, General Benedict Arnold marches from Montreal and overtakes British and Indians under Major George Forster's command at Quinze Chiens, Canada. Negotiations follow, and the two leaders agree to release 487 American captives captured at the Cedars seven days earlier. Arnold's bold dash partially erases their disgrace.

JUNE 4   General Henry Lee arrives at Charleston, South Carolina, and succeeds Colonel William Moultrie as local commander. He then enters into a sharp dispute with local authorities over what to do with Fort Sullivan in the harbor, but Moultrie prevails on him to keep it under construction. When finished, this fort consists of two walls of palmetto logs separated by 16 feet of beach sand. It also mounts 31 cannon and boasts a garrison of 420 men.

JUNE 6–9   A force of 2,000 Americans under General William Thompson ascends the St. Lawrence River intending to capture a strategic British post at Trois Rivieres (Three Rivers). However, they become lost in a swamp soon after landing and are completely unaware that General John Burgoyne is nearby with several thousand crack British troops. Over the next three days the Americans make a valiant attempt to break out of the swamp and are only partly successful; Burgoyne ends up capturing 236 prisoners, once Thompson's main force re-embarks for Sorel.

JUNE 12   In Philadelphia, Congress founds a five-man Board of War and Ordnance, comprising members drawn from that body, to better facilitate management of the Continental Army.

JUNE 14   As Governor General Guy Carleton advances from Trois-Rivieres with 8,000 veteran troops under Generals John Burgoyne and Friedrich von Riedesel, General John Sullivan begins embarking troops, equipment, and supplies at Sorel for a hasty return to Crown Point, New York. This marks the end of America's ill-fated invasion of Canada.

JUNE 16   As superior British forces bear down on American forces in Canada, General Benedict Arnold capably conducts a rearguard action at Chambly, New York, allowing General John Sullivan to safely withdraw to Crown Point.

JUNE 17   Once Montreal is reoccupied by British and Hessian forces, Governor General Guy Carleton begins preparing to invade northern New York. The recent defeat in Canada also prompts the Continental Congress to consider appointing General Horatio Gates as the new commander of northern forces.

JULY 8   In Philadelphia, Colonel John Nixon reads the Declaration of Independence to an excited throng outside the statehouse. The public response is universally favorable, given mounting antipathy toward Great Britain and their hiring of Hessian mercenaries.

JULY 9   General Andrew Lewis orders his artillery to bombard Gwynn Island, Virginia, the headquarters of former royal governor John Murray, Lord Dunmore. Murray is wounded by cannon fire, and, feeling his position cannot be held, he flees with his small fleet up the Potomac River at night.

JULY 20   Cherokee warriors under Chief Dragging Canoe attack Eaton's Station on the Holston River, North Carolina, losing 13 killed before withdrawing. Ironically, the defenders had been alerted in advance by Nancy Ward, the Cherokee war woman. This is the start of another long and bloody conflict between Cherokees and white settlers in the South.

AUGUST 4   The Cherokee settlements of Sugar Town, Soconee, and Keowee, South Carolina, are burned by American militiamen under Major Andrew Williamson. Over the next eight days, they reduce eight more villages to ashes, but the Indians continue fighting.

AUGUST 5   In New York, General Nathanael Greene advises General George Washington that the city is probably indefensible and ought to be burned

to the ground to deprive England of a very useful entrepot. Washington thanks him for his sagacious advice—and declines to take it.

AUGUST 20   On Long Island, New York, General Nathanael Greene falls ill; his replacement is the popular but less capable General John Sullivan.

AUGUST 23   Gravesend Bay, Long Island, is the site chosen by General William Howe to land 8,000 crack troops and resume offensive operations against the Americans. General George Washington counters by deploying six additional regiments along Brooklyn Heights, and a major engagement appears to be in the offing.

AUGUST 25–26   Marching inland, General William Howe becomes aware of a gap in American lines and dispatches 10,000 men under General Henry Clinton and Colonel Hugh Percy to turn their left flank via Valley Grove (Jamaica Pass). These troops stealthily press on through the night and by daybreak are well positioned to attack the complacent defenders.

AUGUST 27–28   On this momentous day, General William Howe launches 32,000 crack regulars against 19,000 poorly trained Americans under George Washington on Long Island. The British easily turn American defenses near Brooklyn, where a major flanking action routs part of Washington's army and captures 2,000 prisoners with a loss of 400 men. The Americans scramble up to their defenses along Brooklyn Heights and dig in, anticipating the worst.

AUGUST 29   General George Washington, determined not to be pinned against Brooklyn Heights, evacuates his army to Manhattan during the night. He is capably assisted by a regiment of soldier-sailors under Colonel John Glover of Massachusetts, who convey 9,500 men and most of their equipment and guns across the East River in only six hours. This is one of Washington's most remarkable escapes, and it enables the Continental Army to fight on.

SEPTEMBER 7   General George Washington convenes a war council and elects to garrison New York City with the divisions of Generals Israel Putnam, Nathanael Greene, and William Heath.

SEPTEMBER 10   In Canada, Governor General Guy Carleton advances his large army of British and Hessian veterans down the Champlain Valley and into northern New York. General Philip J. Schuyler, badly outnumbered, can do little to oppose them once Lake Champlain passes into their hands.

SEPTEMBER 12   General George Washington, facing a rapidly deteriorating strategic situation, opts to abandon Manhattan before he is trapped there and commences ferrying his forces to the mainland. Captain Nathan Hale of Connecticut also volunteers to remain behind as a spy.

SEPTEMBER 15   The American evacuation of New York City is interrupted by General William Howe when he lands his army at Kip's Bay on Manhattan's east side, covered by five Royal Navy warships. The British veterans sweep aside all militia opposition, and General George Washington, riding up to rally his troops, is nearly captured before General Israel Putnam arrives with reinforcements. The shaken Americans withdraw inland and reestablish themselves on Manhattan's west side near Harlem Heights. Kip's Bay is a minor disaster for Washington, who loses

367 men and 67 cannon; British losses prove negligible.

SEPTEMBER 16   British forces begin pursuing General George Washington's forces up Manhattan and enter a defile near Morningside Heights. Washington suddenly turns on them in force, and the Redcoats begin withdrawing, hotly pursued by the reinvigorated Americans. The Battle of Harlem Heights proves that Washington's raw troops can fight effectively if well led; American losses are roughly 60 men to a British tally of 160. Defeat here also prompts General William Howe to postpone offensive operations for a month.

SEPTEMBER 18   In Philadelphia, Congress standardizes Continental Army organization by authorizing 88 battalions of infantry from 13 states. The number of each battalion levied is according to the population of each state.

SEPTEMBER 22   In New York, Captain Nathan Hale is hanged by the British for espionage and goes calmly to the gallows. By declaring "I regret that I have but one life to lose for my country," Hale becomes the first national martyr for independence.

OCTOBER 12   General Charles Cornwallis lands 4,000 troops at Throg's Neck, New York, in a flanking movement to trap American forces still lingering on Manhattan Island. As the British straggle ashore, they are attacked by Colonel Edward Hand's Pennsylvania riflemen, who thwart several attempts to cross a bridge to the mainland. Cornwallis remains bottled up along the shore for the next six days, granting General George Washington sufficient time to evacuate New York City.

OCTOBER 10–13   On Lake Champlain, General Benedict Arnold leads a slap–dash

American armada into action at Valcour Island. Badly outnumbered, Arnold's ships inflict heavy damage on the British fleet under Governor General Guy Carleton before surrendering. Moreover, the British have wasted so much time subduing Arnold that further campaigning appears impractical until the spring.

OCTOBER 14   Crown Point, New York, is abandoned by General Benedict Arnold, who subsequently walks overland to rejoin the garrison at Fort Ticonderoga. Governor general Guy Carleton, meanwhile, suspends further military operations until after winter has passed. This is one of the most telling military decisions of the War for Independence, and it grants tottering American defenses an eight-month respite to strengthen themselves. Carleton thereby transforms Benedict Arnold's naval defeat at Valcour Island into an American strategic victory.

OCTOBER 16   General George Washington convenes a war council which decides to completely evacuate the army from New York City and over to White Plains. General Nathanael Greene nonetheless feels it prudent to leave a 2,000-man garrison behind at Fort Washington, Manhattan, to obstruct British traffic along the Hudson River for as long as possible. Washington, upon further reflection, is undecided.

OCTOBER 18   In Philadelphia, Polish army officer Thadeusz Kosciuszko receives a Congressional Commission as colonel of engineers, and he is immediately dispatched to assist in the defense of Fort Ticonderoga, New York.

OCTOBER 22   General George Washington completes an orderly withdrawal from Manhattan to White Plains, New York. En route, the village of Marmaroneck is subse-

quently occupied by the Queen's Rangers under the celebrated Major Robert Rogers. Colonel John Haslet suddenly turns and attacks the town, seizing Rogers's advance guard, but proves unable to overwhelm the defenders. Losses in this sharp affair are 15 Americans and 66 Loyalists.

OCTOBER 28   At White Plains, New York, General William Howe and 13,500 British and Hessians confront General George Washington's 14,500 Americans. The Americans occupy a three-mile line behind the shallow Bronx River, arrayed in three divisions. Howe promptly drives back the advance guard under General Joseph Spencer. Then the British parade themselves dauntingly before the defenders. At this juncture, Washington concludes that the elevated terrain of Chatterton Hill on his right flank is the key to the whole position. Colonels Joseph Reed and Rufus Putnam are directed there with 2,000 infantry and engineers, who entrench themselves. British General Alexander Leslie tries to storm the position, but the defenders do not fall back until Colonel Johann Rall's Hessians turn their right flank. Washington subsequently falls back in good order to White Castle Heights while Howe is strangely content to simply occupy the battlefield. Americans losses are roughly 150 killed, wounded, and captured; the British sustain roughly twice that number of casualties.

NOVEMBER 4   Governor General Guy Carleton abandons Crown Point, New York, and returns to Canada with his army for the winter. He is rightfully concerned about supply difficulties, but his actions grant the disorganized Americans a badly needed interval to strengthen their defenses.

NOVEMBER 13   In New York City, General Nathanael Greene finally convinces

General George Washington to maintain a 2,800-man garrison at Fort Washington, despite mounting doubts that the position is secure.

NOVEMBER 14 A force of 8,000 British and Hessian troops under General William Howe mount a three-pronged attack on Fort Washington, New York. The 2,800-man garrison under Colonel Robert Magaw resists tenaciously and repulses several Hessian charges, but at length the defenders are driven back into their works. Surrounded, cut off, and lacking fresh water supplies, Magaw surrenders his entire garrison. British/Hessian losses are fewer than 500 men killed and wounded. Tons of important supplies are captured, rendering this a significant American reverse.

NOVEMBER 30 The moment enlistment terms expire, over 2,000 New Jersey and Maryland militia abandon General George Washington's fleeing army. The Americans have little recourse but to continue retreating before a relentless British advance.

DECEMBER 3 General George Washington shepherds the remnants of his Continental Army into Trenton, New Jersey, then prepares to cross the Delaware River into northern Pennsylvania. The American forces are completely demoralized by their recent experiences, and the revolution is imperiled.

DECEMBER 6 General William Howe orders his advanced forces under General Charles Cornwallis to halt at New Brunswick, New Jersey, and then begins dispersing troops into winter quarters. Cornwallis himself is nonetheless dispatched with light troops toward the Delaware River to scour the banks of any remaining American forces.

DECEMBER 12 In Philadelphia, the Regiment of Light Dragoons under

Colonel Elisha Sheldon is authorized by Congress, constituting the start of the American mounted arm.

DECEMBER 13 General Charles Lee, reposing in a tavern three miles from the main American encampment at Morristown, New Jersey, is suddenly captured by a detachment of the 16th Light Dragoons under Lieutenant Colonel Harcourt, a former subordinate. General John Sullivan is picked to succeed Lee.

DECEMBER 14 In New Jersey, General William Howe makes final winter dispositions for his troops at New York and at Amboy, New Brunswick, Princeton, and Trenton, New Jersey. The advanced outposts comprise veteran Hessian troops under Colonel Karl von Donop, who are warned to remain vigilant

DECEMBER 20 Satisfied with the course of the war thus far, General William Howe writes to Lord George Germain and proposes to capture the American capital of Philadelphia the following spring. This constitutes a marked shift in British strategic thinking since the start of the war, which had been centered upon separating New England from the rest of the colonies.

DECEMBER 24 General George Washington, fearing that the game is nearly up, embarks on a spectacular gambit to revive American fortunes. He informs a war council of his intention to conduct a midwinter offensive—unheard of at the time—to capture the Hessian outpost at Trenton. Realizing that few options remain, his officers unanimously agree to Washington's proposal.

DECEMBER 25 On Christmas night, General George Washington ferries his army across the ice-choked Delaware

River and advances in strength upon Trenton, New Jersey. General James Ewing and General John Cadwalader are unable to cross with their respective columns, meaning that Washington proceeds alone with 2,400 shivering men.

DECEMBER 26   General George Washington and his ragged force of 2,400 Americans attack the 1,400-man Hessian garrison of Colonel Johann Rall at Trenton, New Jersey. Covered by a terrible ice storm, Washington deploys two columns under Generals Nathanael Greene and John Sullivan, then strikes the defenders from the north and northeast. Rall, caught flatfooted, attempts to rally his troops but is blasted by Colonel Henry Knox's cannon and outflanked by General Hugh Mercer's brigade. The Hessians continue fighting in an orchard outside of town, but they surrender en masse once Rall is fatally wounded. Hessian losses amount to 1,000 killed, wounded, and captured, and the American lose two killed and five wounded. This single stroke, brilliantly conceived and masterfully executed, keeps the flagging insurrection alive.

DECEMBER 27   In Philadelphia, the Continental Congress extends emergency powers to General George Washington. He now enjoys near dictatorial powers to conduct the war, but he is such a trusted figure that opposition is muted. Colonel Henry Knox, in light of his excellent behavior, is also promoted to brigadier general.

DECEMBER 30   An emboldened General George Washington recrosses the Delaware River into Trenton, New Jersey, and reoccupies the town with 2,000 men. There he learns that generals Charles Cornwallis and James Grant have massed 8,000 men at Princeton and are already advancing upon him. Rather than retreat, Washington orders up 1,600 Pennsylvania militia under General Thomas Mifflin and addresses men whose enlistments have expired, imploring them to remain under arms for at least another six weeks. The majority of them agree.

1777

JANUARY 2   As General Charles Cornwallis advances upon Trenton, New Jersey, seeking to engage General George Washington's main body, he encounters the riflemen of Colonel Edward Hand. They tenaciously resist from the adjoining woods, and it is 5 P.M. before the British reach Assumpink Creek, so Cornwallis, confident he can bag "the Old Fox" on the morrow, encamps for the evening. Washington, however, surmises that the British have stripped the garrisons at Princeton and Brunswick, leaving them vulnerable to attack. Leaving 400 men behind to stoke the camp fires, he leads his 5,500-man army quietly around the unsuspecting Cornwallis and marches rapidly through the darkness. The British, asleep in their camp, are unaware of the ruse until daybreak.

JANUARY 3   American forces under General George Washington surround and gradually envelope the British outpost at Princeton, New Jersey. When the advanced troops under General Hugh Mercer are roughly handled by the British 17th Foot of Lieutenant Colonel Charles Mawhood, Washington appears on the battlefield with the main force and sweeps them away. The victorious Americans abscond with as many British

George Washington at the Battle of Princeton on January 3, 1777. The Battle of Princeton followed shortly after Washington's victory at Trenton and successfully caught the British army unawares. (National Archives)

supplies as possible and depart for Morristown just as General Charles Cornwallis's army approaches. American losses in this little victory are around 40 killed and wounded; the British lose 400, principally captured. Once again, Washington has demonstrated an uncanny knack for timing.

JANUARY 25–29 At Fort Independence, New York, the Hessian garrison sorties and drives off American troops stationed at nearby Lancey's Mills. This action convinces General William Heath that the post cannot be taken, so he abandons the siege. General George Washington harshly reprimands him in consequence.

FEBRUARY 19 In Philadelphia, William Alexander, Thomas Mifflin, Adam Stephen, Arthur St. Clair, and Benjamin Lincoln are all elevated to major general by the Continental Congress. Brigadier General Benedict Arnold, having been passed over for promotion a second time, angrily tenders his resignation, but

General George Washington convinces him to remain in uniform.

MARCH 14 Desertions, illness, and expiring enlistments all whittle down the Continental Army at Morristown, New Jersey, to 3,000 men. General George Washington, faced with starving soldiers, begins requisitioning food from nearby civilians to keep the army fed.

APRIL 7 In Paris, France, the youthful Marie-Joseph du Motier, marquis de Lafayette, and Baron Johann de Kalb are recruited into American service by agent Silas Deane.

APRIL 14 A large military magazine is founded by Congress at Springfield, Massachusetts; it ultimately evolves into the famous Springfield Arsenal.

APRIL 25–28 Loyalist General William Tryon lands 1,850 men at Compo Beach, Connecticut, and burns the village and depot at Danbury. The following day he marches back to his ships via Ridgefield but is intercepted by militiamen under Generals Benedict Arnold, David Wooster, and Gold S. Silliman. Wooster dies in severe fighting, but, on the third day, Arnold attacks Tryon at Compo Beach, pressing him severely until General William Erskine breaks the Americans with a bayonet charge. Tryon's raid concludes with a loss of 200 men and little to show for the loss; American casualties losses are half those of the British force.

MAY 2   In Philadelphia, Benedict Arnold is finally elevated by Congress to major general, but, in another perceived slap, he receives less seniority than the five men promoted ahead of him.

MAY 5   Throughout the spring, General George Washington's recruiting efforts at Morristown, New Jersey, succeed in building the Continental Army up to 9,000 men. His five divisions are commanded by Generals Nathanael Green, Adam Stephan, John Sullivan, Benjamin Lincoln, and William Alexander.

MAY 7   General George Washington, eager to maintain morality among his troops at their winter encampment, summarily bans all cards, dice, and other forms of avarice.

MAY 28   Eager to be back in the fray, General George Washington breaks camp at Morristown, New Jersey, and marches south to the Middlebrook Valley. From there he can monitor British movements in and out of New Brunswick, and possibly attack an isolated detachment.

JUNE 12   General Arthur St. Clair arrives at Fort Ticonderoga, New York, with the three brigades of Generals Alexis Roche de Fermoy, John Paterson, and Enoch Poor, a total of 2,500 men. However, St. Clair is aghast to the fort in dilapidated

condition and surrounded by hills upon which enemy artillery can be mounted.

JUNE 14   In Philadelphia, Congress sanctions a new national flag consisting of thirteen white stars on a blue field, arrayed in a manner representing a constellation, and set against a background of 13 alternating red and white stripes. Consequently, this date becomes popularly known as Flag Day.

JUNE 17   In Canada, General John Burgoyne orders his 7,000 veteran soldiers to march south from Saint Johns, Quebec, toward Crown Point, New York. He embarks on what he presented to British authorities as a decisive campaign, capable of dividing New England from the rest of the colonies and possibly winning the war. Accompanying him on this grand venture are veteran Generals Simon Fraser, William Phillips, and Friedrich von Riedesel, along with 400 Indians, 139 cannon, and 28 gunboats.

JULY 7   The American garrison under General Arthur St. Clair abandons Fort Ticonderoga in the face of superior British forces under General John Burgoyne. However, his rear guard under Colonel Seth Warner disobeys orders and encamps at Hubbardtown where, at daybreak, General Simon Fraser attacks the American encampment. The more numerous defenders begin pressing back upon the British until they are startled by the sudden appearance of General Friedrich von Riedesel's Hessians. Warner, roughly handled, escapes intact with a loss of 350 men to 150 British and Germans.

JULY 9   In Newport, Rhode Island, Major William Barton leads a raiding party of 40 men and captures British general Richard Prescott in his bed. Prescott, trundled back to Providence at night, is subsequently exchanged for General Charles Lee.

JULY 17   The New Hampshire General Court commissions John Stark a brigadier general of militia, although with the understanding that he will summarily ignore orders given by the Continental Congress or Continental Army officers. Such defiance proves popular, and 1,500 militiamen flock to his colors with a week.

JULY 23   At Marblehead, Massachusetts, Polish cavalry leader Count Kazimierz Pulaski arrives and presents Continental authorities with a letter of introduction from Benjamin Franklin.

JULY 25   General Philip J. Schuyler, commanding 2,600 men under brigadiers John Nixon and Arthur St. Clair, concludes that Fort Edward is indefensible in the face of General John Burgoyne's redcoated juggernaut and withdraws farther down the Champlain Valley.

JULY 26   As part of General John Burgoyne's overarching strategy, a column of 1,800 Loyalists and Indians under Lieutenant Colonel Barry St. Leger departs Oswego, New York, and marches up the Mohawk River Valley. St. Leger's first objective is the American outpost at Fort Stanwix, reputed to be in a state of disrepair.

JULY 27   In New York, Indians allied with General John Burgoyne murder settler Jane McCrea, the fiancée of a Loyalist officer. Her killing spurs greater resentment toward the British and boosts Patriot recruitment efforts throughout the region.

JULY 31   In Philadelphia, Congress commissions 19-year old Gilbert du Mortier, Marquis de Lafayette, a major general in the Continental Army. He remains the youngest general in American military history, but lacks a command and volunteers to serve as General George Washington's aide-de-camp.

AUGUST 1   After a hard slog, General John Burgoyne's army reaches the right bank of the Hudson River, New York, having overcome dense woods and obstacles laid in his path by retreating Americans. He then prepares to ferry his 7,000 veterans to the left bank in preparation for a final descent upon Albany.

AUGUST 2   At Fort Stanwix, New York, Colonel Peter Gansevoort of the 3rd New York Infantry is reinforced by 200 men under Lieutenant Colonel Marinus Willett. Minutes later 1,800 British, Loyalists, and Indians under Lieutenant Colonel Barry St. Leger besiege them. The British demand the fort's surrender, lest an Indian massacre result, but Gansevoort, noticing their lack of artillery, flatly refuses.

AUGUST 4   Congress, anguished by General Philip J. Schuyler's refusal to confront a large British invasion force, appoints General Horatio Gates to succeed him as head of the Northern Department.

AUGUST 6   Six miles from Fort Stanwix, New York, General Nicholas Herkimer and 800 militiamen are ambushed at Oriskany Creek by Loyalists and Indians under Sir John Johnson, Chief Cornplanter, and Joseph Brant. Fighting is bloody, and losses are high, but Herkimer, ignoring serious injuries, calmly puffs on his pipe and repels their determined attacks. At length the Indians grow discouraged and withdraw. Oriskany Creek is one of the bloodiest encounters of the entire war, with Americans sustaining 400 casualties and the Indians losing as many as 150 braves.

While the fighting at Oriskany Creek rages, Lieutenant Colonel Marinus Willett sorties from Fort Stanwix and carries the thinly guarded British camp of Lieutenant Colonel Barry St. Leger. They capture five flags and 21 wagons of supplies without the loss of a man. St. Leger's native allies, discouraged by the day's events, begin deserting him.

AUGUST 11 Cornplanter General John Burgoyne, faced with mounting supply shortages, detaches 800 Hessians and Loyalists under Lieutenant Colonel Friedrich Baum to Bennington, Vermont, to procure horses and supplies. Baum is assured that the region is friendly to the crown and that Loyalist reinforcements will join him there.

AUGUST 16 General John Stark, commanding 2,000 rough-hewn frontiersmen, attacks the Hessian encampment at Bennington, Vermont. Lieutenant Colonel Friedrich von Baum wards off the Americans for two hours before his ammunition gives out. Then he leads a charge down the hillside with his dismounted dragoons. Baum is killed, and, for the loss of 30 American casualties, Stark captures 900 of the enemy. The defeat robs General John Burgoyne of valuable manpower at a critical time.

AUGUST 19 At Stillwater, New York, General Horatio Gates arrives to replace General Philip J. Schuyler as commander of the Northern Department. He also brings reinforcements that boost American strength to 4,500. Schuyler, feeling slighted, subsequently demands a court of inquiry to clear his name.

AUGUST 25 At Head of Elk, Maryland, General William Howe disembarks 15,000 men after spending 32 days at sea. His men are quite emaciated by their confinement, so he orders three days of rest before resuming his advance upon Philadelphia.

SEPTEMBER 3 General William Howe commences the Philadelphia campaign by brushing aside American light infantry at Cooch's Bridge, Delaware. General William Maxwell stands his ground until Hessian *Jaeger* (riflemen) turn his position, and then he falls back to White Clay Creek. This is also the first battle waged under the new Stars and Stripes national flag.

SEPTEMBER 11 General William Howe's army, advancing toward Philadelphia, encounters General George Washington's main force of 14,000 men along Brandywine Creek. Howe perceives that the American left is not covered, and he dispatches General Charles Cornwallis with 9,000 men to turn it at Chadd's Ford. A large Hessian contingent under General Wilhelm von Knyphausen is then ordered to demonstrate before the American center as a diversion. Washington fails to notice the turning movement until it is nearly too late, and he dispatches a succession of infantry from his center to stem the tide. Knyphausen then launches a full-scale attack against the newly weakened center, breaks through, and threatens the entire American force. Washington manages to withdraw in good order with 1,200 casualties to a British toll of 600. Philadelphia is now open to the British, but, once again, Washington slips out of their noose and lives to fight another day.

SEPTEMBER 15 Congress commissions Baron Johann DeKalb a major general and Count Kazimierz Pulaski a brigadier general in its never-ending quest to infuse the fledgling Continental Army with European professionalism.

SEPTEMBER 19 Having entered the Hudson Valley, General John Burgoyne orders an attack upon American lines at Freeman's Farm, New York. He draws his army up into three columns: the right flank of 1,800 men under General Simon Fraser, the center of 1,100 men under General James Hamilton, and the left of 1,000 Hessians under General Friedrich von Riedesel. The attack stalls once Fraser encounters riflemen under Colonel Daniel Morgan, while the British center butts up against General Enoch Poor's brigade. An impasse ensues. General Benedict Arnold finally prevails upon General Horatio Gates to commit more troops and charges headlong into the fray. The British give ground and Arnold, ignoring Gates's orders, lunges forward and threatens to crack Burgoyne's center. Fortunately for Burgoyne, General Friedrich von Riedesel makes a sudden appearance on the American right, which saves the day for Burgoyne. The British draw off in good order with 500 casualties, including several regimental commanders picked off by marksmen. The Americans suffer roughly half that number of casualties.

SEPTEMBER 21   Advancing upon Philadelphia, General William Howe orders the highly capable General Charles Grey to attack an American force under General Anthony Wayne, who is shadowing his rear. That evening Grey expertly steals upon the American camp at Paoli, Pennsylvania, routing them with cold steel. Wayne loses 250 men for a handful of British casualties and falls back. With his rear area finally secure, Howe resumes marching toward his objective.

SEPTEMBER 26   The British army of General Charles Cornwallis occupies Philadelphia, Pennsylvania, much to the relief of Loyalist inhabitants. General George Washington discounts the loss, however embarrassing, and positions his army six miles away at Germantown.

From there the Americans are well positioned to strike if an opportunity beckons.

OCTOBER 3   General Henry Clinton marches 4,000 men up the Hudson River into the New York highlands in support of General John Burgoyne. Clinton, however, intends this action as a diversion only, and he has no intention of actually linking up with Burgoyne. Soon after he marches back to New York City.

OCTOBER 4   General George Washington, having judged the moment right, masses 11,000 men and attacks the dispersed British forces of General William Howe at Germantown, Pennsylvania. Three columns under the command of Generals John Sullivan, Anthony Wayne, and Nathanael Greene advance stealthily, hoping to surprise and overpower the defenders in camp. The attack, aided by a morning fog, commences well and drives the enemy back in confusion. However, pandemonium ensues after General Adam Stephan's division begins firing into Wayne's forces. Howe, meanwhile, collects his infantry and sharply counterattacks across the line. Washington deems the battle lost and retreats in good order with a loss of 900 men (including General Francis Nash, killed) to 500 British casualties. Despite the confusion, the Continental Army performs well in battle.

OCTOBER 7   Outnumbered and low on supplies, General John Burgoyne orders another attack against the American right flank at Bemis Heights, New York. The British advance in three columns of 1,500 regulars and are badly outnumbered by 7,000 Americans under General Horatio Gates. Gates, in a rare moment of initiative, promptly counterattacks. Fierce fighting erupts across the front, and the tipping point arrives when General

Benedict Arnold, acting without orders, leads General Ebenezer Learned's brigade in a successful charge that dislodges the Hessians from several strong points. Burgoyne orders a retreat, preparing to make a last stand at his Grand Redoubt, but, fortunately for him, nightfall terminates the contest. British losses total near 600 men and 10 cannon, whereas the Americans lose 200 killed and wounded.

OCTOBER 10 British artillery is trained on the American defenders of Fort Mifflin, a mud-walled position in the middle of the Delaware River. The garrison of 400 men under Lieutenant Colonel Samuel Smith endures a tremendous bombardment with great heroism. Their determined stand holds up the British advance for several weeks.

OCTOBER 12 In New York, General Thomas Conway begins surreptitiously writing critical missives to General Horatio Gates relative to General George Washington's lack of leadership. He also suggests that Gates should consider replacing him as commander in chief; thus begins the infamous Conway Cabal.

OCTOBER 13 At Saratoga, New York, the British army under General John Burgoyne is surrounded by American forces under General Horatio Gates that number three times its size. Burgoyne summons a board of officers, who, upon reviewing the dire facts, votes unanimously to commence surrender negotiations.

OCTOBER 17 History is made at Saratoga, New York, when General John Burgoyne capitulates to fellow Englishman General Horatio Gates, and 5,728 men, 5,000 muskets, and 37 cannon pass into American hands. For the first time in history, an entire British army has been captured intact. Victory at Saratoga also underscores the viability of the American

Revolution, prompting the French government to extend formal diplomatic relations and direct military assistance as an ally.

OCTOBER 22 Colonel Karl von Donop and 1,800 Hessians cross the Delaware River to assault the 1,000-man garrison at Fort Mercer, Pennsylvania. Colonel Christopher Greene calmly allows the enemy to approach within range and cuts them down with musketry fire. The Hessians continue attacking until Von Donop is mortally wounded, and then withdraws with 500 casualties; Greene loses only 35 men.

NOVEMBER 5 In Pennsylvania, General George Washington learns that Brigadier General Thomas Conway harshly criticized his leadership in several letters to General Horatio Gates. Washington composes a stinging rebuke to Conway in return, prompting Conway's resignation to the Board of War.

NOVEMBER 15 On the Delaware River, the Royal Navy slips several large warships within range of Fort Mifflin and begins firing 1,000 heavy balls every 20 minutes. Major Simeon Thayer, the fort's commander, decides his position is untenable and evacuates that evening. The Americans incur over 300 casualties at Fort Mercer, but they delay a British advance upstream by several weeks.

DECEMBER 1 At Portsmouth, New Hampshire, former Prussian officer Baron Friedrich von Steuben arrives with a letter of introduction from Benjamin Franklin.

DECEMBER 19 The Continental Army, 9,000 strong, lumbers into winter quarters at Valley Forge, Pennsylvania. The site is well located only 20 miles from the city and allows General George Washington to both monitor British movements and protect his supply routes. Unfortunately, extreme cold, hunger and deprivation ensue over the winter months. Upwards of 2,500 men—one-third of Washington's force—perish from exposure.

DECEMBER 23   At Valley Forge, Pennsylvania, General George Washington invites Congressional delegates to headquarters to discuss leadership issues. He is not unaware of recent probes into his military affairs, although the so-called *Conway Cabal* fails to trigger any motions for his dismissal.

1778

JANUARY 2   Colonel George Rogers Clark confers with Virginia governor Patrick Henry about the necessity of seizing the Mississippi-Ohio River Valley to keep it from British hands. He is then commissioned a colonel of Virginia militia and proceeds to recruit seven rifle companies needed for his proposed expedition.

JANUARY 13   At Valley Forge, Pennsylvania, General George Washington appeals to the Continental Congress for immediate supplies of food and clothing to prevent his army withering away from exposure and malnutrition

JANUARY 20   While scouting British outposts near Valley Forge, Captain Henry Lee's troopers are suddenly attacked by 200 enemy dragoons. He and seven men seek refuge in Spread Eagle Tavern then trick the British into thinking that American reinforcements are en route by shouting out false orders. The enemy force departs, and Lee's quick-witted action result in his promotion to major.

JANUARY 25   General George Washington orders the strategic position at West Point, astride the Hudson River, fortified against attack. This is the oldest, most continuously occupied military post in the United States. In 1802 it becomes the site of the U.S. Military Academy.

FEBRUARY   In light of recurring manpower shortages, the Rhode Island General Assembly authorizes recruitment of 300 African American slaves to serve in a special light infantry battalion. In time, the Rhode Island Light Infantry is acknowledged as one of the outstanding units in the Continental Army.

FEBRUARY 6   The United States, having survived three years of warfare on its own, formally enters into a military alliance with France. The French king intends to contribute ships and soldiers directly to the cause of American independence, and the Revolutionary War starts to assume a global significance.

FEBRUARY 23   At Valley Forge, Pennsylvania, the American encampment is enlivened by the arrival of former Prussian officer Baron Friedrich von Steuben. Von Steuben, who misrepresented his credentials, and is neither an aristocrat nor a general, institutes the first systematic training routine in American military history. He proves indispensable in transforming the hobbling Continental Army into a disciplined military force.

MARCH 7   In London, Lord George Germain appoints the highly capable, but widely disliked, General Henry Clinton to serve as commander in chief of British forces in North America. He serves

Baron Friedrich Wilhelm von Steuben drills troops at Valley Forge. Steuben's introduction of discipline to the motley assortment of Continental troops of the American Revolution was a major contribution to the success of the army. (National Archives and Records Administration)

longer in this capacity than any other individual.

MARCH 18 At Valley Forge, Pennsylvania, Baron Friedrich von Steuben commences his celebrated regimen by selecting 120 men as a model company and training them thoroughly. These soldiers are subsequently distributed back to their own units to serve as drillmasters. The entire process is continually replicated, and, by the time General George Washington emerges from his winter quarters, his Continental Army possesses discipline and precision in movements that it heretofore lacked. Von Steuben's endeavors are a major factor in the ultimate American victory.

MAY 5 General Friedrich von Steuben is appointed inspector general of the Continental Army upon the recommendation of General George Washington. He then composes the *Blue Book*, the first American drill manual, which is a simplified version of the famous Prussian drill system.

MAY 6 At Valley Forge, the Continental Army stages its first large-scale review in many months and displays an improved military deportment owing to General Friedrich Von Steuben's training regimen.

MAY 8 General Henry Clinton arrives at New York as the new British commander in chief. He is highly capable, though not well liked by many subordinates.

MAY 12 Colonel George Rogers Clark and a handful of frontiersmen depart on a voyage down the Monongahela River. En route they will rendezvous with reinforcements gathering at the falls of the Ohio River, then proceed into the heart of the Illinois Territory.

MAY 19–20 The 20-year-old Marquis de Lafayette takes 2,200 men on a reconnaissance mission between the Delaware and Schuylkill Rivers. At Philadelphia, General William Howe is alerted of the move and detaches General James Grant with 5,000 troops to intercept him at Barren Hill, Pennsylvania. Fortunately, cavalry scout Allan McLane perceives their maneuvers, and Lafayette is forewarned before the trap is sprung. He cleverly conceals his men around Barren Hill until Grant approaches in force, then aggressively deploys his men as if ready to attack. Grant, stymied into assuming the defensive, stands by while the outnumbered Americans slip from his grasp. The youthful marquis skillfully survives his first independent command.

MAY 28 General George Washington appoints General Benedict Arnold, still limping from his Saratoga wounds, to serve as future governor and garrison commander of Philadelphia. This proves a fateful decision with unsavory consequences for both Arnold and the nation.

MAY 30 Mohawks under Chief Joseph Brant burn the settlement of Cobbleskill, New York, initiating a long series of frontier raids. In the wake of the Saratoga debacle, raiding is the only viable tactic left to the British.

JUNE 19 After British general Henry Clinton elects to abandon Philadelphia, rather than risk being cut off by the French fleet, General George Washington rouses the Continental Army from Valley Forge and begins marching to intercept Clinton with 14,500 well-trained men.

General Benedict Arnold arrives at Philadelphia as its garrison commander; he soon becomes entirely distracted by Margaret "Peggy" Shippen, the beguiling daughter of a prominent Loyalist.

JUNE 26 Colonel George Rogers Clark shoots the Ohio River rapids with 175 men in flatboats, then continues sailing west toward the Illinois Territory.

JUNE 28 General George Washington overtakes General Henry Clinton's British army and attacks its rear guard at Monmouth Court House, New Jersey. However, General Charles Lee, commanding

the American advanced forces, carelessly deploys his men and is nearly routed by Clinton's counterattack. Washington personally intervenes to keep his force from collapsing and relieves Lee him of command after a severe dressing-down. The British then make several determined charges, but they are blasted back by the well-trained Americans. It is at this critical juncture that Mary Ludwig Hayes replaces her husband as part of a gun crew and mans a cannon, earning the nickname "Molly Pitcher." Clinton, unable to make headway, retires from the field in good order and continues marching for New York. Both sides lose 400 men apiece, but Monmouth Court House marks the first time that Washington's men withstand the veteran British in a head-on clash.

JULY 3–4 Loyalists under Captain Walter Butler, and Senecas under Chief Cornplanter, attack American settlements in the Wyoming Valley of Pennsylvania, ambushing and routing the militia, After killing and scalping 227 men, Butler goes on to burn several nearby homes and also steals 1,000 head of cattle. The Wyoming Valley massacre is one of the war's biggest frontier atrocities.

JULY 4 General Charles Lee, angered by his treatment after mishandling troops at Monmouth, composes two insulting letters to General George Washington. The commander in chief responds by arresting Lee and charging him with disrespect and insubordination.

JULY 20 Colonel George Rogers Clark's expedition peacefully occupies the French settlements of Vincennes (Indiana), thanks to the support Father Pierre Gibault, a local priest. This places a large tract of the Old Northwest under American control, but it occasions a military riposte from British forces garrisoning Detroit.

AUGUST 29   In Newport, Rhode Island, the division of General John Sullivan breaks off a futile siege and retreats back to Providence. However, they are set upon by aggressive General Robert Pigot, and fighting develops along Butt's Hill when British major general Francis Smith advances upon General John Glover's veteran brigade. A force of Hessians is also directed to storm Quaker Hill on Sullivan's right, but the attack is rebuffed by the Rhode Island Light Infantry, composed mainly of African Americans. Once General Nathanael Greene drives the Germans off, Pigot suspends further action. This is the Revolutionary War's largest battle waged on New England soil; each side lost approximately 300 men.

SEPTEMBER   26   General Benjamin Lincoln is appointed by Congress to succeed General Robert Howe as commander of the Southern Department. General George Washington is not consulted about the appointment.

SEPTEMBER   28   At Old Tappan, New Jersey, General Charles Grey repeats his effective performance at Paoli, Pennsylvania, in 1777, by surprising Lieutenant Colonel George Baylor's detachment of the 3rd Continental Dragoons. The Americans are completely dispersed with a loss of 50 men killed and wounded, whereas the British sustain no casualties.

OCTOBER 1   The court-martial of General Philip J. Schuyler convenes at Pawling, New York, to evaluate his conduct during the loss of Fort Ticonderoga; Schuyler is acquitted of neglect, but he never receives another command.

NOVEMBER 11   Chief Joseph Brant and Captain Walter Butler lead a combined Indian/Loyalist force against the American settlement at Cherry Valley, New York. The garrison of Fort Alden successfully defends its post, but Colonel Ichabod Alden is slain, along with 40 settlers. This action prompts General George Washington to order punitive measures against the Indians of central and western New York.

DECEMBER 4   Newly appointed General Benjamin Lincoln arrives at Charleston, South Carolina, as head of the Southern Department. He immediately begins preparations to eliminate a growing British threat in neighboring Georgia.

DECEMBER 17   Lieutenant Colonel Henry Hamilton, having marched from Detroit with a combined force of Loyalists and Indians, recaptures the distant settlement of Vincennes (Indiana). He intends to attack Kaskaskia the following spring and drive off Colonel George Rogers Clark, but mistakenly allows his Indian and militia contingents to return home for the winter.

DECEMBER 23   The invasion of Georgia begins as a British squadron under Commodore Hyde Parker lands 3,500 soldiers under Lieutenant Colonel Archibald Campbell at the mouth of the Savannah River. General Robert Howe accordingly collects 700 soldiers and 150 militiamen at Sunbury and marches to the defense of the city.

DECEMBER 29   In Georgia, Lieutenant Colonel Archibald Campbell learns that American reinforcements under General Benjamin Lincoln are still in South Carolina, and he elects to attack Savannah, Georgia, with 3,500 men. General Robert Howe, commanding 1,200 soldiers, encamps at Fairlawn Plantation, but Campbell is informed by a local slave of an obscure path around the rear. The Americans are routed in a single charge, and Howe loses nearly 550 killed, wounded and captured, to a British tally of 13 dead. Savannah falls soon after and remains in British hands until the end of the war.

1779

JANUARY 1   A pensive General George Washington warns Congress not to embroil the army in a new campaign against Canada owing to the lack of men and resources. He also fears that France might ultimately gain control of the region.

JANUARY 23   Continental Congress accepts General George Washington's recommendation for a $200 bounty to both new recruits and soldiers who reenlist. This is done to offset continuing and chronic manpower shortages in the Continental Army.

FEBRUARY 5   Colonel George Rogers Clark hastily assembles 127 frontiersmen in mid-winter and sets off from Kaskaskia to recapture Vincennes, in the Illinois Territory. This turns out to be one of the most grueling displays of endurance in the entire war.

FEBRUARY 14   Colonel John Boyd's Loyalists encamp at Kettle Creek, Georgia, for the evening, unaware that American militia under Colonels Andrew Pickens and Elijah Clarke have surrounded him. They lead 350 men in a concerted attack from three directions; Boyd is overwhelmed and routed with a loss of 40 killed and 70 captured. Pickens loses only 32 men and withdraws back into the interior.

FEBRUARY 23–25   The expedition of Colonel George Rogers Clark traverses icy, flooded prairies while advancing on British-held Vincennes. He learns that Lieutenant Colonel Henry Hamilton is unaware of his approach and commands only a small garrison. Clark consequently orders his men to noisily encircle the fort to give an impression of much greater

numbers and, when Hamilton refuses to surrender, the Americans commence peppering the defenders with rifle fire. Two days later Hamilton concludes his position is hopeless, and he surrenders 79 men to Clark. Victory here ensures American control of the entire Illinois Territory, and 20,000 settlers will have migrated there by war's end. This proves a major phase in the opening of the Old Northwest.

MARCH 3   General John Ashe and Colonel Samuel Elbert stop pursuing the British from Augusta, Georgia, and encamp along Briar Creek to await reinforcements. However, they are unaware that 900

George Rogers Clark and his army of volunteers fire on Fort Sackville, near the village of Vincennes, in February 1779. Clark's surprise attack of the British-held fort was a decisive victory for the United States in the American Frontier. (National Archives)

British under Lieutenant Colonel James Prevost have quietly deployed around the American rear. Prevost charges and completely routs 1,200 defenders, who lose 300 men for a British tally of 15. The debacle at Briar Creek halts all American attempts to reconquer Georgia for several months.

MARCH 11 Congress authorizes creation of a Corps of Engineers within the Continental Army, although professionally-trained French officers are also sought to command it.

MAY 11 American troops under General William Moultrie hastily march to Charleston, South Carolina, to prevent its capture by General Augustin Prevost. Moultrie, stiffened by 600 militiamen, rejects Prevost's surrender summons. A standoff ensues until General Kazimierz Pulaski mounts an unauthorized cavalry sortie at Haddrels' Point and is badly repulsed, losing 300 men. Prevost, however, concludes he is badly outnumbered and withdraws to Stono Island before General Benjamin Lincoln's advancing army can arrive.

MAY 23 In Philadelphia, General Benedict Arnold demonstrates his intention to defect by providing detailed information about West Point, New York, to British general Henry Clinton.

JUNE 20 At Stono Ferry, South Carolina, General Benjamin Lincoln leads 1,400 men against the British rear guard, consisting of 900 soldiers under Lieutenant Colonel John Maitland. The American columns, however, are uncoordinated and prove unable to cut through an abattis, so their attack halts in the face of Hessian resistance. Lincoln, judging the battle lost, withdraws with a loss of 300 men to a British tally of 125. Maitland also draws off to join the main British body at Beaufort.

JULY 2 At Poundridge, New York, British cavalry under Lieutenant Colonel Banastre Tarleton surprises Colonel Elisha Sheldon and the 2nd Continental Dragoons. The Americans extricate themselves with the loss of their flag before victorious Tarleton finally withdraws.

JULY 6 In the Hudson Highlands of New York, General George Washington personally reconnoiters the British stronghold at Stony Point, and is convinced it can be stormed at night with cold steel.

JULY 8 Troops under Loyalist general William Tryon lay waste to the coastal community of Fairfield, Connecticut, burning 83 houses, 100 barns, and numerous churches and schools.

JULY 11 Loyalist general William Tryon's forces descend upon Norwalk, Connecticut, burning another 130 homes, 100 barns, and several vessels. Satisfied by this latest round of punitive action, he boards ships and returns to New York.

JULY 15–16 The British bastion at Stony Point, New York, is attacked at night by American forces under General "Mad Anthony" Wayne. His 1,350 soldiers charge in two columns while a third column mounts a diversion. Previously, Wayne ordered his men to remove their musket flints and rely solely on cold steel. The British garrison under Lieutenant Colonel Henry Johnson is fooled by the American diversion and leaves the fort poorly defended, at which point it is carried by Wayne in vicious, hand-to-hand fighting. American losses amount to 100 men killed and wounded; the British sustain 63 killed, 70 wounded, and 543 captured.

JULY 17 General George Washington, after personally inspecting the defenses of Stony Point, New York, declares it indefensible and orders it stripped and abandoned. General Henry Clinton, meanwhile, is hastily assembling an expedition to retake it.

JULY 28   General Solomon Lovell lands Massachusetts militiamen on the western face of the Bagaduce Peninsula, Maine, and prepares to storm British positions with the help of Continental Marines. The attack drives the British back within their fortification at Fort George, Penobscot, whereupon Lovell orders the Americans to construct siege fortifications.

JULY 31   General John Sullivan begins assembling 2,500 crack troops in preparation for a massive sweep against Indian settlements in central and western New York. He commands two brigades under Generals William Maxwell and Enoch Poor, and is shortly joined by a brigade under General James Clinton.

AUGUST 12   American forces deployed to Penobscot, Maine, receive positive instructions from the Massachusetts War Board in Boston, directing Commodore Dudley Saltonstall to sink all British vessels anchored in the harbor. Saltonstall had refused to cooperate with General Solomon Lovell's ground forces thus far, but the Americans finally prepare to make an all-out assault upon British-occupied Fort George.

AUGUST 13   Disaster strikes American forces at Penobscot, Maine, when a British squadron under Commodore George Collier enters the bay, forcing Commodore Dudley Saltonstall's fleet to sail upstream and burn all their vessels. Thus General Solomon Lovell's troops are left high and dry with no recourse but to walk overland back to Boston. This is one of the biggest American reversals of the entire war and Colonel Paul Revere,

the famous town crier, is also court-martialed for neglect of duty.

AUGUST 18–19   In New Jersey, a detachment of 300 American troops under Major Henry Lee marches at night against British forces at Paulus Hook. A stumbling attack is launched in the dark which manages to capture all but 50 Hessians holed up in a blockhouse. A large force of Loyalists pursues Lee as far as Liberty Pole Tavern, but he is rescued by troops under General William Maxwell. Lee, having killed 50 British and captured 150 for a loss of three wounded, receives a special medal from Congress.

AUGUST 29   American troops under General John Sullivan attack 1,200 Indians and Loyalists at the Indian settlement of Newtown (Elmira), New York. Their advance guard walks into an ambush staged by Captain Walter Butler and Chief Joseph Brant and is slaughtered before General Enoch Poor works his brigade behind the defenders. The Americans sustain 36 casualties, while Indian and Loyalist losses are probably as large; neither side is disposed to show any quarter.

SEPTEMBER 10   General John Sullivan's expedition burns the large Indian town of Canandaigua, a settlement so spacious that two days are required to burn it.

SEPTEMBER 13   Captain Walter Butler's Loyalists and Indians ambush a militia detachment under Lieutenant Thomas Boyd near Geneseo, New York, killing 22 men. The Americans quickly retaliate by capturing and burning the entire village.

SEPTEMBER 14   General John Sullivan's punitive expedition lays waste to the Indian capital of Geneseo, New York, by torching 40 Seneca and Cayuga villages in the surrounding area. However, Sullivan's failure to press on against Fort Niagara, an important Loyalist entrepot and staging area for raiding activities, largely negates the purpose of his campaign.

SEPTEMBER 16   General Benjamin Lincoln arrives at Savannah, Georgia, with 1,500 troops to assist French forces under Admiral Charles, Comte d'Estaing. Siege lines are established but d'Estaing grants General Augustin Prevost's request for a 24-hour truce to consider terms. During the interval, Prevost rushes up 800 reinforcements under Lieutenant Colonel John Maitland and strengthens his already-formidable defenses.

SEPTEMBER 30   The army of General John Sullivan marches back from Indian territory in central New York and arrives at Fort Sullivan, Pennsylvania. Over the past four months his punitive campaign dislocated many Iroquois Indians, forcing them to spend the winter months half-starved and exposed to the elements. However, he failed to attack and destroy the major British supply post at Fort Niagara, so the Indians quickly regroup and resume raiding activities.

OCTOBER 2   Continental Congress passes a new regulation mandating that blue cloth will replace green and buff as the official color of the Continental Army. All respective services are trimmed in specific colors: scarlet for artillery, white for light dragoons, and white, buff, red, or blue for the infantry.

OCTOBER 9   British defenses at Savannah, Georgia, are attacked by Franco-American forces under Admiral Charles, Comte d'Estaing and General Benjamin Lincoln. However, General Augustine Prevost is alert and the attempt fails after a diversion by General Isaac Huger's militia fails to materialize, and three out

of four assault columns become tangled in a swamp. General Kazimierz Pulaski then leads an ill-advised cavalry charge against British artillery and is mortally wounded. Allied losses are nearly 1,000 while the British sustain only 155 casualties. Defeat here represents a heavy blow to the nascent French-American alliance and Georgia remains firmly in British hands.

OCTOBER 11   The British base at Newport, Rhode Island, is ordered abandoned by General Henry Clinton, who transfers its 3,000-man garrison to support impending actions in the South.

OCTOBER 17   With winter fast approaching, General George Washington orders the Continental Army back to familiar quarters at Morristown, New Jersey. The supply situation shows little improvement over the previous winter and more hardships are anticipated.

OCTOBER 28   The siege of Savannah, Georgia, having ended disastrously, General Benjamin Lincoln withdraws his battered forces back to Charleston, South Carolina, to rest and refit.

DECEMBER 1   The Continental Army under General George Washington completes its redeployment at Morristown, New Jersey, for the winter. This proves another harsh season of deprivation, exposure, and desertion for the Americans, and their 12,000-man force is greatly depleted by the time spring arrives.

DECEMBER 23   General Benedict Arnold, having been charged with administrative offenses, is court-martialed in Philadelphia, Pennsylvania. Greatly angered by these proceedings, he is further convinced that his best interests lie in supporting the British.

1780

JANUARY 1 At West Point, New York, 100 members of a Massachusetts regiment mutiny over lack of pay and food and depart for home. However, the men are subsequently rounded up by other soldiers, pardoned again, and encouraged to rejoin the army. The ringleaders are also lightly punished, considering the circumstances.

JANUARY 2 At Morristown, New Jersey, the Continental Army endures extremely low temperatures, exacerbated by a lack of blankets, shelter, and clothing. This proves to be the most arduous winter experienced by American forces in the north.

JANUARY 10 A brooding General Charles Lee is summarily dismissed from the service after penning several insulting letters to the Continental Congress; he retires to his estate and plays no further role in the war.

JANUARY 26 In Philadelphia, the court-martial of General Benedict Arnold convicts him of two minor specifications relative to financial speculation and malfeasance while commanding the city garrison. He is also mildly rebuked by his friend General George Washington. Arnold fumes indignantly over the sentence and continues scheming to turn American fortifications at West Point, New York, over to the British.

JANUARY 27 General George Washington, determined to alleviate the incessant suffering of his troops, orders a complete overhaul of supply procedures in New Jersey. He divides the state into 11 separate districts with specific food allotments to be requisitioned from each. The new scheme works well and the influx of food staves off another disastrous winter.

FEBRUARY 1 Near Savannah, Georgia, a British amphibious force of 14,000 men under Admiral Marriot Arbuthnot and General Henry Clinton anchors off Tyler Island for a brief rest and refit. Their intended target, Charleston, South Carolina, musters only 3,200 men under General Benjamin Lincoln. The latter is aware of the coming storm and seeks to remove his army from danger, but he is pressured by Governor John Rutledge to defend the city at all hazards.

FEBRUARY 11 The squadron and army of Admiral Marriot Arbuthnot and General Henry Clinton enter the North Edisto Inlet, South Carolina, and land troops on John's Island. This places them only 30 miles south of Charleston, but General Benjamin Lincoln remains inert within the city.

FEBRUARY 23 Near Charleston, South Carolina, the British Legion under Lieutenant Colonel Banastre Tarleton overruns a patrol of South Carolina militia, killing 10 and capturing 14. This quickly becomes the most feared unit in the British army.

MARCH 3 American forces at Charleston, South Carolina, are reinforced by the arrival of 700 Continental soldiers from North Carolina. Their arrival, however, does little to staunch the flow of fearful militiamen, who are streaming out of the city with their families.

APRIL 1 Outside Charleston, South Carolina, British troops under General Henry Clinton advance their siege works and open a parallel trench within 800 yards of Charleston's defenses. General Benjamin Lincoln, however, remains pressured by politicians to remain within his works.

APRIL 3 Alarmed over developments in the Southern Department, General George Washington orders General Johann de Kalb to Charleston, South Carolina; he marches with a small but veteran brigade of Maryland and Delaware Continentals.

APRIL 14 A roving column of 1,400 cavalry and mounted infantry under Lieutenant Colonel Banastre Tarleton and Major Patrick Ferguson gallops outside the American camp at Monck's Corner, South Carolina, to shut the only remaining exit out of Charleston. Pressing forward, Tarleton surprises the American pickets while Ferguson follows up with a bayonet attack that routs the defenders. American losses are 100 men killed, injured, and taken, along with 200 horses and 42 wagons of supplies captured; three British are wounded.

APRIL 20 By this date British siege trenches are barely 250 yards from the defenses of Charleston, South Carolina, and General Benjamin Lincoln summons a war council to debate what to do next. His officers are leaning toward capitulation but Lieutenant Governor Christopher Gadsden promises a civilian uprising throughout the city should they try to surrender.

APRIL 25 Today, British forces under General Henry Clinton commence digging a third series of parallel trenches, placing their lines only 30 yards from American defenses at Charleston, South Carolina.

APRIL 28 In Boston, Massachusetts, the Marquis de Lafayette returns after a year's absence in France, where he advocated America's cause to the French court. He also bears commissions of lieutenant general and vice admiral for General George Washington.

MAY 6 At Lenud's Ferry, South Carolina, Lieutenant Colonel Banastre Tarleton and 150 troopers of the British Legion pounce on 350 militiamen under Colonel Abraham Buford. Buford was in the act of uniting with Colonel Anthony White's men when the British charged, scattering the defenders. The Americans lose nearly 100 men captured; Tarleton also releases British 18 soldiers seized on the previous day.

MAY 11 By now, British siege guns are firing hot shot directly into the buildings of Charleston, South Carolina. The bombardment's ferocity convinces civilian authorities to ask General Benjamin Lincoln to surrender rather than risk a general assault.

MAY 12 Disaster unfolds for the United States once General Benjamin Lincoln surrenders to General Henry Clinton at Charleston, South Carolina, after a six-week siege. Over 5,400 men, 6,000 muskets, and 400 cannon fall into Clinton's hands. The militiamen are paroled and return home, but the Continentals pass into captivity. Clinton's "Southern strategy" is off to a victorious start, so he prepares to return to New York and entrust the remainder of the campaign to the aggressive General Charles Cornwallis. Charleston also represents the largest single capitulation of American forces until the fall of Bataan in April, 1942.

MAY 18 Brooking no delays, General Charles Cornwallis marches inland from Charleston, South Carolina, with 2,500 veteran troops. He is determined to stamp out all remaining organized resistance in the region.

MAY 25 Two Connecticut regiments, having subsisted on one-eighth of their assigned rations and being five months arrears in pay, mutiny at Morristown,

New Jersey, and march home. The rebellion is subsequently quashed by Pennsylvania troops, but the incident underscores widespread deprivation in the army and Congress's apparent inability to either fund or feed them.

MAY 29 At Waxhaws Creek, South Carolina, British cavalry under Lieutenant Colonel Banastre Tarleton clashes with American forces under Colonels Abraham Buford and William Washington. Though outnumbered two to one, the British commander attacks the American left and center frontally while simultaneously turning their right. A wild melee ensues as troopers slash and saber the fleeing survivors, then Tarleton's horse is suddenly killed under him. Enraged British and Loyalists consequently bayonet several captives before order is restored. Buford suffers losses of 113 killed, 150 wounded, and 203 captured, and the heavy death toll leads to the ominous charge of "Tarleton's Quarter." British losses are three killed and 12 wounded,

JUNE 3 Before departing Charleston, South Carolina, for New York, General Henry Clinton proclaims that all males of military age must declare their allegiance to the Crown. Moreover, they are also obliged to enlist in the Loyalist militia or be considered rebels.

JUNE 7 General Wilhelm von Knyphausen leads a force of 2,500 Hessians and British out of New York City to Connecticut Farms, New Jersey. He there encounters Colonel Elias Dayton's 3rd New Jersey Regiment and some militia, which are slowly driven back until reinforced by General William Maxwell's Continental brigade. Knyphausen, startled by the sheer number of militia opposing him, withdraws, then entrenches at De Hart's Point to maintain a presence in New Jersey.

JUNE 8 General Henry Clinton, satisfied with the progress of his Southern strategy, returns to New York. All further campaigning will be conducted by the General Charles Cornwallis, a brave and aggressive adversary but a belligerent subordinate.

JUNE 13 In Philadelphia, the Continental Congress appoints General Horatio Gates as the new head of the Southern Department. Once more, this is accomplished without consulting General George Washington.

JUNE 21 General Johann de Kalb trudges into Hillsboro, North Carolina, with 1,400 crack Continentals under Colonels William Smallwood and Mordecai Gist. His arrival is welcome, but appeals for food and supplies from the local populace are ignored.

JUNE 22 General George Washington moves the Continental Army back into the field after an exceptionally harsh winter at Morristown, New Jersey.

JUNE 23 At Springfield, New Jersey, a combined British/Hessian expedition under General Wilhelm Knyphausen attacks American positions defended by New Jersey militia under General Philemon Dickinson. General William Maxwell's Continental brigade arrives in time help parry Knyphausen's frontal assault, so the latter brings superior numbers to bear against the defenders. General Nathanael Greene finally orders the men withdrawn to the safety of Short Hills but Knyphausen, stunned by the extent of American resistance, orders a retreat back to Staten Island. The defense of Springfield costs the Americans around 60 men; Knyphausen is presumed to have sustained 300 casualties.

JULY 11 At Newport, Rhode Island, the 5,500-man French expedition under

General Jean, Comte de Rochambeau, lands—only to find the place nearly deserted. General William Heath is eventually ordered from Boston to formally greet the allied commander.

JULY 21 At Bull's Ferry, New Jersey, General Anthony Wayne is dispatched with 2,000 Pennsylvania Continentals to reduce a 70-man British stockade. He bombards the enemy with four 6-pounder cannons, far too light to inflict serious damage, then fails to overcome the plucky defenders and withdraws.

JULY 25 At Coxe's Mill, North Carolina, General Horatio Gates succeeds General Johann de Kalb as commander of the Southern Department. The latter resumes control of his crack brigade of Delaware and Maryland Continentals.

JULY 27 Eager to assume the offense, General Horatio Gates orders his army into motion against the important British supply depot at Camden, South Carolina. Gates, against the advice of his officers, chooses a direct route to Camden that has been previously stripped clean of supplies.

AUGUST 1 At Green Springs, South Carolina, American militia under Colonel Elijah Clarke engage a force of 210 Loyalists. Clarke thoroughly routs his adversary, who had been specifically ordered to capture him, in a sharp engagement of 15 minutes.

AUGUST 5 To further advance his traitorous scheme, General Benedict Arnold lobbies hard to become commander of strategic West Point, New York, and a trusting General George Washington acquiesces. Arnold's intention to betray that post to the British is calculated to horbor serious consequences for the American side.

AUGUST 6 At Hanging Rock, South Carolina, militia under General Thomas Sumter attacks the 500-man Loyalist outpost under Major John Carden. The 800 Americans are initially successful, but then pause to loot the enemy camp. The Loyalist infantry subsequently form a square, supported by two small cannon, and beat back successive attacks. Sumter calls off the attack and retires, having inflicted 192 casualties for a loss of 12 killed and 41 wounded.

AUGUST 8 In the Ohio wilderness, Colonel George Rogers Clark and 1,000 men pursue the Shawnees from their main settlement at Chillicothe, Ohio, to the fortified town at Piqua. There he defeats the Indians, killing 73 at a cost of 20 dead and 40 wounded.

AUGUST 9 General Charles Cornwallis, alerted that General Horatio Gates is advancing upon him, departs Charleston, South Carolina, and hurriedly marches 2,200 battle-hardened veterans to reinforce Lieutenant Colonel Francis Rawdon at Camden. Unlike most British commanders, Cornwallis is a skilled battlefield tactician and eager to come to grips with his adversaries.

AUGUST 15 In South Carolina, General Horatio Gates is reinforced by 100 Maryland Continentals and 300 North Carolina militiamen. However, he errs in issuing molasses rations and green peaches to his hungry men, which play havoc on their digestive tracts. As the Americans proceed toward Camden they also collide head-on with General Charles Cornwallis, moving up the same road. After some skirmishing, both sides establish camps and await daybreak.

AUGUST 16 At Camden, South Carolina, General Horatio Gates and 3,000 Continentals and militia confront 2,200 British veterans under General Charles Cornwallis. A flanking attack by militia fails disastrously on the American left and the British move quickly to turn the American center. The Delaware and Maryland Continentals under Johann de Kalb fight bravely until being over-whelmed, and the American army collapses in a rout. Gates loses 750 killed and cap-tured to a British loss of 68 dead and 245 wounded; moreover, Gates does not stop retreating until reaching Charlotte, North Carolina, 60 miles distant. In a single blow Cornwallis has eliminated the only standing American force in the South.

AUGUST 18 At Fishing Creek, South Carolina, British cavalry under Lieu-tenant Colonel Banastre Tarleton surprise General Thomas Sumter's guerrillas in their camp. For a loss of 16 men, the British kill 150 Americans and capture 300 more. Sumter barely escapes the dis-aster, and immediately begins rallying the survivors to fight again.

SEPTEMBER 9 General Charles Cornwallis, seeking another decisive victory, defies General Henry Clinton and invades North Carolina. Though bold, this consti-tutes a major departure from the system-atic Southern strategy outlined by Clinton and imperils British chances for victory.

SEPTEMBER 20–22 At Hartford, Connecticut, General George Washington and General Jean, Comte de Rochambeau, conduct a preliminary strategy confer-ence. Washington seeks to attack New York City, but Rochambeau demurs until they have a larger fleet and more troops in the area. Rochambeau also speaks of a possible campaign in the Chesapeake Bay region, but nearly a year passes before this becomes possible.

SEPTEMBER 21 General Benedict Arnold, intending to betray strategic West Point to the British, secretly meets with Major John Andre. However, when Andre's ship HMS *Vulture* sails off on the Hudson River, he is stranded behind enemy lines and spends the night at the home of a local Loyalist.

SEPTEMBER 23 Major John Andre dons civilian garb and attempts to pass through American lines, carrying information about West Point's defenses concealed in his boot. However, while walking toward British lines, he is apprehended by three militiamen, who uncover the documen-tation in his boot heel. Word of his arrest quickly passes to General Benedict Arnold's headquarters, and his treacher-ous plot unravels.

SEPTEMBER 25 General Benedict Arnold, his perfidy unmasked, flees to the British warship HMS *Vulture* anchored in the Hudson River and formally joins the British. The unfortunate Major John Andre, however, is slated to be tried as a spy.

SEPTEMBER 26 At Sycamore Shoals (Tennessee), a large gathering of "Over the Mountain Men" (Frontier militia-men) transpires as Colonels Isaac Shelby and John Sevier prepare to confront Major Patrick Ferguson and his Loyalists. They are gradually reinforced by 400 Virginians under Colonel William Campbell, 160 North Carolinians under Colonel Joseph McDowell, and addi-tional soldiers under Colonel Benjamin Cleveland; Campbell is eventually elected "leader" of the unruly force.

SEPTEMBER 27 Major Patrick Ferguson, alerted that western militias are pulling together in strength to oppose him, aban-dons his position along the Catawba River, North Carolina, and marches for the perceived safety of King's Mountain, South Carolina.

OCTOBER 2   Major John Andre, a brave and gallant officer, is hung as a spy at Tappan, New York. Like Nathan Hale, his calmness and stoicism at the gallows impress those witnessing his demise.

OCTOBER 3   In Philadelphia, the Continental Congress streamlines the Continental Army's organization by reducing it to eighty regiments of infantry, four of artillery, and four of cavalry.

OCTOBER 7   The Continental Congress, having finally consulted General George Washington, appoints General Nathanael Greene as commander of the Southern Department. This proves to be one of the war's most fateful decisions.

Patriot militia under Colonels William Campbell entrap Major Patrick Ferguson's Loyalist forces atop King's Mountain, South Carolina. The frontiersmen, numbering 1,100 men, quickly surround Ferguson's position and begin working their way up the slopes, Indian style. Cut off and with men falling fast around him,

General Nathanael Greene of the Continental Army, after a painting by Charles Wilson Peale. (National Archives)

Ferguson rallies a few mounted men and tries escaping but is pierced by six bullets and killed. The Loyalists are annihilated, with 157 dead, 163 wounded, and 698 captured to an American tally of 28 killed and 64 wounded. This disaster strips General Charles Cornwallis of his best light infantry, and he suspends his invasion of North Carolina for several months.

OCTOBER 13   At Hillsboro, North Carolina, the fuming and intermittently ill Daniel Morgan is promoted to brigadier general by the Continental Congress.

OCTOBER 25   At Tearcourt Swamp, South Carolina, General Francis Marion and 150 partisans surprise Loyalists under Colonel Samuel Tynes, and rout them, killing 3, wounding 14, and capturing 23 without loss. Marion also captures 80 horses and valuable supplies.

NOVEMBER 20   General Thomas Sumter and Colonel Elijah Clark, hotly pursued by Lieutenant Colonel Banastre Tarleton and 400 British dragoons, make a determined stand at Blackstock's Plantation, South Carolina. As the British attack develops, a body of mounted militia slips around the rear of the dragoons and delivers a point-blank volley that empties many saddles. At this critical juncture, Sumter is seriously wounded, but the British hurriedly withdraw from the field. Hard-charging Tarleton admits to a loss of 50 men while the Americans sustain three killed and four wounded.

NOVEMBER 22–23   Major Benjamin Tallmadge leads a party of 80 dismounted troopers from Fairfield, Connecticut, crosses Long Island Sound at night, and storms Fort St. George (Brookhaven), New York. The Americans kill seven and seize 54 prisoners before burning 300 tons of hay intended as forage.

NOVEMBER 30 The Continental Congress promotes Major Henry Lee to lieutenant colonel and he receives command of a legion of 300 dragoons and three companies of light infantry. He mercilessly molds them into one of the most effective formations in the Continental Army.

DECEMBER 3 At Charlotte, North Carolina, General Nathanael Greene arrives to assume command of the Southern Department from General Horatio Gates. Possessing only 2,500 Continentals and militia, he boldly intends to initiate offensive operations against superior British forces.

DECEMBER 19 Taking the offensive, General Nathanael Greene daringly splits his forces by sending General Daniel Morgan and 600 light troops on a wide sweep through South Carolina. Morgan is directed to attack the rear of General Charles Cornwallis's army, then rejoin Greene at Cheraw if the British advance upon American forces collected there.

DECEMBER 28 At Hammond's Store, South Carolina, a force of cavalry and mounted infantry under Colonels William Washington and James McCall rout a body of Loyalists under Colonel Thomas Waters, killing or wounding 150 and taking 40 prisoners. General Charles Cornwallis, alarmed by this partisan attrition, dispatches Lieutenant Colonel Banastre Tarleton's British Legion to destroy the raiders.

DECEMBER 30 General Benedict Arnold, now in British employ, lands at Hampton Roads, Virginia, and commences a lengthy and destructive raid up the James River. Such behavior enhances his reputation for villainy among fellow Americans.

1781

JANUARY 1 At Mount Kemble, New Jersey, the Pennsylvania line erupts in mutiny after their enlistments expire. Roughly 2,000 men leave camp determined to march on Philadelphia and present their grievances to Continental Congress. General Anthony Wayne harangues the disgruntled men to return to camp but he is ignored.

JANUARY 6 In South Carolina, General Charles Cornwallis is apprised that General Nathanael Greene has split his forces in two. He counters by ordering Lieutenant Colonel Banastre Tarleton with 1,100 men to pursue light forces under General Daniel Morgan. Tarleton is ordered to destroy Morgan before he can reunite with the main body under Greene.

JANUARY 17 At Cowpens, South Carolina, Lieutenant Colonel Banastre Tarleton and, 1,100 British troops corner General Daniel Morgan's fleeing forces. As Morgan anticipated, the impetuous trooper attacks without proper reconnaissance and plunges headlong into a trap laid for him. The first and second lines of Morgan's force fire two well-aimed volleys apiece, toppling many officers, then quickly withdraw to the rear. The British surge forward to engage Colonel John E. Howard's Continentals, which turn and a deliver a point-blank volley into their disorganized pursuers, stunning them. Colonel William Washington then spurs his dragoons forward, charges over the hill and takes Tarleton in the flank, as does the newly reformed militia on the other side of the ridge. The British army literally disintegrates and Tarleton ignominiously flees with his army, having sustained 110 killed, 229 wounded, and 600 captured, out 1,100 men. Morgan loses only 12 killed and 61 wounded. This is the most startling tactical reversal of the war.

JANUARY 19   An irate General Charles Cornwallis, having lost the bulk of his remaining light troops at Cowpens, pursues General Nathanael Greene across the northernmost reaches of North Carolina. By dint of forced marching he hopes to destroy either Greene or General Daniel Morgan before their forces can unite.

JANUARY 25   General Charles Cornwallis daringly burns his baggage and supplies at Ramsour's Mill, North Carolina, to lighten his army's burdens. He then resumes doggedly pursuing American forces under General Nathanael Greene, now heading toward the North Carolina border.

JANUARY 30   Generals Nathanael Greene and Daniel Morgan unite their forces along the Catawba River, still closely pursued by General Charles Cornwallis.

FEBRUARY 3   An ailing General Daniel Morgan quits the army and returns to Virginia, whereupon Colonel Otho H. Williams assumes command of all light troops. The American army continues retreating toward the Dan River with British forces in hot pursuit.

FEBRUARY 13   The army of General Nathanael Greene quickly crosses the Dan River on boats previously placed there for his utilization and reaches the safety of Virginia. The British, lacking oars and engineers, concede after a 200-mile chase. Cornwallis finally controls all of North Carolina, but his lines of communication stretch back to the coast and are susceptible to guerrilla attacks.

FEBRUARY 23   Once General Nathanael Greene rests, rearms, and is reinforced by 600 Virginia militia, he orders his army back over the Dan River into North Carolina, and begins advancing upon Hillsboro.

FEBRUARY 25   Along the Haw River, North Carolina, American partisans under General Francis Pickens and Colonel Henry Lee bump up against Colonel John Pyle's 300-man Loyalist force. Pyle mistakes Lee's cavalry for Lieutenant Colonel Banastre Tarleton's British Legion, allowing it to approach and intermingle with his men. Pickens, hiding in the nearby woods, opens fire and the American troopers join in the fray, cutting down 93 men and taking 200 captive.

MARCH 6   At Newport, Rhode Island, General George Washington arrives for high-level strategic discussions with General Jean, Comte de Rochambeau. Despite the drama of events transpiring in the South, Washington remains fixed upon an all-out assault upon New York City.

MARCH 15   At Guilford Courthouse, North Carolina, 45 miles west of Hillsboro, the American army of 4,400 Continentals and militia under General Nathanael Greene confronts 1,900 British veterans commanded by General Charles Cornwallis. Though outnumbered two-to-one, the British attack and punch through the first two American lines, only to be stopped by Greene's final line of Continental veterans. At this juncture, Cornwallis orders his artillery fired into the struggling mass, killing several of his own troops, which causes both sides to fall back. The well-disciplined British recover first and resume advancing, and Greene

The Battle of Guilford Courthouse, March 15, 1781, between Continental Army and militia troops under General Nathanael Greene and British regulars under Lord Cornwallis. (Courtesy of the National Museum of the U.S. Army, Army Art Collection)

withdraws in good order. Victory costs the British dearly with 93 killed and 413 wounded, whereas the Americans sustain 78 killed and 183 wounded. Cornwallis cannot tolerate such attrition and abandons his conquest of North Carolina.

MARCH 19 The thoroughly depleted British army of General Charles Cornwallis begins marching back to Wilmington, 200 miles distant. The victorious Americans follow cautiously in his wake, hoping to eliminate detachments.

APRIL 1 The army of General Nathanael Greene, reduced by illness and desertion to 1,500 soldiers, departs Ramsey's Mills, North Carolina, and resumes offensive operations. The British, scattered throughout the South in isolated outposts, are susceptible to being picked off individually, which is exactly what Greene intends to do.

APRIL 7 General Charles Cornwallis shepherds his 1,425 soldiers into Wilmington, North Carolina, where they will rest, refit, and be resupplied by the Royal Navy.

APRIL 23 Fort Watson, South Carolina, is besieged by partisans under General Francis Marion and Colonel Henry Lee, despite a lack of artillery. The problem is resolved solved after Colonel Hezekiah Marham assembles several platformed log-cribs, so elevated that riflemen can deliver a plunging fire into the British camp. The garrison is cowed into surrendering 144 men; American losses total two killed and six wounded.

APRIL 24 At Hobirk's Hill, South Carolina, General Nathanael Greene encamps 1,500 soldiers two miles away from British forces positioned near the old Camden battlefield under Lieutenant

Colonel Francis Rawdon. After resting his command for a few days, Greene intends to attack troops and drive them from the area.

APRIL 25 At Hobkirk's Hill, South Carolina, Lieutenant Colonel Francis Rawdon scrapes together 900 men and attacks General Nathanael Greene first. Marching through the woods, Rawdon avoids detection until he is nearly upon the American encampment. Greene orders part of his Maryland and Virginia Continentals under Colonels Otho H. Williams and Isaac Huger to advance and envelop the British from both flanks, but the usually solid 1st Maryland Regiment inexplicably bolts from the field. Panic ensues along the American line and Greene orders his men to retreat. American losses are 19 dead, 115 wounded, and 136 missing; Rawdon suffers 38 killed and 220 injured, one fourth of his army. He consequently declines to pursue Greene and simply holds his position.

MAY 7 Near Hobkirk's Hill, South Carolina, Lieutenant Colonel Francis Rawdon again advances against the army of General Nathanael Greene. The Americans, however, withdraw nine miles to a strong fortified position that dissuades Rawdon from attacking. The British subsequently retrace their steps back to Camden.

MAY 10 Outnumbered by the enemy and with no prospects of reinforcements, Lieutenant Colonel Francis Rawdon abandons Camden, South Carolina, and withdraws toward Charleston. He also orders all British outposts in the interior evacuated, save for Fort Ninety Six.

MAY 12 Fort Motte, South Carolina, is besieged by partisans under Colonel Henry Lee and General Francis Marion.

To accelerate its capitulation, the Americans assault the fort with fire-tipped arrows, a tactic that was suggested by elderly widow Rebecca Motte, the property owner. British Lieutenant Charles McPherson then surrenders 150 men; the Americans sustain two dead.

MAY 15 Fort Granby, South Carolina, falls to Colonel Henry Lee, along with 352 British and Hessian prisoners under Major Andrew Maxwell. After failing to coax Maxwell's surrender with generous terms, a single cannon shot convinces the garrison to yield.

MAY 20 General Charles Cornwallis marches his army into Petersburg, Virginia, being strengthened to 7,200 men by detachments under General Benedict Arnold. Arnold, never completely trusted by the British, is then relieved and ordered back to New York.

MAY 21 At Fort Galpin, South Carolina, Colonel Henry Lee captures 126 Loyalist prisoners for a loss of one man. This outpost also serves as a depot for the British superintendent of Indian Affairs, so the Americans confiscate considerable amounts of trading goods.

MAY 22 Fort Ninety Six, South Carolina, one of several large British posts still dotting the interior, is besieged by General Nathanael Greene. However, Greene commands less than 1,000 men, lacks heavy artillery, and the 550-man Loyalist garrison under Colonel John Cruger determines to resist.

MAY 23 Fort Grierson in Augusta, Georgia, is taken by Colonel Henry Lee and militia under Colonel Elijah Clarke. The entire 80-man Loyalist garrison is either captured or killed and their commander, Colonel James Grierson, a particularly brutal partisan, is murdered in captivity.

MAY 24 Resuming his offensive with 7,500 men, General Charles Cornwallis departs Petersburg, Virginia, and advances upon the rebel capital at Charlottesville. Given the shortage of Continental troops in the theater, panic ensues.

MAY 26 General Anthony Wayne, a no-nonsense martinet, quells a mutiny at York, Pennsylvania, by executing seven ringleaders. After order is restored, he resumes marching to Virginia.

JUNE 1 In New York City, General Henry Clinton is incensed that General Charles Cornwallis has disobeyed orders and invaded Virginia. He consequently suggests that Cornwallis either advance into the Delaware region or be evacuated by sea and return to New York. Cornwallis, however, enjoys the political backing of Lord George Germain in England, and disobeys orders again by campaigning where he is.

JUNE 3 As part of a deliberate campaign of deception, General Henry Clinton receives intercepted "dispatches" by General George Washington to Congress, outlining his intention to attack New York City shortly. The messages are intended to keep the British from reinforcing General Charles Cornwallis in Virginia.

JUNE 4 Hard-charging Lieutenant Colonel Banastre Tarleton covers 70 miles in only 29 hours and suddenly appears before Charlottesville, Virginia. Governor Thomas Jefferson and the legislature flee for their lives, having been warned moments before by militia captain John Jouett. Tarleton ends up seizing military stores, tobacco, and seven tardy legislators, including Daniel Boone.

JUNE 5 Fort Cornwallis, outside Augusta, Georgia, is captured by partisans under General Andrew Pickens and Colonel Henry Lees. This occurs after three failed assaults, at which point a Maham tower is built and a small cannon is wheeled up. The Loyalists lose heart and capitulate, having sustained 52 killed and 334 taken prisoner to an American loss of 40 men. Colonel Thomas Brown, a heartily despised Loyalist partisan, is also captured.

JUNE 10 In Virginia, General Anthony Wayne arrives with his brigade of 1,000 men and reinforces the Marquis de Lafayette and General Friedrich von Steuben already present. The Americans can now field 4,500 veteran soldiers to oppose General Charles Cornwallis.

JUNE 18 American forces under General Nathanael Greene assault Fort Ninety Six, South Carolina, by striking at Fort Holmes and its attendant star redoubt. They are initially successful and clear the abattis, but a determined Loyalist sortie drives them off. Greene, aware that British reinforcements are approaching, abandons the siege. The Americans suffer 55 killed, 70 wounded, and 20 captured to a Loyalist tally of 27 killed and 58 injured.

JUNE 24 General George Washington marches his soldiers to Peekskill, New York, to await the arrival of General Jean, Comte de Rochambeau, and his own army.

JUNE 26 At Spencer's Tavern, Virginia, the Marquis de Lafayette seeks to destroy a British force under Lieutenant Colonel John G. Simcoe and Hessian major Johann Ewald. The British are surprised in camp by cavalry under Major William McPherson, but British troopers counterstrike the Americans in the flank just as Ewald deploys his jaegers. Pressing ahead, Ewald encounters Continental infantry under Colonel Richard Butler, and

Simcoe, sensing he is badly outnumbered, retreats and abandons his wounded. Lafayette fails to destroy Simcoe's elite force, but both sides conducted themselves admirably: American losses are given as 9 killed, 14 wounded, and 14 missing; the British admit to 10 killed and 23 wounded.

JULY 4 The British army under General Charles Cornwallis crosses the James River at Jamestown Ford, Virginia, and advances toward Williamsburg with 7,000 men. He anticipates that the youthful Marquis de Lafayette will try to obstruct his passage and prepares to surprise him at Green Spring.

JULY 6 At Green Spring, Virginia, General Charles Cornwallis springs his trap on an unsuspecting General Anthony Wayne. However, once the attack is signaled, Cornwallis is startled to find that Wayne orders his 900 men forward on a desperate bayonet charge that momentarily halts their opponents. The Marquis de Lafayette appears with some light infantry at the last possible moment, and Cornwallis, dismayed to see his quarry escape, withdraws back across the James. The Americans suffer 28 dead, 99 injured, and 12 missing to a British tally of 75. Wayne handled himself extremely well under desperate circumstances.

JULY 20 In New York City, General Henry Clinton orders General Charles Cornwallis to march to Williamsburg, Virginia, on the coast. There he is to establish a strong base from which his army can be supplied and reinforced by sea.

JULY 21 Outside New York City, generals George Washington and Jean, Comte de Rochambeau reconnoiter British defenses and conclude that they lack the numbers and equipment necessary for a successful siege. Stalemate in the northern theater continues while the momentum of the war has shifted south to Virginia.

AUGUST 1 At Yorktown, Virginia, British forces under General Charles Cornwallis occupy the tip of the peninsula, astride the York River, and his 7,000 men begin entrenching. He subsequently fortifies Gloucester Point on the opposite shore and appoints Lieutenant Colonel Banastre Tarleton to defend it.

AUGUST 14 In New York, Generals George Washington and Jean, Comte de Rochambeau, receive electrifying news that the French fleet under Admiral Francois, Comte de Grasse, is arriving soon in Chesapeake Bay. Washington immediately proposes abandoning New York City in favor of marching rapidly to Virginia and entrapping General Charles Cornwallis at Yorktown. Rochambeau concurs. The allies prepare to expedite their 400-mile trek in complete secrecy.

AUGUST 21 Outside New York City, Generals George Washington and Jean, Comte de Rochambeau, head south to Virginia with 6,000 men. General William Heath remains behind with 2,500 men and orders to deceive General Henry Clinton into thinking that the city is about to be attacked. To that end false orders are also allowed to "fall" into enemy hands while the construction of bread-baking ovens gives the impression of a permanent French presence there. The unsuspecting Clinton is taken in by this subterfuge, for the moment.

SEPTEMBER 2 In Philadelphia, the combined forces of Generals George Washington and Jean, Comte de Rochambeau, file through the city in an impressive display of force. Washington also allows long-suffering units, with pay months in arrears, to petition the Confederation Congress for redress. Delegate

Robert Morris arranges a loan from Rochambeau to pay the soldiers, and the army resumes marching toward Elk Head, Maryland.

SEPTEMBER 6 In another punitive act, General Benedict Arnold leads 1,732 soldiers on a raid against New London, Connecticut. Fort Griswold, defended by 158 men under Lieutenant Colonel William Ledyard, repels several British attacks and kills Lieutenant Colonel Edmund Eyre before capitulating. The enraged British slay Ledyard with his own sword and massacre 85 soldiers of the garrison. British losses are 48 killed and 145 wounded, and the entire affair further blackens Arnold's reputation.

SEPTEMBER 8 At Eutaw Springs, South Carolina, General Nathanael Greene's 2,450 men encounter a smaller force of 1,800 under Lieutenant Colonel Alexander Stewart. The Americans approach stealthily, surprising and capturing several pickets, then charge directly into the British camp. A severe struggle ensues whereby the militia and Continentals fight exceptionally well and drive the British from their campsite, but cannot evict a party of grenadiers from a fortified house and a thicket off to their right. As they dally, Stewart orders a charge across the field, and the disorganized Americans give way. Greene loses 138 killed, 375 wounded, and 41 missing, a loss rate of 42 percent, while Stewart suffers 85 killed, 351 wounded, and 257 missing, or 42 percent. Eutaw Springs is one of the hardest-fought actions of the war and produces the highest proportional casualties of any battle.

SEPTEMBER 14 In a letter to General Charles Cornwallis, General Henry Clinton assures him that a relief expedition is assembling in New York and should arrive at Yorktown no later than October 5. This knowledge dissuades Cornwallis from cutting his way out of the peninsula

and escaping toward the interior before he is trapped by allied siege lines.

SEPTEMBER 15 At Williamsburg, Virginia, the French and American allies stage an impressive review of 17,000 men, including the divisions of the Marquis de Lafayette, Friedrich von Steuben, and Benjamin Lincoln. The French army is further represented by crack infantry regiments, augmented by engineering, cavalry, and artillery units. General Charles Cornwallis, holed up on the Yorktown peninsula, scarcely musters half that total.

SEPTEMBER 28 At Yorktown, Virginia, the massed Franco-American army advances from Williamsburg and formally invests British positions. General Charles Cornwallis consequently abandons his outer works to save as many soldiers' lives as possible and retires to fortifications nearer the town.

OCTOBER 1 American siege artillery is planted in the captured British outer works and begins shelling British positions at Yorktown, Virginia.

OCTOBER 6 At Yorktown, Virginia, General George Washington takes a shovel and breaks ground for the first parallel trench. Within days his 1,500 sappers and engineers construct a trench 2,000 yards long and 600 yards from the British outer defenses. General Charles Cornwallis is now trapped within his works.

OCTOBER 9 At Yorktown, Virginia, massed firepower from 100 French and American cannons relentlessly pounds British defenses, while hot shot burns the frigate HMS *Charon* and several transports anchored in the York River.

OCTOBER 12 The first allied trench at Yorktown is completed and a second one is commenced 300 yards from British defenses. Work here, however, is compromised because the fatigue parties come under British artillery fire from redoubts Nos. 9 and 10. Plans are made to eliminate this threat as soon as practical.

OCTOBER 14 At Yorktown, Virginia, a combined night assault under colonels Alexander Hamilton and Guillaume de Deux-Ponts storms redoubts Nos. 9 and 10 along the British defensive perimeter. Both posts are subsequently incorporated into allied siege lines, allowing artillery to be mounted at even closer range. American losses are nine killed and 31 wounded; the French lose 15 killed and 77 wounded. The British suffer 18 killed and 73 captured.

OCTOBER 16 At Yorktown, Virginia, General Charles Cornwallis orders a sortie by 350 men under Lieutenant Colonel Robert Abercrombie to buy the defenders additional time. They initially overrun a French battery but are driven back with eight killed and 12 captured. That

evening, Cornwallis attempts to ferry his entire force across the York River to Gloucester and is foiled by bad weather.

OCTOBER 17 With no succor in sight, a drummerboy mounts the British parapet at Yorktown, Virginia, and beats for a parley. An officer is then blindfolded and brought into the headquarters of General George Washington to negotiate surrender terms.

OCTOBER 19 At Yorktown, Virginia, General Charles O'Hara formally surrenders 8,081 British officers to the French and American armies. Commanding General Charles Cornwallis has excused himself from the proceedings. British bands then strike a tune appropriately titled "The World Turned Upside Down," as the defenders dejectedly file out and stack arms. British combat losses at Yorktown total 156 killed, 326 wounded, and 70 missing. The French lose 60 killed and

The Comte de Rochambeau directs General Charles O'Hara to surrender his sword to George Washington at Yorktown. Contrary to popular belief, Cornwallis was not present to deliver over his force of more than 5,000 troops. Instead, pleading ill health, he assigned his second-in-command this odious task. (Library of Congress)

197 wounded; the American tally is 23 dead and 56 injured. This capitulation is an even bigger disaster than Burgoyne's at Saratoga in 1777 for it devastates Britain's political will to continue the struggle.

OCTOBER 30 At West Canada Creek, New York, Colonel Marinus Willett and 460 militiamen and Oneida warriors overtake a body of Loyalists and Indians, routing the rear guard and killing the hated Major Walter Butler. This affair is the last hostile incursion in the region.

NOVEMBER 10 General Arthur St. Clair marches a division down from Yorktown, Virginia, to reinforce General Nathanael Greene, still campaigning in North Carolina.

DECEMBER 22 His mission to America complete, the youthful Marquis de Lafayette embarks at Boston, Massachusetts, and sails back to France. He carries back with him the ideals of the American Revolution which will partly inspire France's own revolution in 1789.

DECEMBER 31 In Philadelphia, the Confederation Congress appoints General Benjamin Lincoln to serve as the nation's first secretary of war.

1782

JANUARY 5 Wilmington, North Carolina, is abandoned by British forces and American troops converge and occupy it from the interior.

JANUARY 12 General Anthony Wayne's army, strengthened by General Arthur St. Clair's division, crosses the Savannah River and commences marching across Georgia.

JANUARY 23 In Georgia, General Anthony Wayne's army is attacked in camp by several hundred Creek warriors under Chief Guristersigo. The Indians are badly repulsed, with 18 killed, and Wayne engages and personally slays the chief in combat.

FEBRUARY 25 At Wambaw Creek Bridge, South Carolina, General Francis Marion, of "Swamp Fox" lore, attacks British forces under Colonel Benjamin Thompson, but withdraws after sustaining 32 casualties.

APRIL 1 A victorious General George Washington relocates his military headquarters to Newburgh, New York, while his officers and men, their pay several months in arrears, begin grousing about Congressional neglect.

APRIL 23 Congress, ever eager to trim expenses, votes to reduce the number of officers in each Continental regiment, along with staff and support positions.

MAY 9 In New York City, General Guy Carleton arrives and replaces General Henry Clinton as British commander in chief in North America. At length he is tasked with orchestrating the withdrawal of all British forces from the former colonies.

MAY 22 At Newburgh, New York, General George Washington angrily dismisses a suggestion from Colonel Lewis Nicola that he install himself as king of the new nation. Stung by the rebuke, Nicola forwards several letters of apology.

JUNE 4–6 Colonel William Crawford, commanding a detachment of 480 Pennsylvania militiamen, conducts an ill-fated campaign against Indians on the upper Ohio River Valley. En route they are ambushed at Sandusky by a mixed Indian/Loyalist force under Captain William Caldwell. The Americans lose eight killed outright and 27 wounded, and several prisoners, including Colonel Crawford, are tortured to death over a fire.

AUGUST 7 General George Washington institutes the Badge of Military Merit (or Purple Heart) at Newburgh, New York, intending to signify distinguished military service to the country; three soldiers are the initial recipients.

AUGUST 14–17 A Loyalist/Indian force of 340 men under Simon Girty and Captain William Caldwell besieges Bryan's Station, Kentucky, but is repulsed. Girty and Caldwell fall back to the ruins of Ruddle's Station and also deliberately mark their trail, as if enticing the Americans to follow.

AUGUST 19 In Kentucky, Colonel Hugh McGary leads a relief column of 182 men to Bryan's Station and pursues Simon Girty's raiding party across the Licking River, despite signs of impending ambush.

AUGUST 19 At the Lower Blue Licks, Kentucky, Colonel Hugh McGary divides his force of 182 mounted Kentuckians into three columns and surges across without proper reconnaissance. Indians and Loyalists under Simon Girty then rise and fire, decimating the attackers. Surviving Kentuckians flee across the river in panic, leaving the Indians to scalp and mutilate their dead and wounded. The Americans lose 77 men in 15 minutes, including noted scout Daniel Boone's youngest son, Israel.

SEPTEMBER 10 In Georgia, General Andrew Pickens leads 316 South Carolina militiamen on a second foray against hostile Cherokees. En route he is joined by additional militia under Colonel Elijah Clarke. The Indians, intimidated by this show of force, fall back.

SEPTEMBER 20 At Lookout Mountain, Tennessee, American militia under Colonel John Sevier defeats the Cherokees under Dragging Canoe. This action finally convinces the Indians to seek peace after a lengthy and costly struggle to both sides.

NOVEMBER 4 Near Johns Island, South Carolina, American and British forces wage a final skirmish, causing the death of Captain William Wilmot, 2nd Maryland Continentals, and four soldiers. Wilmot becomes the final army officer killed in the War for Independence.

NOVEMBER 10 Near Piqua, Ohio, General George Rogers Clark leads 1,500 mounted riflemen on a punitive expedition against Shawnee villages, killing 10 Indians and wounding 10. This action is regarded as the final combat action of the Revolutionary War.

1783

JANUARY 6 Continental Army leaders Alexander McDougal, John Brooks, and Matthias Ogden petition the Confederation Congress for back pay and other amenities. Military officers are frustrated that the Congress is seemingly unable or unwilling to meet its obligations to the army.

MARCH 10–12   In New York, the Newburgh Conspiracy unfolds as Major John Armstrong anonymously circulates letters complaining about Congress's failure to honor its promises to the army. The missives hint at direct action and implore that all like-minded officers convene to discuss the problem on the following day.

MARCH 15   At Newburgh, New York, General George Washington ends the so-called "Newburgh Conspiracy" by strongly denouncing any threats against civilian authority. He personally promises his soldiers that their grievances will be addressed by Congress at the appropriate time. The officers, swayed by Washington's example, disavow their actions and reaffirm their loyalty to the government.

APRIL 19   At Newburgh, New York, a Congressional proclamation declaring the end of hostilities with Great Britain is read. Prayers are then offered, while the troops also receive an extra ration of liquor. Exactly eight years to the day have lapsed since the Revolutionary War commenced at Lexington and Concord.

MAY 2   Alexander Hamilton, heading up a Congressional committee, is tasked with designing plans for a peacetime military establishment. He advocates General George Washington's idea for a small, professional force of four infantry and one artillery regiments. The notion of a national military academy is also toyed with, but Congress is indifferent to military matters and it is not pursued.

MAY 26   The Continental Army demobilizes, save for a small number of troops retained to observe the British evacuation of New York. Soldiers return home without pay, but receive three months' equivalent in promissory notes that are to be redeemed at a later date. The men also retain their firearms.

JUNE 13   In Pennsylvania, a disgruntled Pennsylvania regiment protests their pay being several months in arrears. They angrily threaten to march on Philadelphia to underscore their discontent to Congress in no uncertain terms. Secretary of War Benjamin Lincoln appeals to the men for calm but is ignored.

JUNE 14   In Philadelphia, the Confederation Congress votes to adjourn and flees to Princeton, New Jersey, rather than face a mob of angry Pennsylvania soldiers. General George Washington, meanwhile, dispatches some of his few remaining troops from Newburgh, New York, in support.

SEPTEMBER 3   The Treaty of Paris is signed by dignitaries of the United States and Great Britain in Paris, France, formally concluding eight years of hostilities. The Americans acquire independence along with a huge swath of land east of the Mississippi River as far north as the Great Lakes Region.

OCTOBER 18   At Rocky Hill, New Jersey, General George Washington issues orders to the few remaining soldiers of the Continental Army, thanking them for their service and entreating them to support the American government, whatever form it ultimately assumes.

OCTOBER 29   Secretary of War Benjamin Lincoln, lacking any troops to command, tends his resignation. No new secretary is appointed over the next two years.

NOVEMBER 3   The entire Continental Army disbands by Congressional fiat. Only 500 infantry and 100 artillerymen, consolidated into a single battalion, are fielded under Colonel Henry Jackson. In the absence of standing force, defense of frontier settlements reverts to state militias.

DECEMBER 3   General George Washington authorizes retention of only 500 soldiers to guard military stores and West Point and Pittsburgh. Otherwise, the United States now lacks a standing army.

DECEMBER 4   As British forces depart Staten Island, New York, a tearful George Washington takes leave of his officers at the Fraunces Tavern in New York City. He then intends a final visit to Congress.

DECEMBER 23   At Annapolis, Maryland, General George Washington resigns as commander in chief, and tends his sword to President Thomas Mifflin of the Confederation Congress. General Henry Knox succeeds him as the nation's senior military leader.

1784

JANUARY 1   The only Continental Army unit in existence, the 700-man strong regiment of Colonel Henry Jackson, is divided between garrisons at West Point, New York, and Fort Pitt, Pennsylvania. Their mission is to guard public stores.

APRIL 15   Inspector General Friedrich von Steuben, who did so much to instill the nascent American army with professional-style military discipline, tends his resignation. Congress votes to grant him an elaborate ceremonial sword for services rendered.

JUNE 2   The American military establishment is further reduced when Colonel Henry Jackson is discharged and his regiment is reduced to a company of 80 men. Captain John Dougherty (now the army's senior officer) commands the largest contingent of 55 soldiers at West Point, New York, while the remaining 25 are garrisoned at Fort Pitt, Pennsylvania. However, continuing Indian raids along the frontier and the presence of British forces at Detroit persuade Congress to establish the 1st Regiment with 700 men, divided into eight infantry and two artillery companies. After being recruited in New York, Pennsylvania, New Jersey, and Connecticut, the unit is scattered in forts across the western frontier.

AUGUST 12   Josiah Harmar, a distinguished Continental officer, is reinstated as lieutenant colonel and commander of the 1st Regiment. He then relocates to Fort Pitt, Pennsylvania, to join his regiment and also assumes the title "Commander of the Army."

1785

FEBRUARY 2   Congress offers a $500 reward for the arrest of any person manufacturing counterfeit army pay certificates. They also roundly denounce the practice.

MARCH 8   Former general Henry Knox is appointed by Congress to succeed Benjamin Lincoln as secretary of war. Presently, his staff consists of three clerks and a messenger. Knox is also tasked with overseeing policies as they relate to the military, as well as naval matters, Indian relations, and land grants for veterans.

APRIL 12   Rather than have the 1st Regiment be discharged due to expiring enlistments, Congress authorizes the same 700 men to be recruited again, this time for three years' duration. The regiment remains chronically under-strength after few volunteers step forward to accept the new terms.

JULY 25 In a serious misstep, Congress abolishes the Quartermaster Department; henceforth military supplies are entrusted to civilians. This proves to be a grossly corrupt and inefficient system which nearly hamstrings the army.

1786

JANUARY Lieutenant Colonel Josiah Harmar's 1st Regiment withers away to 200 enlistees once states fail to meet recruitment quotas. In light of this weakness, the Shawnees under Chief Blue Jacket and the Miamis under Chief Little Turtle begin raiding American settlements in Kentucky from their tribal homelands in Ohio.

Little Turtle (ca. 1752–1812)

Little Turtle (Michikinikwa) was born into the Miami tribe near present-day Fort Wayne, Indiana, around 1752. He displayed fine qualities as a warrior, and he was eventually made chief of the Miami by tribal elders. He was also pro-British in outlook, and after the Revolutionary War, Little Turtle advocated armed resistance against white encroachment north of the Ohio River. In 1787 he entered into an alliance with noted Shawnee chief Blue Jacket, and three years later he defeated an armed expedition of 1,400 militia under Colonel Josiah Harmar. Success here rallied other tribes to the cause, and soon Little Turtle become the locus of Native American resistance, much in the manner of his predecessor, Chief Pontiac. President George Washington, however, ordered an even larger effort against them, and in September 1791 General Arthur St. Clair marched into the Ohio territory with 2,600 raw soldiers and militia. Little Turtle watched these developments closely, and on November 4, 1791, he decided to attack the Americans directly in their camp. St. Clair was completely routed on November 4, 1791, and suffered over 600 soldiers killed or wounded, in the Army's largest defeat at the hands of Native Americans. Still, within three years the Americans rebuilt their army under the aegis of General "Mad Anthony" Wayne, who finally cornered and defeated the Indians at Fallen Timbers on August 20, 1794. Little Turtle then submitted to the Treaty of Greenville in 1795 and swore his allegiance to the United States. Once the War of 1812 broke out, the aged chief offered to fight on behalf of the Americans, but he died at the Fort Wayne Indian agency on July 12, 1812. Little Turtle remains one of the most accomplished of Native American chieftains and strategists.

Little Turtle, chief of the Miami tribe, led militant opposition to the influx of settlers in the Ohio country in a conflict known as the Old Northwest Indian War. However, after his defeat at the Battle of Fallen Timbers in 1794, Little Turtle became an ally of the United States. (North Wind Picture Archives)

The brawl between Massachusetts government supporters and rebels known as Shays' Rebellion, 1786–1787. (Bettmann/Corbis)

JULY Secretary of War Henry Knox informs Congress that the entire military establishment has shrunk to 518 rank and file. This is a perilous situation considering ongoing Indian hostilities in Kentucky and elsewhere.

SEPTEMBER 26 In Springfield, Massachusetts, former Continental Army veteran Daniel Shays leads 500 disgruntled farmers in a campaign to force local courts to stop foreclosing farms. Governor James Bowdoin reacts by dispatching General William Shepherd and some state militia to safeguard state courts in the region.

OCTOBER 20 Congress, facing an intractable Indian situation on the frontier, votes to increase the military establishment to 1,340 men. The two artillery companies extant with the 1st Regiment are ordered combined with two new companies and form a battalion commanded by Captain John Dougherty. Recruitment is lackluster, however, and few volunteers step forward.

DECEMBER 26 In western Massachusetts, former army officer Daniel Shays assembles 1,200 "Regulators" (poor farmers) and marches onto Springfield, Massachusetts, to possibly seize the state arsenal there. This hostility induces Governor James Bowdoin to call out 4,400 state militiamen for a period of 30 days and contain the rebellion.

1787

JANUARY The military establishment remains 840 men below authorized strength despite a major recruitment effort and a lessening of the enlistment period to one year. Unfortunately, the government lacks funding to pay soldiers for the next two years.

JANUARY 25 At Springfield, Massachusetts, former army captain Daniel Shays and 1,200 rebellious farmers make an ill-fated attempt to storm the government armory under General William Shepherd. They are driven off by cannon fire after losing three men killed and 20 wounded, at which point their "rebellion" begins to collapse.

JANUARY 27 General Benjamin Lincoln marches into Springfield, Massachusetts, with a large contingent of militiamen to secure the government arsenal. Daniel Shays and his band of rebels, meanwhile, have scattered into the countryside to avoid capture.

FEBRUARY 3 Outside Petersham, Massachusetts, General Benjamin Lincoln orders a nighttime forced march to surprise rebel forces gathered there under former army captain Daniel Shays.

FEBRUARY 4 Massachusetts militiamen under General Benjamin Lincoln surprises rebel forces under Daniel Shays, dispersing them at Petersham. Lincoln takes 140 prisoners but Shays escapes across state lines to Vermont. The insurrection convinces the legislature to lower court costs, not impose direct taxes, and exempt household goods and tools from debt-related confiscations. But the greatest efficacy of Shays' "rebellion" is that of adding greater urgency to creation of a stronger central government, one better capable of defending itself than the Articles of Confederation.

MAY 13 In Philadelphia, former general George Washington makes a rare public appearance by arriving as part of the Constitutional Convention assembled there. Despite America's aversion for military forces, Washington remains hailed as a trusted, popular figure.

JULY 13 Colonel Arthur St. Clair gains appointment as governor of the Northwest Territory, encompassing most of Ohio.

JULY 31 Colonel Josiah Harmar advances to brigadier general, being the only officer of such rank in military service.

OCTOBER 3 Shaken by Shays' Rebellion and mounting Indian hostility, Congress decides to once again enlist recruits for three years of service. They also vote to maintain 700 regular soldiers on the western frontier for protecting settlements, and require the War Department to retain as many troops already in service as possible rather than seek out recruits.

OCTOBER 5 In Ohio, General Arthur St. Clair formally assumes his responsibilities as governor of the Northwest Territory, which also carries concurrent duties as superintendent of Indian affairs for the region. As governor he enjoys authority to raise militia and wage war to secure the frontier from hostile tribesmen.

1788

OCTOBER 2 The ordeals of army life are underscored when the contractor tasked with providing the army with uniforms fails to provide the goods as promised, so soldiers at distant outposts improvise with on-hand supplies. Not surprisingly, Congress also fails to provide funding to pay the soldiers on time.

1789

APRIL 30 In New York City, George Washington is inaugurated as the first president of the United States. Under the new constitution, the position he assumes incorporates the responsibilities of commander in chief of all army, navy, and militia forces.

AUGUST 7 Congress creates the War Department and Henry Knox is reappointed Secretary of War a month later.

As such, he is responsible for military affairs and Indian relations. Knox is also the first military figure of note to endorse a national military academy.

AUGUST 8 Secretary of War Henry Knox, in his first report to President George Washington, informs him that the army's strength is only 672 soldiers, and the bulk of these are serving at posts throughout the Ohio Valley.

SEPTEMBER 29 Congress, increasingly aware of the dangers posed by standing professional forces, mandates that the United States Army be restricted to 1,000 men, divided into eight infantry and four artillery companies. They also approve the earliest veterans' legislation by authorizing pensions for disabled soldiers and sailors.

1790

APRIL 30 Congress, increasingly cognizant of Indian hostilities, authorizes an increase in army manpower ceilings to 1,273 rank and file. The length of service terms remains three years for soldiers and officers alike. In a cost-cutting measure, they also cut the pay of privates from $4.00 to $3.00 per month.

SEPTEMBER 30 At Fort Washington, Ohio, General Josiah Harmar, intent on embarking upon on a punitive expedition against hostile Shawnee and Miami Indians, assembles 353 soldiers and 1,100 Kentucky militiamen. As a whole, Harmar's force is under-strength and inadequately trained.

OCTOBER 14–17 The expedition of General Josiah Harmar, having destroyed one Indian village, dispatches Colonel John Trotter and several soldiers to survey the surrounding region. Trotter turns in only a half-hearted attempt at reconnaissance and is relieved of command.

OCTOBER 21–23 Near Fort Wayne, Indiana, Miamis and Shawnees under Little Turtle and Blue Jacket brush aside an American force under General Josiah Harmar. Harmar, having detached 400 militiamen toward a large Indian village, marches on in search of the warriors. Little Turtle suddenly attacks, routing the militia and massacring the regulars under Major John Wyllys where they stand. Thoroughly bested and low on supplies, Harmar sullenly withdraws back to Fort Washington.

NOVEMBER 3 General Josiah Harmar's army straggles back into Fort Washington, having lost 400 men to Miami chief Little Turtle. The general considers leveling charges against the militia commanders but, on further reflection, does nothing. Little Turtle, however, is emboldened by his victory and raids closer to American settlements.

1791

JANUARY Despite a rather shoddy performance, Congress allows General Josiah Harmar to remain military commander of the Northwest Territory. In fact, given that his small army is badly weakened by defeats, sickness, and desertion, little more could have been expected of him.

MARCH 3 Stung by Harmar's defeat, Congress votes to create the 2nd Infantry at a strength of 995 men. A $6.00 bounty is also proffered to new recruits to help flesh out the ranks.

MARCH 4 Congress promotes Arthur St. Clair, governor of the Northwest Territory, to major general and orders him to replaces the inept Josiah Harmar as military commander. He begins assembling a 3,000-man force for a punitive foray into the heart of Indian territory that summer.

MAY 15   At Fort Washington, Ohio, General Arthur St. Clair is surprised to find only 85 soldiers of the 1st Infantry on station. He spends the next six weeks cobbling together 427 soldiers from the two regiments to serve as the nucleus of his new army.

AUGUST 1–21   A mounted force of Kentucky militia under Brigadier General James Wilkinson raids the Miami village of L'Anguille, Ohio; he completes his mission with the loss of two men, then returns home.

AUGUST 7–29   At Fort Washington, Ohio, General Arthur St. Clair is pressured by the government to begin campaigning, so he marches his recruits six miles into Indian territory. En route the lack of discipline and regular order becomes readily apparent.

AUGUST 16   Lieutenant William Henry Harrison of the 1st Infantry Regiment, a future president and commander in chief, joins the army of General Arthur St. Clair.

SEPTEMBER 15–24   At Fort Washington, Ohio, General Josiah Harmar is court-martialed for his military failure and exonerated after nine days. In light of his severe defeat, he never again receives a military command and finally resigns his commission in January 1792.

OCTOBER 4–13   At Fort Hamilton, Ohio, General Arthur St. Clair advances with 2,300 men, the largest American force assembled since the Revolutionary War. The roster includes the under-manned 1st and 2nd Regiments of Infantry, 80 volunteers, and 600 militiamen. Despite their numbers they are mostly raw, poorly armed, and ill-equipped. St. Clair proceeds with them for 30 miles, then stops to build a fortification.

OCTOBER 14–23   Fort Jefferson, Indiana Territory, is constructed by the army of Arthur St. Clair. However, at this late season, the men continually suffer from the lack of winter clothing and adequate rations. The hardships and deprivations engendered increase an already high desertion rate, which reduces St. Clair's strength.

OCTOBER 31–NOVEMBER 4   General Arthur St. Clair's army, braving cold weather, rampant desertions, and food shortages, pushes deeper into Indian territory and finally arrives on the banks of the Wabash River. The troops, cold and exhausted by their exertions, cannot fortify their campsite and simply sleep on the ground.

NOVEMBER 4   Near Fort Wayne, Indiana, General Arthur St. Clair's army of 1,400 militiamen and soldiers is disastrously defeated by the Miamis under Chief Little Turtle. The Americans are aware of Indians near their camp at dawn, but Colonel William Oldham, when ordered to send out patrols, declines. Little Turtle, judging the moment right, takes the extraordinary move of charging directly into the American camp. The militia scatters immediately, but the 2nd Regiment makes a gallant last stand until it is overwhelmed. The survivors, having sustained 918 dead and 276 wounded, hurriedly repair back to Fort Jefferson. St. Clair's debacle remains the worse defeat ever suffered at the hands of Native Americans.

NOVEMBER 4–8   An ailing General Arthur St. Clair leads his demoralized army past Fort Jefferson and continues onto the perceived safety of Fort Washington. The militia is discharged without pay after arriving and St. Clair dispatches Major Ebenezer Denny to Philadelphia to inform Secretary of War Henry Knox of his misfortune.

1792

MARCH 5 In Ohio, General Arthur St. Clair resigns his commission and General "Mad Anthony" Wayne is appointed military commander in the Northwest Territory to succeed him. Congress also votes to enlarge the military establishment to 5,120 men by strengthening the existing two infantry regiments and artillery battalion while adding three more infantry regiments and four troops of dragoons.

MAY 8 Congress, faced with protracted Indian hostilities and endemic manpower shortages in the U.S. Army, buttresses the defense establishment with the new Militia Act. This authorizes states to draft eligible males, aged 18 to 45, into state service as situations require. Volunteer cavalry and artillery units are likewise allowed, although members are required to provide guns and mounts at their own expense. Actual enforcement of the act is left entirely up to the states, so the end results are less than uniform.

SEPTEMBER 4 At Fort Fayette, Pennsylvania, General Anthony Wayne begins organizing the "Legion of the United States" into four self-contained units. These consist of 1,280 men in two battalions of infantry, one battalion of riflemen, a company of light dragoons, and a company of horse artillery.

NOVEMBER 30 General Anthony Wayne relocates his main camp to Legionville, 22 miles down the Ohio River from Pittsburgh, Pennsylvania. Intent upon revitalizing the moribund American military, he establishes a strict camp of military instruction utilizing Baron Von Steuben's *Blue Book* from the Revolutionary War. Discipline is also rigidly enforced, and several soldiers are executed for major offenses.

1793

APRIL 7 General Anthony Wayne relocates his Legion of the United States to a new camp outside of Fort Washington, Ohio. He also continues high levels of training and preparation, teaching them to actively patrol and, like the Roman legions of old, to entrench every night to thwart surprise attacks on their camp.

OCTOBER 14 Fort Greenville, Ohio, is established by General Anthony Wayne six miles north of Fort Jefferson. Despite the onset of winter conditions, Wayne allows training to continue without interruption.

DECEMBER 24 General Anthony Wayne marches six companies from Fort Greenville, Ohio, to the site of St. Clair's defeat. Once there, burial details are assigned to inter the remains of American soldiers while he supervises construction of Fort Recovery.

1794

APRIL 2 Congress enlarges the weapons procurement system by voting to construct two more arsenals, including Harpers Ferry in western (now West) Virginia. Inventor Eli Whitney, who pioneered the process of interchangeable parts, is offered the position of superintendent but he declines.

MAY 9   The new Corps of Artillerists and Engineers is founded by Congress to garrison the new series of coastal fortifications under consideration. To facilitate this task, a school of engineering instruction also arises at West Point, New York.

JUNE 30–JULY 1   At Fort Recovery, Ohio, the garrison of 140 riflemen and dragoons under Captain William Eaton, is attacked by 1,200 warriors under Little Turtle and Blue Jacket. The defenders repel several daylight assaults and inflict heavy losses before the Indians grow discouraged and withdraw.

JULY 16–AUGUST 8   In the Monongahela Valley of western Pennsylvania, the so-called "Whiskey Rebellion" erupts to protest a new federal excise tax on liquor and stills. The infuriated residents burn the houses of several tax officials, and revenue officials performing their task run the risk of being tarred and feathered.

AUGUST 7   In New York City, President George Washington issues a proclamation demanding that Whiskey Rebels return home or face punitive measures. To that end he commences mobilization of 13,000 militiamen from Maryland, New Jersey, Pennsylvania, and Virginia to suppress the uprising.

AUGUST 8   General Anthony Wayne erects strongly-posted Fort Defiance, Ohio, as an advanced base before campaigning against the Indians.

AUGUST 15–18   In Ohio, General Anthony Wayne's army is reinforced by Kentucky militia and Chickasaw and Choctaw scouts. Thus augmented, he crosses the Maumee River and begins his final drive into the heart of Indian territory. Wayne's force, unlike the previous efforts, is highly-disciplined and led by one of the army's most aggressive

officers. Little Turtle, closely observing Wayne's activities for two years, declares him "the chief that does not sleep" and advises the Indians to make peace. Instead, he is removed from command and the Shawnee Blue Jacket is chosen to lead the warriors into battle.

AUGUST 20   In northwest Ohio, the Battle of Fallen Timbers unfolds as General Anthony Wayne's force of 3,500 well-drilled soldiers and militia defeat a 2,000-man Indian coalition under Blue Jacket. Fighting erupts in areas previously devastated by tornados, and the Americans, having foiled an Indian ambush, rout the milling warriors in a well-executed bayonet charge. Wayne's losses are 33 killed and 140 wounded; the Indians flee to the walls of British-held Fort Miami, whose commander refuses to open the gates. Moreover, Wayne's victory finally clears the way for unobstructed settlement of the Old Northwest.

AUGUST 24   President George Washington, wary of the loyalty of the Pennsylvania militia, elects to muster additional Virginia troops under his two Revolutionary War compatriots Daniel Morgan and Henry Lee.

SEPTEMBER 9–24   Using his authority as commander in chief, President George Washington nationalizes the militias of Pennsylvania, New Jersey, Maryland, and Virginia, and orders 15,450 men into the field. In practice, all four states experience difficulty complying with the order and equipping state troops for service in the Whiskey Rebellion.

SEPTEMBER 12–24   In Indiana Territory, General Anthony Wayne marches to Little Turtle's Miami Town, razes it, and erects a new fortification that will eventually be christened Fort Wayne. Major John Hamtramck eventually garrisons the post with six companies of infantry.

President Washington and his advisers send Confederation Army troops to pacify western counties of Pennsylvania during the Whiskey Rebellion, October 1794. (National Guard)

SEPTEMBER 24 General Henry Lee is instructed by President George Washington to begin marching against the whiskey tax rebels in western Pennsylvania.

OCTOBER 4 George Washington (now acting general) takes to the field for the last time while commanding the newly raised "Army of the Constitution." The force numbers 11,000 militiamen and is divided into two wings under Generals Henry Lee and Daniel Morgan at Carlisle and Cumberland, Pennsylvania, respectively.

NOVEMBER 2–17 In western Pennsylvania, General Henry Lee conducts predawn raids against the "Whiskey rebels," netting several hundred prisoners. The remainder surrender voluntarily, and the "rebellion" collapses. The "Army of the Constitution" disbands without firing a shot, but General Daniel Morgan remains in western Pennsylvania for several months to maintain order. The authorities ultimately detain 200 rebels and 25 are tried, but only two are convicted of treason. Both are subsequently pardoned.

DECEMBER 31 Former general Henry Knox, having served as Secretary of War under both the Articles of Confederation and the Constitution, resigns from office.

1795

JUNE General Daniel Morgan, convinced that the region is finally reconciled to a federal tax on whiskey, disbands his militia force in western Pennsylvania and return home. This act concludes 40 years of distinguished military service.

JUNE 24 At West Point, New York, the Regiment of Artillerists and Engineers organizes under Lieutenant Colonel Stephen Rochefontaine, formerly of the French army. A rudimentary school of instruction for prospective engineering officers is also established.

JULY 11 At Fort Detroit, Captain Moses Porter accepts possession of that post from the British and raises the American flag over the Michigan Territory for the first time. His 65-man artillery company also acts as the garrison.

NOVEMBER 6 A troubled Ensign Meriwether Lewis, having been court-martialed for drunkenness and acquitted, transfers to the "Chosen Rifle Company." There he meets Lieutenant William Clark, and the two become lasting friends.

DECEMBER 14 At Fort Greenville, Ohio, General Anthony Wayne bids farewell to his victorious "Legion of the United States" and rides east to confer with Congress. He is succeeded by the duplicitous and self-serving Brigadier General James Wilkinson, a future Spanish spy.

1796

MAY 30 Congress, finding the existing Legion system top-heavy with brigadier generals and lacking colonels, abolishes it and reinstitutes its prior regimental structure.

AUGUST 14 At Fort Detroit, Michigan Territory, General Anthony Wayne arrives and is saluted by Captain Moses Porter's garrison. Wayne, not enjoying the best of health, remains on station for the next three months.

SEPTEMBER 11 Fort Mackinac, Michigan Territory, reverts to an American garrison under Major Henry Burbeck in accordance with Jay Treaty provisions.

NOVEMBER 1 Congress votes to reorganize the army into four infantry regiments, numbered 1–4, two companies of light dragoons, and the Corps of Artillery and Engineers. Provisions for a single major general and one brigadier general are allowed, along with one paymaster general and one quartermaster general.

DECEMBER 15 At Presque Isle, Pennsylvania, General Anthony Wayne, whose aggressive disposition earned him the sobriquet "Mad Anthony," dies of illness. His death renders Brigadier General James Wilkinson the senior military leader.

1797

MARCH 4 In New York City, John Adams is inaugurated as the second president and commander in chief. In the course of his tenure in office, the appointment of army officers becomes caught in an increasingly ideological struggle between Federalists and a new party, the Jeffersonian Republicans.

JUNE 24 Congress authorizes recruitment of 80,000 militiamen in the event of war with revolutionary France. The army's engineers are also authorized to enlarge and enhance existing harbor defenses.

1798

APRIL 27   Congress, in light of ongoing hostilities with France, enlarges the existing Corps of Artillerists and Engineers by authorizing recruitment of an additional regiment of three additional battalions.

MAY 28   Congress bolsters national defense by authorizing the recruitment of a 10,000-man "Provisional Army" to serve for three years.

JULY 2   Congress appoints former president George Washington commander of the three-year provisional army with a rank of lieutenant general; this is the first use of that rank and it is not invoked again until 1864. Alexander Hamilton becomes both his second-in-command and inspector general with the rank of major general. Most Americans still distrust standing military forces but Washington, a thoroughly trusted figure, is the only man that the polity would accept to hold such rank.

JULY 16   The existing army structure is enlarged by Congress by adding 39 officers and 704 soldiers to the four regiments extant. An additional 12 infantry regiments and 6 troops of light dragoon are also authorized, but these are never raised.

1799

MARCH 2–3   A Medical Department headed by a physician general officer is created by Congress. The Corps and Regiment of Artillerists and Engineers are also redesignated the 1st and 2nd Regiments of Artillerists and Engineers. All ranks are subject to higher pay but smaller whiskey rations.

DECEMBER 14   At Mount Vernon, Virginia, George Washington dies while still holding his commission as a lieutenant general. Congress abolishes that rank, but Alexander Hamilton, the senior major general, now functions as the military's commanding officer.

1800

JANUARY 5   Sensing that greater military professionalism would be desirable, Secretary of War James McHenry suggests that Congress create a national military academy, along with five subordinate schools for the instruction of army and naval officers.

JUNE   The Department of War is relocated from Philadelphia, Pennsylvania, to the new Federal capital at Washington, D.C.

JUNE 15   Congress, convinced that war with France has all but dissipated, releases all new recruits with three month's pay while the army's strength contracts to 3,429 men of all ranks. Once Alexander Hamilton and Charles C. Pinckney have resigned their commissions, Brigadier General James Wilkinson again reigns as the military's senior officer.

1801

MARCH 4   In Washington, D.C., Thomas Jefferson is inaugurated as the third president and commander in chief. Jefferson, who embraces the idea of a smaller military establishment, begins purging the Federalist-dominated officer corps and replaces many with Republican appointees.

APRIL 1   Captain Meriwether Lewis reports to President Thomas Jefferson as his personal secretary. Lewis' first task is to evaluate the professional and political status of the entire officer corps, with a view toward recommending either their retention or discharge.

APRIL 30   New regulations are adopted to cultivate a "more republican" outlook in the military; hence, the traditional long hair of soldiers, tied in a queue, is abolished in favor of short hair. These new regulations stoke the ire of traditionalists and result in the court-martial of at least one colonel.

DECEMBER 14   At West Point, New York, Major Jonathan Williams, a respected scientist and nephew of Benjamin Franklin, assumes command of the small engineering school coalescing there.

1802

MARCH   Andrew Jackson, a garrulous frontier attorney, is appointed a major general of militia in Knoxville, Tennessee.

MARCH 16   President Thomas Jefferson, true to his republican precepts, reduces the size of the U.S. Army by disbanding the dragoon regiment and two infantry regiments. However, Brigadier General James Wilkinson remains on as commanding general, while a bill authorizing the United States Military Academy at West Point, New York, passes. Jefferson has two goals in mind by creating this institution: to acquire a cadre of professionally trained military engineers whose talents will facilitate frontier settlement, and to politically indoctrinate the new officer class, rendering them favorably disposed towards republican governance.

APRIL 1   President Thomas Jefferson pares the U.S. Army down further by ordering the Regiments of Artillerists and Engi-

neers broken up. Henceforth, the former is consolidated into the Regiment of Artillery, and the latter becomes the Corps of Engineers. The trend towards extreme economy reaches ridiculous proportions when no horses are purchased to pull the cannons; these are either dragged by the gunners or hitched to oxen.

JULY 4   At West Point, New York, the United States Military Academy officially opens. This constitutes the genesis of military professionalism in the U.S. Army, and Major Jonathan Williams, a distinguished scientist and nephew of Benjamin Franklin, serves as the first superintendent.

OCTOBER 12   Having taken several courses, Joseph G. Swift and Simon M. Levy become the first two graduates of the U. S. Military Academy, West Point. Both receive second lieutenant's commissions in the elite Corps of Engineers.

DECEMBER 3   New regulations state that the Corps of Engineers be clad in blue jackets with gold-embroidered collars and cuffs denoting their elite status. The motto engraved on their buttons, "Essayons," remains with the present-day formation.

1803

JANUARY 18   In Washington, D.C., President Thomas Jefferson requests Congress to supply $2,500 for a secret exploring/reconnaissance expedition. He does so to strengthen American claims to western territory as far west as the Pacific Northwest; he appoints Captain Meriwether Lewis to lead the endeavor.

MARCH 15   Among the items Captain Lewis Meriwether begins drawing for his proposed western expedition are 15 new Model 1803 rifles. Constructed at the Harpers Ferry arsenal, these are the army's first standard-issue weapons.

MARCH 19   At Pittsburgh, Pennsylvania, Captain Meriwether Lewis contacts his friend, William Clark, inviting him to serve as the expedition's co-commander. If he accepts, Clark will be restored to rank, receive regular army pay, and obtain a veteran's land grant.

JULY 29   Captain Meriwether Lewis is delayed at Pittsburgh, Pennsylvania, awaiting deliveries of specially-designed, 55-foot-long keel boats for river travel. Meanwhile, he receives word that William Clark has signed onto the expedition.

AUGUST 31   Captain Meriwether Lewis departs down the Ohio River on the nation's first government-sponsored exploring expedition. Captain William Clark, meanwhile, is at his brother's home in Clarksville, Indiana Territory, gathering supplies and intending to join him en route. The pair do not return from their epic voyage for three years, and their findings greatly enhance the scientific and geographical knowledge of the continent's interior.

OCTOBER 14   At Clarksville, Indiana Territory, Captains Meriwether Lewis and William Clark are reunited for the first time in seven years.

NOVEMBER 11   Captains Lewis and Clark order their Corps of Discovery paused at Fort Massac, Illinois Territory, to gather up additional supplies. Two days later they move onto the Mississippi River, and the tempo of exploration increases.

1804

MARCH 9–10   Upper Louisiana is transferred to the United States by Captain Amos Stoddard, Regiment of Artillery, who accepts it from the local Spanish commander. Stoddard functions as acting governor until a civilian replacement is appointed that summer.

MARCH 31   Captains Lewis and Clark make final selections for their 33-man

Corps of Discovery at Wood River, Illinois Territory. It now consists of three squads, each headed by a sergeant.

MAY   Spanish spy General James Wilkinson informs his paymasters of the Lewis and Clark expedition. The Spaniards consequently dispatch cavalry patrols along the Platte and Missouri River Valleys to intercept them.

MAY 14   The Lewis and Clark expedition, numbering 33 men, sails from St. Louis, Missouri Territory, in a keelboat and two pirogue boats. They begin paddling up the Missouri River towards the interior of the continent.

JULY   At West Point, New York, the U.S. Military Academy, West Point, accepts its first Native American cadets, including the half-white Charles Gratiot. He is commissioned and serves with distinction for 32 years before ultimately rising to become Chief of the Corps of Engineers.

AUGUST 20   The Corps of Discovery of Lewis and Clark suffers its only fatality when Sergeant Charles Floyd dies from a burst appendix. He is also the first U.S. Army soldier to be buried west of the Mississippi River.

SEPTEMBER 23–25   Captains Lewis and Clark encounter two villages belonging to the Teton Sioux along the Bad River. The two groups mingle peacefully until some excited Indians try seizing one of the pirogues, but the issue is resolved peacefully.

OCTOBER 27–DECEMBER 31   The Lewis and Clark expedition wanders into a village of the Mandan Indians (North Dakota), where they encounter French trader and translator Toussaint Charbonneau. They hire him as a guide along with his Shoshone wife, Sacagawea.

NOVEMBER 2   Near the site of present-day Bismarck, North Dakota, the Lewis and Clark expedition encamps with friendly Mandans along the banks of the Upper Missouri River. They remain there for the winter, having successfully negotiated treacherous western waters.

1805

MARCH 26   Territory acquired from the Louisiana Purchase is divided into the Territory of New Orleans (administered from New Orleans) and the Louisiana Territory (administered from St. Louis). General James Wilkinson, commanding all military forces at New Orleans, is also appointed to serve as governor.

APRIL 7   In North Dakota, the Lewis and Clark expedition departs from their Mandan hosts and resume paddling up the Missouri River. En route they are greatly assisted by their 16-year-old Shoshone guide, Sacagawea.

JUNE 3–JULY 14   The Lewis and Clark expedition discovers the Marias River which contains five steep falls. Rather than risk running them, the men land and portage (drag) their vessels 18 miles around the obstacles. This arduous feat places them a month behind schedule.

JULY 23   Fort Bellefontaine, Missouri, is constructed by Lieutenant Colonel Jacob Kingsbury, 1st Infantry. This is the first American military post west of the Mississippi River and also serves as a government factory for managing the Indian trade.

Sacajawea guides the Lewis and Clark expedition through the Rocky Mountains. Meriwether Lewis and William Clark led the expedition, which was requested by President Thomas Jefferson in order to learn about the western territories that had been secured for the United States by the Louisiana Purchase of 1803. (Bettmann/Corbis)

AUGUST 9   At St. Louis, Missouri, General James Wilkinson instructs Lieutenant Zebulon M. Pike to scout out territory acquired by the Louisiana Purchase and locate the source of the Mississippi River.

AUGUST 12–18   A small party of soldiers under Captain Meriwether Lewis reaches the Continental Divide near the Bitterroot Range and marches overland to a Shoshone camp. There the local chief recognizes their scout Sacagawea as his long-lost sister.

SEPTEMBER 9   At Fort Bellefontaine, Missouri, Lieutenant Zebulon M. Pike

and 20 men depart to locate the source of the Mississippi River. Their travels take them deep into present-day Minnesota.

SEPTEMBER 23–25   The small expedition of Lieutenant Zebulon M. Pike encounters Sioux villages along the Upper Mississippi River. He holds a council, distributes gifts and whiskey, and concludes the first Indian Treaty in the Louisiana Territory. A small plot of land he purchases at the mouth of the Minnesota River becomes the site of Fort Snelling two decades later.

OCTOBER 7   The Corps of Discovery under Captains Lewis and Clark resumes exploring down the Clearwater River, hoping to reach the Pacific Ocean.

OCTOBER 16   Lieutenant Zebulon M. Pike reaches the Swan River, and then ascends to Leech Lake, Minnesota. This he mistakenly assumes is the source of the Mississippi River. He also warns British traders that they are trespassing on American soil and orders them off.

NOVEMBER 7–15   The Lewis and Clark expedition paddles downstream until they reach the Columbia River. After being delayed a week by stormy weather, they continue on for another 20 miles before finally reaching the Pacific Ocean.

DECEMBER 7   Captains Lewis and Clark encounter the Clatsop Indians and construct a small fort christened Fort Clatsop. They remain there among the tribesmen all winter, collecting scientific samples for the return home next spring.

1806

APRIL 10   Congress revises the Articles of War to include two levels of court-martial, general and garrison (or regimental). Each

of these requires a different board of officers, and each imposes differing levels of punishment. Militiamen, however, remain beyond the judicial grasp of the army and can only be tried by militia officers.

APRIL 30 Lieutenant Zebulon M. Pike's expedition returns to St. Louis, Missouri, mistakenly convinced he has identified the source of the Mississippi River in present-day Minnesota.

JUNE 15 Captains Meriwether Lewis and William Clark ascend the Rocky Mountains and begin their return voyage back to St. Louis, Missouri. En route, they divide into three smaller parties to explore as much terrain as possible.

JULY 13 At Fort Bellefontaine, Missouri, Lieutenant Zebulon M. Pike is ordered by General James Wilkinson to explore and chart parts of the Old Southwest (New Mexico and Colorado). He commands 23 men and is instructed to avoid violating Spanish territory.

JULY 26 Captain Meriwether Lewis and three soldiers defeat eight Blackfoot Indians caught stealing guns and horses; two Indians die in the encounter.

SEPTEMBER 3–OCTOBER 28 Lieutenant Zebulon M. Pike's expedition encounters Pawnees along the Republican River, who mention that Spanish soldiers are out scouting for him. Unfazed, Pike continues seeking the headwaters of the Arkansas River.

OCTOBER 8 Aaron Burr, a former vice president, approaches General James Wilkinson with his plan to recruit an armed force, attack Mexico, and establish an independent republic. Burr wants Wilkinson to serve as his deputy.

OCTOBER 21 General James Wilkinson, always eager to save his own skin, contacts President Thomas Jefferson and informs him of Aaron Burr's plan to establish his own independent country.

OCTOBER 23 Captains Lewis and Clark conclude their famous expedition by landing in St. Louis, Missouri, at noon, whereupon Lewis begins composing his final report to President Thomas Jefferson.

NOVEMBER 15 In present-day Colorado, Lieutenant Zebulon M. Pike espies a large mountain 18,000 feet in height; although he never climbs it, the mount is eventually named Pike's Peak in his honor.

NOVEMBER 25 General James Wilkinson imposes martial law in New Orleans and arrests known supporters of Aaron Burr, both in the city and at Fort Adams.

NOVEMBER 27 President Thomas Jefferson issues orders to state militia and army units in the Louisiana Territory to stop the conspiracy of former vice president Aaron Burr.

1807

FEBRUARY 18 Lieutenant Edmund P. Gaines, stationed at Fort Stoddart, Louisiana Territory, is informed that wanted fugitive Aaron Burr is nearby. Gaines rounds up several soldiers, arrests Burr, and brings him back to the fort.

FEBRUARY 26 In present-day New Mexico, Lieutenant Zebulon M. Pike's expedition is accosted by Spanish cavalry along the Rio Grande. The Americans are taken into armed custody and marched to Santa Fe for questioning. Pike insists that he never intended to violate Spanish territory and assumed he was near the Red River.

APRIL   Lieutenant Zebulon M. Pike, having been closely interrogated by Spanish authorities for several weeks, is released and returns to the United States. As a confidant of General James Wilkinson, however, he is viewed as a possible co-conspirator in Aaron Burr's conspiracy.

JULY   6   In Norfolk, Virginia, aspiring attorney Winfield Scott unofficially joins a cavalry unit in the wake of the 1807 attack of HMS *Leopard* on the USS *Chesapeake*. This day Scott energetically surrounds and captures a party of British sailors who have come ashore looking for supplies. This is the beginning of a long and illustrious military career.

1808

APRIL   11   Congress, reacting to the British attack on the American vessel USS *Chesapeake*, responds to President Thomas Jefferson's exhortations and expands the U.S. Army. Consequently, five new infantry regiments (numbered 3rd to 7th) are added along with a regiment of riflemen, a regiment of light dragoons, and a battery of horse (or "flying") artillery. Two additional brigadier generals are also authorized to command them.

MAY–JUNE   Captain George Peter begins experimenting with the first mounted battery of horse artillery possessed by the U.S. Army. He successfully puts his two six-pounder cannons and two five-and-one-half-inch howitzers through their paces at numerous public demonstrations.

MAY 8   Winfield Scott, the six-foot-six-inch-tall former law student, is commissioned a captain in the elite Regiment of

Regiment of Riflemen

Despite a cherished national mythology of American riflemen in the War for Independence, the U.S. Army lacked standing rifle formations for 25 years before President Thomas Jefferson, reacting to the British attack upon the frigate USS *Chesapeake*, reinstituted them in 1808. This new formation, the Regiment of Riflemen, was the military's first self-consciously elite formation. Whereas regular soldiers wore blue uniforms and carried muskets, the riflemen were clad in green jackets with black collars and cuffs and were issued the new Harpers Ferry Model 1803 rifle. Far from the Kentucky "long rifle" of frontier lore, this was a short weapon of jaeger derivation, but could shoot with deadly accuracy out to 250 yards. During the War of 1812, riflemen first made the headlines under Captain Benjamin Forsyth, who led several daring raids across the St. Lawrence River and fought bravely at the captures of York and Fort George in 1813. On May 5, 1814, another company under Major Daniel Appling ambushed a British naval force at Sandy Creek, New York, capturing 200 sailors and Royal Marines. Congress was impressed by the performance of the riflemen, so in 1814 they authorized creation of three additional regiments. On August 4, 1814, Major Ludowick Morgan and several companies from the 1st and 4th Regiments repulsed a determined British attack at Conjockta Creek, New York, thereby sparing the city of Buffalo from capture. All four regiments were consolidated as the Regiment of Riflemen in 1815 under Colonel Thomas Adams Smith, and they spent the next six years performing useful work along the western frontier. The unit was disbanded by Congress in 1821 for economic reasons, but the Regiment of Riflemen is a spiritual forebear of today's Special Forces.

Light Artillery. He remains on active duty until 1861, 53 years hence.

DECEMBER 2   General James Wilkinson, cleared of any complicity with the Aaron Burr conspiracy, is ordered back to New Orleans to take command of the new 3rd, 5th, and 7th Infantries, the Rifle Regiment, and several light artillery companies. This aggregate represent the largest American military force assembled in recent years.

1809

FEBRUARY 15   Revolutionary War veterans Wade Hampton of South Carolina and Peter Gansevoort of New York are appointed the army's newest brigadier generals.

MAY 29   General James Wilkinson, ignoring orders to redeploy his troops north to Fort Adams, encamps them at swampy Terre aux Boeufs, 12 miles south of New Orleans. Consequently, men begin dying off in large numbers due to disease. Captain Winfield Scott grows so disgusted by Wilkinson's neglect that he tends his resignation.

SEPTEMBER   Near New Orleans, General James Wilkinson begins transferring his command from Terre aux Boeufs to Fort Adams. Presently, only 414 sickly soldiers can be mustered for duty and the general is summoned to Washington, D.C., to account for his actions. Brigadier General Wade Hampton, a personal enemy of Wilkinson, is tapped to succeed him.

NOVEMBER   At Fort Adams, Mississippi Territory, Captain Winfield Scott is accused of publicly issuing derogatory remarks about General James Wilkinson. He is ordered to stand trial because of it.

1810

JANUARY 10   At Fort Adams, Captain Winfield Scott is court-martialed for slandering General James Wilkinson in public. He is found guilty of "un-officer like conduct" and sentenced to a 12-month suspension from pay. Scott subsequently duels with the officer who accused him and both men miss; he retires in disgust to Virginia.

1811

JANUARY 11   Back in Virginia, a disenchanted Winfield Scott passes his time studying European military texts. After hearing that his old regimental commander died, he experiences a change of heart and petitions the War Department for reinstatement as senior captain. The request is denied so he continues studying.

JANUARY 15   Eager to secure the southern frontier from Spanish and Indian attacks, Congress surreptitiously authorizes President James Madison to dispatch army troops and seize East Florida. The elite Regiment of Riflemen under Lieutenant Colonel Thomas Adams Smith, assisted by a small party of light dragoons and Georgia militia, begin marching towards the region.

JUNE 1   In Washington, D.C., General James Wilkinson undergoes a general court-martial, facing eight charges and 25 specifications relating to his alleged complicity with the Burr conspiracy. Congress also investigates his mishandling of events at Terre aux Boeufs, which incurred the deaths of several hundred soldiers.

JULY 8   At Vincennes, Indiana Territory, Shawnee chief Tecumseh meets with Territorial Governor William Henry Harrison and denounces the Treaty of 1809 that absconded with millions of acres of Indian land. Harrison, sensing that a fight is brewing, requests that Secretary of War William Eustis dispatch Colonel John P. Boyd's 4th Infantry to the region.

SEPTEMBER   19   Governor William Henry Harrison departs from Vincennes, Indiana Territory, having cobbled together a force of 900 army regulars and militia. He then marches along the Wabash River towards the illegal Indian settlement at Prophetstown on Tippecanoe Creek, intending to evict the inhabitants by force, if necessary.

NOVEMBER 6–7   The Battle of Tippecanoe, Indiana Territory, occurs after the army of General William Henry Harrison encamps near the makeshift Indian village of Prophetstown. Warriors under Tenskwatawa, the Shawnee Prophet and Tecumseh's brother, storm into the American camp and nearly overrun it. Fortunately, they are repulsed by accurate musketry, and at dawn, a charge by mounted troops disperses the attackers. Harrison's losses are 66 killed and 151 wounded, a loss rate of nearly 25 percent; Indian casualties are unknown but presumed equally heavy. The battle also convinces many westerners that Great Britain is arming and inciting the Indians to violence.

1812

JANUARY 2–12   As war fever strikes Washington, D.C., Congress further expands the U.S. Army by adding 10 infantry regiments, 8th–17th, a second regiment of light dragoons, two artillery regiments numbered 2nd and 3rd, and six additional companies of rangers. Two major generals and seven brigadier generals are also authorized.

JANUARY 27   Former Secretary of War Henry Dearborn becomes the army's senior major general; he is assigned to head the Northern Department along the Canadian frontier.

FEBRUARY–MARCH   In Washington, D.C., a militant Congress, headed by a clique of so-called "War Hawks," passes legislation authorizing the recruitment of 30,000 federal volunteers. Funding is also provided to purchase horses for the artillery, although shortages of draft animals persist throughout the War of 1812.

FEBRUARY 14–22   General James Wilkinson is acquitted of all charges relating to the Burr Conspiracy and the Congressional investigation of his Terre aux Boeufs debacle adjourns without further deliberation. Feeling vindicated, the general returns back to his command in New Orleans.

MARCH   In Washington, D.C., Revolutionary War veteran Thomas Pinckney gains appointment as the second major general in charge of the Southern Department, Morgan Lewis becomes the new Quartermaster General, and Joseph Bloomfield, James Winchester, and Thomas Flournoy are installed as brigadier generals. A Commissary General of Purchases position also arises through legislation, but its duties are poorly defined and it remains unfilled for several months.

MARCH 18   In Florida, troops and militia under Lieutenant Colonel Thomas Adams Smith move down the St. Mary's River, and establish a loose blockade of Spanish-held St. Augustine. The ensuing fiasco, conducted by shoestring forces, is known as the "Patriot War" and peters out in embarrassing failure.

APRIL   In Washington, D.C., President James Madison approves General Henry Dearborn's plan for the conquest of Canada. It involved a four-pronged thrust thrusts across Lake Champlain to Montreal, across the Niagara River to York, from Sackett's Harbor, New York, to Kingston, and from Detroit, Michigan Territory, into western-most Upper Canada. To facilitate the latter offensive, Madison orders the 4th Infantry from Vincennes, Indiana Territory, to Detroit, Michigan Territory, to assist Governor William Hull.

APRIL 8   William Hull, governor of the Michigan Territory, is promoted to brigadier general in the U.S. Army and tasked with organizing an expedition from Detroit against Malden, Upper Canada. He commands a small force of one army regiment and three Ohio militia regiments

but Hull, cognizant that success is predicated on American control of Lake Erie, insists on increased naval support. The government promises to oblige him.

APRIL 10   As war clouds with Great Britain gather, Congress authorizes President James Madison to mobilize up to 100,000 state militia for up to six months. Secretary of War William Eustis reminds all 17 states of their requisite manpower quotas, but the governors of New England, citing Constitutional principles, refuse to contribute. This recalcitrance bodes ill for any projected invasion of Canada.

APRIL 23   In Washington, D.C., Congress creates the new civilian-dominated Corps of Artificers under the Quartermaster General. These are to perform specific labors such as carpentry, blacksmithing, and masonry for the army. The Corps of Engineers is also strengthened by a new company of "Bombardiers, Sappers, and Miners."

APRIL 29   At West Point, New York, the U.S. Military Academy is enlarged with additional professors and engineering officers, and a new library with the latest military texts. The number of cadets enrolled at this time is 250.

MAY 14   In Washington, D.C., Congress legislates the Department of Ordnance into existence; this is headed by a colonel wielding the title Commissary-General of Ordnance.

JUNE 1   In Washington, D.C., President James Madison outlines to Congress the necessity of going to war with Great Britain. He cites insults to the American flag at sea in the form of impressment, and arming and inciting Indians to hostilities along the western frontier.

JUNE 9   The 4th Infantry under Lieutenant Colonel James Miller arrives in Ohio, en route to joining the main column under General William Hull. However, Miller's forced march exhausts the troops and requires him to rest them for several days.

JUNE 15   In Ohio, the Northwest Army of General William Hull begins its fateful march to Detroit, Michigan Territory. The three militia regiments clamor loudly about not being paid, but an armed demonstration by the 4th Infantry mutes further protests and the advance resumes.

JUNE 18   As the War of 1812 commences, the U.S. Army consists of 6,700 newly-recruited soldiers, poorly uniformed and equipped, and whose discipline remains problematic at best. However, American political leaders hope that, once backed by thousands of militiamen, the whole can overwhelm the estimated 4,500 British garrisoning Canada.

JUNE 26   Finally at war, Congress further enlarges the U.S. Army by creating eight more infantry regiments, numbered 18th–25th. The military's authorized strength officially stands at 35,603, but the recruits enrolled so far barely constitute a third of that total.

JULY   To flesh out the army's command structure, Congress approves the appointment of Thomas H. Cushing, John Armstrong, Alexander Smyth, and John Chandler as brigadier generals.

JULY 2   Governor John Cotton of Connecticut, a Federalist who opposes war with Great Britain, declares that he will not provide the federal government with militia forces. His defiance eliminates a relatively well-equipped and -trained manpower pool from the war effort.

JULY 12   General William Hull commences offensive operations against Upper Canada by crossing 1,500 militia and regulars across the Detroit River. The Americans occupy Sandwich, where Hull dallies. He is counting on rumors of Canadian discontent to produce large numbers of deserters, but few appear. Worse, 200 of his Ohio militia rest upon their Constitutional scruples and refuse to invade Canada.

JULY 16   Colonel Lewis Cass, commanding a force of Ohio militia and a company of the 4th Infantry under Captain Josiah Snelling, vanquishes the British picket guarding a bridge at Aux Canard River. General William Hull, meanwhile, lacks heavy artillery and uses it as a pretext to halt and not attack the British fortified position at Fort Malden, Amherstburg.

JULY 17   At Fort Mackinac, Michigan, a surprise British raid by 600 British, Canadians, and Indians under Captain Charles Roberts captures the 61-man American garrison of Lieutenant Porter Hanks. Porter was unaware that war had been declared and this bloodless victory encourages increasing numbers of Native Americans to link Britain's cause to their own.

AUGUST 4–7   Near Fort Malden, Upper Canada, General William Hull begins fearing for his lines of communication below Detroit and dispatches a militia force to escort a supply train waiting at the River Raisin. These are subsequently ambushed at Brownstown by Tecumseh's warriors and scattered after losing 17 dead and 11 wounded.

AUGUST 5   In Boston, Massachusetts, Governor Caleb Strong joins Connecticut by refusing the federal government access to militia forces necessary to invade Canada. Moreover, he declares a day of prayer and fasting to protest the war. Public hostility is also directed at Major General Henry Dearborn, tasked with defending New England's coastline with scanty resources.

AUGUST 8   General William Hull, feeling threatened by the approach of British reinforcements under General Isaac Brock from Niagara, abandons Canada and withdraws into the confines of Detroit. This act yields the strategic initiative to Brock, who intends to cow the timid Hull into surrendering.

AUGUST 9   At Detroit, Michigan Territory, General William Hull again dispatches troops to escort a supply train from the River Raisin, only this time he selects Lieutenant Colonel James Miller and his 4th Infantry. Fourteen miles south of Detroit, Miller encounters British and Indians at Maguaga and receives a heavy fire. The Americans nonetheless charge bayonets and rout their opponents, losing 18 dead and 64 wounded. This is the first American land victory of the war, but Hull subsequently orders Miller back to Detroit.

AUGUST 15   At Fort Dearborn (Chicago), Illinois Territory, 400 Potawatomie warriors massacre the small American garrison of Captain Nathan Heald. The Americans evacuate that post under orders from General William Hull and fight valiantly but in vain, losing 53 soldiers, women, and children. Among the slaughtered are noted scout William Wells and Lieutenant George Ronan, the first West Point graduate slain in combat.

AUGUST 15–16   Outside Detroit, Michigan, General Isaac Brock demands that General William Hull surrender, lest his Indian allies massacre the garrison

should fighting break out. He initially rejects the offer and the next day 700 British and Canadians cross the Detroit River and surround the fort. Hull, convinced he is outnumbered, timorously surrenders Detroit and 2,000 men to a decidedly smaller force. Detroit remains the only American city captured by an enemy and its loss shocks public opinion. It also emboldens Indians throughout the region to take up arms on behalf of Great Britain.

AUGUST 23   British general Isaac Brock makes a quick transit from Detroit to Fort George on the Niagara frontier, in anticipation of another invasion. Across the Niagara River, New York militia general Stephen Van Rensselaer struggles to assemble his mixed force of untrained soldiers and raw militia.

SEPTEMBER 4   Fort Harrison, Indiana Territory, is suddenly attacked by Shawnee warriors. Captain Zachary Taylor, the garrison commander, orders his company of the 7th Infantry to hold their ground at all costs, and beats back their assaults.

SEPTEMBER 5   Fort Madison, Iowa Territory, is attacked by 200 Winnebagos. The garrison, consisting of one company of the 1st Infantry, repels several assaults and the Indians gradually abandon their siege.

SEPTEMBER 17   Unable to secure a general's commission in the U.S. Army, William Henry Harrison becomes a major general of the Kentucky militia and makes preparations to retake Detroit, Michigan, as soon as practical.

SEPTEMBER 20–21   At Sackets Harbor, New York, Captain Benjamin Forsyth sails his company of the Regiment of

Riflemen to Upper Canada by boat. Once ashore, they surprise the British supply depot at Gananoque, taking several militia prisoners before returning safely. These are also the first regular army troops in northern New York.

OCTOBER 4   Across from Ogdensburg, New York, British forces under aged Colonel Lethbridge launch a haphazard attack across the St. Lawrence River. They are easily repelled by artillery commanded by militia general Jacob Jennings Brown. This act initiates Brown's highly successful military career.

OCTOBER 13   In western New York, the Battle of Queenstown Heights unfolds as a mixed force of 1,300 U.S. Army troops and New York militia under General Stephen Van Rensselaer crosses the Niagara River to establish a lodgement. General Isaac Brock meets the invaders head on with 1,000 troops and Indians.

Brock is killed in action, but the Americans fail to receive promised reinforcements from the New York side. British general Roger Hale Sheaffe subsequently arrives with reinforcements and the remaining troops under Lieutenant Colonel Winfield Scott surrender. In this second humiliating defeat, American losses are 240 killed and wounded and 958 captured; the British lose 14 killed, 77 wounded, and 21 missing, along with irreplaceable Brock.

OCTOBER 16   In western New York, General Stephen Van Rensselaer, humiliated by his defeat at Queenstown Heights, resigns from command. General Alexander Smyth of the U.S. Army, a pompous braggart, succeeds him and resumes the campaign against Canada.

OCTOBER 17–30   Illinois territorial governor Ninian Edwards attacks hostile Kickapoo villages near Lake Peoria with

The death of General Brock at the Battle of Queenstown Heights in October, 1812. (Metropolitan Toronto Reference Library)

militia and some U.S. Rangers. Resistance is slight, the villages are burned, and the Americans conclude their escapade without further incident. It is one of few offensive successes by Americans in the West.

NOVEMBER 19 In Quebec, Lower Canada, the captured Lieutenant Colonel Winfield Scott learns that the British have captured several Irish deserters serving in the American army and intends to hang them. Scott protests the threat and, following his parole, he calls the captives' plight to the attention of authorities.

NOVEMBER 19–23 At Plattsburg, New York, General Henry Dearborn leads his army of barely-trained U.S. troops and militia north to capture the strategic city of Montreal. At the Canadian border, however, Dearborn's militia rests on their constitutional scruples and refuses to cross. The general, lacking sufficient manpower to proceed further, cancels the invasion. The only fighting occurs when troops under Colonel Zebulon M. Pike are fired on by other Americans in the dark, causing several casualties.

NOVEMBER 21 A protracted artillery duel begins between the garrisons of Fort George and Fort Niagara from the Niagara River. When Betsy Doyle's husband is wounded, she helps man one of the guns.

NOVEMBER 28 Along the Niagara River, General Alexander Smyth begins offensive operations by landing several detachments on the Canadian side. Lieutenant Colonel Charles Boerstler, 14th Infantry, seizes a bridge then hastily returns to the American side, marooning a party of infantry and sailors. A second wave led by Colonel William H. Winder tries to rescue them, but encounters stiff resistance while crossing and retreats. The Americans are captured and Smyth vows to try again.

NOVEMBER 30 At Niagara, General Alexander Smyth makes another fumbling attempt to cross the river by ordering his troops to man their boats—then cancelling the operation on account of a downpour. Chaos ensues in the American camp as the militia runs amok, angrily firing their guns in the air. Smyth is forced to run for his life from the encampment.

DECEMBER 3 In Washington, D.C., Secretary of War William Eustis is blamed for the recent spate of military disasters and resigns from office. He is temporarily succeeded by Secretary of State James Monroe.

DECEMBER 17 A column of Kentucky cavalry, militia, and army regulars under Lieutenant Colonel John B. Campbell, 19th Infantry, braves deep snow and intense cold to attack Miami Indians along the Mississinewa River, Indiana Territory. After burning the village, the Americans withdraw several miles and encamp for the evening along the river bank.

DECEMBER 18 At dawn, Lieutenant Colonel John B. Campbell's encampment is attacked by vengeful Miami warriors at the Mississinewa River. His infantry holds the perimeter against Indian attacks and a cavalry charges finally disperses them in the growing light. American losses are eight dead and 48 wounded, but this successful spoiling attack keeps the Miamis from further mischief on the American left flank.

DECEMBER 20 In Ohio, General William H. Harrison orders the left wing of his army under Brigadier General James Winchester to advance to the Maumee Rapids. Winchester complies but his troops, still clad in summer garments, suffer from intense cold and dwindle down to 1,200 rank and file.

1813

JANUARY 7 Major General Andrew Jackson departs Nashville, Tennessee, with 2,500 militiamen and marches for New Orleans. He intends to assist General James Wilkinson in the capture of Spanish-held West Florida. Wilkinson, however, resents Jackson's interference and asks the War Department to rescind his orders.

JANUARY 10 In Washington, D.C., newly exchanged Lieutenant Colonel Winfield Scott informs President James Madison of the plight of Irish deserters in Canada, presently facing execution. Madison vows to execute the identical number of British soldiers in retaliation if the Irish are harmed.

JANUARY 13 In Washington, D.C., Brigadier General John Armstrong, scheming author of the Newburgh Addresses against Congress in 1783 and a former ambassador to France, is barely confirmed as the new Secretary of War. Though acerbic by nature and a presidential aspirant, he is nonetheless a distinct improvement over his predecessor.

JANUARY 18–19 General James Winchester orders his army out from the Maumee River, Ohio, and makes for the settlement of Frenchtown, Michigan Territory. His shivering Kentuckians rout some British troops they encounter, then occupy the town. Winchester, however, takes no special precautions against being attacked in turn.

JANUARY 22–23 The Battle of Frenchtown (or River Raisin), Michigan Territory, occurs when 1,000 half-frozen Kentucky militia under General James Winchester are overrun by British and Native Americans commanded by Colonel Henry A. Procter. Winchester's entire force

is captured at a loss of 24 British dead and 158 wounded. The Indians, emboldened by the easy victory, take to drinking and massacre 60 wounded prisoners on the following morning. Thereafter, "Remember the Raisin!" becomes a rallying cry for the Kentuckians.

JANUARY 23–FEBRUARY 1 General William Henry Harrison, livid over news of the Frenchtown massacre, falls back from the Maumee River, Ohio, until he reaches the Maumee Rapids. There he orders construction of Fort Meigs, a spacious fortification designed by engineer Captain Eleazar D. Wood, a West Point graduate.

FEBRUARY 6–7 At Ogdensburg, New York, Major Benjamin Forsyth's rifle company dashes across the frozen St. Lawrence River and captures the Canadian settlement of Elizabethtown. The raiders empty the jail of prisoners and return safely to the American side; Forsyth consequently gains promotion to brevet lieutenant colonel.

FEBRUARY 21–22 The British, stung by Lieutenant Colonel Benjamin Forsyth's constant raids, counterattack American forces garrisoning Ogdensburg, New York. Dashing across the ice, they disperse the militia and drive his rifle company from the town. Forsyth retires to Sacketts Harbor while the victorious British plunder the settlement.

MARCH 3 In Washington, D.C., Congress further expands the U.S. Army by adding 18 new infantry regiments numbered 26th–44th. Brigadier General James Wilkinson is promoted to major general, as are William Henry Harrison, Wade Hampton, and Morgan Lewis. Secretary

John Armstrong also pushes through the promotion of younger, capable officers such as George Izard, Zebulon M. Pike, William H. Winder, Duncan McArthur, and Lewis Cass to brigadier general.

MARCH 15   At Natchez, Mississippi Territory, General Andrew Jackson's militia force receives orders from Secretary of War John Armstrong cancelling his march to New Orleans. Moreover, he is ordered to discharge his entire force without pay or supplies. Jackson angrily complies, transporting all his sick and injured troops home through harsh winter conditions. His imposition of strict discipline also earns him a reputation as "Old Hickory."

APRIL 12–15   Mobile, Alabama, is surrounded by American military and naval forces under General James Wilkinson. The Spanish garrison at Fort Charlotte surrenders without a shot, after which Colonel John Bowyer begins construction Fort Bowyer to guard the entrance of Mobile Bay.

APRIL 27   York, Ontario (Toronto), the provincial capital of Upper Canada, is attacked by an amphibious force of 1,700 men under Commodore Isaac Chauncey and General Henry Dearborn. General Zebulon M. Pike, the noted explorer, lands and routs 700 British defenders under General Roger Hale Sheaffe, only to die in a magazine explosion. American losses are 54 dead and around 200 wounded; the British tally is 62 dead, 34 wounded, and 50 missing. Discipline subsequently breaks down and American troops, assisted by Canadian dissidents, burn the settlement.

APRIL 28–MAY 9   Fort Meigs, Maumee River, Ohio, is besieged by British and Indian forces under Brigadier General Henry Procter. General William Henry Harrison, commanding 1,000 defenders, is expecting the arrival of a Kentucky militia brigade under General Green Clay, at which point he intends to sortie against the enemy batteries.

MAY 1   In Washington, D.C., Secretary of War John Armstrong authorizes publication of the *Rules and Regulations of the Army of the United States.* This is the first attempt to systematize military administration in this war, and routine but essential matters such as recruitment, training, payment, and discipline are all addressed. The War Department also issues new regulations for army uniforms; henceforth, the standard blue coat is stripped of all red collars and cuffs, while a new "Belgic" shako, sporting a high false front, is authorized.

MAY 4–5   At Fort Meigs, Ohio, General William Henry Harrison is reinforced by Kentucky militia under General Green Clay and sorties against the British. His men capture the enemy siege battery but Clay's militia is lured inland by the Indians, who quickly surround and massacre them. General Henry Procter, however, lifts the siege four days later returns to Detroit. The Americans, while victorious, suffer losses of 200 killed and 500 captured.

MAY 15   In East Florida, the so-called "Patriot War" ignominiously ends after Congress refuses to approve its annexation. General Thomas Pinckney is ordered to evacuate all American forces back to Georgia, including a detachment of elite riflemen under Colonel Thomas A. Smith.

MAY 16   In Washington, D.C., Congress votes to abolish flogging in the U.S. Army, although the practice will be revived in 1833.

MAY 27   The Battle of Fort George, Upper Canada, unfolds as an amphibious force under General Henry Dearborn and Commodore Isaac Chauncey attacks and captures that noted post. The British under General John Vincent resist handily but are smothered by American firepower; they are chased inland by General Winfield Scott until General Morgan Lewis erroneously halts the pursuit. Vincent is thus enabled to escape in the direction of Burlington Heights and fight another day.

MAY 28–29 The Battle of Sackets Harbor, Lake Ontario (New York), occurs when Governor General Sir George Prevost and Commodore Sir James Lucas Yeo unexpectedly attack this strategic American port while Commodore Isaac Chauncey dallies off Fort George. The 1,200 British initially scatter 500 militia commanded by General Jacob J. Brown, but fail to carry the main works garrisoned by 250 regulars led by Major Thomas Aspinwall, 9th Infantry, and Captain Isaac P. Hayne, 1st Light Dragoons. Once Brown rallies the militia in Prevost's rear, the governor general is unnerved and sounds the retreat. British losses are about 260 men, while the Americans sustain 23 dead and 114 wounded. For his role in this important victory, Brown receives a brigadier general's commission in the regular army.

JUNE 1 In Kentucky, Colonel Richard Mentor Johnson leads his newly recruited mounted riflemen to Ohio, where they join the army of General William Henry Harrison. As militia forces go, these are exceptionally well-trained and eager to fight.

JUNE 6 The Battle of Stoney Creek, Upper Canada, unfolds as 700 British troops under General John Vincent attack an American encampment commanded by Generals John Chandler and William H.

Winder. American security is lax, few sentries are posted, and the British are upon them in force before an alarm is sounded. The 1,600 defenders rally and the British are gradually driven off by daylight but not before capturing both generals. Colonel James Burn, the senior American officer, decides to fall back upon Fort George to regroup. American losses are 17 dead, 30 injured, and 99 missing, while the British sustain 23 killed, 136 wounded, and 55 captured. This battle also marks the furthest American penetration of the Niagara Peninsula from the east.

JUNE 22 In Chesapeake Bay, a British squadron disembarks troops to attack Craney Island off Norfolk, Virginia. They encounter intense artillery fire from batteries designed by Captain Sylvanus Thayer and retreat with heavy losses.

JUNE 24 At Beaver Dams, Upper Canada, an American military expedition of 600 men under Colonel Charles G. Boerstler comes to grief after being surrounded by smaller numbers of British troops and Indians under Lieutenant James Fitzgibbon. Fitzgibbon bluffs Boerstler into believing that he is outnumbered and the American commander, fearing an Indian massacre, timidly complies. This disaster results in the retirement of Major General Henry Dearborn at Niagara.

JUNE 27 In Baltimore, Maryland, Captain George Armistead becomes garrison commander at Fort McHenry. He begins strengthening that position and Armistead, desiring a conspicuous national standard to fly above the ramparts, authorizes Mrs. Mary Pickersgill to sew a larger flag.

JULY 6 At Niagara, General Henry Dearborn, whose lethargic behavior gained him the nickname "Granny," is replaced by General James Wilkinson and reassigned to New York and Boston for the rest of the war. General Wade Hampton, Wilkinson's personal enemy, is also ordered from Virginia to assume command of troops at Plattsburgh, New York.

JULY 10 At Fort George, Colonel Winfield Scott boards 250 soldiers on Commodore Isaac Chauncey's Lake Ontario squadron and recaptures York, Upper Canada. Some military supplies are confiscated; then the invaders depart.

JULY 20–28 Fort Meigs, Ohio, is besieged a second time by British and Indian forces under Brigadier General Henry Procter. Garrison commander General Green Clay is not fooled by a sham battle staged outside the fort by Indians, and the British gradually withdraw.

JULY 27 At Burnt Corn Creek, Alabama Territory, a detachment of Mississippi militia under Colonel James Caller attacks a body of Creek Indians returning from Florida with Spanish arms and gunpowder. The militant "Red Sticks" drive the Americans off, signaling the start of the brief but bloody Creek War.

JULY 29 In Ohio, British general Henry Procter is goaded by Shawnee chief Tecumseh to attack Fort Stephenson on the Sandusky River, Ohio. General William Henry Harrison orders the garrison immediately evacuated but Major George Croghan, commanding 160 soldiers, determines to defend his post to the last.

AUGUST 1 General Henry Procter briefly bombards Fort Stephenson, Ohio, and attacks in broad daylight. He is roundly repulsed by a smaller garrison under Major George Croghan, whose masked cannon, "Old Betsy," is fired point-blank

into their densely packed column. British losses are 90 killed and wounded to an American tally of 1 dead and 7 injured. Croghan receives brevet promotion to lieutenant colonel and becomes a national hero.

AUGUST 9–10 St. Michaels, Maryland, conducts the first "blackout" in American history when it is approached by a British squadron at night. Because the townspeople extinguish all city lights and place lamps in trees and on the masts of vessels, British gunners aim too high, and the town is spared serious damage.

AUGUST 20–SEPTEMBER 4 Major General James Wilkinson arrives at Sackets Harbor, New York, and assumes control of the Northern Army. From here he intends to lead 7,000 recruits down the St. Lawrence River while another force of 3,000 men under General Wade Hampton marches up the Champlain Valley; the two forces will converge in Canada before pressing onto their ultimate objective, Montreal.

AUGUST 30 Fort Meigs, Alabama Territory, is suddenly stormed by 800 Creek warriors under Chief William Weatherford (Red Eagle). The Indians massacre nearly 500 people and the sheer extent of the disaster galvanizes Americans to extract vengeance. The rise of General Andrew Jackson is at hand.

SEPTEMBER 3 Fort Madison, Iowa, is attacked by a large body of Sac and Fox Indians under Black Hawk but are rebuffed by a small garrison of the 1st Infantry.

SEPTEMBER 5 At Sackets Harbor, New York, Secretary of War John Armstrong arrives to confer with General James Wilkinson about the upcoming Montreal campaign. Wilkinson resents his meddling but preparations continue apace.

SEPTEMBER 7 In New York, the expression "Uncle Sam" to denote the United States government first appears in an issue of the Troy *Post*. It is inspired from the practice of stamping all government property "U.S.," as well the name of a local military supplier, Sam Wilson.

SEPTEMBER 18 At Detroit, Michigan, General Henry Procter, reacting to the recent loss of Lake Erie to Commodore Oliver Hazard Perry, orders an immediate evacuation of western Upper Canada. He begins retreating towards the Niagara frontier over the protests of Tecumseh and his Indian allies.

SEPTEMBER 20–25 General William Henry Harrison prepares to sail his army across Lake Erie in pursuit of the fleeing British. Unable to transport horses, he dispatches Colonel Richard M. Johnson's mounted Kentuckians on an end run around the lake to recapture Detroit.

OCTOBER 1 With Detroit secured, General William Henry Harrison departs Fort Malden, Upper Canada, and energetically pursues General Henry Procter's forces up the Thames River Valley. His 3,500 men are spearheaded by Colonel Richard M. Johnson's mounted Kentuckians, who have reunited with the army.

OCTOBER 5 In western Upper Canada, the Battle of the Thames unfolds as 3,000 Americans under General William Henry Harrison overtake fleeing British and Indians under General Henry Procter and Tecumseh. Vengeful Kentuckian cavalry easily disperses the 41st Regiment but have a harder time dislodging 1,000 Indians from nearby woods. Colonel Richard M. Johnson is toppled from his

horse and wounded, but Tecumseh is killed and resistance dwindles. American losses are 12 dead and 22 wounded to a British tally of 12 killed, and 600 captured. Victory here all but eliminates the British threat to the west.

OCTOBER 11 In Nashville, General Andrew Jackson, still hobbled by wounds incurred in a street duel, shepherds his brigade of Tennessee volunteers towards the Coosa River and into the heart of Creek country. Meanwhile, General Thomas Pinckney, empowered by Secretary of War John Armstrong to direct overall operations of the Creek War, adopts a three-pronged approach to crush the insurrection. As one column under Andrew Jackson descends from Tennessee to the north, additional troops will advance from Georgia under General John Floyd while a third column, under General Ferdinand L. Claiborne, marches from the Mississippi Territory.

OCTOBER 26 The Battle of Chateauguay, Lower Canada, occurs when a division of 4,000 Americans under Major General Wade Hampton encounters a force of 1,700 entrenched British, Canadians, and Indians under Lieutenant Colonel Charles De Salaberry. The Americans make a half-hearted attempt to flank the defenders through a swamp, suffers a handful of casualties, then Hampton calls off the invasion and falls back to New York. The retreating force is expertly covered by Brigadier General George Izard.

OCTOBER 29 In Detroit, Brigadier General Lewis Cass is appointed governor the Michigan Territory, a post he occupies for nearly two decades.

NOVEMBER 3 In the Mississippi Territory, 900 Tennessee cavalry under General John Coffee destroy the Creek Indian village of Tallushatchee. The victorious Americans kill 186 warriors and take 86 captives at a cost of five killed and 40 wounded. An orphaned Indian child found on the battlefield is subsequently adopted by General Andrew Jackson.

NOVEMBER 9 The Indian village of Talladega, Mississippi Territory, is destroyed by General Andrew Jackson and 2,000 Tennessee militia. The Indians are nearly annihilated before escaping through a gap in Jackson's line. The Creeks leave 299 warriors dead on the field while the Americans incur 17 killed and 82 wounded. Food shortages then force Jackson back to his main base at Fort Strother.

NOVEMBER 11 The Battle of Crysler's Farm, Upper Canada, transpires when an ailing Major General James Wilkinson sails 2,400 men down the St. Lawrence river, lands, and attacks an 800-man British force shadowing his advance. British colonel Joseph W. Morrison proves tactically astute and skillfully repulses several uncoordinated American thrusts against his line by Brigadier General John P. Boyd, the actual American commander. Brigadier General Leonard Covington is killed before Wilkinson finally calls off the battle and withdraws back to the river to embark. British losses are 22 dead, 148 wounded, and nine missing to an American tally of 102 killed, 237 wounded, and 100 missing. This concludes the American campaign against Montreal, and Wilkinson enters winter quarters in northern New York.

NOVEMBER 13 Major General James Wilkinson lands his soldiers at the Salmon River, New York, where they march overland to French Mills and construct winter quarters.

NOVEMBER 14 Brigadier General Ferdinand L. Claiborne leads a militia column against the Creek village of Econochaca, or "Holy Ground," in the Mississippi Territory. He is assisted by the veteran 3rd U.S. Infantry, which bolsters his untrained militia levies.

NOVEMBER 17–18 At Fort Strother, Mississippi Territory, General Andrew Jackson weathers a mutiny brought on by endemic supply shortages. However, after a supply train arrives and the men are fed, they insist on leaving. A bristling Jackson then deploys a company directly in their path and threatens to shoot anyone attempting to depart. The soldiers, knowing full well their commander's temperament, return to camp.

NOVEMBER 29 General John Floyd leads a detachment of 950 Georgia militia and 400 allied Creeks under Chief William McIntosh engages against Creek Indians at Autosee, Alabama Territory. Floyd suffers 11 killed and 54 wounded to an Indian loss estimated at 200. The Americans burn a nearby village, then withdraw back to the Chattahoochee River.

DECEMBER French Mills, New York, is the scene of suffering comparable to Valley Forge. Incompetence in the Quartermaster Department and Major General James Wilkinson's indifference to the plight to his men results in several hundred deaths through sickness, frostbite, and malnutrition.

DECEMBER 9–12 At Fort Strother, General Andrew Jackson incurs another mutiny brought on by expiring enlistments. After learning his men intend to depart en masse at night, he parades them in front of two armed cannons and vows not one will leave the encampment until reinforcements arrive. After the reinforcements arrive, he discharges the whole save for some willing volunteers.

DECEMBER 10   At Fort George, militia general George McClure hastily evacuates his post in the face of a rumored British attack; before departing he burns the Canadian village of Newark to deny it to the enemy. This singular act harbors unforeseen and unsavory consequences.

DECEMBER 18   A nighttime attack by British forces under newly arrived Lieutenant General Gordon Drummond captures Fort Niagara, New York. The Americans suffer 65 dead, 15 wounded, and 350 captured; British losses are negligible by comparison, six dead and five wounded. This successful action also sets the stage for retaliatory action along the American side of the Niagara River.

DECEMBER 23–24   At Econochaca (Holy Ground), Mississippi Territory, General Ferdinand L. Claiborne attacks and defeats the Creek Indian inhabitants. Resistance is fanatical, stoked by medicine men whose spells supposedly protect the warriors from bullets, but Claiborne clinches the battle with a bayonet charge by the 3rd U.S. Infantry. Chief William Weatherford jumps off a high bluff into the Tallapoosa River below and escapes. American losses are one killed and 20 wounded.

DECEMBER 29–30   British major general Phineas Riall systematically burns American settlements along the Niagara River region, including Black Rock and Buffalo, New York. Militiamen under General Amos Hall fail to mount effective resistance and flee the battlefield. For a loss of 112 men, Riall despoils the frontier and inflicts 30 dead, 40 wounded, and 69 captured.

1814

JANUARY 22   General Andrew Jackson marches from Fort Strother, Mississippi Territory, with 850 newly recruited Tennessee militia to attack a large Indian encampment at Emuckfau Creek. The Indians strike first, however, routing the Americans left under General John Coffee. Severe fighting ensues and Jackson only extricates himself after sustaining 25 dead and 75 wounded. The Americans fall back upon Fort Strother, hotly pursued.

JANUARY 24   In Washington, D.C., Secretary of War John Armstrong continues with his program of military reforms by purging the senior officer corps of deadwood. Younger, more energetic men like Jacob Brown and George Izard rise to major general while Winfield Scott, Eleazer W. Ripley, Alexander Macomb, Edmund P. Gaines, Thomas Adams Smith, and Daniel Bissell advance to brigadier.

The average age of American leadership accordingly drops to a very youthful 36 years, with Scott the youngest at 28.

In the Alabama Territory, General Andrew Jackson's rearguard is roughly handled while crossing Entitachopco Creek and a panic ensues. The general personally intervenes to prevent his retreat becoming a rout and the Creeks finally withdraw. Jackson manages to keep his command intact but the Tennessee militiamen suffer from low morale, food shortages, and their own undisciplined nature. He consequently spends several weeks properly training his charge and is further augmented by the addition of the new 39th U.S. Infantry.

JANUARY 27   In Washington, D.C., Congress increases U.S. Army manpower ceilings to 67,773 men, although only two-thirds of that amount is recruited.

A proposal by President James Madison to raise 100,000 volunteers is immediately voted down.

At Calabee Creek, Alabama Territory, General John Floyd and his 1,300 Georgia and South Carolina militiamen, assisted by 400 allied Lower Creeks, are assailed in their camp by Chief William Weatherford. The Americans sustain heavy losses and are hard pressed to maintain their position. The Creeks are driven off at dawn by artillery. Enemy losses are estimated at around 200, while Floyd suffers 17 dead and 132 wounded. The Americans are forced to withdraw back to their base at Fort Mitchell, Georgia.

FEBRUARY 10   In Washington, D.C., Congress authorizes another four infantry regiments, numbered 45th–48th, for the U.S. Army. Manpower, unfortunately, remains a pressing problem and most battalions remain skeletal at half-strength or less.

MARCH 24   In northern New York, Major General George Izard assumes command of American forces at Plattsburg. Major General Jacob Brown is also ordered by Secretary John Armstrong to take charge of affairs along the Niagara frontier at Buffalo.

MARCH 26   At Albany, New York, former general William Hull is court-martialed for treason relating to his surrender of Detroit. He is found guilty and sentenced to death but, in light of his prior service during the Revolutionary War, President James Madison commutes his sentence.

MARCH 27   In the Alabama Territory, General Andrew Jackson and 2,700 men confront a large Creek force of 1,300 men and women at Horseshoe Bend, a strongly fortified bank of the Tallapoosa River. An artillery bombardment proves ineffective, so Jackson orders the position carried at bayonet point by the 39th Infantry. Resistance is fierce and Lieutenant Sam Houston is severely wounded, but the Creeks are driven into the river. The Americans sustain 47 dead and 159 wounded, while allied Creeks and Cherokees suffer an additional 23 killed and 47 wounded; Creek losses are estimated at 1,000 or more. Victory here dramatically concludes the Creek War, rendering Jackson a national hero.

MARCH 28   General Andrew Jackson, following up his victory at Horseshoe Bend, begins cutting a wide swath of destruction through the heart of Creek territory, burning villages and crops. The general refuses all peace overtures until Chief William Weatherford appears at his camp and surrenders in person.

MARCH 30   At French Mills, New York, Major General James Wilkinson and 4,000 soldiers march against the stone fortification at La Colle Mill, Lower Canada, in freezing weather. The small British garrison easily withstands a bombardment by Wilkinson's light cannon, and he incurs 254 casualties before the action is suspended. This ineptly handled affair causes a public outcry and leads directly to the general's dismissal.

APRIL–JUNE   At Buffalo, New York, Brigadier General Winfield Scott assumes command of the Left Division once Major General Jacob J. Brown returns to Sackets Harbor. He consequently begins an intensive training regimen, and by summer, Scott's men can maneuver with the precision of veterans for the first time in this war. The towering and impetuous leader is eager to confirm their abilities under fire.

APRIL 2   Physician and Surgeon General of the Army James Tilton, seeking to compile better scientific information relative to the health of the troops, orders medical officers to keep meteorological observations on a daily basis.

APRIL 18–19 At Fort Jackson, Alabama Territory, General Andrew Jackson is ordered by Major General Thomas Pinckney to march the bulk of his army back to Tennessee for immediate discharge. Jackson also receives promotion to brigadier general in the U.S. Army.

MAY 1 At Plattsburgh, New York, Major General George Izard begins an intense training regimen for his tattered soldiers. He is among American senior field commanders in possessing professional European training in France, and his resurrection of the Right Division exceeds General Winfield Scott's better-known efforts at Buffalo.

MAY 11 General William Henry Harrison is angered by his treatment by Secretary of War John Armstrong and resigns from the army. Brigadier General Duncan McArthur succeeds him to lead the Northwest Army, although he commands only the merest handfuls of troops.

MAY 12 In Washington, D.C., Congress approves a major reorganization scheme for the U.S. Army, whereby the three artillery regiments are consolidated into the Corps of Artillery, two cavalry units are also brought together into a single Regiment of Light Dragoons, and three additional rifle regiments, numbered 2nd–4th, are recruited.

MAY 22 For his outstanding successes in the Creek War, Andrew Jackson is again promoted to major general in the U.S. Army, and he also receives command of the 7th Military District, headquartered at New Orleans, Louisiana. However, Jackson feels that General Thomas Pinckney is too generously disposed in his dealings with the Creeks, so he conspires with Secretary of War John Armstrong to have him transferred back to South Carolina. As chief negotiator, Jackson negotiates and imposes the harsh Treaty of Fort Jackson and secures millions of acres for the United States.

MAY 30 At Sandy Creek, New York, a detachment of riflemen under Major Daniel Appling ambushes and captures a large detachment of British sailors and Royal Marines. For the loss of one man wounded, the Americans kill, wound, or capture 140 British. The victory spares a valuable shipload of heavy cannons they had been guarding, destined for Commodore Isaac Chauncey's squadron, from imminent capture.

JUNE 28 Near Odelltown, New York, Lieutenant Colonel Benjamin Forsyth, 1st Regiment of Riflemen, dies in a minor skirmish. He refused to retreat when ordered to lure British light troops into an ambush and was fatally shot by an Indian.

JULY 3 At Buffalo, New York, the invigorated Left Division under General Jacob J. Brown crosses the Niagara River and captures Fort Erie, Ontario.

JULY 4 At Detroit, Michigan, Lieutenant Colonel George Croghan sails with 700 men of the 17th, 19th, and 24th Infantries. He is tasked with recapturing strategic Mackinac Island, which fell to the British in August of 1812.

JULY 5 The Battle of Chippewa unfolds as British forces under Major General Phineas Riall attack General Jacob Brown's encampment behind Chippewa Creek, Ontario. While advancing, they encounter the crack brigade of General Winfield Scott, then being exercised, and a stand-up engagement begins. Riall, noticing the grey clothing of Scott's men, assumes they are militia, but the British are quickly outmaneuvered and driven off by their amateur adversaries. The Americans lose 60 dead and 235 wounded to a British tally of 148 killed and 321 wounded. Scott's triumph is the first by Americans on an open field, and proof of growing military professionalism.

JULY 19 On the Mississippi River, Major John Campbell's small flotilla is attacked by large numbers of Indians lining the shore. His 33-man detachment, assisted by 66 U.S. Rangers, fires swivel guns to repel their antagonists, but they are forced back to St. Louis with 30 killed and wounded.

JULY 20 Diminutive Fort Shelby, constructed at distant Prairie du Chien, Wisconsin Territory, is surrendered by Lieutenant Joseph Perkins, 24th Infantry, to prevent an Indian massacre. His small garrison is then paroled by the British and returns to St. Louis under a Canadian escort.

JULY 25 The Battle of Lundy's Lane rages between Major General Jacob J. Brown's 2,800 men and a British force of 3,200 under Lieutenant General Sir Gordon Drummond. The engagement commences when Brigadier General Winfield Scott attacks the advance guard under Brigadier General Phineas Riall, driving him back but then running headlong into reinforcements led by Drummond himself. The Americans take a pounding from British cannon until Brown brings up the rest of his force, and Colonel James Miller, 21st Infantry, storms the British battery atop the lane. Both sides withdraw during the night, although Drummond returns at daybreak and claims victory. The Americans lose 171 dead, 571 wounded, and 110 missing to a British tally of 84 killed, 559 injured, and 235 captured. Lundy's Lane is another fine performance by the Americans, but they cannot readily replace their losses and fall back to Fort Erie.

AUGUST 3 Lieutenant General Gordon Drummond orders 700 picked light infantry to cross the Niagara River at

The culmination of General Jacob Brown's invasion of Upper Canada in 1814, the Battle of Lundy's Lane on July 25, 1814, was a costly, drawn-out battle and a strategic defeat for the Americans. (Library of Congress)

night and capture the American depot at Buffalo, New York. If successful, this would cut the American garrison at Fort Erie off from its supplies. Fortunately, Major Ludowick Morgan and 300 elite riflemen handily repulse them at Conjocta Creek. The British withdraw back to the Canadian side at sunrise, and Drummond is forced to undergo a conventional siege.

AUGUST 4   At Mackinac Island, Michigan Territory, Lieutenant Colonel George Croghan disembarks 700 men on Mackinac Island but fails to overcome stiff resistance from British, Canadians, and Indians. The American suffer heavily, then withdraw back to the fleet; Mackinac remains in British hands until the end of the war.

AUGUST 14   The American encampment at Fort Erie, Upper Canada, is attacked by British forces under Lieutenant General Gordon Drummond. The garrison, commanded by Major General Edmund P. Gaines, was ready and repulse the attacking British columns. Disaster strikes when British troops storm a battery in the fort, accidentally touching off a gunpowder magazine. The ensuing explosion inflicts 900 British casualties; the Americans suffer under 100 killed and wounded, but Drummond determines to maintain the siege.

AUGUST 19   At Benedict, Maryland, British general Robert Ross lands 4,000 veteran troops unopposed. He is intent upon proceeding overland to Washington, D.C., but first destroys the gunboat flotilla of Commodore Joshua Barney anchored in the Patuxent River. Once this is accomplished, the British begin marching against the American capital.

AUGUST 24   The Battle of Bladensburg, Maryland, occurs as Brigadier William

H. Winder's 7,000 poorly-trained militia crumple under an assault by 4,000 British veterans. Only a contingent of U.S. Marines and sailors under Commodore Joshua Barney makes effective resistance before being overrun. American losses are 12 dead and 40 wounded to 249 for the British. The American capital now lies at the mercy of General Robert Ross, while President James Madison becomes the first commander in chief exposed to enemy gunfire and flees with his entourage.

AUGUST 25   In Washington, D.C., British forces under General Robert Ross burn all public buildings. They then withdraw without interference to Admiral George Cockburn's fleet awaiting their return in Chesapeake Bay.

AUGUST 26   Secretary of War John Armstrong, in one of the war's greatest miscalculations, orders Major General George Izard's Right Division from Plattsburgh, New York, to the Niagara frontier, there to assist Major General Jacob J. Brown at Fort Erie. Izard, fearing that Governor General Sir George Prevost is about to invade from Canada, protests that Plattsburg is defended by only 1,500 soldiers and invalids under Brigadier General Alexander Macomb. The orders stand, unfortunately, and Izard departs, effectively removing his Right Division from any impact on military events.

AUGUST 27   In Washington, D.C., President James Madison and his staff filter back to the burned-out remains of the capital. Secretary of War John Armstrong, largely viewed as responsible for the debacle, is pressured to resign from office.

AUGUST 28   Alexandria, Virginia, is occupied by British forces, who come ashore and offer the town a truce in exchange for ransom and supplies. City officials readily acquiesce and even demand that militia reinforcements marching to assist them remain out of town until the British depart.

AUGUST 30 At Caulk's Field, Maryland, a British naval detachment from the frigate HMS *Menelaeus* encounters the 21st Maryland Infantry and attacks in the darkness. Colonel Philip Reed responds with musketry and artillery fire, and the British withdraw with heavy losses, including youthful Captain Sir Peter Parker, killed.

AUGUST 31 As feared, Governor General Sir George Prevost commences his invasion of New York by leading 8,000 crack British troops down the Lake Champlain Valley toward Plattsburg. This is the largest military endeavor along the northern frontier, and the Americans are ill-prepared to contain it.

SEPTEMBER 1 British amphibious forces land at the mouth of the Castine River, Maine, then march overland to capture Castine and Bangor with little resistance. They subsequently chase Captain Charles Morris and the 28-gun frigate *Adams* upstream to Hampden, where the vessel is burned to prevent capture.

SEPTEMBER 5–6 Major Zachary Taylor sails 350 men of his 7th Infantry up the Mississippi River before landing at Credit Island during a storm. He is unaware that 1,200 Sac and Fox Indians under Chief Black Hawk are lurking in the nearby woods. At dawn on the 6th, the Indians attack and drive the outnumbered American back downstream with the assistance of a small detachment of British artillery. The upper Mississippi region remains in British hands for the remainder of the war.

SEPTEMBER 6 Soldiers and riflemen under Major John Ellis Wool and Lieutenant Colonel Daniel Appling engage a large British column marching south along the Beekmantown Road, New York. The Americans are forced back by sheer numbers, but manage to inflict considerable losses upon their opponents.

SEPTEMBER 10 At Plattsburgh, New York, Captain George McGlassin leads a party of 60 volunteers from his 15th Infantry and attacks a British rocket battery being erected across the Saranac River. The defenders scatter, and McGlassin wrecks the battery and returns without suffering a single casualty.

SEPTEMBER 11 As the decisive Battle of Lake Champlain commences, Governor General Sir George Prevost orders his 8,000 Peninsula veterans to attack American fortifications at nearby Plattsburgh, New York. They are opposed by 1,500 regulars and a similar number of militia under Brigadier General Alexander Macomb. The Americans resist fiercely from forts but are on the verge of being outflanked when Prevost, informed of Captain George Downie's squadron's defeat on Lake Champlain, suddenly cancels the attack.

SEPTEMBER 13–14 In Maryland, the Battle of Baltimore begins as General Robert Ross, leading 4,500 crack troops, is shot down by snipers while advancing upon the city. Command reverts to Colonel Arthur Brooke, who attacks American militia gathering under General John Stricker at North Point. Stricker manages to hold his position for several hours before being driven into the city's field works. Brooke then perceives that the victorious British are badly outnumbered by 15,000 defenders under General Samuel Smith and orders his army back to the fleet.

In Baltimore harbor, Admiral Sir George Cockburn's armada begins a fierce bombardment of Fort McHenry, garrisoned by 1,000 troops and militia under Major George Armistead. Despite having over 1,000 rounds fired at him, Armistead loses only 4 killed and 20 wounded. Francis Scott Key, a lawyer visiting the British fleet to release a prisoner, was so moved by the striking imagery presented by the fort's enormous flag that he composes "The Star-Spangled Banner" on the back of an old envelope.

SEPTEMBER 16 At Fort Bowyer, Mobile Bay, Major William Lawrence and 160 soldiers of the 2nd Infantry engage a British squadron taking up bombardment positions. The ships are bested by the American gunners and lose the sloop HMS *Hermes* in a one-sided exchange.

SEPTEMBER 17 At Fort Erie, Major General Jacob J. Brown, having recovered from wounds received at Lundy's Lane, suddenly sorties against British siege positions. His men, mostly militia, successfully storm three of four British batteries before Lieutenant General Gordon Drummond counterattacks and drives them off. Losses are roughly 600 British to 500 American but, with the weather worsening, Drummond finally elects to abandon the siege.

SEPTEMBER 27 In Washington, D.C., John Armstrong resigns as Secretary of War for failing to adequately prepare defense for the capital region. Secretary of State James Monroe once again fills in as acting secretary, only this time for the remainder of the war.

From Mobile, Alabama Territory, General Andrew Jackson requests that the governors of Tennessee, Mississippi, and Kentucky send him militia to help stem an expected British offensive, possibly from Pensacola, Florida. Runners are also sent to Creek, Choctaw, and Cherokee tribes to solicit volunteer warriors.

OCTOBER 5–16 Camp Gaines, Mississippi Territory, is occupied by a militia brigade under Brigadier General John Coffee, who covered 220 miles from Tennessee in only 10 days. He begins training his men on the deck of boats before joining General Andrew Jackson's main army.

OCTOBER 17 At Detroit, Michigan Territory, General Duncan McArthur departs with 650 mounted Kentuckians, Rangers, and Indians on a spectacular mounted raid through western Upper Canada. McArthur aspires to provide a useful diversion for General George Izard's division at Niagara.

OCTOBER 19 At Lyon's Creek, Upper Canada, General Daniel Bissell's brigade advances down Chippawa River until it is attacked by 750 British troops under Lieutenant Colonel Christopher Myers. Maneuvering adroitly, Bissell forces his opponent off the battlefield, then burns nearby Cook's Mills before retiring back to Fort Erie. American losses are 12 dead and 55 wounded to 1 dead Briton and 35 injured; this is the final clash between regular forces in Canada.

NOVEMBER 5 At Niagara, Major General George Izard demolishes Fort Erie, Upper Canada, and evacuates back to Buffalo, New York. The general does so after the British regain control of strategic Lake Ontario with their 120-gun ship-of-the-line HMS *St. Lawrence*. This act signifies the end of the 1814 Niagara Campaign, one of the war's bloodiest. Izard is also highly criticized for abandoning Canada.

NOVEMBER 6 Brigadier General Duncan McArthur's roving cavalry column, informed that Major General George

Izard has crossed over to New York, rides south from the Grand River and towards Malcolm's Mills, Upper Canada. There his troopers disperse a large body of Canadian militia, burn some local mills, and gallop back to Detroit on November 17.

NOVEMBER 7–8 General Andrew Jackson, acting against the wishes of Secretary of War James Monroe, captures Pensacola, Florida, from Spanish forces. Resistance is timorous, and the Americans sustain only 5 killed and 11 wounded. British warships in the harbor are also forced to demolish two forts and immediately depart.

NOVEMBER 22 At Pensacola, Florida, Major General Andrew Jackson becomes convinced that New Orleans is the actual target of a British offensive and hastily departs with troops for that city. He also orders newly released Brigadier General James Winchester to reinforce Mobile, another potential target, with the 2nd, 3rd, and 39th Infantries.

DECEMBER 1 Major General Andrew Jackson's army arrives at New Orleans, Louisiana, from Pensacola, Florida, slightly ahead of a major British invasion.

DECEMBER 8 In West Florida, Major Uriah Blue and part of the 39th Infantry raid hostile Creek villages; little resistance is encountered, and the Americans retire back to Mobile.

DECEMBER 13 At New Orleans, Louisiana, Major General Andrew Jackson declares martial law in Louisiana upon learning that a British armada is approach through nearby Lake Borgne.

DECEMBER 23–24 At Villere's Plantation, Louisiana, Major General Andrew Jackson and 2,000 men engage 1,600 British encamped along the Mississippi River. The attack, assisted by U.S. Navy gunboats, is fiercely pressed but darkness, confusion, and fierce fighting by veteran British troops repel the Americans. General John Keane nonetheless suspends his advance upon New Orleans until reinforcements arrive, allowing Jackson to perfect his defenses. Losses here are 215 Americans and 275 British killed, wounded, and captured.

DECEMBER 24 In Ghent, Belgium, American and British diplomats conclude the Treaty of Ghent, which ends the War of 1812 and restores all captured territory. News of the signing does not reach New York for another seven weeks, however, so fighting continues on land and at sea.

DECEMBER 28 At New Orleans, Louisiana, British forces begin probing Major General Andrew Jackson's line along the Rodriguez Canal and are repelled by accurate rifle and artillery fire.

1815

JANUARY 1 At New Orleans, Louisiana, British artillery under General Sir Edward Pakenham begins bombarding Major General Andrew Jackson's line. A protracted artillery duel ensues, and the British are eventually bested and silenced following a four-hour exchange.

JANUARY 2 Brigadier General John Adair's brigade of poorly trained and equipped Kentucky militia arrives at New Orleans, Louisiana, to reinforce Major General Andrew Jackson's position. They are posted on the opposite bank of the Mississippi River, where little activity is anticipated.

Scott, Winfield (1786–1866)

Winfield Scott was born in Petersburg, Virginia, on June 13, 1786. He briefly attended William and Mary College in 1806, then enlisted as a captain in the U.S. Army. In 1810 he was court-martialed for publicly criticizing General James Wilkinson, receiving a year's suspension. He passed the time studying European military literature, so that when the War of 1812 commenced he was among the most professional officers of his grade. In July 1814, Scott served in the Niagara Campaign as the nation's youngest a brigadier general, aged 28 years. He fought exceedingly well at the battles of Chippewa and Lundy's Lane, being severely wounded, and afterward ventured to Europe to study military establishments there. By this time Scott had acquired the moniker "Old Fuss and Feathers" owing to his insistence upon proper military decorum. Scott rose to be commanding general of the army in 1841, and in this capacity fought brilliantly in the Mexican American War. Commencing with an amphibious landing at Vera Cruz in 1847, Scott marched rapidly inland, defeated larger Mexican

Winfield Scott was the guiding spirit behind America's professional army. Scott served in the War of 1812 and the Black Hawk War, and led the United States through the Mexican War of 1846–1847. (Perry-Castaneda Library)

forces, and occupied the enemy capital in a lightning campaign. Success on the battlefield whetted Scott's appetite for politics, and in 1852 he sought the Whig Party nomination for the presidency but lost badly to Democrat Franklin Pierce. Though Southern-born, Scott was an ardent nationalist, and he sided with the North during the approach of civil war. As President Abraham Lincoln's senior military adviser, Scott promulgated the so-called Anaconda Plan, calling for an offensive down the Mississippi River to divide the Confederacy, while a naval blockade throttled its economy. Scott retired from active duty in the fall of 1861 and spent the rest of his days at the U.S. Military Academy, West Point. He died there on May 29, 1866, a major architect of U.S. Army professionalism.

JANUARY 5   In Washington, D.C., General Winfield Scott heads a new Tactical Board assembled for compiling standard-ized system of military drill. Soon afterward they unveil *Rules and Regulations for the Field Exercise and Maneuvers of Infantry,* which is drawn from existing French tactical systems.

JANUARY 8   In Louisiana, the Battle of New Orleans unfolds as British forces under General Sir Edward Pakenham attack Major General Andrew Jackson's entrenched position and are bloodily repulsed. By comparison, British forces on the Mississippi's west bank completely scatter General John Adair's Kentucky militia, but victory here does not alter the course of events. Pakenham dies along with nearly 2,000 of his men; Jackson only suffers 13 killed, 39 wounded, and 19 missing. New Orleans is the largest battle of the War of 1812, although it happens two weeks after the Treaty of Ghent has been signed in Europe

British and American forces clash at the Battle of New Orleans. A strongly defended left flank anchored on the Mississippi River and a thick cypress swamp on the right forced the British assault to the center of General Andrew Jackson's defense, where Jackson had placed his 3,500 men behind a line of cotton bales. (National Museum of the United States Army)

JANUARY 9–18   Fort St. Phillip on Plaquennes Bend, 70 miles below New Orleans, withstands a rigorous bombardment by Royal Navy warships. Nearly 1,000 projectiles are hurled at the defenders, who sustain two dead and seven wounded.

JANUARY 13   At Point Petre, Georgia, Royal Marines and a West Indian regiment land and engage 80 men of the 1st Regiment of Riflemen and a company of the 42nd Infantry. The victorious British spike their battery and withdraw back to their ships.

JANUARY 23   In New Orleans, Louisiana, Major General Andrew Jackson parades his victorious army, although celebrations are muted once he enforces martial law over the next two months.

FEBRUARY 8   In Washington, D.C., Congress authorizes a colonel of the Ordnance Department to conduct inspection procedures on all weapons purchased for the U.S. Army.

FEBRUARY 9   At Fort Bowyer, Mobile Bay, 6,000 survivors of General Edward Pakenham's army land and commence siege operations. Major William Lawrence, commanding only 370 men, is vastly outnumbered and surrenders once the British trenches approach within a few yards of his works. News of peace arrives the following day, and all prisoners are exchanged.

FEBRUARY 21   At Mobile, Alabama Territory, General Andrew Jackson approves a death sentence for six mutinous Tennessee militiamen, who are executed by firing squad. This act resurfaces as a potent political issue during Jackson's presidential campaigns of 1824 and 1828.

MARCH 3   In Washington, D.C., President James Madison requests a peacetime establishment of 20,000 men, but Congress votes for a force half that size under two major generals and four brigadier generals. Eight infantry regiments, a regiment of riflemen, and the Corps of

Artillery are retained as part of the standing establishment. Still, this represents twice the authorized manpower of Thomas Jefferson's day and is indicative of the growing political acceptance of larger forces. The Regiment of Light Dragoons is also abolished, and the Army lacks a regular cavalry unit until 1833.

MAY 1 The United States is reorganized into Northern and Southern military divisions, headed by Major Generals Jacob J. Brown and Andrew Jackson, respectively.

JULY 9 The War Department, eager to increase military professionalism, dispatches Brevet Major General Winfield Scott to Europe to study and report on the military establishments there.

SEPTEMBER Colonel Thomas Adams Smith and his elite Regiment of Riflemen are transferred to St. Louis, Missouri Territory. Over the next six years they figure prominently in exploration and fort-building across the western frontier.

1816

APRIL Brigadier General Thomas Adams Smith arrives at Cantonment Davis with several companies of riflemen. Shortly afterward he pushes onto to Rock Island, Illinois, and establishes Fort Armstrong.

APRIL 24 In Washington, D.C., the U.S. Army's embryonic general staff increases with the addition of an inspector general and several topographical engineers.

MAY At Detroit, Michigan, General Alexander Macomb commences constructing a military road running south to Fort Meigs, Ohio, 70 miles distant; work continues over the next two years.

MAY 10 Fort Howard at Green Bay, Illinois (Wisconsin) Territory, is constructed by an army garrison; it functions as a major center of the fur trade.

MAY 17 War of 1812 hero Zachary Taylor, having previously resigned to protest a postwar reduction in rank, is recommissioned as a major in new the 3rd Infantry.

JUNE Along the Flint River, Georgia, Lieutenant Colonel Duncan L. Clinch begins construction of Fort Scott, a post intended to protect the southern frontier from hostile Creeks and Seminoles who occasionally cross over from East Florida.

JUNE 20 Fort Shelby at Prairie du Chien, Wisconsin Territory, is reoccupied by a detachment of the Regiment of Riflemen. They subsequently commence construction of Fort Crawford, to confirm American control of the Upper Mississippi region.

JULY 4 Fort Dearborn in Chicago, Illinois Territory, which was destroyed in the War of 1812, is rebuilt by soldiers, along with a new Indian trading post.

JULY 27 Fort Apalachicola in Spanish East Florida, garrisoned by fugitive slaves and hostile Seminole Indians, is attacked by American troops and gunboats under Lieutenant Colonel Duncan L. Clinch. During the siege a lucky cannon shot ignites a powder supply, killing all 270 defenders.

AUGUST At Green Bay, Wisconsin Territory, four companies of the 3rd Infantry, two companies from the Regiment of Riflemen, and some artillery under Colonel John Miller march into Fort Howard, at the mouth of the Fox River.

1817

APRIL 22 In Florida, an angry General Andrew Jackson ignores War Department orders relayed to his subordinates, insisting that all such directives be sent to him directly. Congressmen construe his belligerence as insubordination, at which point Jackson threatens to resign his commission.

JULY 28 At the U.S. Military Academy at West Point, New York, Captain Sylvanus Thayer replaces Captain Alden Partridge as Superintendent. This proves a major development with far-reaching consequences, for Thayer initiates several reforms aimed at modernizing the curriculum and tightening disciplinary standards.

OCTOBER 8 In Washington, D.C., Congressman John C. Calhoun gains appointment as Secretary of War. Happily, he is one of the most effective and efficient secretaries in War Department history and manages to put military administration back on an even keel.

NOVEMBER 20 In Florida, the First Seminole War commences as Indian warriors begin raiding American settlements along the southern Georgia border. They do so to avenge the great loss of life occurring with the destruction of Fort Apalachicola in 1816. Local inhabitants suspect that Spanish authorities have also incited the Indians toward violence in order to keep Florida.

NOVEMBER 21 At Fowltown, Georgia, Mikasukis Seminole warriors strike at a column of 250 soldiers under Major David E. Twiggs. Five Indians are killed and Chief Neamathla escapes back to Florida.

NOVEMBER 30 On the Apalachicola River, Florida, vengeful Seminoles ambush a boatload of U.S. Army troops from the 4th and 7th Infantries, killing 36 soldiers, seven women, and four children.

DECEMBER 26 In Florida, General Andrew Jackson succeeds General Edmund P. Gaines as commander of American forces for the rest of the First Seminole War. Secretary of War John C. Calhoun authorizes him to use whatever force he deems necessary to speedily conclude the matter; Jackson wastes little time obliging him.

1818

JANUARY 6 General Andrew Jackson begins collecting troops for an energetic campaign against hostile Seminole Indians. He had previously written President James Monroe that he could seize the area from Spain within two months; he proceeds to fulfill his offer without authorization.

MARCH 9–10 At Fort Scott, Georgia, General Andrew Jackson and 1,000 Tennessee volunteers arrive after covering 450 miles in only 36 days and join 500 men collected from the 1st, 4th, and 7th Infantries. Eager to push forward, Jackson does not wait for supply wagons to arrive but draws three days' rations and immediately proceeds south into Florida.

MARCH 15–26 General Andrew Jackson's army arrives at Prospect Bluff, East

Florida, and builds Fort Gadsden to guard his line of communications. He subsequently pushes on to St. Marks amidst rumors that British agents and Spanish authorities are providing Seminoles and escaped slaves with firearms.

MARCH 18 In Washington, D.C., Congress votes to allow lifetime pensions for Revolutionary War veterans. A total of $20.00 per month for officers and $8.00 per month for privates is authorized.

APRIL 6 St. Marks, Florida, is seized by a fast-moving column under General Andrew Jackson. There he is joined by 1,500 Creek warriors, bringing his total available manpower up to 4,000 men. From here, Jackson strikes out at the village of Chief Billy Bowlegs on the Suwanee River, 100 miles distant.

APRIL 7 In Florida, soldiers under General Andrew Jackson capture two English traders, Alexander Arbuthnot and Robert Ambrister, along with incriminating evidence that they have been arming the Seminole. Jackson is convinced that Great Britain is fomenting frontier violence against the United States and acts accordingly.

APRIL 8 In Washington, D.C., Secretary of War John C. Calhoun appoints Dr. Joseph Lovell as the first Army Surgeon General; this is a civilian appointment but endowed with military rank.

APRIL 14 In Washington, D.C., Congress authorizes creation of the Army Medical Corps, to be headed by a Surgeon General. Dr. Joseph Lovell is also confirmed to hold that rank and serves with distinction over the next 18 years.

APRIL 29 At St. Marks, Florida, British traders Alexander Arbuthnot and Robert Ambrister are tried and executed by General Andrew Jackson for arming and inciting the Seminole into violence against the United States. This arbitrary act, performed without authorization, triggers a public outcry from Great Britain. In light of Jackson's popularity with the American public, no action is taken to censure him.

MAY In Washington, D.C., Colonel Thomas Sidney Jesup gains appointment as the Army's first Quartermaster General. He is promoted to brigadier general and occupies that position over the next 42 years.

MAY 24–27 In Pensacola, Florida, General Andrew Jackson's troops seize the Spanish-held town and a quick bombardment also induces a nearby Spanish fort to surrender. This act effectively concludes the First Seminole War, and Colonel William King is appointed governor of Pensacola.

JULY 24 At West Point, New York, the first group of 24 cadets trained under the new regimen of Superintendent Sylvanus Thayer graduates from the U.S. Military Academy. The practice of ranking lieutenant's commissions and army seniority relative to academic performance is also initiated.

SEPTEMBER 11 In Washington, D.C., the War Department issues a General Order instructing the garrisons of western military posts to begin extensive farming programs to provide themselves with food and livestock. This is undertaken as much for economic reasons as well as for the health of the troops.

OCTOBER 31 In East Florida, the final contingent of American troops withdraws from Spanish territory and officially concludes the First Seminole War. Of 8,000 regulars and militia mustered to serve, 47 die in action and 36 are wounded.

1819

JUNE 6 In Pittsburgh, Pennsylvania, Major Stephen H. Long of the Topographical Engineers is instructed by Secretary of War John C. Calhoun to explore the region south of the Missouri River. This endeavor lasts two years and thoroughly examines the eastern Rocky Mountains and an area that becomes known as the "Great American Desert."

JUNE 14 At St. Louis, Missouri, Lieutenant Colonel Talbot Chambers leads part of the Regiment of Riflemen in five keelboats up the Missouri River as part of the Yellowstone Expedition. His orders are to establish a fort near the mouth of the Yellowstone River.

JUNE 21 Major Stephen H. Long, Topographic Bureau, leads his small expedition up the Missouri River in the steamboat *Western Explorer*. This is the first time such technology has been employed this far west.

JULY 4–5 At St. Louis, Missouri, eight companies of the 6th Infantry begin ascending the Missouri River as the final phase of the Yellowstone Expedition.

AUGUST In present-day Missouri, Lieutenant Colonel Henry Leavenworth leads 16 boatloads of his 5th Infantry to the confluence of the Missouri and Mississippi rivers. There they stop to construct a fort on land purchased from the Sioux by Lieutenant Zebulon M. Pike in 1804. This new bastion, later christened Fort Snelling, becomes the Army's northernmost military post.

SEPTEMBER 29 At Council Bluffs, present-day Iowa, the Yellowstone Expedition under Colonel Henry Atkinson pauses to construct a post that they call Camp Missouri. Engineers also begin surveying a 330-mile road back to St. Louis, Missouri.

1820

APRIL In Washington, D.C., Congress votes to cut funding for the Yellowstone River expedition, forcing Colonel Talbot Chambers to remain in place at Council Bluffs and construct a fort there. The expedition of Major Stephen H. Long is also curtailed and restricted to exploring the Platte and Arkansas Rivers.

JULY 14–15 Major Stephen H. Long's exploring expedition reaches the eastern Rocky Mountains (Colorado). Here a team under civilian Edwin James ascends Pike's Peak for the first time.

JULY 24 A party of soldiers under Captain John R. Bell, having explored the base of the Rocky Mountains, directs a group of scientists down the Arkansas River. Major Stephen H. Long also ventures down the Canadian River, concluding this phase of the Yellowstone Expedition.

DECEMBER 12 In Washington, D.C., Secretary of War John C. Calhoun responds to mandatory defense cuts by submitting a plan to reduce the army from 8,000 to 6,000 men. Moreover, he calls for an "expandable" force by maintaining the same number of regiments and companies, although with fewer soldiers and the same number of officers. In this manner, the army could be quickly expanded by simply adding new recruits. Congress rejects the scheme.

1821

MARCH 2 In Washington, D.C., Congress reduces the army from 8,000 men to 6,126 by eliminating the 8th Infantry, the Light Artillery Regiment, and the Regiment of Riflemen. The Corps of Artillery is likewise consolidated into four artillery regiments.

MARCH 27 In Washington, D.C., Congress orders that blue be the official color of all U.S. Army uniforms, regardless of branch. The color had been utilized previously by various branches, but only now it is official.

JUNE 1–15 The newly reduced army requires fewer generals in service so Andrew Jackson resigns rather than face demotion to brigadier general. Winfield Scott and Edmund P. Gaines are retained as brigadiers, but Alexander Macomb is reduced to colonel and Chief Army Engineer. Jacob J. Brown remains the sole major general with the grandiose title Commanding General of the Army.

1822

JUNE 6 At Fort Mackinac, Michigan, army surgeon Dr. William Beaumont makes medical history by studying Alexis St. Martin's stomach fluids through an open wound. This constitutes the first-ever direct observations of the human digestive tract.

JULY General Jacob J. Brown instructs General Winfield Scott to establish three centralized recruiting stations within his jurisdiction as an experiment. He does so to obviate long-standing recruiting problems for the army

JULY 6 At Sault Ste. Marie, Michigan Territory, Colonel Hugh Brady, 2nd Infantry, begins construction of Fort Brady. This is part of Secretary of War John C. Calhoun's military construction program along the northern frontier.

1823

JUNE 22–23 Colonel Henry Leavenworth sorties from Fort Atkinson with six companies of the 6th Infantry on a punitive raid against local Arikara Indians. This constitutes the Army's first military action west of the Mississippi River and comes in response to attacks against traders.

JULY 9 At Fort Snelling, Minnesota Territory, Major Stephen H. Long commences his second exploration to explore and find the source of the Minnesota River.

The task takes him across 5,400 miles, and helps to delineate the boundary between the United States and Canada.

AUGUST 9–14 In present-day South Dakota, Colonel Henry Leavenworth conducts 1,000 American troops against hostile Arikara Indians. He bombards their two fortified villages for several days and attempts to negotiate a settlement, but the Indians ultimately escape at night.

1824

MAY 4 In Washington, D.C., Congress passes legislation mandating the construction of civil works by the U.S. Army Corps of Engineers. These are for the most part river navigation, flood control, and harbor dredging activities.

MAY 24 In Washington, D.C., President James Monroe signs a bill allowing the U.S. Army Corps of Engineers to build dams, dredge harbors, and engage in other construction with civilian applications. This is one of the reasons that President Thomas Jefferson created the U.S. Military Institute in 1802.

At Fortress Monroe, Virginia, Secretary of War John C. Calhoun founds the Artillery School of Practice. This constitutes the Army's first professional school of instruction; a one-year tour of duty here is mandatory for new West Point graduates before they are allowed to join their assigned regiments in the field.

1826

MARCH 4 Brigadier Generals Henry Atkinson and Edmund P. Gaines search for a site to construct a new fort that will replace Fort Bellefontaine at St. Louis, Missouri. They settle upon a bluff overlooking the Mississippi River 10 miles from the city.

SEPTEMBER 19–OCTOBER 23 In Missouri, Colonel Leavenworth establishes a new post called Cantonment Miller, which later becomes better known as the Jefferson Barracks. In time this functions as the "Infantry School of Practice" and is the first permanent Army facility west of the Mississippi.

1827

FEBRUARY 17 In Georgia, U.S. Army troops are dispatched to Creek lands to prevent the private surveying of tribal lands. Governor George M. Troup consequently mobilizes the state militia to oppose them. The transfer of land stipulated in the Treaty of Washington, signed the previous January, has not yet occurred, and the governor is pressured to fulfill the terms.

FEBRUARY 27 The U.S. Supreme Court decides the case of *Martin vs. Mott*, confirming that the president, as commander in chief, enjoys sole authority to call out the militia. Moreover, the decision is not subject to judicial review and is binding on all state authorities in question.

MARCH 7 At Jefferson Barracks, Missouri, Colonel Henry Leavenworth is directed to locate a the site for new fort further west of the Mississippi River. He accordingly begins scouting up the nearby Missouri River for a proper venue.

MARCH 27 Congress adopts a pay scale known as "command pay," fixed at $10 a month and implemented for all officers who command companies. The same rate also applies to senior lieutenants who command in the absence of a captain.

APRIL 17 In present-day Kansas, Colonel Henry Leavenworth is joined by men of the 3rd Infantry under Captain William G. Belknap, who assist in choosing the site of Cantonment Leavenworth. This is founded to help improve security along the Santa Fe Trail into northern Mexico, which rapidly develops as a trade route.

MAY 26 Edgar Allen Poe, a future literary notable, enlists in the U.S. Army under the assumed name of Edgar Allen Perry. He serves capably over the next two years, and rises to sergeant major before being honorably discharged.

JUNE 24 Outside Fort Snelling, Minnesota Territory, Winnebago Indians attack settlers and military keelboats after hearing rumors that two of their number have been jailed inside. Governor Lewis Cass mobilizes the Michigan militia while General Henry Atkinson prepares to march with the 6th Infantry from Jefferson Barracks, Missouri.

JUNE 29–28 The Infantry School of Practice at Jefferson Barracks, Missouri, is now home to several infantry companies and is personally inspected by Jacob J. Brown, Commanding General of the Army.

JULY 15–29 General Henry Atkinson conducts troops up the Mississippi River on steamboats as far as Prairie du Chien, Wisconsin Territory, intending to confront hostile Winnebago Indians. Other detachments are en route from Forts Howard and Snelling, while the Illinois and Michigan militias gather at Peoria and Galena, Illinois.

SEPTEMBER 2–33 At Prairie du Chien, Wisconsin Territory, the Winnebago realize that they are badly out-gunned and outnumbered, so they dispatch a white flag to the camp of Major William Whistler to request peace. After handing over two tribal members who had attacked white settlers, General Henry Atkinson allows them to return home.

1828

FEBRUARY 24 In Washington, D.C., Commanding General of the Army Jacob J. Brown dies after serving as the nation's leading military figure for the past seven years. His passing initiates a bitter struggle between Generals Winfield Scott and Edmund P. Gaines to succeed him based on their own perceived seniority.

MAY 29 In Washington, D.C., President John Quincy Adams, embarrassed by the public squabbling of Winfield Scott and Edmund P. Gaines to become Commanding General of the Army, bypasses both in favor of Alexander Macomb. Scott consequently vows never to obey Macomb and tenders his resignation, but it is not accepted. Adams orders him back to Jefferson Barracks, Missouri, to think things over.

DECEMBER 14 At Jefferson Barracks, Missouri, General Winfield Scott's incessant ranting over being bypassed for Commanding General of the Army results in his removal from the Western Department. He is consequently placed on the "waiting orders" list and succeeded by Brevet Brigadier General Henry Atkinson.

1829

MARCH 2 *A System of Exercise and Instruction of Field Artillery* is published and adopted by the Army. As such it is the first military handbook to employ the precise terms "field," "light," and "horse," to denote the specific types of ordnance employed.

MAY 4–14 At Jefferson Barracks, Missouri, Captain Bennett Riley marches with several companies of the infantry as the first military escort for the Santa Fe Trail. Attacks by hostile Kiowa and Comanche warriors have prompted an outcry for help from traders along the trail.

JUNE 5–JULY 1 Captain Bennett Riley's caravan guard is continually attacked by Comanches after they encamp on Chouteau's Island in the Arkansas River. His experience highlights the difficulty of infantry when dealing with mounted raiders.

JULY 18 Command of Fort Crawford, Wisconsin Territory, passes over to Major Lieutenant Colonel Zachary Taylor, who is ordered to construct a new post above a nearby river flood plain.

AUGUST 13 In Washington, D.C., the War Department issues new regulations regarding brevet promotions to ameliorate long-standing confusion relative to seniority. Consequently, officers serving 10 years in one service grade automatically receive brevet promotion to the next rank, although permission to actually wield such authority must come from the War Department.

NOVEMBER 8 At Cantonment, Leavenworth, Captain Bennett Riley's caravan guard returns after suffering four dead at the hands of Comanche raiders. His final report outlines the disadvantages of foot solders when confronting mounted warriors and helps stimulate the rebirth of the U.S. Army's mounted arm.

NOVEMBER 23 General Winfield Scott, having returned from an extended furlough in Europe, withdraws his offer to resign. A forgiving War Department allows him to switch command of the Western Department for the Eastern Department with his bitter rival, Edmund P. Gaines.

1830

DECEMBER 8 In Washington, D.C., the Adjutant General's Office issues Order No. 72 to cease the Army's traditional gill of whiskey given to troops as part of daily rations. Sugar and coffee are added in its place.

1831

FEBRUARY 8 In Washington, D.C., the War Department issues a new regulation requiring that all cantonments and fortifications receive an official designation as "fort."

JUNE 27–30 In Illinois, Chief Black Hawk of the Sac and Fox nation reluctantly agrees with General Edmund P. Gaines to relocate his people from their traditional homelands and across the Mississippi River to Iowa. Once there they nearly starve over the winter, and deprivation prompts an exodus back to their former abode.

NOVEMBER 1 Secretary of War Lewis Cass, cognizant of increasing pressures for the Army to patrol vast reaches of the Western Frontier, calls for reconstitution of the mounted arm. The last U.S. Army cavalry unit in government employ was disbanded in 1815.

1832

APRIL 5 In Washington, D.C., Congress founds a separate Ordnance Department under the aegis of the venerable Colonel George Bomford.

APRIL 6–11 In Illinois, Chief Black Hawk unexpectedly orders the Sac and Fox tribe back across the Mississippi River to their traditional hunting grounds. The so-called Black Hawk War ensues when frightened farmers fire on a group of Indians bearing a white flag and Black Hawk orders them killed.

APRIL 16 In Illinois, Governor John Reynolds mobilizes 1,700 militiamen under Brigadier Samuel Whiteside to confront the Sac and Fox tribes under Black Hawk; one company is commanded by an aspiring attorney, Captain Abraham Lincoln. The men are then marched to St. Louis, Missouri, to draw supplies.

MAY 1 At Fort Osage, Missouri, Captain Benjamin L. E. Bonneville leads a wagon train as far west as the Columbia River, Oregon, then goes off on his own with 100 volunteers to explore for an additional three years. He returns with useful information about Nez Perce and Flathead tribes residing there.

MAY 7–8 Zachary Taylor advances to colonel of the 1st Infantry, whereupon Brevet Brigadier General Henry Atkinson orders him to take charge of troops and militia assembling at Fort Armstrong, Illinois.

MAY 9–10 In Illinois, Brevet Brigadier General Henry Atkinson commences operations against Black Hawk and instructs militia under General Samuel Whiteside to begin scouring the south bank of Rock River as Colonel Zachary Taylor's soldiers move along the north bank.

MAY 11–15 In Illinois, a battalion of mounted volunteers under Major Isaiah Stillman discovers Black Hawk's camp at Sycamore Creek. The major is approached by a truce party bearing a white flag. Suspecting a ruse, the militiamen fire at the party, killing several Indians, then pursue them. They are routed in turn by an Indian ambush and the entire rear guard of 12 men is killed. The remainder flee back to Dixon's Ferry.

MAY 19–29 In Illinois, Brevet Brigadier General Henry Atkinson begins pursuing renegade Indians under Black Hawk, but he is forced to discharge all but 300 volunteers after their enlistments expire.

JUNE 15 Along the Pecatonica River, Illinois, mounted Michigan volunteers under Colonel Henry Dodge defeat a party of Sac and Fox, killing 11 Indians.

JUNE 15–28 In light of increasing activity of the Army on the frontier, Congress votes to grant the Medical Department another 69 surgeons and assistants. A battalion of Mounted Rangers, consisting of 660 men and 25 officers, is also created.

This is the first cavalry unit in federal service since the War of 1812 and frontiersman Henry Dodge is appointed its colonel.

JUNE 16 In Washington, D.C., President Andrew Jackson is angered by General Henry Atkinson's lack of results against Black Hawk. He therefore instructs General Winfield Scott to assume command of affairs in Illinois. Additional companies of infantry and artillery are also dispatched to the theater from New York.

JULY 1–10 On Lake Erie, four steamships carrying 1,000 troops under General Winfield Scott experience an outbreak of cholera. Scott is careful about arresting the progress of the disease, but more than 200 soldiers die and the rest are incapacitated.

JULY 18–21 At Wisconsin Heights, mounted troops under Colonel Henry Dodge encounter Black Hawk's band, and the Indians skillfully delay the Americans as they escape across the Wisconsin River.

JULY 27–31 In Illinois, 1,700 regulars and militiamen under Brevet Brigadier General Henry Atkinson pursue Black Hawk's band to within 20 miles of the Mississippi River. He hopes to engage them before they can cross en masse back to Iowa.

AUGUST 1–2 On the Mississippi River, General Henry Atkinson decisively defeats the Sac and Fox Indians at the Battle of Bad Axe River, Michigan Territory. His troops are assisted by cannon on the armed steamboat *Warrior*, and the Indians lose 150 dead and 50 captured. Thus concludes the final episode of Native Indian resistance east of the Mississippi River.

Depiction of fleeing bands of Sac and Fox Indians caught and attacked by American troops, leading to the Battle of Bad Axe, the final conflict of the Black Hawk War. (North Wind Picture Archives)

AUGUST 7–25   In the Wisconsin Territory, Black Hawk is seized by Winnebagos and surrenders to Brevet Brigadier General Henry Atkinson. The chief is subsequently bound over to Lieutenant Jefferson Davis and transported to the Jefferson Barracks, Missouri, as a prisoner.

SEPTEMBER 14   At Fort Gibson, present-day Oklahoma, Captain Jesse Bean's company of mounted Rangers arrives and commences long patrols of the Pawnee and Comanche territories to enforce the peace.

SEPTEMBER 21   At Fort Armstrong, Illinois, General Winfield Scott negotiates an end to the Black Hawk conflict. The treaty forces the Sac and Fox Indians to cede most of present-day Wisconsin and Iowa to the United States. Chief Keokuk, who is friendly toward the Americans, readily signs it, but Black Hawk, who is released into Keokuk's care, denounces the document as fraudulent.

NOVEMBER 26   At Charleston, South Carolina, General Winfield Scott arrives, ostensibly to inspect coastal defenses and arsenals. He is actually there to evaluate military conditions during the Nullification Crisis with that state. President Andrew Jackson has threatened to employ force if South Carolina makes any attempt to secede from the Union.

1833

MARCH 2   In Washington, D.C., Congress votes to create the 1st Dragoon Regiment, the first mounted regulars since 1815. Henry Dodge is appointed colonel and he commands 749 officers and men.

NOVEMBER 20–DECEMBER 14   At Jefferson Barracks, Missouri, Colonel Henry Dodge arrives with five companies of recruits for his new 1st Dragoons. Once these have been suitably trained, he intends to lead them on a 500-mile winter march to Fort Gibson in the Indian Territory (present-day Oklahoma).

1834

JANUARY 29–MARCH 22   At Williamsport, Maryland, two companies of the 1st Artillery deploy to maintain peace between rival groups working on the Chesapeake-Ohio Canal. This is the first known instance of troops being employed during a labor dispute.

JUNE 17–JULY 4   Brevet Brigadier General Henry Leavenworth departs Fort Gibson, Oklahoma Territory, with eight companies of the 1st Dragoons. He is conducting them on a foray up the upper Red River Valley to arrange treaties with Indians residing there. George Catlin, the noted artist, accompanies them to capture vivid images of Native Americans on his canvas.

JULY 4   Brevet Brigadier General Henry Leavenworth's first dragoon expedition is nearly sidelined by illness and heat exhaustion, forcing him to leave 200 soldiers behind at the Washita River. Colonel Henry Dodge arrives to take command

and leads several companies onto nearby Pawnee and Comanche villages.

JULY 21 In the Oklahoma Territory, Brevet Brigadier General Henry Leavenworth dies of injuries sustained in a riding accident near the Washita River. He becomes also the first general officer to die west of the Mississippi River.

AUGUST 15 At Fort Gibson, Oklahoma Territory, Colonel Henry Dodge shepherds survivors of the first dragoon expedition back into camp. More than 100 troopers have been lost to sickness and heat exhaustion, which underscores the harshness of operating conditions in the west.

1835

MAY 29 Colonel Henry Dodge and his 1st Dragoons depart Fort Gibson, Oklahoma Territory, on a 1,600-mile expedition taking them to the Platte River, then down to Pueblo, New Mexico. En route, he will negotiate trade treaties with local tribes and hopefully impress upon them the power of the United States.

AUGUST 22 Former Army captain Benjamin L. E. Bonneville returns after three years of western exploration and begins writing a detailed account of his experiences. He also applies to have his military rank reinstated, but Secretary of War Lewis Cass refuses.

SEPTEMBER 16 Colonel Henry Dodge and the 1st Dragoons gallop along the Santa Fe Trail and back to Fort Leavenworth. This concludes their successful 1,600-mile sojourn through the heart of Indian country.

NOVEMBER 1 In the Florida Territory, large segments of the Seminole nation under Chief Osceola steadfastly refuse relocation to new homes out west. Moreover, the chief threatens to resist any relocation attempt by force. Brigadier General Duncan L. Clinch nevertheless orders tribal leaders to begin assembling their people for deportation.

DECEMBER 18–25 At Black Swamp, Florida Territory, hostilities flare once militant Seminoles attack tribal members thought to be too accommodating toward the United States. A band of warriors under Osceola also attacks a battalion of mounted militiamen; the Americans lose six dead and eight injured. This is the start of the lengthy Second Seminole War.

DECEMBER 23–27 Near Fort Brooke, Florida Territory, a column of 100 men under Major Francis L. Dade departs to reinforce the garrison at Fort King. He is unaware that large numbers of Seminole warriors are gathering in the nearby woods.

DECEMBER 28 At Fort King, Florida Territory, Indian Agent Wiley Thompson is murdered by Osceola's war band. Meanwhile, Major Francis L. Dade's column is ambushed and annihilated near Wahoo Swamp, losing 110 men killed. Only three soldiers survive the attack; two of these die of wounds.

DECEMBER 29–31 In the Florida Territory, Brigadier General Duncan L. Clinch takes 250 soldiers and 560 mounted militiamen, then advances to the Withlacoochee River. He intends to attack an Indian camp across the river,

Seminole warriors attack a blockhouse, possibly a fort on the Withlacoochee River, at the start of the Second Seminole War in December 1835. (Library of Congress)

but no sooner do they begin fording than the columns come under a heavy fire. Clinch orders a retreat after losing 4 dead and 51 wounded.

1836

JANUARY 17 In the Florida Territory, a body of the Volunteer St. Augustine Guards is ambushed and soundly beaten by Seminoles; they hurriedly retreat after losing nearly half their numbers.

JANUARY 21 General Winfield Scott is authorized to take command of all military forces in the Florida Territory. General Edmund P. Gaines, an old rival, is ordered to remain at New Orleans, Louisiana, but he disobeys and departs for Florida with troops on his own initiative.

FEBRUARY Rising tensions with Mexico prompt the 6th Infantry to depart Jefferson Barracks, Missouri, and relocate to Fort Jesup, Louisiana, to safeguard American interests.

FEBRUARY 9–22 At Tampa, Florida, Brigadier General Edmund P. Gaines lands, with six companies of infantry and marches to the site of the Dade ambush. Once the remains of several soldiers are interred, Gaines pushes onto Fort King only to find that promised food supplies are not there.

General Winfield Scott arrives at Picolata on the St. John's River, Florida Territory, although lacking any troops to command. Ignoring the presence of General Gaines further south, he prepares to mount his own campaign against the Seminoles.

FEBRUARY 26–27 General Edmund P. Gaines orders his 1,000-man force across the Withlacoochee River, Florida Territory, until they are fired upon by nearby

Seminoles. Gaines then orders a log breastwork constructed, christened Camp Izard, and he is besieged there for several days. Once his men begin running low on ammunition and food, he dispatches a messenger to Brigadier General Duncan L. Clinch for assistance.

MARCH 1–8 In the Florida Territory, Brigadier General Duncan L. Clinch disobeys direct orders from General Winfield Scott and marches to assist General Edmund P. Gaines, who is besieged by large numbers of Seminoles. Clinch then departs Fort Drane with a column of infantry and some supplies and plunges into the swamps.

MARCH 9–28 A chastened General Edmund P. Gaines departs Florida for New Orleans, Louisiana, while Brigadier General Duncan L. Clinch assumes command of his forces. Once home, Gaines receives orders placing him in charge of the western frontier while the Texas War for Independence rages.

MARCH 25–31 In the Florida Territory, General Winfield Scott commences a three-pronged offensive against the Seminole. His goal is to have three columns converge on the main Indian villages along the Withlacoochee River. Scott accompanies the right column under Brigadier General Duncan L. Clinch, while Brigadier General William Eustis leads the left column. The center column of 1,250 Alabama and Florida militia under Colonel William Lindsey also advances. The Seminole prove elusive and the Americans, running low on food, withdraw without accomplishing anything.

APRIL Major General Edmund P. Gaines, worried that the Cherokees might ally themselves with the Mexicans in Texas, musters volunteers from Louisiana, Alabama, Mississippi, and Arkansas.

Nonetheless, he remains under strict orders not to cross the Sabine River into Texas unless the Cherokees actually attack.

In Alabama and Georgia, militant members of the Creek nation prepare to resist forced relocation across the Mississippi River. Consequently, a force of 1,000 regulars and 9,000 militiamen are mobilizing to remove them at bayonet point, if necessary.

APRIL 1 In the Florida Territory, the army of General Winfield Scott draws supplies and renews its sweep along the Withlacoochee. Once again, the elusive tribesmen easily evade the American columns in swampy terrain.

APRIL 14 Outside Fort Barnwell, Florida Territory, Seminole warriors ambush a burial detail, routing them. Major William Gates is accordingly court-martialed for not recovering the bodies of slain soldiers from the Indians.

APRIL 20–24 At Fort Drane, Florida Territory, Seminoles launch a rare and unsuccessful night attack but prove unable to capture it. The garrison is successfully relieved four days later.

APRIL 27 In Florida, Alabama militia under Colonel William Chisolm are ambushed by Seminoles at Thonotosassa Creek as they march toward Fort Alabama. After fending off the attack, Chisolm sets a powder charge that destroys the abandoned fort, along with any Seminoles who may have wandered in.

MAY 21 In Washington, D.C., Secretary of War William Cass is displeased by General Winfield Scott's lack of success in the Florida Territory and orders him to Georgia to orchestrate removal of the Creek Indians. Scott, frustrated by his elusive foe, happily complies. Territorial governor Richard Keith Call subsequently requests permission to direct military operations in Scott's absence.

MAY 23   In Washington, D.C., Congress finally acknowledges the utility of mounted formations and authorizes creation of 2nd Regiment of Dragoons under Colonel David E. Twiggs. They also vote funding to secure 10,000 volunteers to bolster the war effort in Florida.

MAY 26–28   At Milledgeville, Georgia, General Winfield Scott begins planning a multi-pronged offensive into the Creek heartland to subdue them as quickly as possible. However, he remains greatly preoccupied by gathering supplies and militia troops.

JUNE 9   At Micanopy, Florida Territory, the garrison of Fort Defiance suddenly sorties against a body of Seminoles, besieging them while a detachment of the 2nd Dragoons assails their flank. The Indians, taken by surprise, melt away back into the woods.

JUNE 10–28   In Georgia, General Thomas S. Jesup advances against hostile Creek Indians and captures the main Indian camp. General Winfield Scott, however, is furious that he twice disobeyed orders to stop. Before Scott can take action against that officer, however, he is summoned back to Washington, D.C.

JUNE 20   In Alabama, civil authorities drag Inspector General Colonel John E. Wool to court for protecting Creek Indians under his control. Wool openly sympathizes with the Indians and he is vindicated by the courts, but he is unable to stop forced relocation of the Creeks.

JUNE 21   In Georgia, the Creek Volunteer Regiment is recruited for service in the Florida Territory. They are to be led by white officers but the regimental major is David Moniac, a native Creek and the first Native American to graduate from the U.S. Military Academy (1822).

In Washington, D.C., Secretary of War Lewis Cass authorizes Florida Governor Richard K. Call to commence military operations against the Seminole. He also receives authority to lead regular forces, even though he is only commander of nearby militia forces.

JULY 2   At Fort Mitchell, Georgia, the forced relocation of Creek Indians begins. Any individuals who resist are shackled by soldiers and dragged away. Consequently, Creek warriors who have volunteered to fight the Seminole in Florida are forced to rejoin their families in the Indian Territory (Oklahoma).

JULY 10   In Louisiana, General Edmund P. Gaines orders a squadron of the 2nd Dragoons and several companies of the 7th Infantry to occupy Nacogdoches on the western frontier. This is in territory disputed by Mexico, but the garrison is eventually withdrawn as tensions subside.

JULY 19   At Micanopy, Florida Territory, Seminoles under Osceola ambush a train of 22 wagons escorted by dragoons and artillerists at Welika Pond. The Indians are driven off after relief forces arrive; the Americans sustain five dead and six injured.

AUGUST 21–24   Near Fort Defiance, Florida Territory, artillerymen and dragoons under Major Benjamin F. Pierce surprise a Seminole encampment near Fort Defiance. They are driven back after losing one killed and 16 wounded; three days later Fort Defiance is deemed untenable and evacuated.

OCTOBER 3 In Washington, D.C., General Winfield Scott arrives, fully expecting to be praised for his handling of the Creek uprising. Instead, he is shocked to find himself under a Court of Inquiry investigating his difficulties with General Edmund P. Gaines. The court eventually clears Scott while Gaines ends up censured for un-officer like behavior.

OCTOBER 8–19 In the Florida Territory, Governor Richard K. Call's militia volunteer force, strengthened by 200 regulars under Major Benjamin K. Pierce, attempts to cross the Withlacoochee River. They are forced back by heavy musket fire and, short on supplies, Call orders his column back to Fort Drane to refit.

NOVEMBER 4 In Washington, D.C., Acting Secretary of War Benjamin F. Butler informs Governor Richard K. Call that he is succeeded in the Florida Territory by General Thomas S. Jesup. This information arrives too late to prevent Call from embarking offensive operations against the Seminole for the time being.

NOVEMBER 17–18 Governor Richard K. Call, returning to the Withlacoochee River, bests the Seminole in two large skirmishes, losing three dead while killing 25 Indians. He remains unaware that Brevet Major General Thomas S. Jesup is en route to succeed him.

NOVEMBER 21 At Wahoo Swamp, Florida Territory, Governor Richard K. Call's column attacks a large Seminole force. They advance to within 50 yards before firing muskets and charging bayonets and the Indians fall back across a stream before rallying. The fighting subsides shortly afterward; among the slain is the Creek David Moniac, the first Native American to graduate from West Point. Again, Call retreats once his supplies of food and ammunition begin running low.

DECEMBER 2–9 In the Florida Territory, Governor Richard K. Call is apprised of his replacement by Brevet Major General Thomas S. Jesup. He protests the move but Jesup ignores him and begins planning his own campaign against the remaining Seminole strongholds.

DECEMBER 12 In the Florida Territory, General Thomas S. Jesup keeps his forces concentrated, rather than dispersing them into roving columns. He also appoints engineering officer Brevet Brigadier General Walter K. Armistead to take charge of northern Florida, while he coordinates military affairs in the southern half.

1837

JANUARY 10–27 Brevet Major General Thomas S. Jesup continues his offensive in the Florida Territory, but he experiences trouble engaging the fast-moving Seminoles. A handful of Indians are killed in and around Lake Apopka, but otherwise fighting is restricted to skirmishing.

FEBRUARY 8 In the Florida Territory, Seminole Indians attack a detachment of the 8th Infantry under Colonel Alexander C. W. Fanning near Lake Monroe, nearly overrunning them during a stiff action. The Indians are finally repulsed by Navy gunboats on the lake.

MAY 19 In Washington, D.C., the War Department adopts a major reorganization by renaming the Eastern and Western Departments as divisions. The

Mississippi River functions as the administrative boundary between them.

JUNE 2   At Tampa, Florida Territory, a daring nighttime raid by Osceola and 200 warriors rescue Seminole Indians confined there for deportation. This act undoes the recent truce and treaty between the tribe and Brevet Major General Thomas S. Jesup; hostilities recommence.

AUGUST 5   In St. Louis, Missouri, Lieutenants Robert E. Lee and Montgomery C. Meigs of the Corps of Engineers report for duty. Both Southerners are destined for highly significant roles in the Civil War, 1861–1865, although on opposite sides.

SEPTEMBER   In the Florida Territory, Brevet Major General Thomas S. Jesup appeals to the War Department for an additional 6,000 army troops to subdue the defiant Seminoles. The swampy nature of the terrain also induces him to requisition numerous small boats and pontoon bridges.

OCTOBER 21–22   At Fort Peyton, Florida Territory, soldiers under General Joseph M. Hernandez treacherously seize Seminole Chief Osceola under a flag of truce. Hernandez is acting under direct orders from Brevet Brigadier General Thomas S. Jesup not to let the chief escape.

DECEMBER 25–28   At Wahoo Swamp, Florida Territory, Colonel Zachary Taylor leads 1,000 troops and militia in a battle against Seminole warriors. A three-hour struggle ensues in knee-deep water and the Americans sustain 26 dead and 112 wounded before the Indians withdraw. Seminole losses are 25 found slain on the field and a further 180 captured; Taylor consequently wins promotion to brevet brigadier general.

1838

JANUARY 4–MARCH 21   General Winfield Scott is dispatched to the Canadian border for talks with the British concerning difficulties engendered by the "Patriot War." This rebellion is waged by discontented Canadians, many of whom operate freely from Buffalo, New York. Colonel William Jenkins Worth is ordered to arrest them, along with any Americans found providing material assistance.

JANUARY 24   In the Florida Territory, Brevet Brigadier General Thomas S. Jesup attacks a concentration of Seminoles discovered at the Lockahatchee River. His Tennessee Volunteers waver in the face of fierce resistance, forcing Jesup to lead them back on foot; he is wounded when a bullet shatters his glasses. The Indians gradually withdraw, leaving seven Americans dead and 31 wounded.

FEBRUARY 8–MARCH 21   In the Florida Territory, Brevet Brigadier General Thomas S. Jesup resorts to diplomacy to resolve Indian hostility and invites several Seminole chiefs to parley with him. The Indians only agree to a cease-fire if they are allowed to remain in unsettled portions of southern Florida. Jesup informs Secretary of War Joel Poinsett of the demand; Poinsett refuses to agree. On March 21st, another deputation of Indians is invited to talks, then seized and imprisoned.

APRIL 24   In the Florida Territory, dragoons and artillerists under Colonel William S. Harney attack a Seminole camp to capture Chief Old Sam. A three-hour battle through the swamp ensues but the Indians withdraw and their chief escapes.

MAY 8   Back in Georgia, General Winfield Scott issues Order No. 35, instructing soldiers to show consideration toward the Cherokees they are forcibly removing. This 1,200-mile sojourn they are about to embark upon becomes reviled as the "Trail of Tears."

MAY 15   In the Florida Territory, Brevet Brigadier General Zachary Taylor succeeds Brevet Major General Thomas S. Jesup as overall commander. The latter returns to Washington, D.C., and resumes his duties as Quartermaster General.

JULY 5   In Washington, D.C., the War Department organizes the Topographical Engineers into a separate corps under Colonel John J. Abert. Funding is also appropriated to establish the new 8th Infantry.

DECEMBER   In Georgia, the "Trail of Tears" begins: the last of 14,000 Cherokees are forcibly relocated from their tribal homelands and marched 1,200 miles overland to Oklahoma. They are escorted by United States troops under Generals Winfield Scott and John E. Wool. Harsh weather conditions encountered result in the deaths of 4,000 Indians en route.

1839

FEBRUARY 15   In Washington, D.C., Secretary of War Joel Poinsett approves Brevet Brigadier General Zachary Taylor's plan for dividing northern Florida into 20-square-mile regions, each possessing a small fort and a 20-man garrison, half of whom are mounted. This strategy requires four full regiments to implement and it will hopefully pacify northern parts of the territory.

MARCH 5–25   General Winfield Scott heads for Maine to help adjudicate a border difficulty arising when Canadian loggers from New Brunswick use the disputed Aroostook region. Scott parleys with Governor John Harvey, another six-foot-six-inch individual whom he encountered during the War of 1812.

MARCH 20   On the Miami River, Florida Territory, Seminole warriors ambush a boatload of troops under Captain Samuel A. Russell. The soldiers fight off their attackers although Russell sustains five wounds in the process.

MARCH 23–25   In Maine, General Winfield Scott and Lieutenant Governor John Harvey of New Brunswick agree to withhold military forces from the disputed Aroostook region. Their cordial agreement lays the foundation for a peaceful resolution of this conflict.

MAY 22   At Fort King, Florida Territory, Commanding General of the Army Alexander Macomb signs a peace treaty with the remaining Seminole leaders and declares the present conflict over. The Indians agree to be settled along the Kissimmee River, provided they bring all their followers in by midsummer.

JULY 21–23 At Fort Andrews, Florida Territory, several bands of Seminoles ignore the recent peace treaty and ambush a company of the 6th Infantry. They subsequently launch a surprise attack on a dragoon encampment along the Caloosahatchee River, almost capturing Lieutenant Colonel William S. Harney. The Americans lose 18 troopers killed out of 26 present, with several captives being tortured to death.

1840

MARCH 28 Near Fort King, Florida Territory, a 16-man patrol under Captain Gabriel Rains, 7th Infantry, is ambushed by a much larger Seminole force. Rains is badly wounded leading a charge, but his command fights its way back to the fort.

MAY 1–6 In the Florida Territory, an ailing Brevet Brigadier General Zachary Taylor hands his command over to Brevet Brigadier General Walter K. Armistead. Armistead can muster a force of 3,400 regulars and 1,500 volunteer militiamen, many of whom are sick. Nonetheless, he continues Taylor's policy of taking the war to the Indians.

MAY 2–28 In the Wisconsin Territory, disgruntled Winnebago Indians leave their reservation and terrorize nearby settlers. Consequently, Colonel William Jenkins Worth is ordered to the region from Sackets Harbor, New York.

DECEMBER 3–24 At Fort Dallas, Florida Territory, Lieutenant Colonel William S. Harney leads 90 men on a foray into the Seminole heartland. Unlike previous endeavors, he moves by canoe at night and his men, dressed in Indian garb, are armed with the latest Colt repeating rifles. In due course, Harney surprises several small encampments, killing Chief Chakaika and some warriors.

1841

MARCH 2–4 Outside of Fort Brooks, Florida Territory, a company under Lieutenant William Alburtis ambushes a detachment of Seminoles, routing them. Two days later a bayonet charge also disperses Indians attacking a supply train that was heading to the fort.

MAY 1–JUNE 4 In the Florida Territory, a youthful Lieutenant William Tecumseh Sherman escorts Chief Coacoochee to Fort Pierce for peace talks. However, when no progress is made, the chief and several consorts are seized and forcibly transported to Louisiana.

MAY 31 The energetic Colonel William Jenkins Worth replaces Brevet Brigadier General Walter K. Armistead as commander of American forces in the Florida Territory. This force has grown so large it is now labeled the Army of the South and consists of 4,800 regulars.

JUNE 25 In Washington, D.C., the soft-spoken Commanding General of the Army Alexander Macomb dies in Washington, D.C. A distinguished War of 1812 veteran, he imposed new and more modern forms of administration on the military's bureaucracy, making it more efficient.

JULY 5   In Washington, D.C., the 55-year-old Winfield Scott is appointed the new Commanding General of the Army. He has served with distinction since 1808 and first garnered national attention during the War of 1812. Brevet Brigadier General John Ellis Wool, another notable veteran, is promoted to full brigadier general to fill the vacancy.

AUGUST 5   The 1st Infantry departs the Florida Territory after three and a half years of grueling campaigns against the Seminoles. Hard service cost the regiment 6 officers and 135 dead, mostly to disease.

OCTOBER 10   At Punta Rassa, Florida Territory, several companies of the 8th Infantry endure a tremendous tropical storm whose floodwaters wipe out their encampment; the 200 soldiers are forced to spend the night in trees.

OCTOBER 17   In the Florida Territory, five companies of the 2nd Dragoons conclude five years of service and are ordered to garrison Forts Towson and Jesup along the western frontier.

DECEMBER 20   In Big Cypress Swamp, Florida Territory, a patrol of the 8th Infantry is ambushed by Seminoles, and two soldiers are killed. Their bodies are subsequently weighed down and sunk in a pond to prevent mutilation by vengeful Indians.

1842

JANUARY 25   Near Dunn's Lake, Florida Territory, several companies of the 2nd Infantry under Major Joseph Plympton surprise a body of Seminoles in their encampment and drive them off.

MARCH 14   Colonel William Jenkins Worth estimates that only 200 Seminoles remain in Florida, whereas several thousand have been deported to new homes west of the Mississippi River. Those remaining show no inclination to abandon their struggle, however.

APRIL 19   At Pelikakaha, Florida Territory, Colonel William Jenkins Worth attacks the encampment of Chief Hallack-Tustenugge. His infantry advances frontally to engage the enemy while part of the 2nd Dragoons sweeps around them from behind; the Seminoles break and flee into the swamps.

APRIL 29–MAY 2   In the Florida Territory, Chief Hallack-Tustenugge arrives at Colonel William Jenkins Worth's camp and requests to parley. Worth invites the chief and several associates for extended talks at Fort King, but when the Indians appear a few days later as arranged, they are seized and imprisoned.

MAY 10   In Washington, D.C., Secretary of War John C. Spencer informs Colonel William Jenkins Worth that the Seminole War has concluded. He is therefore to suspend all offensive operations immediately.

MAY 17   Florida's Second Seminole War, a grueling test of endurance lasting seven years, finally sputters out into two small skirmishes near Fort Wacachoota and Clay's Landing along the Suwanee River.

JUNE 10   In Kansas City, Missouri, Lieutenant John C. Fremont commands a 30-man expedition that will explore the Oregon Trail as a possible route for immigrants heading to the West Coast. The noted scout Christopher "Kit" Carson is among those recruited.

AUGUST In Washington, D.C., Commanding General Winfield Scott issues General Order No. 53, which outlines procedures for adjudicating military offenses. Moreover, it explicitly prohibits arbitrary punishments inflicted upon enlisted men by officers and sergeants.

AUGUST 14 In Florida, Colonel William Jenkins Worth formally announces that the Second Seminole War is over. He also receives brevet promotion to brigadier general as of March 1, 1842, for overseeing the thankless task of finishing up this difficult contest.

AUGUST 23 In Washington, D.C., Congress reduces the standing military establishment by 1,400 soldiers, leaving a total of 8,600 rank and file. The 2nd Dragoons is also converted into a rifle-armed infantry formation for reasons of economy.

NOVEMBER 1 In Florida, Brevet Brigadier General William Jenkins Worth briefly returns to Florida to convince the handful of remaining Seminoles to relocate with their tribesmen across the Mississippi River. To that end, Lieutenant Ethan Allen Hitchcock, 3rd Infantry, is tasked with tracking down any recalcitrant parties, rounding them up, and shipping them west. The seven-year conflict in Florida cost the U.S. Army 1,466 dead—mostly through disease—and 290 wounded while the total number of Seminoles deported does not exceed 6,000.

1843

MARCH 13 At Jefferson Barracks, Missouri, the 2nd Dragoon Regiment is dismounted and retrained as infantry. The transfer goes smoothly save for some grousing among former troopers.

MAY–JUNE At Fort Gibson, Indian Territory (Oklahoma), a patrol of 62 troopers from the 1st Dragoons departs on an extended patrol conducted by Captain Nathan Boone. Boone, son of noted pioneer Daniel Boone, strikes out along the Arkansas River and onto the Santa Fe Trail for the purpose of protecting trade caravans.

MAY 30 In St. Louis, Missouri, Lieutenant John C. Fremont begins his second expedition of the Oregon Trail, during which he also explores regions along the Snake and Columbia Rivers.

JULY 14 In the Indian Territory, Captain Nathan Boone trots back into Fort Gibson after completing an extended patrol to the Santa Fe Trail. En route he also managed to scout along the Canadian and Washita Rivers.

SEPTEMBER 30 At Jefferson Barracks, Missouri, Lieutenant Ulysses S. Grant arrives for duty with the 4th Infantry. Among the young officers he encounters and befriends there is Lieutenant James Longstreet, a future Civil War adversary.

OCTOBER 25 In the Washington Territory, the small expedition of Lieutenant John C. Fremont reaches the Indian village of Walla Walla, thereby completing his reconnaissance of the Oregon Trail.

1844

JANUARY 3–18 Lieutenant John C. Fremont's expedition reaches the fringes of the Sierra Nevada, then turns west to make a dangerous winter crossing of that range into California.

FEBRUARY 4–5 Lieutenant John C. Fremont's expedition, assisted by noted scout Kit Carson, continues trudging through the snow-choked passes of the Sierra Nevada. From this point the men can see California in the distance.

FEBRUARY 10–24 Lieutenant John C. Fremont's expedition forges ahead but runs out of food and has to eat its own horses. At length the cold, weary explorers cross into California and limp into Sutter's Fort to recuperate.

MARCH 4 In Washington, D.C., Congress reverses itself and votes to remount the

John C. Fremont, the "pathfinder" of the U.S. Topographical Corps. (Library of Congress)

2nd Dragoons under Colonel David Twiggs. American interests are presently burgeoning along the Western Frontier and the utility of mounted units is apparent to legislators.

APRIL–MAY In California, Lieutenant John C. Fremont grows aware that Mexican patrols are looking for his expedition, so he orders them across the Mojave Desert and they eventually encamp at Mountain Meadows. En route, one soldier is killed by hostile Indians.

APRIL 22 In Washington, D.C., the War Department reorganizes itself into Eastern and Western Divisions under Generals John E. Wool and Edmund P. Gaines, respectively. Each division is further subdivided into nine departments, each headed by a brigadier general.

APRIL 23–27 Brevet Brigadier General Zachary Taylor is appointed commander of the 1st Military District, headquartered at Fort Jesup, Louisiana. He also receives secret instructions to form an "Army of Observation" and march it to the Sabine River; this is conceived as an independent command and Major General Edmund P. Gaines, Taylor's superior, remains uninformed.

AUGUST 6 Lieutenant John C. Fremont's expedition, having trudged thousands of miles over the past 14 months, ends its journey at St. Louis, Missouri. He relays valuable intelligence about Mexican holdings in the West and also receives a degree of national fame for his daring.

NOVEMBER 30 Once construction of Fort Wilkins on Lake Superior concludes, the military has erected a chain of fortifications along its western periphery, stretching from Texas to the Canadian border.

1845

MARCH 31   In Washington, D.C., Mexico breaks relations with the United States over the issue of Texas annexation; war between the two countries appears imminent.

MAY 18–AUGUST 24   At Fort Leavenworth, Kansas, Colonel Stephen Watts Kearny and several cavalry companies depart on an expedition through Indian country. He is specifically ordered to demonstrate American strength to the inhabitants, and parley with numerous Comanche, Kiowa, and Cheyenne leaders. His sojourn takes him across 2,200 miles in 99 days, across both the Oregon and Santa Fe Trails.

MAY 28   In Washington, D.C., President James K. Polk dispatches General Zachary Taylor from the Sabine River and into southwestern Texas to preclude any chance of Mexican occupation. By the tenets of international law, this territory is Mexican and Taylor's presence there is a provocative act setting the stage for war.

JUNE 3–AUGUST 11   Several companies of the 1st Dragoons under Captain Edwin V. Sumner enter Sioux territory to hold formal discussions with chieftains for the first time.

JUNE 15   In Washington, D.C., Secretary of State James Buchanan assures the government of Texas of military protection once it agrees to the terms of annexation. General Zachary Taylor's "Army of Observation" is accordingly ordered to a point "on or near the Rio Grande."

JUNE 20–AUGUST 12   At St. Louis, Missouri, Lieutenant John C. Fremont conducts his third expedition of 55 men, this time to survey the Arkansas and Red Rivers.

JULY 25   On the Texas coastline, General Zachary Taylor's army is transported to Nueces Bay, Texas, and disembarks on St. Joseph's Island. His presence is a show of force in support a Congressional resolution for the annexation of Texas. Lieutenant George G. Meade, Topographical Engineer, is entrusted with finding land for suitable campsites at Corpus Christi before the army is conveyed to the mainland.

JULY 31   In Texas, General Zachary Taylor's army is reinforced by 3,500 men, prior to marching his army to the Nueces River. Once there, he assumes defensive positions in the vicinity of Corpus Christi.

AUGUST   At New Orleans, General Edmund P. Gaines exceeds his authority by calling out volunteers from Louisiana in anticipation of war with Mexico. He is harshly repudiated by Secretary of War William L. Marcy and ordered to discharge all the levies.

AUGUST 12–16   At Bent's Fort, Indian Territory (Oklahoma), Lieutenant James W. Abert conducts a small detachment from Lieutenant John C. Fremont's expedition and begins exploring Comanche and Kiowa territory. Fremont, probably acting under secret orders, marches his remaining men toward Mexican-held California.

SEPTEMBER–DECEMBER   At Corpus Christi, Texas, the "Army of Occupation" under General Zachary Taylor is continually reinforced to a total strength of 3,900 men, organized in three brigades. His soldiers remain subject to harsh training and discipline, but order lapses once brothels are established outside the camp by local traders.

DECEMBER 5–31 Lieutenant John C. Fremont's expedition advances through the Donner Pass and descends the Sierra Nevada into California. There they again repose at Sutter's Fort for several days before pushing on, although the fort's suspicious owner alerts Mexican authorities.

1846

JANUARY 13 In Washington, D.C., President James K. Polk orders General Zachary Taylor to shift his "Army of Observation" further south from the Nueces River to the north bank of the Rio Grande. This is a move calculated to either induce Mexican authorities into negotiations or spark an armed conflict.

JANUARY 15–27 In California, Lieutenant John C. Fremont's expedition enters the region around present-day San Francisco, which he christens the "Golden Gate." Pushing onward, he finally marches to establish a temporary headquarters at Monterey after obtaining permission from Mexican authorities.

JANUARY 27 Lieutenant Colonel John C. Fremont reaches Monterey, California, with a small body of soldiers. This time, Fremont's "expedition" is not tasked with exploring, but preparing the region for annexation.

FEBRUARY 3 In Texas, General Zachary Taylor begins marching his 3,900 men further down the banks of the Rio Grande and opposite of Matamoros, Mexico. This territory is disputed, and his presence is calculated to provoke a strong reaction from Mexican authorities.

FEBRUARY 22 In California, Lieutenant John C. Fremont violates his prior agreement with Mexican authorities by departing Monterey, scaling Gavilan Peak, and raising the American flag. Mexican soldiers begin assembling nearby to expel him from a log fort he has constructed without authorization.

MARCH 3 In California, Mexican general Jose Castro, commanding at Monterey, formally orders Lieutenant Colonel John C. Fremont's expedition off their territory.

MARCH 19–20 In Texas, General Zachary Taylor confronts Mexican forces drawn up along the opposite bank of the Arroyo Colorado lagoon. Unfazed, he orders his engineers to survey various places to ford under the cover of nearby artillery batteries. Colonel William Jenkins Worth also leads several infantry companies across the lagoon and the Mexicans fall back.

MARCH 28–APRIL 4 In Texas, General Zachary Taylor's army occupies the left bank of the Rio Grande, which is internationally recognized as Mexican territory. Mexican forces at Matamoros, directly across from the Americans, commence building fortifications and entrenching.

APRIL 1 In southern Texas, Mexican forces seize two American dragoons that have accidentally strayed into their territory; both are subsequently released.

APRIL 12 At Matamoros, Mexico, General Pedro de Ampudia issues an ultimatum to General Zachary Taylor and insists that he withdraw his forces back beyond the Nueces River. Ampudia warns the Americans of a general engagement for failure to do so, but Taylor refuses to budge.

APRIL 23 The Mexican government declares war on the United States, initiating a two-year struggle that will cost them the northern third of their country.

APRIL 25 At Carricitos Ranch, Texas, Mexican cavalry ambushes two companies of the 2nd Dragoons under Captain Seth B. Thompson, killing 10 men, wounding four, and capturing the rest. Henceforth, General Zachary Taylor considers that hostilities have commenced and he asks the governor of Louisiana to provide four volunteer regiments.

APRIL 28 Near Point Isabel, Texas, Captain Samuel Walker's company of Texas Rangers is ambushed by Mexican forces, losing five dead and four captured.

APRIL 31 At Matamoros, the 5,700-man Mexican Army of the North surges across the Rio Grande to engage General Zachary Taylor's army. However, Taylor falls back 10 miles to Point Isabel to protect his lines of communication.

MAY At West Point, New York, the U.S. Military Academy graduates 59 new second lieutenants, its largest class to date. Four from the Class of 1846 die in Mexico, but 12 subsequently become Union generals and 10 serve with the Confederacy.

MAY 1–7 Mexican artillery begins bombarding American-held Fort Taylor, directly opposite Matamoros, Mexico. Major Jacob Brown, the garrison commander, returns fire with several pieces until he is mortally wounded on May 6. Meanwhile, the garrison refuses all demands to surrender.

MAY 3–11 Aged General Edmund P. Gaines again violates his authority by calling up volunteer soldiers from four states to reinforce General Zachary Taylor in Texas. The War Department, lacking the money to pay these 15 new regiments, angrily transfers Gaines to the Eastern Division, far away from the scene of operations.

MAY 8 In Texas, the Battle of Palo Alto ensues after General Zachary Taylor's 2,228 troops engage 4,000 Mexicans under General Mariano Arista. Taylor prevails in a protracted artillery duel of three hours, forcing Arista to withdraw to better positions at Resaca de la Palma. Mexican losses are 320 killed and 380 wounded, whereas the Americans suffer only 9 dead and 47 wounded. Major Samuel Ringgold, a noted light artillerist, is among those slain.

MAY 9 In Texas, General Zachary Taylor's army attacks a larger Mexican force at Resaca de la Palma with a combined cavalry and infantry assault. Captain Charles May of the 2nd Dragoons conducts a celebrated charge that seizes a Mexican battery and General Romulo Diaz la Vega. The Mexicans withdraw once General Arista's right flank gives way and they are enfiladed by American artillery while retiring. For a loss of 33 killed and 89 injured, Taylor inflicts 547 dead or wounded on his adversary.

MAY 13 In Washington, D.C., the Senate approves a declaration of war against Mexico, 40 to 2, and authorizes $10 million and 50,000 volunteers. The number of privates assigned to each infantry company also rises to 100 men apiece. However, the war splits the national polity, with Southerners generally in favor of conflict while many Northerners oppose it.

MAY 15 In Washington, D.C., Secretary of War William L. Marcy authorizes state governors to begin recruiting volunteers for service in Mexico. Commanding General of the Army Winfield Scott intends to raise them on a ratio of three infantry to one cavalry, and orders equipment and supplies prepositioned along their routes of movement.

MAY 17–22 In south Texas, General Zachary Taylor's army crosses the Rio Grande and occupies the town of Matamoros. The first volunteer units also begin arriving; Taylor considers them enthusiastic but poorly trained and led.

MAY 19 In Washington, D.C., Congress authorizes the new Regiment of Mounted Riflemen, with Persifor C. Smith as colonel and John C. Fremont as lieutenant colonel. The troopers are to be armed with Model 1841 rifles and sabers, and they are capable of fighting on foot as necessary.

MAY 29 In Washington, D.C., Congress expands the U.S. Army by authorizing an additional major general and two more brigadiers.

JUNE 6–JULY 29 At Fort Leavenworth, Kansas, Colonel Stephen W. Kearny departs on an expedition against Santa Fe, New Mexico. He heads a small cavalry/infantry column of 1,750 men endowed with the grandiose title, "Army of the West." Kearny first marches to Bent's Fort along the Santa Fe Trail to physically inure them to hardship, although several men die due to disease and accidents.

Along the Rio Grande, in Texas, General Zachary Taylor receives orders from the War Department to capture the Mexican city of Monterrey. Taylor, however, elects to first seize Camargo as a supply base before marching further south.

JUNE 11–SEPTEMBER 23 Brigadier General John E. Wool is detached from the Eastern Division and ordered to proceed to Texas. There he will form a division of regulars and volunteers and seize the Mexican town of Chihuahua. Upon reaching San Antonio, Texas, Wool gradually assembles his 3,400 troops as the Division of the Center.

JUNE 26–29 In Washington, D.C., Congress approves eight new general positions: three for the regular Army and five for volunteers. Brevet Brigadier General Zachary Taylor also receives promotion to major general while Stephen Watts Kearny and David E. Twiggs advance to brigadier.

JULY 4 At Sonoma, California, the "Bear Flag Republic" is declared by American settlers. Lieutenant John C. Fremont is also appointed to lead the new "California Army" as a lieutenant colonel and marches off to Monterey to join the squadron of Commodore John D. Sloat anchored there.

JULY 6–SEPTEMBER 19 At Camargo, Mexico, Major General Zachary Taylor's army arrives and encamps, although the local topography and climate prove debilitating to his troops. He also waits several weeks for supplies and reinforcements to trickle in before offensive operations can manifest. By the fall, Taylor possesses four divisions, two regular and two volunteer, and begins advancing toward Monterrey with 6,200 men.

JULY 7 In Havana, Cuba, Commander Alexander S. Mackenzie confers with exiled Mexican general Antonio Lopez de Santa Anna as to a negotiated peace. President James K. Polk believes that if Santa Anna were returned to Mexico City, he would feel obliged to expedite a treaty favorable to the United States.

JULY 15–19 At Monterey, California, Lieutenant Colonel John C. Fremont joins the squadron of Commodore John D. Sloat. The two also begin formulating plans for an amphibious descent upon the settlement of Los Angeles, further south.

AUGUST 2 Having reached the Santa Fe Trail, Brigadier General Stephen Watts Kearny marches his Army of the West from Bent's Fort into the deserts of New Mexico. An epic conquest is now set in motion.

AUGUST 13 In California, the Mexican settlement of Los Angeles surrenders to the naval squadron of Commodore Robert F. Stockton, who has replaced John D. Sloat. It is immediately occupied by military forces under Lieutenant Colonel John C. Fremont.

AUGUST 18 Brigadier General Stephen Watts Kearny's Army of the West, having covered 856 miles of searing desert, occupies Santa Fe, New Mexico. He accepts the surrender of Mexican authorities there and establishes a provisional government without the loss of a man or a single shot fired.

SEPTEMBER 2 At Los Angeles, California, Commodore Robert F. Stockton appoints Major John C. Fremont as military governor and authorizes him to continue recruiting for the California Battalion. Kit Carson, the noted scout, is also dispatched back to Washington, D.C., with information concerning conditions in the region.

SEPTEMBER 12 In Washington, D.C., Secretary of War William L. Marcy denies Commanding General of the Army Winfield Scott a field command. However, to deflate the rising political stock of General Zachary Taylor, a Whig operative, President James K. Polk eventually grants Scott his wish.

SEPTEMBER 14 In Mexico City, the formerly exiled general Antonio Lopez de Santa Anna is appointed commander in chief by his countrymen. He immediately ignores his prior "understanding" with the Polk administration and begins planning to repel the American invaders. His appointment ultimately proves disastrous to Mexico.

SEPTEMBER 20–24 In northern Mexico, the Battle of Monterrey erupts as General Zachary Taylor and 6,640 men attack the 5,000-strong Mexican garrison under General Pedro de Ampudia. Among the defenders is the San Patrico battalion formed from predominately Irish Catholic deserters. The Americans finally flush the defenders from their strong points, including the heavily fortified Bishop's Palace, in four days of hand-to-hand fighting. Ampudia then requests and receives an eight-week armistice in exchange for evacuating the city peacefully. Taylor sustains 120 dead, 368 wounded, and 33 missing to estimated Mexican losses of 430 killed and wounded, along with 28 cannons captured.

SEPTEMBER 22–23 In California, Mexicans inspired by Captain Jose Maria Flores revolt against American rule and besiege their small garrisons at San Diego, Santa Barbara, and Los Angeles. Flores is also appointed acting governor in the absence of Mexican authority.

SEPTEMBER 26 At Santa Fe, New Mexico, Colonel Alexander W. Doniphan is detached from the Army of the West and marches southward to join General John E. Wool. General Stephen Watts Kearny then continues heading for California with an escort of 300 dragoons.

SEPTEMBER 29 At Los Angeles, California, a 48-man detachment of the California Battalion under Marine Corps lieutenant Archibald Gillespie surrenders to a popular uprising, then is allowed to depart.

OCTOBER 6 En route to California Brigadier, General Stephen Watts Kearny encounters scout Kit Carson, heading back to Washington, D.C., who informs him of California's conquest. Kearny consequently sends 200 of his dragoons back to Santa Fe, New Mexico, while he forges ahead with the remaining 100.

OCTOBER 12 In southern Texas, General John E. Wool's Division of the Center crosses the Rio Grande into northern Mexico. Beforehand, he sternly warns his men to strictly respect all non-combatants and their property.

OCTOBER 13 In Washington, D.C., the War Department informs General Zachary Taylor that his recent eight-week armistice is unauthorized and has been disapproved.

OCTOBER 19   At Santa Fe, New Mexico, Lieutenant Colonel Philip St. George Cooke leads his Mormon Battalion west for California. However, their wagons full of family members, including women and children, are ordered to remain in place.

NOVEMBER 5   Off the coast of California, Commodore Robert F. Stockton is ordered by the Navy Department to recognize Brigadier General Stephen Watts Kearny as governor of California. This directive complicates existing matters for Lieutenant Colonel John C. Fremont, who is Stockton's candidate for that same office.

NOVEMBER 13   Saltillo, capital of Coahuilla, Mexico, is occupied by General Zachary Taylor without a shot being fired. Soon afterward he is contacted by General John E. Wool, who feels that a Mexican offensive is brewing and suggests that he relocate his division to Parras to be in supporting distance. Taylor agrees and authorizes the movement.

NOVEMBER 23   In Washington, D.C., President James K. Polk appoints General Winfield Scott to command an amphibious expedition against Vera Cruz. He does so from concerns that General Zachary Taylor, a Whig, does not support his policies and may run against him for the presidency. Scott is ordered to land on the Mexican coast and march overland to the capital of Mexico City.

NOVEMBER 25   Brigadier General Stephen Watts Kearny continues advancing into California with a small column of dragoons. He is unaware that the region has risen in rebellion against the invaders and that his force is badly outnumbered.

DECEMBER 6   In southern California, the Battle of San Pascual rages between 50 dragoons commanded by General Stephen Watts Kearny and 200 California lancers under Major Andreas Pico. The outnumbered Americans are roughly handled in combat, although Pico fails to press his manpower to advantage. A standoff ensues until American reinforcements arrive and the Californios withdraw. This savage little encounter costs the victors 21 dead and 17 wounded; Kearny himself is severely injured by a lance.

DECEMBER 13–16   In northern Mexico, General Zachary Taylor pushes the division of General David E. Twiggs toward the town of Victoria. Meanwhile, General William Jenkins Worth, occupying Saltillo, is apprised of a Mexican offensive bearing down on him and requests reinforcements from Taylor.

DECEMBER 14   At Santa Fe, New Mexico, Colonel Alexander W. Doniphan and 1,000 volunteers march south to Chihuahua to rendezvous with General John E. Wool's division. His route involves crossing 250 miles of desolate desert, and the column is split to help conserve water supplies.

DECEMBER 25   Along the Brazito River, Texas, Colonel Alexander W. Doniphan's column defeats 1,200 Mexican cavalry under Lieutenant Colonel Ponce de Leon, finally securing New Mexico for the United States. The Americans suffer seven wounded.

DECEMBER 27   Having defeated Mexican forces at the Brazito River, American forces under Colonel Alexander W. Doniphan occupy El Paso, Texas, before proceeding south toward Chihuahua.

DECEMBER 29   In northern Mexico, part of General Zachary Taylor's army occupies Victoria, capital of Tamaulipas state. Taylor himself arrives with the balance of the force six days later and awaits developments.

1847

JANUARY 3–16   At Camargo, Mexico, General Winfield Scott begins issuing orders to commandeer 9,000 soldiers from General Zachary Taylor's army. Once accomplished, Taylor's forces will consist mostly of raw and unreliable volunteers.

JANUARY 8   At San Gabriel, California, a force of 607 sailors, Marines, and dragoons under Commodore Robert F. Stockton and Brigadier General Stephen Watts Kearny defeat a Mexican force of infantry and lancers. The Americans form a square and beat back repeated cavalry attacks before advancing up the nearby heights and driving off enemy infantry; the Americans sustain two dead and nine wounded.

JANUARY 9   In southern California, Commodore Robert F. Stockton and Brigadier General Stephen Watts Kearny defeat another Mexican force at the Battle of La Mesa. At this juncture the Californios lose heart and prepare to surrender.

JANUARY 10   In southern California, troops under Brigadier General Stephen Watts Kearny occupy Los Angeles, ending all active resistance to American rule.

JANUARY 13   In northern Mexico, scouts belonging to Mexican general Antonio Lopez de Santa Anna capture American dispatches from General Winfield Scott. Santa Anna now realizes that General Zachary Taylor has been stripped of his best troops and elects to attack him while in this weakened condition.

In southern California, Major Andreas Pico concludes the Treaty of Cahuenga with Major John C. Fremont, which formally brings hostilities to a close. This ushers in a period of American dominance.

JANUARY 14   In northern Mexico, General Zachary Taylor is instructed by the War Department to maintain defensive positions while 9,000 of his soldiers are siphoned off for a forthcoming amphibious expedition under General Winfield Scott. Taylor correctly deduces that Democrat President James K. Polk is determined to weaken his political mettle as a Whig presidential candidate. "Old Rough and Ready" is also angered by Scott's usurpation of his best troops and he disregards orders to remain stationary.

JANUARY 16   In Los Angeles, California, Brigadier General Stephen Watts Kearny produces orders from the War Department which appoint him governor of the territory. However, Commodore Robert F. Stockton, still believing that he enjoys civil authority in California, insists that his candidate—John C. Fremont—be retained as governor. The two leaders are set on a collision course.

JANUARY 19   The inhabitants of Taos, New Mexico, rise against American rule, murdering Governor Charles Bent. Colonel Sterling Price consequently begins marshaling his Missouri Volunteers to punish the insurrectionists.

FEBRUARY 1–27   Colonel Alexander W. Doniphan's column departs El Paso, Texas, and marches south for Chihuahua, Mexico. Progress is dogged by Apache bands, hovering about the flanks for a chance to steal horses.

FEBRUARY 3–4   Taos, New Mexico, is recaptured by Missouri troops under Colonel Sterling Price. The Americans storm the town following an ineffective bombardment, and handily disperse the 1,200 rebels. Price suffers seven dead and

U.S. general John Wool and his staff, in the streets of Saltillo, about 1847. (Yale Collection of Western Americana, Beinecke Rare Book and Manuscript Library)

45 wounded, but New Mexico is again secured for the United States.

FEBRUARY 5 In northern Mexico, General Zachary Taylor defies War Department orders by marching west from Monterrey toward Saltillo. Presently he commands 4,800 raw volunteers stiffened by a handful of regulars under General John E. Wool.

FEBRUARY 11 In Washington, D.C., Congress fleshes out the U.S. Army with several new units including the 3rd Dragoon Regiment, the 9th–16th Infantries, a Voltigeur (rifleman) regiment, and a regiment of mounted riflemen.

FEBRUARY 13 In California, Brigadier General Stephen Watts Kearny receives orders confirming his authority to establish a government in Monterey as commander of the 10th Military District. At Los Angeles, however, John C. Fremont

still considers himself governor and refuses to disband his California Battalion.

FEBRUARY 14 In northern Mexico, General Zachary Taylor's army of 4,800 men advances 17 miles to Agua Nueva, Mexico. He also ignores General John E. Wool's advice to occupy strong defensive positions at St. Juan de la Buena Vista ranch, unaware that a large Mexican army under General Jose Antonio Lopez de Santa Anna is bearing down upon him.

FEBRUARY 19 At Tampico, Mexico, Major General Winfield Scott places the region under martial law, thereby subjecting American soldiers to immediate court-martial for harming Mexican civilians. This act represents the first time that an American military force has imposed martial law on foreign soil.

FEBRUARY 20–21 In northern Mexico, General Zachary Taylor is advised by cavalry scouts that an army of 15,000 Mexicans is marching fast upon him. This intelligence induces him to withdraw to stronger defensive positions at Buena Vista. The outnumbered Americans consist mainly of untried volunteers, backed by a handful of veteran artillery companies and dragoons.

FEBRUARY 22–23 In northern Mexico, the Battle of Buena Vista rages when 15,000 Mexican troops under General Antonio Lopez de Santa Anna attack General Zachary Taylor's force of 4,800 men. Fortunately, the latter are strongly arrayed on good defensive terrain. The enemy troops make several uncoordinated attacks upon Taylor's lines and are beaten back by the adroit tactics of General John E. Wool. After two days of fighting, the demoralized Mexicans retreat back to Mexico. Victory against seemingly insurmountable odds renders Taylor a national hero; he suffers 264 dead and 450 wounded to a Mexican toll of roughly 2,000.

FEBRUARY 28 In northern Mexico, Colonel Alexander W. Doniphan's expedition defeats 3,000 Mexicans at Rio Sacramento. They then occupy the city of Chihuahua after sustaining three killed and eight wounded; Mexican losses are estimated at around 200.

MARCH 1 Off the Mexican coast, General Winfield Scott assembles his invasion force of 13,000 men in three divisions. These soldiers are drawn from among the very best elements in the army.

MARCH 3 In Washington, D.C., Congress expands artillery organization by adding two additional companies to the four existing regiments. Curiously, as in the War of 1812, most artillery formations lack cannons and horses, hence they are trained mostly to fight as infantry.

MARCH 7–9 Off Vera Cruz, Mexico, General Winfield Scott's army, covered by Commodore David E. Conner's squadron, storms Collado Beach with 10,000 men. Once a lodgement is secured, they begin siege preparations to secure the garrison of Castle San Juan de Ulloa. This is the largest American amphibious operation to date, and it proceeds smoothly.

MARCH 25 In California, Major John C. Fremont agrees to disband his California Battalion following a heated confrontation with Brigadier General Stephen Watts Kearny. The two men remain at odds as to who is governor.

MARCH 27 At Vera Cruz, Mexico, General Juan Jose Landero surrenders 3,000 troops to General Winfield Scott, who sustains a loss of only 13 dead and 55 wounded. Scott thereupon insists on proper treatment for all Mexican noncombatants and even attends a Catholic service with his staff.

APRIL 8 Having secured Vera Cruz as a base of operations, General Winfield Scott conducts his 10,000 men down the National Road and toward Mexico City. Scott is anxious to finish campaigning before the onset of the yellow fever season, which could potentially decimate his force. Concurrently, General Antonio Lopez de Santa Anna determines to save his capital and musters every available soldier to defend it.

APRIL 13 Near Cerro Gordo, Mexico, Captain Robert E. Lee of the Corps of Engineers conducts a hazardous reconnaissance of enemy positions. He narrowly escapes capture, but manages to uncover a hidden trail over which troops and cannon can maneuver.

APRIL 17–18 At Cerro Gordo, Mexico, General Winfield Scott attacks 14,000

Mexican soldiers under General Antonio Lopez de Santa Anna. He conducts a series of slashing attacks, inflicting several hundred casualties at a cost of 64 dead and 350 wounded. Mexican losses are unknown but 2,837 captives are taken, along with 83 cannon—and Santa Anna's wooden leg. Scott then resumes his advance upon Mexico City in earnest.

MAY 6 In Mexico, the majority of General Winfield Scott's volunteers depart once their enlistments expire, leaving him with only 7,000 regulars. Meanwhile, General William Jenkins Worth seizes the Mexican city of Puebla as a possible supply base; Scott subsequently appoints him military governor.

MAY 22–JUNE 6 In northern Mexico, Colonel Alexander W. Doniphan's Missourians receive permission to return home after completing an epic 2,100-mile march through hostile deserts. Through effective leadership, Doniphan marches back with 90 percent of his command still intact.

MAY 31 In Monterey, California, General Stephen Watts Kearny arrests Major John C. Fremont after he defies a direct order to step down as governor. Kearny subsequently appoints Colonel Richard B. Mason to head up the 10th Military District, while he transports the unruly Fremont back to Fort Leavenworth under charges of insubordination.

JUNE 4 At Jalapa, Mexico, General Winfield Scott begins concentrating his army by gathering all rear-area security garrisons. Scott has not yet cut himself off from his main base of supply at Vera Cruz and intends to marshal his men at Puebla before resuming his advance upon Mexico City.

JUNE 26 At Pawnee Ford, Indian Territory (Oklahoma), a detachment of the 1st Dragoons is suddenly attacked by Indians,

losing five dead and six injured. The raiders are not identified, but Secretary of War William L. Marcy orders several infantry companies from Fort Leavenworth to patrol the Santa Fe Trail as a precaution.

AUGUST 6–7 In Mexico, General Winfield Scott launches his final drive against Mexico City following the collapse of peace negotiations. His entire army departs, leaving behind only a token garrison of 400 men under Colonel Thomas Childs to guard supplies and invalids there.

AUGUST 11–17 General Winfield Scott's army arrives at Ayolta, Mexico, only 15 miles from Mexico City. Before proceeding further he dispatches teams of engineers to ferret out the best approach. The general must act quickly for he has cut his own supply lines, and his men are down to four days of rations.

AUGUST 19–20 In Mexico, General Winfield Scott edges closer to Mexico City after besting General Antonio Lopez de Santa Anna at the battles of Contreras and Churubusco. The Mexicans included Irish-American deserters from the San Patricio Battalion; they fought capably, knowing that capture meant execution by hanging. The Americans nonetheless carry the Mexican position, losing 137 dead and 865 wounded. In contrast, Santa Anna suffers around 10,000 killed, wounded, and captured. The relentless American drive on Mexico City continues once the army is resupplied.

AUGUST 21–SEPTEMBER 7 At Tucubaya, Mexico, emissaries from General Jose Lopez de Santa Anna arrive in General Winfield Scott's camp and propose an armistice. Scott agrees in principle, although he breaks it off two weeks later after learning that Santa Anna violated the terms by constructing new fortifications. He consequently instructs General William Jenkins Worth to storm Mexican positions at nearby Molino del Rey.

SEPTEMBER 8 In Mexico, the Battle of Molino del Rey unfolds as General Winfield Scott's 8,000 troops carry strong Mexican positions manned by 10,000 soldiers, backed by artillery and cavalry. The initial charge by General William Jenkins Worth is bloodily repulsed, but the Americans regroup and gradually force the defenders back. General Antonio Lopez de Santa Anna suffers more than 2,000 casualties while Scott sustains 117 dead, 653 wounded, and 18 missing. Captain Ulysses S. Grant is among the first American officers to enter the captured town.

SEPTEMBER 12–13 In Mexico, the Battle of Chapultepec rages as 8,000 men under General Winfield Scott disperse a like number of Mexicans directed by General Antonio Lopez de Santa Anna. The Americans carry the city after stiff fighting, losing 450 men killed and wounded; Mexican casualties are around 1,800. Among the defenders are 60 military cadets, many of whom lose their lives in the fighting and are enshrined as national heroes. Mexico City is now defenseless and resigns itself to being occupied by the foreign invaders.

SEPTEMBER 13–OCTOBER 12 At Puebla, Mexico, Colonel Thomas Childs successfully fends off repeated attacks by General Antonio Lopez de Santa Anna with only 400 men. The approach of Colonel Joseph Lane's brigade finally breaks the siege, and the Mexicans withdraw.

SEPTEMBER 14 The victorious army of General Winfield Scott occupies Mexico City after a brilliant campaign of maneuvering. That done, Scott also initiates the first military government in American history. The famous Duke of Wellington, reviewing Scott's achievements, pronounces him "the greatest living soldier."

SEPTEMBER 16 In Mexico City, General Winfield Scott issues General Order No. 20 to proclaim military rule through occupied Mexico. He also assesses the inhabitants $3 million to support the occupation.

NOVEMBER–DECEMBER In Mexico City, the American army settles in for a long stint of occupation duty in Mexico City, although General Winfield Scott is careful to respect local religious and judicial customs. Having uncovered an excess $100,000 in his military accounts, he uses it to found a Soldiers' Home for retired military personnel in Washington, D.C.

NOVEMBER 25 General Zachary Taylor departs northern Mexico and begins his voyage back to the United States, a national hero—and a potential presidential candidate. The veteran General John E. Wool retains command of the army in his absence.

DECEMBER 3 At New Orleans, General Zachary Taylor arrives to thunderous applause. Rumors abound that he intends to parley his national popularity into a run for the presidency.

1848

JANUARY 31 At Fort Leavenworth, Kansas Territory, Major John C. Fremont is court-martialed for disobedience and cashiered. President James K. Polk disapproves of the sentence and restores him to duty in the Regiment of Mounted Riflemen. Fremont, however, resigns his commission on March 15 to continue his career out West.

FEBRUARY 2   In Washington, D.C., President James K. Polk signs the Treaty of Guadalupe Hidalgo and formally ends the Mexican–American War. The United States acquires millions of acres of western land, but skirmishing continues for several weeks.

FEBRUARY 18   In Washington, D.C., President James K. Polk relieves the victorious General Winfield Scott of command and summons him back to Washington, D.C. Previously, Scott had arrested General William Jenkins Worth and several other generals for alleged disrespect. Command of the army now passes to Major General William O. Butler.

MARCH 9   In Chihuahua, Mexico, General Sterling Price's Missourians fight the last pitched engagement of the Mexican War. Having dismissed news of the recent peace treaty as a ruse, he attacks the town of Santa Cruz de Rosales, losing four dead and 19 wounded to a Mexican tally of 40.

MARCH 21–JULY 1   In Mexico City, a huffy General Gideon J. Pillow, angered over treatment by General Winfield Scott, demands and receives a lengthy court of inquiry. He is subsequently exonerated by its findings.

MAY 30   In Washington, D.C., Army Surgeon General Thomas Lawson becomes the first medical officer to reach brevet brigadier general for services during the Mexican War.

JUNE 12   In Mexico City, General William Jenkins Worth holds a final military ceremony, whereby the city is officially turned back over to civilian authorities.

JUNE 19   In Washington, D.C., Congress reduces the military establishment to its pre-1846 levels, although officers are allowed to maintain wartime ranks. It also approves a death plan for families of deceased enlisted men, granting each the equivalent of three months' pay.

JULY 1   At Baton Rouge, Louisiana, Brevet Major General Zachary Taylor becomes commander of the Western Division, despite the fact that he is also the de facto Whig candidate for president.

JULY 6   In Washington, D.C., the War Department issues new regulations to tighten up the standards of military appearance. Henceforth, all long hair is ordered cropped with no whiskers below the ear tip, while mustaches are only allowed in dragoon units.

AUGUST 2   At Vera Cruz, Mexico, the 1st Artillery boards steamers and departs, ending the military occupation of that nation. The Mexican War has cost the U.S. Army 1,010 soldiers killed in combat, 4,899 dead from disease, and 2,745 wounded in action. Volunteer forces sustained a further 711 combat deaths, 6,256 dead from disease, and 1,357 wounded.

AUGUST 7   At Jefferson Barracks, Missouri, the Regiment of Mounted Riflemen is reconstituted as a unit, with many former personnel signing up for another tour of duty.

SEPTEMBER 7   In Washington, D.C., General Winfield Scott is eager to rid himself of politicians and assumes command of the Eastern Division by relocating his headquarters to New York City.

NOVEMBER 7   Brevet Major General Zachary Taylor is elected president of the United States, becoming the first and only standing military officer to occupy the White House. General Winfield Scott, a stickler for military protocol, temporarily resigns as Commanding General of the Army to avoid having a president-elect among his subordinates.

1849

FEBRUARY 12–APRIL 12 Lieutenants Henry C. Whiting and Martin L. Smith, Corps of Engineers, complete a perilous trek through the heart of Indian country. In two months they survey 1,600 miles between San Antonio and El Paso, Texas.

FEBRUARY 28 In accordance with the Treaty of Guadalupe Hidalgo, an army survey team is appointed under Major William H. Emory, who also serves as the head astronomer. They are tasked with accurately fixing the boundary line between the United States and Mexico.

MARCH 3 In Washington, D.C., Congress creates the Department of the Interior and transfers responsibility for Indian affairs from the War Department. The military is nonetheless responsible for enforcing whatever treaties are signed with the tribes.

APRIL 4 At Fort Smith, Arkansas, Captain Randolph B. Marcy and Lieutenant James H. Simpson begin an exploring expedition down the Santa Fe Trail to scout out a railroad route.

APRIL 13 In the Minnesota Territory, Colonel George M. Brooke directs the construction of Fort Ripley along the Mississippi River for the purpose of keeping watch over the Winnebago reservation and protecting them against Sioux and Chippewa raiders.

MAY 10 At Jefferson Barracks, Missouri, the newly reconstituted Regiment of Mounted Riflemen under Colonel William W. Loring gallops off for the Oregon Trail to construct posts and protect settlers moving west.

JUNE 27 In Benicia, California, Captain William H. Warner, of the Topographical Engineers, begins scouting down the Sacramento River as far as the Sierra Mountains and over to the Humboldt River.

AUGUST 16 During a punitive expedition against warring Navajo Indians in the New Mexico Territory, Lieutenant James H. Simpson, Topographical Engineers, becomes the first white man to behold the ancient Indian Pueblos of Chaco Canyon.

AUGUST 31 In the Tunisha Valley, New Mexico Territory, Lieutenant Colonel John M. Washington corners hostile Navajo chieftains, demands the return of all stolen horses, and convinces the Indians to sign a peace treaty. A brief fight ensues, which claims the lives of six Navajos; then the majority of chiefs comply.

SEPTEMBER At Goose Lake, California, hostile Pit River Indians ambush Captain William H. Warner's small expedition, killing him.

SEPTEMBER 11 At Mission San Diego de Aleada, California, Lieutenant Amiel W. Whipple conducts a small expedition to survey the Gila and Colorado Rivers.

OCTOBER 8   In Oregon City, Oregon Territory, Colonel William W. Loring and his
Regiment of Mounted Riflemen become
the first military unit to ride the entire
length of the Oregon Trail, a 2,016 mile
sojourn.

1850

APRIL 12   At Laredo, Texas, two companies of the 1st Infantry fight off an attack
by unidentified hostile Indians, possibly
Comanche; they suffer eight dead and
wounded.

JUNE 17   In Washington, D.C., Congress
expands the size of each infantry company to 74 men, elevating U.S. Army
manpower totals to 12,927. The actual
tally under arms is closer to 8,000.

JUNE 27   Captain Howard Stansbury's
expedition completes the first survey of
the Great Salt Lake, Utah Territory,
while Lieutenant John W. Gunnison
conducts the first detailed observations
of Mormon communities living there.

AUGUST 8   Lieutenant Colonel Edwin V.
Sumner and his 1st Dragoons construct
Fort Atkinson on the Arkansas River,
Kansas Territory, to defend wagon convoys
moving down along the Santa Fe Trail.

SEPTEMBER 16   In Washington, D.C.,
Congress enlarges the U.S. Military
Academy at West Point, authorizing
additional professors for mathematics,
engineering, and ethics.

SEPTEMBER 28   In Washington, D.C.,
Congress votes officers serving in
California and Oregon an additional
$2.00 per diem to help cover expenses,
while enlisted men are to receive double
their usual pay.

1851

JANUARY   In Washington, D.C., veteran
Chief Engineer Joseph G. Totten, mindful
of expanding military commitments in
the West, recommends that the number
of fortifications be increased to 186.

APRIL 12   In Baja, California, the 2nd
Infantry burns two Cocopas Indian villages
and capture 150 warriors. These men are
subsequently enlisted in the fight against
the neighboring Yuma tribes.

JULY 16   Colonel William W. Loring's
Regiment of Mounted Riflemen arrives
back at Jefferson Barracks, Missouri, after
an exhausting tour of duty along the
Oregon Trail. The regiment is in need of
rebuilding and refitting before it can be
redeployed to Texas to fight Indians.

JULY 26   Lieutenant Colonel Edwin
V. Sumner establishes Fort Union on the
Santa Fe Trail, New Mexico Territory, to
protect travelers from Ute and Jicarilla
Apache raiders. This also serves as
the department headquarters and is
the largest Federal post in the entire
Southwest.

1852

JUNE 16 In Baltimore, Maryland, Commanding General of the Army Winfield Scott accepts the Whig Party nomination for the presidency of the United States; however, "Old Fuss and Feathers," a far better general than politician, is defeated by Democrat Franklin Pierce that fall.

JULY 5 Several companies of the 4th Infantry, traveling on the Pacific Railroad across the Isthmus of Panama, are hit by cholera and lose 107 men by the time they transfer to California.

AUGUST In Washington, D.C., a penny-pinching Congress abolishes the $2.00 enlistment bounty, despite lackluster recruiting and persistent manpower shortages.

SEPTEMBER 1 At West Point, New York, Brevet Colonel Robert E. Lee becomes superintendent of the U.S. Military Academy. Many of his cadets subsequently serve as ranking officers that fight for and against him during the Civil War.

1853

MARCH 4 In Washington, D.C., Congress passes the Army Appropriation Act which contains $150,000 for a national survey of the best transcontinental railroad routes; it falls upon the War Department to select the most viable passage.

MARCH 7 In Washington, D.C., Jefferson Davis of Mississippi is appointed the new secretary of war by President Franklin Pierce. Having resigned his U.S. Senate seat to protest the Compromise of 1850, Davis proves surprisingly effective in this role.

MARCH 29 In Washington, D.C., Lieutenant Montgomery C. Meigs, Corps of Engineers, directs final construction of the north and south wings of the U.S. Capitol Building.

JUNE 23 At Fort Leavenworth, Kansas Territory, Captain John W. Gunnison takes several companies of the Regiment of Mounted Riflemen to search for a

Jefferson Davis was a distinguished U.S. senator from Mississippi and secretary of war before becoming president of the Confederate States of America. After the Confederacy's defeat, Davis was indicted for treason. Although he never requested a pardon, he was released from the indictment in 1868. (Library of Congress)

possible railroad route from Kansas through Colorado and to Utah.

OCTOBER   At Carlisle Barracks, Pennsylvania, the Cavalry School packs up and begins relocating to the Jefferson Barracks, Missouri.

OCTOBER 11   In Washington, D.C., Secretary of War Jefferson Davis directs that the curriculum at the U.S. Military Academy be expanded from four to five

years. He does so over the protests of the academy faculty.

OCTOBER 26   Captain John W. Gunnison, exploring along the Sevier River, Utah Territory, is attacked by hostile Paiute Indians, and killed along with several men of the Regiment of Mounted Riflemen. He is succeeded by Lieutenant E. G. Beckwith, who conducts the survivors to a winter camp near Salt Lake City.

1854

FEBRUARY 21   Lieutenant Edward B. Beckwith's small expedition explores the Sierra Nevada looking for a suitable pass for railroads to California. The War Department ignores the route he recommends, but this ironically ends up being the one utilized by the first transcontinental railroad.

MARCH 5   Near Fort Union, New Mexico Territory, Lieutenant Colonel Philip St. George Cooke's 2nd Dragoons defeat a band of hostile Jicarilla Apaches under Lobo Blanco. The chief is killed along with several of his warriors.

MARCH 26–30   At Cieneguila (Taso), New Mexico Territory, Jicarilla Apaches under Chief Chacon ambush a company of the 1st Dragoons under Lieutenant John W. Davidson. Though outnumbered four to one, Davidson fends off the Indians for three hours and retreats with 22 dead.

APRIL 8   At Rio Caliente, New Mexico Territory, Lieutenant Colonel Philip St. George Cooke perceives a Jicarilla

Apache ambush waiting for him, so he suddenly attacks, scattering the would be ambushers. Cooke suffers one dead and one wounded while five Indians are killed and six wounded.

APRIL 14   In Washington, D.C., Congress determines to stimulate flagging military recruitment by restoring the $2.00 enlistment bonus for new recruits.

AUGUST 4   In Washington, D.C., Congress raises the basic military pay of privates by $4.00 per month, while those individuals reenlisting also receive an additional $2.00 per month.

AUGUST 19   Lieutenant John L. Grattan departs Fort Laramie, Wyoming, and enters a Miniconjou Sioux village to demand the arrest of the warrior High Forehead, who has stolen a cow. Chief Conquering Bear refuses to comply, so Grattan fires a cannon into his tent, killing him. All of Grattan's 28 men are then killed on the spot by vengeful Indians.

1855

FEBRUARY 15 Commanding General of the Army Winfield Scott is promoted to brevet lieutenant general through a special act of Congress. He becomes the first American officer since George Washington to wear three stars, but fails to become part of the Army's existing ranking system.

MARCH 3 In Washington, D.C., Secretary of War Jefferson Davis suggests that Congress appropriate funding to acquire 333 camels and experiment with them as pack animals in southwestern deserts. A total of $30,000 is eventually passed and the new U.S. Army Camel Corps is tasked with testing the animals along the frontier.

Congress, acknowledging it has increased security commitments along the western frontier, enlarges the U.S. Army by adding two infantry (9th and 10th) and two mounted (1st and 2nd Cavalry) regiments. Significantly, the latter become the first military units carrying the designation "Cavalry."

MARCH 26 At Jefferson Barracks, Missouri, the new 2nd U.S. Cavalry organizes under Colonel Albert Sidney Johnston and Lieutenant Colonel Robert E. Lee. Its officer corps is so dominated by Southerners that it is popularly referred to as "Jeff Davis's Own."

APRIL 28 At Poncha Pass, Colorado, the 1st Dragoons and some volunteers surprise Ute warriors as they dance around a blazing bonfire. They manage to drop around 40 Indians before the rest flee into the darkness. This stinging reversal

prompts the Utes to sue for peace shortly afterward.

MAY 28 At Louisville, Kentucky, the new 1st Cavalry forms under Colonel Edwin V. Sumner. Among the future Civil War luminaries riding in its ranks are Joseph E. Johnston, John Sedgwick, George B. McClellan, and J. E. B. Stuart.

JULY 29 At Solomon Fork, Kansas Territory, Colonel Edwin V. Sumner leads men of the 1st Cavalry and 2nd Dragoons against 300 Cheyennes. Knowing that the warriors previously washed themselves in magic water for protection against the white man's bullets, Sumner orders his men to charge sabers, routing his opponents.

AUGUST 15 In Washington, D.C., the War Department orders that the venerable felt shako, worn as headgear by soldiers for nearly 50 years, be replaced by a stiff felt hat with the right side distinctly folded up.

AUGUST 24 At Fort Kearney, Nebraska, Colonel William S. Harney leads a punitive expedition of 600 soldiers drawn from the 2nd Dragoons, 6th and 10th Infantries, and 4th Artillery to avenge the Grattan massacre of a year earlier.

SEPTEMBER 3 At Blue Water Creek (Ash Hollow), Nebraska, Colonel William S. Harney attacks Chief Little Thunder's village, killing 86 Sioux and taking 70 prisoner; Harney's losses are four dead and seven wounded. Moreover, he sternly warns the Indians against future attacks against soldiers or settlers.

OCTOBER 31   Near Fort Lane, Oregon Territory, Captain Andrew J. Smith and 250 men from the 1st Dragoons, 4th Infantry, and the 3rd Artillery wage a day-long battle with hostile Indians along Hungry Hill. A stalemate ensues and both sides withdraw.

DECEMBER 29   At Big Cyprus Swamp, Florida, resentful Seminoles under Chief Billy Bowlegs attack Lieutenant George Hartstuff's patrol, killing several soldiers. This act precipitates the Third Seminole War.

1856

MARCH 26–28   Fort Cascades, Washington Territory, is attacked by warriors from the Yakima, Kliktat, and Chinook tribes. Lieutenant Philip H. Sheridan and Colonel George Wright lead 250 men of the 9th Infantry and gradually drive the Indians away from the blockhouse.

APRIL 29   In Texas, the first shipment of camels arrives as part of an extensive experiment to evaluate them as pack animals for the U.S. Army.

MAY 26–28   At Big Meadows, Oregon Territory, Indians attack Captain Andrew J. Smith's detachment of the 1st Dragoons. He manages to keep them at bay with a small howitzer until reinforcements under Captain Christopher C. Augur strike the Indians from behind, scattering them.

JUNE 27   Along the Gila River, Arizona Territory, a party of Coyotera Apaches are surprised by Lieutenant Richard E. Ewell's company of the 1st Dragoons. The Indians suffer 40 dead and 45 captured to 9 Americans wounded.

SEPTEMBER 15   In Kansas Territory, newly appointed governor John W. Geary requests troops to prevent 2,500 Missouri "border ruffians" from invading his charge and illegally voting in elections.

1857

FEBRUARY 21   In Washington, D.C., Congress raises an officer's base pay by $20.00 per month.

MARCH 4–APRIL 23   At Big Cypress Swamp, Florida, several companies of the 5th Infantry corner Seminole warriors under Chief Billy Bowlegs and drive him from the field. This concludes the short-lived Third Seminole War, and those Indians taken into custody are summarily deported to new homes in the Indian Territory (Oklahoma).

MAY 27–28   At Big Meadows, Oregon, 200 Takelma and Tututni warriors, having previously agreed to surrender, suddenly attack a small detachment commanded by Captain Andrew J. Smith. Smith manages to keep the Indians at bay until reinforcements arrive and finally drive them from the battlefield.

MAY 28 At Fort Leavenworth, Kansas Territory, Colonel Albert S. Johnston assembles several companies of his 2nd Dragoons, and the 5th and 10th Infantries, for the purpose of marching to Utah and suppressing unlawful activity by Mormons residing there.

JULY 17 At Fort Davis, Texas, camels imported to Texas for the U.S. Army are ridden overland to Arizona to test their viability as pack animals. Soldiers of the nascent U.S. Camel Corps are unimpressed, finding them smelly and ill-tempered.

OCTOBER 5 In Kansas Territory, U.S. Army troops ensure free and safe elections, thereby allowing an antislavery state legislature to gain power.

NOVEMBER 24 In the Utah Territory, Colonel Albert S. Johnston dispatches a detachment under Captain Randolph B. Marcy to obtain supplies from Fort Massachusetts, New Mexico, 700 miles distant. Mormon raiding parties have burned several Army supply trains, leaving Johnston's force lacking victuals.

1858

JANUARY 9 Lieutenant Joseph Christmas leads a small expedition down the Colorado River, and through the Grand Canyon, until they reach Black Creek. They become the first recorded party to survey the floor of the Grand Canyon.

JANUARY 13 Captain Randolph B. Marcy's detachment surmounts deep snow and freezing weather to reach Fort Massachusetts, New Mexico Territory. He gathers up as many supplies as possible and, escorted by a detachment of Mounted Riflemen, returns to join the main expedition in Utah.

MARCH 27 In Washington, D.C., the Third Seminole War formally concludes when Chief Billy Bowlegs signs a peace treaty agreeing to the relocation of his band from Florida to the Indian Territory (Oklahoma).

MAY 15–18 Outside Fort Walla Walla, Washington Territory, Yakima Indians ambush and engage Lieutenant Colonel Edward J. Steptoe's column of the 9th Infantry, killing two officers.

JUNE 18 In Washington, D.C., Congress confers a local rank and pay of colonel to all superintendents of the U.S. Military Academy, West Point. The commandant of cadets is also elevated to lieutenant colonel.

JUNE 26 Salt Lake City, Utah, is occupied by a column of 5,500 U.S. Army troops under no-nonsense Colonel Albert S. Johnston. This military presence makes church leadership far more tractable, and negotiations bring the so-called "Mormon War" to an end.

SEPTEMBER 1 On the Yakima Plain, Washington Territory, Colonel George Wright takes 600 soldiers against a large force of Northwestern tribesmen, routing them with a single mounted charge. The Americans kill 60 warriors and incur no losses.

SEPTEMBER 15–24 Captain Earl Van Dorn, 2nd Cavalry, departs Fort Belknap, Indian Territory (Oklahoma), on a punitive expedition aimed at renegade Comanche and Kiowa tribesmen. Riding with him are 125 Indian volunteers from the nearby Brazos Reservation.

SEPTEMBER 24   In the Oregon Territory, the Yakima War ends after Colonel George Wright concludes a treaty with tribal representatives.

OCTOBER 1   At Rush Springs, Indian Territory (Oklahoma), Captain Van Dorn's 2nd Cavalry defeats Comanche warriors under Buffalo Hump. The Americans kill 56 warriors at a cost of 5 dead; Van Dorn is the only trooper wounded.

1859

MAY 13   At Crooked Creek, Indian Territory (Oklahoma), Captain Earl Van Dorn's 2nd Cavalry surprises a Comanche encampment, killing 49 and scattering the rest. The Americans and their Indian allies lose six dead and nine wounded; Lieutenant Fitzhugh Lee is severely wounded by an arrow but survives.

JULY 27   San Juan Island in Puget Sound, Oregon Territory, is defiantly occupied by Captain George E. Pickett's company of the 9th Infantry. A British warship anchors nearby and orders Pickett off the disputed territory, but he refuses to budge, vowing to fight.

AUGUST   Several companies from the 4th and 9th Infantries and the 3rd Artillery arrive to reinforce Captain George E. Pickett on disputed San Juan Island, Oregon Territory. A standoff continues between the United States and Great Britain as to its ownership.

OCTOBER 20–NOVEMBER 10   Lieutenant General Winfield Scott arrives at San Juan Island, Oregon Territory, to settle a territorial dispute with Great Britain. Consequently, the Americans are allowed to remain on the southern half of the island, while Royal Marines occupy the northern half.

1860

MARCH 6   In Washington, D.C., Christopher M. Spencer receives a government patent for his highly functional repeating rifle. An estimated 200,000 Spencer carbines are manufactured and issued during the Civil War, which signals the decline of conventional, muzzle-loading ordnance.

APRIL 30   At Fort Defiance, Arizona Territory, a garrison from the 3rd Infantry is attacked by over 1,000 Navajo warriors

in a major uprising; the Indians are eventually driven off.

MAY 3–SEPTEMBER   At St. Louis, Missouri, Major H. A. Blake takes 300 troopers of the 1st Dragoons to scout for a wagon road between Fort Benton, Indian Territory (Oklahoma), and Walla Walla, Washington Territory.

JUNE 21   In Washington, D.C., Major Albert J. Myer is named the Army's first Signal Officer. This officer previously invented communications through flag signaling (wigwag). The U.S. Army is thus the first military establishment to possess an independent Signal Corps.

SEPTEMBER–NOVEMBER At Fort Defiance, Arizona Territory, Major Edward R. S. Canby assembles a punitive expedition of 600 soldiers from the 5th, 7th, 8th, and 10th Infantries, the 2nd Dragoons, and the Mounted Riflemen, then departs. Few skirmishes are fought with the elusive Navajo, although the soldiers end up confiscating over 1,000 horses and 3,000 sheep before tribal elders sue for peace.

NOVEMBER 6 A little-known Illinois politician, Abraham Lincoln, is elected to be the next president of the United States. This event sets in motion a chain of events culminating in a prolonged and costly civil war, 1861–1865.

NOVEMBER 15 Major Robert Anderson, a slave-owning Southerner thought capable of dealing with Southern authorities, is ordered to take charge of Federal troops garrisoning Fort Moultrie in Charleston, South Carolina.

NOVEMBER 23 In Charleston, South Carolina, Major Robert Anderson advises superiors as to the defensive weakness of Fort Moultrie. He strongly suggests transferring his garrison to nearby Fort Sumter, offshore, for better protection.

DECEMBER 11 At Charleston, South Carolina, Major Don Carols Buell arrives at Fort Moultrie bearing War Department instructions for Major Robert Anderson. Secretary of War John B. Floyd, a Virginian and a Southern sympathizer, refuses to send reinforcements to avoid provoking a confrontation.

DECEMBER 12 In Washington, D.C., President James Buchanan declines to reinforce the garrison at Fort Sumter, Charleston, to avoid provoking a fight with local authorities. In light of this timidity, Secretary of State Lewis Cass resigns from office.

With a national crisis brewing, Lieutenant General Winfield Scott transfers his headquarters from New York City to Washington, D.C. Scott functioned at New York City since 1851 owing to his disputes with several secretaries of war and politicians in general.

DECEMBER 26 At Charleston, South Carolina, Major Robert Anderson transfers his small garrison from Fort Moultrie under the cover of darkness and deposits them at the more defensible post of Fort Sumter inside Charleston harbor. This act enrages local authorities.

DECEMBER 27–30 As political tensions rise in South Carolina, South Carolina forces occupy the Federal outposts at Fort Moultrie and Castle Pinckney in Charleston harbor. This constitutes the first act of military aggression against the United States by Southern leaders. They subsequently seize all remaining Federal property in the city with the exception of Fort Sumter in the harbor.

DECEMBER 31 The eve of civil war finds the U.S. Army consisting of 16,000 personnel. However, this total is dispersed around the frontier and, of 197 companies present, only 18 artillery companies remain east of the Mississippi River. The vast bulk of 19 regiments present are scattered in small fortifications throughout the West.

1861

JANUARY 9   At Charleston, South Carolina, state artillery, manned partly by cadets from the Citadel Military School, fires upon the transport *Star of the West* as it approaches the harbor. The vessel thereupon retires back to New York unscathed. This act constitutes the first hostile shots of the Civil War and Major Robert Anderson, commanding Fort Sumter's garrison, protests the deed to Governor Francis W. Pickens.

JANUARY 10   At Fort Barancas at Pensacola, Florida, the Federal garrison under Lieutenant Adam J. Slemmer spikes its cannon and withdraws offshore to Fort Pickens on Santa Rosa Island. Local forces then occupy the navy yard, but Fort Pickens remains in Union hands for the rest of the Civil War.

JANUARY 11   South Carolina governor Francis W. Pickens demands that Major Robert Anderson surrender Fort Sumter, Charleston, to state authorities. Anderson politely yet curtly refuses.

In Louisiana, the U.S. Arsenal at Baton Rouge, defended by Major Joseph A. Haskins and two companies of artillery, refuses to capitulate until it is surrounded by 600 militiamen.

JANUARY 14   At Key West, Florida, army troops preemptively garrison Fort Taylor to forestall its capture; it eventually serves as an important coaling station.

JANUARY 15   At Charleston, South Carolina, Major Robert Anderson receives a second summons to surrender Fort Sumter; again he politely but firmly refuses.

JANUARY 18   In Charleston, South Carolina, state officials issue their third demand for the surrender of Major Robert Anderson and Fort Sumter in Charleston harbor and, once again, he respectfully declines.

JANUARY 24   In Augusta, Georgia, state forces surround a company of U.S. Army troops that refuses to surrender their post. Upon further reflection, the Army troops decide to leave, then salute the flag and are allowed to depart in safety.

FEBRUARY   At St. Louis, Missouri, the forceful Captain Nathaniel Lyon marches men of his 2nd Infantry from Jefferson Barracks and secures the U.S. Arsenal in the city. This preemptive act deprives Confederate authorities of an important source of arms.

FEBRUARY 4–8   At Montgomery, Alabama, the Confederate States of America (CSA) votes itself into existence, underscoring the drift toward secession and civil war.

FEBRUARY 7   In the Indian Territory (Oklahoma), the Choctaw Nation votes to align itself with the new Confederate States of America. Many Indian leaders are also slave holders.

FEBRUARY 9   In Mississippi, former army officer and secretary of war Jefferson Davis is elected president of the Confederate States of America. This appointment completely surprises Davis, who expected a general's commission to lead state forces.

FEBRUARY 4–14   At Apache Pass, Arizona Territory, Lieutenant George N. Bascom accuses Chiricahua chief Cochise of kidnapping a rancher's son. The chief denies it and offers to help find those responsible, but Bascom attempts to seize him and he escapes. Over intervening days, hostages are taken and executed by both sides, signaling the start of a major Apache uprising.

FEBRUARY 13 At Apache Pass, Arizona Territory, Lieutenant George N. Bascom's detachment of the 7th Infantry is trapped by vengeful Apaches until Colonel Bernard J. D. Irwin arrives and rescues him under fire. Three decades later Irwin receives a Congressional Medal of Honor for the deed.

FEBRUARY 18 In the Department of Texas, General David E. Twiggs surrenders all U.S. Army installations, an act widely condemned as treasonous by Union supporters. Twiggs subsequently serves the Confederacy as a general.

MARCH 1 In Charleston, South Carolina, Pierre G. T. Beauregard is commissioned brigadier general, CSA. The Confederate government, having assumed control of events in the immediate vicinity, also begins weighing its options against Fort Sumter. Meanwhile, Major Robert Anderson notifies Washington that Fort Sumter must be either supplied or reinforced soon, lest he be forced to capitulate by default.

MARCH 3 President Jefferson Davis appoints General Pierre G. T. Beauregard as commander of Confederate forces at Charleston, South Carolina. In a fateful move, he also orders Beauregard to prepare for military action against the Federal garrison at nearby Fort Sumter.

MARCH 4 In Washington, D.C., Abraham Lincoln is sworn in as the 16th president; he is an unlikely commander in chief, seeing that his only military experience consists of several weeks in the militia

service during the Black Hawk War of 1832.

MARCH 5 In Washington, D.C., President Abraham Lincoln is informed by Major Robert Anderson that his supplies will run out within four to six weeks, after which he will have to surrender Fort Sumter. Moreover, General Winfield Scott insists that the post can only be defended by no less than 20,000 troops. Lincoln, aware that time is running out, continues balancing the delicate situation.

MARCH 13 At St. Louis, Missouri, Captain Nathaniel Lyon, a pugnacious, aggressive officer by nature, gains appointment as commander of the U.S. Arsenal.

MARCH 28 In Washington, D.C., President Abraham Lincoln orders a sea-borne expedition mounted to succor the Federal garrison at Fort Sumter, Charleston harbor. In effect, Lincoln begins subtly maneuvering his Southern counterpart into firing the first shot.

MARCH 31 In Washington, D.C., President Abraham Lincoln orders another relief expedition, this time to assist the federal garrison at Fort Pickens, Florida. This important post guards the entrance to Pensacola harbor.

APRIL 4 In Washington, D.C., President Abraham Lincoln grants final approval to plans for a relief expedition drawn up by Gustavus V. Fox. He subsequently telegraphs Major Robert Anderson at Fort Sumter, Charleston, of forthcoming events.

APRIL 8 In Charleston, South Carolina, word of a relief expedition prompts Confederate authorities to begin military preparations and plant artillery batteries. A fight of some kind seems in the offing.

APRIL 12   In Charleston, South Carolina, the shoreline erupts in flames as 18 mortars and 30 heavy cannons commence a withering bombardment of Fort Sumter at 4:30 A.M. Major Robert Anderson, commanding only 85 men, 43 civilian engineers, and 48 cannons, can only respond with six guns of his own. Captain Abner Doubleday acquires distinction for firing the first Union shot of the war. Thus the Civil War, a monumental struggle in military history and a defining moment for the United States, commences in earnest.

APRIL 14   At Charleston, South Carolina, Major Robert Anderson surrenders Fort Sumter to Confederate authorities. The 24-hour bombardment produced no casualties, although two Union troops die and four are wounded when some unused ammunition accidently ignites during a final salute to the American flag. The captives depart on the provisional

squadron assembled by Gustavus V. Fox and return north.

APRIL 15   In Washington, D.C., President Abraham Lincoln calls for 75,000 volunteers to serve 90 days and help crush the secessionists. Eventually 90,000 step forward, but the government declines four offers of mounted troops due to their expense.

APRIL 18   At Harpers Ferry, Virginia, Lieutenant Roger Jones burns the U.S. Armory, to prevent its facilities from falling into enemy hands. However, the local population extinguishes the flames before valuable tools, dies, and other equipment are consumed.

APRIL 19   In Baltimore, Maryland, the 6th Massachusetts is violently attacked by pro-Southern rioters in the street. Shots are exchanged, and 4 soldiers die while 36 are wounded. Secessionist

Interior of Fort Sumter in Charleston Harbor, South Carolina, during the bombardment by Confederate shells on April 12, 1861. The Battle of Fort Sumter was the first armed action of the American Civil War. (Library of Congress)

sympathizers also begin cutting rail and telegraph lines leading toward the capital, and for several anxious days Washington, D.C., is temporarily isolated from the rest of the Union.

APRIL 20 Lieutenant Colonel Robert E. Lee tenders his resignation from the U.S. Army. He previously declined an offer to command all Federal forces after his native state of Virginia seceded three days earlier.

APRIL 23 In Richmond, Virginia, General Robert E. Lee is appointed commander of all state forces.

APRIL 25 At St. Louis, Missouri, Captain James H. Stokes and several Union troops arrive by steamer to remove 12,000 rifled muskets from the U.S. arsenal. This daring act denies badly needed arms to Confederate sympathizers gathering in the region.

APRIL 26 At Richmond, Virginia, General Joseph E. Johnston arrives to take charge of Confederate forces guarding the state capital.

MAY 1 General Robert E. Lee orders additional Confederate forces concentrated in the vicinity of Harpers Ferry, western Virginia; these are presently commanded by Colonel Thomas J. Jackson, a known eccentric and religious fanatic.

MAY 3 In Washington, D.C., President Abraham Lincoln issues an additional call for 42,000 three-year volunteers and an additional 18,000 personnel for the Navy. This brings manpower ceilings to 156,000 soldiers and 25,000 sailors.

Meanwhile, aged General Winfield Scott unveils his so-called "Anaconda Plan" for defeating the rebellion. This entails a gunboat-supported drive of 60,000 men down the Mississippi River from Cairo, Illinois, to New Orleans, Louisiana, to cut the Confederacy in half. Concurrently, a tight naval blockade will strangle all Southern trade with Europe. Scott's strategy is not formally enacted until 1864, and Lincoln spends the next three years searching for a general who will execute it forcefully.

MAY 6 Outside of St. Louis, Missouri, the Confederate Missouri State Guard under General Daniel M. Frost establishes a training camp at the behest of Governor Claiborne F. Jackson. Captain Nathaniel Lyon, commanding the Federal garrison, refuses all demands to remove his troops from the city and prepares to neutralize his antagonists.

MAY 10–11 In St. Louis, Missouri, fighting occurs between Southern sympathizers and U.S. Army troops, backed by the local, German-speaking population. Two dozen civilians and two soldiers die as Captain Nathaniel Lyon rounds up General Daniel Frost and 625 Missouri State Guard troops at Camp Jackson. The state remains firmly in Union hands.

MAY 13 Little-known General George B. McClellan assumes command of the Department of the Ohio.

MAY 14 In Baltimore, Maryland, General Benjamin F. Butler consolidates his grip on the city by arresting several secessionists. Governor Thomas H. Hicks also calls for four state regiments to defend both the city and the national capital.

MAY 15 In Baltimore, Maryland, General Benjamin F. Butler relinquishes command of the Department of Annapolis and arrives at Fortress Monroe, Virginia; once there, he rises to major general of volunteers.

Colonel William S. Harney assumes command at St. Louis, Missouri, and implores citizens to ignore secessionist attempts at raising a militia. Curiously, he declines to interfere with ongoing Confederate activities.

MAY 21   In St. Louis, Missouri, Colonel William S. Harney enters into a convention with Missouri State Guard commander General Sterling Price, agreeing not to introduce Federal troops into the state as long as the Southerners maintain order. Congressman Francis P. Blair and Captain Nathaniel Lyon condemn this arrangement as treasonous.

MAY 23   At Fortress Monroe, Virginia, General Benjamin F. Butler refuses to hand over three runaway slaves to their owners, declaring them "contraband of war." This is an important precedent, allowing thousands of slaves to escape to Union lines—and freedom.

MAY 24   As General Samuel P. Heintzelman's 13,000 Federal soldiers occupy Alexandria and Arlington Heights, Virginia, 24-year-old Colonel Elmer E. Ellsworth, 11th New York Regiment (Fire

---

Dix, Dorothea (1802–1887)

Dorothea Dix was born in Hampden, Maine, on April 4, 1802, the daughter of a minister. She overcame a hardscrabble existence to become a school headmistress at the age of 19, and in 1836 Dix visited England to recoup her health. There she observed various social reformers in action and came home determined to duplicate their crusade in the United States. Between 1841 and 1854, Dix campaigned tirelessly in Massachusetts, winning laws that mandated improvements in mental hospitals and state prisons. By 1861, she was one of the best-known women and social reformers in America, and that year she used her reputation to secure appointment as chief of nurses in the Union Army. It was while acting in this capacity that Dix made indelible improvements in both the standards of care for sick soldiers and the training of nurses attending them. She enjoyed less success, however, overcoming her strict, humorless demeanor that garnered the nickname "Dragon Dix." Nor would she mitigate her prejudices against Roman Catholics and other religious minorities who sought to become nurses. Resentment against her moral strictness crested in October 1863, when

Dorothea Dix was world-renowned for her work on behalf of the mentally ill and for her services as a nurse during the Civil War. (Library of Congress)

Congress authorized the Army's surgeon general to appoint nurses. Fortunately, Dix's handling of the Nurse Corps was a resounding success and closely parallels the work of Florence Nightingale during the Crimean War of a decade earlier. As an indication of her personal commitment to aid wounded soldiers, Dix labored throughout the entire war without pay. Afterward she resumed lobbying on behalf of the poor and disadvantaged, and died in Trenton, New Jersey, on July 17, 1887, at a hospital she had founded some 35 years earlier.

Zouaves), removes a Confederate flag from a hotel in Alexandria and is shot dead by the owner. Ellsworth enjoys the melancholy distinction of being the Union's first officer fatality.

MAY 26–29 In Ohio, General George B. McClellan advances three Union columns to Grafton, western Virginia, to secure the Baltimore and Ohio Railroad. This rail line constitutes a strategic link between the capital and the western states.

MAY 28 At Alexandria, General Irvin McDowell is appointed commander of the Department of Northwestern Virginia.

MAY 29 In Washington, D.C., Dorothea L. Dix approaches Secretary of War Simon Cameron and offers to organize hospital services for Federal forces.

MAY 30 In Washington, D.C., Secretary of War Simon Cameron instructs General Benjamin F. Butler that fugitive slaves crossing into Federal lines are not to be returned, but given work around military installations. The Union army is slowly becoming an instrument of emancipation.

MAY 31 At St. Louis, General John C. Fremont supersedes Colonel William S. Harney as Union commander in Missouri. He immediately abrogates the latter's agreement with Confederate leader Sterling Price to forbid the introduction of Federal troops into the region.

JUNE 3 At Philippi, western Virginia, General Thomas A. Morris's Federal troops brush aside a Confederate detachment under Colonel George A. Porterfield, clearing the Kanawha Valley of secessionists. Quick actions by General George B. McClellan, commanding the Department of Ohio, made this small victory possible, and he begins garnering official attention.

JUNE 10 At Big Bethel, Virginia, 4,400 Federal troops under General Ebenezer Pierce engage General John B. Magruder's 1,500 Confederates, but the inexperienced soldiers are committed piecemeal against enemy entrenchments. Pierce loses 76 dead, injured, and missing; among them is Lieutenant John T. Greble, the first West Point graduate killed in the Civil War.

JUNE 11 Two important developments for the Confederacy: Colonel William W. Loring resigns as commander of the New Mexico Territory and is succeeded by Colonel Edward R. S. Canby. Meanwhile, in California, Brigadier General Albert S. Johnson also quits the Department of the Pacific and is replaced by Brigadier General George Wright.

JUNE 13 In Washington, D.C., President Abraham Lincoln authorizes a civilian sanitary commission to assist the military medical corps. It performs useful work, and lends credence to founding the American Red Cross afterward.

JUNE 14 In Richmond, Virginia, Robert E. Lee is promoted to full general, CSA

JUNE 17 In Missouri, General Nathaniel Lyon pursues retreating Missouri State Guard forces under Governor Claiborne F. Jackson to Booneville. After a 20-minute stand the Southerners flee to the southwestern corner of the state, and Lyon warns the inhabitants of stern punishment for any potential acts of treason.

In Springfield, Illinois, an obscure former Army captain named Ulysses S. Grant gains appointment as colonel of the 21st Illinois Infantry.

JUNE 29 In Washington, D.C., President Abraham Lincoln is briefed on strategy by Generals Winfield Scott and Irvin

McDowell. Scott remonstrates against committing raw soldiers to combat so soon and argues, unsuccessfully, against seeking victory in a single battle. Amidst mounting war fever, the administration is prodded into action before the soldiers are ready.

JULY 2   In western Virginia, aged General Robert Patterson directs Union forces across the Potomac River and into the Shenandoah Valley. He is opposed by Confederates under General Joseph E. Johnston, whose attention is increasingly being drawn to events further south.

JULY 4   In Washington, D.C., President Abraham Lincoln requests Congress to authorize 400,000 three-year volunteers and, three weeks later, they raise the amount to 500,000. The sheer magnitude of the conflict begins looming larger.

JULY 5   Near Carthage, Missouri, Colonel Franz Sigel and 1,100 German-speaking volunteers advance upon 4,000 Missouri militia under Governor Claiborne F. Jackson. The Confederates decide to attack Union lines upon a hilltop, at which point Sigel falls back upon Springfield to join Union forces assembling there under Captain Nathaniel Lyon.

JULY 10   In western Virginia, General George B. McClelland dispatches General William S. Rosecrans against Confederates deployed on Rich Mountain. He also orders a second force under General Thomas A. Morris to attack enemy troops at nearby Laurel Hill. This is one of the earliest Union offensives.

JULY 11   On Rich Mountain, Virginia, General William S. Rosecrans and 2,000 Union troops defeat Colonel John Pegram's 1,300 Confederates. They do so after marching all night through a heavy downpour and suffer only 100 casualties. This victory places Union forces astride General Robert S. Garnett's lines of communications, and he withdraws from Laurel Hill with General George B. McClellan's main body in hot pursuit.

JULY 12   At Beverly, western Virginia, a badly outnumbered Colonel John Pegram surrenders 555 Confederates to General William S. Rosecrans. The settlement is subsequently occupied by General George B. McClellan's main army. Southerners under General Robert S. Garnett, anxious to dodge a closing Union pincer movement, hurriedly march to Corrick's Ford.

JULY 13   At Corrick's Ford, western Virginia, General Robert S. Garnett's Confederates are defeated by General Thomas A. Morris's Indiana brigade. Losses are slight on either side, but, significantly, Garnett becomes the first general officer on either side to die in action.

JULY 14   In western Virginia, a Union push under General Robert Patterson stalls south of Harpers Ferry in the face of resistance orchestrated by General Joseph E. Johnston. Aged Patterson, a veteran of the War of 1812, behaves timidly, and his hesitancy to fight gives rise to the unflattering moniker of "Granny."

JULY 16   General Irvin McDowell, having been ordered to take the offensive, leads 32,000 men toward Manassas Junction while cheering throngs in Washington, D.C., shout "On to Richmond!" However, his recruits only cover six miles and another two days are required to reach Centreville, 22 miles distant. This dilatory movement grants Confederates under General Pierre G. T. Beauregard time to collect forces and reposition themselves to meet him.

JULY 17   In Richmond, Virginia, President Jefferson Davis orders General Joseph E. Johnston to reinforce General Pierre G. T. Beauregard. This is first time that large numbers of troops are strategically shuttled from one front to another by train. Johnston handles his charge capably and brings Confederate numbers at Manassas Junction nearly up to par with the Union army. His movements are further expedited by Union general Robert Patterson, who fails to detect or respond to Johnston's transfer.

JULY 20   General Joseph E. Johnston arrives at Manassas Junction, Virginia, with Confederate reinforcements, although he diplomatically allows General Pierre G. T. Beauregard to retain overall command. General Irvin McDowell, having personally reconnoitered Confederate positions, concludes that their right is too strong to assail frontally. Instead, he elects to use an unguarded crossing point nearer to Beauregard's left flank. His plan is tactically sound, but still complicated for inexperienced officers and men to execute properly.

JULY 21   At Bull Run, 30 miles west of Washington, D.C., the first major land engagement of the Civil War commences as 32,000 raw Union troops under General Irvin McDowell attack 30,000 equally green Confederate forces under General Pierre G. T. Beauregard. The initial Union advance makes good progress, then stalls in the vicinity of Henry House Hill when General Thomas J. Jackson's Virginia brigade makes a determined stand. Beauregard, sensing confusion in Union ranks, rushes up reinforcement and orders a sudden advance across the entire line; McDowell's tired, demoralized soldiers withdraw in confusion. Bull Run is a tactical triumph for the Confederacy, but both sides are so completely disorganized that no effective pursuit is mounted. Southern losses are 1,982 to a Union tally of 2,896.

JULY 22   The three-month enlistment of many Union volunteers begins expiring, allowing many of them to be discharged. President Abraham Lincoln consequently signs two bills authorizing one million three-year volunteers.

In Washington, D.C., General George B. McClelland is ordered to succeed the now-disgraced General Irvin McDowell. "Little Mac's" star is in the ascent.

JULY 25   In St. Louis, Missouri, noted explorer John C. Fremont is formally appointed to command the Department of the West with a rank of major general.

JULY 27   In Washington, D.C., President Abraham Lincoln confers with newly-appointed General George B. McClellan in Washington, D.C., for the first time. The commander in chief urges a strategic offense by advancing into Tennessee by way of Virginia and Kentucky, but McClellan, intent on honing his troops to a fine edge, demurs.

JULY 28   In light of the deteriorating situation in western Virginia, little-known General Robert E. Lee is ordered to take command of Confederates forces stationed there.

JULY 31   In Washington, D.C., President Abraham Lincoln elevates an obscure Colonel Ulysses S. Grant to brigadier general of volunteers in Illinois. Unforeseen at the time, this is one of the most decisive military appointments in military history, and a leading factor in the Union victory.

AUGUST   1   In Richmond, Virginia, President Jefferson Davis urges General Joseph E. Johnston to maintain the strategic initiative by attacking any Union forces still in Virginia. Johnston, feeling his recruits are not up to the task, declines to act.

AUGUST 5   In Washington, D.C., Congress again abolishes flogging as punishment in the army; to enhance enlistments, a private's pay also rises from $11.00 to $13.00 per month.

AUGUST 7   Newly promoted Brigadier General Ulysses S. Grant assumes command of the District of Southeast Missouri.

AUGUST 10   In Missouri, General Nathaniel Lyon initiates the Battle of Wilson's Creek by storming Confederate campsites in the morning hours. Concurrently, General Franz Sigel stealthily advances upon the Southerners from below until General Ben McCulloch drives him off. Lyon, unaware of Sigel's debacle, holds his ground as General Sterling Price makes two frontal assaults. Once Lyon is killed in action, the Federals draw off in orderly fashion and the exhausted Confederates remain on the field. Losses are 1,317 Union casualties to a Southern tally of 1,230.

AUGUST 20   In northern Virginia, General George B. McClellan takes charge of the newly constituted Department and Army of the Potomac. This force becomes a permanent fixture in the Eastern Theater over the next four years.

AUGUST 25   At St. Louis, Missouri, General John C. Fremont orders the word "Springfield" added to regimental colors of all units present at the Battle of Wilson's Creek. Thus begins the U.S. Army system of awarding battle streamers.

AUGUST 26   In northwestern Virginia, newly arrived General Robert E. Lee wins a minor engagement at Kessler's Cross Lanes, then begins gathering strength for an offensive in the region.

AUGUST 27–29   Assisted by a large naval squadron, General Benjamin F. Butler lands 900 soldiers and occupies Forts Hatteras and Clark at Hatteras Inlet, North Carolina. Victory here creates the first Union toehold in the South; the inlet also performs useful service as a coaling station for blockading squadrons offshore.

AUGUST 30   At St. Louis, Missouri, General John C. Fremont declares both martial law and a conditional emancipation declaration. Henceforth all slaves belonging to Confederate sympathizers in Missouri are considered freed. President Abraham Lincoln, alarmed by this action, declares Fremont's actions dictatorial and fears it might upset slave-owning Union sympathizers throughout the region.

AUGUST 31   In western Virginia, General William S. Rosecrans and 6,000 Ohio troops march south from Clarksburg to attack Confederate troops gathered at Carnifex Ferry under general and former secretary of war John B. Floyd.

SEPTEMBER 3   In Tennessee, General Leonidas K. Polk orders Confederate forces to violate Kentucky neutrality by occupying the heights of Hickham, Clark Cliffs, and Columbus. This precludes any chance of Union forces deploying there and also establishes a continuous war front reaching from Missouri to the Atlantic Ocean. By violating Kentucky neutrality, however, Polk induces that state to throw its lot in with the Union.

SEPTEMBER 5   At Cairo, Illinois, General Ulysses S. Grant prepares his forces for an immediate occupation of Paducah, Kentucky, to secure the Ohio River. Control of the Tennessee and Cumberland Rivers, which flow directly into the Confederate heartland, also appear in the offing.

SEPTEMBER 6   General Ulysses S. Grant advances south from Cairo, Illinois, and captures Paducah, Kentucky, at the mouth of the Tennessee River. This move would not have been feasible had not Confederate forces first violated Kentucky's neutrality. Grant then appoints General Charles F. Smith commander of

Union forces in western Kentucky, then hastens back to Cairo to organize additional troops.

SEPTEMBER 10   In western Virginia, General William S. Rosecrans and 6,000 men attack 2,000 Confederates deployed at Carnifex Ferry. The Federals press into a bend of the Gauley River, capturing many Southern supplies. General John B. Floyd hastily withdraws across the river under the cover of darkness, destroying the ferry to thwart pursuers.

SEPTEMBER 11–12   In western Virginia, General Robert E. Lee masses 15,000 Confederates against Union General J. J. Reynolds and 2,000 Union troops at Cheat Mountain. The assailants are hampered by rough terrain and are misled by prisoners into thinking that they are outnumbered. Lee, alarmed by the supposed approach of Union reinforcements, cancels his attack and unceremoniously withdraws.

SEPTEMBER 15   General Robert E. Lee, bested at Cheat Mountain, orders Confederate forces to abandon the westernmost counties of Virginia. Consequently, he earns the unflattering sobriquet of "Granny." Authorities in Richmond are displeased with his performance as a leader and plans are afoot to transfer him to a quiet sector in South Carolina.

SEPTEMBER 20   At Lexington, Missouri, Colonel James Mulligan surrenders 2,800 Union troops to General Sterling Price following a nine-day siege. The Confederates ingeniously employed dampened bales of hemp as moveable breastworks, rolling them ahead of their advance. General John C. Fremont's inability to relieve the garrison causes officials in St. Louis and Washington, D.C., to question his abilities.

OCTOBER 1   At Centreville, Virginia, President Jefferson Davis and Generals Joseph E. Johnston and Pierre G. T. Beauregard hotly debate military strategy. They finally agree to restrain from launching offensive operations into Northern territory until the following spring, when greater resources are available.

OCTOBER 9   In Florida, 1,000 Confederates under General Richard H. Anderson cross Pensacola Bay to attack Union troops on Santa Rosa Island. The maneuver stalls outside of Fort Pickens, and a counterattack by the garrison nets several Southern captives as they withdraw.

OCTOBER 11   Brigadier General William S. Rosencrans gains appointment as commander of the Department of Western Virginia. His exceptional performance to date is one of the few bright spots in military affairs.

OCTOBER 14   In Washington, D.C., President Abraham Lincoln orders General Winfield Scott to suspend writs of habeas corpus in the region stretching from the capital up to Maine. He does so to quickly squelch all seditious or treasonous activities by Confederate sympathizers.

OCTOBER 18   In Washington, D.C., President Abraham Lincoln confers with Cabinet members over mounting dissatisfaction with General-in-Chief Winfield Scott, and begins pondering his retirement. He also has trouble encouraging Generals William T. Sherman and George B. McClellan to willingly transfer troops for the pending expedition against Port Royal, South Carolina.

OCTOBER 21   In Virginia, Colonel Isaac D. Baker ferries 1,700 men of his brigade across the Potomac River at Ball's Bluff, a

100-foot-high ledge overlooking that waterway. He does so without proper reconnaissance and is unaware that Confederates under Colonel Nathan G. Evans are positioned in the woods above him. An unequal battle ensues for three and a half hours, until the Federals succumb to panic. Baker is killed and loses nearly 1,000 men, either drowned or captured.

OCTOBER 22 In another fateful assignment, General Thomas J. "Stonewall" Jackson is ordered to command Confederate forces in the Shenandoah Valley of western Virginia.

OCTOBER 24 President Abraham Lincoln decides it is politically expedient to relieve General John C. Fremont in Missouri and replace him with General David Hunter, a less-volatile abolitionist. The president remains very concerned about keeping Missouri in the Union fold.

OCTOBER 28 At Bowling Green, Kentucky, formidable General Albert S. Johnston arrives to replace General Simon B. Buckner as commander of the Confederate Army Corps of Kentucky.

OCTOBER 31 In Washington, D.C., ailing and elderly Lieutenant General Winfield Scott, once the doyen of his age, resigns as head of Union forces. He then retires to the U.S. Military Academy at West Point, New York, for the remainder of the war.

NOVEMBER 1 Dashing, 34-year-old General George B. McClellan succeeds Lieutenant General Winfield Scott as the new general-in-chief of Union forces. In light of his youth and reputation for brilliance, much is expected of him.

At Cairo, Illinois, General Ulysses S. Grant arrives to take charge of the District of Southeast Missouri. Unlike many contemporaries, Grant is aggressively disposed and begins making plans to evict Confederates from their nearby strong point at Columbus, Kentucky.

NOVEMBER 4–7 Union troops under General Thomas W. Sherman land under the cover of a naval squadron and capture Port Royal, South Carolina, along with Fort Walker on Hilton Head and Fort Beauregard on Philips Island. The Federal army thus acquires another lodgement on the Southern coastline from which power can be projected inland.

NOVEMBER 5 At its St. Louis headquarters, the Department of the West orders General Ulysses S. Grant on a diversionary attack against Confederate troops deployed along the heights of Columbus, Kentucky. This maneuver is intended to distract Southern forces and preclude their crossing the Mississippi River into Missouri. Grant is all too willing to oblige superiors and makes immediate preparations.

NOVEMBER 6–7 General Ulysses S. Grant and 3,000 Union troops debark at Hunter's Farm, three miles above Belmont, Missouri, and they rapidly overrun General Gideon Pillow's 2,500 Confederates in camp. However, a plundering spree ensues and allows General Leonidas K. Polk to cross the Mississippi with Southern reinforcements and counterattack. Grant cuts his way back to the riverbank and escapes intact. Belmont is a technical defeat but demonstrates his willingness to undertake offensive operations.

NOVEMBER 9 At St. Louis, Missouri, General Henry W. Halleck takes charge of the newly designated Department of

Missouri (Missouri, Arkansas, Illinois, and western Kentucky). In Ohio, General Don Carlos Buell replaces the unpopular and highly irritable General William T. Sherman as head of the Department of the Cumberland.

NOVEMBER 13 Outside Washington, D.C., George B. McClellan contemptuously snubs President Abraham Lincoln when the latter calls upon his headquarters, and he retires to bed. Henceforth, an understandably angry Lincoln summons the general to the White House whenever consultations are sought.

NOVEMBER 15 In Washington, D.C., President Abraham Lincoln and his cabinet focus their attention on New Orleans, Louisiana, the Confederacy's second largest city, which is also vulnerable to an attack from the sea. Secretary of the Navy Gideon Welles selects Captain David G. Farragut, a 60-year-old Tennessean known for his aggressive disposition. He will seconded by the Army's General Benjamin F. Butler.

NOVEMBER 20 A superb organizer and disciplinarian, General George B. McClellan reviews 70,000 men of the Army of the Potomac near Washington, D.C. Observers comment favorably on the military deportment and appearance of all ranks, which are quite a departure from the amateurish force hastily gathered the previous summer.

NOVEMBER 24 At Caseyville and Eddyville, Kentucky, Colonel Nathan B. Forrest mounts a prolonged cavalry raid against Union forces, initiating his spectacular career as the Confederacy's greatest cavalry leader.

DECEMBER 2 In Washington, D.C., Secretary of War Simon Cameron reports that the United States Army presently consists of 20,334 federal soldiers and 640,637 state volunteers.

DECEMBER 4 In St. Louis, Missouri, General Henry W. Halleck authorizes punitive measures against Southern sympathizers cooperating with Confederate forces within his jurisdiction. These measures include the death penalty for anyone caught assisting rebel guerrillas.

DECEMBER 14 In west Texas, General Henry H. Sibley assumes control of Confederate forces along the Upper Rio Grande, including the New Mexico and Arizona Territories. He begins military preparations for an offensive, intent upon securing that region for the South.

DECEMBER 20 In Washington, D.C., the Joint Committee on the Conduct of the War arises in Congress following the disastrous rout at Ball's Bluff the previous October. Composed of Radical Republicans like Benjamin F. Wade and Zachariah Chandler of Michigan, it is tasked with scrutinizing the conduct of senior army commanders throughout the war and exerts a most unwelcome presence.

DECEMBER 28 Outside Sacramento, Kentucky, Colonel Nathan B. Forrest and 300 Confederate cavalrymen encounter 168 Union troopers under Major Eli Murray and give battle. The Federals are quickly struck on both flanks and scattered in this first of many scrapes. The future "Wizard of the Saddle" then gallops back to Greeneville in triumph.

DECEMBER 31 In Washington, D.C., President Abraham Lincoln notes the lack of activity by Union forces in the West and cables General Henry W. Halleck at St. Louis, Missouri, to prod him into some kind of offensive operation.

1862

JANUARY 1 In western Virginia, General Thomas J. Jackson orders 8,500 Confederates under General William W. Loring to depart their winter encampment at Winchester and secure the lightly defended town of Romney. No sooner does Loring march than temperatures plunge to below zero; his men, lacking heavy overcoats, suffer greatly from exposure.

JANUARY 6 In Washington, D.C., President Abraham Lincoln ignores demands to replace General George B. McClellan, then ill with typhoid fever, for his military inactivity. Lincoln also urges General Don Carlos Buell, commanding the Army of the Ohio in Kentucky, to assume offensive operations.

JANUARY 10 In western Virginia, Union forces hastily abandon the strategic settlement of Romney to advancing Confederates under General William W. Loring. However, that leader enters into a bitter contretemps with General Thomas J. Jackson over marching his ill-clad soldiers during bitterly cold weather.

JANUARY 11 In Washington, D.C., Secretary of War Simon Cameron resigns from office after being charged with corruption and mismanagement. President Abraham Lincoln subsequently nominates former attorney general Edwin M. Stanton to succeed him. The appointment is fortuitous, for Stanton infuses his military administration with energy and efficiency.

JANUARY 13 President Abraham Lincoln again entreats Generals Henry W. Halleck and Don Carlos Buell to initiate offensive operations in the western theater. Neither leader is willing to comply at present.

JANUARY 16 In Kentucky, General Felix K. Zollicoffer disobeys orders from General George B. Crittenden and positions Confederate troops north of the Cumberland River, where they stand with a river to their backs. Crittenden arrives with reinforcements shortly after and concludes that the water is running too high to recross. He elects to make the most of his subordinate's mistake by attacking a Union force gathered at nearby Mill Springs.

JANUARY 19 At Mill Springs (Logan's Cross Roads), Kentucky, 4,000 Confederates under General George B. Crittenden and Felix K. Zollicoffer attack the Union encampment of General George H. Thomas. Thomas repels his antagonists with a well-directed enfilade fire that kills Zollicoffer and drives Crittenden from the field. Confederate losses are 125 killed, 309 wounded, and 99 missing, along with most of their supplies and artillery. Thomas sustains only 40 dead, 207 wounded, and 15 missing in this first of many well-executed victories.

JANUARY 23 In western Virginia, General William W. Loring smolders once his command has been deliberately left in an exposed position only 20 miles from Union lines. Consequently, he and other officers violate the chain of command by petitioning friends in the Confederate Congress to have their orders amended.

JANUARY 26 In light of ongoing difficulties with President Jefferson Davis, General Pierre G. T. Beauregard transfers to the Western Theater as a subordinate of General Albert S. Johnston. Military command in Virginia reverts back to General Joseph E. Johnston, who also has an uneasy relationship with Davis.

JANUARY 27   In Washington, D.C., President Abraham Lincoln issues General Order No. 1, mandating a general offensive against the Confederacy from various points along the line. Lincoln is exasperated by the lack of initiative displayed by Union commanders, but General George B. McClellan simply ignores the directive.

JANUARY 31   In Richmond, Virginia, Confederate Secretary of War Judah P. Benjamin instructs General Thomas J. Jackson to relocate those portions of his command still at Romney, western Virginia, back to Winchester. Jackson is livid that General William W. Loring has violated the chain of command behind his back and resigns from the Army. President Jefferson Davis refuses to accept and he gradually persuades Jackson to remain in uniform.

FEBRUARY 1   In west Texas, Confederate forces under General Henry H. Sibley advance from El Paso and into New Mexico, intending to conquer that region for the South. Scattered Union forces begin scrambling to oppose him.

FEBRUARY 2   In Cairo, Illinois, General Ulysses S. Grant boards 17,000 troops of the Army of West Tennessee on river transports. He intends to seize Confederate-held Fort Henry on the Tennessee River, assisted by Commodore Andrew H. Foote's gunboats.

FEBRUARY 4   In Washington, D.C., Congress authorizes President Abraham Lincoln to seize control of the railroads. He begins organizing rail transportation into a single unit, administered by the War Department, for the benefit of the U.S. Army.

FEBRUARY 6   Outside Confederate-held Fort Henry, Tennessee, General Ulysses S. Grant commences a flanking movement that prompts Southern general Lloyd Tilghman to evacuate his 3,400-man garrison to Fort Donelson, 10 miles away on the Cumberland River. Grant's bloodless victory allows Union forces free movement along the upper Tennessee River.

FEBRUARY 8   On Roanoke Island, North Carolina, General Ambrose Burnside orders three brigades under Generals Jesse Reno, John G. Parke, and John G. Foster to attack Confederate defensive works on its northern tip. Southern resistance crumbles and 2,500 men are taken prisoner. Burnside's victory now impedes overland communications with Norfolk, Virginia, and causes its eventual abandonment.

FEBRUARY 9   In Tennessee, General Gideon J. Pillow supersedes Generals Bushrod J. Johnson and Simon B. Buckner as commander of Confederate-held Fort Donelson, Tennessee. General Ulysses S. Grant knew Pillow from his Mexican War days and heartily despises his leadership abilities.

FEBRUARY 10   At Rolla, Missouri, General Samuel R. Curtis orders 12,000 men from his Army of the Southwest to march against the Missouri Home Guard under General Sterling Price. He is intent on driving them into Arkansas to preclude any chance of them interfering with a forthcoming thrust down the Mississippi River.

FEBRUARY 11   In Washington, D.C., Secretary of War Edwin M. Stanton establishes the U.S. Military Rail Road under former railroad executive Daniel McCallum. This becomes the largest, unified railroad system in the world and rail-borne Union logistics achieve a degree of effectiveness unmatched by the South.

FEBRUARY 12 In Tennessee, General Ulysses S. Grant directs 15,000 Union troops overland to invest Fort Donelson on the Cumberland River, Tennessee, now defended by 21,000 Confederates under General John B. Floyd. After arriving, Generals John A. McClernand and Charles F. Smith begin probing Southern defenses in concert with gunboats offshore.

FEBRUARY 15 At Fort Donelson, Tennessee, the 15,000 Confederate defenders under Generals John B. Floyd and Gideon J. Pillow sortie against Union lines to escape capture. Their attack penetrates the division of General John A. McClernand, but they begin arguing among themselves about what to do next. General Ulysses S. Grant hastily repairs back to camp and organizes a sharp coun-terattack that drives the milling Southerners back inside their works.

FEBRUARY 16 Fort Donelson, Tennessee, surrenders to General Ulysses S. Grant after Confederates John B. Floyd and Gideon J. Pillow ignominiously flee their command, leaving General Simon B. Buckner to capitulate. The victorious Grant takes 15,000 Southerners, 20,000 stands of arms, 48 field pieces, 57 heavy cannon, and tons of supplies. Hereafter he is also lionized in the press as "Unconditional Surrender" Grant. This victory also opens up the northern tier of Confederate defenses and allows for invasions further south.

Outside Fort Craig, New Mexico Territory, General Henry H. Sibley's Confederate column arrives and confronts Colonel Edward R. S. Canby, his brother-

Battle of Fort Donelson and the capture of General Simon Buckner and his army on February 16, 1862. Forts Donelson and Henry comprised the strategic center of Confederate operations in the West during the Civil War. General Ulysses S. Grant set out to capture the forts in early 1862, and by February 16, 1862, Buckner conceded to Grant's demand for an unconditional surrender. (Library of Congress)

in-law. However, Sibley considers the position too strong to attack directly and bypasses it, hoping to lure the garrison out into the open.

FEBRUARY 19 In the New Mexico Territory, 3,000 Confederate troops under General Henry H. Sibley cross the Rio Grande at Valverde Ford, five miles north of Union-held Fort Craig. As anticipated, Colonel Edward R. S. Canby sorties his 2,000-man garrison and marches to prevent the Southerners from crossing.

FEBRUARY 21 At Valverde, New Mexico Territory, Union troops under Colonel Edward R. S. Canby engage General Henry H. Sibley's marauding Confederates as they cross the Rio Grande. A stout and indecisive fight ensues, at which point Canby disengages and returns to Fort Craig, five miles distant. His garrison still constitutes a threat to Confederate communications, a fact that Sibley appears to ignore.

MARCH 2 General Leonidas K. Polk orders Confederate positions at Columbus, Kentucky, abandoned due to the Union capture of Fort Donelson. The large garrison and its 140 cannons subsequently cross the Mississippi River and deploy at New Madrid, Missouri, and Island No. 10.

MARCH 4 In Arkansas, General Earl Van Dorn marches 16,000 men from the Boston Mountains toward the Missouri border. He seeks to engage the smaller Union army of General Samuel R. Curtis, then operating in the northwest corner of the state. If Curtis can be destroyed, then Missouri is also likely to fall.

MARCH 6 In northern Arkansas, General Samuel R. Curtis and 10,000 Union troops entrench along Pea Ridge in

anticipation of a major Confederate assault. General Earl Van Dorn arrives with superior numbers, probes Union positions, and concludes they are too strong to be assailed frontally. He subsequently orders his men on a night march around Curtis to cut him off from Missouri and take him from behind.

MARCH 7 In Arkansas, Confederate forces under General Earl Van Dorn execute a complicated night march around Pea Ridge to catch the Union Army of the Southwest in the rear. General Samuel R. Curtis, however, quickly perceives the danger and simply orders his entire command to "about face." General Sterling Price's Missourians then commence the action by launching two desperate charges that are heavily repelled. A final assault at sunset pushes the Union line back 800 yards, but fails to break it.

MARCH 8 Fighting resumes at Pea Ridge, Arkansas, as Confederate artillery bombards defiant Union positions. General Samuel R. Curtis orders his 11,000 men to constrict and consolidate their lines and also deduces that the Southerners are nearly out of ammunition. He orders an attack across the line, driving Van Dorn's 18,000 soldiers off in confusion. Pea Ridge is the first major Union victory in the far West, and it thwarts Confederate hopes for invading Missouri for two years.

MARCH 11 General Henry W. Halleck becomes commander of all Union forces in the West once the Departments of Kansas, the Missouri, and the Ohio are amalgamated into the new Department of the Mississippi. He now wields authority over Union forces in 11 states and three territories as far west as Colorado.

In Washington, D.C., President Abraham Lincoln despairs of General George

B. McClelland's lack of aggressiveness and issues War Order No. 3, removing that reluctant leader as general in chief. McClellan still retains command of the Army of the Potomac, which he continues training to a fine edge.

MARCH 13 At Fairfax Court House, Virginia, General George B. McClellan finalizes his strategy against Richmond by proposing to transport his Army of the Potomac up the York and James Rivers to outflank strong Confederate defenses. His force presently consists of five corps: I Corps (General Irvin McDowell), II Corps (General Edwin V. Sumner), III Corps (General Samuel P. Heintzelman), IV Corps (Major General Erasmus D. Keyes), and V Corps (General Nathaniel P. Banks). The men are well-trained and in fine spirits.

At Slocum's Creek, North Carolina, General Ambrose E. Burnside lands 12,000 Union troops along the Neuse River, supported by 13 gunboats. He then marches inland, intending to capture New Bern, the state's second-largest city and a strategic railhead.

MARCH 14 In North Carolina, General Ambrose E. Burnside advances 12,000 Union troops toward New Bern, North Carolina, despite heavy rain and muddy conditions. Confederates under General Lawrence O. Branch resist doggedly until a militia unit suddenly panics, and they retreat. New Bern is occupied, and the Union gains an important base for projecting military strength deeper inland. Burnside is promoted to major general of volunteers for his victory.

MARCH 16 On the Mississippi River, General John Pope, in concert with Commodore Henry H. Foote's gunboat flotilla, initiates combined operations against Confederate batteries on Island No. 10. This post is well armed and

situated, presenting a formidable obstacle to all river navigation.

MARCH 17 In Virginia, the Army of the Potomac, numbering 105,000 men in five corps, embarks from Alexandria for an amphibious transit to Fortress Monroe. Once landed between the York and James Rivers, General George B. McClellan begins maneuvering to outflank Confederate defenses guarding the Confederate capital at Richmond.

MARCH 20 On Ship Island, Mississippi, General Benjamin F. Butler gains command of the Department of the Gulf, prior to combined operations against New Orleans, Louisiana.

MARCH 21 In western Virginia, Colonel Turner Ashby alerts General Thomas J. Jackson that General Nathaniel P. Banks is withdrawing two Union divisions from the Shenandoah Valley. Jackson correctly assumes that these soldiers will reinforce the Army of the Potomac before Richmond, so he determines to lure them back.

MARCH 22 In western Virginia, General Thomas J. Jackson is mistakenly informed by Colonel Turner Ashby's Confederate cavalry that Union strength at Kernstown is roughly 4,000—the same as his own. Unfortunately, General James Shields commands at least twice as many men, with most of them hidden in nearby copses.

MARCH 23 In western Virginia, General Thomas J. Jackson's force marches 41 miles in two days and attacks Union positions at Kernstown. However, Union General James Shields continuously feeds additional men into the fray and Jackson's entire line falls back in confusion out of town. However, Kernstown, while a Confederate tactical defeat, induces

President Abraham Lincoln to detain General Irvin McDowell's I Corps at Washington, D.C. This, in turn, deprives the Army of the Potomac of reinforcements during the upcoming Peninsula Campaign. It also heralds the start of Jackson's legendary Shenandoah Valley Campaign.

MARCH 25 Near Santa Fe, New Mexico Territory, Major John M. Chivington is ordered to attack Confederate forces lodged in his vicinity. He marches to the far end of Glorietta Pass that evening, capturing several sentinels, and prepares to storm the enemy camp at dawn.

MARCH 26 At Glorietta Pass, New Mexico Territory, Colonel John M. Chivington attacks Major Charles L. Pryon's Confederates as they repose at Johnson's Ranch. Fighting is inconclusive until a last-minute charge by Union cavalry against the Southern rearguard nets several prisoners, then Chivington withdraws to Kozlowski's Ranch to regroup.

MARCH 28 Union troops at Johnson's Ranch near Glorietta Pass, New Mexico, are reinforced by Colonel John P. Slough, and Major John M. Chivington, 1st Colorado Volunteers, orders his force back through Glorietta Pass. The Federals happily stumble upon the lightly guarded Confederate baggage train, capturing it intact. This disaster spells the end of General Henry H. Sibley's offensive, and the Confederates retreat back to Texas.

MARCH 29 At Corinth, Mississippi, General Albert S. Johnston assembles the Army of Mississippi by amalgamating Confederate forces in Kentucky and Mississippi into a single structure under his command. Present are Generals Leonidas K. Polk (I Corps), Braxton Bragg (II Corps), William J. Hardee

(III Corps), and George B. Crittenden (Reserve), while Johnston is also seconded by General Pierre G. T. Beauregard. This is the largest concentration of Confederate forces in the West to date.

APRIL 2 On the Tennessee River, skirmishing breaks out between opposing videttes at Pittsburg Landing (Shiloh), Tennessee, as Union forces under General Ulysses S. Grant consolidate their bridgehead. General Pierre G. T. Beauregard subsequently draws up an overly complex order of battle, placing all three Confederate corps in distinct waves of attacks, a tactic guaranteed to exacerbate confusion in the heat of battle.

APRIL 3 In Washington, D.C., President Abraham Lincoln upbraids General George B. McClellan for failing to officially assign a corps of 20,000 men to the defenses of Washington, D.C. He reiterates that General Irvin McDowell's I Corp must be retained to defend the nation's capital.

APRIL 4 General George B. McClellan, having finally assembled his army of 112,000 men on the York Peninsula, Virginia, begins his long anticipated drive against Richmond. Happily, his Army of the Potomac is well-trained, well-led, and eager to prove its mettle in combat.

APRIL 6 On this momentous day the Battle of Shiloh, southwestern Tennessee, erupts as 44,000 Confederates under General Albert S. Johnston surprise 39,000 Union troops under General William T. Sherman. However, General Johnston is fatally injured while directing combat from his saddle and General Pierre G. T. Beauregard assumes tactical control of events. At one point he orders up 62 cannons to blast Federal defenders in the so-called Hornet's Nest into surrendering. Meanwhile General Ulysses

S. Grant arrives and begins organizing a coherent defense, backed by gunboats on the Tennessee River. Beauregard briefly tests Grant's position and judges it too strong to be carried by his exhausted soldiers. Fighting ceases at nightfall.

APRIL 7 The struggle at Shiloh, Tennessee, resumes as General Ulysses S. Grant, now heavily reinforced, mounts a spirited counterattack to regain ground lost in the previous day's fighting. General Pierre G. T. Beauregard resists gamely, but yields to superior numbers and withdraws back to Corinth, Mississippi. Grant, with 65,000 men engaged, loses 13,047 while the 44,000 Confederates sustain 10,694. The casualty list stuns public opinion, North and South alike, and Grant is attacked in the press as a "butcher."

APRIL 8 In the Mississippi River, General William W. Mackall surrenders Island No. 10 and 4,500 Confederates to General John Pope. Considering the intricacy of the terrain and the tricky currents involved, Pope performed well. President Abraham Lincoln subsequently brings him east to command the newly organized Army of Virginia.

General Ulysses S. Grant advances from Pittsburg Landing, Tennessee, in pursuit of General Pierre G. T. Beauregard. General William T. Sherman engages them briefly, but is capably contained by a rearguard directed by General Nathan B. Forrest. The Southerners continue trudging back to Corinth, Mississippi.

APRIL 9 In Washington, D.C., President Abraham Lincoln agonizes over General George B. McClellan's apparent lack of aggressiveness and confers with Cabinet members over how to prod him on. The chief executive suggests several lines of attack for the Army of the Potomac, and entreats the recalcitrant leader to attack immediately. McClellan continues advancing on Richmond, Virginia, although at a snail's pace.

APRIL 10 In Virginia, General Joseph E. Johnston assumes command of Confederate forces in the Peninsula district. He eventually leads 34,000 troops, but remains pessimistic about resisting the Army of the Potomac, thrice his size, indefinitely.

APRIL 11 Confederates at Fort Pulaski, Georgia, surrender to Captain Quincy A. Gillmore following a heavy bombardment of 5,725 shells from nearby Cockspur Island. This battle marks the first employment of long-range, rifled ordnance which yields impressive results against older masonry defenses.

At Pittsburg Landing, Tennessee, General Henry W. Halleck arrives to supersede General Ulysses S. Grant over allegations of drunkenness. Command of the Army of the Tennessee also temporarily reverts to General George H. Thomas.

APRIL 12 At Big Shanty, Georgia, Major James J. Andrews and 22 Union volunteers steal the Confederate locomotive *General*, then head northward toward Chattanooga, Tennessee, to destroy railroad bridges leading to the city. Once the *General* finally runs out of steam, the men flee into the woods where most are captured. Andrews and seven volunteers are executed as spies on June 7, 1862, but they became the first recipients of the new Congressional Medal of Honor.

APRIL 15 In Richmond, Virginia, President Jefferson Davis breaks the strategic impasse by ordering General Joseph E. Johnston to move his army to Yorktown and reinforce General John B. Magruder's troops holding the line. Johnston, heavily outnumbered, is pessimistic that he can stave off defeat for long.

APRIL 16   In Richmond, Virginia, President Jefferson Davis authorizes forced conscription to maintain existing Confederate manpower levels, and all white males aged 18 to 35 are now eligible for three years of service. This is also the first military conscription act in American history.

APRIL 28   The Confederate garrisons of Forts Jackson and St. Philip, on the Mississippi River, mutiny against General John K. Duncan; they surrender 900 prisoners to Union forces under Commander David D. Porter, who had previously captured New Orleans.

APRIL 29   At Pittsburg Landing, Tennessee, General Henry W. Halleck concentrates the Armies of the Tennessee, Ohio, and Mississippi, and advances upon Confederate defenses at Corinth, Mississippi. However, he proceeds with such caution that General Pierre G. T. Beauregard easily evacuates the premises ahead of time.

APRIL 30   Confederate forces under General Thomas J. Jackson advance from Elk Run, western Virginia, to Staunton in driving rain. This proves one of the war's most impressive forced marches and bequeaths to troops involved the sobriquet of "Jackson's foot cavalry."

MAY 1   After New Orleans, Louisiana, surrenders to Admiral David G. Farragut, the town is occupied by Union troops under General Benjamin F. Butler, who also serves as military governor. Butler enjoys a stormy and controversial tenure throughout his stay.

MAY 3   Heavily outnumbered, General Joseph E. Johnston begins withdrawing 55,000 Confederates from Yorktown, Virginia, before heavy Union ordnance bombards them into submission. The Army of the Potomac under General George B. McClellan, stalled a month while planting siege guns, resumes moving slowly up the peninsula in pursuit.

MAY 4–5   In Virginia, General George B. McClellan's Army of the Potomac attacks Confederate forces under General Joseph E. Johnston as they funnel through Williamsburg. Heavy fighting results, especially after a flank attack by General Winfield S. Hancock disrupts Confederate reinforcements. Fortunately, General James Longstreet extricates his forces by nightfall and retires in the direction of Richmond. Williamsburg, the first pitched battle of the Peninsula Campaign, proves indecisive and characterized by heavy casualties: Union losses are 2,239 while the Confederates sustain 1,703.

MAY 8   In western Virginia, General Thomas J. Jackson leads 10,000 Confederates against 6,000 Federals under General Robert H. Milroy at McDowell. Union troops manage to charge up a heavily wooded hill where the Southerners are deploying and inflict heavy loss. Confederate General Edward Johnson and his Army of the Northwest still repulse several attacks while Jackson rushes up additional troops. At length Milroy retreats up the Shenandoah Valley, while Colonel Turner Ashby's cavalry rounds up Union stragglers.

MAY 9   In Washington, D.C., President Abraham Lincoln diplomatically yet determinedly admonishes General George B. McClellan for not moving against the Confederate capital at Richmond, Virginia, with vigor. The general, as always, ignores the president and continues as planned.

MAY 20   In the Luray Valley, western Virginia, General Thomas J. Jackson's command swells to 17,000 men following the arrival of General Richard S. Ewell's contingent. Jackson is determined to prevent General Nathaniel P. Banks from reinforcing the Army of the Potomac and resumes offensive operations.

MAY 21 Only eight miles from the Confederate capital of Richmond, Virginia, and ignoring numerical superiority over its defenders, General George B. McClellan halts and calls for reinforcements. To that end, the I Corps of General Irvin McDowell prepares to march overland from Washington, D.C., to join him.

In western Virginia, General Thomas J. Jackson directs Confederate movements north through the Luray Valley and approaches the isolated Union outpost at Front Royal. His march is effectively masked by Colonel Turner Ashby's cavalry, whose antics completely confound General Nathaniel P. Banks.

MAY 23 Front Royal, Virginia, is attacked by 23,000 Confederates under General Thomas J. Jackson. He bursts upon the surprised Union garrison, driving them out. At one point, General Richard Taylor is hailed by Belle Boyd, the female spy, who relays useful intelligence about Union dispositions. The town succumbs to Jackson's onslaught and the Federals retreat after losing 1,063 men captured.

MAY 24 In Washington, D.C., President Abraham Lincoln is alarmed by Confederate activity in the Shenandoah Valley and again orders General Irvin McDowell's I Corps halted at Fredericksburg. He also instructs General John C. Fremont to gather his forces and drive Confederates from the region altogether. General George B. McClellan is consequently advised that his promised

reinforcements are not forthcoming at this time.

MAY 25 The Army of the Potomac, edging ever closer to Richmond, Virginia, becomes divided by the rain-swollen Chickahominy River, with three corps lodged on its northern bank and two below. Consequently, General Joseph E. Johnston contemplates an offensive stroke against the commands of Generals Edwin V. Sumner, William B. Franklin, and Fitz John Porter on the northern bank, possibly defeating each one in detail.

In western Virginia, General Thomas J. Jackson hurriedly marches toward another engagement at Winchester. General Richard S. Ewell's division attacks the Union left while the Louisiana Brigade of General Richard Taylor simultaneously strikes the right, and General Nathaniel Banks is overpowered with a loss of 2,019 casualties. The Southerners sustain only 400. In three days Jackson's command has won three victories, netted 3,030 prisoners, 9,000 firearms, and a trove of quartermaster stores. They also begin referring to their defeated adversary as "Commissary Banks."

MAY 28 General J. E. B. Stuart arrives at Richmond, Virginia, with intelligence that the much-feared approach of General Irvin McDowell's I Corps from Fredericksburg is nonexistent. General Joseph E. Johnston is thus prodded into canceling his proposed lunge against the three Union corps north of the Chickahominy River, and plans to overpower the two corps marooned on the south bank.

At Harpers Ferry, western Virginia, 50,000 Union troops under Generals Irvin McDowell, John C. Fremont, and Nathaniel P. Banks assemble to cut off and possibly annihilate the fast-marching Confederates of General Thomas J. Jackson. All are goaded on by an anxious President Abraham Lincoln, who urges them to move and strike with all possible haste.

MAY 30 General Joseph E. Johnston makes a close reconnaissance of Union forces looming within 10 miles of Richmond, Virginia. He elects to concentrate 51,000 men against the combined III and IV Corps of Generals Samuel P. Heintzelman and Erasmus D. Keyes on the south bank. In practice, the execution of Johnston's sensible plan is compromised by over-reliance on verbal commands, which his inexperienced officers manage to bungle.

At Corinth, Mississippi, General Henry W. Halleck's forces secure the town and 2,000 Confederates prisoners. A vital transportation link is thus secured and severs the Memphis and Charleston, and the Mobile and Ohio Railroads. However, Halleck's dilatory pace was glacial and has taken him 30 days to cover only 22 miles.

MAY 31 Federal troops under General George B. McClellan continue creeping toward Richmond, Virginia, but topography requires him to further split his forces along either bank of Chickahominy Creek. General Joseph E. Johnston suddenly attacks the isolated III and IV corps under Generals Samuel P. Heintzelman and Eramus D. Keyes at Fair Oaks on the south bank. Hard fighting evicts the division of General Silas Casey and captures several batteries, but the Federals reform and establish new lines. A secondary attack at nearby Seven Pines fares little better and Union troops under redoubtable Phil Kearny resist several Southern onslaughts. Johnston is then seriously wounded by a ball in the shoulder and is succeeded by General Gustavus W. Smith, who orders the Southerners withdrawn.

JUNE 1 At Seven Pines, Virginia, Confederate forces resume their offensive against the Army of the Potomac. The Southerners deliver their charges fiercely but in piecemeal fashion, and are driven off before General Robert E. Lee gallops up from Richmond to succeed General Gustavus W. Smith in command. Lee orders the fighting stopped; the Confederates, who did most of the attacking, lose 6,134 men to a Union tally of 5,031. However, a corner is turned in the course of events once Lee seizes the reins as the new Confederate field commander.

JUNE 7 In New Orleans, Louisiana, General Benjamin F. Butler orders William B. Mumford hung for tearing down an American flag from the city mint. He also issues his controversial Order No. 28, requiring Southern women who act disrespectfully toward Union soldiers to be treated like prostitutes.

JUNE 8 At Port Republic, western Virginia, the Army of the Valley under General Thomas J. Jackson reposes before advancing against Union forces commanded by General James Shields. General Richard S. Ewell's 5,000 men also assume defensive positions at Cross Keys in anticipation of an attack by General John C. Fremont's army. Fremont eventually approaches Ewell's position with 12,000 men, but he suddenly disengages and withdraws back down the Keezletown Road.

JUNE 9 In western Virginia, General Thomas J. Jackson's soldiers cross a wagon bridge over the North River and attack General Erasmus B. Tyler's brigade at Port Republic. Tyler, heavily outnumbered, orders a withdrawal which degenerates under pressure into a rout. Union losses are 1,108, including 558 prisoners, while the Southerners incur roughly 800 casualties.

Port Republic is the sixth and final victory of Jackson's remarkable

Shenandoah Valley Campaign. Since March his famous "foot cavalry," who never exceeded 17,000 men, has slogged 676 miles and defied all attempts by 60,000 Federals to ensnare them. Jackson also siphoned off valuable Union manpower that might have proved decisive before Richmond. All told, it is a remarkable display of economy of force.

JUNE 10   In Mississippi, General Henry W. Halleck authorizes Generals Ulysses S. Grant, John Pope, and Don Carlos Buell to resume independent command of their respective armies. Grant, as senior officer present, reigns again as theater commander, which promises to increase the tempo of events.

JUNE 12   Outside Richmond, Virginia, General J. E. B. Stuart rouses his sleeping men and orders them into the saddle. He then departs with 1,200 Virginian troopers to ascertain if General George B. McClellan's right flank is "in the air." If so, this would facilitate a daring offensive envisioned by General Robert E. Lee.

JUNE 14   In Virginia, General J. E. B. Stuart's Confederate cavalry destroys a bridge over the Chickahominy River to prevent a Union pursuit, completing its legendary ride around the Army of the Potomac's left flank. The Federal cavalry pursuing Stuart was commanded by Brigadier General Philip St. George Cooke, his father-in-law.

JUNE 15   General J. E. B. Stuart dashes into Richmond, Virginia, with important military intelligence about the Army of the Potomac. Apparently, the V Corps under General Fitz John Porter is presently unsupported on the north bank of the Chickahominy River. General Robert E. Lee, determined to end the impasse near Richmond, concocts a plan to crush Porter in detail.

JUNE 17   In Mississippi, General Braxton Bragg succeeds the ailing General Pierre G. T. Beauregard as commander of the Confederate Western Department. Bragg, a friend of President Jefferson Davis, is a capable strategist and logistician, but is also saddled with a garrulous disposition that alienates subordinates.

JUNE 23   Outside Richmond, Virginia, General Robert E. Lee outlines his offensive against the Army of the Potomac's right wing under General Fitz John Porter. He will concentrate no less than 55,000 men against the 30,000-man V Corps by throwing the divisions of Thomas J. Jackson, James Longstreet, Daniel H. Hill, and Ambrose P. Hill at it in a coordinated strike.

JUNE 25   The Army of the Potomac edges to within six miles of the Confederate capital at Richmond, Virginia, the closest Union forces will approach in three years. General George B. McClellan, desiring to place heavy cannons on the city's outskirts, orders Oak Grove wrested from the enemy. The position is carried at a cost of 626 men, while the Confederates suffer 441 casualties; this is also McClellan's last offensive move against the Southern capital.

JUNE 26   Near Mechanicsville, Virginia, the Confederate divisions of Generals James Longstreet, Daniel H. Hill, and Ambrose P. Hill concentrate to overpower the 30,000 Federal troops of General Fitz John Porter's V Corps. Porter, strongly entrenched behind Beaver Dam Creek, effectively repels all Southern attacks with a loss of 1,484 Confederates to 361 Federals. However, Lee's unexpected pugnaciousness confounds General George B. McClellan, and he directs Porter to relocate to Gaines' Mill, five miles distant. This is the beginning of what becomes known as the "Great Skedaddle."

JUNE 27   At Gaines' Mill, Virginia, General Fitz John Porter's V Corps assumes strong defensive positions along a swampy plateau. Confederates under General Robert E. Lee attack repeatedly for several hours before Porter has to withdraw in good order toward Chickahominy Creek. Gaines's Mill is the most costly of the so-called Seven Days' Battles, with Confederate losses of 7,993 to a Union tally of 6,837. However, General George B. McClellan is convinced he is outnumbered and continues withdrawing to the James River.

At Tupelo, Mississippi, General Braxton Bragg directs General John P. McCown's division to transit to Chattanooga, Tennessee, by rail and reinforce the army of General Edmund Kirby-Smith. The movement takes only six days and convinces Bragg that larger transfers could be effected before Union forces can respond effectively.

JUNE 28   In Virginia, hard-fighting Major General Philip Kearny institutes the so-called "division patch" for his 3rd Division, III Corps, Army of the Potomac. This is a piece of red cloth pinned to the top of all caps and is the beginning of unit identification patches.

JUNE 29   A division of Confederates under General John B. Magruder attacks the Union rearguard of General Edwin V. Sumner's II Corps at Savage Station, Virginia. Heavy casualties result. Union troops retreat after suffering 900 casualties and a further 2,500 captured when a field hospital surrenders; Magruder sustains only 400 killed and wounded but fails to pursue. The Union withdrawal continues apace.

JUNE 30   General Robert E. Lee, intent upon destroying at least a portion of General George B. McClellan's Army of the Potomac, hopes to ensnare them in a pincer movement at White Oak Swamp. The initial attack goes off well and General George A. McCall is captured, but before the Southerners can seize the vital crossroads, they are evicted in vicious hand-to-hand fighting. Lee's losses are 3,673 while McClellan sustains 3,797 casualties, including Generals George A. McCall and John F. Reynolds taken prisoner. Lee resolves to try again.

JULY 1   In Virginia, General Robert E. Lee maneuvers to deliver one last and possibly crushing blow against the Army of the Potomac at Malvern Hill. This is a 150-foot-high rise flanked by swamps, ably manned by General Fitz John Porter's V Corps, and crowned by artillery. Lee nevertheless commits his army to several costly frontal assaults and only quits after sustaining 5,650 casualties to a Union tally of 3,007. This is one of the most mismanaged attacks of his career.

The Seven Days' Campaign ends with Union forces pushed far from the Southern capital of Richmond, Virginia, thereby preserving the Confederacy for another three and a half years. Victory costs the Southerners 20,141 casualties while the Army of the Potomac loses 15,849. The campaign also defines General Robert E. Lee as a capable and offensive-minded battle captain, much given to taking calculated risks. Two costly years will pass before the North can find an effective foil.

At Booneville, Mississippi, Colonel Philip H. Sheridan's cavalry, armed with the latest Colt revolving rifles, rebuffs 4,700 Confederates under General James R. Chalmers. Sheridan's aggressive handling of troops comes to the attention of General Henry W. Halleck, who subsequently arranges his promotion to brigadier general.

JULY 2   In Washington, D.C., Congress passes the Morrill Act, which sets aside federal land for engineering and agricultural colleges where military science constitutes part of the student curricula. This is the origin of today's Reserve Officer Candidate Training (ROTC).

JULY 10 In the Shenandoah Valley, Virginia, General John Pope of the newly designated Army of Virginia reminds inhabitants of their obligation to assist Union efforts. He also warns that swift justice will be meted out for all treasonable deeds.

JULY 11–17 In Mississippi, General Henry W. Halleck is summoned from the Department of the Mississippi by President Abraham Lincoln to Washington, D.C, to serve as the new General in Chief of the Army. He proves himself an excellent military administrator, and his departure allows General Ulysses S. Grant to resume command of military operations throughout the District of Western Tennessee.

JULY 12 The Congressional Medal of Honor, established in 1861 to honor naval personnel, is expanded to include soldiers. During the present struggle no less than 1,198 are presented.

JULY 15 In the New Mexico Territory, Apaches under Mangas Coloradas and Cochise ambush Colonel James H. Carleton's "California Column" at Apache Pass. However, the advance guard of Captain Thomas Roberts drives them off with well-aimed howitzer fire, and Carleton continues on.

JULY 17 In Washington, D.C., Congress approves the Second Confiscation Act which allows the recruitment of African American soldiers directly into the Army for the first time. Political pressure had been building among abolitionist groups to introduce and formalize this process.

JULY 22 At Murfreesboro, Tennessee, Colonel Nathan B. Forrest's Confederate cavalry seizes a Union garrison of 1,200 men. He accomplishes this by overrunning the 9th Michigan and 7th Pennsylvania Cavalries, then bluffing the still-intact 3rd Minnesota Cavalry into surrendering.

Confederate raiders under Colonel John H. Morgan canter back into Livingston, Tennessee, after a spectacular jaunt through Kentucky. The Federals are subsequently apprised that Confederate operatives working for Morgan had tapped into their telegraph lines and intercepted army dispatches over the past 12 days.

JULY 23 At Tupelo, Mississippi, General Braxton Bragg orchestrates the transfer of 31,000 Confederate troops to Chattanooga, Tennessee. This is the largest Southern rail movement of the war and covers 776 miles without major mishap. Bragg, unfortunately, leaves behind two feuding commanders, Sterling Price at Tupelo and Earl Van Dorn at Vicksburg; each commands 16,000 men, and cooperation between them is problematic.

AUGUST 5 At Baton Rouge, Louisiana, Confederate general and former vice president John C. Breckinridge attacks Union positions with 2,600 men, supported by the ironclad *Arkansas*. General Thomas Williams deploys 2,500 men to receive him, and heavy fighting erupts in very dense fog. Six hours later Breckinridge concedes defeat, once his naval support is lost, and he retreats back to Vicksburg, Mississippi.

AUGUST 6 In Minnesota, starving Mdewkanton Santees (Sioux) arrive at the Lower Agency, Minnesota, and Chief Little Crow (Taoyateduta) pleads with agent Andrew F. Myrick for promised foodstuffs. Myrick rebuffs the Indians, telling them to eat grass, and the chief angrily departs.

AUGUST 9 At Cedar Mountain, Virginia, General Thomas J. Jackson's Confederates converge upon the Union II Corps, 9,000 men under General Nathaniel P. Banks. Jackson attacks without proper reconnaissance and Banks commits his entire reserves to battle, which nearly roll up the Confederate line. Fortunately, General A. P. Hill's division comes trudging up the road and stabilizes Jackson's position. Banks then concedes the field and withdraws in good order. Southern losses are 1,334 men to a Union tally of 2,353, a toll leading participants to dub the engagement "Slaughter Mountain."

AUGUST 16 At Knoxville, Tennessee, General Edmund Kirby-Smith takes 10,000 men and plunges through the Cumberland Gap into Kentucky. This action initiates a concerted Southern attempt to reclaim that state for the Confederacy.

AUGUST 17 Half-starved Sioux tribesmen kill five settlers at Acton Township, Minnesota Territory, whereupon Chief Little Crow, realizing that war with the whites is unavoidable, orders his braves on the warpath.

AUGUST 18 In the Minnesota Territory, rampaging Sioux warriors attack the Upper and Lower Indian Agencies, killing 20 people including agent Andrew J. Myrick, whose mouth is stuffed with grass. Captain John Marsh's detachment of the 5th Minnesota is also ambushed at Redwood Ferry with a loss of 24 soldiers.

AUGUST 20 Fort Ridgely, Minnesota Territory, is attacked by Mdewkanton Santee (Sioux) warriors under Chief Little Crow. The garrison of Lieutenant Timothy Sheehan loses six killed and 20 wounded, while Santee casualties are

Federal battery fords a tributary of the Rappahannock River at the Battle of Cedar Mountain on August 9, 1862. (Library of Congress)

considerably heavier. The Indians draw back but continue their siege.

AUGUST 22 At Fort Ridgely, Minnesota Territory, Chief Little Crow is joined by 400 warriors of the Sisseton and Wahpeton bands, then makes another ill-fated attack upon the 180-man garrison. The Indian are again repulsed with 100 casualties, while the soldiers sustain 3 killed and 13 wounded. Little Crow orders the siege abandoned.

AUGUST 23 In Virginia, General J. E. B. Stuart attacks Catlett's Station, the headquarters of General John Pope. He seizes 300 captives, Pope's personal baggage and uniform, and valuable military correspondence. From the latter General Robert E. Lee learns that Pope's 51,000-man Army of Virginia is to unite with the 100,000-strong Army of the Potomac under General George B. McClellan; Lee plans to crush Pope in detail before the two forces can merge.

AUGUST 25 In Virginia, General Thomas J. Jackson's corps departs the Army of Northern Virginia and advances to the Rappahannock River. In one of the most impressive marches of the entire war, Jackson covers 56 miles in only two days and arrives behind General John Pope's Army of Virginia. The Confederates are also interposed between Pope and the Union capital at Washington, D.C.

In Washington, D.C., Secretary of War Edwin M. Stanton authorizes recruitment of 5,000 African American soldiers, and General Rufus Saxton, military governor of the South Carolina Sea Islands, is instructed to raise five regiments of black troops. This pilot program is done much less out of altruism than to placate Radical Republicans and alleviate manpower shortages.

AUGUST 26 At Manassas Junction, Virginia, General Isaac Trimble's Confederates capture General John Pope's main supply base. The nominally malnourished Confederates, looking famously more like scarecrows than soldiers, gleefully gorge themselves. The attack also evokes a sharp response from the embarrassed Pope.

AUGUST 27 At Fort Sibley, Minnesota Territory, Colonel Henry H. Sibley's column arrives from distant Fort Snelling and relieves the garrison. Meanwhile, another detachment of troopers is ambushed at Birch Coulee, losing 16 killed and 44 wounded.

In Virginia, General John Pope hurriedly marches from behind the Rappahannock River to search General Thomas J. Jackson's Confederate Corps. Jackson, meanwhile, deploys along the Warrenton Turnpike and awaits the arrival of General James Longstreet. Having divided his army in two, the most perilous part of General Robert E. Lee's strategy is at hand.

AUGUST 28 In Virginia, General Thomas J. Jackson's corps attacks 2,800 Union troops under General Rufus King at Groveton, Virginia. They charge headlong into the "Black Hat" brigade of General John Gibbon at Brawner's Farm and a fierce stand-up fight of two hours ensues before both sides withdraw. Jackson loses 1,200 men out of 4,500 committed while Union forces sustain 1,100 casualties out of 2,800 present. Gibbon's force subsequently becomes known as the "Iron Brigade."

AUGUST 29 Near Groveton, Virginia, the Second Battle of Manassas begins as General John Pope masses 65,000 men to attack the isolated corps of General Thomas J. Jackson. As the battle rages, General Fitz John Porter detects the approach of General James Longstreet's 30,000 Confederates on Pope's left flank and immediately notifies his superior—Pope nonetheless orders him to attack Jackson's men immediately. Porter, however, disobeys and prepares to receive Longstreet; his insubordination probably saves the Army of Virginia from annihilation.

AUGUST 30   In Virginia, the Second Battle of Manassas continues as Union troops resume attacking the isolated Confederate corps of General Thomas J. Jackson. General Fitz John Porter's V Corps surges forward and assails Jackson's right when a massed charge, spearheaded by General John B. Hood's Texan Brigade, suddenly rolls up the Union left. At this precise moment Jackson orders his own men forward and Pope's army dissolves in chaos. Union losses are severe at 16,054 casualties; Lee sustains only 9,197. More importantly, the Confederates are now poised to take the war north into Maryland.

Outside Richmond, Kentucky, General Mahlon D. Manson deploys his 6,500 Federal soldiers into defensive positions. However, General Patrick R. Cleburne's Confederates dislodge the defenders, who abandon the town and fall back toward Louisville. Southern losses are 98 killed, 492 wounded, and 10 missing, while Manson suffers 206 killed, 844 wounded, and 4,303 captured.

SEPTEMBER 1   Near Chantilly, Virginia, General Thomas J. Jackson's Confederates are suddenly accosted by Union forces from General Joseph Hooker's division. Confused fighting results until the appearance of General Philip Kearny's brigade, which closes a gap in Union lines. Kearny, one of the North's bravest soldiers, then stumbles into a Confederate picket line and is shot dead. Losses in this hard-fought affair are 500 Confederates and 700 Federals killed, wounded, or captured.

SEPTEMBER 2   In light of the new military emergency, President Abraham Lincoln ignores his Cabinet and restores General George B. McClellan as head of the Army of the Potomac. This decision is welcome news to the soldiers, who still respect and adore their "Little Mac."

SEPTEMBER 3–5   In Virginia, General John Pope remonstrates to General in Chief Henry W. Halleck that his debacle at Second Manassas is due to General Fitz John Porter's insubordination and General George B. McClellan's failure to provide timely support. Porter, a highly accomplished fighter, will face a court-martial for it.

SEPTEMBER 4   At White's Ford, Virginia, General Robert E. Lee's Army of Northern Virginia marches 40,000 men across the Potomac River and filters into Maryland. The invasion of the North commences, and panic ensues in Washington, D.C.

SEPTEMBER 7   Confederates forces under General Robert E. Lee occupy Frederick, Maryland, within striking distance of the national capital. General George B. McClellan, reappointed as commander of the Army of the Potomac, dutifully advances to engage the invaders.

SEPTEMBER 9   In Maryland, General Robert E. Lee grows concerned about the large Union garrison holding Harpers Ferry toward his rear. He consequently issues Special Order No. 191, detaching General Thomas J. Jackson's corps back to the Shenandoah Valley to capture that strategic post, while General James Longstreet's corps advances toward Hagerstown. Ever the gambler, Lee again daringly splits his forces in two, leaving

the Army of Northern Virginia danger-
ously dispersed.

SEPTEMBER 12 The Army of Northern
Virginia is officially disbanded and reorganized into the new XI, XII, and XIII
Corps of the Army of the Potomac. General John Pope, meanwhile, is reassigned
back to the western frontier.

SEPTEMBER 13 In Maryland, Private Barton W. Mitchell, 27th Indiana, finds a
copy of General Robert E. Lee's Special
Order No. 191 wrapped around a cigar.
General George B. McClellan suddenly
realizes that the Southerners are hope-
lessly scattered and subject to defeat in
detail. Still, the lethargic leader wastes 16
hours before putting the Army of the
Potomac in motion.

Harpers Ferry, western Virginia, is
enveloped by a three-pronged Confeder-
ate maneuver once General Lafayette
McLaw's division occupies neighboring
Maryland Heights, and General John G.
Walker positions his force on nearby
Loudoun Heights. Union colonel Dixon
S. Miles is speedily trapped by 23,000
Confederates enjoying superiority in
numbers and position.

SEPTEMBER 14 In Maryland, General
George B. McClellan sorties the Army of
the Potomac to catch General Robert E.
Lee's dispersed Confederates. The corps
of Generals Jesse L. Reno and Joseph
Hooker are ordered forward through Fox
and Turner's Gaps near South Mountain,
but encounter General James Longstreet's
command. Several hours pass before the
Federals clear South Mountain after
heavy fighting and proceed. Losses in this
severe engagement total 2,325 Union
(including General Reno, slain) to 2,685
Confederate.

General George B. McClellan also dispatches the VI Corps of General William
B. Franklin to proceed with all haste

through Crampton's Gap, Maryland, to
relieve Harpers Ferry. Franklin engages a
smaller Confederate force and requires all
day to flush them from the heavily
wooded slopes. Franklin is finally positioned to pitch into General Lafayette
McLaws division at Harpers Ferry, but he
overestimates the size of Southern forces
opposing him and encamps for the night.

In Mississippi, General Sterling Price
occupies Iuka with 15,000 soldiers prior
to uniting with General Braxton Bragg in
Kentucky. General Ulysses S. Grant, however, sees an opportunity to trap and
destroy the exposed Confederates and
orders Generals William S. Rosecrans and
Edward O. C. Ord toward Iuka to catch
the defenders in a strategic pincer.

SEPTEMBER 15 Near Sharpsburg,
Maryland, General Robert E. Lee
instructs his Army of Northern Virginia
to consolidate, now that Union forces
are on the move. He also orders General
Thomas J. Jackson's corps to depart the
Shenandoah Valley and rejoin him
immediately.

At Harpers Ferry, western Virginia, the
Union garrison surrenders to General
Thomas J. Jackson. For a loss of 39 dead
and 247 injured, the Southerners kill 44,
wound 173, and seize 12,520 prisoners,
along with innumerable small arms, 73
cannons, tons of supplies and equipment,
and livestock. This is the largest Federal
capitulation of the Civil War, but Jackson
has no time to celebrate. Rounding up
the bulk of his men, he force marches
them back to General Robert E. Lee
with all speed.

SEPTEMBER 16 In Maryland, General
Robert E. Lee is buoyed by the recent
seizure of Harpers Ferry and determines
not to leave Maryland without a fight. He
therefore deploys the Army of Northern
Virginia along a series of low hills at
Sharpsburg and is reinforced by the two

divisions of General Thomas J. Jackson's corps. General Ambrose P. Hill's light division remains at Harpers Ferry, 17 miles distant, processing thousands of prisoners. Meanwhile, General George B. McClellan masses 75,000 troops against Lee's 38,000.

SEPTEMBER 17 In Maryland, the Battle of Antietam commences when 12,000 soldiers of General Joseph Hooker's I Corps advance against the Confederate left under General Thomas J. Jackson. A bloody see-saw stalemate ensues for several hours until Union forces switch and hit the Confederate center guarded by General Daniel H. Hill's division. Heavily pressed, Hill retires though a deadly enfilade fire, dropping men in clumps, before the battle shifts again to the Confederate right. Here General Ambrose Burnside repeatedly attempts to cross the stone bridge over Antietam Creek. He finally succeeds at 3:00 P.M., but Burnside's own left is suddenly assailed by General Ambrose P. Hill's "Light Division" and the Federals withdraw back to their starting positions. General George B. McClellan, with 25,000 fresh troops in reserve, declines to attack further and Lee retires back into Virginia. Antietam is the single bloodiest day in American military history with Union losses of 12,410 men and a Confederate tally of 11,172. However, the first Confederate invasion of the North ends in costly defeat. It also provides President Abraham Lincoln the military pretext he sought to announce his Emancipation Proclamation.

SEPTEMBER 18 General Robert E. Lee disengages and begins ferrying the Army of Northern Virginia across the Potomac River at Blackford's Ferry, Maryland, while superior forces under General George B. McClellan fail to intervene or even pursue. The Union commander is again roundly criticized for lethargy.

SEPTEMBER 19 Near Iuka, Mississippi, Union columns under Generals William S. Rosecrans and Edward O. C. Ord attempt to crush 15,000 Confederates under General Sterling Price. However, Price's cavalry alerts him of their approach and he attacks Rosecrans before the two forces can unite. After stiff combat, Price abandons his offensive at nightfall and marches off to join General Earl Van Dorn's army outside Corinth. The Southerners sustain 86 killed, 408 wounded, and 200 captured to a Union tally of 141 men dead, 613 injured, and 36 missing.

SEPTEMBER 23 In the Minnesota Valley, Little Crow's band of 800 Mdewkanton Santees (Sioux) are pursued by 1,600 volunteers and troops under Colonel Henry H. Sibley. Sibley encamps for the evening at Lone Tree Lake (reported as Wood Lake), and Little Crow suddenly springs on his pursuers, attacking at dawn. The Santees are subsequently repulsed by artillery, and Chief Mankato is killed, along with 30 warriors. Sibley presses ahead and the Santees surrender en mass. The soldiers rescue 269 white hostages while 2,000 Native Americans are seized, many of whom face execution for atrocities against settlers.

SEPTEMBER 27 At New Orleans, Louisiana, the *Chasseurs d'Afrique*, the first black regiment recruited from former slaves, is mustered into Union service by General Benjamin F. Butler. There is no shortage of enthusiasm among blacks to serve in the military, and two infantry regiments and one of artillery are also recruited.

SEPTEMBER 28 At Ripley, Tennessee, the armies of Generals Sterling Price and Earl Van Dorn unite prior to attacking the vital railroad junction at Corinth, Mississippi. Van Dorn, who enjoys seniority, asserts his authority over the resentful Price, so cooperation proves sullen.

OCTOBER 1 General Don Carlos Buell conducts his 50,000-man Army of the Ohio from Louisville, Kentucky, in four columns; three of these will concentrate at Perryville while a fourth demonstrates toward Confederate-held Frankfort. En route their movements are aggravated by incessant heat and water shortages.

General John C. Pemberton arrives at Vicksburg, Mississippi, to supersede General Earl Van Dorn. Unknown at the time, his tenure commanding the Department of Mississippi and East Louisiana proves disastrous for Confederate fortunes.

OCTOBER 2 President Abraham Lincoln, in a less-than-subtle hint, establishes his tent right next to General George B. McClellan's headquarters. He is determined to spur that officer into greater efforts.

OCTOBER 3 At Corinth, Mississippi, Confederates under Generals Earl Van Dorn and Sterling Price attack Union forces commanded by General William S. Rosecrans. The Federals are carefully deployed along mutually supporting lines of defense, with all intervals covered by carefully sited cannons. The Southerners, taking heavy losses, grind the defenders back toward their second line of entrenchments. That evening Van Dorn redeploys his weary men in a semi-circle around the town and prepares to attack its chain of batteries.

OCTOBER 4 At Corinth, Mississippi, General Earl Van Dorn's Confederates resume attacking General William S. Rosecrans's defensive works. Part of General Martin E. Green's division storms and seizes the Robinson lunette, while his remaining brigades force their

way into the town. However, Union resistance cannot be overcome and Van Dorn finally withdraws back to Ripley. Federal casualties are 2,520 while Van Dorn sustains 4,233, a butcher's bill that the Confederacy can ill-afford in this theater.

OCTOBER 6 A frustrated President Abraham Lincoln again orders General Henry W. Halleck to prod dithering General George B. McClellan into action. The latter composes a tersely worded message to advance, but McClellan, true to form, ignores it.

OCTOBER 7 Near Perryville, Kentucky, General Charles C. Gilbert's III Corps, Army of the Ohio, trudges down the Springfield Road and encamps. His arrival prompts General Braxton Bragg to begin massing his Army of Mississippi, 16,000 strong, for an attack. However, Bragg remains unaware that two additional corps under General Don Carlos Buell also deploy that evening, raising Federal manpower to 25,000.

OCTOBER 8 Near Perryville, Kentucky, General Don Carlos Buell arranges 25,000 men to do battle with General Braxton Bragg's Army of Mississippi. General Leonidas K. Polk's Confederates, infiltrating through an unguarded ravine, suddenly turn the Union left and drive it back. Fighting rages on until darkness and Bragg, having won a tactical victory, finally perceives he is outnumbered and withdraws back to Harrodsburg. Perryville proves a costly encounter for both sides: Buell records 4,211 casualties, while Bragg sustains 3,405.

OCTOBER 13 In Kentucky, Confederates under Generals Braxton Bragg and Edmund Kirby-Smith filter back through the Cumberland Gap and back into Tennessee. Their invasion of Kentucky, the high tide of Confederate fortunes in the center region, has failed, although more to Union numbers than Union generalship.

OCTOBER 16 General Ulysses S. Grant assumes command of the Department of the Tennessee. He immediately begins marshaling men and resources for a campaign against Vicksburg, Mississippi.

OCTOBER 17 Southeast of Richmond, Kentucky, Colonel John H. Morgan and 1,800 Confederates gallop off on their second major raid of the war. This time he heads for the lightly defended town of Lexington, intending to take it by storm.

OCTOBER 24 In Ohio, General Don Carlos Buell is sacked for failing to aggressively pursue General Braxton Bragg's retreating Confederates. He is replaced by General William S. Rosecrans, a proven leader of some ability.

OCTOBER 26 General George B. McClellan finally crosses his Army of the Potomac back into Virginia, but so cautiously that General Robert E. Lee easily interposes his Army of Northern Virginia between the invaders and the Confederate capital at Richmond.

NOVEMBER 5 In Washington, D.C., President Abraham Lincoln, exasperated by General George B. McClellan's dilatory movements, removes him as head of the Army of the Potomac. His replacement is General Ambrose E. Burnside, who initially declines the appointment.

NOVEMBER 8 At New Orleans, Louisiana, General Benjamin F. Butler concludes his stormy and controversial tenure as head of the Department of the Gulf, and he is replaced by General Nathaniel P. Banks. Before leaving, Butler peremptorily closes all breweries and distilleries within his jurisdiction to preclude any celebrations by the populace.

NOVEMBER 9 In Virginia, General Ambrose E. Burnside assumes command of the Army of the Potomac, a position he never sought and tried twice to refuse. His first act is to order Union cavalry under Colonel Ulric Dahlgren to attack Confederate positions at Fredericksburg, Virginia, where he takes 54 prisoners. Convinced that the town's defenses are weak, Burnside begins planning an offensive in that area.

NOVEMBER 15 In Virginia, General Ambrose E. Burnside advances upon Falmouth by first feinting in the direction of Warrenton. The Army of thePotomac covers 40 miles in two days and arrives opposite Fredericksburg along the Rappahannock River. Burnside's movements temporarily confound the Confederate high command as to his intentions.

NOVEMBER 18 General Ambrose E. Burnside remains at Falmouth, Virginia, behind the Rappahannock River and directly opposite the heights of Fredericksburg. He takes no offensive actions over the next three weeks while waiting for pontoon bridges to arrive, which allows the Confederates ample time to receive him.

NOVEMBER 21 General Ambrose E. Burnside demands that the mayor of Fredericksburg, Virginia, surrender. When he refuses, Burnside threatens to bombard the city and advises him to evacuate women and children.

NOVEMBER 22 Outside Fredericksburg, Virginia, General Ambrose E. Burnside reverses himself and assures the mayor that he will not fire into the town. In return, he expects no hostile actions from its inhabitants.

NOVEMBER 29   In Texas, General John B. Magruder arrives to take charge of the District of Texas, New Mexico, and Arizona. He considers recapturing the city of Galveston an immediate priority and begins gathering the men and ships necessary for a surprise attack.

NOVEMBER 30   At Falmouth, Virginia, General Ambrose E. Burnside receives pontoons and other bridging equipment he had requested three weeks earlier. The Army of the Potomac is preparing to cross the Rappahannock River to Fredericksburg, but General Robert E. Lee rushes James Longstreet's corps of 35,000 men to fortify the nearby heights.

DECEMBER 3   At Van Buren, Arkansas, General Thomas C. Hindman marches the Confederate Army of the Trans-Mississippi to destroy the outnumbered Union division of General James G. Blunt at Cane Hill. Blunt is apprised of the danger and requests General Francis J. Herron at Springfield, Missouri, for reinforcements.

DECEMBER 5   Two Union divisions from the Army of the Frontier under General Francis J. Herron conduct an impressive forced march and cover the 100 miles from Springfield, Missouri, to Fayetteville, Arkansas, in only two days. General James G. Blunt's force is now suitably disposed to engage the approaching Confederates under General Thomas C. Hindman.

DECEMBER 7   The Battle of Prairie Grove, Arkansas, commences as General Thomas C. Hindman's Confederates attack General Francis J. Herron outside of Fayetteville. Hindman achieves a strategic surprise, but then inexplicably assumes defensive positions as the outnumbered Union force attacks. General James G. Blunt's Army of the Frontier

also hurriedly marches to Prairie Grove with fresh troops and pitches into the Confederates, fighting them to a draw. Hindman ultimately withdraws after suffering 1,317 casualties to a Union loss of 1,251. Herron's impressive march undoubtedly saved Arkansas for the Union.

DECEMBER 11   In Virginia, General Ambrose E. Burnside orders the Army of the Potomac to bridge its way across the Rappahannock River to Fredericksburg. As the fog lifts, his engineers receive heavy sniper fire from General William Barksdale's Mississippi brigade. Seven boatloads of volunteers then row themselves across the river under fire and flush the Southerners from the town, which is then occupied.

At Columbia, Tennessee, General Nathan B. Forrest orders 2,500 Confederate troopers out to wreck portions of the Mississippi Central and Mobile and Ohio Railroads.

DECEMBER 12   In Virginia, the Army of the Potomac engages in a looting binge at Fredericksburg, while General Robert E. Lee summons the corps of General Thomas J. Jackson to occupy the right flank of Confederate defenses. That evening, General Ambrose E. Burnside finishing crossing the Rappahannock River and deploys 112,000 men below Southern positions.

DECEMBER 13   In Virginia, the Battle of Fredericksburg, Virginia, commences as a dense fog lifts and reveals to General Robert E. Lee the serried ranks of blue-coated infantry advancing up the slopes toward him. The thrust against Lee's right makes good progress until being contained by General Thomas J. Jackson's corps. Burnside's main attack then commences up a steep hill called Marye's Heights, ably defended by General James

Longstreet's corps. A force of 60,000 men bravely charges Confederate entrenchments and are mowed down with great slaughter. By nightfall Burnside has sustained 12,653 casualties while the well-protected Confederates endure 5,377. This is a one-sided slaughter of which Lee aptly remarks, "It is well that war is so terrible. We should grow too fond of it."

DECEMBER 14 In Virginia, the battered Army of the Potomac under General Ambrose E. Burnside begins withdrawing back across the Rappahannock River. General Thomas J. Jackson suggests to Robert E. Lee that the Southerners should attack and destroy Burnside completely, but Lee allows them to withdraw unmolested.

DECEMBER 15 At Fredericksburg, Virginia, General Ambrose E. Burnside sends a flag to General Robert E. Lee requesting a temporary truce to recover the Union dead—and those surviving two days of exposure to rain and cold. Lee magnanimously grants his request.

DECEMBER 16 At Falmouth, Virginia, General Ambrose E. Burnside issues a directive accepting full responsibility for the disaster at Fredericksburg. On balance, the Army of the Potomac performed well under heavy fire.

DECEMBER 18 Lexington, Tennessee, is overrun by General Nathan B. Forrest and 2,500 Confederate cavalry. Forrest's men clatter across an unburned bridge on the Lower Road and flank a portion of the defenders. The Union garrison of Colonel Robert G. Ingersoll repels three headlong charges by the Southerners, but is eventually forced to surrender.

DECEMBER 20 Utilizing superb marching discipline, the Confederate cavalry under General Earl Van Dorn captures a primary Union stockpile at Holly Springs, Mississippi, netting $1.5 million worth of supplies and 1,500 prisoners. Van Dorn orders the supplies burned, tracks torn up, and telegraph wires cut. Holly Springs is one of the most devastating cavalry raids of the war and completely negates General Ulysses S. Grant's impending offensive against Vicksburg, Mississippi.

DECEMBER 21 In Mississippi, General Ulysses S. Grant cannot overcome the loss of supplies incurred at Holly Springs, so he evacuates Oxford and marches back to Memphis, Tennessee. His first attempt to attack the Confederate bastion of Vicksburg ends ignominiously.

DECEMBER 26 General William S. Rosecrans directs the 43,000 men of his Army of the Cumberland from Nashville, Tennessee, and toward General Braxton Bragg's Confederates at Murfreesboro. His advance is dogged by cold, wet weather and stout resistance by Southern cavalry under General Joseph Wheeler.

Near the mouth of the Yazoo River, Mississippi, General William T. Sherman's XIII Corps disembarks 32,000 men at Johnson's Plantation. Landing here places Union forces only six miles from the northern outskirts of Vicksburg. He is unaware that the 6,000 defenders present are being reinforced to a total strength of 14,000.

DECEMBER 28 Near Selectman's Fort, Virginia, General J. E. B. Stuart successfully tangles with Federal cavalry on Occoquan Creek, taking 100 captives. He then gallops off for Burke's Station and telegraphs a humorous message to Quartermaster General Montgomery C. Meigs, complaining about the poor quality of Union mules.

Outside Chickasaw Bluffs, Mississippi, General Frederick Steele's 4th Division makes a preliminary probe of Confederate defenses, but is halted by artillery fire and defensive works in his path. General William T. Sherman determines to attack in force, but is ignorant of the Union disaster at Holly Springs and General Ulysses S. Grant's subsequent withdrawal back to Tennessee.

DECEMBER 29 Along Chickasaw Bluffs, six miles north of Vicksburg, Mississippi, the XIII Corps under General William T. Sherman attacks prepared Confederate defenses. They withstand a maelstrom of Southern rifle and artillery fire pouring down upon them from the heights and are bloodily repelled. Union losses total 1,776 to a Confederate tally of 207, so the first Federal attempt to capture Vicksburg ends in total defeat.

DECEMBER 30 General William S. Rosecrans and his Army of the Cumberland trudge into Murfreesboro, Tennessee, having taken three days to cover 30 miles in bad weather. He establishes a line running north to south along Stone's River, behind which sit 37,000 Confederates of General Braxton Bragg's Army of Tennessee. Ironically, both leaders intend to attack the next day by hitting the other's right flank.

DECEMBER 31 Outside Murfreesboro, Tennessee, General Braxton Bragg launches an all-out assault against the Army of the Cumberland along Stone's River. The defenders are routed initially and flee three miles before General William S. Rosecrans energetically brings up reinforcements and consolidates his defenses. Bragg, far behind at headquarters, allows the attack to peter out, despite the fact that General John C. Breckinridge's fresh division is uncommitted. However, Bragg is convinced that he has won a victory and telegraphs word to authorities in Richmond, Virginia.

At Parker's Cross Roads, Tennessee, General Nathan B. Forrest's 1,200 Confederate cavalry engage the 2nd Union Brigade under Colonel Cyrus L. Dunham. The Southerners are suddenly overturned by the unexpected appearance of John W. Fuller's 3rd Brigade, which takes them from behind. Forrest instantly orders his command to charge and cut their way through Union lines. Parker's Cross Roads proves a rare setback for the "Wizard of the Saddle" and both sides suffer 300 casualties apiece.

1863

JANUARY 1 Outside Murfreesboro, Tennessee, combat is suspended along Stone's River as both sides redress ranks and attend their wounded. General Braxton Bragg is nonetheless surprised to find the Army of the Cumberland standing its ground defiantly before him. Fighting will resume on the morrow.

At Galveston, Texas, a surprise attack by General John B. Magruder captures a Union garrison consisting of 250 men of the 42nd Massachusetts. The port remains in Confederate hands for the rest of the war.

JANUARY 2 Along Stones River, Tennessee, General Braxton Bragg surveys the new line held by General William S. Rosencrans and renews the struggle. He commits General John C. Breckinridge's

Kentucky division to strike the Union left flank, which runs directly into massed Union artillery posted across the river. Breckinridge is bloodily repelled with 1,700 casualties, after which many Confederate leaders implore Bragg to retreat. Rosecrans loses 13,249 casualties among 41,000 men present, while the Confederates suffer 10,266 out of 34,739 engaged. The Southerners cannot sustain such attrition in this theater.

JANUARY 10 In Washington, D.C., General Fitz John Porter is court-martialed and cashiered for disobeying orders at the Battle of Second Manassas. This verdict deprives the Union army of a highly capable leader, and the verdict remains in contention until being overturned in 1879.

JANUARY 11 General John A. McClernand and Admiral David D. Porter attack Confederate Fort Hindman (Arkansas Post) under General Thomas J. Churchill. Churchill, outnumbered and outgunned, capitulates that evening. McClernand captures 4,791 Confederates, who also lose 2 dead, 81 wounded, 17 cannons, thousands of weapons, and tons of ammunition.

JANUARY 20 In Virginia, General Ambrose E. Burnside orders the Army of the Potomac to begin its infamous "mud march" up the Rappahannock River to turn General Robert E. Lee's left flank. No sooner does his maneuvering commence than heavy rain falls, while troops, supplies, and the all-important pontoon bridges bog down in the ankle-deep mud.

JANUARY 22 General Ambrose E. Burnside's offensive across the Rappahannock River stumbles and finally ends due to inclement weather and impassible mud. He then concludes his "master stroke" by ordering the long-suffering troops back

into camp at Falmouth, Virginia. There, agitated by the performance of subordinates, Burnside issues General Order No. 8 and strips Generals Joseph Hooker, Edwin V. Sumner, and William B. Franklin of their commands.

JANUARY 25 In Washington, D.C., President Abraham Lincoln relieves General Ambrose E. Burnside as commander of the Army of the Potomac; he is replaced by flamboyant General "Fighting Joe" Hooker, one of Burnside's loudest critics.

JANUARY 27 In Idaho Territory, Colonel Patrick E. Connor leads the 1st California Cavalry on an expedition against the encampment of Chief Bear Hunter on the Bear River, Idaho Territory. Bear Hunter and 224 Indians are slain in battle, while an additional 124 women and children are taken prisoner. Connor loses 21 dead and 46 wounded, but his action induces many local chiefs to arrange peace talks.

JANUARY 30 General Ulysses S. Grant, arriving at Milliken's Bend, Louisiana, begins formulating a new strategic campaign against Vicksburg, Mississippi, one freeing him from concern about supply depots.

MARCH 2 In Washington, D.C., Congress authorizes four new major generals and nine new brigadiers for the U.S. Army. An additional 40 major generals and 200 brigadiers are also assigned to the volunteers while 33 senior military officials are dismissed for a variety of reasons.

MARCH 3 In Washington, D.C., President Abraham Lincoln signs the Enrollment or Federal Draft Act, rendering all able-bodied males from 20 to 45 eligible for military service. Prospective candidates are allowed to find substitutes to take their place, or simply pay a $300 fine to escape the draft.

MARCH 5 At Thompson's Station, Tennessee, General Earl Van Dorn advances with 6,000 Confederates against a Union position consisting of 2,857 soldiers and cavalry, supported by six cannons. However, a determined charge by Colonel Nathan B. Forrest breaks all resistance, and the garrison surrenders.

MARCH 8 At Fairfax County Court House, Virginia, Captain John S. Mosby and his Confederate rangers capture General Edwin H. Stoughton in his headquarters, along with 32 prisoners and 58 horses. The general was sleeping in his bed and rudely awakened by a slap to his backside—delivered by Mosby himself.

MARCH 10 In Washington, D.C., President Abraham Lincoln signs a general amnesty for soldiers presently absent without leave (AWOL). They are pardoned by rejoining their units by April 1, 1863.

MARCH 21 In Virginia, General Daniel Butterfield is tasked with creating a system of unit badges and other identifications to encourage unit esprit d'corps in the Army of the Potomac. Hereafter, each corps possesses its own unique design, with different divisions designated by differing color schemes.

MARCH 25 At Brentwood, Tennessee, General Nathan B. Forrest and his Confederate cavalry column attack 800 Union troops under Colonel Edward Bloodgood posted south of the town. The Federals surrender, but as the marauders withdraw they are set upon a third force of Union cavalry, losing captured wagons and supplies in the chase.

APRIL 1 The Draft Act of 1863 goes into effect as the first conscription law in United States history and it ultimately accounts for 6 percent of the Army's manpower.

APRIL 2 On the Mississippi River, General Ulysses S. Grant and Admiral David D. Porter finalize a plan of operations against Vicksburg, Mississippi. They decide that General William T. Sherman's force will mount large-scale diversions along Hayne's Bluff in the north, while Grant marches south along the west bank of the Mississippi River with the bulk of his army. Once positioned, they will be carried across by Porter's fleet and land below the city.

APRIL 5 At Fredericksburg, Virginia, President Abraham Lincoln confers with General Joseph Hooker over strategy. Both leaders concur that military operations should focus on destroying the Army of Northern Virginia, while the Confederate capital at Richmond is a secondary concern.

APRIL 12 In Louisiana, General Nathaniel P. Banks marches the XIX Corps up the Teche River toward Irish Bend to capture Fort Bisland. Banks moves two divisions overland while ordering General Curvier Groves's division to land north of the fort and cut the garrison's retreat.

APRIL 13–14 At Irish Bend, Louisiana, Confederates under General Richard Taylor deliver an early morning strike against the XIX Corps of General Nathaniel P. Banks. The Southerners get the better of it and the garrison of Fort Bisland manages to escape. The fort is subsequently occupied by Banks's Federals.

APRIL 15 At Milliken's Bend, Louisiana, General Ulysses S. Grant masses 45,000 troops only 10 miles north of the Confederate bastion of Vicksburg, Mississippi. He commences his Vicksburg campaign by ordering General James B. McPherson's corps to march south along the west bank to New Carthage while General William T. Sherman's forces mount demonstrations to the north along Chickasaw Bluff. The Confederate defenders are completely taken in by the deception.

APRIL 17 At La Grange, Tennessee, Colonel Benjamin H. Grierson takes 1,700 men on a daring diversionary raid through the heart of Mississippi and on to Baton Rouge, Louisiana. He undertakes it to divert Southern attention from the main Union drive on the Mississippi River; Union cavalry has never been utilized in such a strategic manner before.

APRIL 21 At Palo Alto, Mississippi, Colonel Benjamin H. Grierson skirmishes with Confederates and cleverly splits his column by sending Colonel Edward Hatch's 2nd Iowa off to threaten the Mobile and Ohio Railroad. The Confederates take the bait and chase after Hatch, leaving Grierson to complete his drive toward Mississippi unopposed.

APRIL 24 On this fateful day, the Army of the Tennessee under General Ulysses S. Grant reaches Hard Times Plantation, Louisiana, on the left bank of the Mississippi River. Grant immediately orders the troops embarked on transports, provided by Commodore David D. Porter, and ferried across to Bruinsville, Mississippi, on the Confederate shore.

APRIL 27 At Falmouth, Virginia, General Joseph Hooker places the 134,000-man Army of the Potomac into motion by moving the banks of the Rappahannock River. He intends to deploy them in the wooded region known as the Wilderness,

10 miles behind Confederate lines. No Union commander has enjoyed such numerical superiority over General Robert E. Lee before.

APRIL 29 In Virginia, General John Stoneman's Union cavalry division crosses the Rappahannock River and commences a major raid. However, this maneuver mistakenly strips the Army of the Potomac of its cavalry and the ability to effectively reconnoiter the densely wooded terrain.

APRIL 30 In Virginia, the Army of the Potomac covers 30 miles down the banks of the Rappahannock River, then crosses and arrives 10 miles behind General Robert E. Lee's position at Fredericksburg, Virginia. Considering the size and complexity of the operation, General Joseph Hooker pulls it off brilliantly and catches the Southerners off guard.

At Bruinsburg, Mississippi, General Ulysses S. Grant ferries the XIII and XVII Corps of his Army of the Tennessee across the Mississippi River. With this single stroke, Grant bypasses Confederate defenses at Vicksburg and gains a lodgement only 35 miles below the city. The Confederates prove slow to react.

MAY 1 General Thomas J. Jackson's corps arrives near Chancellorsville, Virginia, and tangles with advanced Union pickets nearby. This aggressive display apparently unnerves General Joseph Hooker, who inexplicably orders his Army of the Potomac back into the woody morass known as the Wilderness. Southern cavalry under General J. E. B. Stuart also perceives that the Union right flank is "up in the air" and subject to be turned. General Robert E. Lee consequently orders Jackson to take 30,000 men on a 14-mile end-run around Hooker's exposed right to possibly cripple his more numerous adversary.

General Ulysses S. Grant masses advances inland from Bruinsburg, Mississippi, with 23,000 men and attacks 8,000 Confederates under General John S. Bowen at Port Gibson. The Southerners are forced from the field and Grant's offensive begins gathering momentum. He also takes the bold and risky expedient of carrying all essential impedimenta on the backs of his soldiers, foraging off the land, and cutting his own supply line to gain greater mobility.

MAY 2 In Virginia, General Thomas J. Jackson's 30,000 Confederates steal their way around the Army of the Potomac's right flank at Chancellorsville, and at 6:00 P.M. his men slash into the unsuspecting Federals while they prepare dinner. The largely German-speaking troops crumble under the onslaught and flee two miles before rallying. Jackson, ignoring the confusion around him, rides forward to personally reconnoiter, and is accidently shot by men of the 18th North Carolina.

Colonel Benjamin H. Grierson's cavalry column fights its final skirmish with Confederate forces at Robert's Ford on the Comite River, Louisiana, before clattering into Baton Rouge. His spectacular raid of 800 miles concludes after suffering three dead, seven injured, and nine missing; Confederate losses are estimated at 100 dead, 500 captured, 2,000 weapons taken, and over 50 miles of railroad track and telegraph lines destroyed. More importantly, Grierson's raid distracted the Southerners long enough for Union forces to cross the Mississippi River below Vicksburg.

MAY 3 In Virginia, the struggle around Chancellorsville, Virginia, resumes as General J. E. B. Stuart mounts 50 cannons at Hazel Grove and bombards the Union forces of General Joseph Hooker. Hooker, though still outnumbering his opponents two to one, clings to his defensive posture,

then orders the Army of the Potomac back to the Rappahannock River. General Robert E. Lee, watching Hooker withdraw, daringly divides his force again and marches off to meet a new Union threat developing in his rear. Chancellorsville occasions heavy losses to both sides: Hooker suffers 17,287 casualties, while Lee sustains 12,463. Moreover, the South is deprived of General Thomas J. "Stonewall" Jackson, who dies of his wounds shortly afterward.

At Fredericksburg, Virginia, General John Sedgwick's VI Corps, numbering 19,000 men, attacks and storms the heights. It takes three charges, but Sedgwick orders his men to settle the issue with cold steel alone. The Confederates are finally ejected from their works and the VI Corps proceeds toward Chancellorsville. En route it collides with General Cadmus M. Wilcox's brigade at Salem Church, and heavy fighting ensues; Sedgwick suffers 1,523 casualties to a Southern tally of 674.

MAY 4 In Virginia, the Battle of Salem Church continues as General John Sedgwick attacks Confederate positions until General Richard H. Anderson's division reinforces the defenders. Outnumbered and nearly outflanked, Sedgwick skillfully withdraws toward the Rappahannock River; Union casualties number 4,700; Confederate losses are unknown but presumed lighter.

MAY 10 At Guiney's Station, Virginia, General Thomas J. Jackson, publicly renowned as "Stonewall" and admired by soldiers on both sides, dies of pneumonia. His passing is an irreparable loss to the Confederate war effort, and General Robert E. Lee loses his most accomplished subordinate.

MAY 12 At Raymond, Mississippi, General James B. McPherson's XVII

Corps encounters strong resistance from General John Gregg's Confederates, so he orders his entire force of 12,000 men forward, cracking the Southern right wing. Gregg subsequently falls back in good order toward Jackson. General Ulysses S. Grant consequently alters his strategy toward Vicksburg: with General John C. Pemberton potentially advancing on him from the west and General Joseph E. Johnston from the east, he intends to seek each out individually and defeat them in detail.

MAY 13 General Joseph E. Johnston arrives at Jackson, Mississippi, to find a small garrison of 6,000 men under General John Gregg. He realizes two full Union corps are marching toward the city, and orders his troops and supplies evacuated immediately. Johnston also instructs General John C. Pemberton at Vicksburg to march hurriedly with his 22,000 men and catch General Ulysses S. Grant between them in a pincer.

MAY 14 In Richmond, Virginia, General Robert E. Lee attends a high-level strategy conference to advocate a risky but potentially rewarding scheme for invading Pennsylvania. Once Federal forces are defeated on their own soil, President Abraham Lincoln will be discredited and England or France might possibly intervene on the Confederacy's behalf.

At Jackson, Mississippi, General James B. McPherson's XVII's Corps makes contact with Confederate outposts, while General William T. Sherman sends additional men forward to seize several poorly guarded cannons. General John Gregg's Confederates disengage and escape north from the city, handing General Ulysses S. Grant a strategic railroad junction east of Vicksburg.

MAY 16 At Champion's Hill, Mississippi, General John C. Pemberton deploys

22,000 troops along a commanding position halfway between Jackson and Vicksburg. General Ulysses S. Grant then arrives and orders the XIII Corps of General John A. McClernand on his right and the XVII Corps of General James B. McPherson on his left. Within hours Pemberton is in full flight across Baker's Creek, burning the bridge behind him. Union losses are 1,838 to a Southern tally of 3,840.

MAY 17 Surviving Confederates under General John C. Pemberton deploy along the west bank of the Big Black River, 12 miles east of strategic Vicksburg, Mississippi. Soon after, General John A. McClernand's XIII Corps encounters Confederate pickets and charges their position. Southern forces are soon streaming across the Big Black and they keep running until they reach the outskirts of Vicksburg, Mississippi. Confederate losses are 1,751 killed, wounded, and missing, along with 18 artillery pieces captured. Union casualties are only 279. Engineers quickly throw pontoon bridges across the river, and the advance toward Vicksburg continues on schedule.

MAY 18 General Ulysses S. Grant takes up storming positions outside the Confederate bastion of Vicksburg, Mississippi. Southern defenses appear outwardly hopeless, yet General John C. Pemberton declares his intention to fight to the last. General Joseph E. Johnston also frantically wires Pemberton and warns him not to become trapped within the city.

MAY 19 A preliminary Union attack upon Vicksburg, Mississippi, is repelled with heavy loss. General Ulysses S. Grant simply realigns his forces and prepares to try again.

MAY 21 General Nathaniel Banks commences the siege of Port Hudson,

54th Massachusetts Volunteer Infantry

The onset of civil war in 1861 was seen by abolitionist activists as an opportunity for African Americans to prove their worth to the nation by joining the military. It fell upon Governor John A. Andrew of Massachusetts to authorize creation of the 54th Massachusetts Volunteer Infantry in March 1861, although not until after the Emancipation Proclamation the following year did recruitment begin in earnest. Captain Robert Gould Shaw, son of a prominent abolitionist family, gained appointment as colonel, and he spent several months organizing and training his charge at Camp Meigs, outside of Boston. Among the blacks recruited were two sons of noted abolitionist Frederick Douglass. The 54th departed Boston in December 1862, despite a proclamation by Confederate president Jefferson Davis that armed African Americans and their white officers would be put to death if captured. Shaw led his regiment to Charleston, South Carolina, where, on July 16, 1863, it fought well against a Confederate assault on James Island, losing 42 men but gaining official praise. On July 18, 1863, the 54th Massachusetts gained national renown by spearheading the ill-fated second assault against Battery Wagner outside Charleston. The Federals were bloodily repulsed, and the 54th, which gained a foothold on the fort, lost Colonel Shaw and 272 other casualties. These were mostly buried in a mass grave, but the unit's heroic sacrifice spurred the recruitment of other additional African American units. Sergeant William H. Carney also became the first African American soldier to win a Congressional Medal of Honor by rescuing the regimental flag under fire. The 54th saw additional action in Florida and South Carolina before mustering out in August 1865. The unit was reactivated on November 21, 2008, as a National Guard ceremonial unit, the 54th Massachusetts Volunteer Regiment.

The storming of Fort Wagner in July 1863. The Battle of Fort Wagner was a poorly planned frontal assault launched by Union brigadier general Quincy A. Gillmore, whose largely African American 54th Massachusetts Volunteer Infantry Regiment was decimated by Confederate defenders. The only consolation the Northern public found in the disaster was the self-sacrificing bravery displayed by the regiment, which was cited as proof that black soldiers could fight as well as whites. (Library of Congress)

Louisiana; on paper, the 30,000 Union troops committed should have easily dispatched the 6,500 defenders, but Banks's ineptitude transformed what should have been an easy victory into a 48-day ordeal.

MAY   22   At Vicksburg, Mississippi, General Ulysses S. Grant again launches a frontal assault upon Confederate defenses. The Federals charge hard but cannot surmount a three-mile stretch of entrenched positions, despite a continuous and heavy bombardment. The 45,000 Union troops committed suffer 3,199 casualties in minutes, while Confederate losses are around 500. Grant resigns himself to commencing the formal siege operations while food shortages, intense summer heat, and civilian discomfiture take their toll on the defenders.

In Washington, D.C., the War Department establishes the Bureau of Colored Troops to coordinate recruitment of African Americans from all regions of the country. Such units receive the official designation of United States Colored Volunteers and, subsequently, United States Colored Troops. Ultimately, the bureau enlists 186,017 soldiers who are organized into 120 infantry regiments, 12 heavy artillery regiments, one light artillery regiment, and seven cavalry regiments. They prove a valuable source of trained manpower for the Union army.

MAY   27   At Port Hudson, Louisiana, General Nathaniel P. Banks launches his long-anticipated attack upon Confederate defenses. The combined assaults by Generals Christopher Auger and Godfrey Wetzel are defeated piecemeal, while an advance by General Thomas W. Sherman is also repelled. Union losses are 1,995 killed and wounded to a Confederate tally of 235. Port Hudson also witnesses the combat debut of African American troops, who acquit themselves well.

MAY   28   In Boston, Massachusetts, the 54th Massachusetts Infantry, composed of African American soldiers and white officers, parades under Colonel Robert G. Shaw, a wealthy Brahmin and devoted abolitionist. Shortly after, they ship out for South Carolina to serve at the siege of Charleston.

MAY 30   General Robert E. Lee reorganizes his Army of Northern Virginia into four corps: General James Longstreet (I), General Richard S. Ewell (II), General Ambrose P. Hill (III) and General J. E. B. Stuart (Cavalry Corps).

JUNE 3   In Virginia, General Robert E. Lee begins his second invasion of the North by moving the Army of Northern Virginia, 75,000 strong, from Fredericksburg and into the Shenandoah Valley. For the North, another national crisis is at hand.

JUNE 8   The Army of Northern Virginia under General Robert E. Lee arrives at Culpepper Court House, Virginia, where General J. E. B. Stuart stages an elaborate cavalry review for enthralled spectators. However, he is slated to receive some rather unexpected visitors within hours.

JUNE 9   At Beverly, Virginia, General John Buford's Union cavalry splashes across the Rappahannock River, and General David M. Gregg's force crosses at Kelly's Ford against the headquarters of General J. E. B. Stuart to catch that wily trooper in a pincer movement. Stuart, mustering 9,500 troopers, hurriedly assembles his command at Brandy Station to receive them. Fierce and indecisive fighting erupts before General Alfred Pleasonton assumes that Confederate reinforcements are approaching and signals his men to withdraw. Brandy Station is the largest mounted action of the war and a tactical victory for the Confederates, who inflict 936 Union casualties for a loss of 523 men. The 10-hour struggle nonetheless underscores the excellent progress Union cavalry has made under capable leadership.

JUNE 14 At Port Hudson, Louisiana, General Nathaniel P. Banks hurls another assault against Confederate defenses. General Halbert E. Payne's division charges the strong entrenchments at Priest Cap and is repelled with 1,805 casualties; the well-protected Confederate defenders lose only 22 killed and 25 wounded.

At Winchester, western Virginia, General Richard S. Ewell's II Corps engages General Robert H. Milroy's Federals. In time the latter realizes that the entire Army of Northern Virginia is bearing down on him, so he spikes his artillery, burn all baggage trains, and evacuates Winchester in the darkness. Ewell, however, anticipated such a move and instructs General Edward Johnson to position himself along Martinburg Turnpike to intercept them.

JUNE 15 At Stevenson's Depot, four miles north of Winchester, Virginia, General Edward Johnson's Confederates ambush Union forces under General Robert H. Milroy. The Southerners bag 2,500 prisoners, 300 wagons, 300 horses, and 23 cannons. This action clears Federal forces from the Shenandoah Valley and facilitates General Robert E. Lee's invasion of Pennsylvania.

In Mississippi, a frantic Confederate general Joseph E. Johnston again wires General John C. Pemberton at Vicksburg that his position is hopeless and that he must evacuate immediately to save his army. Pemberton never receives the missive, owing to cut telegraph wires, and remains trapped within his works by General Ulysses S. Grant.

JUNE 17 General Robert E. Lee advances north into Maryland; he dispatches General J. E. B. Stuart's cavalry to screen his right flank from prying Federal eyes. Colonel Thomas Munford of 5th Virginia Cavalry is also scouting near Aldie, Virginia, when he brushes up against Union troopers under General Hugh J. Kilpatrick. Fighting is intense but inconclusive; Union losses total around 300 to a Confederate tally of 100.

JUNE 18 In Mississippi, General Ulysses S. Grant relieves General John A. McClernand from command of the XIII Corps for insubordination after he issued unauthorized, laudatory statements to his men, praising them for their role at Vicksburg, Mississippi, and denigrating the performance of other units.

JUNE 22 In Virginia, General J. E. B. Stuart receives discretionary and somewhat vague instructions from General Robert E. Lee. He is directed to raid Union supply lines and guard the army's right flank as it lurches northward into Pennsylvania.

JUNE 23 In Pennsylvania, General Robert E. Lee's army nears Chambersburg as several disparate Union columns grope along in pursuit.

JUNE 25 At Salem Depot, Virginia, General J. E. B. Stuart directs three cavalry brigades north to join the main Confederate army across the Potomac River. However, his discretionary orders end up deflecting him from the main theater of operations, and he gallops off. The whereabouts of pursuing Union forces remains unknown to General Robert E. Lee.

JUNE 27 In Washington, D.C., President Abraham Lincoln appoints General George G. Meade to replace General Joseph Hooker as commander of the Army of the Potomac.

JUNE 28 In Maryland, General Robert E. Lee is startled to find Union forces concentrating at Frederick, threatening his communications with Virginia. As a precaution, he orders his dispersed command assembled at Gettysburg, Pennsylvania, an important road junction.

At Vicksburg, Mississippi, General John C. Pemberton is petitioned by his soldiers to surrender rather than starve to death. Having endured a seven-week siege, the final curtain lowers on Confederate fortunes in the West.

JUNE 30 A Union cavalry corps under General John Buford arrives and occupies the vital road junction at Gettysburg, Pennsylvania. He briefly skirmishes with Confederates belonging to General Henry Heth's division, and calls for reinforcements from General John Reynolds's corps. Heth, meanwhile, alerts General Ambrose P. Hill of Federal troops at the junction, but Hill blithely dismisses it.

At Hanover, Pennsylvania, General J. E. B. Stuart's cavalry skirmishes with Union troopers under General Elon Farnsworth. After an inconclusive fight, Stuart orders his command on an even wider detour around pursuing Union forces. The Army of Northern Virginia remains blinded in his absence.

JULY 1 At Gettysburg, Pennsylvania, General Henry Heth's Confederate division stumbles headlong into the Union troopers of General John Buford as the former was foraging for shoes. Sharp fighting commences as both sides rush up reinforcements, and at length Union troops are streaming through Gettysburg in confusion. Disaster is only averted when General Winfield S. Hancock arrives and deploys his II Corps along the high ground at Cemetery Hill. Casualties for the day amount to 9,000 Federals and 6,800 Confederates.

A Confederate staff officer locates the elusive cavalry of General J. E. B. Stuart and orders him to repair back to General Robert E. Lee's headquarters at Gettysburg immediately.

In Tennessee, General William S. Rosecrans climaxes his successful Tullahoma Campaign by bloodlessly occupying Chattanooga once General Braxton Bragg's Confederates are strategically out-maneuvered and withdraw.

JULY 2 At Gettysburg, Pennsylvania, General Robert E. Lee's 75,000 Confederates confront 85,000 Federals under General George G. Meade, then arrayed along good defensive terrain. Lee intends to bring the Federals to battle, but does so over the objections of General James Longstreet, who advises him to withdraw. Bloody fighting erupts along the line and the Southerners are gradually repelled with little to show for their losses. A crisis develops on the extreme Union left as Colonel Joshua L. Chamberlain's 20th Maine drive an Alabama brigade down the slopes of Little Round Top at bayonet point. That evening, Meade anticipates that Lee will direct his next attack against the Union center on the morrow, and heavily reinforces it.

JULY 3 At Gettysburg, Pennsylvania, 140 Confederate cannons bombard Union positions for several hours, after which the divisions of Generals George E. Pickett, Johnston Pettigrew, and Isaac Trimble advance upon them. They are quickly decimated by intense rifle and artillery fire and withdraw after a gallant dash that carries them directly into Union lines. Eventually thousands of wounded and stunned survivors stream back across the field toward Seminary Ridge in abject defeat. General Robert E. Lee's gamble had failed, and the debacle at Gettysburg represents the high tide of Confederate military fortunes. Three days of ferocious combat depletes the Army of Northern Virginia by an estimated 20,451 men while the Army of the Potomac suffers losses of 23,049.

JULY 4 The Confederate citadel of Vicksburg, Mississippi, surrenders to

General Ulysses S. Grant; the South is now cut in two along the Mississippi River. Union losses for the campaign total 800 killed, 3,900 wounded, and 200 missing, while the Southerners lost 900 dead, 2,500 wounded, 200 missing, and 29,491 captured.

At Helena, Arkansas, Federals under General Benjamin M. Prentiss withstand Confederate attacks from Generals Theophilus H. Holmes and Sterling Price. The Southerners endure a withering cannonade and concede defeat after losing 380 dead and 1,100 wounded; Federal losses are only 239 killed, wounded, and missing.

JULY 8 At Cumming's Ferry, Kentucky, General John H. Morgan crosses the Ohio River with 2,500 mounted soldiers; this is intended as his largest and most daring raid mounted to date.

JULY 9 Port Hudson, Louisiana, surrenders to General Nathaniel P. Banks's Army of the Gulf. Southerners under General Franklin Gardner lost 146 killed, 447 wounded, and 6,400 captured, while Union casualties topped 708 dead, 3,336 injured, and 319 missing.

JULY 10 Outside Charleston, South Carolina, General Quincy A. Gilmore lands 3,700 Federal troops on Morris Island, overpowering Confederate forces there. He prepares to carry nearby Battery Wagner defended by General William B. Taliafero.

JULY 11 At Charleston, South Carolina, General Quincy A. Gillmore launches a determined Union assault upon Battery Wagner in the harbor, unaware that the garrison had been recently enlarged to 1,200 men. His attack is bloodily repelled with losses of 49 killed, 123 wounded, and 167 missing; the Southerners sustain only six dead and six wounded.

JULY 13–17 In New York City, violent anti-draft riots erupt as a seething mob of 50,000 Irish émigrés attacks the draft office, burning it to the ground. Over 1,000 people, principally African Americans, are either killed or injured.

JULY 14 At Williamsport, Maryland, General Henry Heth acts as rear guard for the retiring Army of Northern Virginia. However, an impatient General Hugh J. Kilpatrick orders two companies of the 6th Michigan Cavalry to charge the Confederates, who capture 719 prisoners, three battle flags, and two cannons.

JULY 18 Colonel Robert G. Shaw's 54th Massachusetts Infantry, an African American formation, spearheads the attack against Battery Wagner, South Carolina. Sergeant William H. Carney becomes the first black soldier awarded a Congressional Medal of Honor; however, the attempt is repulsed with 1,515 casualties, including Colonel Shaw; the Confederates sustain 36 dead, 133 injured, and five missing.

JULY 26 At Salineville, Ohio, General John H. Morgan and his remaining 364 troopers surrender after a continuous running fight of several days. Morgan is confined at the Ohio State Penitentiary in Columbus as a common criminal.

AUGUST 20 In the New Mexico Territory, Colonel Kit Carson commences a scorched-earth policy against hostile Navajos with the assistance of Ute, Zuni, and Melscalero Apache tribesmen. All captives are subsequently transferred to a new reservation at Bosque Rendondo.

AUGUST 21 At Lawrence, Kansas, William C. Quantrill and 450 Confederate irregulars seize the town and systematically execute 180 men and boys before burning 185 buildings. This is the Civil War's largest atrocity against civilians.

SEPTEMBER 3 At Whitestone Hill, Dakota Territory, General Alfred Sully's cavalry attacks a hostile Santee (Sioux) village, killing an estimated 200 inhabitants. A further 156 captives are taken.

SEPTEMBER 6 At Charleston, South Carolina, Confederate forces abandon Battery Wagner upon the orders of General Pierre G. T. Beauregard. This act concludes 60 days of continuous bombardment by Union land and naval forces.

SEPTEMBER 9 Chattanooga, Tennessee, surrenders to the Army of the Cumberland under General William S. Rosecrans without a shot being fired. General Braxton Bragg's Army of Tennessee consequently retires 28 miles to Lafayette, Georgia, and awaits reinforcement.

SEPTEMBER 13 At Gordon's Mills, northern Georgia, General Braxton Bragg orders General Leonidas K. Polk to attack the isolated Union XXI Corps; Polk, however, dithers, and General William S. Rosecrans orders his dispersed forces concentrated near Chickamauga Creek.

SEPTEMBER 17 Congress awards 12-year-old Musician Willie Johnson a Congressional Medal of Honor for bravery during the Seven Days Battle of 1862; he remains the youngest recipient.

SEPTEMBER 19 In Georgia, the Battle of Chickamauga begins once General Braxton Bragg and General William S. Rosecrans continually feed units in to an ever-expanding fray; severe combat occasions serious losses to both sides. Bragg, fortunately, is reinforced that evening by the timely arrival of General James Longstreet's veteran I Corps.

SEPTEMBER 20 General Braxton Bragg renews combat at Chickamauga, Georgia, although a bloody stalemate ensues until General William S. Rosecrans orders General Thomas J. Wood's division to plug a supposed breach in his line. General James Longstreet's I Corps suddenly bursts onto the scene and completely sweeps away the Union center and right. Only the XIV Corps of

Union brigadier general William Rosencrans and Confederate general Braxton Bragg command the fighting at the Battle of Chickamauga in Tennessee, September 1863. (Library of Congress)

General George H. Thomas holds its ground before retiring. This is the bloodiest battle of the Western theater, with Union casualties of 16,179 to a Southern tally of 17,804.

SEPTEMBER 22   At Chattanooga, Tennessee, General William S. Rosecrans rallies his Army of the Cumberland as General Ulysses S. Grant dispatches three divisions of the XV Corps from Vicksburg, Mississippi, to assist him. Meanwhile, General Braxton Bragg's Army of Tennessee commences a siege.

SEPTEMBER 24   In Virginia, Colonel Daniel C. McCallum of the U.S. Military Railroad transports 20,000 men of XI and XII Corps to Chattanooga, Tennessee. This masterful display of logistics underscores the North's industrial and organizational superiority over the South.

SEPTEMBER 27   At Chattanooga, Tennessee, General Braxton Bragg determines to starve out the Army of the Cumberland from Chattanooga, and orders General Joseph Wheeler's cavalry to raid Union supply lines in the Sequatchie Valley.

OCTOBER 6   In Tennessee, General Joseph Wheeler concludes his spectacular raid in the Sequatchie Valley by recrossing the Tennessee River at Muscle Shoals, Alabama. He nearly guts Union supply lines, inflicts 2,000 casualties, captures more than 1,000 wagons, tears up miles of track, and ruins millions of dollars in equipment.

OCTOBER 14   At Bristoe Station, Virginia, General Ambrose P. Hill perceives General George G. Meade's rearguard fording the Broad Run. He attacks, unaware that General Gouverneur K. Warren's II Corps is deployed behind a railroad embankment nearby. The Confederates are thoroughly enfiladed, losing

1,361 men, while the Federals sustain 548 casualties.

OCTOBER 17   At Chattanooga, Tennessee, General William S. Rosecrans is relieved from the Army of the Cumberland and replaced by General George H. Thomas, who declares that the city will be held until they starve.

OCTOBER 18   In Louisville, Kentucky, General Ulysses S. Grant confers with Secretary of War Edwin M. Stanton, and learns of his appointment as commander of the Military Division of the Mississippi. This encompasses the Army of the Tennessee, the Army of the Cumberland, and the Army of the Ohio.

OCTOBER 19   At Warrenton, Virginia, Union cavalry under General Hugh J. Kilpatrick attacks General J. E. B. Stuart's troopers, but no sooner does fighting commence then General Fitzhugh Lee's 2nd Virginia Cavalry strikes the rear of General George A. Custer's brigade, while Stuart attacks from the front. Kilpatrick is routed and the embarrassing affair becomes known as the "Buckland Races."

OCTOBER 23   At Chattanooga, Tennessee, General Ulysses S. Grant arrives and inspects Confederate lines below Lookout Mountain. Perceiving a gap, Grant orders a new supply route established from Bridgeport, the so-called "Cracker Line." This keeps the Army of the Cumberland fed while Grant plans his masterstroke.

NOVEMBER 7   In Virginia, the Army of the Potomac crosses the Rappahannock River, Virginia, and runs into stiff fights at Kelly's Ford and Rappahannock Station. North Carolina troops guarding the ford are overwhelmed by the sudden attack and largely captured. Five miles upstream, General John Sedgwick routs the vaunted "Louisiana Tigers," taking 1,600 prisoners.

NOVEMBER 14 At Loudoun , Tennessee, General James Longstreet's 15,000 Confederates cross the Tennessee River, as General Ambrose E. Burnside gallops into the town to evacuate 5,000 Union troops there. A parallel race unfolds as the two forces slog through ankle-deep mud to reach Knoxville first.

NOVEMBER 19 Outside of Knoxville, Tennessee, General Ambrose E. Burnside orders General William P. Sanders's cavalry brigade to contest General James Longstreet's advance. Sanders contains the Confederates for several hours before being killed, being the only Southern-born Union general slain in combat.

NOVEMBER 23 At Chattanooga, Tennessee, General Ulysses S. Grant orders General George H. Thomas's IV Corps paraded in full view of enemy at Orchard Knob, whereupon they suddenly charge, upending their astonished opponents. Grant subsequently deploys troops at the foot of Lookout Mountain; Orchard Knob serves as his headquarters for the rest of the campaign.

NOVEMBER 24 At Lookout Mountain, Tennessee, General Joseph Hooker begins scaling toward the 1,100-foot summit with 12,000 men. The Confederates, scarcely mustering 2,693 men, resist fiercely but ultimately yield to the Federal juggernaut.

NOVEMBER 25 At Chattanooga, Tennessee, General Ulysses S. Grant and 64,000 men attack General Braxton Bragg's command of 46,000. General William T. Sherman's attack stalls on the Southern right, so Grant orders General George H. Thomas to seize Confederate rifle pits along Missionary Ridge. Thomas, however, charges up the slope without orders, driving the enemy before him. Bragg's stranglehold on Chattanooga is decisively crushed, with Union casualties of 5,335 and a Confederate tally of 6,687.

NOVEMBER 26 In Virginia, General George G. Meade throws his Army of the Potomac across the Rapidan River, covered by a fog. He is counting on his 85,000 men to crush the widely dispersed right wing of the Army of Northern Virginia before it can concentrate.

NOVEMBER 27 In Virginia, General William H. French's III Corps marches down the wrong road, allowing the Army of Northern Virginia to deploy General Edward Johnson's division at Payne's Farm. Heavy fighting erupts as Southern reinforcements appear, at which point Meade suspends the action. Confederate losses are 545; the Union tally is not recorded.

General Patrick R. Cleburne's Confederate rearguard confronts General Joseph Hooker's corps at Ringgold Gap, Georgia. The Federals are blasted back with loss until Cleburne is ordered to withdraw. This well-conducted action inflicts 507 Union casualties, while Cleburne sustains one-third that total.

DECEMBER 16 President Jefferson Davis appoints General Joseph E. Johnston to succeeded General Braxton Bragg as commander of the Army of Tennessee. General Leonidas K. Polk is also appointed as head of the Army of Mississippi.

DECEMBER 23 In Washington, the government issues a patent for the single-shot Remington carbine. This weapon fires the same ammunition as the more expensive Spencer carbines, and 15,000 are acquired.

DECEMBER 27 General Joseph E. Johnston arrives at Dalton, Georgia, to assume control of the Confederate Department of Tennessee and its battered army. The disgraced General Braxton Bragg, meanwhile, repairs back to Richmond, Virginia, where he serves as a military adviser to President Jefferson Davis.

1864

JANUARY 15   Emaciated by a ruthless, scorched-earth policy, many Navajos begin surrendering to Kit Carson in the Canyon de Chelly, New Mexico Territory.

FEBRUARY 1   In Washington, D.C., the House of Representatives resurrects the rank of lieutenant general, U.S. Army, for Ulysses S. Grant.

FEBRUARY 9   In Richmond, Virginia, Union prisoners under Colonel Thomas E. Rose burrow out of notorious Libby Prison and dash for freedom; 59 escapees make it to Union lines, and 48 are recaptured, including Rose.

FEBRUARY 14   Meridian, Mississippi, falls without resistance to Union forces under General William T. Sherman. Sherman then systematically destroys all buildings, supplies, and railroads in his grasp; this is the earliest application of what becomes known as "total war."

FEBRUARY 20   At Olustee, Florida, Union forces under Generals Thomas Seymour attack General Joseph Finnegan's Confederates. The attackers are repelled with considerable loss and Seymour uses a remaining brigade to cover his retreat. He loses 1,861 men—a staggering loss rate of 34 percent, while Finnegan sustains 946, or 20 percent.

FEBRUARY 22   At Okolona, Mississippi, General Nathan B. Forrest's Confederate cavalry attacks a larger Union rear guard under General William Sooy Smith. Forrest engages the main Union body, and several of his charges are bloodily repelled, but Smith retreats in the direction of Pontotoc. Union loses are 319 killed, wounded, and missing; Forrest loses fewer men.

FEBRUARY 27   Near Americus, Georgia, Andersonville Prison, a 16-acre log stockade, receives its first Union captives. In time it acquires infamy as the worst prison site in the Confederacy.

MARCH 2   In Washington, D.C., the Senate confers Ulysses S. Grant with the rank of lieutenant general; the last individual so honored was George Washington during the Quasi-War with France.

MARCH 9   In Washington, D.C., General Ulysses S. Grant succeeds General Henry W. Halleck as general in chief. However, Grant diplomatically allows General George G. Meade to remain in command of the Army of the Potomac.

MARCH 12   In Washington, D.C., leadership changes are finalized with the issuance of General Order No. 98; henceforth General Ulysses S. Grant is in overall command of military operations while General William T. Sherman leads the Military Division of the Mississippi and General James B. McPherson heads the Army and Department of the Tennessee.

MARCH 25   Paducah, Kentucky, is captured by General Nathan B. Forrest and 2,800 Confederate troopers. However, garrison commander Colonel Stephen G. Hicks refuses to surrender and withdraws his 665 men into the safety of nearby Fort Anderson.

APRIL 1   At Arkadelphia, Arkansas, General Frederick Steele marches for the Red River, Louisiana, after reinforcements under General John M. Thayer fail to arrive. His command is dogged by supply shortages, and progress is obstructed by Confederate cavalry under

Grant, Ulysses S. (1822–1885)

Hiram Ulysses Grant was born in Point Pleasant, Ohio, on April 22, 1822, and attended the U.S. Military Academy in 1839. His name was mistakenly registered as Ulysses S. Grant, and he adopted it. Grant graduated in the middle of his class four years later and subsequently fought well in the Mexican War under General Winfield Scott, winning a brevet promotion to captain. However, he grew increasingly disenchanted with military life and resigned his commission in 1854. Grant failed at several business ventures and was living in near-poverty when the Civil War erupted in 1861. He quickly secured promotion to brigadier general of volunteers, and by February 1862 he had captured Fort Donelson, Tennessee, along with 14,000 Confederate prisoners. He next landed at Shiloh, Tennessee, on April 6, 1862 and was nearly defeated with heavy casualties. Rumors of heavy drinking resulted in his subordination to General Henry W. Halleck, and it was not until the spring of 1863 that he could focus again on the Confederate bastion of Vicksburg, Mississippi. Grant isolated this post following a

Ulysses S. Grant commanded the Union armies in the latter half of the American Civil War and would later become president of the United States (1869–1877). (National Archives)

brilliant series of maneuvers, and on July 4, 1863, he accepted the city's unconditional surrender. President Abraham Lincoln prized Grant's aggressive, no-compromise approach to war and arranged his promotion to lieutenant general in the spring of 1864. He next set about subduing the Army of Northern Virginia under General Robert E. Lee, which was finally accomplished in April 1865, victoriously ending the Civil War for the Union. Grant was hailed as America's savior. In 1868 and 1872 he parleyed his tremendous popularity into two successful terms as president. He died at Mount McGregor, New York, on July 23, 1885, the only other individual, next to Lincoln, most responsible for preserving the United States.

Generals Joseph O. Shelby and John S. Marmaduke.

APRIL 8 At Mansfield, Louisiana, General Nathaniel P. Banks and 18,000 men are attacked by 8,000 Confederates under General Richard Taylor at Sabine Crossroads. The rebels crash through two Federal lines, overrunning their artillery and wagon train. Banks retreats with 2,235 casualties while Taylor sustains less than 1,000.

APRIL 9 In Washington, D.C., General Ulysses S. Grant finalizes Union strategy to finally crush the Confederacy. General Nathaniel P. Banks is to capture Mobile, Alabama; General William T. Sherman will seize Atlanta, Georgia; General Franz Sigel is to capture the Shenandoah Valley, and General Benjamin F. Butler will attack Richmond, Virginia, from the James River. Meanwhile, the Army of the Potomac under Grant is to seek out General Robert E. Lee and his Army of Northern Virginia.

At Pleasant Hill, Louisiana, General Nathaniel P. Banks consolidates 15,000 men. General Richard Taylor's Confederates attack again with 12,000 men. The rebels are repulsed in stiff fighting, and Taylor withdraws; Union losses are 1,506 to a Confederate tally of 1,621. However, this concludes the Red River Campaign.

APRIL 10–14   At Prairie D'Ane, Arkansas, General Frederick Steele's Union column encounters General Sterling Price's Confederates and a running battle ensues. Following the defeat of General Nathaniel P. Banks in Louisiana, Steele finds himself marooned behind enemy lines with few supplies and reinforcements.

APRIL 12   Fort Pillow, Tennessee, falls to General Nathan B. Forrest's Confederate cavalry, and the garrison, partly consisting of African American soldiers, is massacred. Confederate losses are 14 dead and 86 wounded, a pittance compared to the Federal tally of 231 killed, 100 wounded, and 226 captured.

APRIL 17   In Virginia, General Ulysses S. Grant orders all prisoner exchanges suspended until Confederates release identical numbers of Union captives. This proves an impossible demand, and the South halts prisoner exchanges altogether.

APRIL 18   Near Poison Springs, Arkansas, General John S. Marmaduke's Confederate cavalry detects a smaller party of Union soldiers and attacks. The Federals break in panic and flee, which forces General Frederick Steele's Union army at Camden to remain on the defensive. The enraged Southerners murder several African American captives in cold blood.

APRIL 25   At Camden, Arkansas, General Frederick Steele's Union army,

outnumbered and nearly surrounded by Confederates, begins retreating back to Little Rock. He methodically evacuates his camp that night, slipping past Confederate outposts without detection, and gains a head start.

APRIL 29   At Jenkin's Ferry, Arkansas, General John S. Marmaduke's Confederate cavalry attacks the Union rearguard as General Frederick Steele passes his army over the Sabine River. The Southerners are repulsed, and soldiers from the 2nd U.S. Colored Infantry murder several Southern prisoners following atrocities inflicted on them at Poison Springs.

MAY 2   At Winchester, Virginia, General Franz Sigel's 6,500 Union troops proceed down the Shenandoah Valley Pike toward New Market. His goal is to deny Southerners any foodstuffs from this region, the "breadbasket of the Confederacy."

MAY 4   In Virginia, General Ulysses S. Grant directs the Army of the Potomac across the Rapidan River toward the heavily forested Wilderness area. He musters 122,000 men, organized into General Winfield S. Hancock's II Corps, General Gouverneur K. Warren's V Corps, General John Sedgwick's VI Corps, and General Ambrose E. Burnside's IX Corps. The soldiers are well-trained, equipped, and share their commander's confidence.

At Chattanooga, Tennessee, General William T. Sherman advances his 110,000 men south into Georgia to confront General Joseph E. Johnston. Sherman's goal is Atlanta, an important rail and communications hub.

MAY 5   In Virginia, the Battle of the Wilderness erupts as General Gouverneur K. Warren's V Corps engages General

A preliminary clash between Union and Confederate troops just prior to the Battle of the Wilderness in Virginia, May 5–6, 1864. (Library of Congress)

Richard S. Ewell's II Corps along the Orange Turnpike Road. Two miles south, General Winfield S. Hancock's II Corps also engages General Ambrose P. Hill's III Corps in fierce fighting. Hill's counterattack gains ground initially, but is halted by the VI Corps, which rallies long enough for Hancock to bring up reinforcements.

MAY 6 In Virginia, the Battle of the Wilderness continues as General Winfield S. Hancock's II Corps smashes into General Ambrose P. Hill's III Corps, nearly breaking it. General James Longstreet suddenly makes a belated appearance, striking Hancock's left and rear and forcing him back. Longstreet is accidentally wounded by his own troops, and when the Confederates finally resume advancing, they are repulsed by entrenched Federal troops and artillery. General John Sedgwick's VI Corps also attacks General Richard S. Ewell's II Corps along the Orange Turnpike, but Union forces are repulsed. The dry vegetation is set ablaze by the fighting, and

hundreds of wounded soldiers are burned to death.

The Wilderness is a dazzling tactical upset for General Robert E. Lee, who inflicts 17,666 on Union forces while Confederate casualties are in the range of 8,000. Grant, however, is undeterred by heavy losses, and begins sidestepping around Lee's right flank and inches closer to Richmond, Virginia.

MAY 7 At Dalton, Georgia, the armies of the Cumberland (General George H. Thomas), the Ohio (General John M. Schofield), and the Tennessee (General James B. McPherson), the whole comprising 112,000 men under General William T. Sherman, confront General Joseph E. Johnston, leading 62,000 Confederates of the Army of Tennessee. The two skillful leaders are well-matched, and an intricate game of military chess unfolds between them.

MAY 9 In southwest Virginia, General George Crook advances 6,155 Union troops to destroy a portion of the Virginia and Tennessee Railroad. He encounters 2,400 Confederates under General Albert G. Jenkins at Cloyd's Mountain and attacks. A stalemate ensues, until a Union column turns the Southern left and rolls up their line. Crook then burns the New River Bridge and achieves his objective.

MAY 10 In Virginia, General Ulysses S. Grant attacks near Spotsylvania Court House to test Confederate defenses. He singles out a position known as the "Mule Shoe" and dispatches Colonel Emory Upton, who arrayed his 12 regiments in a densely-packed assault column, to attack. Upton penetrates the Mule Shoe's left flank, but he is not supported and ultimately fails. Grant is nonetheless impressed by the new tactic, and intends to try again with an entire corps.

MAY 11 At Spotsylvania Court House, Virginia, General Ulysses S. Grant orders General Winfield S. Hancock's II Corps drawn up into dense attack columns, for an attack against the Confederate center. General Robert E. Lee mistakenly interprets Union movements by concluding that Grant is attempting sidestep his left flank, and orders all artillery removed from the Mule Shoe and redeployed elsewhere.

At Yellow Tavern, Virginia, a cavalry fight erupts as 4,500 Confederates under General J. E. B. Stuart defend themselves against General Philip H. Sheridan's division. The Federals retire with 704 casualties while the Southerners lose 300 men, including irreplaceable Stuart, who is fatally wounded.

MAY 12 In Virginia, the Struggle at Spotsylvania Court House renews as General Ulysses S. Grant launches General Winfield S. Hancock's II Corps, arrayed in dense columns, against the Mule Shoe.

General Edward Johnson's "Stonewall Brigade" is overrun with 3,000 prisoners, but a vicious, point-blank musketry duel breaks out, and at length Grant cancels the attack. Union losses are 18,339 men to 10,000 Confederates.

MAY 15 At New Market, Virginia, General Franz Sigel and 6,500 men engage 5,500 Confederates under General John C. Breckinridge. The Confederates throw two infantry brigades forward and drive Sigel's men before them. At one point Breckinridge commits 264 cadets (or "Katydids") from the Virginia Military Institute, and several are killed and injured. The Federals withdraw across the Shenandoah River, and the disgraced Sigel is replaced by Major General David Hunter.

MAY 15–16 In Georgia, the Battle of Resaca unfolds as General Joseph Hooker's Federals engage the Confederates of General John B. Hood on the Union left, while General William T. Sherman orders a division across the Oostanaula River to seize a strategic railroad bridge. General Joseph E. Johnston expertly disengages and withdraws to safety; losses in the two-day struggle are 6,000 Union and 5,000 Confederates, and Sherman resumes advancing into Georgia.

MAY 16 Near Drewry's Bluff, Virginia, General Pierre G. T. Beauregard attacks General Benjamin F. Butler's Army of the James. He seizes General Charles A. Heckman and 400 prisoners before ammunition shortages force the Southerners to halt. General Robert F. Hoke also strikes the Union center, but stalls in a heavy fog. Butler withdraws behind fortifications, and the Federals are corked into the peninsula. Confederate losses are 2,506 while the Union sustains 4,160 casualties.

MAY 20 In Virginia, General Pierre G. T. Beauregard again attacks the Army of the James in the Bermuda Hundred Peninsula by striking at Ware Bottom Church. Union divisions under Generals Alfred H. Terry and Adelbert Ames are hard-pressed, but finally drive their antagonists back. Union losses are roughly 800 to 700 for the Confederates, but Butler remains unable to assist the main drive outside Richmond.

MAY 21 In Virginia, General Ulysses S. Grant begins probing Confederate lines near Milford Station. The lack of strong resistance convinces him to slip around General Robert E. Lee's left flank and cross the nearby Anna River.

MAY 25 At New Hope Church, Georgia, General Joseph Hooker's XX Corps attacks General John B. Hood's Confederates. Two Union divisions charge the troops of General Alexander P. Stewart, who cling to their positions and force the Federals off with 1,600 casualties. Nonetheless, Union forces are now only 25 miles northeast of Atlanta.

MAY 31 In Virginia, Confederates under General Robert E. Lee rush across the North Anna River and again stymie General Ulysses S. Grant's overland campaign to Richmond. Grant, however, succeeds at the strategic level by forcing the redoubtable Army of Northern Virginia from field positions along the Rapidan River to the gates of the Confederate capital. By remaining there for the rest of the war, Grant has acquired the strategic initiative.

JUNE 3 In Virginia, the Battle of Cold Harbor unfolds as General Ulysses S. Grant orders 108,000 Federal troops against General Robert E. Lee's 59,000 men behind a continuous, seven-mile front dotted by earthen fortifications and interlocking fields of fire. Within 30 minutes 7,000 Federals are casualties, while the Confederates sustain roughly 1,500. This is the biggest military blunder of Grant's career and the Northern press begins assailing him as a "butcher."

JUNE 5 In western Virginia, General David Hunter leads 15,000 Union troops down the Shenandoah Valley and engages 5,600 Confederates under General William E. Jones at Piedmont. The Federals charge through a gap in the Southern line, capturing all their artillery. Jones is killed rallying his command, which loses 1,600 men; Union losses are 780.

JUNE 10 At Brice's Cross Road, Mississippi, General Nathan B. Forrest and 3,500 Confederate cavalry put on a display of tactical virtuosity by routing General Samuel D. Sturgis with twice as many men. Forrest accomplishes this by orchestrating simultaneous attacks striking the Union left, right, and center, while a small force maneuvered around Sturgis' rear. The Federals bolt from the field and abandon their own wagon and artillery train. Forrest suffers 492 casualties and inflicts 2,240.

JUNE 11 At Trevilian Station, Virginia, General Philip H. Sheridan's column encounters the dismounted division of General Wade Hampton deployed in the woods. General George A. Custer's Michigan brigade turns Hampton's flank, then exceeds orders by dashing between Hampton and General Fitzhugh Lee's divisions, capturing 50 wagons, 800 prisoners and 1,500 horses. Lee begins pressing the unsupported Custer from all sides, but Sheridan gallops up with reinforcements, and the Southerners retire with 500 prisoners in tow.

JUNE 12 In Virginia, General Philip H. Sheridan renews his clash with Confederates Wade Hampton and

Fitzhugh Lee at Trevilian Station. The Federals charge hard, but Hampton repels seven Union attacks. Sheridan then concludes his raid and returns to Petersburg. At Trevilian Station, he admits to 735 casualties, while Confederate losses are 1,000.

JUNE 14 In Virginia, Union engineers construct the 2,100-foot long James River bridge from Windmill Point to Fort Powhatan, Virginia. The feat takes 450 engineers eight hours to construct, and General Ulysses S. Grant now shifts his army across the river and threatens Petersburg.

JUNE 15 In Washington, D.C., Congress passes legislation granting equal pay to African American soldiers. Previously, black personnel protested this inequity by refusing to accept less pay than white counterparts.

JUNE 18 General Robert E. Lee leads 50,000 men, to Petersburg, Virginia, and prepares for a lengthy siege. He now defends a line 26 miles in circumference and guards four railroads that constitute his supply line. Heavy fighting along the city's outskirts costs the Union 10,586 casualties, while the Southerners lose 4,000.

At Lynchburg, western Virginia, General David Hunter's 18,000 Union troops attack 14,000 newly arrived Confederates under General Jubal A. Early. A draw ensues and Hunter concludes that the enemy has been reinforced, so he retreats back up the Shenandoah Valley. The energetic Early immediately pursues his larger adversary.

JUNE 22 At Petersburg, Virginia, General Ulysses S. Grant shifts troops around Southern defenses to weaken their lines. General David B. Birney's II Corps and General Horatio G. Wright's VI Corps attack the Weldon Railroad, but General

Cadmus M. Wilcox's division holds fast in their path. The veteran division of General John Gibbon is routed and loses 1,600 prisoners, forcing the Federals to withdraw.

At Kennesaw Mountain, Georgia, General John B. Hood attacks Union positions at Kolb's Farm with 11,000 men. General Joseph Hooker, commanding 14,000 troops and 40 cannons, mows down charging Confederates. Hood withdraws with 1,500 casualties to a Union total of 250.

JUNE 23 In Virginia, Union forces under David B. Birney and Horatio G. Wright again attack the Weldon Railroad. The II and VI Corps recover ground lost on the previous day, but General William Mahone's stubborn defense prevents them from reaching their objective. The Federals withdraw below Jerusalem Plank Road with 2,962 casualties.

JUNE 25 Outside Petersburg, Virginia, miners from the 48th Pennsylvania begin tunneling beneath Confederate defenses. They run a 511-foot shaft beneath Elliott's Salient and plant 8,000 pounds of gunpowder below it. General Ambrose E. Burnside also trains General Edward Ferrero's African American division to spearhead the assault after the charges are detonated.

JUNE 27 In Georgia, General William T. Sherman attacks General Joseph E. Johnston at Kennesaw Mountain. The Confederates hold high ground strewn with large boulders and respond with rifle and artillery fire, dropping Federals in clumps. The main thrust against Johnston's line at Cheatham's Hill, defended by General William J. Hardee's corps, is raked by fire from above. Sherman cancels the attack after losing 3,000 men; Johnston suffers 750 casualties.

JULY 8   Near Frederick, Maryland, General Lew Wallace collects a hodge-podge assortment of Union troops behind the Monocacy River to defend the national capital from General Jubal A. Early's advancing Confederates. General Ulysses S. Grant also dispatches a division from the Army of the Potomac to Baltimore by rail.

JULY 9   At Monocacy, Maryland, General Lew Wallace and 6,000 Union troops confront 14,000 Confederates under General Jubal A. Early. The Southerners turn the Union left, and a charge by General William R. Terry's Virginia brigade dislodges the defenders. Wallace retreats up the Baltimore Pike in good order with 1,800 casualties, while Early sustains around 700. However, Monocacy delays the Confederates by 24 hours, and allows the veteran VI Corps time to arrive at the capital.

JULY 11   Outside Washington, D.C., Major General Jubal A. Early's Confederates test defenses of Fort Stevens. This constitutes the first military threat to the capital since 1814, and more than 20,000 of the city's inhabitants are put under arms to resist any attack.

JULY 13–14   At Tupelo, Mississippi, 7,500 Confederates under Generals Stephen D. Lee and Nathan B. Forrest attack Federal troops under General Andrew J. Smith. However, Lee insists on charging the Federals head on, and Forrest's men are decimated by rifle and artillery fire. Tupelo proves a surprising Union victory, and they suffer 674 casualties to a Confederate tally of 1,326.

JULY 17   In Georgia, General Joseph E. Johnston is preparing to attack the isolated Army of the Cumberland at Peachtree Creek, Georgia, when a telegram arrives from President Jefferson Davis, announcing his replacement by General John B. Hood. Davis was angered by Johnston's Fabian tactics, and the change marks a strategic turning point in the course of the war.

JULY 20   At Peachtree Creek, Georgia, the 20,000-man Army of the Cumberland of General George H. Thomas crosses three miles north of Atlanta, where it is attacked by 19,000 Confederates under General John B. Hood. Heavy fighting and losses ensue but Hood's gambit fails and he orders a retreat. Peachtree Creek, the first of several audacious offensives, costs Hood 2,500 men to a Union tally of 1,779.

JULY 22   In Georgia, the Battle of Atlanta commences as General William J. Hardee's corps strikes at the Army of the Tennessee. However, he errs by mistakenly attacking General James B. McPherson's troops frontally and is bloodily repelled. McPherson then stumbles onto a Confederate picket line and is shot dead; he is the sole Union army commander killed in combat. Hood's second sortie depletes his army of 8,000 men, while Union losses are 3,722.

JULY 23–24   At Kernstown, western Virginia, General Jubal A. Early's 14,000 Confederates engage General George Crook's Union VIII Corps of 8,500. The Federals withstand several charges until flanked by General John C. Breckinridge; they are driven off with 1,185 casualties. Early's success convinces the political establishment in Washington, D.C., that vigorous leadership is needed to secure the Shenandoah region.

JULY 28   At Killdeer Mountain (North Dakota), General Alfred Sully engages hostile Lakotas (Sioux) in their camp while looking for the Santees (Eastern Sioux) responsible for the bloody uprising in Minnesota two years earlier. He deploys his 3,000 men in a hollow square, and their firepower evicts the Tetons from their campsite. The Indians lose 150 warriors; Sully suffers five dead and 10 wounded.

At Ezra Church, Georgia, General Oliver O. Howard's Army of the Tennessee advances to sever the final rail links to Atlanta. General John B. Hood consequently dispatches corps under Stephen D. Lee and Alexander P. Stewart to hit the Union left flank and roll it up. However, the Southerners mistakenly veer into the front of General John A. Logan's XV Corps, which routs them. Confederate losses are 5,000 men to a Union tally of only 562.

JULY 30   At Petersburg, Virginia, the Battle of the Crater begins as fuses to an explosive-laden tunnel beneath Confederates lines are lit beneath Elliot's Salient, destroying an artillery emplacement. However, awe-struck Union forces pause 15 minutes before charging into the smoking crater, while the Confederates rush reinforcement to the threatened point. Milling Federal troops are shot down in droves and suffer 3,798 casualties while the Southerners suffer 1,491.

Outside Macon, Georgia, General George Stoneman's Union cavalry attempts circling around the city to cross the Ocmulgee River. However, he is surrounded by General Alfred Iverson's Confederate troopers at Sunshine Church and surrenders 700 men. Stoneman's defeat paralyzes General William T. Sherman's mounted arm for several weeks.

AUGUST 4   West of Atlanta, Georgia, General William T. Sherman orders General John M. Schofield's Army of the Ohio to storm Confederate earthworks near Utoy Creek. They succeed,

and Union troops are now within two miles of East Point, a strategic railroad junction.

AUGUST 6   At Harpers Ferry, western Virginia, 33-year old General Philip H. Sheridan assumes command of the Army of the Shenandoah. President Abraham Lincoln and Secretary of War Edwin M. Stanton fear that he is too inexperienced for so important a task, but Grant is happy to have this headstrong firebrand in charge.

AUGUST 15   In western Virginia, General Philip H. Sheridan withdraws toward Winchester, inducing Confederates under General Jubal A. Early to follow. Sheridan is ordered to move cautiously and avoid any embarrassing defeats so close to President Abraham Lincoln's reelection bid. Early, however, misinterprets this behavior as timidity.

AUGUST 18   At Deep Bottom Run, Virginia, Confederates attack General Winfield S. Hancock's II Corps, and are repelled with loss. General Ulysses S. Grant, however, is convinced that Southern defenses north of the James River are strong, so Hancock is recalled to Petersburg with 2,901 casualties, while the Confederates sustain 1,500.

Outside Petersburg, Virginia, General Gouverneur K. Warren's V Corps attacks portions of the Weldon Railroad. General Pierre G. T. Beauregard dispatches General Henry Heth's division to slash Warren's left flank, but Union reinforcements drive the Southerners back into the city. General Robert E. Lee must now recapture the Weldon Railroad to preserve his supply line.

AUGUST 19   At Weldon Station, Virginia, General Gouverneur K. Warren's V Corps is reinforced by three divisions of the IX Corps, plus General Gershom Mott's

The Battle of Ream's Station in Virginia on August 25, 1864. Union soldiers successfully destroyed eight miles of the Confederate Weldon Railroad before Confederate major general Henry Heth attacked and defeated the Union troops. (Library of Congress)

division from the II Corps. A large Southern counterattack is then orchestrated by General Ambrose P. Hill and Warren is heavily jostled, but the Weldon Railroad remains in Union hands. Federal losses are 4,455, while Confederates sustain around 1,600.

Memphis, Tennessee, briefly falls to a surprise raid by 2,000 Confederate cavalry under General Nathan B. Forrest. General Cadwallader C. Washburn, the garrison commander, escapes in his night clothes. Forrest raids Federal supply lines over the next two months with near impunity.

AUGUST 25 At Ream's Station, Virginia, General Ambrose P. Hill's Confederates assault General Winfield S. Hancock's Union II Corps. Hill's advance rebounds off the divisions of Nelson A. Miles and David M. Gregg, until parts of General John Gibbon's veteran division stumbles in combat and runs. The Union loses 2,372 men while the Southerners sustain only 700 casualties.

AUGUST 31 At Jonesboro, Georgia, General William J. Hardee leads 20,000 Confederates against General Oliver O. Howard. The Federals, posted on high ground with clear fields of fire, handily repulse Hardee's piecemeal attacks. He withdraws after suffering 2,000 casualties; Howard suffers a mere 178.

SEPTEMBER 1 The struggle at Jonesboro, Georgia, continues once General William J. Hardee's Confederates are attacked by General William T. Sherman. He orders an intricate advance by several corps, but Union attacks are poorly coordinated and repulsed with loss. Union casualties are 1,274 out of 20,460 present; the Confederates suffer 911 out of 12,661 engaged.

SEPTEMBER 2 In Georgia, General William T. Sherman telegraphs President Abraham Lincoln that Atlanta has surrendered to the XX Corps of General Henry W. Slocum; victory here rekindles President Abraham Lincoln's sagging election prospects. In four months

Sherman sustained 4,432 dead and 22,822 wounded, while the Confederates lose 3,044 killed and 18,952 injured.

SEPTEMBER 7 Total war manifests once General William T. Sherman issues Special Order No. 67 to the inhabitants of Atlanta, Georgia. This act requires all 1,600 families to abandon their homes and evacuate the city immediately.

SEPTEMBER 16 At Coggin's Point, Virginia, General Wade Hampton's cavalry disperses elements of the 1st D.C. Cavalry and the 13th Pennsylvania Cavalry, and then absconds with 2,486 head of cattle. Hampton returns to Confederate lines the next day after committing the largest single incident of cattle rustling in American history.

SEPTEMBER 19 At Winchester, western Virginia, General Philip H. Sheridan's army of 35,000 men attacks 12,000 Confederates under General Jubal A. Early. The outnumbered Southerners strike back in a vicious counterattack that stuns the XIX Corps, but when General Fitzhugh Lee fails to stop Union cavalry under Generals Wesley Merritt and William W. Averill, Confederate resistance collapses. Union losses are 5,018 to a Confederate tally of 3,611; Early withdraws his survivors south to Fisher's Hill.

SEPTEMBER 22 In western Virginia, the Battle of Fisher's Hill erupts after General Philip H. Sheridan probes General Jubal A. Early's line with 28,000 men. Early, commanding only 9,000 men, is preparing to retreat when two divisions of Union cavalry come streaming down the hillside on his left flank. The Confederates are thoroughly thrashed, losing 1,235 men and 14 cannons to a Union tally of 456.

SEPTEMBER 27 At Centralia, Missouri, Confederate guerrillas under William

"Bloody Bill" Anderson plunder the town and rob its inhabitants. He also apprehends 23 Union musicians on a train and executes them. Major A. V. E. Johnson then arrives with 158 recruits of his 39th Missouri Infantry, most of whom die in an ambush. By the time "Bloody Bill" departs Centralia, 116 Federals have been murdered in cold blood.

SEPTEMBER 29 Near Poplar Springs Church, Virginia, General Gouverneur K. Warren's V Corps attacks Confederate positions along the Squirrel Level Road. The position is overrun, but General Ambrose P. Hill rushes up Generals Henry Heth and Cadmus M. Wilcox, and the Federals fall back to Peeble's Farms.

At New Market Heights, Virginia, General David B. Birney's X Corps attacks up the slopes, spearheaded by General Charles A. Paine's division of African Americans. The black troops lose 800 men in an hour, but they carry the Confederate earthworks in tremendous display of courage. Of 16 Congressional Medals of Honor received by African American in the Civil War, 14 are granted for this action.

Outside Richmond, Virginia, General Edward O. C. Ord's XVIII Corps captures Fort Harrison, garrisoned by 800 artillerists, and also defeat a Confederate counterattack by troops retreating from New Market Heights. Ord then orders his troops to entrench for the inevitable Southern counterattack expected on the morrow.

SEPTEMBER 30 Outside, Richmond, Virginia, General Robert E. Lee arrives with eight infantry brigades and attacks Fort Harrison. Generals Robert F. Hoke and Charles Field charge, but the entrenched Federals easily repel four determined attacks. Lee suspends the action after suffering 2,000 casualties;

Union losses over the past two days exceed 3,300.

OCTOBER 2   At Saltville, Virginia, Confederate forces repulse a Federal attack by General Stephen G. Burbridge. A detachment of the 5th U.S. Colored Cavalry suffers heavily, and the following day vengeful guerrillas under Champ Ferguson stalk the battlefield and kill about 100 wounded African Americans and several white officers.

OCTOBER 5   General Samuel O. French leads 3,276 Confederates forward against the Union depot at Alltoona Pass, Georgia. That post is held by 2,025 Union soldiers under General John M. Corse, who counts on the rugged terrain and rapid-fire Henry repeating rifles to thwart them. The Southerners attack for several hours, but Corse sweeps them down the slopes with concentrated firepower. Union losses are 706, while the Confederates sustain 897.

OCTOBER 7   General Robert E. Lee determines to recapture Fort Harrison, Virginia, to restore his siege lines outside Richmond. The overworked divisions of Robert F. Hoke and Charles W. Field then advance to drive Union forces from the Darbytown Road, encountering stiff opposition from General Alfred H. Terry's division, X Corps, and the attack stalls. Hoke also fails to advance in time, at which point Lee calls off the action with 1,350 Confederate casualties; Union losses are 399.

OCTOBER 9   Union cavalry brigades under Generals George A. Custer and Wesley Merritt engage General Thomas L. Rosser's Confederate cavalry at Tom's Brook, Virginia. Custer, leading 2,500 troopers to confront Rosser's 3,500 men, recognizes his old West Point roommate and doffs his hat before engaging.

Merritt, meanwhile, crashes headlong into opposing troops, and routs them while Custer chases Rosser for 20 miles. This is the biggest triumph of the Union cavalry and celebrated as the "Woodstock Races."

OCTOBER 17   In western Virginia, General John B. Gordon steals upon the Union encampment at Cedar Creek to examine their deployment and discerns that General Horatio G. Wright's left flank is subject to a sudden flanking attack. General Jubal A. Early, once apprised, begins planning an attack.

OCTOBER 19   The Battle of Cedar Creek erupts as the Confederate divisions of Clement A. Evans, Stephen Ramseur, and John Pegram plow into into the camp of General Horatio G. Wright. The Federal VIII and IX Corps crumble before the Southern onslaught but, fortunately, General Philip H. Sheridan is returning from a strategy session and spurs his horse 12 miles to rally his men. The exhausted Confederates wilt in the face of Sheridan's unexpected counterattack with 2,810 casualties. Sheridan's losses are 5,671, but the Shenandoah Valley is finally free of Confederate resistance.

OCTOBER 23–24   The Battle of Westport, Missouri, unfolds as General Sterling Price's fends off numerous Union forces. General James G. Blunt brushes up against Southern cavalry led by Joseph Shelby, and is rebuffed. However, General Alfred Pleasonton looms across Big Blue River and begins pressing upon Sterling's rear. General Samuel R. Curtis then reinforces Blunt and forces his way across Brush Creek just as Pleasonton closes in from behind. Price's army flees in confusion; casualties are roughly 1,500 apiece in this last major engagement of the Trans–Mississippi region.

OCTOBER 26 Confederate outlaw William "Bloody Bill" Anderson is killed in a Union ambush at Richmond, Missouri.

OCTOBER 27 Below Petersburg, Virginia, 43,000 Union troops advance against the South Side Railroad in an early morning drizzle. General Geoffrey Weitzel is halted by heavy fighting, while General John Holman's brigade slips around the Southern flank and charges. Holman's progress is subsequently stymied by General William Mahone's Southerners, and Weitzel, conceding the engagement, withdraws. Union losses are 1,103 to a Confederate tally of 451.

An even larger operation unfolds when General Winfield S. Hancock's II Corps, General Gouverneur K. Warren's V Corps, and General John G. Parke's IX Corps march seven miles southwest of Petersburg to Hatcher's Run. Parke encounters heavy resistance from General Cadmus M. Wilcox's Confederate division and stalls. The Federals retire in good order with 1,700 casualties; Confederate losses are estimated at 1,000. General Ulysses S. Grant then concludes offensive operations around Petersburg and settles into winter quarters.

OCTOBER 28 At Newtonia, Missouri, General James G. Blunt's Union division surprises General Sterling Price's retreating Confederates. However, quick reactions by General Joseph O. Shelby and his "Iron Brigade" allow the bulk of Southern forces to escape to safety.

NOVEMBER 9 At Atlanta, Georgia, General William T. Sherman organizes his army into two wings under Generals Oliver O. Howard (XV, XVII Corps) and Henry W. Slocum (XIV, XX Corps). Sherman also declares that the army is at liberty to forage on the countryside while marching on Savannah; in terms of

destruction, this endeavor proves a bigger application of "total war" than the Atlanta campaign.

NOVEMBER 13 General Jubal A. Early is ordered back to New Market, Virginia, and dispatches parts of his army to the defense of Petersburg. Thus ends the celebrated Valley Campaign of 1864, whereby Confederates marched 1,670 miles and fought 75 battles of various sizes.

NOVEMBER 15 General William T. Sherman departs Atlanta, Georgia, and advances toward Savannah with 62,000 men. He also initiates a 60-mile wide swath of destruction across the state, destroying anything and everything of possible use to the Confederacy.

NOVEMBER 21 General John B. Hood leads 31,000 men and 8,000 cavalry from Florence, Alabama, toward Nashville, Tennessee. By threatening Union lines of communication, Hood hopes to force General William T. Sherman back into Tennessee. His timetable has been delayed three weeks by General Nathan B. Forrest's absence, whereby General George H. Thomas strengthens the defenses of Nashville.

NOVEMBER 25 Near Adobe Walls, Texas, Colonel Christopher "Kit" Carson leads 200 cavalry through a hostile Kiowa encampment, while his Ute and Apache allies steal warriors' horses. However, the survivors flee into nearby Comanche lodges and soon hundreds of angry warriors begin massing to attack the intruders. Carson ducks behind the ruins of Adobe Walls, where two 12-pounder mountain howitzers keep the milling warriors at bay. After several hours of long distance fire, the Americans and their allies escape to New Mexico at night. Carson suffers two dead and 10 wounded; Indian losses are between 50 and 150, due mainly to cannon fire.

NOVEMBER 29   In Colorado, militiamen under Colonel John M. Chivington attack a peaceful Cheyenne camp at Sand Creek. Chief Black Kettle had been directed there with an understanding that they would be safe. Nonetheless, vengeful militiamen sweep down upon the camp at dawn, killing Black Kettle and 149 Cheyennes, including women and children. Chivington loses nine dead and 40 wounded.

NOVEMBER 30   General John M. Schofield arrives at Franklin, Tennessee, with 15,000 men and within hours he is confronted by 23,000 Confederates of General John B. Hood's Army of Tennessee. Hood's charge catches two Union brigades out in the open, and he surges directly into Federal trenches beyond. The defenders hold their fire until the cheering Southerners are nearly on top of them, then unleash a concentrated fusillade that topples hundreds. The battle costs the Confederates 6,252 men, including the talented Patrick L. Cleburne; Union losses total 2,326. Hood gathers up his survivors and marches against Nashville.

DECEMBER 9   General Ulysses S. Grant, frustrated by the perceived lack of aggressiveness by General George H. Thomas at Nashville, Tennessee, orders General John M. Schofield to succeed him. The directive is suspended after Thomas informs Grant that his attack has been cancelled on account of heavy snowfall. The onset of freezing weather also causes General John B. Hood's unsheltered Confederates to shiver in their trenches.

DECEMBER 15   The Battle of Nashville commences as General George H. Thomas

unleashes the XVI and IV Corps against the Confederate left wing. Simultaneously, a diversionary attack by General James B. Steedman's African American troops pins down the Confederate right. General John B. Hood furiously shifts troops to support his overextended line, but it crumbles under the weight of Union numbers. Hood is badly drubbed, but he defiantly determines to make another stand nearby.

DECEMBER 16   The Battle of Nashville resumes as General George H. Thomas renews his drive against General John B. Hood's reformed left wing. In the ensuing rout, the Federals capture General Edward Johnson and nearly all Hood's artillery. Hood's losses total 5,962, while Thomas, a methodical pugilist, loses 3,057. This victory also eliminates the Confederate Army of Tennessee.

DECEMBER 21   Savannah, Georgia, falls to Union forces under General William T. Sherman after his 285-mile "March to the Sea." He then telegrams President Abraham Lincoln, stating, "I beg to present to you as a Christmas gift the city of Savannah with 150 heavy guns and also about 250,000 bales of cotton."

DECEMBER 25   General Benjamin F. Butler orders an attack upon Fort Fisher, Wilmington, North Carolina, by his Army of the James. He lands 2,200 men and advances inland; Confederate gunners unleash a torrent of shot that keeps the attackers 50 yards from their objective. Butler summarily cancels the entire operation and withdraws back to the Union fleet offshore.

DECEMBER 28   General Ulysses S. Grant concedes to President Abraham Lincoln that operations against Fort Fisher, North Carolina, have been a complete fiasco. Moreover, he insists that General

Benjamin F. Butler to sacked for "Gross and culpable failure."

DECEMBER 31   Union forces have settled comfortably into their siege lines around Petersburg and Richmond, Virginia, being constantly reinforced to a strength of 110,000 men. On the other hand, the Army of Northern Virginia of General Robert E. Lee, which still musters 66,000 men, withers away in its trenches through illness, desertion, and combat.

1865

JANUARY 3   General Alfred H. Terry is appointed to succeed General Benjamin F. Butler as commander of the joint expedition against Fort Fisher, Wilmington, North Carolina. Even Butler's most vocal political allies cannot salvage his military career.

JANUARY 7   In the Colorado Territory, Cheyenne and Sioux warriors attack the frontier settlement of Julesburg and Valley Station. The Indians send a small detachment forward to lure the 7th Iowa Cavalry out into the open, but the intended ambush is sprung too early and the troopers escape. The warriors loot and burn nearby settlements before retiring.

JANUARY 11   At Beverly, West Virginia, General Thomas L. Rosser's 300 Confederate troopers brave freezing weather and attack a Union encampment. The defenders are overwhelmed before serious resistance is mounted, and Rosser secures 587 captives, 100 horses, 600 rifles and 10,000 rations.

JANUARY 15   At Wilmington, North Carolina, General Alfred H. Terry commences an all-out assault on Fort Fisher. Generals Newton M. Curtis, Galusha Pennypacker, and Louis H. Bell encounter fierce resistance, and all three leaders are either killed or wounded in eight hours of combat. General Joseph C. Abbott's remaining brigade finally attacks and overpowers the defenders. Union losses are 1,341, while the Confederates sustain 2,000 killed, wounded, or captured.

JANUARY 16   In Richmond, the Confederate Congress passes a resolution to appoint General Robert E. Lee as general in chief, and to also restore General Joseph E. Johnston as commander of the Army of Tennessee. They do so out of fading confidence in President Jefferson Davis's military leadership.

JANUARY 24   In Virginia, General Ulysses S. Grant reverses himself and approves renewed prisoner exchanges. This influx of new Confederate manpower is calculated to exacerbate existing food shortages throughout the South.

FEBRUARY 5   In Virginia, General Gouverneur K. Warren's V Corps renews its offensive near Hatcher's Run, while General Andrew A. Humphrey's II Corps occupies nearby Vaughan Road. The Confederates launch several strong counterattacks but are repulsed. Humphrey's corps is reinforced overnight by General David M. Gregg's cavalry division.

FEBRUARY 6   In Virginia, heavy fighting resumes along Hatcher's Run as General John B. Gordon's Confederates slam into General Gouverneur K. Warren's V Corps. Southern general John Pegram falls in heavy fighting, but General Clement A. Evans and his forces gradually push the Federals back from Boydton Plank Road.

FEBRUARY 7 Fighting continues at Hatcher's Run, Virginia, as Union forces successfully extend their siege lines at a cost of 1,512 casualties. Southern losses are unknown but presumed as heavy. General Robert E. Lee's defensive perimeter now stretches 37 miles in length, and General Ulysses S. Grant prepares to stretch it thinner by shifting his forces leftward.

FEBRUARY 17 In South Carolina, General William T. Sherman accepts the surrender of Columbia. Previously, General Wade Hampton's Confederate cavalry burned stockpiles of cotton bales, and the sparks ignite several uncontrollable fires. Southerners are convinced that Charleston was torched on Sherman's orders.

FEBRUARY 18 Charleston, South Carolina, is occupied by Union forces under General Alexander Schimmelfenning. The fall of the "fire eater" center of the Confederacy is sweet revenge, and the 567-day siege of Fort Sumter in the harbor also concludes.

FEBRUARY 21 General Robert E. Lee alerts Confederate Secretary of War John C. Breckinridge that he will abandon Richmond, Virginia, to maintain communication with Confederate forces in the Carolinas. He also requests that General Joseph E. Johnston be returned to active duty.

FEBRUARY 22 General John M. Schofield's Union troops occupy Wilmington, North Carolina, closing the last remaining port of the Confederacy, and begin directing military operations toward the interior by ordering all railroads in the vicinity repaired.

FEBRUARY 25 General Joseph E. Johnston arrives at Charlotte, North Carolina, to resume command of the Army of Tennessee, now reduced to a skeleton force of 25,000 ragged, hungry men. They are unequal to the task of confronting General William T. Sherman's Federal army.

MARCH 2 General George A. Custer's 3rd Cavalry Division clatters up to Waynesboro, Virginia, and observes that General Gabriel C. Wharton's division lacks sufficient manpower to cover both flanks. Custer dispatches three dismounted regiments to encircle their left and leads his two remaining brigades on a thunderous charge through the Confederate center. He seizes 1,600 prisoners, 11 cannons, and 200 wagons as General Jubal A. Early flees from the field.

MARCH 3 In Washington, D.C., President Abraham Lincoln instructs General Ulysses S. Grant to ignore any of General Robert E. Lee's gestures toward peace unless he first surrenders.

MARCH 9 The Battle of Kinston, North Carolina, unfolds as Confederates under General Braxton Bragg attack General Jacob D. Cox's XXII Corps. General Robert F. Hoke's division outflanks the Federal left under General Samuel P. Carter, while General Daniel H. Hill executes a similar move against the Union right. Once the second Union line commanded under General Thomas H. Ruger holds fast, the Southern offensive stumbles. Union losses are 1,257, while the Confederates suffer only 134.

MARCH 10 At Monroe's Crossroads, North Carolina, Confederate cavalry under generals Wade Hampton and Joseph Wheeler attack General Hugh J. Kilpatrick's campsite. Kilpatrick, clad only in a nightshirt, narrowly evades capture as the Southerners sweep all in their path. The Federals rally and gradually recapture their bivouac, as Hampton withdraws back to Fayetteville. The affair becomes popularly known as the "Battle of Kilpatrick's Pants."

MARCH 17 General Edward R. S. Canby advances on Mobile, Alabama, with 32,000 men of the XVI and XII Corps; his opponent, General Dabney H. Maury, only musters 2,000 rank and file. Another column under General Frederick Steele proceeds from Pensacola, but progress is slow owing to the muddy condition of the roads.

MARCH 19 The Battle of Bentonville, North Carolina, commences as General William P. Carlin's division marches down the Goldsborough Road toward Cole's Plantation. He encounters heavily entrenched Confederates, and desperate fighting breaks out once the Southerners fail to break Union lines. The conflict recedes by nightfall, and both sides bring up reinforcements.

MARCH 20 At Bentonville, North Carolina, General Oliver O. Howard's Union forces reinforce General Henry W. Slocum, and his arrival boosts their numbers to 60,000—three times the size of Confederates under General Joseph E. Johnston. Johnston, meanwhile, continues strengthening his fortifications and determines to protect Mill Creek Bridge to his rear from capture.

MARCH 21 The Battle of Bentonville resumes as General William T. Sherman dispatches General Joseph A. Mower's division to turn the Confederate left, while Union forces demonstrate to their front. Mower makes good progress and nearly reaches Mill Creek Bridge before being assailed on both flanks and withdrawing. General Joseph E. Johnston lacks the manpower to pursue, however, and orders

his army withdrawn toward Smithville. Bentonville is the last conventional clash of the Civil War; Union casualties are 1,646 to a Confederate tally of 2,606.

MARCH 22 General James H. Wilson leads 13,500 Union cavalry across the Tennessee River to seize the Confederate munitions center at Selma, Alabama. This is also the largest cavalry force ever fielded in American military history, consisting of divisions under Generals Edward M. Cook, Eli Long, and Emory Upton.

MARCH 23 Union forces under Generals William T. Sherman and John M. Schofield unite at Goldsborough, North Carolina. Sherman has covered 425 miles from Savannah, Georgia, in only 50 days, a logistical and organizational triumph far exceeding his "March to the Sea" in complexity and difficulty.

MARCH 24 At Petersburg, Virginia, General Robert E. Lee orders General John B. Gordon to cobble together elements of several Confederate corps and seize a portion of nearby Union lines. A break though would impel General Ulysses S. Grant to transfer forces, allowing the Army of Virginia to slip out of the city and join General Joseph E. Johnston in North Carolina.

MARCH 25 General John B. Gordon launches 11,000 Southerners into Union trenches near Fort Stedman, surprising the defenders and capturing several batteries. A swift counterattack by General John Hartranft recaptures Fort Stedman and forces Gordon's veterans back. The outnumbered Confederates withdraw in disorder, losing 3,500 men to a Union tally of 1,044. Lee prepares to abandon Petersburg altogether.

MARCH 31 General Philip H. Sheridan's cavalry turns the Confederate left flank at Dinwiddie Court House, Virginia, when he is assailed by General George E. Pickett's division and driven off. Pickett withdraws to Five Forks that evening, and General Robert E. Lee explicitly instructs him to hold that position at all cost.

APRIL 1   The Battle of Five Forks, Virginia, begins once General Philip H. Sheridan orders George A. Custer and Thomas C. Devlin to slash at the Confederate right while his remaining cavalry engages them frontally. Confederate generals George E. Pickett and Fitzhugh Lee are absent, attending a fish bake several miles to the rear, and Southern defenses buckle. The Union suffers 986 casualties, while the Confederates lose 4,400 men and four cannons. General Robert E. Lee has no recourse but to abandon Richmond and save his army from encirclement.

Generals Eli Long and Emory Upton press 1,500 Confederate cavalry under General Nathan B. Forrest at Ebenezer Church, Alabama, as he awaits the arrival of General James R. Chalmer's division. The first Union wave gallops forward and is repulsed until Forrest's center-left, held by Alabama militia, bolts from the field and his entire line collapses. Federal losses amount to 12 dead and 40 wounded to a Confederate tally of 300.

APRIL 2   General Ulysses S. Grant orders an all-out assault upon Confederate defenses ringing Petersburg, Virginia. General Horatio G. Wright's VI Corps storms the Southern right at Fort Fisher, fatally rupturing General Robert E. Lee's lines. The XXIV Corps also charges down Boydton Plank Road, where the redoubtable General Ambrose P. Hill is killed rallying his shaken men. Lee, meanwhile, orders the immediate evacuation of Petersburg and advises President

Jefferson Davis to relocate the seat of Confederate governance. Petersburg costs the Union 5,100 killed, 24,800 wounded, and 17,500 captured; Southern casualties are variously estimated at between 28,000 and 38,000.

General James H. Wilson attacks Selma, Alabama, defended by 5,000 men under General Nathan B. Forrest. General Eli Long's division is sent to attack the Confederate right while Wilson decides the issue with a thundering charge down the Selma Road that scatters the defenders. Forrest loses 2,700 men captured and 102 cannons seized, while Union casualties are 46 dead, 300 wounded, and 13 missing.

APRIL 3   Richmond, Virginia, is occupied by General Godfrey Weitzel's largely African American XXV Corps. He sends forward an advance party under Major Atherton H. Stevens, and civil authorities formally capitulate. The Stars and Stripes is raised over the state capitol for the first time in four years,

APRIL 5   At Amelia Court House, Virginia, General Robert E. Lee is joined by General Richard S. Ewell's forces, bringing his strength up to 58,000. He determines to attack Union forces directly in their path and cut themselves free, then decides in favor of a night march around their left flank. Meanwhile, victorious Federal forces continue milling around their fortifications, until General Ulysses S. Grant arrives to supervise a pursuit of the fleeing Confederates.

APRIL 6   The Battle of Sayler's Creek, Virginia, unfolds as the Army of Northern Virginia inadvertently separates into three parts, and pursuing Union forces exploit the gaps. The Southerners initially repulse their advance, but General George W. Getty's division suddenly flanks the defenders. General Richard S.

Ewell's entire line is promptly enveloped, and he surrenders 3,400 prisoners. On the right, General Richard H. Anderson's corps also dissolves in the face of General George A. Custer's mounted charge. Anderson's survivors flee into the woods and Federal troops round up another 2,600 captives, 300 wagons, and 15 cannons. On the Confederate left, General Andrew A. Humphrey's II Corps overruns General John B. Gordon's rear guard of 7,000 men, and additional 1,700 men are taken. All told, the Army of Northern Virginia loses 7,700 men and eight generals; Union casualties are 166 killed and 982 wounded.

APRIL 8   General Robert E. Lee gathers his surviving men and plans to break through General Philip H. Sheridan's cavalry at Appomattox Court House. During a council of war held that night, Lee and his generals agree to brush Sheridan aside that morning before pressing on to Lynchburg.

APRIL 9   General Robert E. Lee directs Generals John B. Gordon and Fitzhugh Lee to attack General Philip H. Sheridan's forces at Appomattox Court House, Virginia. The Federal troopers are gradually dislodged whereupon Lee discerns General Edward O. C. Ord's Army of the James drawn up behind them. Crestfallen, he acknowledges the futility of combat and parleys with Union authorities about surrender terms. Accompanied by his secretary, Lee meets with General Ulysses S. Grant and formally surrenders the Army of Northern Virginia. Grant proffers generous terms, whereby Lee's 30,000 survivors are paroled and return home in possession of their horses and mules. Union forces also issue 25,000 rations to the half-starved Southerners.

Fort Blakely, Mobile, Alabama, is besieged by 45,000 Federal troops under General Edward R. S. Canby. An assault force of 16,000 attacks the Confederate defenses at noon, and General St. John R. Liddell surrenders after 20 minutes of fighting. Union losses are 113 killed and 516 wounded while the Southerners incur 629 casualties with 3,423 men and 40 cannons captured.

APRIL 10   In Washington, D.C., President Abraham Lincoln, after receiving word of General Robert E. Lee's surrender, orders a military band to strike up "Dixie."

APRIL 12   At Appomattox Court House, Virginia, the Army of Northern Virginia lays down its arms to General Joshua L. Chamberlain. General John B. Gordon leads the weather-beaten 28,000 Southerners along the Richmond Stage Road, whereupon Chambers orders his men to present arms; the salute is returned in kind.

APRIL 13   In Washington, D.C., Secretary of War Edwin M. Stanton orders the military draft suspended and also reduces supply requisitions.

APRIL 14   At Charleston, South Carolina, General Robert Anderson hoists the identical American flag over the battered remnants of Fort Sumter which was previously lowered on April 14, 1861.

APRIL 16   General James H. Wilson's army occupies Columbus, Georgia, after brushing aside Confederate militia and taking 1,200 captives. The victorious troopers, unaware that the war is over, burn several factories, 100,000 bales of cotton, and 200 rail cars.

APRIL 18   At Durham Station, North Carolina, General Joseph E. Johnston surrenders 37,000 men to General William T. Sherman. However, the surrender terms are viewed as overly generous and are disavowed. The War

Department accuses Sherman of over-stepping his authority and ordered him to renegotiate the identical terms used at Appomattox.

APRIL 20 In Washington, D.C., General Henry W. Halleck is removed as chief of staff and is reassigned to the Military Division of the James in Virginia.

APRIL 26 Generals Joseph E. Johnston and William T. Sherman meet again at Durham Station, North Carolina, and renegotiate a surrender agreement with terms offered at Appomattox, Virginia.

APRIL 30 General Edward R. S. Canby holds preliminary surrender talks with General Richard Taylor at Mobile, Alabama. Afterward, Taylor returns to his headquarters at Meridian, Mississippi, and prepares to capitulate.

MAY 1 In Washington, D.C., the War Department issues General Order No. 79 and begins demobilizing the 1,052,038 soldiers and volunteers comprising the Union army. The Army will not approach this size again until 1918.

MAY 4 At Citronelle, Alabama, General Richard Taylor surrenders Confederate forces east of the Mississippi River to General Edward R. S. Canby. He receives identical terms offered at Appomattox and is allowed to send his men home by steamship.

MAY 10 Near Abbeville, Georgia, President Jefferson Davis and his wife Varina are captured by the 1st Wisconsin Cavalry under Lieutenant Colonel Benjamin Pritchard. His arrest signals the end of Confederate governance.

Confederate guerrilla William C. Quantrill is mortally wounded in a Union ambush near Taylorville, Kentucky, and dies in prison shortly afterward.

MAY 13 In Texas, Colonel Theodore H. Barrett leads Union troops into combat at Palmetto Ranch. They engage Confederate cavalry under Colonel John S. Ford, who deftly outflanks Barrett and forces him fall back 17 miles. Union losses are 130 killed, wounded, and captured; the Confederates suffered far less. Palmetto Ranch is also the last encounter west of the Mississippi River.

MAY 23 In Washington, D.C., the Grand Army of the Republic parades in a mass review while flags are permitted to fly at full mast for the first time in four years. Significantly, not one of the 166 African American regiments raised are allowed to join the festivities.

The army of General William T. Sherman, sporting a much looser appearance than the spit-and-polish Army of the Potomac, also tramps its way through Washington, D.C. Sherman seethes over his recent contretemps with Secretary of War Edwin M. Stanton and refuses to shake his hand.

Grand review of the great veteran armies of Grant and Sherman at Washington, D.C., on May 23, 1865; however, a number of distinguished African American regiments were deliberately excluded from the parade. (Library of Congress)

MAY 26 At New Orleans, Louisiana, General Simon B. Buckner surrenders to General Edward R. S. Canby's deputy, General Peter J. Osterhaus. This eliminates all remaining Confederate forces west of the Mississippi River. General Joseph O. Shelby, however, spurs 1,000 followers into Mexico to found a military colony.

JUNE 2 At Galveston, Texas, General Edmund Kirby-Smith formally capitulates to General Edmund J. Davis. The articles of surrender are signed aboard the warship *Fort Jackson*.

JUNE 23 At Doaksville, Indian Territory (Oklahoma), General Stand Watie surrenders the Confederate Cherokees, being the final Southern general to lay down his arms.

JULY 6 General Ulysses S. Grant attempts to curb rising racial violence against former African American slaves by ordering military personnel to arrest any civilians suspected of crimes against blacks or soldiers.

JULY 7 In Washington, D.C., the Army hangs Mary Suratt, Lewis Paine, David Herold, and George Atzerodt for their roles in the assassination of President Abraham Lincoln.

JULY 11 Near Fort Laramie (Wyoming), Sioux war bands attack part of the 7th Iowa Cavalry and are repelled after losing 20 warriors.

JULY 27 In the Wyoming Territory, Sioux warriors attack the Platte Bridge Station and are repulsed by men of the 11th Ohio and 11th Kansas Cavalry with loss.

NOVEMBER 10 Confederate captain Henry Wirz is hung for his role as commandant of notorious Andersonville Prison, Georgia. During his tenure, over 10,000 Union prisoners perished under squalid conditions; he is the only Confederate so punished.

1866

JANUARY 9 At Nashville, Tennessee, Union troops open a school for freed African Americans in an Army barracks. It is named in honor of General Clinton B. Fisk, head of the Freedman's bureau, and is eventually chartered as Fisk University.

JANUARY 24 Dr. Mary E. Walker becomes the first woman awarded a Congressional Medal of Honor for her services during the Civil War in 1864. She functioned as a spy and spent several months in a Confederate prisoner of war camp.

MARCH 21 In Washington, D.C., Congress authorizes the first two national soldiers' homes at Dayton, Ohio, and Togus, Maine. These are founded for the relief of disabled officers and men.

APRIL 6 In Decatur, Illinois, Dr. B. F. Stephenson and Rev. W. J. Rudolph organize the first chapter of the Grand Army of the Republic, a national veterans' organization rising to 409,498 members.

MAY 13 In the Wyoming Territory, Colonel Henry B. Carrington advances up the Bozeman Trail to commence construction of Fort Phil Kearney. His incursion is resented by Chief Red Cloud, who begins mobilizing the Lakota Sioux to take up arms.

Red Cloud (1822–1909)

Red Cloud (Mahpiua Luta) was born along the North Platte River, Nebraska, in 1822, part of the Oglala Sioux nation. He matured into a fierce warrior and head of the Bad Face military society. He had risen to prominence by 1865, just when the United States was constructing a road through Nebraska and Wyoming into Montana. Red Cloud angrily departed peace talks at Fort Laramie and declared they would fight rather than allow his territory to be violated. Commencing with the Fetterman Massacre of December 21, 1866, he led a devastating guerrilla war that thwarted all attempts to contain it. A peace treaty was reached at Fort Laramie in November 1868, but Red Cloud did not sign until all three forts had been abandoned and burned. Only then did he agree to lay down his arms and relocate to a reservation, the so-called Red Cloud Agency, in Nebraska. Thereafter he served as a peace missionary and frequently visited Washington, D.C., to plead for better treatment of his people. Consequently, the Fort Laramie treaty was revised and rendered more favorable towards the Oglala. However, white encroachment on the Black Hills region of South Dakota resulted in the large Indian uprising of 1876 as restive warriors under Crazy Horse and Sitting Bull took to the field to fight. Red Cloud, fearing disaster, forbid people from his reservation from taking the war path. However, the government suspected Red Cloud was assisting the rebels, and in 1878 they ordered his band relocated to the Pine Ridge Agency of South Dakota. There Agent Trant V. McGillycuddy arranged Red Chief's dismissal as chief. Nonetheless, Red Cloud opposed participating in the Ghost Dance religion and steered clear of fighting at Wounded Knee in December 1890. Red Cloud continued living among his people at Pine Ridge until his death there on December 10, 1909. He was one of few Native Americans able to dictate peace terms to the United States.

Red Cloud was a Lakota leader and warrior who organized what has been termed the most successful Indian war against the United States. (National Archives)

MAY 29 At West Point, New York, Winfield Scott, hero of the War of 1812 and Mexican War, and progenitor of the Civil War's "Anaconda Strategy," dies at the U.S. Military Academy, West Point, aged 80 years.

JUNE At Fort Laramie, Wyoming Territory, a peace council transpires between Army representatives and Lakota chiefs Red Cloud, Man-Afraid-of-his Horse, and Spotted Tail. However, once the government makes clear its intention to construct forts throughout the region, Red Cloud and his entourage storm out.

JUNE 15 Captain William G. Rankin and men of the 31st Infantry begin constructing Fort Buford on the Missouri River, North Dakota. Being located in the heart of essential buffalo hunting grounds, this deeply angers nearby Sioux.

JUNE 16 Colonel Henry B. Carrington's column, guided by noted scout Jim Bridger, arrives at Fort Laramie, Montana Territory, to rest and refit. Carrington continues onto the Bozeman trail to construct several forts.

JUNE 28 Colonel Henry B. Carrington trudges into a fortified position along the Powder River, Wyoming Territory, and reinforces the garrison. The post is christened Fort Reno, and Carrington retains one-fourth of his command there while pushing ahead.

JULY 13 In Washington, D.C., Congress passes legislation allowing Army officers of any branch to head up the U.S. Military Academy, West Point. Prior to this arrangement, the superintendent had to be an engineer.

JULY 15 Along the Bozeman Trail, Montana Territory, Colonel Henry B. Carrington begins building Fort Phil Kearny. Lakota Sioux and Northern Cheyenne warriors retaliate by attacking a wagon train along Crazy Woman Creek. They are repelled by accompanying soldiers, but Red Cloud's war against the United States commences.

JULY 17 Near Fort Phil Kearny, Wyoming Territory, resentful Oglala braves try stampeding the horses and mules belonging to Colonel Henry B. Carrington's command. The soldiers briefly pursue their antagonists, but are driven back by superior numbers.

JULY 25 In Washington, D.C., Congress honors Ulysses S. Grant by promoting

him to four-star, lieutenant general. He is the first officer since George Washington to hold such a stellar rank.

JULY 28 In Washington, D.C., President Andrew Johnson fixes the postwar military establishment at 45 infantry and six cavalry regiments, totaling 54,302 men. This force plays a prominent role in Reconstruction activities throughout the South.

AUGUST 1 The War Department issues orders for hiring 1,000 Indian scouts to work along the western frontier. Prospective recruits receive the same pay and allowances of regular cavalry troopers; 474 braves join in the first year.

SEPTEMBER 1 On the Tongue River, Montana, Brigadier General Patrick E. Connor directs 250 cavalry and 80 Pawnee scouts to attack a hostile Arapaho village under Little Horse. The Pawnees abscond with 1,000 Indian ponies and Connor withdraws after killing 50 Indians.

In the New Mexico Territory, Navajo leader Manuelito surrenders his 23-man band to pursing Army troops. The chief and his followers are relocated to new homes on the Bosque Redondo Reservation.

SEPTEMBER 8 Along the Powder River, Montana Territory, 2,000 troopers under Colonels Samuel Walker and Nelson Cole encounter a force of 400 Sioux warriors led by Sitting Bull. The Indians, noting the dilapidated condition of their opponents' horses, attack at once, but a sudden sleet storm forces the contestants to quit. Afterward the Indians find hundreds of sickly mounts shot dead by their riders.

SEPTEMBER 21 The 9th and 10th U.S. Cavalries are activated under Colonels Edward Hatch and Benjamin H. Grierson. Being recruited entirely from African Americans, they gain renown as the

"Buffalo soldiers," a title acquired from the Plains Indians opposing them.

DECEMBER 6 Outside Fort Phil Kearny, Wyoming Territory, Oglala Sioux warriors under Miniconjou attack a wagon train to lure out a relieving force. Captain William J. Fetterman pursues the elusive Indians as far as Lodge Trail Ridge before turning back, swearing to fight to the Indians wherever they are found.

DECEMBER 21 Outside Fort Phil Kearny, Wyoming Territory, 2,000 Lakota (Sioux), Arapaho, and Cheyenne warriors under Red Cloud lure Captain William J. Fetterman's 80-man troop into a deadly ambush where he is wiped out by superior numbers. This is the worst defeat suffered at the hands of Plains Indians thus far and, because troopers are armed with single-shot weapons, the Army begins issuing newer, rapid-fire carbines.

1867

The army updates its drill manual for the first time in 20 years by adopting Colonel Emory Upton's new *Infantry Tactics*. This year 50,000 obsolete Springfield rifled muskets are also modified to accept breech-loaded metallic cartridges.

MARCH 2 In Washington, D.C., Radical Republican senator Thaddeus Stevens forces the Command of the Army Act through Congress. Henceforth, any military order issued by the President must first pass through the Commanding General of the Army for his approval. This measure aims to halt President Andrew Johnson's dealings with military governors in his capacity as commander in chief.

MARCH 11 In Washington, D.C., President Andrew Johnson appoints commanders to the five military districts established under the First Reconstruction Act. These leaders will direct 20,000 occupation troops, including several hundred black militiamen. They are also tasked with registering former slaves to vote and ensuring that they participate in elections without violence.

MARCH 27 The Alabama legislature fails to ratify the 14th Amendment, so military rule (Reconstruction) is imposed on that former Confederate state.

APRIL 7 At Fort Larned, Kansas Territory, General Winfield S. Hancock directs 1,400 cavalry into the Central Plains region to halt indigenous tribesmen from harassing the Kansas Pacific Railroad. Several bands of Lakotas and Cheyennes are singled out for punishment, but the mobile Native Americans easily evade their antagonists. Moreover, they counter Hancock's advance by attacking wagon trains and stagecoaches.

APRIL 12 In Kansas, General Winfield S. Hancock unsuccessfully parleys with Cheyenne and Sioux chiefs Tall Bull and Pawnee Killer. The talks fail and the Indians slip out of their village, which Hancock vindictively burns. The Indians regard this act as a declaration of war and commence large-scale raiding of settlers and stagecoaches.

APRIL 19 In Kansas, General Winfield Scott Hancock's troops burn abandoned Cheyenne and Sioux villages at Pawnee Fork, Kansas, in retribution for their incessant raiding activities.

JUNE   The garrison at Fort Phil Kearny is the first force equipped with new .50-caliber Springfield breech-loaders. These weapons quadruple the amount of firepower available during engagements with hostile Indians.

JUNE 1   At Fort Hays, Kansas, Lieutenant Colonel George Armstrong Custer leads his 7th U.S. Cavalry into the area between the Platte and Arkansas Rivers. He intends to clear it of hostile Sioux and Cheyenne raiding parties, but the splendidly mounted Plains Indians easily evade the Americans over the next two weeks.

JUNE 24   Along the Republican River, Kansas, Pawnee warriors attack Lieutenant Colonel George A. Custer's encampment as his 7th Cavalry reposes. The intruders are repulsed, then reappear in the distance to taunt the troopers. Custer dispatches Captain Louis Hamilton and 50 troopers in pursuit, but he is ambushed and hastily gallops back to the main camp.

JULY 7   In the Kansas Territory, Lieutenant Colonel George A. Custer departs his encampment along the Republican River and marches for Fort Wallace. He is subsequently alerted that three soldiers have deserted and orders them hunted down and shot—which is done. He also anticipates a detachment of cavalry under Lieutenant Lyman Kidder with orders for him from General William T. Sherman.

JULY 11   In Kansas Territory, Lieutenant Colonel George A. Custer stumbles upon the remains of Lieutenant Lyman Kidder's detachment, which has been massacred by hostile Plains Indians.

JULY 12   Lieutenant Colonel George A. Custer's 7th Cavalry command trots into Fort Wallace, Kansas, frustrated and thoroughly exhausted from chasing elusive Plains Indians.

JULY 15   At Fort Wallace, Kansas, Lieutenant Colonel George A. Custer summarily decides to march back to Fort Hays, Kansas without orders. They arrive two days later after covering 150 miles—then Custer personally rides an additional 60 miles to Fort Harker to stay with his wife. Consequently, he is arrested for taking absence without leave and is suspended from command for a year.

AUGUST 1   Outside Fort C. F. Smith on the Bozeman Trail, Montana Territory, Sioux and Cheyenne warriors under Dull Knife and Two Moon attack 20 woodcutters under Lieutenant Sigismund Sternberg. They Indians try overwhelming the defenders, but are repulsed by newly issued rapid-fire Springfield rifles in what becomes knows as the "Hayfield Fight." The Indians quit after six hours, their losses unknown; Sternberg suffers three dead and three injured.

AUGUST 2   Outside Fort Phil Kearny, Wyoming Territory, 1,500 Sioux under Red Cloud attack a 30-man detachment. Fortunately, Captain James W. Powell circles his wagons and repels the warriors with heavy fire from breech-loading Springfield rifles. The "Wagon Box Fight" is the last pitched encounter of Red Cloud's War; American losses are six dead and two wounded, while the Indians sustain 60 dead and 120 wounded. Hereafter, Red Cloud avoids direct confrontations with army troops in favor of raiding settlers and supply lines.

AUGUST 17   At Plum Creek, Nebraska, Major Frank North's cavalry, assisted by 48 Pawnee scouts, discovers a Cheyenne encampment whose inhabitants had been tearing up railroad tracks recently. The Americans and their allies suddenly charge, routing their opponents; 15 Cheyennes are slain with no loss to the victors.

OCTOBER 21–28   At Medicine Lodge Creek, Kansas Territory, 7,000 Southern Plains Indians gather to sign treaties with the new Peace Commission. The signatories are to be relegated to new reservations with the Kiowa and Comanche tribes taking up residence between the Red and Washita Rivers, while the Southern Cheyenne and Arapaho tribes are lodged between the Cimarron and Arkansas Rivers. The peace commissioners are accompanied by 600 Army troops as a precaution.

OCTOBER 29   Major Charles O. Wood's detachment of the 9th Infantry becomes the first American troops to occupy Alaskan soil since its purchase from Russia. They arrive at the Russian governor's mansion in Sitka for ceremonies marking the official transfer of that vast territory to the United States.

DECEMBER   In Kentucky, the Army disbands its 125th Colored Infantry, the last such African American infantry unit. Thereafter the few remaining blacks transfer over to the 9th and 10th Cavalry, the famous "Buffalo Soldiers."

1868

APRIL 29   At Fort Laramie, Wyoming, General William T. Sherman signs the Treaty of Fort Laramie with representatives of the Sioux nation. Victorious Red Cloud demands that the government disband all Army posts along the Bozeman Trail, Wyoming Territory. Furthermore, the region east of the Big Horn Mountains and north of the North Platte River are reaffirmed as Indian territory. In exchange, several bands of Sioux and Cheyenne are resettled on reservations in Montana, Wyoming, and the Dakotas. For the first time, Red Cloud obtains a significant victory for the Plains Indians.

MAY 30   Memorial Day is celebrated for the first time and General John A. Logan, commanding the Grand Army of the Republic, calls upon Union veterans to decorate military graves with flowers.

General Ulysses S. Grant, commanding general of the Army, is nominated for the presidency by the Republican Party;

he campaigns in uniform up though the November election.

JULY 1   At Fort Harney, Oregon, Colonel George Crook successfully concludes the three-year struggle with the Northern Paiute (Snake) Indians after Chief Old Weawea surrenders. The Americans prevail largely because of the tracking and scouting abilities of their Shoshone allies.

AUGUST 29   At Fort Hays, Kansas Territory, Major George A. Forsyth departs with 50 mounted volunteers as part of an experimental program employing civilian scouts against the Indians. He is tasked with preventing Cheyenne, Arapaho, and Sioux war bands from raiding along the Saline and Solomon Rivers.

SEPTEMBER 17–25   In the Colorado Territory, Major George A. Forsyth and 50 civilian scouts are attacked by 600 mounted Cheyenne, Lakota, and Arapaho Indians under Chiefs Tall Bull, White

Horse, and Bull Bear. Forsyth deploys his men on Beecher's Island in the Republican River. For nine days the Americans drive off their numerically superior opponents with their repeating Spencer rifles. They are finally rescued by a party of African American troopers, the famed 10th Cavalry or "Buffalo soldiers," under Captain Louis Carpenter. Among the many slain are Roman Nose, a celebrated Cheyenne warrior, and Lieutenant Frederick Beecher, nephew of abolitionist Henry Ward Beecher, for whom the battle is named.

SEPTEMBER 24 In Michigan, Lieutenant Colonel George A. Custer receives a telegram cancelling his one-year suspension and ordering him to rejoin the 7th Cavalry at Fort Hays, Kansas Territory. Because of the Army's recent and dismal performance on the plains, Custer is viewed as an effective, hard-hitting commander.

NOVEMBER 12 At Fort Hays, Kansas Territory, an army column under Colonel Alfred E. Sully, including Lieutenant Colonel George A. Custer's 7th Cavalry, rides south to curtail raiding Cheyenne and Arapaho Indians. The campaign begins a month behind schedule, owing to the tardiness of supplies.

NOVEMBER 15 At Fort Bascom, New Mexico Territory, Major Andrew W. Evans leads six companies of the 3rd Cavalry, accompanied by infantry and artillery, against suspected Comanche raiders.

NOVEMBER 23 At Camp Supply, Indian Territory (Oklahoma), General Philip H. Sheridan departs on a long winter raid to locate and eradicate Indian war bands. His campaign is spearheaded by Lieutenant Colonel George A. Custer, who has enjoyed less-than-brilliant success combating Plains Indians.

NOVEMBER 27 At Washita, Indian Territory (Oklahoma), Lieutenant Colonel George A. Custer's 7th Cavalry attacks the Southern Cheyenne of Chief Black Kettle in their camp. Black Kettle, noted for his accommodation with whites, desperately tries to surrender and is killed along with his wife and 103 tribesmen. American losses are 21 killed—including Captain Louis M. Hamilton (grandson of Alexander Hamilton)—and 14 wounded. Continuing resentment among neighboring Arapaho, Cheyenne, and Comanche bands triggers a frontier war lasting several years.

DECEMBER 25 In the New Mexico Territory, Major Andrew Evans attacks a Comanche camp near Soldier Spring on the Red River. Once the settlement is carried, Evans faces a major counterattack by 200 angry Comanche and Kiowa warriors, who are repulsed with a loss of 30 men; Evans sustains one killed.

1869

JANUARY 7 Fort Sill, Oklahoma, is founded as a base for supplying operations against the nearby Kiowa and Cheyenne; it remains active as home of the U.S. Army's artillery school.

FEBRUARY 18 The School of Instruction for Light Artillery opens at Fort Riley, Kansas, although it folds in March 1871.

MARCH 4 In Washington, D.C., Ulysses S. Grant is inaugurated as the eighteenth president of the United States and commander in chief. In power, he pursues a "Peace Policy" with frontier Indians to placate frontier tensions.

MARCH 8 President Ulysses S. Grant appoints General William T. Sherman to succeed him as the four-star, commanding general of the army. In practice, Sherman remains studiously neutral toward governmental politics, and also begins a system of schools to enhance military professionalism.

MARCH 15 At Sweetwater Creek, Texas, Lieutenant Colonel George A. Custer rides into the Cheyenne camp of Chiefs Medicine Bow and Little Robe to parley. When several chiefs subsequently visit the American camp they are taken hostage, at which point Custer demands the release of three white hostages. The Cheyennes comply and promise to return to their reservation once their ponies regain strength.

MARCH 28 The Washita Campaign ends as Lieutenant Colonel George A. Custer's 7th Cavalry rides back to Camp Supply. The effort removed many hostile Indians between the Platte and Arkansas Rivers.

APRIL 5 Daniel F. Blakeman, the oldest surviving veteran of the American Revolution, dies at the age of 109.

APRIL 6 Lieutenant Colonel George A. Custer directs the 7th Cavalry back to Fort Hays, Kansas, concluding General Philip H. Sheridan's winter campaign against recalcitrant Plains Indians.

At San Francisco, California, Captain Charles W. Raymond departs on the first leg of his Alaska Expedition, which ultimately takes him along the Yukon River.

MAY 10 At Promontory Point, Utah, a battalion of the 21st Infantry under Major Milton Cogswell serves as the honor guard during ceremonies marking the joining of the Central Pacific and Union Pacific railroads. The 21st continues onto the Presidio in San Francisco, California, being the first Army unit to cross the nation entirely by rail.

MAY 24 Major John Wesley Powell departs Green River City, above the Colorado River, and conducts the first exploration of the Grand Canyon region.

JUNE 9 At Fort McPherson, Nebraska Territory, Major Eugene Carr leads the 5th Cavalry and three companies of Pawnee scouts in search of hostile Cheyenne bands under Tall Bull.

JULY At Camp Halleck, Nevada, Lieutenant George M. Wheeler departs on a five-month sojourn to find the best routes for military roads to various sites in Arizona and Nevada.

JULY 4 Captain Charles W. Raymond arrives at British Fort, Lower Yukon, below the Arctic Circle. There he employs astronomical observations to prove that the post is on American soil, whereupon British traders residing there are evicted, and the post is renamed Fort Hamilton.

JULY 8 On the Republican River, Kansas, three soldiers led by Corporal John Kyle are attacked by eight hostile Indians. Kyle's Indian Scout, Sergeant Co-Rux-Te-Chod-Ish (Mad Bear) charges ahead to secure a prisoner, is wounded by friendly fire, yet keeps on fighting. He becomes the first Native American to receive a Congressional Medal of Honor.

JULY 11   At Summit Springs, Colorado Territory, Major Eugene A. Carr's 5th Cavalry, assisted by Pawnee scouts under William "Buffalo Bill" Cody, overrun a Cheyenne village on the South Platte River. The Dog Soldiers, a military order within the tribe, suffer 52 dead, including Chief Tall Bull; one American is wounded. This defeat demoralizes remaining Cheyenne war bands, who straggle back to their reservations.

AUGUST 19   At the lower end of the Grand Canyon, Major John Wesley Powell's expedition safely emerges. Powell consequently becomes head of the U.S. Topographical and Geological Survey in the following year.

1870

JANUARY 23   In the Montana Territory, Major Eugene M. Baker directs the 2nd Cavalry to attack a Piegan (Blackfoot) village on the Marias River in retribution for past raids. The troopers kill 173 Native Americans and take an additional 143 captive. The public reacts badly to the massacre, however, so Congress scuttles a bill transferring the Bureau of Indian Affairs to the War Department.

MAY 19   At Kickapoo Springs, Texas, Sergeant Emanuel Stance distinguishes himself in a surprise attack upon Apache raiders. He consequently becomes the first African American to win a Congressional Medal of Honor in the post–Civil War era.

JUNE 30   At West Point, New York, Lieutenant Colonel Emory Upton gains appointment as commandant of cadets at the U.S. Military Academy, and his invigorated regimen greatly abets the growth of military professionalism.

AUGUST 22   Lieutenant Gustavus C. Doane leads a small expedition from Fort Ellis, Montana, to Lake Yellowstone. They are the first white men to investigate what ultimately becomes Yellowstone National Park.

NOVEMBER 1   Sergeant-observers from the Signal Service are deployed at 22 cities to monitor and telegraph weather conditions from around the country. This constitutes the first networked weather observations, and the origins of the National Weather Service.

1871

JANUARY 19   In the Arizona Territory, General George Stoneman commences a winter campaign against Apache war bands who have been attacking settlers.

APRIL 30   At Camp Grant, Arizona Territory, settlers angered by a spate of scalpings attack an Apache community and massacre 100 inhabitants. This act ignites another Indian war which lasts intermittently until Geronimo's capture in 1886.

MAY 3   At Camp Halleck, Nevada, Lieutenant George M. Wheeler, Corps of Engineers, leads a small expedition to continue mapping the area south of the Central Pacific Railroad. He is ordered to provide accurate information relative to Indian tribes in the region, and possible routes for roads or railroad tracks.

MAY 18 At Salt Creek, Texas, hostile Kiowas under Satanta attack a military wagon train as it plods along to Fort Griffin, Texas. The Indians kill seven men and abscond with 41 mules. Just hours before, they had allowed a smaller caravan carrying General William T. Sherman, then checking on Indian pacification efforts, to pass. Sherman subsequently orders the arrest of Satanta, Big Tree, and Satank.

MAY 27 Kiowa chief Satanta, having boasted of his role in the Salt Creek Massacre, is accosted at the Fort Sill Agency by General William T. Sherman and arrested. Nearby Indians appear determined to resist, but Colonel Benjamin H. Grierson deploys his 10th Cavalry in a show of force, and three tribal leaders are taken into custody.

JUNE 4 Lieutenant Colonel George Crook, soon to be known as one of the Army's premier Indian fighters, assumes command of the Arizona Territory.

SEPTEMBER 4 Outside Fort Crittenden, Arizona Territory, Apaches under Cochise steal up on the garrison and rustle their herd of 54 horses and seven mules.

SEPTEMBER 16 In California, Lieutenant George M. Wheeler's expedition begins working its way up the Colorado River, assisted by a dozen Mojave guides.

SEPTEMBER 19 Major John W. Powell's expedition of soldiers and scouts commences the first known raft expedition down the Colorado River to explore the Utah Territory.

OCTOBER 10 On the Brazos River, Texas, Lieutenant Robert G. Carter's detachment of the 4th Cavalry is attacked by large numbers of hostile Indians. However, the troopers form a skirmish line and hold off their antagonists until reinforcements arrive.

OCTOBER 20 Lieutenant George M. Wheeler's small expedition, marooned on the Colorado River near Diamond Creek, Arizona, by leaking boats and nearly out of food, is rescued by a search party.

1872

APRIL 3 At Lost River Gap, Oregon, Major Elmer Otis confers with Modoc leader Captain Jack in a failed attempt to induce the Indians to return to their reservation peacefully.

APRIL 20 In Crockett County, Texas, Kiowas under Big Bow and Comanches under White Horse attack a wagon train and kill 16 teamsters. They then skirmish with two cavalry companies under Captain N. Clooney before riding off; one soldier and one officer are killed.

JULY 6 In the Oregon Territory, Superintendent of Indian Affairs T. B. Ordenal is ordered by the Bureau of Indian Affairs to relocate the Modoc band to their Klamath reservation by force, if necessary. The stage is being set for a bloody little war.

JULY 26 At Fort Rice, North Dakota, Colonel D. S. Stanley takes a large military expedition, supported by Gatling guns and a brass cannon, on an expedition to survey land east of Bozeman, Montana. There they are constantly harassed by Hunkpapa Sioux warriors, who consider his presence a provocation.

JULY 27   Hunkpapa Sioux attack the camp of Major Eugene M. Baker, 2nd Cavalry, who is scouting ahead of Colonel D. S. Stanley's main column. Two soldiers are killed in the so-called Battle of Poker Flat, and the expedition turns back.

AUGUST 14   Along Arrow Creek, Montana Territory, Sioux warriors under Crazy Horse attack Major Eugene M. Baker's 2nd Cavalry as they escort a survey party. The Indians simply taunt their enemies by riding close by, and Crazy Horse has his horse shot from beneath him, but escapes unhurt.

SEPTEMBER 29   Along the Red River, Texas, Colonel Ranald S. Mackenzie's 4th Cavalry, assisted by 20 Tonkawa scouts, surprise a large Comanche encampment at McClellan's Creek. The troopers kill 50 Indians, capture 130 prisoners, and seize 3,000 valuable ponies for a loss of one dead and three wounded.

OCTOBER 1–11   In the Dragoon Mountains, General Oliver O. Howard and noted scout Thomas Jeffords gain an audience with renegade Chiricahua (Apache) leader Cochise. The chief agrees to relocate to a reservation in his Chiricahua homeland, but only if Jeffords, a personal friend, serves as his agent.

NOVEMBER 28   Along the Lost River, Oregon, fighting breaks out between Captain James Jackson's detachment of the 1st Cavalry and Modoc Indians under Kintpuash (Captain Jack). Jackson retreats after losing one dead and seven wounded, while the Indians flee into nearby lava beds, a natural strong point.

DECEMBER 21   Lieutenant Colonel Frank Wheaton, 21st Infantry, arrives outside the Tule Lake lava beds, northern California, intending to storm hostile Modocs hiding there. A Modoc war party also ambushes an ammunition train at Land's Ranch en route to join Wheaton; five soldiers are killed.

DECEMBER 28   In the Arizona Territory, Captains William M. Brown and James Burn, 5th Cavalry, attack some Yavapai Apaches at Skull Cave along Salt River Canyon. The American attack falters until Brown orders his men to shoot at the roof of the cave, whereupon bullets ricochet down, striking 76 men, women, and children. The Americans secure 20 captives, then depart.

1873

JANUARY 13   In northern California, Modoc Indians commence firing at Army troops and volunteers gathered outside the Tule Lake lava beds. This hostile reception forces them to move farther off.

JANUARY 16–17   In northern California, Colonel Frank Wheaton and 400 soldiers attack Modoc positions in the Tule Lake lava beds. Though covered by artillery fire, Indian resistance is tenacious, and the Americans retreat with nine killed and 28 wounded; Indian losses are nil. Considering the disparity of forces, this is an embarrassing defeat.

JANUARY 22   At Scorpion Point, northern California, Modoc raiders attack a wagon train escorted by 22 soldiers; the escorts run, and the grain-filled wagons are burned.

APRIL 6 At Camp Verde, Arizona, Colonel George Crook accepts the surrender of 300 Yavapai Apaches. These are subsequently dispatched to reservations in New Mexico, and Crook is promoted to brigadier general.

APRIL 11 In northern California, General Edward R. S. Canby attempts to placate warring Modoc Indians by meeting tribal leaders at the Tule Lake lava beds. However, he is murdered there by Captain Jack (Kintpuash), along with a peace commissioner. This treachery leads to renewed efforts by the army to crush the insurgents. Significantly, Canby is the only regular army general killed in the Indian wars.

APRIL 15 In northern California, Colonel Alvin C. Gillem, supported by howitzers and Tenino mercenaries, attacks Modoc positions in the Tule Lake lava beds. The well-protected Indians suffer no casualties and repulse the Americans with seven dead and 13 wounded.

APRIL 26 Outside Tule Lake, northern California, Modoc warriors under Scarfaced Charley surprise Captain Evan Thomas's cavalry company in its camp, killing 18 soldiers and wounding 16. The embarrassing defeat leads to Colonel Alvin C. Gillem's replacement by Brigadier General Jefferson Davis.

MAY 2 In northern California, Modocs attack an army wagon train carrying supplies at Scorpion Point near Tule Lake; several soldiers are wounded, but they repel their antagonists.

MAY 4 General Philip H. Sheridan instructs Lieutenant Colonel Ranald S. Mackenzie to relocate his 4th Cavalry to Fort Clark, Texas, and pursue marauding Apache bands into Mexican Territory if necessary.

MAY 10 In northern California, Modoc Indians sortie from the Tule Lake lava beds and surprise troops of the 4th Artillery; five Americans die and another 12 are wounded. However, the Indians lose five killed, among them Ellen's Man, an important leader. The ensuing dissension forces the band of Hooker Jim to break off on its own.

MAY 13 At Bracketville, Texas, Colonel Ranald S. Mackenzie departs Fort Clark with the 4th Cavalry, and gallops south into Mexican Territory to attack renegade Indian bands encamped along the San Rodrigo River.

MAY 18 At Nacimiento, Mexico, Colonel Ranald S. Mackenzie, guided by Seminole scouts, attacks a hostile Kickapoo settlement. The Americans kill

A Modoc named Scarfaced Charley (Chikchikam Lupatkuelatko), photographed about 1873. The Modocs inhabited the area around the Lost River, near the California-Oregon border, before being relocated to the Klamath Reservation as stipulated in the 1864 U.S.-Modoc Treaty. Dispute over this treaty led to the Modoc War of 1872–1873. (National Archives)

19 Indians at a cost of one dead and two wounded. The 317 survivors are then forced back onto reservations in Kansas.

MAY 22   At Willow Creek Ridge, northern California, Army troops attack and capture the war band of Hooker Jim. He subsequently offers to help them capture the elusive Captain Jack.

JUNE 3   Modoc bands under Hooker Jim assist in the capture of Kintpuash (Captain Jack) near the Lost River, California.

JUNE 20   At Fort Rice, Dakota Territory, Lieutenant Colonel George A. Custer leads his 7th Cavalry up the Yellowstone River to scour the region for hostile Cheyennes and Sioux who have been harassing the Northern Pacific Railroad. After Colonel David S. Stanley is removed for drunkenness, Custer assumes command of the ensuing campaign.

AUGUST 4   Along the Tongue River, Montana Territory, Lieutenant Colonel George A. Custer, accompanied only by his brother and 20 mounted scouts, is attacked by 300 Sioux and Cheyenne warriors. Custer's men rise in the grass and deliver several point blank volleys, driving them back in confusion. The men are then rescued by the 7th Cavalry, which gallops up to their rescue. Typical of "Custer's luck," his bold handling of men in combat averts what might have been a disaster.

AUGUST 11   In the Montana Territory, Lieutenant Colonel George A. Custer's 7th Cavalry engages a Sioux village near the mouth of the Rose Bud River. Suddenly, warriors under Crazy Horse begin closing in from the rear. Custer signals his men to about face, then charges the enemy forming to their new front. The Indians scatter before the onslaught, while Custer recrosses the Yellowstone River and escapes. American losses are three killed and four wounded to an estimated 40 Indians dead. Another close call resolved by aggressive tactics.

OCTOBER 3   At Fort Klamath, Oregon, Kintpuash (Captain Jack) and three other Modoc leaders are hung for the murder of peace commissioners. The remaining 150 tribal members are transferred to Fort Quapaw, Indian Territory (Oklahoma), where they languish until 1909.

NOVEMBER 24   In Washington, D.C., the government issues a patent for barbed wire, which becomes a fixture in future land warfare.

1874

JUNE 8   In Arizona, noted Chiricahua Apache leader Cochise dies and is succeeded by his son Taza.

JUNE 16   In Washington, D.C., Congress reduces the Army down to 25,000 men, and eliminates all recruiting efforts. Not until personnel levels dip below this assigned strength are recruiting efforts resumed.

JULY   In Washington, D.C., Commanding General William T. Sherman announces the end of President Ulysses S. Grant's "peace policy" toward Native Americans. He thereupon instructs General Philip H. Sheridan to punish all hostile tribes in the western plains. Sherman also relocates his headquarters to Chicago, Illinois, following continual disagreements with Secretary of War William W. Belknap.

JULY 2   At Fort Abraham Lincoln, Dakota Territory, Lieutenant Colonel George A. Custer leads his 7th Cavalry out to begin exploring the Black Hills region to verify the presence of valuable mineral deposits in the region, especially gold. To that end he is accompanied by civilian specialists in geology, topography, and paleontology, along with a large party of Crow scouts under Bloody Knife.

JULY 22   Lieutenant Colonel George A. Custer's cavalry column enters the Black Hills region of the Dakotas, looking for gold. However, this region is regarded as sacred to the Sioux, and his Crow scouts, fearing retaliation, recuse themselves from the expedition.

JULY 27   At Fort Leavenworth, Kansas, General John Pope orders the 6th Cavalry and 5th Infantry to assemble at Fort Dodge, Kansas, and begin sweeping the southern plains for hostile Indians.

AUGUST 2   Lieutenant Colonel George A. Custer confirms the discovery of gold in the Black Hills region of the Dakota Territory. This announcement results in an influx of miners and prospectors onto Sioux land, greatly angering the inhabitants.

AUGUST 30   Lieutenant Colonel George A. Custer trots back into Fort Abraham Lincoln, Dakota Territory, after covering 1,205 miles in 60 days without violence or major mishap. However, the intrusion exacerbates tensions with the Sioux, who claim the hills as sacred land, and matters get worse after hungry prospectors begin swarming into the region.

In the Oklahoma Territory, Colonel Nelson A. Miles leads a lengthy pursuit of Cheyenne and Kiowa war parties along the Red River. Their running skirmish lasts five hours and culminates with a determined stand by the warriors at Tule Canyon. Miles, however, orders his troopers to withdraw due to lack of provisions.

SEPTEMBER 9–12   In Texas, Kiowas and Comanches under Lone Wolf, Satanta, and Big Tree attack Major William R. Price's supply train along the Washita River. The Indians are rebuffed after a three-day siege.

SEPTEMBER 26   In Texas, Comanche warriors attack the bivouac of Colonel Ranald S. Mackenzie's 4th Cavalry and attempt to stampede its horses. The raiders are quickly detected by alert sentinels and driven off by gunfire.

SEPTEMBER 28   At Palo Duro Canyon, Texas, Colonel Ranald S. Mackenzie's 4th Cavalry attacks a body of Kiowas, Cheyennes, and Comanches, destroying their winter camp and food supplies, and stampeding 1,500 ponies. Such a demoralizing defeat induces many warriors to surrender at nearby reservation agencies, ending the Red River War.

1875

APRIL 12   Sergeant Alchesay and Corporal Elsatsoou of the Indian Scouts receive Congressional Medals of Honor for services rendered against the Apaches in 1872–1873.

APRIL 25   In the Black Hills region of the Wyoming Territory, geologists, prospectors, and scientists begin conducting a four-month expedition to find additional sources of gold. Their presence is greatly resented by the indigenous Sioux, so an armed escort of 400 cavalrymen is provided.

MAY At Fort Sill, Indian Territory (Oklahoma), Comanche war bands under Quanah Parker surrender to military authorities. Parker, who is half white, strikes up cordial relations with Colonel Ranald S. Mackenzie.

JUNE 2 In Texas, Lieutenant Adolphus W. Greely runs the first telegraph wire through Indian Territory (Oklahoma) and establishes the direct link between Fort Bliss, Texas, and Fort Sill.

JUNE 12 In the New Mexico Territory, Chief Taza of the Chiricahua Apaches relocates his people to the San Carlos Reservation. However, 400 hold-outs, including the militant Geronimo, opt to flee to Mexico instead.

NOVEMBER 9 Indian Inspector E. C. Watkins identifies Hunkpapa Sioux under Sitting Bull and Oglala Sioux under Crazy Horse, and hundreds of their followers, as potentially hostile. He urges the government to have them relocated to designated reservations by January 31, 1876, or face direction action by the War Department.

DECEMBER The Federal government orders the Sioux nation to return to its reservations no later than January 31, 1876, or face military action. Undeterred, Sitting Bull and Crazy Horse begin marshaling their warriors for action.

1876

In Washington, D.C., Congress establishes Army manpower levels at 27,442 rank and file, a number that remains stable until the Spanish-American War of 1898. The Secretary of War also subordinates all inspectors general to local commanders instead of the War Department, thereby ending their reputation as "spies" for higher headquarters.

FEBRUARY 1 In Washington, D.C., Secretary of the Interior Chandler confirms that hundreds of Sioux under Sitting Bull and Crazy Horse have failed to report to reservations as ordered. He consequently turns matters over to the War Department for resolution.

FEBRUARY 8 Lieutenant General Philip H. Sheridan, heading up the Division of the Missouri, issues orders for subjugation of the Sioux and their relocation to reservations. One column under Brigadier General George Crook will proceed north from Fort Fetterman, Wyoming, while a second column under Brigadier General Alfred H. Terry will advance along the Yellowstone River. A final column under Colonel John Gibbon will march from Fort Ellis, Montana. Sheridan anticipates that these converging forces will trap the Indians and force their immediate surrender.

MARCH 2 In Washington, D.C., the House of Representatives votes in the affirmative to impeach Secretary of War William W. Belknap on corruption charges. His ensuing Senate trial declares him not guilty, but he nonetheless resigns from office.

MARCH 17 In the Montana Territory, Colonel Joseph Reynolds's 3rd Cavalry surprises a combined Sioux/Cheyenne village along the Powder River. The defenders are stampeded, then rallied by Chief Crazy Horse, and charge back into battle. Reynolds is so unnerved that he retreats, abandoning several dead soldiers and one wounded trooper to the Indians. General George Crook is furious, and orders him court-martialed.

MAY 17   General Alfred H. Terry departs Fort Abraham Lincoln, Dakota Territory, with a column of cavalry and infantry. His orders have him marching westward to the Yellowstone River, then move in a southwesterly direction toward the hostile tribes. Lieutenant Colonel George A. Custer is nearly sacked owing to command difficulties, but a last-minute intercession by Terry keeps him in the saddle.

MAY 29   Brigadier General George Crook departs Fort Fetterman, Wyoming Territory, with 1,500 troopers and gallops north to ensnare hostile Indians in the Little Big Horn Region. Crook is to rendezvous with 260 Shoshone and Crow scouts who volunteer to fight the Sioux, a traditional enemy.

JUNE 17   At Rosebud Creek, Montana Territory, General George Crook leads 1,700 cavalry, infantry, and allied Indians into battle with Lakotas and Cheyennes under Crazy Horse. The latter forsakes the usual tactic of skirting the army's flanks, and unexpectedly charges the troopers head-on. The ensuing struggle lasts six hours and ends in a draw, but Crook's column is so incapacitated that it is effectively neutralized; Indian losses are not known but presumed heavy.

JUNE 21   In the Yellowstone River, Wyoming Territory, General Alfred H. Terry confers with Colonels John Gibbon and George A. Custer on the steamboat *Far West*. Custer is subsequently ordered south along Rosebud Creek to the headwaters of the Little Bighorn River, while Gibbon and Terry will proceed upstream to the Bighorn River before jointly ascending the Little

Bighorn. Terry aspires to catch the Indians in a pincher movement, but he remains unaware of General George Crook's retreat after Rosebud Creek.

JUNE 22   In the Montana Territory, Lieutenant Colonel George A. Custer's 7th Cavalry rides down the Little Big Horn River to rendezvous with Colonel John Gibbon's force. However, General Alfred H. Terry has specifically ordered impetuous Custer not to engage the enemy until Gibbon appears within supporting distance.

JUNE 24   In the Montana Territory, Lieutenant Colonel George A. Custer happens upon the large encampment of Gall, Crazy Horse and Two Moons and warriors from the Cheyenne, San Arc, Miniconjoux Sioux, Oglala Sioux, Blackfeet, and Hunkpapa Sioux nations. This is the largest collection of Native American might ever assembled, but Custer disobeys orders and prepares to divide up his small force and attack.

JUNE 25   In the Montana Territory, the Battle of Little Big Horn unfolds as Lieutenant Colonel George A. Custer and 12 companies of his 7th Cavalry, slightly more than 250 men, attack an Indian encampment housing an estimated 15,000 Indians, including 2,000–3,000 warriors. Repulsed, Custer hastily forms a skirmish line on a nearby hilltop while the Indians surround the Americans and whittle them down before settling the issue in a final rush. The 7th loses 268 dead—Custer among them—and 50 wounded in less than two hours. This defeat stuns the government, and prompts them to pursue the war more vigorously.

JUNE 26   At Little Big Horn, Montana Territory, companies of the 7th Cavalry under Major Marcus Reno and Captain Frederick Benteen successfully defend their hilltop position. The Indians are aware that reinforcements are approaching and begin dismantling their camp.

JUNE 27   General Alfred E. Terry arrives at Little Big Horn and rescues Major Marcus A. Reno's survivors. The mass of victorious Indians have since split up into various groups and dispersed.

JULY 5   In Washington, D.C., Congress approves expanding the number of army officers teaching military science at colleges from 20 to 30.

JULY 9   At Big Horn, Montana Territory, Private William Evans volunteers to serve as a courier to deliver messages to Brigadier General George Crook. He rides through the heart of hostile Sioux territory, winning a Congressional Medal of Honor.

JULY 17   At Warbonnet Creek, Nebraska Territory, Colonel Wesley Merritt's 5th Cavalry defeats a war party of Northern Cheyennes under Chief Yellow Hair. The chief is killed and then scalped by scout William F. Cody, who later restages the encounter at his Wild West Show under the name Buffalo Bill.

AUGUST 15   In Washington, D.C., Congress authorizes an additional 2,500 cavalrymen to the Army, but instead of raising new units, the recruits are used to flesh out the cavalry companies extant.

SEPTEMBER 7   Brigadier General George Crook details Captain Anson Mills to depart from the main column with 150 men and proceed to Deadwood, South Dakota Territory, to procure kindling. While marching, Anson comes upon a large Indian village at Slim Buttes and prepares to attack.

SEPTEMBER 9   In the South Dakota Territory, Captain Anson Mills and his 3rd Cavalry attack Oglala and Minneconjou Sioux under American Horse at the Battle of Slim Buttes. The Indians scatter and take up defensive positions in a gulch, but Chief American Horse, who has taken refuge in a cave, is fatally wounded in the stomach before Crazy Horse can arrive with reinforcements. The battle continues until General George Crook's main column appears, then the Indians disengage and escape. American Horse's death is touted revenge for Custer's death, even through his participation at Little Big Horn remains problematic.

OCTOBER 21   At Cedar Creek, Montana Territory, Colonel Nelson A. Miles and the 5th Infantry engage Sitting Bull and a large body of Sioux. Miles advances to attack and orders the Indians to surrender, but Sitting Bull simply withdraws and makes for Canada.

NOVEMBER 14   At Fort Fetterman, Wyoming Territory, Colonel Ranald S. Mackenzie departs with 2,200 men to search for Crazy Horse. His column proceeds through deep snow for the Powder River region, assisted by 400 Indian scouts from various allied tribes.

NOVEMBER 25   In the Wyoming Territory, General George Crook dispatches Colonel Ranald S. Mackenzie, the 4th Cavalry, and Pawnee mercenaries to attack a Cheyenne village along the Red Fork of the Powder River. The troopers storm into the sleeping village, killing 40 inhabitants and scattering the rest. American losses are 6 dead and 26 wounded, but the tribesmen, especially women and children, endure sub-zero weather with only the clothing on their backs.

DECEMBER 18   At Ash Creek, Montana Territory, soldiers under Lieutenant Frank D. Baldwin advance upon a Sioux village. The inhabitants flee following a preliminary exchange of fire, and the Americans seize their encampment along with 60 horses.

1877

JANUARY 8   Near Wolf Mountain, Montana Territory, Colonel Nelson A. Miles is attacked by 500 Sioux and Cheyenne warriors under Crazy Horse. Miles receives them with artillery, and the Indians are repulsed with few losses to either side. The battle unfolds in the middle of a raging snowstorm.

JANUARY 13   Near Elkhorn Creek, Wyoming, a five-man detachment from the 3rd Cavalry is ambushed by 14 hostile Indians. The defenders suffer three wounded, but manage to hold off their antagonists until the Indians withdraw.

APRIL 3   In Mexico, Lieutenant Colonel William R. Shafter leads a column of troops from across the border to Piedras Negras. There he secures the release of two jailed Mexican nationals who had previously assisted Army efforts. The Mexican government files an official protest over the incident.

APRIL 20   On the Ojo Caliente Reservation, Arizona Territory, Indian agent John P. Clum arrests Geronimo for agitating his fellow Apaches and transfers him to the San Carlos Reservation.

APRIL 24   In Washington, D.C., President Rutherford B. Hayes orders the last remaining Army troops out from New Orleans, Louisiana. This act concludes the process in Southern history known as Reconstruction.

MAY 3   In the Oregon Territory, General Oliver O. Howard orders the "non-treaty" Nez Perce Indians off their ancestral homes along the Snake River region and onto reservations. Chief Joseph and others seek compliance from their people, but resentment mounts.

MAY 6   At Camp Robinson, Nebraska Territory, Lakota chief Crazy Horse surrenders himself and 1,000 warriors to Army authorities. Observers noted he did not appear broken in spirit and continued chanting war songs with his followers.

MAY 7   At Little Muddy Creek, Montana Territory, Colonel Nelson A. Miles defeats hostile Lakotas under Lame Deer and Iron Star in their camp. Sioux losses are 14 dead, including both chiefs, while the Americans sustain four killed and seven wounded. This marks the final encounter of the Great Sioux War, which has proved disastrous to the Plains Indians.

JUNE 1   In Washington, D.C., Secretary of War George W. McCrary intends to combat lawless marauders along the southern border by authorizing Army

Chief Joseph of the Nez Perce. An extremely capable strategist, he eluded thousands of army troops sent after him for several months. (Library of Congress)

units to perform "hot pursuit" into Mexican territory, as necessary.

JUNE 13   In the Wallowa Valley, Washington Territory, Nez Perce warriors kill four settlers, then flee northward with Chief Joseph's band. General Oliver O. Howard orders troops to undertake an immediate pursuit.

JUNE 14   At West Point, New York, Henry O. Flipper becomes the first African American commissioned from the U.S. Military Academy, West Point. He is posted as a second lieutenant with the 10th Cavalry, the famous "Buffalo Soldiers."

JUNE 17   At White Bird Canyon, Idaho Territory, Chief Joseph's band engages Captain David Perry's 1st Cavalry by ambushing them. Indian fire kills 24 Americans and wounds 10, while Nez Perce losses are 3 wounded. The 400 tribesmen then flee east over the Rocky Mountains before reinforcements arrive.

JUNE 26   In the Idaho Territory, Brigadier General Oliver O. Howard enters White Bird Canyon expecting a fight, only to discover that the Nez Perces are long departed. He pauses long enough to bury those slain in the June 17 battle, then marches on.

JULY 4–5   At Cottonwood Creek, Idaho Territory, Lieutenant S. M. Rains's 12-man patrol stumbles upon the main Nez Perce encampment and is killed to a man. The tribe quickly departs the area.

JULY 11–12   At Clearwater River, Idaho Territory, General Oliver O. Howard surprises the Nez Perce encampment and attacks with 500 soldiers backed by artillery and Gatling guns. The Indians fight tenaciously and hold their ground long enough for their families to flee toward the Bitterroot Mountains.

American losses are 13 dead and 27 injured to an Indian tally of four killed and six wounded. Hereafter, Chief Joseph orders the tribe to seek refuge among the Crow Indians further east.

AUGUST 9–10   At Big Hole River, Montana Territory, Colonel John Gibbon's soldiers surprise the Nez Perce fugitives in camp. The Indians quickly regroup and drive Gibbon off with 31 dead and 38 wounded. Nez Perce losses total 77, including women and children, and they escape into the night. Chief Looking Glass, who had insisted that the tribe stop to rest, loses much of his influence.

AUGUST 20   At Camas Meadows, Idaho Territory, a Nez Perce raiding party surprises an Army encampment at night and absconds with 150 mules. Pursing cavalry chases the marauders for eight miles, until they are pinned down near a lava bed for several hours by sniper fire. The Nez Perce escape, while American losses are one dead and seven wounded.

SEPTEMBER 2   At the San Carlos Reservation, Arizona Territory, Mimbreno Apache leader Victorio, angered by horrid living conditions, escapes with 300 followers and begins raiding across New Mexico.

SEPTEMBER 5   At Fort Robinson, Nebraska, Chief Crazy Horse is bayoneted by troops after resisting arrest. The commanding officer was apparently unnerved by unrest among Indians at the fort and suspected the chief of complicity.

SEPTEMBER 13   At Canyon Creek, Montana Territory, Colonel Samuel D. Sturgis launches a slow, dismounted advance while exchanging rifle fire at long range, but the Indians drive them back with losses of 3 dead and 11 wounded. Sturgis is roundly criticized for his mishandling of affairs.

SEPTEMBER 30 At Bear Paw Mountain, Montana, cavalry under Colonel Nelson A. Miles overtakes Chief Joseph's Nez Perce warriors, and a bloody battle ensues. Miles launches a frontal assault and is repulsed by accurate Indian fire, losing 21 killed and 38 wounded. He then elects to besiege them and let starvation and cold run their course. The Nez Perce, only 40 miles short of the Canadian border, spend the next five days in freezing weather.

OCTOBER 5 At Bear Paw Mountain, Montana Territory, Chief Looking Glass is killed while skirmishing with Army troops, and Chief Joseph is finally moved to surrender his half-starved band to Brigadier General Oliver O. Howard. This act concludes an epic 1,300 mile trek, at the end of which Joseph eloquently declares, "I am tired; my heart is sick and sad. From where the sun now stands I will fight no more forever." The surviving 800 men, women, and children are subsequently dispatched to a reservation in Oklahoma.

OCTOBER 17 In Canada, Chief Sitting Bull parleys with General Alfred A. Terry, whereupon the general urges his band to lay down their arms and return home. Sitting Bull angrily denounces Terry for the hardships endured by his people, and tells him to "go back home where you came from."

1878

MAY 30 On the Camas Prairie, Idaho Territory, Bannock Indians take to the warpath under Buffalo Horn and commence raiding the vicinity. General Oliver O. Howard is ordered to round up the entire tribe and deport them en masse to the Yakima Indian Reservation in eastern Washington.

JUNE 8 At Clark's Fork, Idaho Territory, 200 Bannock Indians under Buffalo Horn encounters stiff resistance from 60 volunteers and are repulsed; the chief is among those slain. The raiders are nonetheless swelled by Paiute Indians under Oyte and Egan, which raise their numbers to 450.

JUNE 23 In the Steens Mountains, Oregon Territory, Captain Reuben F. Bernard's cavalry troop surprises Bannock and Paiute raiders under Egan, although the Indians escape and flee into the night.

JULY 8 At Birch Creek, Oregon Territory, Captain Reuben F. Bernard's 1st Cavalry encounters Bannocks and other tribesmen in entrenched positions, but he outflanks their position, forcing them to flee south. Bernard attributes his success to his Indian scouts.

JULY 13 In Idaho, Captain Evan Miles's cavalry confronts Bannock Indians encamped outside the Umatilla Reservation. The ensuing combat drives the Indians off into the Mountains, and an Umatilla scout returns to Miles, bearing Chief Egan's scalp.

JULY 20 Along the John Day River, Oregon Territory, Brigadier General James W. Forsyth attacks a party of Bannock Indians, scattering them with little resistance. Many of the fugitives are rounded up and sent to reservations.

SEPTEMBER 9 In the Indian Territory (Oklahoma), 300 Northern Cheyennes under Dull Knife and Little Wolf break free and march back to ancestral homes in Wyoming and Montana. The army pursues them with 10,000 soldiers for six weeks before the fugitives are overtaken.

SEPTEMBER 12 East of Yellowstone, Wyoming Territory, Colonel Nelson A. Miles intercepts fleeing Bannock Indians attempting to head to Canada, and cuts them off. The defeated Indians finally sue for peace.

SEPTEMBER 29 Little Wolf and Dull Knife conduct the Northern Cheyennes to Smoky Hill, Kansas Territory, where

they are surprised at Punished Woman's Creek by pursuing army troops. Fighting proves inconclusive, and the Cheyennes escape their tormenters and continue retreating north.

OCTOBER 23 Northern Cheyennes under Dull Knife, exhausted and starving, surrender to U.S. Cavalry and are taken to Fort Robinson, Nebraska Territory, for interment. A party of diehards under Little Wolf refuses to give up and continues heading north.

1879

JANUARY 2 At the Fort Robinson army barracks, Nebraska Territory, Dull Knife refuses to return the Northern Cheyennes back to reservations in the Indian Territory (Oklahoma). The commanding officer cuts off all food and water to the tribesmen in return, and the Indians make plans to spring themselves from confinement.

JANUARY 9 Cheyenne refugees under Dull Knife and Little Wolf, confined to army barracks for a week without food or water, escape en masse from Fort Robinson, Nebraska Territory. Only half elude recapture, and the fugitives are hunted down by troops over the next three weeks.

MARCH 27 At the Little Missouri River, Montana Territory, Little Wolf's band of Northern Cheyennes surrenders to Lieutenant William Philo Clark, 2nd Cavalry. Consequently, 33 warriors, 43 women, and 43 children are rounded up and escorted to Fort Keogh. There Little Wolf and several warriors volunteer to serve as scouts for the U.S. Army.

MAY 9 Sitting Bull's band attempts to return to the United States from Canada,

but they are blocked by Colonel Thomas H. Rutger at Fort Assiniboine, Montana Territory.

JUNE 14 The largely African American 25th Infantry Bicycle Corps under Lieutenant James A. Moss embarks on a mobility test from Fort Missoula, Montana Territory, to St. Louis, Missouri, 900 miles distant. This strenuous endeavor is successfully completed in 40 days.

JUNE 30 In the Department of California, General E. O. C. Ord places renewed emphasis on marksmanship by directing weekly target practice for all troops. The best shots are relieved from guard duty for a week.

JULY 29 In Washington, D.C., the War Department follows General E. O. C. Ord's example by instituting new target-practice regulations. Hereafter, each soldier is allotted 20 rounds per month, and the best shots are rewarded with prizes and furloughs.

SEPTEMBER 4 Apache leader Victorio attacks an encampment of the 9th Cavalry at Ojo Caliente, Arizona Territory, then vanishes across the Mexican border.

SEPTEMBER 10 At the White River Agency in Colorado, Indian Agent Nathan C. Meeker becomes embroiled in a dispute with nearby Ute Indians and requests military assistance to preserve order.

SEPTEMBER 16 At Fort Steele, Wyoming Territory, Major Thomas T. Thornburgh departs with 400 men for the White River Indian Agency, Colorado Territory, to assist civil authorities there.

SEPTEMBER 18 In the Black Range, New Mexico Territory, Victorio's Apaches ambush Captain Byron Dawson's patrol of the 9th Cavalry, killing eight troopers and stealing horses. This action commences a prolonged cross-border conflict between settlers and Native Americans in the Southwest.

SEPTEMBER 29–OCTOBER 2 At Milk Creek, Colorado Territory, Ute Indians under Chief Jack (Nicaagat) ambush an army column under Major Thomas T. Thornburgh, killing him and 12 soldiers, and wounding 43 others. The Indians, having sustained 23 dead, return to the White River Agency and massacre Indian agent Nathan C. Meeker and his family.

OCTOBER 11 At White River Agency, Colorado Territory, Colonel Ranald S. Mackenzie's 4th Cavalry deploys and forces the Ute Indians gathered to surrender and release several white hostages. The tribesmen are then forcibly relocated to the Uintah Reservation in the Utah Territory.

OCTOBER 31 At the Ponca Indian Agency, Indian Territory (Oklahoma), Chief Big Snake is accosted by soldiers for attempting to relocate his tribe onto land reserved for the Cheyennes; he resists orders to arrest him and is killed by soldiers.

1880

MAY 14 Outside Fort Tularosa, New Mexico Territory, Sergeant George Jordan's detachment of the 9th Cavalry repels an attack by hostile Indians.

JULY 29 Colonel Benjamin H. Grierson leads the African American 10th Cavalry out from Fort Quitman, Texas, and begins a long pursuit of Apache raiders under Victorio, who eventually cross the border back into Mexico.

AUGUST 6 At Rattlesnake Springs, New Mexico, Colonel Benjamin H. Grierson's 10th Cavalry and Apaches under Victorio begin skirmishing. The Indians gradually draw off and attack a nearby supply train, only to be pursued by Grierson's troopers. Victorio thereafter returns to his refuge in Mexico.

OCTOBER 15–16 Colonel George Buell's cavalry, assisted by Colonel Joaquin Terrazas and 350 Mexican militiamen, corner the renegade Victorio at Tres Castillos, Mexico. The Americans are discretely sent home before the Mexicans attack, killing the chief and 78 Apaches, while 62 survivors are used as slaves.

MAY 7 General William T. Sherman establishes the Infantry and Cavalry School at Fort Leavenworth, Kansas, to promote continuing professionalism in the military. Today it serves as the Army Command and General Staff College.

JULY 19 At Fort Buford, Dakota Territory, Sitting Bull surrenders himself to Federal authorities, with 45 warriors, 67 women, and 73 children. The captives are detained two years at Fort Randall, South Dakota, before relocating onto a reservation.

AUGUST 30   At Cibecue Creek, Arizona Territory, Colonel Eugene A. Carr arrests White Mountain Apache spiritualist Nakaidoklini for agitating his fellow tribesmen. However, resentful Apaches from the nearby San Carlos Reservation begin swarming around Carr's campsite and fighting breaks out. Nakaidoklini is gunned down along with six soldiers and one officer.

AUGUST 31   Colonel Eugene A. Carr's 6th Cavalry arrives back at Fort Apache, Arizona Territory, and is attacked by throngs of angry White Mountain Apaches.

SEPTEMBER 30   At the San Carlos Indian reservation, Arizona Territory, the death of medicine man Nakaidoklini the previous August still rankles Apache living there. This evening 74 warriors under Juh, Nachise, and Chato escape toward Mexico, along with a little-known individual named Geronimo.

1882

APRIL 19–23   At the San Carlos Reservation, Arizona Territory, Apaches kill the local police chief and force members of the nearby Warm Spring Reservation to join their band. Lieutenant Colonel George A. Forsyth pursues them to Horseshoe Canyon and wages an indecisive skirmish, whereupon the renegades gallop into Mexico. Forsyth's 6th Cavalry pursues them across the border until a Mexican infantry unit orders them out.

JULY 6   A party of avenging Apaches under Natiotish, still smarting over the death of a medicine man the year before at the hands of Army troops, attacks the settlement of San Carlos, Arizona Territory, killing three white men.

JULY 17   At Big Dry Fork, Arizona Territory, Captain Adna Romanza Chaffee

perceives an Apache ambush set for him along East Clear Creek. He then out-flanks the Indians and charges, killing 22 including Chief Natiotish; two soldiers are killed. The remaining war bands return to their reservations after this, the final clash with Apaches in Arizona.

JULY 26   In Washington, D.C., the United States signs onto the Geneva Convention of 1864, mandating that wounded soldiers will receive medical attention, buildings are spared from destruction, and prisoners are well-treated.

SEPTEMBER   General George Crook, commanding of the Department of Arizona, secures the San Carlos Reservation, then crosses into Mexico with 50 troopers and 200 Apache scouts to capture Geronimo.

1883

MARCH 21–APRIL 1   An Apache raiding party of 25 warriors under Chato, Chihuahua, and Bonito raids across the Mexican border into the Arizona Territory and

kills 26 settlers without interference from the Army, which has turned out in force looking for them.

MAY 1 In northern Mexico, Captain Emmet Crawford leads a column of the 4th Cavalry to flush out a renegade Apache band under Geronimo. Crawford is ably assisted by 193 Apache scouts working for the army.

MAY 15 Captain Emmet Crawford's 4th Cavalry surprises Apaches under Chato and Benito at San Bernardino Springs, Arizona, killing 30 warriors. This defeat convinces the Indians to voluntarily return to the San Carlos Reservation in the Arizona Territory.

JUNE Apache scouts working for General George Crook locate Geronimo's band in the Sierra Madre. The chief meets with the general and finally agrees to give up. The event reflects highly upon Crook, who maintained that the Indians must be dealt with fairly to curtail otherwise avoidable violence.

AUGUST At Fort Conger, Alaska, Lieutenant Adolphus W. Greely's expedition, short on food, marches south to winter at Camp Sabine. Promised supply ships have yet to arrive.

NOVEMBER 1 Hard-charging Lieutenant General Philip H. Sheridan replaces William T. Sherman as commanding general of the army. However, he does not officially obtain his fourth star until June 1888.

1884

MARCH Apache leader Geronimo voluntarily returns to the San Carlos Reservation, Arizona Territory, but begins agitating among his fellow tribesmen once more.

MAY 18 At Fort Apache, Arizona Territory, Lieutenant Britton Davis learns from Apache scouts that Geronimo has again fled the San Carlos Reservation and is on the loose again.

JUNE At Camp Sabine, Alaska, the expedition of Lieutenant Greely and six men is finally rescued; Greely is subsequently exonerated from charges of recklessness.

DECEMBER 6 In Washington, D.C., Colonel Thomas L. Casey, Corps of Engineers, sets the marble capstone atop of the 300-foot tall Washington Monument. This venerated landmark has been under construction since July 4, 1848.

1885

FEBRUARY 21 In Washington, D.C., the iconic Washington Monument is finished by the Army Corps of Engineers. It is 300 feet in height and weighs in excess of 90,000 tons.

MARCH 3 In Washington, D.C., Congress authorizes the Board of Fortifications and Coast Defenses to evaluate defenses along America's coastline and make recommendations. They also create the rank General of the Army for the senior military officer.

MARCH 4 Former president Ulysses S. Grant is reappointed a general on the retired list, enabling him to receive financial assistance during a period of personal impoverishment.

MAY 17   At the San Carlos Reservation, Arizona Territory, Geronimo, Nachise, and Nana lead 42 Chiricahua men and 92 women for refuge in the Sierra Madre of Mexico. Brigadier General George Crook accordingly relocates his headquarters to Fort Bowie, New Mexico Territory, and begins searching for him.

JUNE 2   In the New Mexico Territory, the 6th and 10th Cavalries fan across the Mogollon Mountains to locate Geronimo and his Apache band. The 4th Cavalry is also authorized to enter the Sierra Madre in Sonora, Mexico. Brigadier General George Crook ultimately deploys 2,000 troopers to catch the elusive warrior.

JUNE 8   Captain Henry W. Lawton's patrol is ambushed at Guadalupe Canyon, Arizona Territory, by the Apache band of Chihuahua. Five soldiers die, and the Indians abscond with two horses and five mules.

JULY 13   Captain Wirt Davis and his 4th Cavalry cross the Mexican border in search of the renegade Apache Geronimo; they are assisted by 100 Indian scouts. Brigadier General George Crook now has 2,000 troops fanning across the countryside, but the wily warriors evade their pursuers.

JULY 23   Ulysses S. Grant, a former president and one of history's most successful military leaders, dies at his summer cottage. With the encouragement and assistance of Mark Twain, Grant publishes his memoirs, which provide a financial windfall to his impoverished family.

AUGUST 7   In northern Mexico, Captain Wirt Davis attacks an Apache camp thought to contain Geronimo; 15 captives are taken. The chief, however, was not present.

NOVEMBER 9   At Cajon Pass, California, Army troops guard railroad personnel as they drive the final spikes on the newly finished California Southern Railroad.

NOVEMBER 23–24   A band of Apaches under Josanie slips past over the Mexican border to raid white settlements in Arizona and New Mexico, killing 38 whites. This is despite the presence of Brigadier General George Crook and 2,000 soldiers on the lookout for them. Josanie also raids a nearby White Mountain Apache reservation, killing 20 Indians who had opposed Geronimo.

DECEMBER 9   Near Papanosas, New Mexico Territory, the 8th Cavalry under Lieutenant Samuel W. Fountain attacks a group of Apaches; the Indians evade capture and escape.

DECEMBER 10   In the Arizona Territory, Apache raiders under Josanie murder several settlers and subsequently attack a nearby detachment of soldiers, slaying five and wounding two.

DECEMBER 27   In the Chiricahua Mountains, Arizona Territory, Josanie's Apache war band takes refuge after winter storms block the passes with deep snow. To date the raiders have covered 1,200 miles and killed 40 people.

1886

JANUARY 8   In northern Mexico, Captain Emmett Crawford's 6th Cavalry initiates a 48-hour forced march to snare Geronimo at his last-known location.

JANUARY 9   From his sanctuary along the Aros River, northern Mexico, Geronimo sends a messenger to Brigadier General George Crook declaring his intention to surrender within a few weeks. His party also flees the approach of Captain Emmett Crawford's cavalry.

JANUARY 10 In the Sierra Madre, Mexico, the 6th Cavalry under Captain Emmett Crawford attacks Geronimo's encampment. The position is overrun and supplies captured, but the elusive Indians escape.

JANUARY 11 Near the Aros River, northern Mexico, Captain Emmett Crawford's cavalry scouts about for the renegade Apache Geronimo. They are suddenly ambushed by Mexican guerrillas; Crawford is fatally wounded and dies a week later.

MARCH 25 At Canyon de los Embredos (Canyon of the Tricksters), northern Mexico, Brigadier General George Crook meets again with renegade Apache chief Geronimo and persuades him to return to the San Carlos Reservation, Arizona Territory.

MARCH 29 Geronimo, having agreed to surrender, is entrusted to a small cavalry troop for conveyance to Fort Bowie, New Mexico Territory. However, the Apaches change their minds at the last moment and disappear into the Sonoran Mountains of Mexico. Consequently, the War Department decides to sack Brigadier General Crook and replace him with hard-bitten General Nelson A. Miles.

APRIL 27 In the Santa Cruz Valley, New Mexico Territory, Geronimo's Apaches attack Peck Ranch, killing several settlers and taking hostages. U.S. Army cavalry is again ordered in pursuit of the renegades.

MAY 3 At Pinto Mountain, Sonora, Mexico, Lieutenant H. P. Clark's 10th

Cavalry engages Geronimo's Apaches in an extended skirmish, but fail to corner them.

MAY 5 At Fort Huachuca, Arizona Territory, Captain Henry Lawton takes a troop of the 4th Cavalry and 100 Apache scouts to look for the renegade Apache Geronimo. They spend four months searching in vain for his elusive band.

MAY 16 In Washington, D.C., Congress authorizes graduates of the U.S. Military Academy, West Point, to automatically be commissioned second lieutenants.

JULY 9 Cognizant that his pursuit of Geronimo has failed, Brigadier General Nelson A. Miles resurrects his predecessor's policy of a negotiated surrender.

JULY 20 In northern Mexico, Captain Henry W. Lawton's 4th Cavalry, guided by 20 Apache scouts, surprises Geronimo's Apaches in camp, but they escape into the nearby hills.

AUGUST 17 In the Wyoming Territory, Captain Moses Harris, 1st Cavalry, establishes the Fort Yellowstone Guards to protect Yellowstone Park from illegal poaching.

AUGUST 24 At the Bavispe River, Mexico, Apache chief Geronimo confers with Lieutenant Charles B. Gatewood, and agrees to surrender, but then only to Brigadier General Nelson A. Miles in person.

SEPTEMBER 4 At Skeleton Canyon, Arizona Territory, Geronimo concludes his legendary 1,600-mile pursuit and surrenders to Brigadier General Nelson A. Miles. The chief, 20 warriors, and 13 accompanying women are subsequently deported to new homes at Fort Pickens, Florida.

1887

JANUARY 29 In Washington, D.C., Congress authorizes construction of the Cavalry and Light Artillery School at Fort Riley, Kansas. However, five years lapse before the facilities are finished and instruction can begin.

MARCH 1 Congress authorizes the Army Hospital Corps to provide a professional cadre of enlisted soldiers to assist surgeons in the field. This is accomplished to relieve line units from assigning personnel from their ranks to do the job.

JULY 26 At Buffalo, New York, the 12th Infantry is assembled and conducts regimental-level exercises as an integrated unit for the first time since 1866. The small size of the American army and the vast frontier it guards requires units to be dispersed at various forts.

NOVEMBER 5 At the Crow Agency, Montana Territory, General T. H. Ruger arrives with troops to suppress a perceived uprising. A party of Crow warriors under Sword Bearer had been celebrating a successful raid on a Blackfoot camp when a gun was accidently fired into the local agent's house. A scuffle with the troops ensues, and Sword Bearer and eight Crows are slain.

1888

AUGUST 14 Following the death of Lieutenant General Philip H. Sheridan, Major General John M. Schofield is chosen to succeed him as commanding general of the army. However, Schofield does not receive the grade of lieutenant general.

1889

MARCH 5 In Washington, D.C., Redfield Procter, a noted Civil War veteran, gains appointment as the new Secretary of War. He will revise the military justice code and introduce a system of efficiency reports and examinations for all officers.

MAY 11 In the Arizona Territory, bandits attempt to seize an Army paymaster's wagon but are repelled by soldiers commanded by Sergeant Benjamin Brown. Brown, severely wounded, wins a Congressional Medal of Honor.

1890

JANUARY Congress authorizes a pound of vegetables to the daily ration of all soldiers, although the Secretary of War will determine the exact proportions these new rations will assume.

JUNE 16 In Washington, D.C., Congress modifies the promotion system for all officers under the grade of brigadier general. Henceforth, all ranks can be transferred within a given branch without loss of rank or seniority. Additionally, regimental officers below major will be regularly examined to ensure minimum levels of competence.

OCTOBER 1 In Washington, D.C., Congress transfers the Weather Service from the U.S. Army Signal Corps to the Department of Agriculture as an economy measure. The Signal Corps is also enlarged by one major, four captains, and four lieutenants.

NOVEMBER 20 At Pine Ridge, South Dakota, the "Ghost Dance" religion preached by Wokova Sioux is seen as provoking an uprising among fellow Sioux. Brigadier General Nelson A. Miles therefore dispatches troops and Apache Indian police to the agency to restore order.

DECEMBER 15 At the Standing Rock Reservation, South Dakota Territory, Apache Indian police attempt to arrest Sitting Bull. A struggle ensues and the police end up killing him, after which enraged tribesmen open fire; 13 Native Americans die in the exchange. This altercation initiates the "Ghost Dance War," a final conflict between the Army and the Plains Indians.

DECEMBER 27 Major Samuel M. Whiteside's 7th Cavalry overtakes Big Foot's band of Miniconjou Sioux and orders them to Wounded Knee, South Dakota Territory, for internment. Big Foot, ill

with pneumonia, peacefully submits and Whiteside kindly dispatches his surgeon to tend to the ailing chief. The troops also issue rations to the hungry Indians.

DECEMBER 28–29 At Wounded Knee Creek, South Dakota, tensions between the Lakota Sioux and Colonel James W. Forsyth's 7th Cavalry explode. Forsyth begins disarming several Indian leaders associated with the Ghost Dance religion, but fighting breaks out after an angry brave fires upon the soldiers, who then open fire into the crowd. A one-sided slaughter ensues for the Native Americans with 84 men (including Big Foot), 44 women, and 18 children slain, and a further 51 wounded. American losses are 19 dead and 33 wounded, mostly from friendly fire.

DECEMBER 30 At White Clay Creek, South Dakota Territory, Sioux ambush a patrol of the 7th Cavalry under Colonel James W. Forsyth until a detachment of the 9th Cavalry marches to its relief. Brigadier General Nelson A. Miles consequently deploys 3,500 men around the Pine Ridge Reservation to contain the "rebellion."

DECEMBER 31 Major James Forsyth's 7th Cavalry is dispatched to Drexel Mission Church on White Clay Creek, 15 miles north of the Pine Ridge Agency, South Dakota. There the troopers are attacked by renegade Sioux and pinned in a valley until the 9th Cavalry rescues them.

1891

JANUARY 1 At Little Grass Creek, South Dakota Territory, Sioux war bands attack Captain John B. Kerr's encampment, and the fight continues until the soldiers are rescued by the 6th Cavalry under

Lieutenant Colonel Eugene A. Carr. American losses are one dead and one wounded; six Indian dead are found on the battlefield.

JANUARY 15   The Pine Ridge Reservation, South Dakota Territory, is surrounded by Army troops under Brigadier
General Nelson A. Miles. Chief Kicking
Bear and 5,000 Sioux tribesmen capitulate peacefully, concluding nearly three
centuries of internecine conflict between
whites and Native Americans.

MARCH 1   In Washington, D.C., the War
Department authorizes recruitment of
26 companies of Indian scouts, one for
each army regiment, and 1,071 scouts
are enlisted over the next six years.
Allied tribes such as the Crow and former enemies like the Sioux are all
solicited.

1892

At Coeur d'Alene, Idaho, Army troops
restore order in the wake of violence
between striking silver miners and strike
breakers.

1893

This year the Army adopts the Danish .30 caliber Krag-Jorgensen rifle. This is the first American firearm possessing a five-round clip and it replaces the single-shot Spring Model 1873 rifle.

JANUARY 9   At Fort Riley, Kansas, the
School for Cavalry and Light Artillery
finally opens for instruction after its facilities are completed. Hereafter, units are
rotated through a year-long course of
practical training and instruction.

JUNE 24   The Army Medical School opens
under the auspices of General George M.

Sternberg, Surgeon General. It is tasked
with imparting proper instruction and procedures on all Medical Corps personnel.

NOVEMBER 3   In Washington, D.C., Congress authorizes the War Department to
assign 100 officers for the purposes of
teaching military science at various colleges.

1894

JULY 3   In Chicago, Illinois, Army troops
deploy to enforce a court injunction
against a strike against the Pullman Company. Governor John P. Atgeld protests
the move on constitutional grounds, and
the militant American Railway Union
strikers under by Eugene V. Debs are

unmoved. The troops are there to see that
delivery of mail is not interrupted.

JULY 8   At Hammond, Indiana, Army
troops fire upon an unruly mob of strikers,
killing one and wounding a dozen. The
troops are withdrawn two weeks later.

1895

OCTOBER 5   In Washington, D.C., Major
General Nelson A. Miles replaces John

M. Schofield as commanding general of
the U.S. Army.

1896

JULY 31 At Jackson Hole, Wyoming, white settlers kill three Bannock Indians and the government orders Major Adna R. Chaffee to restore order and prevent the outbreak of further fighting.

1897

MAY 31 The Army discharges the last of its Indian scouts, although many Native Americans continue serving in the ranks as regular soldiers.

1898

FEBRUARY 18 In Alaska, the 14th Infantry act as a peacekeeping force to protect miners and public property during the ongoing gold rush there. The soldiers establish a "safety zone" to root out criminals and troublemakers.

MARCH 8 In Washington, D.C., Congress expands the Army by adding the 6th and 7th Artillery Regiments to the standing establishment.

APRIL 11 In Washington, D.C., President William T. McKinley requests Congress to declare war on Spain.

APRIL 15 In light of a possible war with Spain, the War Department orders troops and equipment concentrated in several ports along the Gulf of Mexico. However, the order is countermanded when facilities there are found lacking. Eight corps are ambitiously planned with each commanded by a major general, but the VI Corps is never raised.

APRIL 22–23 In Washington, D.C., Congress passes the Volunteer Army Act to raise and equip 125,000 men. This includes the 1st Volunteer Cavalry in which Colonel Leonard Wood is appointed ranking officer.

Assistant Secretary of the Navy Theodore Roosevelt also resigns from office to serve as its lieutenant colonel. The Army almost doubles in size to 65,000 for the duration of hostilities.

APRIL 25 War is officially declared on Spain.

APRIL 26 In Washington, D.C. Congress augments existing infantry regiments by authorizing a third battalion, along with two additional companies per unit. All companies extant are also enlarged to 100 men apiece.

MAY 8 Major General Nelson A. Miles begins preparing and organizing 70,000 regulars and volunteers for an amphibious descent upon Havana, Cuba.

MAY 19 In Washington, D.C., President William McKinley authorizes Brigadier General Greely, chief of the Signal Corps, to assume control of the nation's telephone and telegraph systems. Furthermore, he is tasked with intercepting Spanish communications for intelligence purposes.

MAY 25 At San Francisco, California, troopships depart for Manila carrying

2,000 troops of General Thomas M. Anderson's 2nd Division. They act as the vanguard of the VIII Corps, then assembling under General Wesley Merritt.

MAY 26–JUNE 14 At Tampa Bay, Florida, General William R. "Pecos Bill" Shafter is ordered to prepare his invasion force of 25,000 men by collecting the requisite supplies and equipment, then loading everything on transports.

MAY 28 In Washington, D.C., Congress mandates that all officers transferring from the regulars to the volunteers do so with losing any accumulated seniority.

JUNE 14 At Tampa, Florida, a force of 17,000 troops and volunteers under the command of Major General William R. Shafter sails for Santiago, Cuba. This is also the largest expeditionary force dispatched from the United States to date.

JUNE 20 The 17,000-man V Corps under Major General William R. Shafter arrives off Santiago, Cuba. Shafter subsequently confers with Rear Admiral William T. Sampson as to strategy.

JUNE 22 Major General William R. Shafter disembarks 17,000 men off Daiquiri, Cuba, and only 15 miles from his main objective at Santiago. Because of the lack of boats and other landing craft, all horses and mules are forced to jump into the surf and wade ashore.

JUNE 23 Siboney, Cuba, is seized by American troops, and becomes their base for attacking Santiago, eight miles distant. They are assisted by Cuban rebels, who pin down Spanish troops opposing their line of march.

JUNE 24–25 At Las Guasimas, Cuba, General Joseph Wheeler (a former Confederate) pushes forward his cavalry division and defeats Spanish forces under General Antero Rubin, driving them back to Santiago. The Americans lose 16 killed and 52 wounded, while Spanish losses approach 250. They also encounter German-made Mauser rifles, firing smokeless ammunition, for the first time.

JUNE 27–29 At San Francisco, Brigadier General Arthur McArthur's division begins steaming west for the Philippines. Major General Wesley Merritt also departs two days later on the cruiser *Newport*.

JUNE 28 In Cuba, Major General William R. Shafter learns that the 8,000-man Spanish garrison of Manzanillo has broken through guerrilla lines and is hurrying toward their main position at Santiago. This intelligence prompts Shafter to attack the city before such reinforcements can arrive.

JUNE 30 At Cavite, south of Manila, Philippines, General Thomas M. Anderson's 2nd Division comes ashore They are also transporting guerrilla leader Emilio Aguinaldo to rally his people against the Spanish.

JULY 1 Near Santiago, Cuba, the battles of El Caney and San Juan Hill unfold as the Americans try surrounding the city. In the former engagement, the brigades of Generals Adna R. Chaffee and William Ludlow attack Spanish defenders commanded by General Joaquin Vara de Rey, whose valiant defense holds them at bay for seven hours. General Henry Lawton's 2nd Division finally carries the heights at a cost of 81 killed and 360 wounded; the Spanish lose 248 killed and wounded along with 300 captured. Meanwhile, the balance of the V Corps attacks San Juan Hill, overlooking Santiago. General Jacob F. Kent's division moves forward but is shot down in large numbers by Mauser-wielding snipers.

Frederic Remington's painting Charge of the Rough Riders on San Juan Hill *was very popular and helped foster the image of his friend Lieutenant Colonel Theodore Roosevelt as a war hero. (Wildside Press)*

The "Rough Riders" under Lieutenant Colonel Theodore Roosevelt also falter and are saved by the 9th Cavalry, the famous "Buffalo Soldiers." The Americans subsequently regroup and charge, seizing both objectives at a loss of 140 killed and 940 wounded.

JULY 2   In Cuba, Major General William T. Shafter, discouraged by heavy casualties sustained at El Caney and San Juan Hill, implores Admiral William T. Sampson to reduce Santiago by bombardment. Sampson agrees to confer with Shafter at Siboney on the following day.

JULY 9   In Cuba, General William R. Shafter orders a general advance upon Santiago once the Spanish fleet has been destroyed. He then closes off all possible escape routes by occupying the western shores of the bay.

JULY 11   A naval convoy arrives off Siboney, Cuba, with additional soldiers under Major General Nelson A. Miles. They are not needed on Cuba at present, and are subsequently detailed to attack Puerto Rico.

JULY 15   As in the Civil War, the Army authorizes corps and division patches to bolster unit identity and esprit de corps.

JULY 17   At Santiago, Cuba, General Jose Toral surrenders 24,000 prisoners and 97 cannons to General William R. Shafter; the conquest of Cuba has cost the United States 243 dead and 1,445 injured. General Leonard Wood is subsequently installed as Santiago's military governor.

JULY 18   The Quartermaster Department, determined to sort through organizational chaos, creates the Division of Transportation. This department oversees all matters pertaining to the transport of men and matériel over rail and water.

JULY 21   At Guantanamo, Cuba, Major General Nelson A. Miles sails with 3,400 volunteers for Puerto Rico. He commands the 6th Massachusetts and 6th Illinois Volunteer Infantries, along with five army batteries.

JULY 25   Guanica, Puerto Rico, falls to Major General Nelson A. Miles with little resistance. This is also the last time that a senior military commander accompanies troops into combat

At Cavite, Philippines, General Wesley Merritt arrives with 11,000 men of VIII Corps. His goal is the conquest of Manila, and the Americans are counting aid from Filipino guerrilla leader Emilio Aguinaldo who, as things turn out, entertains designs of his own.

JULY 27 At Guanica, Puerto Rico, American forces are stiffened by the arrival of 3,300 volunteers under Major General James H. Wilson. General Nelson A. Miles then prepares to advance on nearby Ponce. The reinforcements remain on their vessels and proceed directly to their objective by sea.

JULY 28 General G. Garretson's forces occupy Yaucho, Puerto Rico, without resistance. He also pronounces the inhabitants free from Spanish rule, triggering a joyous, friendly reception.

JULY 29 Once ashore, General Wesley Merritt's VIII Corps passes effortlessly through guerrilla lines and assumes siege positions around the capital of Manila, Philippines.

JULY 31 On the island of Puerto Rico, Brigadier General Theodore Schwan arrives with 2,900 regular soldiers of the 11th and 19th Infantries as reinforcements.

AUGUST 1 In Washington, D.C., the War Department learns that 4,200 soldiers on Cuba have contracted illness, principally yellow fever, out of a total force of 17,000. These are subsequently ordered into quarantine at Montauk Point, Long Island. By war's end, 90 percent of American casualties result from non-combat causes, such as disease and poor sanitation.

AUGUST 3 At Arroyo, Puerto Rico, Major General Peter C. Hains arrives with 3,700 volunteers. General Nelson A. Miles, now commanding 17,000 men, begins directing a four-pronged advance against the 8,000-man Spanish garrison.

AUGUST 4 In Cuba, Colonel Theodore Roosevelt writes General William R. Shafter and declares that the American Army is riddled by malaria and is on the verge of losing all combat effectiveness. He insists that the soldiers be immediately relocated to a healthier clime.

AUGUST 7 In the Philippines, Major General Wesley Merritt issues an ultimatum to General Fermin Jaudenes y Alvarez to surrender the city of Manila, Philippines, or face attack. Jaudenes y Alvarez, for his part, demands a minimum battle of some kind to assuage Spain's honor. He also insists that the rebels not be allowed to enter the city.

AUGUST 8 General Theodore Schwan probes the outlaying defenses of San Juan, Puerto Rico, before military activity on the island ceases. Spanish resistance quickly crumbles and the island is secured.

AUGUST 9 General James H. Wilson defeats Spanish forces at Coamo, Puerto Rico, then captures several towns. American losses are six wounded to a Spanish tally of 40 killed and wounded and 170 captured.

AUGUST 13–14 At Manila, Philippines, the Spanish garrison of General Fremin Jaudenes y Alvarez resists combined forces under Commodore George Dewey and Major General Wesley Merritt, unaware that the war has ended. They capitulate the following day, surrendering 13,000 prisoners and 22,000 stands of arms. American losses are five killed and 38 wounded. The Spanish-American War cost $250 million, 5,462 American lives (overwhelmingly through disease) and an additional 1,604 wounded. The United States also acquires an overseas empire and is thrust into an unfamiliar role as a global power.

AUGUST 26 In the Philippines, Major General Wesley Merritt is ordered to Paris, France, to participate in peace negotiations. His successor, General Elwell S. Otis, proves unpopular, and officers begin requesting other assignments.

AUGUST 31 Volunteer troop strength crests at 216,029 officers and men. Once combined with the army regulars, the total military establishment stands at 275,000, the largest it has been since 1865.

OCTOBER 5 Near Leech Lake, Minnesota, Army troops wage their final pitched battle with Native Americans when a band of Chippewas opens fire on a detachment of the 3rd Infantry. A two-day siege ensues until reinforcements arrive; American losses are six dead

and 14 wounded. Private Oscar Burkhard is the last soldier of the Indian Wars to receive a Congressional Medal of Honor.

OCTOBER 7 The War Department issues new regulations, whereby khaki-colored field uniforms replace the two-tone blue woolen Army outfit dating back to the Civil War era. The lethality of modern weaponry necessitates better camouflage for all ranks.

NOVEMBER 16 In Washington, D.C., the Transport Corps is established under the aegis of the Quartermaster General of the Army. Its designated official home ports are San Francisco, California, and New York City.

DECEMBER 26 Brigadier General Marcus P. Miller's force arrives at the island of Mindoro, Philippines, but fails to negotiate a landing site with heavily armed locals; they eventually sail back to Manila.

1899

JANUARY 9 Outside Manila, Philippines, General Elwell S. Otis meets with guerrilla leader Emilio Aguinaldo to circumvent an outbreak of hostilities. However, he has no authority to grant Filipinos voting rights or any other vestiges of independence.

FEBRUARY 4 Angered that the Philippines have received immediate independence, Emilio Aguinaldo orders his guerrillas to attack American outposts along the San Juan River, Manila. No sooner does the United States acquire its first overseas possession than it finds itself embroiled in an Asian land war.

FEBRUARY 5 North of Manila, Philippines, Brigadier General Arthur

MacArthur's brigade drives Filipino guerrillas back into the brush and captures a fortified ridge overlooking the city. He sustains 44 dead and 194 wounded.

FEBRUARY 10 At Caloocan, Philippines, Brigadier General Arthur MacArthur's troops again attack Filipino guerrilla forces. The town and a railroad station with several hundred cars falls quickly, and extends American lines six miles from the center of town.

MARCH 2 In Washington, D.C., Congress authorizes an additional 35,000 two-year volunteers to suppress the Philippine insurgency. In a major change, all officers receive federal, not state, commissions.

American soldiers ride into the captured Filipino insurgent capital of Malolos in 1899. (Library of Congress)

This is a complete departure from traditional state militia practices. The Army can also recruit an additional 3,000 men to flesh out existing regiments.

MARCH 25–31   Colonel Frederick Funston leads his Kansas and Nebraska volunteers to capture the first rebel capital at Malolos, suffering 500 casualties in the process. Insurgent leader Emilio Aguinaldo eludes his antagonists and withdraws to upon Tarlac to regroup.

APRIL 15   At Catubig, Samar, Philippines, rebels attack an American outpost in overwhelming strength but are held at bay by Corporal Anthony J. Carson, 3rd Infantry, and a handful of survivors. Reinforcements rescue them two days later.

APRIL 27   Colonel Frederick Funston and the 20th Kansas Volunteer Infantry attack rebels along the Rio Grande del Pampanga, routing the defenders in a one-sided action. Funston and two of his men

receive the Congressional Medal of Honor for their victory.

APRIL 28   In Manila, Philippines, Major General Elwell S. Otis rejects rebel peace terms and insists on their unconditional surrender. The guerrillas refuse.

MAY 13   At San Miguel de Mayumo, Luzon, Philippines, a body of 300 rebels is dispersed by a 13-man contingent under Captain William E. Birkhimer, 3rd Artillery, and Corporal Frank L. Anders, 1st North Dakota Volunteer Infantry. Both win Congressional Medals of Honor.

JUNE 13   At the Zapote River, Luzon, Philippines, a 10-man detachment under Captain H. Sage, 23rd Infantry, holds its ground and repeatedly repulses a much larger guerrilla force.

JUNE 30   The Army Signal Corps purchases several electrical-driven trucks to test them as potential transport vehicles.

However, the effort is abandoned two years later when their batteries prove incapable of holding a charge for sufficient periods of time. Nascent gasoline-powered vehicles, only now beginning to make their appearance, are the key to the future.

JULY   In the Philippines, General Elwell S. Otis's VIII Corps loses 8,000 volunteers when their enlistments expire. The Army thus wages its protracted guerrilla war with only 20,000 men until reinforcements can arrive that fall.

JULY 19   On Negros Island, Philippines, Captain Bernard A. Byrne and two companies of the 6th Infantry drive bolo-wielding tribesmen from the village of Bobong.

SEPTEMBER 28   At Porac, Luzon, Philippines, the 33rd Infantry sweeps against enemy positions, driving guerrillas from their positions and taking several prisoners.

OCTOBER 19   At San Isidro, Luzon, Philippines, a small detachment of men from the 22nd Infantry defends a bridge against superior numbers of guerrillas. The soldiers hold out until the main body arrives and rescues them; Sergeant Charles W. Ray and Private Charles H. Pierce receive Congressional Medals of Honor.

NOVEMBER 11   At San Jacinto, Philippines, the 33rd Volunteer Regiment is ambushed by Filipino guerrillas, but Major Peyton C. March turns the tables on the attackers, defeating them. The Americans sustain 21 dead and wounded.

NOVEMBER 13   At Tarlac, Philippines, General Arthur MacArthur's division storms into the last capital of Filipino guerrillas. The insurgents quickly melt away into the jungle, and thereafter resort to small-scale raids and ambushes.

NOVEMBER 24   General Elwell S. Otis's troops sweep through Luzon, Philippines, and capture the renegade president of the Philippine Congress, along with his secretary of state and treasurer. Luzon, the main northern island of the Philippines, is safely in American hands, but fanatical Muslim guerrillas continue causing problems further south.

DECEMBER 4   At Vigan, Luzon, Philippines, a patrol of the 33rd Infantry is besieged by superior guerrilla forces until Lieutenant Colonel Webb Hayes arrives with his 31st Infantry to relieve them. During the fight, Private Joseph L. Epps sneaks up on a group of rebels behind a wall, surprises them, and singlehandedly captures the entire band.

DECEMBER 9   On Luzon, Philippines, Lieutenant Colonel Robert L. Howze and the 34th Volunteer Infantry score a sizable victory over Filipino insurgents during a three-hour engagement. The Americans destroy a brigade-sized unit of guerrillas.

DECEMBER 18   Near San Mateo, Philippines, Major General Henry W. Lawton, a tall individual made even more conspicuous by a white raincoat and pith helmet, is killed by a sniper. He becomes the highest-ranking fatality of the insurgency.

DECEMBER 19   Near San Mateo, Philippines, skirmishing breaks out between men of the 7th Infantry and nearby guerrillas. Sergeant Edward H. Gibson, ignoring heavy enemy fire, swims across the river and captures a canoe that is subsequently used to cross troops downstream and outflank their adversaries.

1900

JANUARY 7   At Patol Bridge, Cavite, Philippines, the 38th Volunteer Infantry routs a larger body of Filipino irregulars, killing over 100 insurgents in a two–hour battle. American casualties are eight wounded.

MARCH 4   At Tinuba, Luzon, Philippines, the 9th Infantry charges and disperses a large guerrilla force. By now, the Americans control all of southern Luzon and the Visaya Islands.

MARCH 24   At San Juan, Puerto Rico, the Army creates the Puerto Rico battalion to assist in security matters on the island.

APRIL 15–17   At Catubig, Samar, Philippines, a detachment of the 43rd Infantry is attacked and nearly overwhelmed by superior insurgent forces. The defenders manage to hold out for two days until reinforcements arrive.

MAY 6   At Hillongas, Philippines, the 43rd Infantry clashes with guerrilla forces and carries enemy positions in hand–to–hand fighting. Navy Coxswain William Thordesen and Private William P. McClay win Congressional Medals of Honor for heroism in combat.

MAY 15   In Manila, Philippines, Governor General Elwell S. Otis, who is derided by the troops as "Granny," is replaced by Brigadier General Arthur MacArthur. He has 63,000 soldiers and volunteers on hand to crush the rebellion.

MAY 26   In Washington, D.C., the War Department issues Order No. 155 which establishes the Army War College for regular commissioned officers. This is a graduate-level institution for enhancing military professionalism in the upper

ranks, and General Samuel B. Young serves as its first president.

MAY 29   At Labo, Luzon, Philippines, a company of the 45th Infantry is pinned down by enemy fire, until Private Joseph A. Nolan volunteers to run through enemy lines and summon a relief detachment. He succeeds, and his detachment is rescued.

JUNE 5   At Payapay, Philippines, a patrol from the 28th Volunteer Infantry engages guerrillas, killing 14 insurgents; the American company commander is also slain.

JUNE 6   In Washington, D.C., Congress resurrects the title of lieutenant general for Major General Nelson A. Miles, who has been the commanding general of the Army since 1895.

JUNE 19–20   In light of a mass uprising at Peking (Beijing), China, General Adna R. Chaffee assembles an expeditionary force in the Philippines consisting of the 9th and 14th Infantries, two troops of the 6th Cavalry, and a battery from the 5th Artillery. These immediately begin embarking for China.

JUNE 21   In Manila, Philippines, Brigadier General Arthur MacArthur determines to undermine guerrilla resistance by offering an amnesty to Filipino insurgents.

JULY 8   At Dagu, China, Colonel Emerson H. Liscum and the 9th Infantry arrive from the Philippines and march 40 miles to join the main allied force concentrating inland at Tianjin.

JULY 13–14   The city of Tianjin, China, falls to allied forces. Colonel Emerson H. Liscum leads the 1st Marines and 9th

Chaffee, Adna R. (1842–1914)

Adna Romanza Chaffee was born in Ashtabula, Ohio, on April 14, 1842, and in 1861, he joined the 6th U.S. Cavalry as a private. He rode with his regiment for the next 27 years. Chaffee proved himself a capable soldier and participated in 54 major battles and skirmishes. He continued in the peacetime establishment and fought under Generals George Crook and Nelson Miles in campaigns against the Comanches and Apaches in the Old Southwest. In 1888 he transferred to the 9th U.S. Cavalry, the famous "Buffalo Soldiers," as brevet lieutenant colonel and in 1897 took up teaching responsibilities at the Cavalry School at Fort Leavenworth, Kansas. When war with Spain commenced in 1898, Chaffee gained appointment as a brigadier general of volunteers and fought with distinction at El Caney, Cuba. In 1900 Secretary of War Elihu H. Wood directed him to lead American forces throughout the so-called "Boxer Rebellion" in China. Landing with troops from the Philippines, Chaffee marched overland to Beijing, helped storm the city gates on August 14, 1900, and rescued the diplomatic legation besieged there. He then advanced to major general in 1901, relieved General Arthur MacArthur as commanding general of the Philippines, and

Army brigadier general Adna Romanza Chaffee distinguished himself in the Battle of El Caney in Cuba and was later Chief of Staff of the Army. He was one of the few senior officers to rise from the rank of private. (Library of Congress)

conducted closing operations against the militant Moro rebels. Once home, Chaffee pinned on his third star as a lieutenant general and, as the first-ever U.S. Army Chief of Staff, he ventured to Europe in 1904 and observed military maneuvers there. Chaffee resigned on February 1, 1906, and settled in Los Angeles, California, to serve as president of the Board of Water Works. He died there on November 1, 1914, the only American soldier to have risen from the rank of private to lieutenant general.

Infantry in storming the walls, losing 18 dead and 22 wounded. The overall effort is directed by British brigadier general A. R. F. Dorward; this represents the first occasion that Americans have assisted a foreign military power in the field since 1779.

JULY 16   At Barrio de Talaug, Luzon, Philippines, a detachment of the 28th Volunteer Infantry attacks and drives 400 Filipino insurgents from their stronghold.

JULY 21–AUGUST 14   In China, American troops are closely engaged by Boxers (rebels) as they advance from Tientsin to Peking (Beijing). Despite heavy fighting, the force pushes onward.

JULY 26–29 At Dagu, China, General Adna R. Chaffee's American Expeditionary Force, consisting of elements from the 14th Infantry, the 6th Cavalry, and 5th Artillery, debarks and marches to join allied forces inland at Tianjin.

AUGUST 5–6 In China, Brigadier General Sir Alfred Gaselee's allied column storms Chinese defenses along the Pei-Ho River and the city of Yangtsun; victory costs the Americans seven dead and 65 wounded.

AUGUST 13–14 At Peking (Beijing), China, Major General Adna R. Chaffee's force captures the gates of the city and secures the foreign dignitaries sequestered there. He is assisted by 12,000 German, British, Austrian, Russian, and Japanese soldiers.

AUGUST 15 In Peking (Beijing), China, Lieutenant Charles P. Summerall's two-gun detachment blasts open the gates of the Forbidden City, whereupon troops rush in and dispose of remaining Boxers. Battery commander Captain Henry J. Reilly dies in action.

SEPTEMBER 14 Near Carig, Philippines, a 23-man detachment commanded by Sergeant Henry Schroeder, 16th Infantry, surprises and routs a much larger force of guerrillas, killing 36 and wounding 90.

SEPTEMBER 17 On Luzon, Philippines, the 15th Infantry and 37th Volunteers storm a fortified insurgent village while sustaining heavy casualties.

OCTOBER In the Philippines, General Elwell S. Otis leads a concerted sweep north of Manila with 12,000 soldiers. Intense bush fighting erupts, whereby hundreds of soldiers and thousands of Filipinos are killed or wounded.

OCTOBER 3 In China, General Adna R. Chaffee's American Expeditionary Force embarks and sails back to the Philippines. A force of 2,100 soldiers remains behind to guard various railroads.

OCTOBER 21–23 At Loac, Luzon, Philippines, a patrol from the 28th Volunteers is ambushed by 400 Filipino rebels and successfully defends itself. The Americans kill 75 insurgents for a loss of four wounded, and Captain George W. Biegler wins the Congressional Medal of Honor.

1901

JANUARY 31 In Cuba, Major Walter Reed and the U.S. Army Medical Corps under Major Walter Reed experiments to identify and isolate the cause of yellow fever. The culprit turns out to be mosquitoes.

FEBRUARY 2 In Washington, D.C., Congress approves the Army Reorganization and fixes the standing establishment at 30 infantry regiments, 15 cavalry regiments, 50 field batteries, and 126 companies of coastal artillery. Manpower ceilings are set at 88,619. The Army is also authorized to enroll Filipinos directly into the new Philippine Scouts, where they serve under regular Army officers.

FEBRUARY 21 In Washington, D.C., Vice President-elect Theodore Roosevelt conducts groundbreaking ceremonies for the new Army War College.

MARCH 23 At Palawan, Luzon, Macabebe scouts under Colonel Frederick Funston capture guerrilla leader Emilio Aguinaldo. The colonel, posing as a prisoner of war, was led directly to his intended quarry by the unsuspecting rebels. The Americans still confront a Muslim-based insurgency on the southern islands of Samar, Mindanao, and Jolo.

APRIL 19 The Philippine Insurrection is formally declared over; American public opinion feels that the conflict was unnecessary and that the islands should have received independence.

JULY 1 In Puerto Rico, indigenous forces are reorganized as the Provisional Regiment of Infantry and activated on the Regular Army roster.

SEPTEMBER 23 At Balangiga, Samar Island, Philippines, Company C, 9th Infantry, is overrun by Moro rebels who kill 48 Americans, while the remaining 36 escape and flee to safety. The massacre triggers a harsh retaliatory measure from General Jacob M. Smith.

NOVEMBER 27 In Washington, D.C., Secretary of War Elihu Root initiates classes at the Army War College for post-graduate training of military officers. This school arises from the Army's relatively poor performance in the war against Spain.

1902

FEBRUARY 18 At Lukban, Samar, Philippines, Army forces capture the final rebel outpost, which eliminates all organized resistance on that island.

MARCH 3 The Corps of Artillery is founded by merging the coastal, light, and heavy artillery into a single entity. At this time, this also constitutes the largest single branch in the U.S. Army.

MARCH 17 The Army Corps of Engineers receive a new full-dress uniform that is so favorably received that it stimulates new uniforms for all branches of the military by year's end.

MAY 2 At Pandapatan, Bayang, Mindanao, Colonel Frank D. Baldwin leads the 27th Infantry against Moro fortifications and captures fierce Muslim warriors at bayonet point. Baldwin suffers 10 dead and 40 wounded to some 300–400 Moro casualties.

MAY 20 In Cuba, military government ends as Governor General Leonard Wood withdraws the last of his troops once President Tomas Estrada Palma is sworn into power. Wood previously proved instrumental in modernizing Cuban schools and establishing a new constitution and other laws.

JULY 4 In Washington, D.C., President Theodore Roosevelt declares the Philippine insurgency officially over. In three years of fighting, it consumed the lives of 4,000 Americans and 20,000 Filipinos in 2,811 recorded actions. However, the southern island of Mindanao still seethes with Muslim unrest for independence.

JULY 14 In Washington, D.C., the War Department introduces new, russet-colored footwear, ushering in the age of the "Brown shoe" army.

1903

JANUARY 21   In Washington, D.C., Congress passes the Dick Act to completely overhaul the Militia Act of 1792. Hereafter, the new National Guard receives the same training, discipline, and weapons of the regular establishment.

FEBRUARY 14   In Washington, D.C., Congress authorizes creation of a General Staff Corps. This is undertaken at the urging of Secretary of War Elihu Root to impose greater centralization of the Army along German lines, and to promote better relations between the top military ranks and the civilian secretary of war.

APRIL 7   At Bacolod, Philippines, Captain John J. Pershing attacks Moro positions with a massive artillery bombardment, then sweeps in at bayonet point. The defenders flee, but Pershing allows the Moros to escape and describe the power of the Americans to fellow rebels.

JUNE 11   At West Point, New York, Secretary of War Elihu Root presents 64 diplomas to the graduating class of the U.S. Military Academy; Lieutenant Douglas MacArthur graduates at the head of his class.

JUNE 23   The Army adopts the Springfield M-1903 rifle as its first semiautomatic infantry weapon. This durable and highly accurate .30-caliber weapon remains in service up through the beginning of World War II.

AUGUST 8   Lieutenant General Nelson A. Miles, Commanding General of the Army, retires from active service after 42 years in the field.

AUGUST 15   The Division of Military Information, a precursor to the Intelligence Division, transfers from the Adjutant General's Office to the Office of the Chief of Staff.

AUGUST 16   In Washington, D.C., Lieutenant General Samuel B. M. Young becomes the Army's first Chief of Staff and serves only six months in this capacity. The new general staff he heads is tasked with organizing, administering, and equipping the field army, collecting, analyzing, and disseminating military intelligence, and facilitating war planning, military education, and coastal defense. It is inspired by the highly successful German model.

1904

JANUARY 9   In Washington, D.C., Major General Adna R. Chaffee becomes the second Army Chief of Staff, replacing General Samuel B. M. Young.

APRIL 24   In Washington, D.C., Congress introduces a new Medal of Honor policy; hereafter, all claims are to be accompanied by official documents specifying the act for which the medal is merited.

JUNE 27   In Washington, D.C., the War Department directs seven Army Service Schools at Fort Leavenworth, Kansas, to be consolidated into a single entity. This is done upon the urging of Colonel Arthur L. Wagner, an influential proponent of military education.

1905

JANUARY 11   In Washington, D.C., Congress authorizes the Certificate of Merit medal for Army privates who have distinguished themselves in combat since 1854.

JANUARY 12   In Washington, D.C., the War Department issues General Order No. 5, authorizing service medals for the China and Philippine campaigns.

MAY 1–24   On Jolo Island, Philippines, the Muslim Moros revolt against American attempts to end traditional practices such as slavery and tribal feuding. Three campaigns are required to quell their fanatical resistance.

MAY 13   In Brooklyn, New York, Hiram Cronk, the oldest surviving veteran of the War of 1812, dies at the age of 105.

AUGUST 25   In Washington, D.C., Secretary of War Elihu Root authorizes the new Army Signal Corps School at Fort Leavenworth. This is for the benefit of junior officers and includes courses in such pioneering fields as photography, electricity, and acoustics.

1906

MARCH 6–8   At Bad-Dajo, Jolo Island, Philippines, Lieutenant Gordon Johnson's 6th Infantry attacks and destroys a Moro fort, routing the defenders. This is one of the final major actions of the Philippine Insurrection.

APRIL 18   At San Francisco, California, Brigadier General Frederick Funston organizes the California National Guard and his own 22nd Infantry and 6th Cavalry as a relief force, following the destructive earthquake there.

JUNE 25   In Washington, D.C., Congress expands the U.S. Army Ordnance Corps by adding a brigadier general. The Picatinny Arsenal in Dover, New Jersey, also opens the Army's first gunpowder-production facility.

JULY 25   On Samar Island, Philippines, African American soldiers of the 25th Infantry, assisted by the Philippine Constabulary, defeat sword-wielding Pulahane tribesmen.

AUGUST 3   In Washington, D.C., President Theodore Roosevelt orders the "Army of Cuban Occupation" sent to the island to restore order during a period of political unrest. This consists of five infantry regiments, two cavalry regiments, and several artillery batteries; they remain in place until February 1, 1909.

AUGUST 13–14   In Brownsville, Texas, civilians accuse men from the African American 25th Infantry of nighttime gunfire near the town. The three companies present are arrested, court-martialed, and dismissed from the service.

SEPTEMBER 20   At the behest of President Theodore Roosevelt, Captain John J. Pershing is promoted to brigadier general over the heads of 862 officers enjoying more seniority.

OCTOBER 6   At Havana, Cuba, Brigadier General Frederick Funston arrives with advanced elements of a 6,000–man occupation force. His task is made easier after resistance from rebels fails to materialize.

DECEMBER 30   In Washington, D.C., the War Department orders all soldiers to be issued metal identification with individual serial numbers, the infamous "dog tags."

1907

JANUARY 15   President Theodore Roosevelt orders 167 African American soldiers discharged after three of their number were accused of engaging in a shooting spree in Brownsville, Texas. The president feels the soldiers are maintaining a conspiracy of silence to protect the accused.

JANUARY 25   The Coastal and Field Artillery are separated and reconstituted as individual branches of service.

FEBRUARY   In Washington, D.C., President Theodore Roosevelt selects Lieutenant George Goethals, Corps of Engineers, to direct the Panama Canal project. He is assisted by Colonel William C. Gorgas of the Medical Department, who labors to eliminate yellow fever from the region.

MARCH 2   In Washington, D.C., Congress abolishes the rank of lieutenant general, but reconstitutes the Adjutant General's Department.

1908

MARCH 1   In another sign of growing military professionalism, the new Quartermaster School is established at Philadelphia, Pennsylvania.

APRIL 23   In Washington, D.C., Congress establishes the Army Medical Reserve Corps to provide a steady pool of medically trained personnel as needed.

MAY 11   In Washington, D.C., Congress authorizes a military pay increase for the

first time since 1876; the base pay of privates is $15.00 per month, while corporals receive $21.00, and sergeants $45.00.

MAY 14   The Army adopts new fitness regulations, requiring all infantry officers to be capable of riding horseback 30 miles a day for three days, Coast Artillery officers must also walk 50 miles in three days, and all regimental officers must pass an annual physical exam.

1909

MARCH 3   In Washington, D.C., Congress orders a complete investigation of the August 1906 shooting "incident" at

Brownsville, Texas. Most of the dismissed African American soldiers are reinstated and allowed to return to the 25th Infantry.

JUNE 11 At West Point, New York, George S. Patton is among the 103 cadets who graduate from the U.S. Military Academy.

1910

APRIL 22 In Washington, D.C., General Leonard Wood gains appointment as the new Army Chief of Staff. A vocal proponent of military preparedness, he is a major force behind the creation of four-week "citizen camps" to impart basic military skills upon businessmen and other professionals.

1911

JANUARY 1 In another sign of growing professionalism among the officer class, *The Field Artillery Journal* begins publication.

FEBRUARY 14 The Army adopts the iconic M1911 Colt .45 automatic pistol. This is a clip-fed weapon firing with tremendous stopping power, and remains in service over half a century.

MARCH 3 In Washington, D.C., Congress authorizes the U.S. Army Dental Corps as a division of the Army Medical Service.

MARCH 7 President William H. Taft grows concerned over rising instability in Mexico and orders 20,000 Army troops deployed along the Southern border.

JUNE 11 The Army founds the School of Fire at Fort Sill, Oklahoma, and in 1919 it is redesignated the Field Artillery School.

JUNE 24 Once the regime of Mexican dictator Porfiro Diaz is overthrown, President William Howard Taft orders the 20,000 American troops lining the southwestern border withdrawn.

SEPTEMBER 8 The Army authorizes a new campaign hat, which gains renown as the "Montana Peak" or "Smokey the Bear" hat. It is usually associated with drill instructors to present times.

1912

JANUARY 14 On Jolo Island, Philippines, Captain E. G. Peyton's cavalry, assisted by Philippine Scouts, captures several bands of renegade Moros for a loss of two wounded.

JANUARY 22 Tianjin, China, is occupied by Army troops to protect American lives and property, as the overthrow of the Manchu dynasty continues and the Republic of China is born.

FEBRUARY Aged General Fred C. Ainsworth, Adjutant General of the Army, composes an insulting memo to Army Chief of Staff Leonard Wood concerning the pace of military reforms. Secretary of War Henry Lewis Stimson relieves Ainsworth, but the elderly officer is retired rather than court-martialed.

JUNE 12 The so-called "Munson Last," designed by Colonel Edward L. Munson, Medical Corps, is adopted by the Army as its standard footgear.

AUGUST 24–26 In Washington, D.C., Congress creates the Quartermaster Corps by consolidating the Quartermaster, Pay, and Subsistence Departments.

1913

JUNE 13–15 At Bud Bagsak, Jolo Island, Philippines, Brigadier General John J. Pershing captures the final Moro stronghold and crushes their rebellion at the cost of 27 casualties. Despite his rank, Pershing distinguishes himself under fire.

1914

JANUARY 1 Administration of Moro Province, Mindanao, Philippines, is turned over to civil authorities by the Army.

APRIL 28 In Washington, D.C., President Woodrow Wilson orders Army troops across the Mexican border to restore order at Veracruz, Mexico, after American sailors have been seized.

APRIL 30 At Veracruz, Mexico Brigadier General Frederick Funston arrives with an infantry brigade and relieves Marines and naval forces already there.

MAY 2 At Veracruz, Mexico, Brigadier General Frederick Funston takes charge of all American forces present, 3,607 soldiers and 3,446 Marines.

MAY 5–6 In Mexico, Captain Douglas MacArthur leads a nighttime reconnaissance through the lines outside Veracruz and returns with three captured locomotives.

JUNE 28 World War I commences in Europe, following the assassination of Archduke Franz Ferdinand in Sarajevo.

AUGUST 3 In Panama, Colonel George W. Goethals completes construction work on the Panama Canal, six months ahead of schedule. His task was facilitated by the elimination of malaria and yellow fever by Colonel William C. Gorgas.

OCTOBER The 9th and 10th Cavalries are dispatched to Naco, Mexico, after that town is besieged by revolutionaries under Pancho Villa, whose wild firing kills one American soldier and injures 18.

NOVEMBER 23 The United States disengages itself from Mexico by withdrawing Brigadier General Frederick Funston's force from Veracruz. President Woodrow Wilson instructs Funston not hand power over to any particular faction within the city.

1915

JANUARY 7 At Naco, Mexico, Major General Hugh Scott negotiates with guerrilla leader Pancho Villa in an attempt to end fighting along the border.

MARCH 1 In Washington, D.C., Captain George Van Horn Moseley, of the Army General Staff's War College Division, submits a plan for universal military training to the Senate's Military Committee. No action is taken.

AUGUST 16–17 Men of the 27th Infantry are rushed into Texas City, Texas, when that town is suddenly inundated by floodwaters brought on by a sudden storm.

1916

FEBRUARY 24 Acting Secretary of War Hugh Scott asks the War College Division if any comprehensive war plans exist for dealing with Germany. He is informed that none exist.

MARCH 9 At Colombus, New Mexico, General Francisco "Pancho" Villa attacks the town and kills 18 Americans before being rebuffed by the 13th Cavalry under Colonel H. J. Slocum. The guerrillas suffer 100 casualties during the subsequent pursuit back to Mexico.

MARCH 15 President Woodrow Wilson orders Brigadier General John J. Pershing to lead 12,000 American troops on a punitive expedition into Mexico to apprehend the guerrilla Francisco "Pancho" Villa. They begin fanning out across the countryside, but are ordered to proceed no further south than Chihuahua.

MARCH 28–29 After a 17-hour forced march, the 7th Cavalry surprises a force of 500 Mexican guerrillas at Guerrero, Mexico, killing 40 and driving off the rest.

APRIL 8 In northern Mexico, Brigadier General John J. Pershing pushes south toward Colonia Dublan, Mexico, in his search for Mexican guerrillas. Being denied the use of national railroads, he employs motor-transport companies to ensure a steady flow of supplies and ammunition. This is the first time that the Army relies on gasoline-powered trucks in the field.

APRIL 12 At Santa Cruz de Villegas (Parral), Mexico, the 13th Cavalry under Major Frank Tompkins engages Mexican irregulars; American losses are three dead and seven wounded to an estimated 40 Mexican casualties.

MAY 5 At Ojos Azules, Mexico, Apache Scouts under Major Robert Le Howze disperse a larger force of guerrillas, killing 60 without loss; Howze wins the Congressional Medal of Honor.

MAY 9 President Venustiano Carranza orders all American forces inside his country to leave immediately, just as President Woodrow Wilson orders additional National Guard troops deployed along the U.S./Mexican border.

MAY 22 In southwestern Texas, "Pancho" Villa's guerrillas slip across the American border and attack Glen Springs, killing three soldiers and a child. He is determined to provoke a war between the United States and Mexico at any cost.

JUNE 3 In Washington, D.C., Congress passes the National Defense Act which raises personnel levels of the Army from 175,000 to 225,000, and that of the National Guard to 2.4 million; office training courses (ROTC) are also established on many college campuses.

JUNE 21 At Carrizal, Mexico, the 10th Cavalry engages Mexican regulars and

sustains 10 killed, 10 wounded, and 23 captured. Mexican casualties total 74 dead, including General Felix U. Gomez.

JUNE 25 In Mexico City, President Venustaino Carranza seeks to defuse mounting tensions with the United States by releasing 17 captured African Americans taken at Carrizal.

AUGUST 31 Monthly Returns indicate that 111,954 men of the National Guardsmen are deployed along the U.S./Mexican border. These also employ over 60,000 horses and mules.

1917

JANUARY 28 In Washington, D.C., President Woodrow Wilson orders General John J. Pershing to withdraw from Mexico, ending, in effect, the futile pursuit of Francisco "Pancho" Villa. Pershing presently deploys 11,500 men in the vicinity of Colonia Dublan, supported by 170 trucks.

JANUARY 31 In Berlin, the German government resumes unrestricted warfare against neutral shipping, an act placing the United States on the path to war.

FEBRUARY 5 In Mexico, General Frederick Funston withdraws the final Army detachment back to American territory, officially concluding the Punitive Expedition.

APRIL 6 In Washington, D.C., President Woodrow Wilson requests a declaration of war from Congress against the Central Powers. The Army presently numbers around 200,000 men, lacks tanks or armored vehicles, has no capacity to produce modern artillery, and possesses only a handful of obsolete aircraft.

MAY 18 In Washington, D.C., President Woodrow Wilson signs the Selective Service Act. Henceforth, all men between 21 and 30 are eligible to be called to the colors, commencing June 5, 1917. This is the first military conscription since 1863, and ultimately inducts 3 million men out of 24 million registered.

MAY 26 Major General John J. "Black Jack" Pershing is appointed commanding officer of the new American Expeditionary Force (AEF) slated for deployment in France. He is specifically ordered to keep the AEF unified as a fighting force and not parceled out in detachments to bolster the allies.

MAY 29 At New York City, Major General John J. Pershing sails with his staff on the SS *Baltic,* while the American Expeditionary Force (AEF) is being organized from scratch.

JUNE 5 By this date, 10 million young American men between the ages of

21 and 30 have registered for military service, although only 2.8 million are actually inducted into uniform.

JUNE 13 Major General John J. Pershing and his entourage arrive at Pas-de-Calais, France, before moving onto Paris, future headquarters of the American Expeditionary Force (AEF).

JUNE 14 Major General John J. Pershing arrives in Paris, France, with the advanced detachment of his American Expeditionary Force (AEF). His first task is to establish an extensive series of training camps for his anticipated 1.1 million soldiers.

JUNE 23 The War Department authorizes the U.S. Army Ambulance Service for direct attachment to French combat divisions. This releases thousands of French soldiers for service at the battlefront.

JUNE 26 At St. Nazaire, France, the 1st Infantry Division under Major General William L. Sibert arrives—the first of over one million troops to follow.

General John J. Pershing arrives at the Paris railroad station in June 1917. Pershing commanded a force of one million U.S. soldiers, insisting that they remain a "distinct and separate component" of the campaign on the Western Front. Although inexperienced, the sheer number of U.S. soldiers overwhelmed the already-weary German troops, leading to the Armistice on November 11, 1918. The success of the Pershing expedition made the general a national hero upon his return to the United States in 1919. (Library of Congress)

JULY 4 In Paris, France, the 1st Infantry Division parades down the Champs Elysee before marching off to various training grounds. Colonel Charles E. Stanton, delivering a speech at the grave site of the Marquis de Lafayette, boldly declares, "Lafayette, nous voici!" (Lafayette, we are here!)

JULY 14 At Arras, France, Lieutenant Louis J. Genella, serving alongside British forces with the Medical Corps, is the first American soldier wounded in Europe.

JULY 16 At Le Valdahon, France, Brigadier General Peyton C. March assembles the 1st Artillery Brigade and commences an intensive training routine.

JULY 19 The Signal Corps is instructed to make an extensive photographic record of combat operations; it ultimately takes 30,000 still pictures and shoots 350,000 feet of motion picture film. It also maintains 15,000 carrier pigeons to be used as messengers.

AUGUST 14 At Camp Mills, New York, the 42nd Division—a National Guard formation—begins organizing under General William A. Mann. His chief of staff is Colonel Douglas MacArthur. Being composed of units from 26 states, it acquires the nickname "Rainbow Division."

SEPTEMBER 1 At Chaumont, France, Major General John J. Pershing transfers his AEF field headquarters to the French army's old Damremont caserne.

SEPTEMBER 4 At Dannes-Camiers, France, four members of the U.S. Base Hospital become the first American servicemen killed in action after German airplanes bomb their facility.

SEPTEMBER 23 In Washington, D.C., Major General Tasker H. Bliss receives his fourth star and replaces Major General Hugh L. Scott as Army Chief of Staff.

OCTOBER 2 In France, Major General Peyton C. March is appointed as commander of all AEF artillery.

OCTOBER 6 In France, General John J. Pershing is promoted to full general (four stars), after the American Expeditionary Force (AEF) exceeds 90,000 soldiers and is approaching combat readiness.

OCTOBER 9 In England, Major General George T. Bartlett is appointed commander of all American forces stationed on that island.

OCTOBER 15 At Des Moines, Iowa, the initial batch of African American officers is commissioned, the first of 1,300 so honored. Ultimately, 400,000 blacks serve in the ranks and perform well when allowed to fight.

OCTOBER 21 The 1st Division assumes advanced positions in the vicinity of Luneville (Nancy), France, and is attached to a seasoned French division in line.

OCTOBER 23 Near Sommervillier, Lorraine, Sergeant Alex Arch, 6th Field Artillery, fires the first American artillery shells of the war at German lines.

OCTOBER 26 At Borumont, France, the 2nd Division organizes under Major General Omar Bundy; it consists of a brigade of Army soldiers and another of U.S. Marines.

OCTOBER 31 At Neufchateau, France, the 26th ("Yankee") Division assembles

under General Clarence Edwards. It boasts 28,000 men—roughly twice the strength of worn-out British, French, or German divisions.

NOVEMBER 2–3 At Bathelemont, along the Rhine-Marne Canal, 3 American soldiers from Company F, 16th Infantry, 1st Division, die in a nighttime German trench raid, while an additional 5 are wounded and 12 captured.

NOVEMBER 20–DECEMBER 4 In the Cambrai sector, the 11th, 12th, and 14th Engineers accompany a large British offensive; this is the first offensive involving American troops, and "Cambrai" becomes the first campaign streamer of the war.

NOVEMBER 28 At Langres, France, the General Staff College is founded, for the benefit of field grade officers. The First Army Tank School also arises there under Major George S. Patton.

DECEMBER 12 At Hoboken, New Jersey, the African American 93rd Division begins embarking on ships for the Western Front. However, black soldiers remain a low priority, and most are outfitted with equipment provided by France.

DECEMBER 14 In France, Major General Robert Lee Bullard assumes command of the 1st Infantry Division.

DECEMBER 31 By this date American military strength along the Western Front is 174,664 officers and men, although few of the troops have undergone real combat experience.

1918

JANUARY 9 At Atacosa Canyon, Arizona, soldiers from the 10th Cavalry trade shots with a small band of Yaqui Apaches from

Mexico. No casualties result, and the transgressors are arrested and jailed for 30 days.

JANUARY 15 At Neufchateau, France, the I Corps forms, being the first unit of its size to reach operational status.

JANUARY 20 Major General Hunter S. Liggett is ordered to take command of the new I Corps. The raw Americans are girding themselves for a more active combat role.

JANUARY 26 In France, Brigadier General Samuel D. Rockenbach assumes command of the U.S. Army Tank Corps. Tanks are in their mechanical infancy, and the machines operated by the Americans are obtained from the French.

FEBRUARY 8 General John J. Pershing authorizes a service newspaper named *Stars and Stripes* to be published by and for the troops weekly; 71 issues are issued from Paris before the war ends.

FEBRUARY 16 American soldiers on leave in Aix-les-Bains are serenaded by a band from the African American 369th Infantry, the famous "Harlem Hellfighters."

MARCH 12 At Givry-en-Argonne, France, the African American 369th Infantry under Colonel William Hayward is assigned to the French 16th Division and fights alongside of them. They acquire a distinguished record under fire.

MARCH 16 At Chateauvillain, France, the 3rd Division under Major General Joseph T. Dickman arrives at the 9th Training Area.

MARCH 21 At this date, the American Expeditionary Force boasts 300,000 troops preparing for action.

MARCH 21–APRIL 6 Field Marshal Paul von Hindenberg unleashes his famous "Kaiserschlact" across the Western front to crush the allied powers. Elements of the 6th Engineers, attached to British units

near Peronne, France, hold their position at Warfusee-Abancourt until relieved, losing 78 men, including 25 killed.

MARCH 23 In the Pas-de-Calais Region, France, U.S. Army II Corps assembles and is deployed within the British 1st Army Area. Because no commanding general has been assigned, the troops continue with their training activities.

APRIL 3 American forces along the Ansauville sector near St. Mihiel have sustained 549 casualties to date, principally from German gas attacks and trench raids.

APRIL 10 Troops from the 32nd Division are utilized as a replacement source for the 41st Division, which then advances into the combat zone.

APRIL 14 Marshal Ferdinand Foch, supreme allied commander, requests President Woodrow Wilson to transfer more troops to the Western Front as soon as possible. General John J. Pershing, however, is adamant that the American Expeditionary Force not be parceled out to plug gaps in allied lines.

APRIL 20–21 At St. Mihiel, France, the 26th Division receives its baptism of fire when a German attack secures the village of Seicheprey. This is retaken by a counterattack that same afternoon; then the Americans also advance into the adjoining woods, driving the Germans back. They suffer 634 casualties and 136 prisoners; the Germans leave 160 dead behind.

MAY 3–4 At Villers-Tournelles, France, German mustard gas shells surprise the 18th Infantry, inflicting 900 casualties.

MAY 28 At Cantigny, France, General Robert Lee Bullard's 1st Division launches a determined attack against German positions. The enthusiastic

Americans drive the German 82nd Reserve Division from the town, then hold it against repeated counterattacks. For a cost of 1,067 casualties, the "Doughboys" inflict 1,600 on the Germans, including 225 captured.

MAY 30 As the German offensive rumbles toward the Marne River, the 3rd Division is brought up by rail to help defend Chateau-Thierry. The 2nd Division also deploys astride the Paris-Metz road, directly in the German line of advance.

MAY 31–JUNE 5 Along the Marne River, France, the 3rd Division successfully repels German attacks along its sector and gains the nickname "Rock of the Marne."

JUNE 3–4 At Chateau-Thierry, France, the 2nd Division is instrumental in halting the German drive toward Paris. Losses are 187 dead and 636 wounded.

JUNE 15 In the Pas-de-Calais region, France, Major General George W. Read assumes command of the II Corps and prepares to support the British Army's Somme offensive.

JUNE 16–17 At Juarez, Mexico, the 24th Infantry and the 5th and 7th Cavalries suddenly storm across the Mexican border, attacking irregulars under Francisco "Pancho" Villa; several hundred are killed.

JULY 1 Near Chateau-Thierry, France, units of the 2nd Division storm into Vaux, after prolonged bombardment. This textbook attack only costs the Americans 46 lives, a sharp contrast to the costly frontal assault tactics employed by Marines elsewhere.

JULY 4 In France, General John J. Pershing declares American troop strength at over one million men; the Americans commit 19 divisions into combat fray, each twice the size of their veteran but depleted German counterparts.

At Hamel, France, Corporal Thomas A. Pope, 131st (Illinois) Infantry, distinguishes himself by singlehandedly wiping out a German machine gun nest; he wins the first Congressional Medal of Honor of this conflict.

JULY 13 At Meaux, France, Major General Robert Lee Bullard is appointed commander of the III Corps, and begins moving troops west of Soissons to support the French 10th Army.

JULY 15–18 In the vicinity of Reims, France, eight American divisions (85,000 troops) engage in the Second Battle of the Marne, which finally blunts the waning German offensive. The 3rd and 28th Divisions distinguish themselves in combat and seal off several breeches before enemy troops can pour through. By now over one million American troops are present in Europe and are beginning to impact military events.

JULY 17 In Washington, D.C., President Woodrow Wilson agrees to deploy American forces in Russia, to protect military stores and evacuate the Czech Legion as it flees from Bolshevik forces. The 85th Division and a like number of Japanese deploy in Siberia to deter the revolutionaries.

JULY 18–AUGUST 2 Along the Aisne-Marne Salient, France, the 4th and 26th Divisions support a large French offensive by capturing several strategic positions and forcing a gradual German withdrawal in that sector.

JULY 19–31 During the ongoing Aisne-Marne counteroffensive, the 1st and 2nd Divisions overpower German reinforcements and seize land west of the Soissons/Chateau-Thierry highway. The

4th and 26th Divisions also advance, capturing 3,500 prisoners and 68 cannons. Nine American divisions, totaling 310,000 men, are committed to battle and sustain 67,000 casualties.

JULY 21   Bersy-le-Sec, France, falls to the 1st Division within three miles of Soissons. The exhausted troops, having lost nearly half their number, halt to await French reinforcements.

JULY 24   At Melun, France, an allied conference orders General John J. Pershing to reduce the German-held salient near St. Mihiel, thereby freeing up the railroad network northeast of Paris. This becomes the first purely American offensive of the war.

JULY 28–AUGUST 5   Along the Somme River, France, allied forces, including 54,000 Americans, begin probing the weakened German salient. The 42nd "Rainbow" Division then crosses the Ourcq River, seizes its objectives, and is relieved by the 4th Division. The 32nd Division also captures Fismes on the south bank of the Vesle. Within a month of heavy fighting, the Aisne-Marne Salient is eliminated.

AUGUST 7   In Washington, D.C., Chief of Staff General Peyton C. March harmonizes relations between the regular Army, the National Guard, and the wartime National Army by consolidating all these elements into what he calls "one army."

AUGUST 10   At Chaumont, France, General John J. Pershing orders his headquarters transferred to Neufchateau to be closer to the front. A relatively unknown Colonel George C. Marshall is also installed as his chief of staff.

AUGUST 15   The 27th and 31st Infantries land at Vladivostok, Russia, to guard the Trans-Siberian railroad and allow the

Czech Legion to escape from the Bolsheviks. They are also there to dissuade Japan from attempting to dominate Russia's Far Eastern Maritimes.

AUGUST 17   In France, 85,000 American troops join French forces in attacking north of the Soissons-Reims line and begin grinding toward the Belgian border.

AUGUST 18   In Lorraine, France, Major General Joseph T. Dickman departs the 3rd Division to command the IV Corps, comprised of the 1st, 82nd, and 90th Divisions.

AUGUST 21   Brigadier General Samuel D. Rockenbach, Chief of the Tank Corps, declares the 326th, 327th, 344th, and 354th Tank Battalions ready for combat in the St. Mihiel offensive.

SEPTEMBER 1   At Vladivostok, Russia, Major General William S. Graves assumes command of 4,500 American troops deployed in Siberia. He is to assist the evacuation of Czech soldiers, and not get embroiled in the Russian civil war.

SEPTEMBER 3–4   After a month of fighting, the 28th and 77th Divisions evict German forces from the Aisne-Marne salient, and the latter abandons the Vesle River region.

SEPTEMBER 4   A force of 4,500 American soldiers are rerouted by the British from Archangel to Murmansk, to protect railroad and supply dumps against Bolsheviks. They remain there over the next nine months.

SEPTEMBER 7   In the Ussuri Valley, Siberia, the 27th Infantry assists Japanese troops to clear the region of Bolshevik troops. The city of Habarovsk falls soon after, and the flags of both nations fly side by side at the railroad station.

SEPTEMBER 12–16 At the St. Mihiel salient south of Verdun, France, General John J. Pershing directs the First Army of 550,000 men to storm Germany positions. This is America's first independent offensive, which crushes all resistance and takes 15,000 prisoners, 443 guns, and 7,000 casualties after four days of intense combat. Pershing seeks to capture Metz and maintain the initiative, but Marshal Ferdinand Foch redirects him toward the Meuse-Argonne sector, east of Verdun.

SEPTEMBER 13 At Vieville-sous-les-Cotes, France, Captain Ernest N. Harmon's 2nd Cavalry conducts the AEF's only mounted charge by breaking up a German withdrawal in St. Mihiel. The U.S. Army Tank Corps, spearheaded by the 304th Tank Brigade under Major George S. Patton, also receives its baptism under fire, despite thick mud and mechanical failures.

SEPTEMBER 21 Pressing forward, the First Army under General John J. Pershing relocates its headquarters to Souilly, France. Fourteen Choctaw code talkers are also involved in Army communication throughout the Meuse-Argonne Campaign. The French are so impressed at their ability to baffle German intelligence that they are inducted as Chevaliers de l'Orde National du Mérite.

SEPTEMBER 26 Along the Meuse-Argonne front, France, General John J. Pershing's First Army unleashes 896,000 Americans attack along a 200-mile front. German resistance is stubborn, but the defenders are slowly forced back by sheer numbers. This conflict represents the largest number of Americans committed to a single engagement until 1944.

SEPTEMBER 28–30 The African American 370th Infantry, attached to the French XXX Corps, fights with distinction in the lines between Vauxaillon and Canal de l'Oise à l'Aisne.

OCTOBER 2–6 In the Charlevaux Valley, France, Major Charles W. Whittelsey advances with the 307th and 308th Infantry Regiments and takes his objectives, but is surrounded by Germans and isolated. The Americans cling to their position tenaciously over five days, as Whittelsey uses the carrier pigeon Cher Ami to alert headquarters of his plight. By the time "Lost Battalion" is rescued, only 194 men remain; Whittelsey receives a Congressional Medal of Honor.

OCTOBER 4–12 General John J. Pershing's First Army rumbles forward across the Meuse-Argonne line, sweeping the region clear of German defenders. The I, III, and V Corps perform superbly, pausing only on October 12 to rest and regroup. Beforehand, they make several lodgments in Germany's last-ditch "Hindenberg Line."

OCTOBER 8 At Chatel Chehery, Argonne Forest, France, Corporal Alvin York singlehandedly captures a 132-man German patrol. Previously, York stole around the enemy positions and, with superb marksmanship, shot down two dozen Germans before they capitulated. He becomes the war's iconic hero and wins a Congressional Medal of Honor.

OCTOBER 14–16 On the east bank of the Meuse River, the 29th and 33rd Divisions advance in concert with French forces. Men of the 42nd Division also storm the town of Cote de Chatillon, gaining another lodgement on the Hindenberg Line.

OCTOBER 16 In France, Major General Hunter Liggett assumes tactical control over the First Army, while General John J. Pershing advances to command the

York, Alvin (1887–1964)

Alvin York was born in Pall Mall, Tennessee, on December 13, 1887, one of 11 children from a poverty-stricken family. Forced to hunt and provide food at an early age, he became a superb marksman. York was also much given to drinking, gambling, and fighting until 1911, when he underwent a religious conversion and joined the Church of Christ and Christian Union. As a committed pacifist, York applied for conscientious objector status in 1917, which was denied by the draft board, and he was inducted into the U.S. Army. He made clear to superiors his unease about fighting in combat. And his battalion commander, Major George E. Buxton, a Bible scholar, debated chapter and verse with him for three days as to war and the moral obligations it posed to men of conscience. York agonized but sided with his superior and decided to fight. He arrived in France as a corporal and part of G Company, 328th U.S. Infantry, 82nd Division, and fought in the Argonne Forest. On October 8, 1918, York led 17 men that captured a small enemy detachment, then came under fire from several emplacements. York immediately crept forward to engage the enemy and single-handedly shot down 17 enemy gunners. When the Germans realized their opponent was a single American, seven soldiers rushed him until York

Originally a conscientious objector, the humble and pious Alvin York was the most famous American doughboy (soldier) of World War I. His exploits as a marksman were legendary and were further popularized by a noted 1940 movie. But true to his religious leanings, York shunned wealth and fame, led a life of modesty, and died in obscurity. (Library of Congress)

fired his pistol and expertly shot them down. A captive German major pleaded with him to stop; then York and his men rounded up 132 prisoners and marched them back to battalion headquarters. General John J. Pershing subsequently lauded York as "the greatest civilian soldier of the war." Consequently he received a Congressional Medal of Honor and 50 other decorations, but York returned to Tennessee and lived the rest of his life in semi-seclusion. He allowed his biography to be published in 1928 and also advised the film *Sergeant York* (1940), starring Gary Cooper, but continually gave away any money accruing from his celebrity. York died in near-poverty at Nashville on December 2, 1964, a modest American hero.

new American Group of Armies. This is in addition to serving as commander in chief of the AEF.

OCTOBER 20 At Romagne, France, new 155mm cannons of the 11th Artillery Regiment commence firing in support of the 89th Division; these are the

heaviest field pieces deployed in Europe by the AEF.

OCTOBER 22–31 In the Meuse–Argonne sector, France, the First Army continues driving eastward, with the 3rd Division capturing Bois de Foret, and the 89th Division capturing Romagne Heights.

General John J. Pershing keeps attacking and determines to maintain the strategic initiative.

OCTOBER 27   In Italy, the 332rd (Ohio) Infantry becomes the only American combat formation deployed on the Italian Front, and captures several bridgeheads across the Piave River.

OCTOBER 28–NOVEMBER 4   On the Italian front, the 332nd Infantry pursues Austrian troops north as far as the Tagliamento River before halting.

NOVEMBER 1   In France, General John J. Pershing orders a breakthrough on the Meuse-Argonne front, with a view toward seizing Sedan. The First Army seizes Barricourt Heights and advances into the heavily defended Hindenberg Line, forcing the Germans to fall back from the Meuse line.

NOVEMBER 4   In France, III Corps throws bridges across the Meuse River and begins pushing toward Montmedy. Beaufort falls soon after, and the German army starts retreating from the Meuse region.

NOVEMBER 5   At Sedan, France, the I Corps storms a communications center in the heart of the city, while elements of the V Corps take the high ground to its front. General John J. Pershing orders Major General William Lee Bullard's Second Army to advance between the Moselle River and Etang de Lachaussee.

NOVEMBER 5–8   At Sedan, France, General John J. Pershing allows the Fourth French Army the honor of regaining their city. Meanwhile, the First Army continues pressing toward Longwy and Briey.

NOVEMBER 10   In France, the First Army crosses the Meuse River and approaches the city of Verdun, while gunners of Battery E, 11th Field Artillery, fire the final artillery salvo of the war at Beaufort, France. To date, the First Army has sustained 26,000 dead and 95,000 wounded in exchange for 100,000 German casualties, 25,000 prisoners, and 874 guns captured.

NOVEMBER 11   The Armistice is signed at Compiegne, France, ending World War I. The American Expeditionary Force (AEF) loses 130,174 dead (50,604 in combat and the rest by disease) and 203,460 wounded. The American war effort deploys 1,078,222 combat men in Europe, which decisively tips the military balance in favor of the Allies.

DECEMBER 1   Major General Joseph T. Dickman's Third Army begins military occupation duties in Germany, and is responsible for the region between Luxembourg and the Rhine River near Coblenz.

DECEMBER 8   In Coblenz, Germany, the Third Army forms a bridgehead across the Rhine River and crosses over. The American zone of occupation is 35 kilometers wide and 30 kilometers deep.

1919

JANUARY 19   At Shenkhursk, northern Russia, American forces repel a major attack by Bolsheviks.

MARCH 15   At Cirque de Paris, France, the American Legion is formed as the nation's premier veteran's organization.

The first meeting is attended by nearly 1,000 delegates.

MARCH 28–29 At Genoa, Italy, men of the 332nd Infantry embark for the United States. This is the only Army unit to win an Italian battle steamer for its role at Vittorio-Veneto.

MARCH 31–APRIL 4 At Bolshie Ozerki, northern Russia, Bolshevik forces launch a heavy assault upon allied defenses, and the 339th Infantry and the British Yorkshire Regiment repulse them with heavy loss.

MAY 1 Along the Vaga River, northern Russia, the 339th Infantry is preparing to hand its position over to the White Russians, when superior Bolshevik forces attack. Again they are defeated with little loss to the Americans.

MAY 30 At Archangel, northern Russia, the Army Expeditionary Force conducts Memorial Day services at the city cemetery before departing Russia for good.

JUNE 12 At West Point, New York, General Douglas MacArthur, aged 39 years, becomes the youngest superintendent of the U.S. Military Academy.

JUNE 25 At Romanovka, Siberia, the 31st Infantry engages large Bolshevik forces and loses 19 dead and 25 wounded. This is one of the costliest encounters of the occupation.

JULY 3 The American Force in Germany (AFG) is created to replace the Third Army; Major General Hunter Liggett is ordered back to the United States.

JULY 7 A convoy of army trucks under Lieutenant Colonel Dwight D. Eisenhower rumbles out from Washington, D.C., to San Francisco, California, to evaluate its motorized mobility. It arrives nine weeks later, having attained an average speed of 6 miles per hour.

AUGUST 5 At Archangel, Russia, the Army Expeditionary Force finally withdraws and departs on ships; they suffered 400 casualties while fighting the Bolshevik Seventh Army.

SEPTEMBER 3 General John J. Pershing is promoted to General of the Armies of the United States with five stars, becoming the only officer in American military history entrusted with such rank while still on active duty.

1920

JANUARY 16–19 In Verhnudinsk, Siberia, the 27th Infantry prepares for a 2,000-mile trek across the Gobi Desert, Mongolia, when they are ordered to evacuate the region. The 27th acquires the nickname "Wolfhounds" after the noted Siberian breed.

APRIL 1 At Vladivostok, Russia, the last remaining Army unit troops embark and sail away. American involvement in this region limits Japanese expansion there.

JUNE 4 In Washington, D.C., Congress passes the Army Reorganization Act which sets Army manpower at 300,000. The standing establishment is formally divided into three distinct but interrelated components: the Regular Army, the National Guard, and the Organized

Reserve. The Infantry, Artillery, and Cavalry all receive their own chiefs, while the Tank Corps is formally abolished.

1921

FEBRUARY 25 At Schofield Barracks, Hawaii, the Hawaiian Division assembles from various combat elements. This is the origin of the 24th Infantry Division.

JUNE 8 In Manila, Philippines, the Army organizes the Philippine Division from various combat elements, including the famous Philippine Scouts.

JULY 1 In Washington, D.C., General John J. Pershing becomes Army Chief of Staff to replace outgoing Major General Peyton C. March.

NOVEMBER 11 At Arlington National Cemetery, Virginia, an unknown soldier from World War I is laid to rest; the shrine subsequently becomes known as the Tomb of the Unknown Soldier.

NOVEMBER 17 The 3rd Infantry ("The Old Guard") is ordered to march from Camp Sheridan, Ohio, to Fort Snelling, Minnesota. The regiment successfully covers the 950-mile trek at an average of 30 miles per day under winter conditions.

1922

JANUARY 25 At Fort Hunt, Virginia, Army Chief of Staff General John J. Pershing orchestrates creation of the U.S. Army band; it gains renown as "Pershing's Own."

JUNE 30 In Washington, D.C., Congress exercises budgetary belt-tightening by cutting Army manpower levels to 175,000 men, discharging 600 officers and 100,000 soldiers.

JULY 1 In Washington, D.C., Secretary of War John W. Weeks and Army Chief of Staff General John J. Pershing protest recent Congressional manpower cuts, insisting they jeopardize national security.

1923

JANUARY 24 At Fortress Ehrenbreitstein, Koblenz, Germany, Major General Henry T. Allen attends ceremonies marking the end of American occupation duty; they are replaced by French troops.

APRIL 1 "U.S. Forces in China" is created to expand its military contacts in Asia. This serves as the headquarters for troops assigned to Tianjin and along the railroad to Peking (Beijing).

1924

FEBRUARY 21 In Washington, D.C., the Army Industrial College is founded in recognition of the growing importance of technology to warfare.

SEPTEMBER 13 In Washington, D.C., Chief of Staff General John J. Pershing concludes 42 years of distinguished service by retiring, and he is succeeded by Major General John L. Hines.

1926

JUNE 21 At Fort Leavenworth, Kansas, Major Dwight D. Eisenhower is among 245 officers to complete the prestigious Command and General Staff School.

1927

APRIL 29 In New Orleans, Louisiana, Army engineers dynamite a large section of the Mississippi River levee to divert raging flood waters threatening the city.

1930

JANUARY 20 In Washington, D.C., the War Department bans alcoholic beverages on all military bases in concert with the new Volsted Act (Prohibition).

JULY 20 In Washington, D.C., the Veterans Administration (VA) is created by an executive order. This entity amalgamates several existing federal agencies currently dealing with former servicemen.

1931

MARCH 31 In Managua, Nicaragua, Army engineers conduct relief work after an extensive earthquake and use demolition charge to bring down buildings in the path of raging fires.

1932

FEBRUARY 1 In China, the recent outbreak of fighting between Japan and China prompts the 31st Infantry to reinforce the 4th Marines in Shanghai, China, and secure the International Settlement.

In 1932, some 12,000 World War I veterans banded together as the Bonus Army to march on Washington, D.C., and demand bonus payments to alleviate their suffering during the Great Depression. After the bonus bill failed to pass in Congress, the Bonus Army was dispersed by U.S. troops led by Brigadier General Perry Miles and General Douglas MacArthur, and their camp was burned. (UPI-Bettmann/Corbis)

FEBRUARY 22   The Purple Heart medal is designated by the Army for soldiers who have received wounds in combat.

MAY 29   In Washington, D.C., 17,000 unemployed veterans, the so-called "Bonus Army," demand that they be allowed to cash in World War I bonus certificates at face value.

JULY 28–29   In Washington, D.C., the "Bonus Army" comes to a tragic end when 2,000 troops and six tanks dislodge the remaining protestors. Army Chief of Staff Major General Douglas MacArthur evicts the squatters, when orders forbidding him to do so fail to arrive in time.

AUGUST 9   The War Department creates four Field Armies within the continental United States: the First Army (headquartered at Governor's Island, New York), the Second Army (Chicago, Illinois), the Third (Fort Sam Houston, Texas), and the Fourth (Omaha, Nebraska).

1933

JUNE 15   The National Defense Act renders state militia part of the federal National Guard. However, they remain under the control of state governors until federalized by the president.

1934

JUNE 15   In Washington, D.C., Congress passes the National Guard Act, rendering that formation part of the United States Army in war or a declared national emergency.

1935

MARCH 21   In light of his long career in exploration, retired Major General Adolphus W. Greely receives the second peacetime Congressional Medal of Honor.

OCTOBER 1   In Washington, D.C., General Douglas A. MacArthur resigns as Army Chief of Staff and sails to the Philippines to serve as military adviser to President Manuel Quezon. Major Dwight D. Eisenhower had served as his chief of staff.

1938

JANUARY 7   The use of spiral canvass leggings (puttees) is abolished in all services but the cavalry.

1939

JANUARY 9   The Army begins issuing the famous semi-automatic M-1 Garand rifle to replace the bolt-action Springfield. The M-1 can loose an 8-round clip in 20 seconds.

AUGUST 8   At Plattsburg, New York, Brigadier General Adna R. Chaffee, Jr.'s 7th Cavalry Brigade (Mechanized) rolls into town after completing an overland journey from Fort Knox, Kentucky.

SEPTEMBER 1   In Washington, D.C., President Franklin D. Roosevelt appoints Brigadier General George C. Marshall to replace outgoing General Malin Craig as the new Army Chief of Staff. Marshall also jumps to four-star rank, being the first individual so promoted in Army History. He commands 174,000 men that are dispersed across 130 locations.

SEPTEMBER 16   The Army adopts Major General Walter Krueger's "triangular" divisional structure, consisting of three infantry regiments assisted by field artillery and support units, which is believed to enhance tactical flexibility.

SEPTEMBER 23   At Camp Holabird, Maryland, the American Bantam Car

Company delivers its prototype quarter-ton truck. This becomes affectionately known as the "Jeep" and 650,000 are constructed over the next five years.

NOVEMBER 1   Lowly Army chow is upgraded with the issuance of the new "C-Ration" for feeding troops under service conditions.

1940

JULY 6   In Washington, D.C., Major General John F. Williams, chief of the National Guard Bureau, reports that he has 235,000 under arms and ready for active duty.

JULY 10   Major General Adna R. Chaffee, Jr. is appointed head of the new Armored Force. It consists of 242 officers, 7,015 enlisted men, and 393 light tanks, all obsolete by contemporary European standards.

JULY 18   At Fort Benning, Georgia, the first experimental parachute test platoon is culled from 48 volunteers from the 29th Infantry.

JULY 25   In Washington, D.C., a General Headquarters is authorized at the Army War College under Major General Lesley J. McNair. This is primarily concerned with training and combat readiness.

AUGUST 16   At Fort Benning, Georgia, the Army Parachute Test Platoon makes its first successful test jump under Lieutenant William T. Ryder.

SEPTEMBER 6   At Fort Benning, Georgia, Brigadier General George S. Patton assumes command of the new 2nd Armored Division, christened "Hell on Wheels."

SEPTEMBER 16   In Washington, D.C., President Franklin D. Roosevelt signs the Selective Service and Training Act into law. This requires males between the age of 21 and 35 to sign up for military training. This is also the first peacetime draft in American history, and mandates that all services enlist African Americans for the first time.

OCTOBER 2   At Fort Benning, Georgia, the 501st Parachute Battalion is constituted under Major William M. Miley. The men are deployed from Douglas C-33 (DC-2) transports.

OCTOBER 29   In Washington, D.C., Secretary of War Henry Stimson initiates the military draft by drawing number 158.

DECEMBER 29   In Washington, D.C., President Franklin D. Roosevelt declares the state of world affairs "as serious as war," and encourages the American public for continuing patriotism and sacrifice. At this time the U.S. Army has expanded to 1 million men; this breaks down into 500,000 Regular Army, 270,000 National Guard, and 630,000 draftees.

1941

FEBRUARY 7   At Fort Shafter, Hawaii, Lieutenant General Walter C. Short becomes commander of the Hawaiian Department, with headquarters at Pearl Harbor.

MAY 3   In Washington, D.C., the Army's senior leadership slots are filled by Lieutenant Generals Walter Krueger (Third Army), Hugh A. Drum (First Army), Benjamin Lear (Second Army), and John L. DeWitt (Fourth Army).

MAY 19   In London, United Kingdom, Major General James E. Chaney is appointed Special Army Observer and reports directly to the Army Chief of Staff.

JUNE 9   At Fort Benning, Georgia, the new M-1 helmet, patterned after football helmets and carefully fitted to each individual's head, begin replacing the old World War I-style "tin hat."

JULY 1   To date, the U.S. Army has grown eight-fold and boasts 1.4 million members. The whole force is divided into 4 armies of 9 corps, 29 infantry divisions, and 4 armored divisions.

JULY 3   Army Chief of Staff George C. Marshall initiates the American Military Mission to China (AMMISCA) to directly supply Chinese armies through the lend-lease program. Major General John Magruder is selected to lead the mission.

JULY 7   The Army begins planning on "Blue West" to construct its first subpolar base on Greenland. This region is of considerable strategic significance to Western Hemispheric defenses, so Colonel Benjamin F. Giles lands a preliminary force of 469 men at Narsarssock to organize airfields and antiaircraft emplacements.

JULY 26   In Washington, D.C., President Franklin D. Roosevelt nationalizes all military contingents of the Philippine Commonwealth. General Douglas MacArthur, presently serving in the Philippine army, returns to active service; he is appointed commander in chief of the U.S. Forces in the Far East (USAFFE) as a lieutenant general.

SEPTEMBER 11   In Washington, D.C., construction begins on the "Pentagon" building, future home of the War Department. It is completed in 18 months at a cost of $83 million, becoming the largest office building in the world.

SEPTEMBER 15–16   Major General Charles H. Bonesteel's "Indigo Force" arrives at Reykjavik, Iceland, and unloads heavy equipment in the face of severe weather.

SEPTEMBER 15–20   In Louisiana, General Ben Lear's Second Army is pitted against Lieutenant General Walter Krueger's Third Army in the largest single war game held in the United States. It involves 22 divisions (350,000 troops) and four Air Corps wings. The exercise highlights gross deficiencies in training and equipment.

OCTOBER 1   The Army begins acquiring sufficient transport vessels to ship General Douglas MacArthur 500,000 tons of supplies, and 20,000 additional troops to protect the Philippines.

OCTOBER 10   At Schofield Barracks, Hawaii, the new 25th Infantry Division is formed from elements of the 24th Infantry Division. In time it acquires the nickname "Tropic Lightning."

NOVEMBER 15   At Fort Lewis, Washington, the 1st Battalion, 87th Infantry becomes the first unit designated to operate in mountainous terrain; this is also the origin of the famous 10th Mountain Division.

NOVEMBER 20   At Manila, General Douglas MacArthur is reinforced by the 192nd Tank Battalion. It joins the 194th Tank Battalion to form the 1st Provisional Tank Group.

DECEMBER 1   At Manila, Philippines, General Douglas MacArthur incorporates 10 poorly trained Philippine National Army divisions into his command structure. The Northern Luzon Force is headed by Major General Jonathan Wainwright.

DECEMBER 7   The surprise Japanese air raid on Pearl Harbor, Hawaii, plunges the unprepared United States into World War II. General Walter C. Short is cashiered in the wake of the attack.

DECEMBER 8   Congress declares war on the Japanese Empire. Consequently, the discharge of all draftees stops, and National Guard units revert over to Federal control.

DECEMBER 12   At Legaspi, Luzon, Philippines, Japanese forces successfully land, then begin driving north unopposed. Brigadier General George M. Parker's Southern Luzon Force gradually gives ground before them.

DECEMBER 14   In Washington, D.C., Chief of Staff General George C. Marshall approves plans expanding the Army by 2 million men and 100 divisions over the next two years; by 1945, military manpower peaks at 8 million men and women arrayed in 89 divisions.

DECEMBER 19–20   On Luzon, Philippines, Japanese forces begin driving southward from Aparri and toward the Lingayen Gulf. Other units land at Davao, Mindanao, southern Philippines,

meeting light resistance from Colonel Roger B. Hilsman's Philippine army units.

DECEMBER 20   In Washington, D.C., President Franklin D. Roosevelt signs the Draft Act mandating all males between 18 and 65 to register for military service, although only men from 20 to 44 are taken.

DECEMBER 22   In the Philippines, General Douglas MacArthur advances to full general, as his forces wage a losing battle against superbly disciplined Japanese troops, backed by sea and air power. The first American troops also arrive at Brisbane, Australia, as part of Brigadier General Julian F. Barnes's Task Force South Pacific.

DECEMBER 22–24   In the Philippines, General Masaharu Homma's 14th Army lands at Lingayen Gulf, while Major General Jonathan Wainwright's men try stemming their advance.

DECEMBER 23   In the Philippines, General Douglas MacArthur declares Manila an open city, whereupon all American and Philippine forces begin an immediate evacuation into the Bataan Peninsula. This marks the beginning of a final stand.

DECEMBER 24   At Binalonan, Philippines, Colonel Clinton S. Pierce's 26th Cavalry (Philippine Scouts) charges Japanese forces to slow their advance. The regiment loses half its men, and yields the village by dusk.

DECEMBER 31   At Bataan, Philippines, the 192nd Tank Battalion covers the final American withdrawal across the Calumpit Bridge. Eight tanks are lost as General Jonathan Wainwright prepares to demolish the bridge.

1942

JANUARY 1   With the nation at war, the U.S. Army contains 29 infantry divisions, 5 armored divisions, and 2 cavalry divisions.

JANUARY 7   On the Bataan Peninsula, General Douglas MacArthur directs that the Northern Luzon Force be redesignated I Philippine Corps (western sector) while the Bataan Defense Force becomes the II Philippine Corps (eastern sector). MacArthur employs 47,500 troops, short on food, ammunition, and suffering from disease.

JANUARY 9   On Bataan, Philippines, Japanese forces heavily probe the Abucay Line, stretching from Manila Bay to Mount Natib. Demolitions are employed to slow them down, and the Japanese gradually withdraw with considerable loss.

JANUARY 11   At Surabaya, Java, the 131st Field Artillery, Texas National Guard, lands to assist the assorted Dutch, British, and Australian troops already there.

JANUARY 12   At Bataan, Philippines, Lieutenant Alexander R. Nininger, 57th Infantry (Philippine Scouts), leads three counterattacks along the Abucay Line. He dies in hand-to-hand fighting, winning the first Congressional Medal of Honor awarded in this war.

JANUARY 16   On Bataan, Philippines, Japanese forces cross the Batalan River to outflank the Abucay defense line. Lieutenant Edwin P. Ramsey, 26th Cavalry (Philippine Scouts), leads the final mounted charge of American military history. The Japanese are finally halted, the

surviving cavalry horses are destroyed, and the dismounted troopers are employed as infantry.

JANUARY 22   On Bataan, Philippines, General Douglas MacArthur orders the Mauban-Abucay Line abandoned and a new defensive position assumed behind the Pilar-Bagrac Road, further south.

JANUARY 26   Company B, 133rd Infantry Regiment, arrives in Belfast, Northern Ireland; these are the first American troops deployed to Europe since 1917.

FEBRUARY 1   At Fort Benjamin Harrison, Indiana, the Army Chaplain School is founded to prepare civilian preachers for the rigors of military service.

MARCH 4   At Chongqing, China, Lieutenant General Joseph W. Stillwell arrives to take charge of the China-Burma-India (CBI) theater; he is greeted by Generalissimo Jiang Jieshi, although the two will enjoy a contentious relationship.

MARCH 9   At Surabaya, Java, the 131st Field Artillery surrenders to Japanese forces once the Dutch East Indies is conquered. In time, the men are forced to construct the famous bridge over the River Kwai.

MARCH 11   In Washington, D.C., President Franklin D. Roosevelt orders General Douglas A. MacArthur to depart the Philippines with his command staff and establish a new headquarters in Australia. He complies, with the greatest reluctance.

MARCH 13   At Front Royal, Virginia, Secretary of War Robert P. Patterson approves creation of the Canine (K-9)

Corps. During the war, 10,526 dogs are accepted into service, and 2,290 are killed in the line of duty.

MARCH 17 At Corregidor, Philippines, General Douglas MacArthur departs on Navy PT boats and sails to Australia. Beforehand, he promises the Filipino people, "I will return," and appoints Major General Jonathan M. Wainwright to succeed him.

MARCH 25 In Washington, D.C., the War Department announces that General Douglas MacArthur will receive the Congressional Medal of Honor, and within days he also gains appointment as Allied Supreme Commander, Southwest Pacific.

APRIL 9 At Bataan, Philippines, half-starved U.S. Army and Filipino units surrender to superior Japanese forces. The 75,000 captives (12,000 Americans among them) are harshly treated in the infamous "Bataan Death March"; over 5,200 Americans perish through abusive treatment.

APRIL 9–11 At Seymour, Australia, the 41st Infantry Division arrives to erect a training center 65 miles from Melbourne for the incoming 32nd Infantry Division. These divisions constitute the new I Corps under Major General Robert L. Eichelberger.

APRIL 25 Acting upon an executive order signed by President Franklin D. Roosevelt in January, Army troops begin rounding up 110,000 Japanese American citizens for interment at various relocation camps scattered throughout the West.

APRIL 30 The Army contracts with General Motors to produce the amphibious 2-ton truck DUKW, of which 37,000 are acquired during the war.

MAY 2 In Burma, Lieutenant General Joseph Stillwell, accompanied by 26 Americans, 13 British, and 16 Chinese, walks into the jungle and toward allied territory in India. The Japanese have won another stunning land campaign.

MAY 5–6 On Corregidor, Manila Bay, Philippines, Japanese forces launch a nighttime offensive against the remaining American detachments. Once they land a handful of tanks on the island, Major General Jonathan M. Wainwright surrenders his 3,500 American to Lieutenant General Masaharu Homma.

MAY 14 In Washington, D.C., President Franklin D. Roosevelt signs the Women's Auxiliary Army Corps (WAAC) Act into law. This allows large numbers of women to contribute directly to the war effort by joining.

MAY 15 At Fort Benning, Georgia, the Parachute School commences a separate training apart from other Infantry School programs.

MAY 20 Lieutenant General Joseph W. Stillwell and his small party walk out of the Burmese jungle and into the safety of allied lines at Imphal, India.

MAY 27 On New Caledonia, Major General Alexander M. Patch organizes his Americal Division with National Guard regiments from Illinois, Massachusetts, and North Dakota. This becomes the only infantry division with a name instead of a numerical designation.

JUNE 14 At Bridgeport, Connecticut, the General Electric factory designs and constructs its famous M1 2.75-inch rocket launcher, better known as the bazooka.

Devil's Brigade

The 1st Special Service Force arose from a suggestion by British scientist Geoffrey Pike, who felt that the Allies needed a commando-style unit capable of executing raids for attacking German facilities in Norway which produced heavy water for their atomic bomb. The idea was run by U.S. Army Chief of Staff George C. Marshall in March 1942, who approved creation of a half-American/half-Canadian unit capable of special operations. Thus was born the 1st Special Service Force under Colonel Robert T. Frederick, the officer who sponsored a concept paper for the Army's Operations Division. Frederick recruited his unit from diverse American and Canadian soldiery, some of the best and most talented individuals available, then subjected them to a rigorous training regimen at Fort William Henry Harrison in Helena, Montana. Once completely proficient at parachuting, skiing, infiltration, and hand-to-hand combat, they were initially deployed to fight the Japanese on Kiska in August 1943. Because that island had been evacuated, Frederick's force shipped to Italy and was assigned to help crack the formidable German defensive lines there. On December 6, 1943, they expertly infiltrated and stormed German positions at Monte La Difensa, overcoming incredibly difficult terrain, and seizing all objectives. After other successful missions, the 1st Special Service Force transferred to Anzio beachhead, where their aggressive patrolling earned them the name "Black Devils" from the Germans. Henceforth, the "Devil's Brigade" was among the first Allied units to enter Rome on June 4, 1944, and subsequently fought well as part of the 1st Airborne Task Force in southern France. They were disbanded there on December 5, 1944, the spiritual forebear of the U.S. Army's Green Berets and the Canadian army's top secret JTF2 military unit.

JUNE 16   At Camp Hale, Colorado, the First Special Service Force arises when U.S. and Canadian Light Infantry forces are merged into a single unit. To signify their special status, they wear a collar insignia of crossed arrows instead of crossed rifles. In time they gain renown as the "Devil's Brigade."

JUNE 19   At Carrickfergus, Northern Ireland, Major William O. Darby organizes his 1st Ranger Battalion before detailing them to train at the famous British Royal Commando School in Scotland.

JUNE 22   In Washington, D.C., the War Department designates General Joseph Stillwell's command the grandiose title of "American Army Forces in China, Burma, and India," or simply CBI.

JUNE 24   Major General Dwight D. Eisenhower replaces Major General James E. Chaney as commanding general of the European Theater of Operations (ETO). Eisenhower, unlike many contemporaries, did not see combat during World War I.

JUNE 28   At Salamuna, New Guinea, the first American land assault in the South Pacific transpires, as commandos raid the Japanese garrison there.

AUGUST 7   In England, the 1st Infantry Division becomes the first unit of its kind to deploy. It is commanded by Major General Terry de la Mesa Allen and seconded by Brigadier General Theodore Roosevelt, Jr., son of the late president.

AUGUST 16   At Camp Claiborne, Louisiana, the 101st Airborne Division ("Screaming Eagles") is activated under Major General William C. Lee.

AUGUST 19   At Dieppe, France, 50 American commandos under Colonel Lucien K. Truscott assist British and Canadian troops during a major raid. These are the first American to fight in Europe since 1918.

SEPTEMBER 17   In Washington, D.C., Brigadier General Leslie R. Groves gains appointment to head the highly secret "Manhattan Project," which produces the first atomic bomb in 1945.

SEPTEMBER 24   At Rockhampton, Australia, Major General Robert L. Eichelberger receives the first Army command of the Pacific Theater of Operations (PTO) by rising to lieutenant general in charge of I Corps.

OCTOBER 7–24   On New Guinea, the 2nd Battalion, 126th Infantry, departs Port Moresby and begins hiking across the Owen Stanley Mountains. This is the first large American offensive of the Pacific War.

OCTOBER 22   Off the coast of Algeria, Major General Mark W. Clark and a small party debark from a submarine and paddle ashore to confer with French officials prior to the allied invasion there.

NOVEMBER 8   On the North African coast, OPERATION TORCH unfolds as Major General Dwight D. Eisenhower lands 400,000 men against light Vichy French resistance. The 2nd Battalion, 509th Parachute Infantry, commits the first American airborne assault of the war by capturing an airfield near Oran, Algeria.

NOVEMBER 16–19   At Natunga, New Guinea, the 32nd Division has a difficult time against rough terrain and fanatical Japanese defenders. General Douglas MacArthur nonetheless orders them to continue "regardless of cost."

NOVEMBER 18   In Washington, D.C., the Selective Service Act lowers the draft age to 18 years. The burgeoning American military establishment soon numbers 10 million men.

NOVEMBER 20   In Alaska, Army engineers finish the Alaska Military Highway, which reaches from Dawson Creek, Alberta (Canada), to Soldier's Summit, Alaska, a total of 1,532 miles.

DECEMBER 1–14   In New Guinea, General Douglas MacArthur is dissatisfied with progress by the 32nd Division, so he sacks the commander and instructs Lieutenant General Robert Eichelberger to "take Buna or not come back alive."

DECEMBER 9   On Guadalcanal, General Archive Vandegrift's 1st Marine Division is withdrawn from combat and sent to Australia to refit. Major General Alexander M. Patch and his Americal Division succeed them and conduct mop-up operations.

DECEMBER 15–31   On Guadalcanal, the 132nd Infantry succeeds in securing the base of the mountain after several days of intense fighting. Combat on the island is nearing an end.

DECEMBER 31   At Buna, New Guinea, the 32nd Infantry Division finally begins encircling Japanese defenders in a mopping-up operation. The 41st Infantry Division arrives in strength from Port Moreby to assist.

1943

The Army begins recruiting the all–Nisei (Japanese America) 100th Battalion—a precursor of the famous 442nd Regimental Combat Team. The response in Hawaii is overwhelmingly positive, as forced relocation to camps has not occurred there.

JANUARY 2–3 In New Guinea, the 32nd Infantry Division, widely criticized for earlier failures to seize Buna, finally storms that village in the face of determined Japanese resistance.

On Guadalcanal, Solomon Islands, Major General Alexander M. Patch assumes command of the new XIV Corps, consisting of his American Division, the 25th Infantry Division, and the 2nd Marine Division.

JANUARY 5 At Oujda, Morocco, Major General Mark W. Clark is appointed commander of the new Fifth Army. This consists of the I Armored Corps of Major General George C. Patton, and VI Corps under Major General Ernest J. Dawley.

JANUARY 22 In New Guinea, the Papuan Campaign ends once U.S. and Australian troops wipe out the last pockets of Japanese resistance at Buna. This constitutes the first Allied land victory in the Pacific.

JANUARY 27 In Algiers, North Africa, the unit, the 149th Post Headquarters Company, Women's Army Auxiliary Corps (WAAC), deploys for service. These are the first American women sent overseas.

FEBRUARY 9 On Guadalcanal, the American and 25th Infantry Divisions link up at Tenaru Village, ending a bloody campaign on the island. Japanese forces stage a brilliantly conducted evacuation beforehand, rescuing their last remaining 11,000 troops.

FEBRUARY 14–25 At Kasserine Pass, Tunisia, the inexperienced I Corps is nearly routed by the veteran Panzerarmee Afrika under Marshal Erwin Rommel, losing half its armor to adroitly handled German counterparts.

FEBRUARY 26 In Tunisia, the I Corps sorts itself out under better leadership and counterattacks, retaking Kasserine Pass from the Germans.

FEBRUARY 28 In Burma, Army engineers begin working on the ambitious Ledo road to connect India to southern China and relive acute supply difficulties.

MARCH 5 In Tunisia, Major General George S. Patton, Jr., replaces Major General Lloyd R. Fredendall as commander of the badly battered II Corps.

MARCH 17 At El Guettar, Tunisia, aggressive Major General George C. Patton attacks with his reinvigorated II Corps and defeats part of the vaunted Panzerarmee Afrika (formerly Afrika Korps) for the first time.

APRIL 16 In Tunisia, Major General Omar N. Bradley succeeds Major General George C. Patton as commander of the II Corps.

MAY 3 In Iceland, Lieutenant General Frank M. Andrews, commanding the European Theater of Operations (ETO), dies when his plane crashes into a mountain.

MAY 3–4 In Tunisia, Major General Omar N. Bradley's II Corps drives German defenders from their positions at

Bizerte and Tunis. Bizerte falls on the following day.

MAY 11–31   On the Aleutian Island of Attu, the 7th Infantry Division stages an amphibious assault and gradually overcomes a determined Japanese garrison of 2,500 men. American losses are 600 dead and 1,200 wounded.

MAY 13   In Tunisia, Field Marshal Jurgen von Arnim surrenders 250,000 men of the Fifth Panzer Army to Allied forces. This disaster is as costly to the Third Reich as Stalingrad four months earlier; American losses are 18,500 men.

JULY 1   In Washington, D.C., President Franklin D. Roosevelt signs a bill dissolving the Women's Army Auxiliary Corps (WAAC) and authorizing the Women's Army Corps (WAC) as part of the regular Army establishment. Henceforth, females now enjoy full military status and can accept over 300 different types of jobs.

JULY 10   Lieutenant General George C. Patton is appointed head of the new Seventh Army in preparation for the upcoming invasion of Sicily.

JULY 10–AUGUST 17   In Sicily, General Dwight D. Eisenhower directs OPERATION HUSKY by landing eight American and British divisions, totaling 470,00 men, to confront 300,000 Italian and 50,000 German troops under General Alfredo Guzzoni.

JULY 23   In Sicily, the Lieutenant General George C. Patton's Seventh Army

U.S. tank landing ships line up and wait for tanks to come aboard at La Pecherie, a French naval base in Tunisia, two days before the invasion of Sicily in July 1943. The tank landing ship (LST, for "Landing Ship, Tank") was created during World War II to support amphibious operations by carrying significant quantities of vehicles, cargo, and troops directly onto an unimproved shore. (National Archives)

captures Palermo ahead of schedule, then maneuvers eastward to take Messina.

JULY 25–AUGUST 7   On New Georgia Island, the Solomons, the 37th and 45th Infantry Divisions (XIV Corps) inch toward Munda Airfield, braving jungle terrain and fanatical Japanese resistance.

AUGUST 15   Kiska, Aleutian Islands, falls to 34,000 Americans and Canadians under Major General Charles H. Corlett without a shot being fired. The Japanese had stealthily evacuated their garrison on July 28. The First Special Service Force under Colonel Robert T. Frederick also makes its combat debut here.

AUGUST 17   In Sicily, Lieutenant General George C. Patton's Seventh Army captures Messina, ending the campaign. British and American casualties are 25,000 casualties to an Axis tally of 167,000 killed, wounded, and captured. The island subsequently serves as a springboard for invading the Italian Peninsula.

SEPTEMBER 4   In Oran, North Africa, the Nisei 100th Infantry Battalion is assigned to the 34th (Red Bull) Infantry Division before shipping over to Italy.

SEPTEMBER 9–16   At Salerno, Italy, Lieutenant General Mark W. Clark's Fifth Army commences OPERATION AVALANCHE by splashing ashore. The Germans under Field Marshall Albert Kesselring resist tenaciously, but at length they are gradually repulsed by naval gunfire, and withdraw into the hills.

OCTOBER 1   Naples, Italy, falls to the Fifth Army under Lieutenant General Mark W. Clark. The first unit in is the 82nd Airborne Division, and within days the Americans have advanced forces north to the Volturno River.

OCTOBER 26–NOVEMBER 4   In Italy, the VI Corps crosses the Volturno River and fights its way to the entrance to the Liri Valley.

NOVEMBER 1   On Bougainville, Solomon Islands, the 37th and 43rd Infantry Divisions conduct mop-up operations on the northern part of the chain, although the sizable Japanese garrison resists tenaciously and mounts a major counterattack.

NOVEMBER 5–15   In southern Italy, the Fifth Army stalls after it encounters the fearsome German Winter Line near Migano Gap. Resistance at Mount la Difensa is so insurmountable that the First Special Service Force under Colonel Robert T. Frederick is ordered in to reduce entrenched pockets of resistance.

NOVEMBER 20–23   On Makin, Gilbert Islands, the 27th Infantry Division performs the Army's first large amphibious assault in the Pacific, by landing and gradually reducing dug-in Japanese defenders.

DECEMBER 2–8   Mount la Difensa, Italy, site of a German blocking position, falls to the First Special Service Force of Colonel Robert T. Frederick, assisted by the 36th Infantry Division. Advances elsewhere are slow and costly.

DECEMBER 8–11   In Italy, an attack by Army Rangers and the 36th Infantry Division up the slopes of Mount Sammucro stalls in the face of insurmountable German resistance, and is cancelled.

DECEMBER 10   In Tehran, Iran, the Persian Gulf Service Command is renamed the Persian Gulf Command. It is tasked with constructing a modern transport route from Khorramshahr to

Andimesk, Soviet Union, to facilitate the flow of war matériel.

DECEMBER 15–17 At Ceppagna, Italy, the 36th Infantry Division, now reinforced by the 504th Parachute Infantry and a battalion of tanks, finally

takes San Pietro after heavy fighting and losses.

DECEMBER 30 At Fort Benning, Georgia, the 555th Parachute Infantry Company is activated. This is the first-ever African American airborne unit.

1944

JANUARY 2 At Saidor, New Guinea, part of the 32nd (Red Arrow) Infantry Division makes a surprise landing and quickly captures a port. A 12,000-man Japanese garrison at Sio, 75 miles to the east, is now cut off.

JANUARY 6 In Burma, Brigadier General Frank D. Merrill takes charge of the 3,000-man 5307th Composite Unit, better known as "Merrill's Marauders." They are especially trained for deep penetration missions behind Japanese lines.

JANUARY 15 In Italy, Lieutenant General Mark Clark's Fifth Army captures strategic Mount Trocchio after a protracted battle with skilled German defenders. To date, operations against the so-called "Winter Line" have cost 15,864 casualties.

JANUARY 16 In London, England, General Dwight D. Eisenhower establishes new headquarters as Supreme Commander of the forthcoming Allied Expeditionary Force. Over two million tons of war matériel and 50,000 vehicles of various types are en route to Britain by summer.

JANUARY 20–22 Near San Angelo, Italy, the 36th Infantry Division claws out a small lodgement across the Rapido River, then halts in the face of dogged German resistance.

JANUARY 22 At Anzio, Italy, Allied forces under Major General John P. Lucas outflank German defenses along the Rapido River by landing at Nettuno, 30 miles west of Rome. The Allies place 36,000 men ashore, but the Germans recover quickly and begin fighting back. The result is a costly impasse lasting five months.

JANUARY 24–FEBRUARY 11 In Italy, severe fighting breaks out along the Rapido River line as the 34th Infantry Division fails to overcome stout resistance. Other forces begin probing German defenses below Monte Cassino, taking heavy casualties.

JANUARY 29–30 Near Anzio beachhead, Italy, the 1st and 3rd Ranger Battalions are ambushed by the Hermann Goering Panzer Division at Cisterna, and withdraw after heavy losses.

FEBRUARY 11 In England, Army forces are bolstered by the 5th and 6th Armored Divisions. To date nearly one million Americans are training in the United Kingdom.

FEBRUARY 15–18 In Italy, the II Corps again fails to cross the Rapido River south of Monte Cassino, after which Major General Mark W. Clark orders the historic abbey destroyed to deny any possible use to German forces.

Merrill's Marauders

In August 1943, Allied leaders decided to create a special U.S. Army long-range penetration unit for active duty in Burma. Tactically, it was to be patterned after the British "Chindits" of Colonel Orde Wingates, and lightly equipped to move rapidly across difficult terrain. At length 3,000 volunteers were gathered at Bombay, India, as the 5307th Composite Unit (provisional) under newly promoted Brigadier General Frank D. Merrill, a former cavalry officer with no experience in jungle fighting. Consequently, the 5307th was dubbed "Merrill's Marauders" by the press, a name they never used themselves. Happily, Merrill proved a competent, adaptable leader, and commencing in February 1944, they blazed a trail of glory through the Burmese jungle, marching across 750 miles of some of the roughest terrain in Southeast Asia, and bested veterans of the Japanese 18th Division in five major engagements. Success for the 5307th was predicated upon stealth and surprise in the jungle for, as light infantry, they were not expected to engage in conventional stand-up battles. The strategic towns of Walawbum, Shaduzup, Inkangahtawng, Nhpum Ga, and Myitkina all fell to their clever tactics, which invariably inflicted far heavier casualties on the Japanese than they themselves suffered. However, the Marauders were decimated by disease throughout their five-month ordeal, so much so that by the time the unit disbanded and was transferred to the 475th Infantry on August 10, 1944, only 130 soldiers out of the original 3,000 remained combat capable. General Merrill was himself sidelined by a heart attack and malaria, and General Joseph Stillwell was roundly criticized for pushing the unit far beyond reasonable expectations. In consequence of their exceptional performance, the 5307th received the Distinguished Unit Citation, and every surviving soldier was awarded the Bronze Star. Its lineal descendent is today's 75th Ranger Regiment.

American ground forces known as "Merrill's Marauders" are led by a column of Burmese villagers as they move in to attack a Japanese position in Burma, March 19, 1944. (AP Photo)

FEBRUARY 16–19   At Anzio, Italy, German forces launch a massive counterattack that forces the Allies to divert air power in support of the 3rd and 45th Infantry Divisions, and the British 56th Division. The panzers advance close to the beachhead, but are driven back in heavy fighting.

FEBRUARY 18–23   In the Pacific, OPERATION CATCHPOLE unfolds as Marines and the 106th Regimental Combat Team storm Eniwetok Atoll, Engebi, and Parry Islands, northwest of Kwajalein. All are secured four days later.

FEBRUARY 23   At Anzio, Italy, Major General John P. Lucas is replaced by the Major General Lucian K. Truscott, 3rd Infantry Division, a highly aggressive commander.

MARCH 3   At Anzio, a final German counterattack is rebuffed by the 3rd Infantry Division as Major General Lucian K. Truscott prepares a counteroffensive of his own.

MARCH 15   In Italy, the Fifth Army surges forward in another attempt to break the German "Gustav" line, centered at the ancient monastery at Monte Cassino. Heavy fighting and severe losses ensue, so the Allies regroup and prepare to try again.

APRIL 9   At Nhpum Ga, Burma, the 2nd Battalion—Merrill's Marauders—is rescued by the 1st and 3rd Battalions. American losses during the 10-day siege are 59 dead and 314 wounded. A further 379 soldiers are incapacitated by illness.

APRIL 22   At Hollandia, New Guinea, American and Australian forces catch Japanese defenders off guard, when two divisions of Lieutenant General Robert L. Eichelberger's I Corps storm ashore. This places them 300 miles behind Japanese front lines, and the garrison at Wewak, 90 miles to the east, is cut off.

MAY 8   In England, General Dwight D. Eisenhower declares that June 5 is D-Day for OPERATION OVERLORD, the invasion of Western Europe.

MAY 11–16   At the Gulf of Gaeta, Italy, the 88th and 85th Infantry Divisions again attack the German Gustav Line, and make good progress while pressing through the Formia corridor.

MAY 17   In North Burma, Merrill's Marauders attack and seize an important air field at Myitkyina, but stubborn Japanese resistance prevents them from taking the nearby town.

MAY 18–19   At Monte Cassino, Italy, the Germans defenders finally withdraw and abandon their vaunted "Gustav" line. The centuries-old monastery there, dating back to the 5th Century, has been reduced to rubble.

MAY 25   At Anzio, Italy, Major General Lucian K. Truscott's VI Corps breaks through German defenses and drives toward Rome. Five months of static warfare have cost the Allies 5,000 dead, 17,000 wounded, and 6,800 captured.

MAY 29   On Biak Island, New Guinea, the first armored battle of the Southwest Pacific rages as American Sherman tanks destroy eight Japanese light tanks.

JUNE 4–5   The Fifth Army under Major General Mark W. Clark liberates Rome from the Germans. The 88th Reconnaissance Troop, 88th Infantry Division, is the first American unit to arrive, and occupies Piazza Venezia that evening.

JUNE 6   At Normandy, France, OPERATION OVERLORD unfolds, and five American,

442nd Regimental Combat Team

In consequence of the Japanese attack on Pearl Harbor, Hawaii (December 7, 1941), President Franklin D. Roosevelt signed executive orders forcibly uprooting 110,000 citizens of Nisei ancestry to relocation camps. However, this practice was never carried out in the Hawaiian Islands, where one-third of the population was Japanese American, and in early 1942 several thousand National Guardsmen of Asian ancestry petitioned the military to fight in the war. The War Department eventually approved their petition, and the soldiers were transferred to Camp McCoy, Wisconsin, as the 100th Infantry battalion (Separate). The unit impressed superiors during training, so in September 1943 it was sent to Salerno, Italy, to fight as part of the 34th Infantry Division. The 100th Battalion fought superbly in battles up the Italian Peninsula, so in 1944 it was expanded into the three-battalion 442nd Regimental Combat Team (RCT). Their unofficial slogan was "Go for broke," which is gambling slang for staking everything on one throw of the dice. Like its predecessor, the 442nd fought well in many severe engagements in Italy, southern France, and Germany, and at one point suffered 800 casualties rescuing the "Lost Battalion" of the 141st Infantry in the Vosges Mountains. By war's end the 442nd RCT had become the U.S. Army's most decorated unit, with 18,143 medals awarded, including 21 Congressional Medals of Honor and 560 Silver Stars. Its 93 percent casualty rate also earned it the nickname of "Purple Heart battalion." The 442nd RCT was disbanded in 1946, then resurrected in 1947 as the 442nd Infantry. It is currently stationed in Hawaii, Guam, and Samoa, and has also seen service in Iraq (2004–2006).

Japanese-American infantrymen of the 442nd Regimental Combat Team run for cover as a German artillery shell is about to land in Levine, Italy, on April 4, 1945. For its size and length of service, the 442nd Regimental Combat Team was one of the most highly decorated in the history of the U.S. military. (National Archives)

British, and Canadian beachheads are carved out after severe combat. A total of 66,000 troops land in a matter of hours, preceded by a massive airdrop by American and British paratroopers, which disrupts German rear areas. The two American fronts are Omaha Beach (V Corps) and Utah Beach (VII Corps). Brigadier General Theodore Roosevelt, Jr., son of the former president, fights all day directing the 4th Infantry Division, and wins a Congressional Medal of Honor.

JUNE 8 At Normandy, France, the Allies consolidate their beachhead once British and American forces establish contact at Bayeaux. Major General Lawton J. Collins's VII Corps next presses toward Cherbourg, while Major General Leonard Gerow's V Corps advances inland from Omaha Beach. German resistance remains tenacious.

JUNE 10 At Cicitavechchia, Italy, the 442nd Regimental Combat Team joins the 34th ("Red Bull") Division and expands by absorbing the Nisei 100th Infantry Battalion, veterans of the Salerno campaign.

JUNE 16–17 On Saipan, Marianas Islands, the 27th Infantry Division lands to assist Marines on the beachhead during a fierce Japanese counterattack. The attackers withdraw after losing 31 tanks and 300 men.

JUNE 17–18 At Barneville-sur-mer, France, Major General Manton S. Eddy's 9th Infantry Division battles to break into the Cotentin Peninsula and cut off German defenders. The XIV Corps also presses out of the beachhead area by advancing as far as Villiers-Fossard.

JUNE 19–23 On Saipan, Marianas Islands, the 27th Infantry Division begins secur-

ing Nafutan Point on the southern coast, and attacks Japanese positions along Purple Heart Ridge and Death Valley.

JUNE 22 In Washington, D.C., President Franklin D. Roosevelt signs the Serviceman's Adjustment Act, infinitely better-known as the G.I. Bill of Rights. This landmark legislation provides veterans with assistance in education and housing, and dramatically expands the middle class during the postwar period.

JUNE 23–26 At Cherbourg, France, the 9th infantry Division begin threading through German defenses while the 4th and 79th Infantry Divisions stall in the face of stubborn resistance. Cherbourg finally falls after hard fighting, and serves as a major entrepot for the rest of the war.

JULY 13–14 At Normandy, France, the 102nd Cavalry Reconnaissance Squadron demonstrates an ingenious hedgerow cutter for General Omar N. Bradley. These are subsequently mass-produced in time to be fitted to many medium and light tanks.

JULY 15–18 At Normandy, France, the 29th and 35th Infantry Divisions fight past the hedgerows to within a mile of St. Lo, which falls on the 18th. The First Army then prepares for OPERATION COBRA, the long-awaited breakout from the landing zone.

JULY 18–20 Near Pisa, Italy, the 34th, 88th, and 91st Infantry Divisions storm into Leghorn and approach the formidable German Gothic line.

JULY 22 At Colombieres, France, Lieutenant General Omar N. Bradley assumes command of the Twelfth Army Group, which includes the First Army under Lieutenant General Courtney H. Hodges and the Third Army under Lieutenant

General George S. Patton. The latter has been restored to command following a one-year hiatus.

JULY 24   In Guam, Marianas Islands, the 77th Infantry Division goes ashore to help relieve the 1st Provisional Marine Brigade. They also confront savage Japanese resistance.

JULY 25   At St. Lo, France, General George S. Patton's Third Army initiates OPERATION COBRA, assisted by waves of heavy bombers flattening German defenses in their path. Lieutenant General Lesley J. McNair, Ground forces commander, is accidentally killed when American bombers undershoot their target; he is the highest-ranking officer killed by "friendly fire."

JULY 27   At Myitkina, Burma, a Japanese air field falls to the exhausted remnants of Merrill's Marauders. The 209th and 236th Engineer Battalions are then rushed forward to thwart Japanese counterattacks.

JULY 30–AUGUST 9   At Sansapor, New Guinea, Major General Franklin C. Sibert's 6th Infantry Division lands on the northern coast, while the 32nd Infantry Division encounters heavy resistance during the advance to Aitape.

AUGUST 5   At Myitkina, Burma, the 475th Infantry Regiment organizes itself as a long-range penetration unit assigned to the 5332nd Brigade (Provisional). This is the beginnings of the future Mars Task Force under the Northern Combat Area Command (NCAC).

AUGUST 8   At Brest, France, Lieutenant General George S. Patton orders the 6th Armored Division to make an all-out assault against stubborn German defenses. Near St. Malo, the 83rd Infantry

Division moves slowly on Dinard, but Le Mans is quickly overrun by the XV Corps and the 2nd French Armored Division.

AUGUST   15   In   southern   France, OPERATION DRAGOON unfolds as Lieutenant General Alexander M. Patch's Seventh Army splashes ashore on the Riviera. The VI Corps, under General Lucian K. Truscott, spearheads the drive up the Rhone River Valley.

AUGUST 21   In France, American and Canadian forces maneuver to close the Falaise-Argentan Gap, and 50,000 Germans are captured. Fighting around Normandy has ended, so the French 2nd Armored Division is tasked with liberating their capital of Paris.

The famous "Red Ball Express" is organized by the Transportation Corps, which is 75 percent manned by African American soldiers and employs over 6,000 trucks and other vehicles. They are created to provide front line units with sufficient food and ammunition for protracted fighting.

AUGUST 27   In Paris, France, General Dwight D. Eisenhower and his staff arrive to observe the 28th (Keystone) Division parade through the city; then it promptly marches off to the front lines.

AUGUST 30   Along the French Riviera, Major General Robert T. Frederick's 1st Airborne Task Force seizes Nice, as the Eleventh Army continues up the Rhone River Valley to Lyon. Lieutenant General Alexander M. Patch wants to link up with American forces driving east from Normandy.

AUGUST 31   In France, Lieutenant General George S. Patton's Third Army surges across the Meuse River and pursues retreating German forces. Patton has to stop, however, after outrunning his own lines of supply.

SEPTEMBER 1–5 In northern Italy, General Mark W. Clark orders the Fifth Army against the Gothic line from the Serchio River to Pisa; after four days of heavy fighting, the city of Lucca is liberated.

SEPTEMBER 2 In Belgium, the XIX and VII Corps begin driving towards Tournai, while the 9th Infantry Division hovers on the outskirts of Charleroi. In France, the 3rd Armored Division also approaches Mons.

In southern France, newly promoted Lieutenant General Lucian K. Truscott is ordered back to Italy to succeed Lieutenant General Mark W. Clark as commander of the Fifth Army.

SEPTEMBER 12–16 In France, the 5th Armored Division and 4th and 28th Infantry Divisions lurch towards Schnee Eifel, Germany, along a 30-mile front. Resistance stiffens once the terrain militates against armored units, and the drive falters.

SEPTEMBER 12–OCTOBER 27 In northern Italy, the Fifth Army incurs heavy losses as it attacks the Gothic Line around Bologna. These defenses are not penetrated until the spring of 1945.

SEPTEMBER 13 Near Roetgen, Germany, Major General Maurice Rose's 3rd Armored Division advances into the heavily forested area of the Monschau corridor. Once joined by the 9th Infantry Division, a bloody struggle known as the Battle of Huertgen Forest unfolds over the next four weeks.

SEPTEMBER 16 At Myitkina, Burma, the 5307th Composite Group, "Merrill's Marauders," disbands. They are one of the most successful ad-hoc formations of the war.

SEPTEMBER 17–27 In the Netherlands, OPERATION MARKET GARDEN commences as the American 82nd and 101st Airborne Divisions, along with the famous British "Red Devil" parachutists, drop behind German lines. They fight valiantly but are unable to surmount strong German defenses; Allied forces near Arnhem subsequently withdraw after suffering heavy losses.

SEPTEMBER 24 On Peleliu, the 321st Regimental Combat Team presses up the west coast of the island, while the 7th Marines move against the coral ridges from the south and west.

OCTOBER 5–9 In the Huertgen Forest, Germany, the VII Corps attacks the city of Schmidt, from which the region between the Roer River and the Schwammenauel Dam can be controlled. Movement is hampered by rough terrain, poor weather, and effective German defenses. The 9th Infantry Division is forced to extricate itself, aided by armored units.

OCTOBER 17 At Leyte Gulf, Philippines, the islands of Suluan and Dinagat are stormed by the 6th Ranger Battalion. However, success here alerts the main Japanese garrison on Luzon that an attack is pending.

OCTOBER 19 In China, CBI commander Lieutenant General Joseph Stillwell, contentious in his relations with Generalissimo Jiang Jieshi, is replaced by Major General Daniel Sultan.

At Aachen, Germany, the 1st and 28th Infantry Divisions, backed by the 3rd Armored Division, isolates the city by cutting the Aachen-Laurensburg highway.

Enemy resistance gradually yields to superior numbers and firepower.

OCTOBER 20 At Leyte, Philippines, General Douglas A. MacArthur comes ashore with his armies and declares, "People of the Philippines, I have returned!" The force consists of the Sixth Army under General Walter P. Krueger, 132,000 men strong, including the X Corps (1st Cavalry Division, 24th Infantry Division) and XXIV Corps (7th and 96th Infantry Divisions). The soldiers are conveyed ashore by 700 naval vessels.

OCTOBER 21 The ancient city of Aachen, Germany, former capital of Charlemagne's Holy Roman Empire, falls to the VII Corps; Colonel Thomas Lancer, 1st Infantry Division, becomes the new military governor.

OCTOBER 31 At Camp Landis, Burma, Brigadier General John P. Willey assembles his Mars Task Force and begins pushing northward to the Burma Road.

NOVEMBER 1–3 Around Schmidt, Germany, the V Corps launches its second all-out attack to capture that strategic point. Part of the 28th Infantry Division crosses the Kall River and takes the city, cutting Germany supply routes through the Lammersdorf Corridor.

NOVEMBER 2 On Leyte, Philippines, General Walter Krueger's Sixth Army overcomes tenacious Japanese defenders and secures several landing areas. The soldiers begin bracing for a counterattack.

NOVEMBER 3 Along the Serchio River, Italy, Major General Edward M. Almond's predominately African American 92nd Infantry ("Buffalo") Division undertakes it first combat operations.

NOVEMBER 9 In France, Lieutenant General George S. Patton's Third Army commences an all-out drive across the Moselle River to capture the strategic city of Metz.

NOVEMBER 16 In Germany, the furthest penetration achieved by an American combat unit is the VII Corps, First Army, when it reaches Schevenhuette. From here the 104th and 4th Infantry Divisions will occupy Cologne and the Roer River.

NOVEMBER 21–27 In Germany, the V Corps makes another concerted effort to capture the Huertgen Forest. The 5th Armored Division and 8th Infantry Division brave bad weather and fierce resistance, and Huertgen village itself is stormed by the 121st Infantry Regimental Combat Team.

NOVEMBER 22 Metz, France, falls to Lieutenant General George S. Patton's Third Army, which sustains 29,000 casualties; 37,000 Germans are captured.

NOVEMBER 27 On Peleliu, the 81st Infantry Division completes mop-up operations. American losses are 1,460 dead and 7,711 wounded, while the 10,000-man Japanese garrison chooses annihilation to surrender.

NOVEMBER 29–DECEMBER 5 At Huertgen Forest, Germany, the 5th Armored Division advances to assist the 13th and 121st Infantries, whose combined losses total 1,200 men. These grind their way to the banks of the Roer River, despite strong German counterattacks.

DECEMBER 4 In France, Lieutenant General George S. Patton's Third Army pushes across the Saar River, then halts before heavily fortified sections of the Siegfried Line.

761st Tank Battalion

The U.S. Army entered World War II harboring traditional prejudices against African Americans, viewing them as unsuited for the intricacies of modern warfare and distinctly "inferior" to their white counterparts. However, the exigencies of war led to the creation of the all-black 761st Tank Battalion on March 15, 1942, principally at the behest of Army Ground Forces commander General Lesley J. McNair, who felt that they should fight as a segregated unit under white officers. The 761st endured a troubled gestation, being trained at Southern bases in Kentucky, Louisiana, and Texas, where members often bore the brunt of racial hostility. The Army did little to advance their fortunes by restricting them to training at Fort Hood, Texas, for two years, even though all-white units were deemed combat-ready in only a few weeks. Consequently, by the time the 761st deployed in Europe in the fall of 1944, it was particularly well-trained, and General George S. Patton, impressed with their martial demeanor, requested them for his crack Third Army. The tanks of the 761st performed particularly useful work in the closing phases of the campaign in western France and fought exceptionally well up through the Rhineland Campaign in Germany. Unlike many white units, which were continually rotated to and from the front, the 761st fought continuously at the front lines for 183 days without relief. They did so without complaint, and two of their members, Sergeants Ruben Rivers and Warren G. H. Crecy, received Congressional Medals of Honor; a total of 11 Silver Stars and 69 Bronze Stars were also awarded. However, the unit suffered from lack of recognition from white peers, even though mounting civil rights pressure forced President Harry S. Truman to desegregate the military in 1947. It fell upon President Jimmy Carter to finally award the 761st Tank Battalion a Presidential Unit Citation on January 24, 1978, for bravely surmounting obstacles both on and off the battlefield.

The 761st Tank Battalion was one of few all-black armored formations in the U.S. Army, and it acquitted itself exceptionally well in prolonged combat action. (U.S. Army Military Center for Military History)

DECEMBER 5–21 At Deposito, Leyte, Philippines, the 77th Infantry Division commences a drive on Ormoc, which falls on the 10th. The 38th Infantry Division and 11th Airborne Division also claw their way towards Buri airfield, giving the Americans full control of the Ormoc Valley.

DECEMBER 6 In Germany, the costly Huertgen Forrest campaign concludes, once the badly battered 4th Infantry Division is replaced on the lines by the 83th Infantry Division. The five infantry divisions and one armored division involved suffered average losses of 5,000 men apiece.

DECEMBER 14 At Palawan, Philippines, Japanese troops at the Puerto Princesa Prison round up 150 American prisoners, douse them with gasoline, and then set them afire. This is one of the most horrific atrocities committed by Japanese soldiers in the war.

DECEMBER 15 In Washington, D.C., Congress promotes George C. Marshall, Douglas MacArthur, Dwight D. Eisenhower, and Henry H. Arnold to the newly created rank General of the Army (or five-star general).

DECEMBER 16 In Belgium, German forces unleash a surprise attack on American forces in the Ardennes region, the so-called Battle of the Bulge. The 28th Infantry Division and 14th Cavalry Group are badly battered, while the green 106th Division is completely overrun. German progress nonetheless slows, as American defenses congeal in increasingly rough terrain.

DECEMBER 18–19 In Belgium, Brigadier General Anthony McAuliffe's 101st Airborne Division, backed by elements of the 9th and 10th Armored Divisions, forms a defensive perimeter around the crucial road junction at Bastogne. The defenders brace themselves for the oncoming attack.

DECEMBER 20 At Metz, France, Lieutenant General George S. Patton rotates his Third Army 90 degrees to strike northward against the German flank. He deploys the 4th Armored Division and the 26th and 80th Infantry Divisions by skillfully realigning them by 90 degrees.

DECEMBER 22 Bastogne, Belgium, is encircled by superior German forces, but is nonetheless held by Brigadier General Anthony McAuliffe's 101st Airborne Division. When pressed to surrender, he responds to a German deputation by telling them "Nuts!"

DECEMBER 25 On Leyte-Samar Island, Philippines, the Eighth Army relieves the battle-worn Sixth Army and prepares for a final show down with Japanese forces. The ensuing mop-up continues over the next six months.

DECEMBER 26 At Bastogne, Belgium, the 37th Tank Battalion of Colonel Creighton Abrams breaks the German siege by advancing from the south. Lieutenant General George S. Patton's Third Army is right behind them, and the allies begin counterattacking across the line.

DECEMBER 28 Near Saar, Germany, Army Group G launches a counteroffensive against Lieutenant General Alexander M. Patch's Seventh Army, which yields some territory along the Rhine River.

DECEMBER 30 In Belgium, Army forces press forward through the Ardennes, erasing the "bulge" in their lines caused by the recent German offensive.

DECEMBER 31 Private Eddie Slovik, 28th Infantry Division, becomes the only American soldier executed for desertion in World War II. He is also first to face a firing squad since the Civil War.

1945

JANUARY 8–16 In Burma, the Mars Task Force traverses rugged, mountainous jungle terrain and prepares to attack Japanese troops blocking the Burma Road between Hsenwi and Wanting.

JANUARY 9 On the Lingayen Gulf, Luzon, Philippines, Lieutenant General Walter Krueger's Sixth Army commences OPERATION MIKE 1 as he lands the 6th, 37th, 40th, and 43rd Infantry Divisions (68,000 men). American forces are now 100 miles north of Manila, yet resistance by Lieutenant General Tomoyuki Yamashita's 250,000 Japanese is deceptively light at first.

JANUARY 12–22 In Burma, the Ledo Road is finished, which reopens a supply route running directly into southern China from India. The first U.S./Chinese convoy rolls into Kunming, China, this day amid celebrations.

U.S. soldiers of the 289th Infantry Regiment on their way to cut off the Saint Vith-Houffalize road in Belgium in January 1945. The Battle of the Bulge in the Ardennes Forest was the largest battle on the Western Front in World War II and the largest engagement ever involving U.S. troops. (National Archives)¡

Murphy, Audie (1924–1971)

Audie Murphy was born in Hunt County, Texas, the son of an impoverished sharecropper. His father abandoned his family, and Murphy had only acquired a fifth-grade education before quitting school to work in the fields. America's entry into World War II induced Murphy to escape his plight through military service, but the Marine Corps rejected the five-foot five-inch, 112-pound recruit as too small, while the Army declined until he reached the legal age of 18. In June 1942, Murphy passed through basic training, rose quickly to corporal, and was assigned to Company B, 1st Battalion, 15th U.S. Infantry, as part of the 3rd Infantry Division. He first saw action in Sicily, then fought well in a succession of savage battles, including Salerno, the Volturno River, and the march on Rome. At Anzio, Murphy won a Bronze Star for single-handedly destroying a German tank after most of his company was wiped out. His unit next participated in the invasion of southern France, and he fought his way through the Vosges Mountains. Distinguished service in the Comar Pocket of western Germany resulted in his battlefield commission to second lieutenant, but Murphy would only accept a promotion if allowed to remain with his men. His greatest moment under fire occurred on January 16,

Youthful Audie Murphy was America's most decorated soldier in World War II, receiving 24 medals in 28 months as a combat rifleman. After the war, Murphy wrote a best-selling memoir and became a popular movie actor. (Library of Congress)

1945, near the German village of Holtzwir, when a large force of Germans overran his advanced positions. Murphy manned a machine gun on a damaged American tank and singlehandedly slew 50 enemy troops. He consequently won a Congressional Medal of Honor and, having already received 24 medals, the 21-year-old Texan became the most decorated hero of World War II. Murphy parleyed his celebrity into a Hollywood career and the film *To Hell and Back* (1955), based on his autobiography, was one of the highest-grossing films of the decade. He died in a plane cash near Roanoke, Virginia, on May 28, 1971.

JANUARY 13   In the Ardennes, Belgium, the 87th Infantry Division, Third Army, contacts the British Army along the Our-the River, restoring the "Bulge" from which the battle derives it names. Since December 16, 1944, the Army has sustained 19,000 killed and 15,000 captured.

JANUARY 15   At Compiegne, France, 2,800 African American volunteers are assigned to the 5th Reinforcement Regiment. By March, 4,562 blacks have been integrated into understrength front line units, a feat unthinkable prior to the Battle of the Bulge.

JANUARY 16   In Belgium, the First and Third Armies link up at Houffalize, concluding maneuvers associated with the "Battle of the Bulge." German losses throughout this period are estimated at 250,000.

JANUARY 17–18   In Burma, the Mars Task Force captures Namhkam village, only three miles from the Burma Road. On the following day the Americans scale Loi-kang ridge, overlooking their objective.

JANUARY 26   On Luzon, Philippines, the XIV Corps, Sixth Army, crosses the Pampanga River and liberates the former Clark Field. Other troops encircle Japanese defenders at Bamban and Cabantuan.

JANUARY 29   In Burma, Lieutenant General Dan Sultan commences a major offensive, which culminates in the capture of Rangoon that May.

JANUARY 29–31   At Luzon, Philippines, Major General C. P. Hall's XI Corps lands at the neck of the Bataan Peninsula and advances; no resistance is encountered.

JANUARY 31   On Luzon, Philippines, Major General Oscar W. Griswold's XIV Corps begins its drive on Manila. The 37th Infantry Division and the 1st Cavalry Division vie with each other to enter the city first.

FEBRUARY 3   At Manila, Philippines, 1st Cavalry Division and 37th infantry Division engage 18,000 men of Special Naval Detachment Force under Rear Admiral Sanji Iwabuchi in brutal house-to-house combat. The Japanese commit terrible atrocities against civilians during the encounter.

FEBRUARY 4   In Manila, Philippines, the 37th Infantry Division batters its way across the Quezon Bridge and reaches infamous Bilibid prison, rescuing 3,700 malnourished prisoners of war.

FEBRUARY 5   In Germany, Major General Frank W. Milburn's XXI Corps cuts the Colmar Pocket in half, and a protracted mop-up operation ensues.

FEBRUARY 13   At Luzon, Philippines, the 38th and 6th Infantry Divisions eliminate Japanese defenders on the Bataan Peninsula, while artillery belonging to the XI Corps begins bombarding Corregidor Island in Manila Bay.

FEBRUARY 16–27   Corregidor, Manila harbor, is assaulted by the 503rd Parachute Infantry, while part of the 34th Infantry attacks from the sea. "The Rock" is soon again in American hands, at a cost of 225 killed and 405 wounded.

FEBRUARY 18   In Sarasiccia-Campana, Italy, soldiers of 10th Mountain Division scale a steep cliff in the darkness, then attack and overwhelm German defenders guarding Monte Belvedere.

FEBRUARY 22–24   At La Serra, Italy, the 10th Mountain Division drives German defenders from the slopes of Monte Belvedere, before advancing on Monte Torraccia, which falls on the 24th.

FEBRUARY 23   At Los Banos, Luzon, Philippines, Lieutenant Colonel Henry A. Burgess's 511th Parachute Infantry rescues American captives in a prisoner of war camp. The Japanese were planning to execute their captives.

FEBRUARY 24   Manila, capital of the Philippines, falls to a combined assault by the 37th Infantry Division and the 11th Airborne Division. An estimated 12,000 Japanese lie dead among its ruble.

FEBRUARY 28   Puerto Princesa, southern Philippines, falls to Brigadier General Harold H. Haney's Palawan Task Force, as

American troops and Filipino guerrillas overrun nearby Samar.

MARCH 1   In Germany, the VII Corps, First Army, crosses the Erft River and advances upon Cologne, Germany. Further south, the XX Corps, Third Army, also seizes Trier, ending a contest that commenced on January 29.

MARCH 7   At Remagen, Germany, the 9th Armored Division, III Corps, storms across the Rhine River and captures the intact bridge, then drives the remaining German defenders deep into the Ruhr region. These are the first foreign troops to invade Germany proper since Napoleon's time.

MARCH 8   In France, Lieutenant General Jacob L. Devers, commanding the Sixth Army Group, gains his fourth star to full general.

MARCH 10   In the southern Philippines, the 41st Infantry Division drives out Japanese defenders on the Zamboanga Peninsula before advancing against Mindanao City.

MARCH 12   In Germany, Lieutenant General Omar N. Bradley, commanding the 12th Army Group, is promoted to four-star, or full, general.

MARCH 14   At Luzon, Philippines, the 6th Infantry Division attacks the Japanese "Shimbu" line. Major General Edwin D. Patrick is killed in action, becoming the first of two ranking leaders to fall in the Pacific.

MARCH 15   In France, Lieutenant General George S. Patton's Third Army and Lieutenant General Alexander M. Patch's Seventh Army maneuver to jointly attack the triangular Saar-Palatine region, which is bounded on three sides by the Rhine, Moselle, and Lauter-Sarre rivers.

MARCH 17   In Washington, D.C., the 101st ("Screaming Eagles") Airborne Division receives a Presidential Unit Citation for its defense of Bastogne during the Battle of the Bugle. This is the first division to receive such distinction.

MARCH 18–21   In Germany, the Third Army, consisting of two armored divisions and four infantry divisions, crashes through German defenses in the Palatine. The 4th Armored Division and 90th Infantry Division subsequently press towards Mainz and Worms, while, further south, the Seventh Army probes the heavily defended Siegfried Line.

MARCH 22–23   At Oppenheim, Germany, the 5th Infantry Division, Third Army, forces its way across the Rhine River on rafts and boats. They move at night and arrive on the opposite bank before the defenders can react.

MARCH 25   In Germany, in the Saar Palatine region, the Third and Seventh Armies destroy the German First and Seventh Armies (Army Group G), taking 81,692 captives. The Rhine River is cleared as far south as Speyer, while VI Corps drives enemy units from northern Alsace.

MARCH 26   On Iwo Jima, Japanese forces launch a nighttime counterattack, inflicting four soldiers dead and 89 wounded before recoiling. The Army is then entrusted with administrative control of the island, following the departure of the Marines's V Amphibious Corps.

In the Philippines, Major General William H. Arnold's Americal Division lands at Cebu Island, encountering sharp resistance from a 14,500-man Japanese garrison.

MARCH 28   In Germany, General Dwight D. Eisenhower orders the Allied thrust directly south to Leipzig, leaving Berlin as a Soviet objective. This move also transfers the bulk of fighting from Field Marshal Bernard Montgomery's 21st Army Group to General Omar N. Bradley's 12th Army Group.

MARCH 30   Near Paderborn, Germany, Major General Maurice Rose of 3rd Armored Division becomes only the second divisional leader to be killed in combat.

APRIL 1   At Okinawa, Ryukyu Islands, OPERATION ICEBERG commences, as Lieutenant General Simon B. Buckner's 10th Army lands at Higashi Beach unopposed. His 165,000 men gradually encounter fierce resistance inland from 115,000 Japanese Army troops and naval infantry, under Lieutenant General Mitsuru Ushijima and Rear Admiral Minoro Ota.

APRIL 4   At Okinawa, Ryukyu Islands, Major General John Hodge's XXIV Corps (7th, 27th, 77th, and 96th Infantry Divisions) encounters several belts of entrenched Japanese defenders, and it maneuvers southward.

APRIL 5   At Okinawa, Ryukyu Islands, the XXIV Corps encounters stout resistance as it advances into the so-called Shuri Line. Resistance is fanatical, and casualties are high.

APRIL 10   In Germany, the Third Army occupies the Ohrdruf death camp, the first of several such institutions liberated by American forces. The soldiers are horrified by what they behold.

APRIL 11   In Germany, elements of the 2nd Armored Division reach the Elbe River, 80 miles west of Berlin, and begin looking for Soviet troops nearby.

APRIL 12   At Warm Springs, Georgia, President Franklin D. Roosevelt dies, whereupon Harry S. Truman is sworn in as the new commander in chief.

APRIL 14   In the Po Valley, Italy, the Fifth Army begins a long-delayed offensive as the 10th Mountain Division advances into the valley, while the 1st Armored Division moves towards Vergato on Highway 64.

APRIL 16–21   Near Iwo Jima, Ryukyu Islands, Major General A. D. Bruce's 77th Infantry Division is ordered to storm the small island of Ie Shima. It falls after five days of fanatical resistance.

APRIL 17   At Mindanao, southern Philippines, Major General Franklin C. Sibert's X Corps lands and engages 41,000 Japanese defenders. The region is not cleared of enemy troops until June 30.

APRIL 18   At Ie Shima, Ryukyu Islands, the beloved war correspondent Ernie Pyle dies of wounds received in battle. He had been the constant companion of Americans since the North African and Italian campaigns.

APRIL 19   In Germany, the V Corps (2nd and 69th Infantry Divisions) pushes eastward and captures Leipzig, while the 1st Infantry Division (VII Corps) advances through the Hartz Mountains and contacts friendly units beyond.

APRIL 24   At Okinawa, Ryukyu Islands, General Simon B. Buckner's XIV Corps punches through the Machinato Line, and Japanese forces fall back to the next line of prepared positions.

APRIL 25   At Torgau, Germany, patrols of the 69th Infantry Division encounter the

Soviet 59th Guards Division at the Elbe River. Soldiers from both sides openly embrace each other.

APRIL 26 At Verona, Italy, Task Force Darby presses onto Lake Gardia to cut German escape routes, and Colonel William O. Darby is killed by a mortar fragment. The 85th Infantry Division also forces a bridgehead on the Adige River, while the 1st Armored Division moves onto Lake Como.

APRIL 28 In Italy, the northern cities of Alessandria, Brescia, and Vicenza are captured by the Fifth Army, whose soldiers learn that Italian dictator Benito Mussolini was executed by partisans near Lake Como.

APRIL 29 The infamous death camp at Dachau, Germany, is liberated by the 42nd and 45th Infantry Divisions, Third Army, who release 30,000 starving captives.

APRIL 30 At Elienberg, Germany, General Courtney H. Hodges meets the commander of the Soviet 5th Guard Army. Adolf Hitler also commits suicide in his bunker, and is succeeded by Grand Admiral Karl Doenitz.

MAY 1 In northern Italy, Lieutenant General Lucian K. Truscott's Fifth Army clears German troops out of the Piave and Brenta Valleys, prior to a final drive up the Brenner Pass into Austria.

MAY 2 German forces surrender to the Fifth Army in Italy, ending 604 days of nonstop fighting since the attack on Salerno in 1943.

MAY 3 At Augusburg, Germany, the 103rd Infantry Division drives down the Brenner Pass to contact the Fifth Army,

pressing northward. The XV Corps also advances towards Salzburg, while the XXI Corps crosses into Bavaria and approaches Hitler's hideout at Berchtesgaden.

MAY 7–8 At Reims, France, Field Marshal Alfred Jodl surrenders to General Dwight D. Eisenhower, who accepts on behalf of the allied powers. American casualties in France and Germany total 114,000. V-E Day is subsequently proclaimed by President Harry S. Truman.

MAY 21 At Okinawa, advances by the 96th Infantry Division and the 6th Marine Division force Japanese defenders out of the Shuri Line, and they occupy final defensive positions along the Yaeju Dake Escarpment.

MAY 25 In Washington, D.C., the Joint Chiefs of Staff formulate an initial plan for invading Japan. This consists of OPERATION OLYMPIC, the invasion of Kyushu on November 1, followed by OPERATION CORONET, the reduction of the main island of Honshu, on March 1, 1946. Heavy casualties are expected.

JUNE 5 In Germany, the United States, Great Britain, France, and the Soviet Union arrange Central Europe into occupation zones, while the city of Berlin, deep with the Russian sector, is likewise divided among the victors.

JUNE 18 At Okinawa, Lieutenant General Simon B. Buckner is killed when his observation post is struck by a Japanese shell; he is the senior Army officer to fall in the Pacific.

JUNE 21 Japanese resistance on Okinawa ceases; the Tenth Army suffers 7,613 killed and 31,807 wounded, equally divided between Army troops and

Marines. Japanese losses amount to 107,500 killed and 7,400 captured.

JULY 5 General Douglas MacArthur completes his reconquest of the Philippines, following 10 months of combat and 12,000 casualties. The Japanese sacrificed 400,000 soldiers in a futile defense.

JULY 14 In Germany, Supreme Headquarters Allied Expeditionary Forces (SHAEF) is disbanded and General Dwight D. Eisenhower steps down as "Allied Commander." He next serves as commander of United States Forces in Europe (USFET) and Military Governor over the next few months.

JULY 23 At Okinawa, Ryukyu Islands, Lieutenant General Joseph W. Stillwell takes command of the Tenth Army and prepares for the future invasion of Japan.

JULY 31 In Germany, General Omar N. Bradley's 12th Army Group (First, Third, and Seventh Armies) disbands, and command of American ground troops passes to United States Forces, European Theater (USFTF).

AUGUST 1 At Okinawa, Lieutenant General Joseph W. Stillwell receives his fourth star to become a full general; he is the 17th officer so decorated during World War II.

AUGUST 15 In Tokyo, Emperor Hirohito goes on the airwaves for the first time to announce Japan's capitulation. The actual surrender date is September 2. General Douglas A. MacArthur is also appointed Supreme Commander of the Allied Powers for the ensuing occupation.

AUGUST 20 Near Sian, Northeast Manchuria, OSS agents locate Major General Jonathan M. Wainwright, who was captured at Bataan in April 1942. He is immediately flown to Tokyo, Japan.

AUGUST 30 At Yokohama, Japan, General Robert L. Eichelberger arrives at Atsugi Field to establish his Eighth Army as an occupation force.

SEPTEMBER 2 In Tokyo Bay, representatives from Japan and the victorious allies gather onboard the deck of the battleship *Missouri* to sign surrender documents. General Douglas A. MacArthur signs on behalf of the Allies while his friend, newly freed Major General Jonathan W. Wainwright, stands nearby. The 1st Cavalry Division also arrives in Tokyo, becoming the first American unit in the Japanese capital.

SEPTEMBER 3 At Baguio, Philippines, Lieutenant General Jonathan M. Wainwright accepts General Tomoyuki Yamashita's surrender; he is thereupon arrested and shipped to Japan to face charges of war crimes.

OCTOBER 1 At Khorramshahr, Iran, the Persian Gulf Service Command is activated to replace the Persian Gulf Command. It is tasked with disbanding American installations throughout the region.

OCTOBER 7 At Bad Tolz, Germany, General George S. Patton is relieved as military governor of Bavaria for contesting occupation policies. He is replaced by General Lucius K. Truscott.

NOVEMBER 19 In Washington, D.C., General Dwight D. Eisenhower replaces General George C. Marshall as Army Chief of Staff.

DECEMBER 9 Near Mannheim, Germany, General George S. Patton is critically injured when his staff car collides with an Army vehicle.

DECEMBER 15 General George C. Marshall is appointed special ambassador to China by President Harry S. Truman, and is tasked with arranging a truce between Nationalists under Jiang Jieshi and Communists under Mao Zedong.

DECEMBER 21 At Bad Neuheim, Germany, General George S. Patton dies from injuries received in an auto accident.

DECEMBER 31 In Japan, the Eighth Army assumes total responsibility for occupation duties, allowing the Marine Corps V Amphibious Corp to depart.

1946

JANUARY 4–15 In Washington, D.C., the War Department announces demobilization will be slowed to preserve sufficient personnel for current international obligations. This change results in an outpouring of anger from soldiers deployed overseas, and Congress is besieged by letters.

MARCH 3 In Berlin, Germany, Ordnance officer Lieutenant James Wilson is killed by a Soviet sentry. This is the first sign of increasing hostility between the Free and Communist camps.

APRIL 27 In Washington, D.C., the Gillem Report is released by the War Department, which calls for the end of racial discrimination.

JUNE 25 In Washington, D.C., the Selective Service Act is extended by Congress to March 31, 1947, for men between 19 and 34, but the length of service is reduced to 18 months.

AUGUST 12 At Yohyon, northern Korea, three American soldiers belonging to the 32nd Infantry Regiment are seized by Soviet forces; they are detained for 13 days.

OCTOBER 2 In Washington, D.C., the War Department reveals plans to replace the Selective Service with the Universal Military Training program. The plan is not adopted, after vocal resistance from civic groups and veteran organizations.

1947

MARCH 31 In light of high rates of voluntary enlistment, the War Department allows the military draft to expire; this is the first time since 1940 that conscription is not enforced.

APRIL 16 In Washington, D.C., President Harry S. Truman signs the Army-Navy Nurses Act of 1947, which makes the Army Nurse Corps part of the regular Army establishment.

JUNE 18 Colonel Florence Blanchfield, Army Nurse Corps, becomes the first woman tended a regular Army commission.

JULY 26 In Washington, D.C., President Harry S. Truman signs the National Security Act of 1947 into law; this mandates a "National Security Establishment" consisting of the Army, Navy/Marines Corps, and a new, independent Air Force.

SEPTEMBER 15 In Italy, the Army-led occupation of Italy ends, and, because that country is now a member of the new North Atlantic Treaty Organization (NATO), American forces remain at several leased bases.

1948

FEBRUARY 19 Lieutenant General James A. Van Fleet assumes command of the new Joint U.S. Military Advisory and Planning Group (JUSMAPG), which proves instrumental in orchestrating the Greek victory over Communist insurgents on October 16, 1948.

MAY 10 President Harry S. Truman orders the Army to seize control of all U.S. railroads, until labor peace is restored on July 19.

JUNE 24 In Washington, D.C., President Harry S. Truman signs a new Selective Service Act, requiring all males between 18 and 25 to register for possible military service.

JULY 26 President Harry S. Truman signs Executive Order 9981, mandating an end to segregation in all United States armed forces. However, the last segregated unit is not integrated until 1954.

AUGUST 15 In newly created South Korea, the Provisional Military Advisory Group (PMAG) is established to handle logistical support for South Korean constabulary force.

1949

JUNE 30 In South Korea, the 5th Regimental Combat Team is the last Army unit to depart and conclude the American occupation. Only the 472 officers and men attached to the Korean Military Assistance Group (KMAG) remain behind.

AUGUST 10 In Washington, D.C., President Harry S. Truman amends the National Security Act by establishing the new Department of Defense (DoD) to replace the National Military Establishment.

AUGUST 16 In Washington, D.C., General Omar Bradley is appointed the first Chairman of the Joint Chiefs of Staff (JCS).

1950

JUNE 25 In South Korea, 135,000 men of the North Korean People's Army (NKPA), backed by 150 Russian-built tanks, roll south of the 38th Parallel. This is the first military challenge of the Cold War period.

JUNE 27 In Washington, D.C., President Harry S. Truman authorizes General Douglas MacArthur to commit air and naval forces against Communist forces in South Korea. However, the Eighth Army is in poor shape after five years of occupation duty in Japan, and lacks heavy tanks and other essential equipment.

JUNE 29   At Suwon, South Korea, five soldiers of the 507th Antiaircraft Artillery Battalion are the first American casualties of the Korean War.

JULY 1   In South Korea, the 1st Battalion, 21st Regiment, 24th Infantry Division, arrives from Japan and is designated Task Force Smith, under Lieutenant Colonel Charles B. Smith.

JULY 5   At Osan, South Korea, Task Force Smith is attacked by the North Korean 4th Division. They manage to destroy four T-34 tanks and delay the enemy's advance by seven hours while losing 181 dead, wounded, and missing.

JULY 6–12   At Pyongtaek, South Korea, the 34th Infantry wages a desperate rear-guard action that delays the Communist advance for several hours. The 21st Infantry performs similar work at Chochiwan before retreating. Several American captives are bound and executed by Communist forces, who also shoot thousands of South Koreans. Such treatment will be paid back in kind.

JULY 8   In Washington, D.C., President Harry S. Truman appoints General Douglas MacArthur supreme commander of United Nations forces in Korea, and head of the United Nations Command (UNC).

JULY 10   At Pusan, South Korea, Major General William F. Dean's 24th Infantry Division begins arriving and assuming defensive positions.

JULY 13   At Taegu, South Korea, Lieutenant General Walton H. Walker establishes headquarters and assumes control of U.S. forces in the peninsula.

JULY 14–26   At Taejon on the Kum River, South Korea, the 24th Infantry Division wages an ill-fated struggle to stop North Korean forces from crossing. Major General William F. Dean picks up a bazooka and personally destroys an enemy tank. At length the Americans give way, and Dean is separated from his men; he is taken captive on August 25.

JULY 20   In Washington, D.C., Congress passes the Army Reorganization Act of 1950, which removes size limits on the Army General Staff, consolidates the field, coast, and anti-aircraft artillery into a single Artillery branch, merges tanks and mechanized cavalry into the Armor branch, and recognizes a total of 14 specialist branches.

JULY 25–27   At Chinju, South Korea, the 19th and 29th Infantry Regiments are decimated in combat by the North Korean 6th Division. The surviving troops are reassigned as part of the 25th Infantry Division.

JULY 27   In Washington, D.C., President Harry S. Truman extends the enlistment period for all armed forces by 12 months; 50,000 men are also ordered to report for training in September.

JULY 29   At Pusan, South Korea, General Walton H. Walker issues his famous "Stand or Die" order to the Eighth Army. "There will be no Dunkirk, there will be no Bataan," he insists.

JULY 31–AUGUST 1   At Pusan, South Korea, the Eighth Army is stiffened by the arrival of the 5th Regimental Combat Team, the 555th Field Artillery Battalion, and Major General Laurence B. Keiser's 2nd Infantry Division.

AUGUST 3   Outside Pusan, South Korea, General Walton H. Walker's Eighth Army establishes its perimeter behind the

Naktong River, occupied by the 1st Cavalry Division, the 2nd, 24th, and 25th Infantry Divisions, the 1st Provisional Marine Brigade, the 27th British Brigade, and eight Republic of Korea (ROK) divisions.

AUGUST 5–19   In South Korea, the First Battle of the Naktong Bulge unfolds as North Korean forces begin probing the 24th Infantry Division. They are driven off with 8,500 casualties and large amounts of equipment destroyed; UN losses amount to 1,800 killed, wounded, and missing.

AUGUST 16   In Japan, Major General Edward M. Almond's X Corps is activated for upcoming OPERATION CHROMITE, an amphibious descent upon Inchon, South Korea.

AUGUST 18–25   Outside Pusan, North Korean forces attack through a series of narrow valleys dubbed the "Bowling Alley." The 23rd and 27th Infantry Regiments easily hold their ground, inflicting an estimated 4,000 casualties.

AUGUST 23   In Tokyo, Japan, General Douglas MacArthur presents his case for an amphibious assault upon Inchon, on the west coast of South Korea. He convinces Admiral Forrest P. Sherman, Chief of Naval Operations, and General Joseph L. Collins, Army Chief of staff, to proceed, then sets the invasion date for September 15.

AUGUST 25   In Washington, D.C., President Harry S. Truman orders the Army to take control of the railroad system to thwart a possible strike; they remain in charge until May 1952.

Commander of the United Nations Command, General Douglas MacArthur observes the Inchon landing from the command ship Mount McKinley *on September 15, 1950. From left to right are Brigadier General Courtney Whitney, Major General Edwin Wright, MacArthur, and Major General Edmond Almond. Disputes with President Truman over the conduct of the war resulted in MacArthur's recall in April 1951. (National Archives)*

AUGUST 31–SEPTEMBER 9 Outside Pusan, North Korean forces launch a second attempt to penetrate the Naktong Bulge, but Army and Marine units counterattack and drive the Communists off with an estimated 10,000 casualties.

SEPTEMBER 15 At Inchon, South Korea, General Douglas MacArthur launches the audacious OPERATION CHROMITE, overcoming tricky tides and tough defenses to land the X Corps of Major General Edward M. Almond. The attack succeeds brilliantly, and the 1st Marine Division, backed by Major General David G. Barr's 7th Infantry Division, presses inland towards the capital of Seoul. MacArthur's gambit has turned the tide of war decisively in the UN's favor.

SEPTEMBER 16 At Pusan, South Korea, General Walton H. Walker orders the Eighth Army to break out of the Naktong Perimeter. North Korean forces hastily retreat northward.

SEPTEMBER 20 In Washington, D.C., Congress promotes Chairman of the Joint Chiefs of Staff (JCS) Omar N. Bradley to the rank of General of the Army (five stars), the first so honored since the end of World War II, and also the last.

SEPTEMBER 24–25 At Kimpo Air Base, Seoul, Soul Korea, the 187th Airborne Regimental Combat Team becomes the first parachute unit deployed in the war.

SEPTEMBER 26 At Suwon, South Korea, the 7th Infantry Division (X Corps), pushing west, and the 1st Cavalry Division (Eighth Army), marching north, link up, while Communist forces flee back to North Korea.

SEPTEMBER 27 In Washington, D.C., President Harry S. Truman, acting upon the advice of the Joint Chiefs of Staff (JCS), orders UN forces north of the 38th parallel into North Korea to unify the country under UN auspices. This fateful decision sparks a sharp reaction from the People's Republic of China.

OCTOBER 9 Near Kaesong, South Korea, the Eighth Army crosses the 38th parallel and advances on Pyongyang, North Korea, the Communist capital. The advance is spearheaded by the 1st Cavalry Division.

OCTOBER 15 On Wake Island, President Harry S. Truman and General Douglas MacArthur convene to discuss military strategy in Korea. At the time, MacArthur discounts any possibility of Soviet or Chinese intervention.

OCTOBER 19 In North Korea, Pyongyang, the Communist capital, is occupied by the 1st Cavalry Division and the 1st ROK Division.

OCTOBER 20 At Sukchon and Sunchon, North Korea, the 187th Airborne Regimental Combat Team makes the first parachute drop of the Korean War, but fails to snare the retreating North Koreans.

OCTOBER 24 In South Korea, General Douglas MacArthur removes all restrictions on UN forces and orders them up to the border with Red China.

OCTOBER 25 North of Unsan, North Korea, ROK forces are attacked by the Chinese 50th Field Army for the first time. General Douglas MacArthur nonetheless allows the X Corps and the Eighth Army to continue to operate independently of each other.

NOVEMBER 1 At Chonggodo, North Korea, the 21st Infantry Regiment deploys 18 miles south of the Yalu River separating Korea from China. This is the northernmost point UN forces reach during this war.

Ridgway, Matthew B. (1895–1993)

A man of war and peace, Matthew B. Ridgway is regarded as one of the finest high-level strategists of the Cold War, and an all-around American hero. (National Archives/Corbis)

Matthew Bunker Ridgway was born in Fort Monroe, Virginia, on March 3, 1895, the son of an army colonel. He graduated from West Point in 1917 and spent several months patrolling the Mexican border. Over the next two decades Ridgway fulfilled a typical regimen of far-ranging appointments in China, Nicaragua, and the Philippines, and in 1935 he was chosen to pass through the elite Army War College. Following American entry into World War II, Ridgway rose to major general, commanding the 82nd Airborne Division, and in July 1943, he spearheaded the invasion of Sicily and seized strategic points until relieved. In June 1944 Ridgway jumped with his men over Normandy, France, spearheading OPERATION OVERLORD. He subsequently assumed control of the Allied 18th Airborne Corps of American, British, and Polish units during the ill-fated OPERATION MARKET GARDEN in the Netherlands. In December 1944 Ridgway's paratroopers blunted the northern shoulder of the German "Battle of the Bulge," then crossed the Rhine River into Germany in 1945 and linked up with Soviet forces along the Elbe River. In December 1950 Ridgway was ordered to replace the late General Walton Walker as head of the Eighth Army in Korea. The following spring he launched Operations KILLER and RIPPER, which promptly drove Chinese forces back across the 38th Parallel. In May 1952 he succeeded General Dwight D. Eisenhower as commander of the North Atlantic Treaty Organization (NATO), supervising its enlargement from 12 to 80 divisions. Eisenhower then picked him to serve as army chief of staff in Washington, D.C., and he urged the president not to get involved in French Indochina. Ridgway retired from active service in 1955, and he died in Pittsburgh, Pennsylvania, on July 26, 1993, one of the most adept American military leaders of the 20th century.

NOVEMBER 2–6 Near Unsan, North Korea, a sudden attack by the 116th Chinese Division annihilates the 3rd Battalion, 8th Cavalry Regiment, 1st Cavalry Division. The Communists just as quickly withdraw; the action is meant as a warning to UN forces, but General Douglas MacArthur decides to ignore it.

NOVEMBER 21 Disregarding Chinese warnings, the 17th Infantry, 7th Infantry Division, marches into Hyesanjin along the Yalu River—and directly on the Chinese border.

NOVEMBER 25–27 Throughout North Korea, the Chinese 13th Army Group of 300,000 men successfully counterattacks the Eighth Army, overrunning the 2nd and 25th Infantry Divisions and several South Korean formations. The Eighth Army immediately withdraws down the peninsula to prevent encirclement and destruction.

NOVEMBER 27 In North Korea, the Chinese 9th Army Group begins an offensive of its own in the Chosin Reservoir area. They overrun the 31st Regimental Combat Team; only 1,000 soldiers of the original 2,500 make it back to Marine lines at Hagaru-ri by December 1.

NOVEMBER 28–29 At Kunri, North Korea, the 2nd Division, rear guard of the retreating Eighth Army, are ambushed by thousands of Chinese and overrun. American losses are 5,000 killed, wounded, and captured. It is a devastating defeat.

NOVEMBER 30 Major General Edward M. Almond, staggered by the Chinese onslaught, orders the X Corps (3rd and 7th Infantry Divisions, 1st Marine Division, and ROK I Corps) back to the port of Hungnam for evacuation by sea.

DECEMBER 15 In South Korea, General Walton H. Walker orders the battered Eighth Army into new defensive lines along the Imjin River, north of Seoul, to stem the Chinese onslaught.

DECEMBER 19 In Europe, the North Atlantic Council approves General Dwight D. Eisenhower to serve as supreme commander of all Western European defense forces.

DECEMBER 23 Near Uijongbu, South Korea, hard-charging Lieutenant General Walton H. Walker dies in an unfortunate jeep accident. The new M-41 light tank is subsequently christened the "Walker Bulldog" in his honor.

DECEMBER 25 Communist Chinese forces flood en masse over the 38th parallel and into South Korea. They intend to drive UN forces into the sea.

DECEMBER 26 In South Korea, Lieutenant General Matthew C. Ridgway assumes command of the Eighth Army.

1951

JANUARY 3 In South Korea, Chinese forces press hard upon the Han River east and west of Seoul, so the Eighth Army abandons the capital and falls back to new lines further south.

JANUARY 4–5 In South Korea, General Matthew B. Ridgway orders the Eighth Army and X Corps back to Line D, 50 miles below the 38th parallel. The Chinese impulsively follow, inadvertently extending their supply lines and exposing themselves to aerial interdiction.

JANUARY 7–14 In South Korea, the X Corps and Eighth Army absorb the latest Chinese offensive 50 miles south of the 38th parallel, until the 2nd Infantry Division gives ground, leaving a 20-mile salient on the UN's right flank. General Matthew B. Ridgway directs the 1st Marine Division to this threatened position.

JANUARY 15–17 In western South Korea, OPERATION WOLFHOUND commences as General Matthew B. Ridgway unleashes 6,000 troops, tanks, and artillery against nearby Chinese Communist units, who suffer 1,800 casualties for an American loss of 3 dead and 7 injured.

JANUARY 25 In South Korea, General Matthew B. Ridgway initiates OPERATION THUNDERBOLT as I and IX Corps advance and recapture Inchon and Suwon. Their methodical advance grinds down Chinese forces, which retreat behind the Han River.

FEBRUARY 1 At Sinchon, South Korea, the 23rd Infantry Regiment and a French battalion rout the Chinese 125th Division, inflicting 5,000 casualties for a loss of 225 dead and injured.

FEBRUARY 5–9 South of Seoul, South Korea, OPERATION PUNCH commences as General Matthew B. Ridgway orders the 25th Infantry Division, backed by artillery, tanks, and air power, to seize the Hill 440 complex. They inflict 4,200 casualties on Chinese forces, in exchange for 70 killed and wounded.

FEBRUARY 11–13   At Hoengsong, South Korea, the 2nd Infantry Division is attacked by superior Chinese forces, and suffers heavy losses. However, a determined stand by the Dutch Battalion allows the Americans to withdraw safely to Wonju.

FEBRUARY 13–15   In South Korea, the Battle of Chipyong-ni unfolds as the 23rd U.S. Infantry, the French battalion, and supporting armor and artillery units defend against superior Chinese forces. UN forces lose 350 men killed, wounded, and missing, and are completely surrounded, but refuse to surrender. Chinese failure to take Chipyong-ni proves that their latest offensive is losing impetus.

FEBRUARY 21–MARCH 6   In South Korea, General Matthew B. Ridgway initiates OPERATION KILLER by ordering the IX and X Corps to eliminate a large Chinese-held salient in UN lines. The operation successfully concludes two weeks later, having inflicted 10,000 casualties on the Communists.

MARCH 6–31   In South Korea, General Matthew B. Ridgway commences OPERATION RIPPER as the 25th and 7th Infantry Divisions cross the Han River, and recapture Seoul on March 14. However, the State Department complains about the aggressive names given to Ridgway's offensives and insists they receive less menacing titles.

MARCH 15   In South Korea, UN forces occupy the much-battered capital of Seoul, only this time for good.

MARCH 22–31   In South Korea, General Matthew B. Ridgway unleashes OPERATION COURAGEOUS against Chinese forces confronting the I Corps. The maneuver succeeds in pushing them and their North Korean allies north of the 38th parallel.

MARCH 23   Near Munsan-ri, South Korea, the 187th Airborne Regimental Combat Team makes the second and final airborne assault of the war. They attempt to cut off retreating Communist forces, but the majority of the enemy escape; 1 American is killed while 84 suffer jump-related injuries.

APRIL 5   In North Korea, OPERATION RUGGED unfolds as the Eighth Army again crosses the 38th parallel to establish lines Kansas and Utah; American losses are 1,000 killed, wounded, and missing.

APRIL 11   In Washington, D.C., President Harry S. Truman relieves General Douglas MacArthur as UN supreme commander, Far East, and appoints General Matthew B. Ridgway to succeed him. MacArthur was publicly tactless about expanding the war into Manchuria and using atomic weapons.

APRIL 14   Lieutenant General James Van Fleet, succeeds Lieutenant General; Matthew B. Ridgway as the commander of the Eighth Army.

APRIL 22   In South Korea, the Chinese Communists unleash their Fifth Offensive against the Eighth Army, and the Americans withdraw to a new defensive line north of Seoul, dubbed "No Name Line." The Chinese are contained after suffering 70,000 casualties. UN losses are 1,900 killed, wounded, and missing.

MAY 3   In Vienna, Austria, a military policeman from the 769th Military Police Battalion is killed by Soviet troops.

MAY 16   In South Korea, the Chinese hurl 175,000 soldiers at the center of UN lines by striking the X Corps, the ROK III Corps, and the right flank of the 8th Army. The Allies give ground initially, but gradually contain the attack with massed artillery and air power. Chinese losses are estimated at 90,000, while the Americans suffer 1,200 killed, wounded, and missing.

MAY 31   In Washington, D.C., traditional Army-Navy-Marine-Air Force legal systems are all replaced by the Uniform Code of Military Justice.

JUNE 3–12   In South Korea, General James A. Van Fleet commences OPERATION PILEDRIVER by ordering the Eighth Army into the Iron Triangle, just north of the 38th parallel. This is the final UN offensive of the war, and the Americans fail to take all their objectives.

JUNE 19   In Washington, D.C., President Harry S. Truman signs the Universal Military Training and Service Act, which increases the length of service to two years and lowers the draft age to 18 years.

AUGUST 18–SEPTEMBER 5   In Korea, Bloody Ridge becomes the focus of the 2nd Infantry Division, assisted by several ROK units. The position is taken at a loss of 2,700 UN casualties; Chinese losses are estimated at 15,000.

SEPTEMBER 13–OCTOBER 15   In Korea, the 2nd Infantry Division attacks Heartbreak Ridge in concert with several ROK formations and the French Battalion. Fighting is fierce, and UN forces suffer 2,700 casualties before driving the enemy off; Chinese losses are estimated at 25,000 men. Significantly, UN artillery expends so many shells that ammunition shortages persist for several days.

OCTOBER 3–9   In Korea, OPERATION COMMANDO unfolds as five divisions from I Corps secure Line Jamestown in the Old Baldy area. The Americans suffer 2,500 casualties, mostly in the 1st Cavalry Division.

NOVEMBER 12   In Korea, General Matthew B. Ridgway halts offensive operations and substitutes a new policy of "Active defense." Here, UN units constantly employ patrols, raids, and ambushes instead of remaining static.

1952

APRIL 17   In Washington, D.C., President Harry S. Truman signs Executive Order 10345, extending army enlistments by nine months.

APRIL 27   In Japan, the United States terminates its occupation, and civilian authority is restored. The Americans still retain basing rights on the mainland, and the Ryukyu Islands are still under U.S. jurisdiction.

APRIL 28   General Matthew B. Ridgway is appointed the new NATO supreme commander of Allied forces in Europe,

following the resignation of General Dwight D. Eisenhower.

MAY 7–JUNE 10   On Koje-do Island, South Korea, Communist prisoners stage an uprising and seize camp commander Brigadier General Francis Dodd. On June 10 the 187th Regimental Combat Team restores order, killing 150 captives; one American is killed.

MAY 19   At Panmunjom, Korea, Major General William K. Harrison, Jr., gains appointment as the senior UN negotiator. He immediately declares a recess after Chinese and North Korean delegates recite propaganda speeches.

JUNE 11 At Fort Bragg, North Carolina, the 10th Special Forces Group becomes the Army's first designated special forces outfit.

JUNE 14 In Korea, the Chinese attack the hill complex called Old Baldy, defended by the 2nd and 45th Infantry Divisions. For the remainder of the war, this position changes hands with considerable loss to both sides.

JULY 16 In Washington, D.C., Congress passes the Korean War G.I. Bill of Rights, conferring educational benefits, loan guarantees, and similar perquisites for veterans.

OCTOBER 14–NOVEMBER 5 In Korea, General James A. Van Fleet orders the 7th Infantry Division to capture Triangle Hill; their attack, spearheaded by the 31st Infantry and backed by 16 field artillery battalions and waves of Air force fighter bombers, fails after 12 days of fierce combat. The 7th Division suffers 2,000 casualties to an estimated Chinese loss of 19,000.

1953

JANUARY 20 In Washington, D.C., Dwight D. Eisenhower is inaugurated as the 34th president and commander in chief of all armed forces.

FEBRUARY 10 In Korea, Lieutenant General Maxwell D. Taylor replaces General James A. Van Fleet as commander of the Eighth Army.

MARCH 23–25 In Korea, Chinese forces capture the hill known as Old Baldy. The 31st Infantry Regiment is ordered to recapture it, but fails to overcome stout defenses. General Maxwell D. Taylor, perceiving the position as unessential to UN defenses, cancels future operations to regain it.

APRIL 20–MAY 3 In Korea, OPERATION LITTLE SWITCH begins as the UN repatriates 6,670 Communist captives and the Chinese return 684 prisoners, including 149 Americans.

MAY 25 At Fort Sill, Oklahoma, the Army successfully tests its new 280-mm atomic cannon in Nevada. The warhead flies 10,000 meters and detonates 160 meters above the ground with a force of 15 kilotons. Outwardly impressive, it does not enter into production.

JUNE 10 In South Korea, the Chinese attack Outpost Harry, defended by troops of the 74th Infantry Division, who repel their antagonists and inflict an estimated 4,200 casualties in exchange for 550 killed, wounded, and missing.

JULY 6–10 In North Korea, the Chinese seize the position called Pork Chop Hill. The 7th Infantry Division goes in to take it back, but they fail after four days of intense combat. General Maxwell D. Taylor, who regards the position as unimportant, orders the struggle abandoned. The Americans suffer 232 killed, 805 wounded, and 9 missing; the Chinese losses are estimated in the range of 6,500.

JULY 13–20 In Korea, Chinese forces mount a final offensive by attacking along the Kumsong River with six divisions. These engage the 2nd, 3rd, 40th and 45th infantry Divisions, and are repelled with losses estimated at several thousand men. American casualties are 243 dead, 768 wounded, and 88 missing.

JULY 27 At Panmunjom, the guns fall silent in Korea as the armistice is signed. United States and the United Nations have successfully met the first armed challenge of the Cold War. American losses are 29,856 killed and 77,596 wounded; Chinese and North Korean loses are estimated as high as 1.5 million.

AUGUST 5–DECEMBER 23 At Panmunjom, Korea, OPERATION BIG SWITCH gets underway, once the Communists repatriate 12,773 UN prisoners in exchange for 75,823 Chinese and North Koreans.

AUGUST 16 In Washington, D.C., General Matthew B. Ridgway becomes the new Army Chief of Staff, to replace outgoing General Joseph L. Collins.

DECEMBER 26 The United States announces the withdrawal of two infantry divisions from the Korean Peninsula.

1954

APRIL 1 At Fort Bragg, North Carolina, the first Army helicopter battalion is activated; this promising technology will play an expanded role in upcoming conflicts.

MAY 30 At Fort Meade, Maryland, the Army activates its first Nike Ajax surface-to-air missile battery to guard the nation's capital against air attacks.

JUNE 1 The Army acquires eight batteries of Honest John rockets, its first tactical nuclear weapon.

SEPTEMBER 3 On Quemoy Island, Republic of China, a Communist artillery bombardment kills two American military advisers.

1955

FEBRUARY 1 General John E. Dahlquist becomes the first commander of the U.S. Army Continental Army Command (CONARC), tasked with supervising all military matters within the United States.

JUNE 30 In Washington, D.C., General Maxwell D. Taylor gains appointment as Chief of Staff, U.S. Army, to replace outgoing General Matthew D. Ridgway. Taylor

opposes President Dwight D. Eisenhower's policy of emphasizing nuclear weapons at the expense of conventional forces.

NOVEMBER 1 In South Vietnam, Lieutenant General Samuel T. Williams becomes head of the new Military Assistance Advisory Group Vietnam (MAAG-Vietnam). This body is tasked with supplying arms and advice to the new government.

1956

FEBRUARY 1 At Huntsville, Alabama, the Army initiates the Missile Agency at the Redstone Arsenal, for developing new Thor and Jupiter intermediate range ballistic missiles (IRBMs).

JUNE 12 At Independence Hall, Philadelphia, President Dwight D. Eisenhower

presides over ceremonies, whereby the U.S. Army adopts its first official flag in 181 years.

AUGUST 2 In Duluth, Minnesota, Albert Woolson, the oldest surviving Union soldier of the Civil war, dies at the age of 109.

AUGUST 14   Over Fort Rucker, Alabama, the first aerial refueling between an H-21 helicopter and a fixed-wing aircraft is successfully completed.

SEPTEMBER 21   At Fort Campbell, Kentucky, the 101st Airborne Division adopts the new Pentomic structure. Here the traditional triangular organization of three regiments is replaced by five battle groups, each slightly larger than battalion-sized.

DECEMBER 1–4   The Army decommissions its last mules and carrier pigeons for transport and communication purposes.

1957

APRIL 29   At Fort Belvoir, Virginia, SM1, the Army's first nuclear reactor, is dedicated by Secretary of the Army William M. Bruckner. It becomes the first American reactor activated to power an electrical grid.

MAY 1   The Army begins issuing the M14 automatic/semi-automatic rifle, which is chambered to fire the standard NATO 7.62-mm round. It replaces the M-1 semi-automatic rifle, which has been a standard-issue weapon since 1939.

SEPTEMBER 24   In Little Rock, Arkansas, National Guard Troops and units of the 101st Airborne Division assist desegregation efforts at the city's Central High School. They have been so ordered by President Dwight D. Eisenhower.

1958

JANUARY 31   At Cape Canaveral, Florida, the Army launches Explorer I, America's first space satellite, atop a Jupiter C rocket.

JULY 19   In Lebanon, Task Force 201, consisting of the 187th Battle Group, 24th Infantry Division, lands to support the Marines and prevent an outbreak of civil war.

AUGUST 6   President Dwight D. Eisenhower signs the Defense Reorganization Act, so that the Secretary of Defense can enjoy more administrative control over the departments of the Army, Navy, and Air Force.

1959

JULY 8   At Bienhoa, South Vietnam, Viet Cong rockets kill Army advisers Major Dale Buis and Master Sergeant Chester Ovnard. These are the first American fatalities in Southeast Asia.

OCTOBER 16   At Walter Reed Army Hospital, Maryland, former General of the Army George C. Marshall, a major architect of American victory in World War II, dies.

1960

APRIL 20 The new M-60 Patton tank, sporting a large 105-mm cannon, enters production and replaces the earlier M-48 tank. It sees continual front line service over the next four decades.

1961

APRIL In Laos, the Military Assistance Advisory Group—Laos (MAAG-Laos) forms under Lieutenant Colonel Arthur D. Simons. He commands 430 soldiers, divided up into 48 mobile "White Star" training teams.

MAY 11 In Washington, D.C., President John F. Kennedy signs National Security Action Memorandum No. 52 to explore ways of increasing the Army's counterinsurgency abilities. He also authorizes 400 Special Forces deployed to Laos, with a further 100 military advisers sent into South Vietnam.

DECEMBER 26 In Saigon, South Vietnam, Viet Cong capture Army Specialist George Fryett as he rides his bicycle. He is the first American prisoner of the war, although the Communists release him the following June.

DECEMBER 31 To date, the tally of Army casualties in Southeast Asia amounts to 14 killed and wounded.

1962

JANUARY 10–11 In Berlin, the American government removes its tanks from the sector containing the Berlin Wall; the Soviets reciprocate two days later.

FEBRUARY 4 South of Saigon, South Vietnam, an Army H-21 ferrying South Vietnamese soldiers is shot down by the Viet Cong; this is the first helicopter lost in Southeast Asia, and all four American crewmen are killed.

FEBRUARY 8 In South Vietnam, the Military Assistance Command, Vietnam (MACV) is created under Major General Paul D. Harkins, for funneling advisers and supplies to that struggling nation.

APRIL 3 In Washington, D.C., the Defense Department orders all army reserve and National Guard units fully integrated.

MAY 12 At Tuy Hoa, South Vietnam, the 57th Medical Detachment performs its first helicopter evacuation. Over the next 10 years, helicopters will carry 900,000 wounded soldiers to safety.

SEPTEMBER 21 At Fort Bragg, North Carolina, the 5th Special Forces Group, 1st Special Forces, is activated. President John F. Kennedy takes a keen interest in counterinsurgency matters.

SEPTEMBER 30–OCTOBER 1 In Oxford, Mississippi, President John F. Kennedy federalizes the National Guard and dispatches them to restore order after racial rioting breaks out at the University of Mississippi.

Green Berets

The U.S. Army can trace its modern special forces back to June 1952, when the 10th Special Forces Group (Airborne) was established at Fort Bragg, North Carolina. Drawing upon the experience of Office of Strategic Services (OSS) units of World War II, these were envisioned as purveyors of unconventional warfare, whose manifest included airborne insertion, demolition, reconnaissance, and foreign language training for working with indigenous forces. They were a direct reaction to the "Wars of National Liberation" instigated and abetted by the Soviet Union, especially in the Third World, and the demand for special forces resulted in the expansion of the force. In 1957 the 1st Special Force Group was activated on Okinawa for service in Asia, but in 1962 they came to the attention of President John F. Kennedy, who sought unconventional warfare as a means of combating Communism. That year he authorized special forces personnel to wear distinctive green berets as part of their dress and field uniforms; hence they became unofficially known to the world at large as the "Green Berets." Special forces were extremely active in Southeast Asia throughout the 1960s and into the following decade, and the Green Berets acquired a near-mythic reputation for efficiency in combat, infiltration, long-range reconnaissance, and the ability to win "hearts and minds" of the local populace they worked with. Since Vietnam they have seen active duty world-wide, not simply in combat functions, but as military instructors proficient in foreign languages and cultural nuances. In 1986 Congress authorized creation of no less than seven Special Forces Groups, with two National Guard Groups added in 2001. Green Berets were among the first American forces in Afghanistan in 2001 and Iraq in 2003, where they function as one of the world's premier purveyors of unconventional warfare.

OCTOBER 12 In Washington, D.C., President John F. Kennedy approves Brigadier General William P. Yarborough's suggestion that Special Forces wear green berets as part of their standard uniform.

1963

JANUARY American troop strength in South Vietnam stands at 7,900 soldiers and advisers. To date, Army aviation units have performed 50,000 sorties on behalf of ARVN, nearly half of them during combat operations.

FEBRUARY 24 In South Vietnam, an American soldier is killed by Viet Cong ground fire that also downs three H-21 helicopters. Hereafter, soldiers are authorized to shoot back in their own defense.

NOVEMBER 1–2 In Southeast Asia, the CIA turns over its border surveillance program to the 5th Special Forces Group. These erect 18 border camps along strategic infiltration routes by the following summer.

1964

JANUARY Presently, there are 10,100 Army personnel in South Vietnam; of these 489 have become casualties, with 45 killed in action.

JANUARY 16 In Washington, D.C., the Joint Chiefs of Staff authorize creation of the MACV Studies and Observation Group (SOG), a highly classified operation employing Special Forces for secret operations throughout Southeast Asia.

FEBRUARY 3 In Kontum, South Vietnam, Viet Cong sappers attack an Army advisory compound and kill an American soldier. This marks the first time that Americans have been targeted in their own facilities.

JUNE 20 In Saigon, South Vietnam, General William C. Westmoreland succeeds General Paul D. Harkins as head of MACV.

JULY 6 At Nam Dong, Central Highlands, South Vietnam, a Viet Cong battalion is repelled by Captain Roger A. Donlon and 11 men of Detachment A-726, as it attempts to storm their camp. Donlon wins the first Congressional Medal of Honor in Vietnam, and is the first soldier so honored since the Korean War.

OCTOBER 1 In South Vietnam, the 5th Special Forces Group establishes its headquarters, but, because many field teams are undermanned, their tour of duty is extended to 12 months.

1965

JANUARY Army personnel in South Vietnam hit 14,700 officers and men. Since fighting began in 1961, the United States has sustained 1,300 dead and 6,100 wounded in action.

FEBRUARY 7 At Pleiku, South Vietnam, a Viet Cong raid on an Army barracks results in 8 Americans killed and 126 wounded. President Lyndon B. Johnson orders retaliatory air raids in North Vietnam in consequence.

MARCH 21 In Selma and Montgomery, Alabama, President Lyndon B. Johnson federalizes the Alabama National Guard, and deploys 2,200 Army troops to protect 25,000 marching civil rights protestors.

APRIL 28 In the Dominican Republic, the 82nd Airborne Division deploys in the wake of a military coup and the onset of civil war. It is not until the installment of a provisional government in September that the Americans depart.

MAY 3–12 At Bien Hoa, South Vietnam, the 173rd Airborne Brigade becomes the first Army combat unit in theater. It is accompanied by the 319th Artillery, also the first unit of its kind to arrive.

JUNE 7 In Saigon, South Vietnam, General William Westmoreland requests 44 additional battalions to counter North Vietnamese troops infiltrating down the Ho Chi Minh trail. He calculates that this show of force will convince Communist leaders that they cannot win the war.

JUNE 9–12 In Phuoc Long Province, South Vietnam, 1,500 Viet Cong attack a Special Forces camp at Dong Xoai. The defenders repulse four heavy attacks until they are evacuated by helicopter. Eight Americans die, and Lieutenant Charles Q. Williams wins a Congressional Medal of Honor.

JUNE 26 In Washington, D.C., the government allows General William C. Westmoreland to commit American forces into combat whenever deemed necessary. A new offensive phase of the war commences.

JULY 26 In Washington, D.C., President Lyndon B. Johnson announces an increase in military manpower from 75,000 to 125,000. The draft is also doubled from 17,000 to 35,000 men per month.

AUGUST 3 In Saigon, Army Military Police units deploy the first sentry dogs used in the Vietnam War. No less than 2,200 dogs are employed as scouts, sentries, and mine detectors.

SEPTEMBER 11 At An Khe, South Vietnam, the 1st Cavalry (Airmobile) Division arrives to test the theory of vertical envelopment with helicopters. Their success grants troops a quantum leap in terms of mobility.

SEPTEMBER 20 In Washington, D.C., the Joint Chiefs of Staff authorize Project Shining Brass, which involves classified cross-border operations into Laos for gathering military intelligence along the Ho Chi Minh Trail. The teams involved consist of three Special Forces troops and nine Montagnard tribesmen; they perform over 1,200 missions by 1970.

OCTOBER 10–14 Near An Khe, Central Highlands, South Vietnam, the 1st Cavalry Division performs its first airmobile operation against Viet Cong troop concentrations. The elusive enemy

escapes, but the Americans reopen a highway from the coast to Pleiku.

NOVEMBER 14–20 In Pleiku Province, South Vietnam, the Battle of Landing Zone X-Ray unfolds once the 1st Cavalry Division deploys deep inside enemy territory near the Cambodia border. The 1st Battalion, 7th Cavalry, lands at "position X-Ray" and is attacked by 2,000 of the North Vietnamese 33rd and 66th Regiments. The Americans gradually send reinforcements, and the Communists run for sanctuary in Cambodia. This represents the first major engagement of the Vietnam War; American losses are 240 killed and 470 wounded, while the Communists suffer around 2,000.

NOVEMBER 17 The 1st Cavalry Division deploys the 2nd Battalion, 7th Cavalry, at Ia Drang two miles to the northeast of Landing Zone X-Ray. There they are ambushed by Communist forces and nearly overrun until rescued by the 1st Battalion, 5th Cavalry. American losses are 276 men to an estimated 400 Viet Cong.

NOVEMBER 27–DECEMBER In the final months of the year, American troop strength in South Vietnam rises to 116,800 officers and men who are now engaged in combat operations. They have sustained 898 killed in action. The Defense Department estimates that an active strategy of seeking out enemy units over so vast a country requires an additional 400,000 men.

1966

JANUARY 28–MARCH 6 In Binh Dinh Province, South Vietnam, the 3rd Brigade, 1st Cavalry Division, commences OPERATION MASHER, the war's first "search and

destroy" mission. Communists on the Bong Son Plain offer light resistance, and quickly reclaim most of the lost territory once the Americans depart.

MARCH 16 In the A Shau Valley, South Vietnam, Viet Cong overrun a Special Forces camp, killing or wounding 200 Americans and South Vietnamese. This is the last such camp established in the valley, which is of great strategic importance to the Communists.

APRIL 11–12 In the III Corps region, South Vietnam, the 1st Infantry Division moves into the heart of Viet Cong territory, and a company of the 2nd Battalion, 16th Infantry, is ambushed 40 miles east of Saigon, losing 35 dead and 71 wounded.

JUNE 2–13 In Bien Long Province, South Vietnam, the 1st Infantry Division begins OPERATION EL PASO II by sweeping north and west of Saigon. Heavy fighting develops near the Cambodian border; for a loss of 200 dead and wounded, the Americans inflict 1,000 Communist casualties.

JUNE 2–20 Near Dak To, Konum Province, the 101st Airborne Division commences OPERATION HAWTHORNE, whereby Lieutenant Colonel David Hackworth's 1st Battalion, 327th Infantry, defeats a force of Viet Cong besieging a Special Forces camp. The Communists are reinforced and counterattack, mauling one of Hackworth's companies.

JUNE 7 In Kontum Province, South Vietnam, Company C, 2nd Battalion, 503rd Infantry, is besieged by superior numbers of Viet Cong, until Captain William Carpenter calls down a napalm strike on his own position. The Americans hold their ground with a loss of 6 dead and 25 injured.

JUNE 11 In Washington, D.C., Secretary of Defense Robert McNamara declares U.S. troop strength in South Vietnam at 285,000 men; total fatalities since the year began are 2,100.

JULY 11 Sergeant Major William O. Woodridge, a highly decorated, 25-year veteran of two wars, is sworn in as the first Sergeant Major of the Army.

SEPTEMBER 8 At Bien Hoa, South Vietnam, the 11th Armored Cavalry ("Blackhorse"), equipped with numerous tanks, helicopter, and flamethrower units, deploys as an independent tactical unit. It is tasked with escorting convoys along dangerous roads.

SEPTEMBER 13–FEBRUARY 12 In Binh Dinh Province, South Vietnam, the 1st Cavalry Division deploys 120 helicopters and 5 battalions in its biggest maneuver to date. OPERATION THAYER is aimed at Viet Cong strongholds in the Kim Son Valley, but Communist units escape intact.

NOVEMBER 2 Along the Demilitarized Zone (DMZ), South Korea, North Koreans ambush part of the 23rd Infantry, 2nd Infantry Division; six Americans are killed.

NOVEMBER 6–25 In the Central Highlands, South Vietnam, OPERATION ATTLEBORO is the first multi-divisional endeavor of the war effort, as the 1st Infantry Division and a brigade from the 25th Infantry Division sweep assigned areas clean of Viet Cong forces. For a loss of 155 dead and 494 wounded, the Americans kill 300 Communists and take several large weapon caches.

DECEMBER 2 On the road near Suoi Cat, South Vietnam, Viet Cong ambush the 1st Squadron, 11th Armored Cavalry; the "Blackhorses" respond with artillery and tank canister rounds that rout the enemy.

DECEMBER 16 In the Mekong Delta, South Vietnam, the 2nd Brigade, 9th Infantry Division, joins the Mobile Riverine Force. This is the Army's first amphibious force employed since the Civil War.

DECEMBER 27 In the Lim Som Valley, South Vietnam, Company C, 1st Battalion, 12th Cavalry, is attacked by North Vietnamese at Landing Zone Bird. Battery B, 2nd Battalion, 19th Artillery, then fires "Beehive" rounds into the enemy's ranks, routing them.

1967

JANUARY 5 In Washington, D.C., the State Department admits that, to date, 5,008 Americans have been killed in South Vietnam, and 30,093 wounded in the year 1966. Total casualties since January 1961 are higher; 6,664 dead and 37,738 injured.

JANUARY 8–26 Northwest of Saigon, South Vietnam, a force of 16,000 Army troops and 14,000 South Vietnamese commence OPERATION CEDAR FALLS in region known as the Iron Triangle. Elements of the 175th Airborne Brigade and the 1st and 25th Infantry Divisions advance, but the Viet Cong melt away into the jungle. The Communists lose 750 dead and 280 captured to an American loss of 72 soldiers killed.

JANUARY 16 In Saigon, South Vietnam, MACV orders the construction of a fortified line along the northern border to halt Communist infiltration along the Demilitarized Zone (DMZ).

FEBRUARY 11–FEBRUARY 21 In Binh Dinh Province, South Vietnam, OPERATION PERSHING begins as the 1st Cavalry Division begins a year-long sweep of the region, assisted by the South Korean Capital Division and the ARVN 22nd Division; 9000 Viet Cong are claimed dead.

FEBRUARY 12 Along the Demilitarized Zone (DMZ), South Korea, North Koreans ambush another patrol of the 23rd Infantry; one American soldier is killed.

FEBRUARY 22 In War Zone C, near the Cambodian border, OPERATION JUNCTION CITY unfolds as the 2nd Brigade, 173rd Airborne Brigade, performs the first and only airborne operation of the Vietnam War to halt Communist infiltration there.

MARCH 19–20 Near Bau Bang village, northwest of Saigon, South Vietnam, Viet Cong strike part of the 5th Cavalry, but are repelled after a successful night action.

APRIL 1 At Firebase George, South Vietnam, the 1st Battalion, 26th Infantry of Lieutenant Colonel Alexander M. Haig repels a Viet Cong night attack.

APRIL 29 Along the Demilitarized Zone, South Korea, men of the 2nd Division exact revenge by ambushing North Korean infiltrators, killing one.

MAY 11–AUGUST 2 In the southern I Corps region, OPERATION MALHEUR I commences destroy Communist units in the vicinity. In three months they account for 869 Viet Cong killed, but 9,000 civilians are forcibly evacuated.

MAY 18–26 In Kontum Province, Central Highlands, South Vietnam, the 4th Infantry Division commences OPERATIONS SAM HOUSTON and FRANCIS MARION. The soldiers account for more than 2,000 enemy dead, but are worn out by constant fighting over nine days.

MAY 22 Along the Cambodian border, American and Vietnamese Special Forces begin OPERATION DANIEL BOONE, to gather intelligence, take prisoners, and commit sabotage where possible; 1,825 such missions are launched over the next four years.

JULY 15   At Da Nang, South Vietnam, the Viet Cong fire 50 122-mm rockets against aviation facilities; 8 Americans die, 175 are wounded, and 42 parked aircraft are destroyed or damaged.

AUGUST 10   Below the Demilitarized Zone (DMZ) in South Korea, Communist infiltrators attack a party of the 13th Engineers, killing three Americans.

OCTOBER 7   Along the Imjim River, South Korea, Communist infiltrators attack a patrol boat belonging to the 2nd Infantry Division.

OCTOBER 14   In Washington, D.C., the United States charges North Vietnam with mistreating prisoners in violation of the Geneva Convention.

OCTOBER 30–NOVEMBER 4   At Loc Ninh on the Cambodian border, a Special Forces outpost resists a Viet Cong siege. In the course of the battle, they are heavily assisted by artillery and air strikes.

NOVEMBER 3–DECEMBER 1   In Kontum Province, Central Highlands, South Vietnam, Viet Cong prepare to storm the Special Forces camp at Dak To. A spoiling attack launched by the 4th Infantry Division's 3rd Battalion, 12th Infantry, suddenly drives enemy forces from Hill 1338, and they retreat toward Cambodia.

NOVEMBER 8   In Washington, D.C., President Lyndon B. Johnson signs legislation granting women equal opportunities for promotion throughout the U.S. military.

NOVEMBER 11   In the southern I Corps tactical zone, South Vietnam, the 1st Cavalry Division commences OPERATION WALLOWA to crush North Vietnamese units lurking in the Que Son Valley. Enemy forces are decimated, but they filter back in after the Americans depart.

NOVEMBER 19–22   In Kontum Province, South Vietnam, the Communists post forces atop Hill 875 as a rear guard, and the 2nd Battalion, 503rd Infantry, drives them off after heavy fighting. The Communists flee after suffering 1,000 casualties; American losses are 115.

DECEMBER 8   In Tay Ninh Province, northwest of Saigon, South Vietnam, the 25th Infantry Division commences OPERATION YELLOWSTONE while, in Binh Duong Province, the 1st Infantry Division sorties into the Iron Triangle. The Americans account for 5,000 Communist troops killed, well into the new year.

DECEMBER 31   At this date, no less than 9,378 American soldiers have been killed in action; to this must be added an additional 6,782 combat-related deaths between 1961 and 1966.

1968

JANUARY 22–29   Along the Demilitarized Zone (DMZ), South Korea, North Korean infiltrators continue harassing attacks against outposts manned by the 2nd Infantry Division.

JANUARY 30–31   At midnight on Tet, the Vietnamese New Year, Communist forces strike at 36 provincial and 64 district capitals. A Viet Cong sapper team breaches the wall of the U.S. Embassy before Military Police kill them. American losses over the next nine days total 546 dead and 6,000 wounded, while Communist casualties are at around 20,000. Tet proves a costly tactical defeat for the Communists, but the American public begins turning against continued involvement in Southeast Asia.

FEBRUARY 2–24 The old imperial capital of Hue, South Vietnam, becomes the site of intense combat as Army troops and Marines wrest it back from the Viet Cong. The 2nd Brigade, 101st Airborne Division, attacks south of the city, while the 7th and 12th Cavalry Regiments sweep in from the north and west. Before departing, the Communists execute 5,000 political opponents in the war's biggest atrocity.

FEBRUARY 7 At Lang Vei, near Khe Sanh, a Special Forces camp is overrun by North Vietnamese Army troops, employing Soviet-made PT-76 tanks for the first time.

MARCH 2 North of Tan San Nhut, South Vietnam, Company C, 4th Battalion, 9th Infantry, is ambushed and nearly annihilated, losing 49 dead and 29 wounded. This is one of the worst American defeats of the war.

MARCH 11 Lieutenant General Frederick C. Weyland charges into action along the III Corps front with the 1st, 9th, and 25th Infantry Divisions, clearing out numerous pockets of enemy troops and killing 2,658 Communists for a cost of 105 American dead. A second sweep near Saigon accounts for an additional 3,542 enemy troops, clearing the region of Viet Cong.

MARCH 16 At My Lai, South Vietnam, a platoon of Americans under Lieutenant William L. Calley goes on a rampage after being sniped at and kills men, women, and children. The massacre serves as a rallying point for the antiwar movements around the globe.

MARCH 27 Along the Demilitarized Zone (DMZ), South Korea, a patrol from the 2nd Division ambushes North Korean infiltrators, killing three.

APRIL 14 At Khe Sanh, I Corps zone, the 1st Air Cavalry Division establishes contact with Marine defenders during OPERATION PEGASUS/LAM SOM 207, ending the siege there.

APRIL 19–MAY 17 In the A Shau Valley, South Vietnam, OPERATION DELAWARE commences, as the 1st Cavalry Division commits an air assault that loses 10 helicopters to severe antiaircraft fire.

APRIL 21 Along the Demilitarized Zone (DMZ), South Korea, a company from the 31st Infantry engages a similar-sized unit of North Korean infiltrators.

APRIL 24–MAY 3 In the A Shau Valley, South Vietnam, the 1st Cavalry Division begins air assaults into the southern entrance of the valley, meeting stiff resistance. However, the Americans establish a logistics foothold capable of supplying additional sorties further up the valley.

APRIL 29–MAY 17 In the A Shau Valley, South Vietnam, the 101st Airborne Division engages in several firefights, but most enemy units desert the area, abandoning valuable caches of food, supplies, and weapons.

JUNE 10 In Saigon, South Vietnam, General Creighton W. Abrams replaces General William C. Westmoreland as commander of U.S. Forces in South Vietnam. This change reflects dissatisfaction with the course and conduct of the war.

Abrams, Creighton W. (1914–1974)

Creighton Williams Abrams was born in Springfield, Massachusetts, on September 15, 1914, and he passed through the U.S. Military Academy in 1940. He rose to major in 1942 and subsequently commanded the 37th Tank Battalion throughout World War II, fighting with distinction under General George S. Patton. After the war he attended the Command and General Staff School at Fort Leavenworth, and during the Korean War he served as chief of staff with the I, X, and XI Corps. He rose to brigadier general in 1956 and major general in charge of the 3rd Armored Division in 1960, and faced off against Soviet armor during the Berlin Crisis of 1962. Later that he faced a crisis of another kind when ordered to quell desegregation unrest at the University of Mississippi, and his adroit handling of the situation won him praise from Secretary of the Army Cyrus Vance and Attorney General Robert F. Kennedy. In 1967 Abrams fulfilled his most daunting task, that of commanding the U.S. Military Assistance Command, Vietnam (MACV), where he trained and equipped thousands of South Vietnamese soldiers for their struggle with the Communist north. In July 1968 Abrams succeeded General William Westmoreland as supreme commander

U.S. Army general Creighton Williams Abrams Jr. commanded the Military Assistance Command Vietnam (MACV) during 1968–1972. As Chief of Staff of the Army during 1972–1974, Abrams helped rebuild the U.S. military establishment. (Herbert Elmer Abrams/Center for Military History)

in Vietnam and shifted military priorities from search-and-destroy missions to aggressive small-unit operations, while also accelerating "Vietnamization" to allow the South Vietnamese to fight their own war. He next oversaw the draw-down of American forces until July 1972 before reporting back to Washington, D.C., as the new Army Chief of Staff. In this capacity he initiated remedial programs to end drug use and racial problems in the Army, and oversaw the transition to an all-volunteer force. Abrams died in Washington on September 4, 1974, whereupon the Army christened its latest turbine-power tank the M-1 tank Abrams.

JUNE 23   As of today, the Vietnam War has become the longest-running conflict in American history.

JULY 3   In Washington, D.C., the recently dismissed General William C. Westmoreland becomes the new Army Chief of Staff.

JULY 20   Along the Demilitarized Zone (DMZ), South Korea, patrols from the 2nd and 7th Infantry Divisions engage

North Koreans firing at them from the other side.

AUGUST 5   Along the Demilitarized Zone (DMZ), South Korea, North Koreans fire upon a patrol from the 38th Infantry.

SEPTEMBER 1   In South Vietnam, Brigadier General Frederic M. Davison becomes the first African American general to lead a combat brigade, after assuming control of the 199th Infantry Brigade.

SEPTEMBER 13 Major General Keith L. Ware, 1st Infantry Division, dies in a helicopter crash.

SEPTEMBER 19 Along the Demilitarized Zone (DMZ), South Korea, a detachment of North Korean infiltrators is ambushed and destroyed by American troops.

SEPTEMBER 25 In Tay Ninh Province, South Vietnam, artillery attached to the 25th Infantry Division is equipped with new motion-detection equipment. They fire off shells to interdict North Vietnamese infiltration movements. As the war continues, interdiction missions constitute half of all artillery shells fired.

SEPTEMBER 30 In Southeast Asia, Special Forces personnel reach an all-time record of 3,542 officers and men deployed.

OCTOBER 11–22 Along the Demilitarized Zone (DMZ), South Korea, a 2nd Infantry Division patrol ambushes Communist infiltrators, killing two.

OCTOBER 27–NOVEMBER 9 In South Vietnam, General Creighton W. Abrams anticipates future troop reductions by shifting the 1st Cavalry Division to the Saigon in III Corps region to prevent enemy infiltration of the capital region.

NOVEMBER 19 In South Vietnam, 9th Infantry Division snipers score their first confirmed kills, and Sergeant Adelbert F. Waldron ends the war with 109 kills and two Distinguished Service Crosses.

DECEMBER 1 In the northern Mekong Delta, South Vietnam, the 9th Infantry Division commences OPERATION SPEEDY EXPRESS against Viet Cong infiltration. Here Air mobility is used to land troops in the vicinity of enemy troops as quickly as possible. By June an estimated 10,899 Communists are claimed killed for a loss of 267 Americans.

1969

JANUARY 1–AUGUST 31 In the Mekong Delta, South Vietnam, OPERATION RICE FARMER is launched by the 9th Infantry Division against local Viet Cong units; the Americans claim 1,861 Communists killed.

JANUARY 13–JULY 21 In the Batangan Peninsula, Quang Ngai Province, South Vietnam, two Americal Division battalions and two Marine Corps battalions advance to clear out Viet Cong units and weapon caches. Army losses are 56 dead and 268 wounded, mostly to mines and booby traps.

JANUARY 23 Along the Demilitarized Zone (DMZ), South Korea, 2nd Infantry Division outposts are attacked by North Korean infiltrators, but they are repulsed.

FEBRUARY 15 In South Vietnam, the new M551 Sheridan tanks deploy with the 3rd Squadron, 4th Cavalry. Armed with a 152-mm main gun/rocket launcher, it is a lighter, more mobile alternative to the heavier M-48 Patton tanks in service.

MARCH 1–APRIL 14 In Kontum Province, South Vietnam, OPERATION WAYNE GRAY is conducted by the 4th Infantry Division, and results in 608 dead Communists.

MARCH 1–MAY 8 In the A Shau Valley, South Vietnam, the 101st Airborne

Division cuts a vital infiltration route despite stiff resistance. By May the paratroopers have uncovered several large caches of weapons and supplies.

MARCH 18–APRIL 2 In the II Corps, South Vietnam, OPERATION ATLAS WEDGE is conducted by the 1st Division to interdict Communist traffic along Highway 13. Colonel George S. Patton Jr.'s 11th Cavalry kills over 400 North Vietnamese at a cost of 20 killed and 100 wounded.

APRIL 3 By this date, Vietnam combat deaths stand at 33,641, slightly higher than the toll suffered in the Korean War (33,629).

MAY 6 Landing Zone Carolyn, War Zone C, on the Cambodian border is attacked by superior North Vietnamese forces, and the 442 defenders, consisting of detachments from the 19th Artillery and 21st Artillery, call in support from AH-1G Cobra helicopter gunships. The Communists draw off, leaving behind 172 dead; American losses are 10 killed and 80 injured.

MAY 10–JUNE 7 In the A Shau Valley, South Vietnam, OPERATION APACHE SNOW commences as the 3rd Battalion, 187th Infantry, 101st Airborne Division engages two North Vietnamese battalions on Ap Bia Mountain, soon to be dubbed "Hamburger Hill." The Americans drive them off after a bloody, 10-day struggle, and at a cost of 56 dead and 300 wounded. This toll is so controversial that the action triggers a Congressional investigation.

MAY 16–AUGUST 13 In Quang Tin Province, South Vietnam, OPERATION LAMAR PLAIN commences. The 101st Airborne Division and the Americal Division sweep through the southern I Corps to root out any Communist units; 542 dead enemy soldiers are claimed.

JUNE 5–7 At Firebase Crook, South Vietnam, the garrison is alerted by seismic detectors of enemy forces massing nearby. Over the next two nights, detachments from the 3rd Battalion, 22nd Infantry, repel the attackers with beehive rounds

A wounded U.S. soldier is rushed to an evacuation helicopter amid fierce fighting against North Vietnamese forces during the Battle of Ap Bia Mountain on May 18, 1969. Known as the Battle of "Hamburger Hill," it was one of the bloodiest engagements of the Vietnam War. (UPI-Bettmann/Corbis)

fired at point-blank range; the Americans suffer one killed and seven injured.

JUNE 8 At Chu Lai, Vietnam, Lieutenant Sharon A. Lane becomes the first Army nurse killed after a Communist rocket strikes the 312th Evacuation Hospital; she receives a posthumous Bronze Star. By war's end a total of eight nurses die from various causes.

JULY 8–AUGUST 31 In South Vietnam, the Army's personnel draw down commences with OPERATION KEYSTONE EAGLE, involving two brigades of the 9th infantry Division and 15,700 officers and men.

AUGUST 17 Over the Demilitarized Zone (DMZ), South Korea, a helicopter from the 59th Aviation Company strays into North Korea and is shot down; three crewmen are taken prisoner.

SEPTEMBER 5 At Fort Benning, Georgia, Lieutenant William Calley is charged with murder for the My Lai Massacre of March 16, 1968. His subsequent court-martial becomes a rallying point for opposing viewpoints on the war.

SEPTEMBER 16 In Washington, D.C., President Richard M. Nixon declares that an additional 35,000 servicemen will be removed from Vietnam by December 15.

SEPTEMBER 18–DECEMBER 15 In South Vietnam, OPERATION KEYSTONE CARDINAL withdraws the 3rd Brigade, 82nd Airborne Division, back home.

OCTOBER 18 Along the Demilitarized Zone (DMZ), South Korea, a jeep from the 7th Division is ambushed by North Koreans; four Americans are killed.

NOVEMBER 26 In Washington, D.C., President Richard M. Nixon signs legislation establishing a lottery based on birthdays for the selective service. This new system commences on December 1

DECEMBER 15 In Washington, D.C., President Richard M. Nixon announces that American troop strength in South Vietnam will be cut to 434,000 by April, following the withdrawal of 110,000 combat soldiers.

1970

JANUARY 28 In Washington, D.C., the Department of Defense announces a third wave of troop withdrawals from South Vietnam, involving 50,000 military personnel from all four branches. All are to depart no later than April 19.

FEBRUARY 1–APRIL 15 In South Vietnam, OPERATION KEYSTONE BLUEJAY removes the 1st Infantry Division and the 3rd Brigade, 4th Infantry Division, in quick succession.

FEBRUARY 17 In Washington, D.C., President Richard M. Nixon declares that the

process of Vietnamization proceeds on schedule. The South Vietnamese are assuming the bulk of responsibility for the fighting.

MARCH 18 In southern I Corps, a helicopter crash injures Americal Division commander Major General Lloyd B. Ramsey during a survey mission.

APRIL 1 In Tay Ninh Province, South Vietnam, Firebase Illingsworth, three miles from the Cambodian border, is attacked by the Viet Cong. A battalion of the 8th Cavalry and several field batteries repel their antagonists, who leave 75 dead on the ground; American losses are 24 killed and 54 wounded.

In Binh Tuy Province, South Vietnam, Brigadier General William R. Bond is killed by enemy fire while accompanying a resupply convoy.

APRIL 29–JUNE 30   In Washington, D.C., President Richard M. Nixon authorizes Americans to attack Communist sanctuaries in Cambodia; this represents a major escalation of the ground war.

MAY 1   Along the Cambodian border, American forces begin OPERATION ROCK-CRUSHER, as the 1st Cavalry Division, assisted by the 11th Armored Cavalry and 5,000 South Vietnamese troops, advance into the so-called Fishhook region.

MAY 3–4   In Cambodia, the 1st Squadron, 9th Cavalry, discovers an enemy supply dump nearly a square mile in length; Communist forces simply melt away into the jungle.

MAY 4   At Kent State University, Ohio, National Guard troops fire upon rioting student demonstrators, killing four and wounding nine.

MAY 4–16   In the III Corps tactical area, South Vietnam, the 4th Division and the 22nd South Vietnamese Division commence OPERATION BINH TAY by crossing the into Cambodia. They overcome foreboding terrain, and a North Vietnamese hospital complex is overrun without resistance.

MAY 6–14   West of Tay Ninh Province, South Vietnam, the 25th Infantry Division pushes into the Cambodian region known as the Dog's Head, while the 3rd Brigade, 9th Division, advances upon the Parrot's Beak.

MAY 28   In Washington, D.C., the Army issues Regulation 350–216 regarding war crimes, illegal orders, and the responsibility of individual soldiers under such circumstances. This is a byproduct of the My Lai massacre.

JUNE 11   Colonel Anna M. Hayes, Chief of the Army Nurse Corps, and Colonel Elizabeth P. Hoisington, Director of WAC, become the military's first female brigadier generals.

JUNE 30   The Cambodian incursion draws to a close and American forces withdraw. They suffer 338 dead and 1,525 wounded, while Communists losses are estimated at 11,000 dead and 2,328 captured, along with mounds of equipment and supplies destroyed.

JULY 1–23   In Thua Thien Province, South Vietnam, Firebase Ripcord is attacked by superior numbers of North Vietnamese. The defenders stand their ground until July 18, when a helicopter crash ignites the base ammunition dump. Major General John J. Hennessy, 101st Airborne Division, orders the firebase evacuated, which is accomplished by airlift under heavy fire. American losses are 61 dead and 325 wounded.

JULY 1–DECEMBER 31   In South Vietnam, increments IV and V of the drawdown remove brigades from the 4th, 9th, and 25th Infantry Divisions, totaling 57,000 men.

JULY 7   Major George W. Casey, commander of the 1st Cavalry Division, dies when his helicopter crashes; his replacement is Major General George W. Putnam.

AUGUST 21   In Washington, D.C., Secretary of Defense Melvin Laird introduces the Total Force Concept. Under this regimen, the Reserves and National Guard are the first recourse for augmenting active forces, instead of resorting to a draft.

NOVEMBER 21 In North Vietnam, helicopter-borne Special Forces under Colonel Arthur "Bull" Simons mount OPERATION KINGPIN, a daring raid against Son Tay prison, 23 miles west of Hanoi. The raiders kill 25 North Vietnamese in the camp, only to find it abandoned.

1971

JANUARY 1 In South Vietnam, OPERATION KEYSTONE ROBIN removes parts of the 1st Cavalry Division, the 11th Armored Cavalry Regiment, and the 25th Infantry Division.

JANUARY 6 In Washington, D.C., Secretary of War Melvin Laird declares that Vietnamization is ahead of schedule, and all combat missions for U.S. troops will cease by mid-summer.

JANUARY 28 In Washington, D.C., President Richard M. Nixon seeks a two-year extension of the draft and requests Congress to provide a 50 percent pay raise for new recruits. He seeks an all-volunteer force by the middle of the decade.

JANUARY 30–FEBRUARY 7 In the I Corps, OPERATION LAM SON 719/DEWEY CANYON II unfolds as the 5th Infantry Division moves west 9 miles toward the old Marine Corps base at Khe Sanh, while the 101st Airborne Division advances back into the A Shau Valley. Both moves are diversionary measures to mask the impending South Vietnamese thrust into Laos.

FEBRUARY 8–MARCH 6 OPERATION LAM SON 719, consisting of 16,000 South Vietnamese troops, backed by American air power, attacks Communist sanctuaries in neighboring Laos. Lieutenant General James W. Sutherland directs the movements of XXIV Corps, which operates 700 helicopters supporting ARVN units.

MARCH 1 The 5th Special Forces Group, having acquired a distinguished combat record, departs South Vietnam. A handful of personnel remain behind as instructors with the Special Advisory Group.

MARCH 4–APRIL 6 In Laos, South Vietnamese forces commence a hurried withdrawal, and many have to be evacuated by air. The incursion ends with 108 Army helicopters downed and a further 618 damaged. American losses are 215 dead and 1,200 wounded.

MARCH 15 At Bien Hoa, South Vietnam, two lieutenants die after an African American soldier rolls a grenade into an officers' barracks. Racial altercations and attacks against officers ("fraggings") are becoming common, resulting in 86 deaths and 788 injuries.

MARCH 28 In Quang Tin Province, South Vietnam, Firebase Mary Ann is attacked by Viet Cong sappers, and the 231 defenders from Company C, 1st Battalion, 46th Infantry, are caught flat-footed; they suffer 30 killed and 82 injured. Americal Division commander Major General James L. Baldwin and 196th Brigade commander Colonel William S. Hathaway are consequently relieved of duty.

MARCH 29   At Fort Benning, Georgia, a military court finds Lieutenant William Calley guilty of murdering 22 Vietnamese at My Lai; he receives life imprisonment at hard labor, but is finally pardoned in November 1974.

MAY 1–NOVEMBER 30   In South Vietnam, OPERATION KEYSTONE ORIOLE unfolds; the Americal Division, the 173rd Airborne Brigade, and other units totaling 71,000 men, return home.

NOVEMBER 12   In Washington, D.C., President Richard M. Nixon declares that another 45,000 combat troops will be withdrawn from Vietnam by February 1, 1972. Combat-related deaths for the year also total 1,302, in contrast to 14,592 for the same period in 1968.

DECEMBER 1   In South Vietnam, OPERATION KEYSTONE MALLARD unfolds as the 101st Airborne Division, the famed "Screaming Eagles," redeploys back to Fort Campbell, Kentucky.

1972

JANUARY 13   In Washington, D.C., President Richard M. Nixon announces the withdrawal of an additional 70,000 American combat troops from South Vietnam by the end of the year, reducing overall troop strength to 69,000.

MARCH 30–MAY 1   In South Vietnam, Communist forces pour across the Demilitarized Zone (DMZ) into Quang Tri Province and commence their so-called "Easter Offensive." Quang Tri city becomes the first provincial capital to fall to the Communists since Hue in 1968.

APRIL 5–MAY 12   In Binh Long Province, South Vietnam, An Loc is attacked by North Vietnamese regulars, backed by Soviet-made PT-76 and T-54 tanks. Major General James F. Hollingsworth calls in major air strikes and sweeps by AH–1G Cobra helicopter gunships, which decimate Communist armor and drive them back into the jungle.

MAY 1–JUNE 30   In South Vietnam, OPERATION PHEASANT removes the final Army combat unit: the 3rd Brigade, 1st Cavalry Division, and the 19th Infantry Brigade.

JUNE 1   To test the appeal of an all-volunteer force, Defense Secretary Melvin Laird announces that Army recruits will receive a $1,500 bonus for a four-year enlistment. This is a temporary expedient.

JUNE 29   In Saigon, South Vietnam, MACV commander General Creighton W. Abrams is replaced by General Frederick C. Weyand.

JULY 9   At An Loc, South Vietnam, Brigadier General Richard Tallman is killed by enemy mortar fire.

AUGUST 11–26   Task Force Gimlet, consisting of the 3rd Battalion, 21st Infantry, and assorted units, is the last combat unit withdrawn from South Vietnam.

AUGUST 28   In Washington, D.C., President Richard M. Nixon declares that the draft will cease as of June 30, 1972.

OCTOBER 12   In Washington, D.C., General Creighton Abrams becomes Chief of Staff of the Army. He confronts rebuilding a force suffering from poor discipline, drug use, lower defense appropriations, and fashionable anti-military sentiment.

DECEMBER 1 For the first time since January 1965, MACV is able to announce

that no American serviceperson died in Vietnam during the week.

DECEMBER 31 American troop strength in South Vietnam stands at 24,200 officers and enlisted men.

1973

JANUARY In South Vietnam, OPERATION ENHANCE unfolds as the Army turns over 70,767 guns, 383 artillery pieces, 622 tracked vehicles, and 2,035 wheeled vehicles over to its ARVN allies.

JANUARY 27 At An Loc, South Vietnam, Lieutenant Colonel William B. Nolde is the final American soldier killed, when he is struck by shrapnel from an artillery round. His dies only 11 hours before the cease-fire.

MARCH 16 In North Vietnam, Army Captain Floyd J. Thompson is finally released after nine years of captivity. He is the longest-held American captive of the war.

MARCH 29 In Washington, D.C., General Frederic C. Weyand warns Congress that the survival of South Vietnam depends on the continuance of American economic and military aid.

APRIL 26 In Washington, D.C., the Department of Defense raises the combat arms enlistment bonus from $1,500 to $2,500.

JULY 1 Conscription ends in the United States, but the Selective Service still registers young men of military age.

AUGUST In South Korea, Lieutenant Colonel Colin Powell takes charge of a battalion within the 2nd Infantry Division.

1974

JANUARY As part of its rebuilding program, the Army activates the 75th Infantry Regiment (Ranger) of three battalions. Greater emphasis is being placed on mobile, light infantry formations.

SEPTEMBER 4 In Washington, D.C., General Frederick C. Weyand becomes Army Chief of Staff to replace ailing General Creighton Abrams.

1975

MARCH 27 Army Chief of Staff General Frederick C. Weyand ventures to Saigon, South Vietnam, for a high-level conference with governmental officials. He remains convinced that the country cannot survive without continuing military assistance from the United States.

APRIL 8 In Washington, D.C., Army Chief of Staff General Frederick C. Weyand informs Congress that the fall of South Vietnam is imminent without major American military assistance. No such intervention is forthcoming.

AUGUST 27 In Ohio, Governor James Rhodes and 27 National Guardsmen are cleared of charges stemming from the deaths of four students at Kent State University in May 1970.

OCTOBER 7 In Washington, D.C., President Gerald R. Ford signs legislation allowing women to enroll at all four service academies for the first time.

1976

MAY 7 At South Dakota State University, Martha Hahn becomes the first female lieutenant commissioned through ROTC.

JULY 1 At Fort Monroe, Virginia, the new Army Field Manual FM-100–5 is issued. This new version emphasizes aggressive, small-unit tactics coupled with rigorous training and heavy firepower. This is also the conceptual beginning of the "Air-Land Battle," whereby air power and ground forces are closely integrated to overpower an enemy.

JULY 7 At the U.S. Military Academy, West Point, New York, the first female cadets are enrolled in the class of 1980.

JULY 12 Secretary of the Army Martin R. Hoffman, after learning that the Soviet Union is placing renewed emphasis on chemical and biological warfare, overturns an earlier decision to eliminate the Chemical Corps.

AUGUST 18 At Panmunjom, South Korea, Captain Arthur Bonifas and Lieutenant Mark Barrett are attacked and killed by North Koreans while pruning a tree in the Demilitarized Zone (DMZ).

American forces are placed on full alert in consequence.

AUGUST 21 OPERATION PAUL BUNYON, a show of force that includes fully armed soldiers, helicopter gunships, and B-52 bombers, commences as American soldiers return to the Demilitarized Zone (DMZ) and prune several trees under North Korean noses.

AUGUST 23 In Washington, D.C., Secretary of the Army Martin R. Hoffman declares that 149 West Point cadets implicated in a cheating scandal can regain admittance following a one-year probationary period for "reflection."

OCTOBER 1 In Washington, D.C., General Bernard W. Rogers gains appointment as the new Army Chief of Staff, being the last World War II veteran so honored.

DECEMBER 15 The Borman Commission, headed by former astronaut Frank Borman, releases its final report relative to the West Point cheating scandal. It recommends that all accused students be readmitted, and places greater emphasis on Cadet Honor Code.

1977

JANUARY 1 At Arlington Hall, Virginia, Army intelligence activities are consolidated into the new U.S. Army Intelligence and Security Command (INSCOM) under Brigadier General William I. Rolya.

FEBRUARY 14 In Washington, D.C., Clifford Irving becomes the first African American appointed as Secretary of the Army.

JUNE 10 In Washington, D.C., Secretary of the Army Clifford Alexander restores a Congressional Medal of Honor to Mary Walker, which she received for distinguished service during the Civil War; she remains the only female recipient.

NOVEMBER 18 At the White Sands Missile Range, New Mexico, the new Pershing II ballistic missile test is successfully conducted. It is designed to counter a threat posed by the Soviet SS–20 missile to NATO.

NOVEMBER 21 At Fort Bragg, North Carolina, the 1st Special Forces Operational Detachment–Delta (1st SFOD-D) is created. In contrast with Special Forces, which are instructional and reconnaissance units, Delta Force is a counterterrorist unit specializing in rescuing hostages.

DECEMBER 20 In Washington, D.C., Secretary of the Army Clifford Alexander announces that while many positions within the Army are open to women, they remained excluded from combat arms.

1978

JANUARY 24 In Washington, D.C., the 761st Tank Battalion, an African American unit, receives a Presidential Unit Citation, 33 years after World War

Delta Force

The 1st Special Forces Operational Detachment Force, popularly known as Delta Force, is one of the world's premier clandestine military units. Created in 1977 by Colonel Charles Beckwith, who had trained with the British Special Air Service (SAS) squadrons, it functions as an elite, anti-terrorist organization recruited from successful infantry rangers and Special Force (Green Beret) veterans. Prospective members undergo grueling psychological and physical endurance testing at undisclosed locations, and only a handful of the toughest, most intelligent recruits are allowed to join. Once accepted, Delta recruits receive special training in weapons handling, communications, reconnaissance, hostage rescue, and intelligence operations. The deaths of certain high-level narcotics figures and terrorists across the globe over the past two decades are also attributed to Delta assassination squads, but the U.S. Army, which controls them exclusively, denies any such actions. So classified are their missions and personnel rosters that Delta Force members wear no special insignia on their uniforms, and occasionally wear long hair and beards to promote a distinctly unmilitary appearance. In terms of operations, Delta members frequently act in concert with the Navy's DEVGRU (SEAL Team Six) anti-terrorist unit and the Central Intelligence Agency's Special Operations Group. To date, Delta members have been known to have participated in OPERATION EAGLE CLAW, the failed 1980 attempt to rescue American hostages in Iran, and operations against Somalia warlords in Mogadishu in October 1993. However, recent operations against al-Qaeda and the Taliban in Afghanistan and Iraq, while rumored to be highly successful, remain undiscussed. In addition to combat operations, Delta Force members routinely train with elite special forces from Australia, England, Germany, France, and Canada. This lethal and shadowy organization remains America's point men in the war against global terrorism.

II. It fought exceptionally well during the dash across northern France in 1944.

FEBRUARY 9 The Army adopts a new Kevlar helmet, strongly reminiscent of German helmets of World Wars I and II, to replace the old M1 "steelpot."

SEPTEMBER 25 At the Redstone Arsenal, Alabama, the Hellfire AGM-114 laser-guided missile is successfully tested; this lethal device will arm the next generation of helicopter gunships.

OCTOBER 20 In Washington, D.C., President Jimmy Carter abolishes the Women's Army Corps (WAC) as a separate entity within the U.S. Army. Henceforth, all female personnel will be directly integrated into standing, noncombat Army formations. Brigadier General Mary E. Clarke also becomes the first female major general in Army history.

1979

JANUARY 1 In Washington, D.C., Army Chief of Staff Bernard W. Rogers issues orders allowing berets to be worn by Rangers (black) and Green Berets (green).

NOVEMBER The Army adopts the camouflage Battle Dress Uniform (BDU) worn by paratroopers, rangers, and Special Forces, to replace standard green fatigues.

DECEMBER 7 Near the Demilitarized Zone (DMZ), South Korea, a 2nd Infantry Division patrol wanders into a North Korean minefield; one soldier dies and two are wounded.

1980

FEBRUARY 28 In a major development, the Army deploys its first turbine-powered M1 Abrams tanks to replace the older M60 Patton tanks. Both are armed with the same 105-mm main gun, but the M1A1, which arrives in 1985, boasts a powerful, German-designed 120-mm cannon.

MARCH 1 In Washington, D.C., President Jimmy Carter authorizes the new Rapid Deployment Joint Task Force (RDF), consisting mostly of the 82nd Airborne Division, with Special Forces and Rangers units attached as needed.

APRIL 24 After failed negotiations to secure American hostages held in Teheran, Iran, President Jimmy Carter authorizes OPERATION EAGLE CLAW, a helicopter-borne commando mission to rescue them by force. They are conveyed inland by eight RH-53 helicopters launched from the carrier *Nimitz*, but when three helicopters malfunction after encountering a dust storm, the mission is aborted. Disaster strikes at Landing Zone Desert One, when a EC-130 transport and a helicopter collide, killing eight Americans and wounding five. Consequently, the U.S. Central Command (CENTCOM) is created to better orchestrate future operations in this strategic theater.

MAY 28 At West Point, New York, the Military Academy graduates its first 61 female cadets.

JUNE The lowly Army C-ration is replaced by the new Meals-Ready-to-Eat (MREs). These consist of dehydrated food in airtight pouches, and pack higher nutritional content.

JUNE 27 In Washington, D.C., President Jimmy Carter signs legislation reactivating draft registration for 19- and 20-year-old men in response to the Soviet invasion of Afghanistan.

OCTOBER 16 At Fort Irwin, California, the new National Training Center (NTC) opens for service. This facility covers 1,000 square miles of the Mojave Desert, is highly automated, and becomes the Army's premier testing and training ground.

1981

JANUARY In an attempt to boost recruiting, the U.S. Army Recruiting Command unveils its "Be all that you can be" campaign. This proves to be one of the most successful advertising efforts of the 20th Century, and brings in numerous high-quality recruits.

JANUARY 22 In Washington, D.C., Alexander M. Haig is appointed the new Secretary of State. He is only the second soldier to hold that position, after George C. Marshall.

FEBRUARY 27 The Army deploys its new Stinger shoulder-launched, surface-to-air missile to infantry units across Europe. It replaces the earlier and less-capable Redeye missile system, and proves devastating against

Soviet aircraft and helicopters in Afghanistan.

APRIL 3 Colonel Harry G. Summers publishes his seminal text *On Strategy: The Vietnam War in Context*, which maintains that the United States should have waged conventional war against the North Vietnamese, instead of gradually escalating pressure that allowed the enemy to adapt.

APRIL 8 In New York City, General Omar N. Bradley dies; he is still the Army's senior officer and last five-star general.

OCTOBER 20 At Fort Myer, Virginia, the Army officially christens its new armored personnel carrier the M2/3 Bradley. This replaces the aluminum-hulled M-113 of the Vietnam War.

1982

JANUARY The 82nd Airborne Division accepts the role of UN Multinational Force and Observers (MFO) in the Sinai

Peninsula separating Egypt and Israel. This remains the Army's longest-running peacekeeping mission.

AUGUST 30   In Japan, Lieutenant General Roscoe Robinson, Jr., is the first African American elevated to full (four-star) general.

NOVEMBER 13   In Washington, D.C., the Vietnam Veterans Memorial is dedicated, on which the names of all 59,800 servicemen and women killed are etched. It is part of the national healing process to move on from this divisive conflict.

1983

JANUARY 1   At MacDill Air Force Base, Florida, the Rapid Deployment Joint Task Force (RDF) is redesignated the U.S. Central Command (CENT-COM). This unified body coordinates military operations in over 25 countries.

MARCH 22   The U.S. Army Tank, Automotive, and Armaments Command concludes seven years of testing, and decides to obtain 55,000 High-Mobility Multipurpose Wheeled Vehicles (HMMWV, or Hum-Vees) to replace the legendary M551 "Jeep."

MARCH 31   At Fort Riley, Kansas, the first battery of M270 Multiple Launch Rocket Systems (MLRS) deploys with the 1st Infantry Division. This is the first multiple-rocket system acquired by the Army since the Korean War.

APRIL   The Army assigns its first Bradley armored fighting vehicles (AFVs) to cavalry and mechanized infantry units. Heavily armed and armored, these machines are capable of firing TOW antitank weapons, a 25-mm chain gun (cannon) and several machine guns. Each Bradley also carries a squad of infantry in comparative safety.

OCTOBER 25–30   President Ronald W. Reagan unleashes OPERATION URGENT FURY to rescue 1,100 American medical students taken hostage in Grenada by Marxist revolutionaries. The attack begins at dawn with a low-altitude parachute assault by the 2nd Ranger Battalion, 75th Infantry, against the unfinished Soviet airstrip at Port Salinas. They overcome Cuban and Grenadian forces, and quickly secure their objective.

OCTOBER 27   On Grenada, American forces round up 638 Cubans, who have also suffered 24 killed and 59 wounded. An

U.S. paratroopers stand by artillery pieces after the Invasion of Grenada on October 27, 1983. (AP Photo)

additional 45 Grenadian soldiers are also slain, while American losses are 18 dead and 166 wounded, mostly through friendly fire.

DECEMBER On Grenada, the bulk of American forces involved in OPERATION URGENT FURY are gradually withdrawn. This small but successful action witnessed the combat debut of UH–60 Black Hawk helicopters, and over 100 female military personnel directly participated.

1984

MAY 28 In Washington, D.C., this Memorial Day, President Ronald Reagan pays homage to the only unidentified serviceman killed in Vietnam.

SEPTEMBER 10 The School of the Americas is relocated from Fort Gulick, Panama Canal Zone, to Fort Benning, Georgia. This academy fosters close cooperation between the U.S. Army and military establishments of Latin American nations.

NOVEMBER 23 Along the Demilitarized Zone (DMZ), South Korea, a Communist defector suddenly breaks for American lines, triggering a huge fire fight; one soldier is injured.

1985

JANUARY 31 The Army replaces its iconic Browning M1911A1 .45-caliber automatic pistol, in service since 1911, with the smaller Beretta M9 9-mm pistol.

MARCH 24 In Ludwiglust, East Germany, a Soviet sentry shoots Major Arthur D. Nicholson of the U.S. Military Liaison Mission. He is the last American killed in the Cold War, and receives a posthumous Purple Heart.

AUGUST 27 In Washington, D.C., Secretary of Defense Casper Weinberger halts production and development of the controversial M988 Sergeant York anti-aircraft system, after prolonged developmental costs of $1.8 billion.

OCTOBER 12 At Fort Drum, New York, the 10th Mountain Division is activated while the National Guard 29th Division (Maryland and Virginia) is reorganized as a light infantry division.

1986

APRIL 14–15 At Fort Monroe, Virginia, the new U.S. Army ROTC Cadet Command begins under Major General Robert E. Wagner. It oversees ROTC programs at more than 400 colleges and universities, and 800 high schools with Junior ROTC programs.

DECEMBER 4 In the Panama Canal Zone, U.S. Army South is activated to coordinate the multi-service U.S. Southern Command through a single headquarters at Fort Clayton.

1987

MARCH 31 In El Paraiso, El Salvador, Special Forces Sergeant Gregory Frontius dies, killed in a firefight with FMLN guerrillas receiving military aid from Communist Nicaragua.

APRIL 9 The Special Forces are established as a basic branch of the U.S. Army. The military is placing renewed emphasis on special operations around the world to combat Communism and terrorism.

NOVEMBER 1 At Fort Benning, Georgia, the Ranger Training Brigade is established along with four Ranger Training Battalions. The Army is rediscovering its light infantry roots.

1988

MARCH 16–28 In Washington, D.C., President Ronald W. Reagan responses to Nicaraguan Sandinista (Communist) incursions into Honduras by deploying 3,200 Army troops during OPERATION GOLDEN PHEASANT. Their presence deters Communist aggression, and they are eventually withdrawn.

1989

APRIL 21 In Quezon City, the Philippines, Colonel James N. Rowe of the Joint United States Military Advisory Group (JUSMAG) is assassinated by Marxist guerrillas.

OCTOBER 1 In Washington, D.C., President George H. W. Bush appoints General Colin Powell as Chairman of the Joint Chiefs of Staff; he is the first African American so honored and, at 52 years of age, the youngest.

DECEMBER 20–24 President George H. W. Bush responds to Panamanian aggression with OPERATION JUST CAUSE, a concerted invasion by U.S. Armed forces that quickly overruns General Manuel Noriega's self-defense forces. The Americans lose 18 dead and 255 wounded. Captain Linda Bray, 988th Military Police Company, also becomes the first woman to direct American troops in combat.

1990

FEBRUARY 21 In Colon Province, Panama, two helicopters crash in a driving rainstorm, killing 11 soldiers of the 7th Infantry Division.

MARCH 1 In the Fulda Gap, West Germany, the 11th Armored Cavalry performs the last border patrol of the Cold War.

JULY 30 The Central Intelligence Agency declares that at least 100,000 Iraqi troops are poised on the borders of Kuwait; invasion seems imminent.

Powell, Colin L. (1937–)

Colin Luther Powell was born in the Harlem district of New York City on April 5, 1937, a son of Jamaican immigrants. He enrolled in the local ROTC program while attending the City College of New York and was commissioned a second lieutenant in the U.S. Army in 1958. He rose to brigadier general in 1979, served as a national security adviser under President Ronald Reagan, and in 1989 made history when President George H. W. Bush appointed him the nation's first African American chairman of the Joint Chiefs of Staff (JCS). Here Powell helped orchestrate OPERATIONS DESERT SHIELD and DESERT STORM in response to the 1991 Iraqi invasion of Kuwait, and worked closely with General H. Norman Schwarzkopf during the run-up to the ensuing Gulf War. Powell was reappointed to the JCS in 1991 after President Bush awarded him a Presidential Medal of Freedom for his services. However, he disagreed strongly with cuts in military spending proposed by President Bill Clinton and resigned from office in September 1993. Powell continued on as a private citizen for several years, and in 1995 he published his best-selling memoir, *My American Journey*. Moreover, in 2001 President George W. Bush appointed him the nation's first African American secretary of state. His task grew increasingly complex in the wake of the September 11, 2001, attack upon the World Trade Towers in New York, whereupon Bush intended to invade Iraq to depose dictator Saddam Hussein. Powell skillfully articulated the American position to a skeptical United Nations with verve and style, although American claims of Iraqi weapons of mass destruction (WMDs) were never verified. Powell was stung by criticism leveled at him that he failed to weld together a large-enough coalition for OPERATION IRAQI FREEDOM, and he concluded half a century of devoted service by retiring in January 2005. His replacement was Condoleezza Rice, another African American.

Colin Powell was a U.S. Army general and the first African American to serve as chairman of the Joint Chiefs of Staff. He later became the first African American to serve as secretary of state, appointed by President George W. Bush in 2000. (Stocklight)

AUGUST 2   Iraqi dictator Saddam Hussein orders his forces to invade Kuwait, an American ally and major oil exporter. President George H. W. Bush declares a national emergency, while the Joint Chief of Staff reviews CENTCOM Operations Plan 1002–90 for transferring American forces into the region over the next three to four months.

AUGUST 4   In New York City, General H. Norman Schwarzkopf briefs the National Security Council as to military options available for Kuwait. He holds that a minimum of 17 weeks is necessary to acquire sufficient military force to drive the Iraqis out. Saddam Hussein's potential use of chemical weapons is also reviewed.

AUGUST 6–7   The Army receives deployment orders to Saudi Arabia, and the 82nd Airborne Division and the 24th Infantry Division are placed on alert. Within the next 24 hours, the 1st Cavalry Division, the 1st Brigade, 2nd

Armored Division, the 101st Airborne Division, and the 3rd Armored Cavalry Regiment are likewise shipped out as part of OPERATION DESERT SHIELD.

AUGUST 8–9 In Dhahran, Saudi Arabia, the 2nd Brigade, 82nd Airborne Division, becomes the first large American unit air-lifted into the theater. They are joined by staff officers of the XVIII Airborne Corps, slated to arrive shortly.

AUGUST 12–14 In Saudi Arabia, OPERATIONS DRAGON I and II unfold, as the 82nd Airborne Division assumes defensive positions around the ports of al-Jubayl, Dhahran, and ad-Damman.

AUGUST 13 In Saudi Arabia, the Army deploys it first PAC-2 Patriot surface-to-air missile unit, Battery B, 2nd Battalion, 7th Air Defense Artillery. These will counter hundreds of SCUD Soviet-made ballistic missiles owned by Iraq.

AUGUST 22 In Washington, D.C., President George H. W. Bush signs Executive Order 12727, mobilizing 200,000 Army reservists for six months of active service. This is the largest activation of Reserve forces since the Korean War.

AUGUST 31 Colonel Jesse Johnson leads the 5th Special Forces Group to Saudi Arabia to help train Arab coalition armies. They are joined by the 3rd and 10th Special Forces Group, as well as Delta Force contingents.

SEPTEMBER 16 At Fort Hood, Texas, the 1st Cavalry Division ships men and equipment to Saudi Arabia. It will operate with the 1st Brigade, 2nd Armor

Division, until the 155th Armored Brigade is ready for service overseas.

NOVEMBER 6 The Army begins replacing its M1 Abrams tanks with the newer, more powerfully armed M1A1s, sporting a German-made 120-mm cannon.

NOVEMBER 8 In Washington, D.C., President George H. W. Bush orders American forces in the Persian Gulf increased to 430,000 men. Reinforcements include the entire VII Corps from Germany. A total of 200,000 men, 6,000 tracked vehicles, and 59,000 wheeled vehicles are relocated by mid-February, 1991.

NOVEMBER 13–14 In Washington, D.C., President George H. W. Bush extends the term of service for Reservists by an additional 180 days. Secretary of Defense Dick Cheney also mobilizes 80,000 additional Reservists and National Guard troops for OPERATION DESERT SHIELD.

NOVEMBER 27 At Fort Bragg, North Carolina, the 1st Special Operations Command is redesignated the U.S. Army Special Operations Command (Airborne).

DECEMBER 1 In Washington, D.C., Secretary of Defense Dick Cheney enlarges the call-up of Reservists to 115,000 men and women.

DECEMBER 27 In Riyadh, Saudi Arabia, General Colin Powell and Secretary of Defense Dick Cheney are briefed by General H. Norman Schwarzkopf. When the push comes, he intends to send the VII Corps and XVIII Airborne Corps on a flanking movement that will decisively turn the Iraqi right flank.

1991

JANUARY In the Persian Gulf, the Army has deployed 710,821 officers and men in

18 divisions, with 200,000 of these deployed in the Arabian Desert.

JANUARY 1   At Tactical Assembly Area (TAA) Thompson, Saudi Arabia, the 1st Armored Division, VII Corps, deploys and begins extensively drilling and maneuvering with live gunnery.

JANUARY 2   In Florida, the U.S. Central Command (CENTCOM) reveals U.S. military strength in the Persian Gulf to be 325,000. Over 200,000 additional troops are en route to the same destination.

JANUARY 7   In Florida, the U.S. Central Command's (CENTCOM) intelligence section states that Saddam Hussein has 452,000 Iraqi troops (35 divisions) in and around Kuwait, bolstered by 4,300 tanks and 3,100 artillery pieces.

JANUARY 10   In Saudi Arabia, the 1st Brigade, 2nd Armored Division ("Tiger Brigade") is removed from the 1st Cavalry Division and reassigned to the 2nd Marine Division, I Marine Expeditionary Force, to provide them with enhanced firepower from their ultra-modern M1A1 Abrams tanks. The Marines are still employing older M60A3 Patton tanks.

JANUARY 14   The 1st Armored Division reconnoiters the terrain west of the Saudi-Iraqi border, proving it is passable for tanks and other tracked vehicles. This information permits the 1st and 3rd Armored Divisions to deploy further west and avoid troop congestion on the ground.

JANUARY 16   In Florida, the U.S. Central Command (CENTCOM) declares that 425,000 U.S. troops are in the Persian Gulf region, along with military forces of 19 nations and naval forces of 14 nations.

JANUARY 17   In Saudi Arabia, the 2nd Battalion, 34th Armor Regiment (1st Division) rehearses attacks on Iraqi earthen positions (sand berms) using plows and armored earthmovers.

JANUARY 18   In Washington, D.C., President George H. W. Bush extends the tour of Army reservists beyond 180 days, and authorizes the call-up of one million reservists as needed.

JANUARY 31   In Iraq, two soldiers of the 233rd Transportation Company stray into enemy territory and are taken prisoner. Specialist Melissa A. Rathbun-Nealy becomes the first American female prisoner of the conflict.

To prevent further Scud attacks upon Saudi Arabia and Israel, the Joint Special Operations Task Force (JSOTF) is ordered to destroy the launchers or point them out to Coalition air forces. They employ two squadrons from Delta Force, a company from the 1st Battalion, 75th Rangers, some Navy SEALS, and elements of the Army 160th Special Operations Aviation Regiment ("Night Stalkers").

FEBRUARY 1   At Phase Blue Line, Saudi Arabia, a 15-minute fire fight erupts between Iraqi forces and the 4th Battalion, 325th Infantry, 82nd Airborne Division. No losses are incurred.

FEBRUARY 3   In Saudi Arabia, OPERATION DESERT SHIELD concludes as most ground units are deployed to their assigned assembly areas. The VII Corps and the XVIII Airborne Corps figure prominently in upcoming OPERATION DESERT STORM.

FEBRUARY 7   Along the Kuwaiti-Iraqi border, artillery belonging to the VII Corps and 1st Cavalry Division fire the first shots of OPERATION DESERT STORM. This action marks the debut of laser-guided Copperhead missiles, which knock out an enemy observation tower.

FEBRUARY 13   In Saudi Arabia, the 42nd Field Artillery Brigade and the 1st Cavalry Division commence another large artillery raid as MLRS missile batteries unleash 216 rounds which, in turn, drop 140,000 "bomblets" upon exposed enemy positions.

FEBRUARY 14 In Saudi Arabia, the 1st Armored Division, 9,000 vehicles strong, rumbles toward Tactical Assembly Area (TAA) Garcia, just below the 2nd Armored Cavalry's position.

FEBRUARY 15 In Saudi Arabia, Coalition commander General H. Norman Schwarzkopf is apprised of Iraqi morale through prisoners, learning that the enemy soldiers are tired of incessant warfare and would surrender, except for execution by the Republican Guard and possible threats against family members.

FEBRUARY 17 In Saudi Arabia, the VII Corps unleashes five battalions of artillery that smash various Iraqi air defenses. This enables AH-64A Apaches of the 6th Cavalry to slip through enemy lines unopposed, destroying several communication facilities.

FEBRUARY 19 In Saudi Arabia, the 24th Infantry Division (Mechanized) rumbles forward to engage Iraqi troops. Meanwhile, an Iraqi border post is eliminated by a Copperhead missile fired by Battery B, 4th Battalion, 41st Field Artillery.

FEBRUARY 20 At Wadi al Batin, Kuwait, part of the 1st Cavalry Division forces its way through Iraqi sand berms and fans out into the desert, looking for enemy positions. They are attacked by Iraqi artillery and antitank guns, and withdraw with three killed and nine injured.

FEBRUARY 23 In the Euphrates River Valley, Iraq, Special Forces deploy and seek intelligence concerning Iraqi troop movements. A three-man team under Master Sergeant Jeffrey Sims is discovered and battles superior forces for several

hours, until MH-60 Black Hawks of the 160th Special Operations Aviation Regiment (SOAR) extract them.

FEBRUARY 24 In Kuwait, General H. Norman Schwarzkopf decides that the Iraqis have been have been sufficiently "softened up," and launches an all-out offensive. At 4:00 A.M., the XVIII Airborne Corps, supported by the 82nd Airborne Division and French 6th Light Armored Division, moves forward and easily seizes its objectives. VII Corps, the main strike force under Lieutenant General Tommy Franks, is preceded by a massive bombardment of 11,000 artillery rounds and 414 MLRS rockets, then advances to breach Iraqi defenses. All objectives are reached in only two hours instead of the 18 hours anticipated.

FEBRUARY 25 In Saudi Arabia, General H. Norman Schwarzkopf grows concerned that the Iraqi Republican Guard is trying to escape, so he orders Lieutenant General Franks eastward to cut them off. At this juncture, Saddam Hussein takes to the air waves and instructs his forces out of Kuwait.

FEBRUARY 25–26 The 101st Airborne Division undertakes a 150-mile penetration of Iraqi territory. This is the longest air assault in history and it cuts off Highway 8 from enemy supplies and reinforcements moving below it.

FEBRUARY 26 At 73 Eastling, M1A1 Abrams tanks of the 2nd Armored Cavalry Regiment engage the Republican Guard Tawakalna Division; they destroy 28 Russian-built T-72 tanks and 16 other armored vehicles at a cost of three dead.

FEBRUARY 26–27 The Battle of Objective Norfolk unfolds as the 1st and 3rd Brigades, 1st Infantry Division, race ahead and engage the Republican Guard's Tawakalna Division and the 37th Brigade of the 12th Armored Division. The swirling battle results in the destruction of scores of tanks, and hundreds of killed and injured. American losses are six dead and the destruction of a handful of Abrams and Bradleys, all through friendly fire.

FEBRUARY 27 Along Medinah Ridge, the 1st Armored Division rolls forward and attacks the Republican Guard's Medinah Division and the remnants of the 12th Armored Division. The Americans, amply supported by artillery and helicopter fire, devastate their opponents and destroy over 300 vehicles; one American is killed and a handful of vehicles are damaged.

The 24th Infantry Division (Mechanized) dashes into Iraqi territory near Basrah, capturing Jalibah Air Base and destroying several MiG-29 fighters in their reinforced hangars. They then dash down Highway 8, sweeping aside remnants of the al-Faw, Nebuchadnezzar, and Hammurabi Divisions.

FEBRUARY 28 In Washington, D.C., President George H. W. Bush declares a unilateral cease-fire after 100 hours of combat. OPERATION DESERT STORM is a striking success, and its toll is astonishingly light: 98 Americans dead (21 through friendly fire) and 352 wounded. A further 126 were killed in non-combat related accidents.

MARCH 2 In Iraq, the Hammurabi Division fires upon the 24th Infantry Division as it retreats. The Americans return fire, bagging an additional 185 Iraqi armored vehicles, 400 trucks, and 34 pieces of artillery.

MARCH 3 At Safwan, Iraq, General H. Norman Schwarzkopf and Saudi Lieutenant General Khalid ibn Sultan meet with Iraqi counterparts to hammer out cease-fire terms and the repatriation of all captives. The U.S. Central Command (CENTCOM) estimates that Coalition Forces have accounted for 3,300 Iraqi tanks, 2,100 armored vehicles, and 2,200 artillery pieces. No less than 80,000 Iraqi prisoners are in custody and their death toll is estimated at 100,000.

MARCH 4–12 At Khamisiyah, Iraq, engineers from the 82nd Airborne Division destroy a huge Iraqi bunker/weapons cache, unaware that chemical and nerve agents are present. Many soldiers are exposed to low-level doses, which leads to what becomes known as Gulf War Syndrome, a malady ultimately affecting 100,000 personnel.

MARCH 31 In Western Europe, the 1987 IMF Treaty between the United States and the Soviet Union means that all remaining Pershing II Missiles deployed there are removed and sent home for destruction.

APRIL 6–JULY 24 In northern Iraq, OPERATION PROVIDE COMFORT unfolds to assist thousands of Kurdish refugees. Elements of the 3rd Infantry Division (Mechanized) arrive from Turkey and distribute 17,000 tons of relief supplies.

APRIL 23 In Washington, D.C., Congress votes to award Generals Colin Powell and H. Norman Schwarzkopf special gold medals. Success in Kuwait has completely cured the United States of the so-called "Vietnam Syndrome."

APRIL 24 In Washington, D.C., President George H. W. Bush posthumously awards a Congressional Medal of Honor to Corporal Freddie Stowers, 371st Infantry, who died leading a squad in France on September 28, 1918. He remains the first African American of either world war so recognized.

JUNE 13 In Kuwait, the 11th Armored Cavalry Regiment arrives and assumes responsibility for the continuing defense of that nation.

1992

MAY 1–10 In Los Angeles, California, parts of the 7th Infantry Division (Light) and the National Guard 40th Infantry (Mechanized) deploy to restore order, following the acquittal of police charged with the beating of Rodney King.

AUGUST–OCTOBER In South Florida, troops from the 82nd Airborne and 10th Mountain Divisions assist National Guard troops in disaster relief operations, following destructive Hurricane Andrew.

AUGUST 18 In Washington, D.C., President George H. W. Bush orders U.S. forces into Somalia to thwart a humanitarian crisis there.

DECEMBER 3 The 10th Mountain Division (Light) prepares to deploy to Somalia, to participate in OPERATION RESTORE HOPE and assist that war-ravaged nation.

1993

JANUARY 15 In Baledogle, Somalia, Company E, 2nd Battalion, 87th Infantry (10th Mountain Division) engage in a firefight with heavily armed militiamen, or "technicals." The Somalis lose six members.

FEBRUARY 24–26 In Kismaayo, Somalia, the 2nd Battalion, 87th Infantry (10th Mountain Division), trades fire with local militias; 23 Somalis are slain.

MAY 4 In Somalia, Army forces under Major General Thomas M. Montgomery deploy and enact OPERATION CONTINUE HOPE, to provide humanitarian relief. The Americans enforce their peacekeeping mission with a Quick Reaction Force of 60 helicopters and 1,000 aviation personnel.

AUGUST 8 In Medina, Somalia, a peacekeeping Army humvee strikes a mine; four soldiers are killed.

AUGUST 28 In Washington, D.C., President William J. Clinton orders Army troops in Somalia to capture senior Somali militia leader Mohamed Farah Aidid. Task Force Ranger, consisting of Rangers, Delta Force, Navy SEALS, and Air Force Special Operations personnel is created for that purpose. However, Clinton refuses to provide them with tanks for fear of alienating the population.

OCTOBER 3–4 In downtown Mogadishu, Somalia, Task Force Ranger arrives by MH-6 Little Bird and MH-60 Blackhawk helicopters, and captures one of Mohamed Farah Aidid's lieutenants downtown. However, two Blackhawks are downed by rocket-propelled grenades. Delta Force snipers Master Sergeant Gary Gordon and Sergeant First Class Randall Shugart arrive at the second crash site and resist Somali militia until they are killed, winning posthumous Congressional Medals of Honor. Additional troops, backed by Pakistani tanks, subsequently rescue the 100 rangers and Deltas trapped in the city. American losses are 19 dead and 100 wounded; Somali casualties are estimated in the range of 1,000.

OCTOBER 6 At Mogadishu Airport, Somalia, a mortar round kills Special Forces Sergeant Matt Rierson; he is the last American soldier to die in Somalia.

1994

MARCH 8   In Washington, D.C., the Army announces Force XXI, an ambitious project incorporating the latest digital technology into current weapons systems. It intends to modernize the Army for the challenges of the 21st Century.

MARCH 12   In Somalia, the 2nd Battalion, 22nd Infantry (10th Mountain Division), withdraws, ending the failed, two-year mission to restore stability to a war-torn nation. A total of 27 American soldiers die in action, 4 are killed in accidents, and over 100 are wounded.

AUGUST 31–SEPTEMBER 6   In Berlin, Germany, American, British, French, and Russian forces are withdrawn from their respective sectors in the city. The Army's Berlin Brigade is disbanded, after seeing active service since 1945.

SEPTEMBER 19   OPERATION UPHOLD DEMOCRACY unfolds in Haiti to restore a constitutionally elected government under President Jean-Bertrand Aristide. The XVIII Airborne Corps, 10th Mountain Division (Light), 3rd Special Force Group, and 25th Infantry Division all contribute units.

OCTOBER 10   President Bill Clinton, responding to Iraqi movements toward the Kuwaiti border, initiates OPERATION VIGILANT WARRIOR, and deploys 36,000 American troops to the Persian Gulf, backed by warships and hundreds of aircraft. Elements of the 24th Infantry Division (Mechanized) are also activated there as a precaution.

1995

DECEMBER 14   The 1st Armored Division deploys in Bosnia-Herzegovina as an international peacekeeping force under the aegis of Task Force Eagle. A total of 60,000 NATO troops, of which 20,000 are American, replace UN peacekeepers in this volatile region.

DECEMBER 21   At Fort Bliss, Texas, the 7th Air Defense Artillery receives the new patriot PAC-3 missiles, with enhanced capabilities against ballistic missiles.

DECEMBER 31   In Bosnia-Herzegovina, engineers from the 1st Armored Division construct the world's longest pontoon bridge—620 meters—across the rain-swollen Sava River.

1996

FEBRUARY 3   Near Gradacac, Bosnia-Herzegovina, Sergeant First Class Donald A. Dugan, 1st Cavalry (1st Armored Division), is killed by a land mine.

AUGUST 22   In Utah, the Army begins destroying its stockpile of chemical weapons, a process that is slated to take seven years.

NOVEMBER 13   At Fort Stewart, Georgia, the 24th Infantry Division (Mechanized) is deactivated. The Army now stands at 10 divisions, its smallest size since before the Korean War.

1997

APRIL 2 In Washington, D.C., Major General Claudia J. Kennedy is promoted to lieutenant general. She is the first female three-star general in Army history, and functions as Deputy Chief of Staff for Intelligence.

OCTOBER 1 At Fort Hood, Texas, the 4th Infantry Division (Mechanized) is the first unit to begin conversion to new, digital electronics.

1998

JANUARY 12 In the Persian Gulf, 27,000 American and British troops are arrive for possible action against Iraq, following Saddam Hussein's refusal to admit a UN weapons inspection team.

NOVEMBER 11 In Kuwait, OPERATION DESERT THUNDER unfolds with the 1st Brigade, 3rd Infantry Division, arriving at the Iraq border to counter threatening moves by Saddam Hussein.

1999

MARCH 24–JUNE 10 In former Yugoslavia, the commander of OPERATION ALLIED FORCE is General Wesley K. Clark, U.S. Army. This is also the first wartime action in NATO history.

MARCH 31 On the Macedonian-Serbian frontier, three American soldiers are captured by Serbian forces; they are abused and held in custody until May 2.

APRIL 21 At Tirana, Albania, Task Force Hawk deploys as part of OPERATION ALLIED FORCE. This consists of 5,100 heavily armed soldiers and equipment, but, despite a dangerous military environment, they never fire a shot in anger.

JUNE 11 In Kosovo, OPERATION JOINT GUARDIAN unfolds, as the 82nd Airborne Division and elements of the 1st Infantry Division (Mechanized) occupy select positions in that war-torn region.

JUNE 21 In Washington, D.C., General Eric K. Shinseki gains appointment as the Army's Chief of Staff; he is also the first Japanese-American holding that position.

AUGUST 13 In Panama, U.S. Army South headquarters transfers to Fort Buchanan, Puerto Rico, once sovereignty of the canal zone is transferred. Nearly a century of Army occupation duties in this strategic region concludes.

OCTOBER 12 In Washington, D.C., General Eric K. Shinseki unveils a radical reorganization scheme to transform the Army into a lighter, faster, and more flexible strategic ground force, using a new generation of wheeled vehicles.

2000

JANUARY 21 In Washington, D.C., President William J. Clinton awards Congressional Medal of Honors to 21 Asian American soldiers of the 442nd Regimental Combat Team, who were denied such honors in World War II on account of race.

OCTOBER 16 In Washington, D.C., Army Chief of Staff General Eric R. Shinseki allows all ranks to wear black berets to raise unit esprit de corps. Rangers, who already wear black berets, switch over to tan to preserve their unique identity, while Green Berets continue with green and Airborne forces wear maroon.

2001

JANUARY 16 In Washington, D.C., former president Theodore Roosevelt receives Congressional Medal of Honor for heroism in the Battle of San Juan Heights, 1898. The medal is accepted on his behalf by his great-grandson.

SEPTEMBER 11 Two hijacked airliners, commanded by Muslim terrorists, crash into New York's World Trade Center, killing 3,000 people. Another airliner crashes into the Pentagon Building in Washington, D.C., killing 125 military and civilian personnel, including Lieutenant General Timothy J. Maude, Deputy Chief of Staff for personnel, the highest-ranking fatality since World War II. A fourth plane crashes into a field in rural Pennsylvania after passengers attempt to wrest control from their abductors.

SEPTEMBER 14 In Washington, D.C., President George W. Bush calls up 50,000 reservists for active duty in the war on terror, and most are deployed in domestic security settings. He also insists that the Taliban regime of Afghanistan surrender fugitive Saudi terrorist Osama bin Ladin—or face war.

OCTOBER 7 OPERATION ENDURING FREEDOM commences once Special Forces teams arrive in northern Afghanistan to coordinate anti-Taliban efforts with the Northern Alliance. Advanced echelons of the 10th Mountain Division (Light) also deploy in Uzbekistan to guard an airfield; this constitutes the first American unit to serve on territory of the former Soviet Union.

OCTOBER 20 Southwest of Kandahar, Afghanistan, the 75th Ranger Regiment deploys at a deserted Taliban-held airfield and searches adjoining buildings for possible military intelligence.

NOVEMBER 5–18 In Afghanistan, the Northern Alliance, buttressed by Special Forces and Coalition air power, begins an offensive that quickly overruns half the country.

NOVEMBER 13 In Afghanistan, the Northern Alliance rolls into the capital, Kabul, while Taliban forces are in full retreat. Saudi fugitive Osama bin Laden disappears from view.

NOVEMBER 14–DECEMBER 2 In southern Afghanistan, Pashtun tribes drive Taliban forces from their spiritual capital at Kandahar. Both columns receive Coalition air support directed by Special Forces.

NOVEMBER 25–28 During a prison uprising in Mazar-e-sharif, Afghanistan, Air Force bombs accidentally wound five Special Forces soldiers, who are immediately evacuated to medical facilities at Landstuhl, Germany.

NOVEMBER 28 At Mazar-e-sharif, Afghanistan, advanced elements of the 10th Mountain Division are the first regular Army units deployed in theater.

DECEMBER 16 In Afghanistan, the Pashtun-based Eastern Alliance clear al-Qaeda pockets from their Tora Bora stronghold, killing 200 and capturing 11. American and British Special Forces subsequently comb the caves, but no trace of Osama bin Laden is found.

DECEMBER 22 In Kabul, Afghanistan, General Tommy Franks arrives to attend ceremonies marking the inauguration of a new interim government under Hamid Karzai. He assumes power only 78 days following the commencement of OPERATION ENDURING FREEDOM.

2002

JANUARY 10 In the Philippines, an advanced team of soldiers arrives to assist the Philippine military combat the violent Abu Sayyaf, a Muslim group with ties to al-Qaeda. A total of 600 Americans gradually deploy there.

JANUARY 29 At Kandahar Airport, Afghanistan, the 3rd Brigade, 101st Airborne Division, replaces Marines forces. As Task Force Rakkaan, it consists of the 187th Infantry Regiment's three battalions.

FEBRUARY 21 At Basilan Island, Philippines, an MH-47E Chinook transport helicopter of the 160th Special Operations Aviation regiment crashes, killing eight soldiers.

FEBRUARY 27 At Fort Lauderdale, Florida, the Army's new assault vehicle, the Stryker, is revealed. Fast and heavily armed, these form the core of new Stryker Brigade Combat Teams (SBCTs); a total of five SBCTs are planned.

MARCH 2–10 In the Shah-i-Kot Valley, Afghanistan, 1,200 Army troops and special forces conduct OPERATION ANACONDA, forcing Taliban remnants from their mountain strongholds. Units present include the 10th Mountain Division, the 101st Airborne Division, and the 75th Ranger Regiment. They account for 500 enemy dead at a cost of 8 killed and 40 wounded.

MAY 8 In Washington, D.C., Secretary of Defense Donald H. Rumsfeld cancels the Army's new Crusader artillery system This is a self-propelled 155-mm gun with its own resupply vehicle, but it is subject to cost overruns.

MAY 31 In Bagram, Afghanistan, Lieutenant General Dan K. McNeill assumes command of Combined Joint Task Force 180 and is tasked with coordinating coalition forces throughout the country.

AUGUST 18–26 In southeastern Afghanistan, OPERATION MOUNTAIN SWEEP is conducted by men of the 82nd Airborne Division and the 75th Rangers; Taliban weapon caches are captured, but the fighters evade contact.

U.S. Army soldiers assigned to the 82nd Airborne Division prepare to enter and clear a house in the Paktika province of Afghanistan, during OPERATION MOUNTAIN SWEEP, *August 21, 2002. (Department of Defense)*

SEPTEMBER 7–11 In the Bermel Valley, Afghanistan, the 504th Parachute Infantry (82nd Airborne Division) seizes suspected Taliban agents, weapons, and many documents.

SEPTEMBER 29 In southeastern Afghanistan, OPERATION ALAMO SWEEP, the 82nd Airborne Division, the 75th Rangers, and other units are airlifted to the Afghanistan-Pakistan border to root out all Taliban forces lurking there.

DECEMBER 18 In the Persian Gulf, the United States begins deploying 50,000 additional troops in anticipation of a possible attack against Iraqi dictator Saddam Hussein.

2003

JANUARY 16 In Colombia, South America, men from the 7th Special Forces Group arrive to help train Colombian troops in anti-terrorists tactics. They reinforce 10 Green Berets already present.

JANUARY 28 In Spin Boldak, Afghanistan, Special Forces and 82nd Airborne Divisions soldiers clear out caves in the Adi Gahr Mountains; 18 al-Qaeda terrorists die without loss.

FEBRUARY 19–MARCH 3 In the Baghran Valley, Afghanistan, the 504th parachute Infantry, 82nd Airborne Division, searches for Taliban and al-Qaeda weapon caches. None are encountered.

MARCH 1 In Ankara, Turkey, parliament denies the 4th Infantry Division access to its soil for the purpose of invading Iraq. The unit is then rerouted to Kuwait by 30 ships.

MARCH 15 In Saudi Arabia, the Army deploys 57,500 men of the 3rd Infantry and 101st Airborne Divisions, while the 4th Infantry Division (Mechanized) is en route by water. The 3rd U.S. Army in theater is commanded by Lieutenant General David D. McKiernan.

MARCH 19 In the Persian Gulf, OPERATION IRAQI FREEDOM begins as coalition forces invade Iraq; Special Forces are already in theater gathering military intelligence. President George W. Bush declares that his goal is the removal of Saddam Hussein from power, the destruction of Iraqi weapons of mass destruction (WMDs), and the elimination of terrorist elements within that country.

MARCH 20 In Iraq, the 3rd Infantry Division begins the ground offensive by

Petraeus, David H. (1951–)

David Howell Petraeus was born in Cornwall-on-Hudson, New York, and he graduated from the U.S. Military Academy in 1974. His first assignment was with the 509th Airborne Battalion Combat Team in Vicenza, Italy, and he became closely identified with light infantry. Petraeus attended the Command and General Staff College in 1983, graduating top in his class, and also received a doctorate in International Relations from Princeton University in 1987. In 2003 Petraeus next commanded the 101st Airborne Division during OPERATION IRAQI FREEDOM, overcame stiff enemy resistance, and occupied the city of Mosul. He was successful at counterinsurgency warfare and civic relations to isolate insurgents from the greater population. In February 2004, Petraeus accompanied his men back to the States, and the following June he was promoted to lieutenant general commanding the Multi-National Security Transition Command Iraq. Petraeus was now tasked with rebuilding that nation's shattered military and security apparatus. His methodical techniques made considerable progress to that end, but at too slow a rate for many in Congress, who wanted to withdraw from Iraq and abandon the inhabitants to their fate. On January 27, 2007, Petraeus became a full general, replaced General George C. Casey as head of the Multi-National Force-Iraq, and employed an additional 20,000 soldiers sent to Iraq as a military "surge." The results were spec-

Lieutenant General David H. Petraeus was nominated by George W. Bush to head the U.S. armed forces in Iraq. In the fall of 2008 he gained appointment as commander of the U.S. Central Command, tasked with orchestrating the war against terrorism in both Iraq and Afghanistan. (U.S. Army)

tacular, and terrorist violence declined nearly 80 percent from the previous year. On September 16, 2008, Petraeus handed over his responsibilities to General Raymond T. Odierno and accepted command of the U.S. Central Command, headquartered in Tampa, Florida. He is presently tasked with directing military operations in 20 nations stretching from Egypt to Pakistan, as well as the ongoing OPERATIONS ENDURING FREEDOM in Afghanistan and IRAQI FREEDOM in Iraq.

crossing over from Kuwait. Resistance is light and easily dispatched by AH-62 Apache gunships, while the 15th Infantry (3rd Division) neutralizes enemy armored vehicles.

MARCH 20–MARCH 27 In southern Afghanistan, the 504th Parachute Infantry (82nd Airborne Division) conducts OPERATION VALIANT STRIKE in the Sami Ghar Mountains. Several weapons caches are seized.

MARCH 21 In southern Iraq, the 101st Airborne Division under Major General David H. Petraeus crosses the border, while the 3rd Infantry Division comes under attack at An Nasiriyah. Their counterfire destroys the Iraqi 11th Infantry Division, and the Jalibah Airfield quickly falls.

MARCH 22 In Kuwait, General Tommy R. Franks, Commander, Central Command (CENTCOM), declares that OPERATION IRAQI FREEDOM is a campaign of "overwhelming force."

MARCH 23 Near An Nasiriyah, Iraq, an 18-vehicle convoy from the 507th Maintenance Battalion is ambushed; 11 soldiers are killed and 6 are captured.

MARCH 24 Near Najaf, Iraq, the 1st Brigade, 3rd Infantry Division repels waves of Iraqi Fedayeen, or suicide attackers. The soldiers expend so much ammunition that they employ captured enemy weapons to keep fighting.

MARCH 26 Najaf, Iraq, is surrounded by two brigades of the 3rd Infantry Division; American losses are two M1A1 Abrams tanks and one M2 Bradley disabled, with one crewman killed. Meanwhile, the 173rd Airborne Brigade drops 1,000 infantry over Bashur Airfield, Iraq, that unit's first combat jump

since Vietnam. Another 150 men of the 10th Special Force Group (Airborne) also direct air strikes against nearby targets.

MARCH 27 In Iraq, the 3rd Infantry Division resumes its advance upon Karbala, while Fedayeen fighters engage in severe fighting near Najaf.

In Afghanistan, the 505th Parachute Infantry (82nd Airborne Division) commences OPERATION DESERT LION in the Kohe Safi Mountains near Bagram Air Base. Resistance is minimal, and a large cache of 107-mm rockets is uncovered.

MARCH 28 Around Karbala, Iraq, AH-64 Apache Longbow helicopters of the 101st Airborne Division engage tanks of the Republican Guard Medina Division; several are damaged by intense antiaircraft fire.

MARCH 29 Outside Najaf, Iraq, the 3rd Infantry Division battles the Republican Guard Medina Division while being harassed by Fedayeen fighters. These fire at them from schools, hospitals, and mosques, and also employ women and children as human shields.

MARCH 30–31 The American advance on Baghdad, Iraq, continues as the 3rd Infantry Division seizes a bridge at Al Handiyah, 50 miles from the capital. Meanwhile, the 101st Airborne Division captures the airfield at An Najaf, while the 82nd Airborne Division, tasked with keeping American lines of supply open, destroys several Iraqi artillery batteries.

APRIL Throughout the United States, OPERATION NOBLE EAGLE commences as 1.4 million National Guard and Army Reserve forces deploy at various sensitive areas and border regions to thwart possible terrorist attacks.

APRIL 1   At Nasiriya, Iraq, Special Forces free Private First Class Jessica Lynch, who had been wounded and captured when the 507th Maintenance Company was ambushed.

APRIL 3   The 1st Brigade, 3rd Infantry Division, rumbles through the Karaba Gap, seizes the Yasin al Khudayr bridge over the Euphrates River, and occupies Saddam International Airport.

APRIL 4   Near Baghdad, Iraq, the 3rd Infantry Division destroys members of the Special Republican Guards as they make a stand at Saddam International Airport. In a 12-hour battle, the Americans lose one dead and eight wounded, while enemy losses are estimated at 250. Sergeant First Class Paul R. Smith, 11th Engineer Battalion, is killed while manning a .50-caliber machine gun and becomes the only soldier from OPERATION IRAQI FREEDOM recommended for a Congressional Medal of Honor.

APRIL 5   In Baghdad, Iraq, the 3rd Infantry Division dispatched two battalions on a quick raid into downtown Baghdad. Meanwhile, U.S. Central Command (CENTCOM) announces that 6,500 Iraqis are in captivity.

APRIL 6   On a plain between Ibril and Makhmur, northern Iraq, 31 men from the Special Forces, reinforced by Kurdish guerrillas, repel Iraqi infantry and armor with Javelin missiles.

APRIL 7   The 3rd Infantry Division advances into the heart of central Baghdad and crushes the remaining Republican Guards. 4 Americans die and 30 are wounded, while an estimated 600 Iraqis are killed. The Republican Palace, the seat of Saddam Hussein's regime, is captured and occupied.

APRIL 8   The 3rd Division consolidates its grip on Baghdad, Iraq, and occupies the west bank of the Tigris River. Two journalists die when an M1A1 Abrams tank, informed that Iraqis are sniping from the Palestine Hotel, fires on their room.

APRIL 9   In Baghdad, Iraq, Marines advance to link up with elements of the 3rd Division, while jubilant Iraqis tear down a massive statute of Saddam Hussein. This iconic image is broadcast around the world.

APRIL 10   Organized Iraqi resistance collapses as Special Forces and Kurdish fighters occupy the northern city of Kirkuk. The 82nd and 101st Airborne Divisions continue with mopping up operations around Samawah and Karbala.

APRIL 11   In Baghdad and Kirkuk, Iraq, soldiers and Marines actively patrol to discourage widespread looting. Near Mosul, Special Force teams arrange a truce between themselves and the Iraqi V Corps. An active hunt for weapon caches turns up several tons of ballistic missiles and heavy weapons.

APRIL 12   An epidemic of looting in Baghdad, Kirkuk, and Mosul, Iraq, despite the presence of American forces. General Amir Saadi also becomes the highest-ranking Iraqi captured, while the 3rd Infantry Division continues skirmishing with militia groups.

APRIL 14   In Iraq, U.S. CENTCOM leader General Tommy Franks declares all organized resistance ended and all major towns and cities under Coalition control. Special Forces and 3rd Infantry Division soldiers also capture Mohammed Abas (Abu Abbas) who hijacked the Italian liner *Achille Lauro* and murdered an American citizen. Meanwhile the 4th Infantry Division, under Major General Raymond T. Odierno, finally reaches Iraq from assembly areas in Kuwait and forms the core of Task Force Iron Horse.

APRIL 16   In Baghdad, Iraq, General Tommy Franks, the senior American ground commander, enters the city for the first time.

APRIL 19   In southern Iraq, the 4th Division encounters pocket of resistance from Iraqi paramilitaries between Taji and Samarra; they destroy eight armed trucks and seize 30 prisoners.

MAY 14   In Baghdad, Iraq, redeployment of the 3rd Infantry Division halts amid continuing unrest and violence. Security of the city is entrusted to Major General Ricardo S. Sanchez's 1st Armored Division, but the 3rd Infantry will assist them in that task.

MAY 15   In northern Iraq, the 4th Infantry Division executes OPERATION PLANET X against a village south of Tikrit. They seize 260 suspected Baath Party members along with fugitive general Mahdi Adil Abdallah.

JUNE 1   Along the Shatt al Arab waterway separating Iran from Iraq, four soldiers of the 1092nd Engineer Battalion are seized by Iranians. The men are interrogated then released the following day.

JUNE 9–13   In Balad, Iraq, OPERATION PENINSULA STRIKE unfolds as Task Force Iron Horse, including the 4th Infantry Division, the 173rd Airborne Brigade, and the 7th Cavalry (3rd Infantry Division), raid suspected hideouts of Baath Party members. The troops engage a party of armed Iraqis, killing 20 without loss.

JUNE 14   In Baghdad, Iraq, Major General Ricardo S. Sanchez is promoted to lieutenant general in charge of V Corps and succeeds General Tommy Franks as head of the Multi-National Force-Iraq.

JUNE 18   North of Baghdad, Iraq, the 4th Infantry Division raids two farmhouses and uncovers $8.5 million in U.S. dollars and $400 million in Iraqi dinars. They also accost 20 of Saddam's personal bodyguards, weapons, and $1 million in stolen jewelry.

JUNE 29–JULY 7   North of Baghdad, Iraq, OPERATION SIDEWINDER is undertaken by the 4th Division, to apprehend the Iraqi terrorists. A total of 282 prisoners are secured, along with weapons and ammunition.

JULY 7   In Baghdad, Iraq, General John P. Abizaid, former deputy head of Combined Forces Command, replaces General Tommy Franks as U.S. CENTCOM commander.

JULY 12–17   In northern Iraq, OPERATION SODA MOUNTAIN is launched by the 4th Division, the 101st Infantry Division, and the 3rd Armored Cavalry against local insurgents. A total of 141 raids are conducted, 600 prisoners are seized (including 62 former regime leaders), along with weapons and ammunition.

JULY 16   In Baghdad, Iraq, General John P. Abizaid declares that the Americans are engaged in a guerrilla war with supporters of the previous regime and that foreign Muslims are arriving to fight for the al-Qaeda terror network.

JULY 22   In Mosul, northern Iraq, the 101st Airborne Division tracks down and kills Saddam Hussein's two brutal sons, Uday and Qusay, following an anonymous tip from the local populace.

AUGUST 18   At Fort Benning, Georgia, Specialist Liana Bombardier is the first woman to win the National Long-Range Rifle Championship in the century-long history of the competition. She consequently walks off with the prestigious Billy C. Atkins Trophy.

AUGUST 26 In Khalis, Iraq, the 2nd Brigade, 4th Infantry Division commences OPERATION IVY NEEDLE to corral a gang of criminals who have attacked Coalition forces and Iraqi police; 24 members of the gang are apprehended.

SEPTEMBER 12 At Fort Stewart, Georgia, the 3rd Infantry Division receives a Presidential Unit Citation to for its lengthy service in the Iraq.

OCTOBER 1 The Army reacts to the new National Call to Service Act passed by Congress in 2002 with a pilot program allowing recruits to sign on for only 15 months of active duty.

OCTOBER 31 In Iraq, a protracted Sunni-based insurgency rages, resulting in 120 Americans killed and 1,100 wounded as of this date. The weapons of choice in this struggle are roadside bombs, or improvised explosive devices (IEDs), detonated as military convoys pass by.

NOVEMBER 2 Over Fallujah, Iraq, an insurgent missile brings down an Army CH-47 Chinook helicopter, killing 16 soldiers and injuring 26.

NOVEMBER 12 In Kuwait, the 3rd Brigade, 2nd Infantry Division, is the first Stryker brigade deployed abroad. Many of the wheeled Strykers feature slatted armor

to protect them against rocket-propelled grenades fired by Iraqi insurgents.

NOVEMBER 15 Over Mosul, Iraq, a pair of UH-60 Black Hawk helicopters collide, killing 17 soldiers and injuring five.

NOVEMBER 27 In Iraq, President George W. Bush makes a surprise Thanksgiving appearance at Baghdad International Airport and enjoys dinner with the 101st Airborne Division.

DECEMBER 4 At Abu Ghurayb, Iraq, OPERATION BULLDOG MAMMOTH unfolds as the 70th Armor (4th Division), the 325th Airborne Infantry (82nd Airborne Division), and the 70th Military Police Battalion raid apartments of terror suspects; 40 individuals are seized, along with weapons and explosives.

DECEMBER 8 In Ad Duluiyah, Iraq, two soldiers from the 2nd Infantry Division die when their Stryker vehicle rolls down an embankment and into a canal; these are the division's first fatalities.

DECEMBER 13 Southeast of Tikrit, Iraq, the 1st Brigade, 4th Division (Mechanized), commences OPERATION RED DAWN by searching the village of Ad Dawr. They capture fugitive Iraqi president Saddam Hussein hiding away in his "spider hole."

DECEMBER 29 *Time* votes "The American Soldier" as "Person of the Year." The Iraqi insurgency has cost 450 American lives, while 8,000 have been wounded.

2004

JANUARY 2 Near Fallujah, Iraq, ground fire downs an OH-58D Kiowa helicopter of 82nd Aviation Regiment. Captain

Kimberly N. Hampton becomes the first female helicopter pilot killed in OPERATION IRAQI FREEDOM.

JANUARY 8 Over Fallujah, a medivac UH-60 Black Hawk helicopter from the 17th Cavalry is hit by a ground-launched missile; all nine occupants die.

JANUARY 16 In Seoul, the United States and South Korea reach an agreement whereby the American redeploy their troops south of the Demilitarized Zone (DMZ) for the first time since 1953.

JANUARY 28 In Washington, D.C., General Peter J. Shoemaker explains the Army's new organization plan to the House Armed Services Committee. Henceforth, each of the 10 divisional headquarters is retained, but each division now consists of four brigades with their own field artillery, signal, and engineering units.

FEBRUARY 1 In Wuerzburg, Germany, the 1st Infantry Division departs for a tour in Iraq. Their heavy equipment remains behind, as they will utilize armored humvees to combat the insurgency. In concert with the 2nd Brigade, the 25th Infantry Division, and the 30th Separate Heavy Brigade, they now constitute Task Force Iron Danger.

FEBRUARY 12 At Fallujah, Iraq, General John P. Abizaid comes under hostile rocket and small arms fire while visiting the 82nd Airborne Division fire; no casualties are incurred.

FEBRUARY 14 At Fort Campbell, Kentucky, the 101st Airborne Division rotates home after a lengthy tour of duty in Iraq, during which it sustained 58 fatalities.

FEBRUARY 16 At Fort Benning, Georgia, the prototype XM-8 rifle undergoes field testing at the Infantry Center. The Army seeks a replacement for its aging M-16 rifle, in service since the Vietnam War.

FEBRUARY 23 In Washington, D.C., Army Chief of Staff General Peter J. Shoemaker cancels the Army's RAH-66 Comanche helicopter program after 20 years and several billion dollars in development.

MARCH 6 Near the Afghan-Pakistani border, nine Taliban fighters are killed after they attack a Special Forces outpost.

MARCH 26–APRIL 10 At the National Training Center, Fort Urwin, California, the 3rd Infantry Division becomes the first unit to be reorganized under the new tactical structure. It deploys in Iraq that fall.

MARCH 28 In Ghazni, Afghanistan, the 10th Mountain Division uncovers a cache of Taliban grenades, mines, and mortar rounds. A detachment from the 6th Field Artillery also seizes 2,000 rifles and stores of ammunition at a house in Kandahar.

MARCH 31 In Baghdad, Iraq, the 1st Cavalry Division arrives to replace the 1st Armored Division. Meanwhile, the 1st Infantry Division and the National Guard 81st Armored Brigade join the 1st Marine Expeditionary Force and sweep insurgent strongholds at Fallujah and Ramadi.

APRIL 2 The Army announces that recruitment goals have been met for the previous year, despite the ongoing conflicts in Iraq and Afghanistan.

APRIL 4 In Baghdad, Iraq, the 1st Cavalry Division engages insurgents in the downtown area; seven Americans die and 51 are injured. Enemy losses are unknown.

APRIL 9 In Iraq, two soldiers from the 724th Transportation Company are captured by insurgents; both are subsequently murdered in captivity. In Baghdad,

Specialist Michelle Witmer, 32nd Military Police Company, is killed by an improvised explosive device, becoming the first female National Guard (Wisconsin) soldier killed in Army history.

APRIL 15 In Iraq, an upsurge in violence results in extended tours for 20,000 soldiers previously scheduled to be rotated home; their tours are extended by 90 days.

APRIL 16 Near Kharbut, Iraq, two CH-47 Chinook helicopters crash in a sandstorm, but the crews are rescued by MH-53Js despite near-zero visibility. The

rescue crews win the Mackay Trophy for outstanding flight of the year.

APRIL 22 At Fort Hood, Texas, the 4th Infantry Division (Mechanized) returns from a tour in Iraq; 79 soldiers died in combat operations.

NOVEMBER 7–18 At Fallujah, Iraq, 15,000 Army troops surround a Sunni insurgent stronghold and attack, systematically killing 1,600 terrorists at a cost of 38 dead and 275 wounded. This action breaks the back of terrorist networks in the region.

2005

JANUARY 12 In Iraq, United States forces conclude their search for weapons of mass destruction (WMDs), one of the main reasons for the American invasion there; none are uncovered.

APRIL 28 In Fort Bragg, North Carolina, Sergeant Hasan Akbar is sentenced to death by a court-martial for the murder of two fellow soldiers at Camp Pennsylvania, Kuwait, in March 2003.

JUNE 28 In Afghanistan, an Army helicopter attempting to rescue a party of Navy SEALS in Afghanistan is shot down and crashes, killing 19 service members.

OCTOBER 1–7 Near Sadah, Iraq, on the Syrian border, 1,000 Army troops commence OPERATION IRON FIST to root out terrorists operating nearby, killing 50.

2006

MARCH 16 Near Samarra, Iraq, Army troops attack Iraqi insurgents, utilizing the largest air strike since the beginning of the war.

JULY 31 In Kabul, Afghanistan, the United States formally transfers military control to NATO, which assumes responsibility for fighting Taliban extremists and drug lords.

SEPTEMBER 3 In Iraq, Army troops apprehend Hamid Juma Faris, a senior

al-Qaeda operative, best known for orchestrating a deadly bombing of the Shi'ite Askariya Shrine.

OCTOBER 3 In Iraq, eight American soldiers die from numerous roadside bombs.

NOVEMBER 17 In Washington, D.C., General John Abizaid, U.S. Central Command (CENTCOM) testifies before the Senate Armed Service Committee. He pushes for an increase of troop strength in

Iraq and against a fixed timetable for an American withdrawal.

NOVEMBER 25 North of Baghdad, Iraq, American troops and Iraqi security forces kill 22 insurgents.

DECEMBER 31 The death toll of U.S. forces in Iraq reaches 3,000; the estimated toll of Iraqi civilians killed by numerous insurgent groups ranges from 30,000 to a high of 650,000. (The higher totals are viewed to have come from special interest groups that oppose the occupation.)

2007

JANUARY 20 Over northern Baghdad, Iraq, a UH-60 Black Hawk helicopter crashes; all 13 passengers are killed.

JANUARY 23 In Washington, D.C., President George W. Bush reiterates his plan to deploy 20,000 additional troops to Iraq to combat the insurgency. He is confident that the "surge" will bring ongoing violence there to a halt.

JANUARY 28 Near Najaf, Iraq, Army troops and Iraqi security forces battle Sunni insurgents bent on attacking and killing Shia religious pilgrims celebrating the festival of Ashura; around 250 terrorists are slain.

FEBRUARY 10 In Iraq, Lieutenant General David H. Petraeus replaces Lieutenant General George W. Casey, Jr., as head of Coalition occupation forces.

MARCH 2 In Washington, D.C., Secretary of Defense Robert M. Gates relieves Army Secretary Francis J. Harvey over allegations of poor conditions at Walter Reed Army Medical Center. General Kevin Kiley is also dismissed as Army Surgeon General.

MARCH 16 In Tampa, Florida, Admiral William J. Fallon replaces General John P. Abizaid as head of the U.S. Central Command (CENTCOM).

APRIL 11 In Washington, D.C., Secretary of Defense Robert M. Gates announces that military tours in Iraq and Afghanistan are extended 3 months, for a total of 15 months.

MAY 13 In Helmand Province, Afghanistan, Army, NATO, and Afghan security forces kill Mullah Dadullah, one of the highest-ranking Taliban leaders to die in combat.

MAY 15 In Washington, D.C., President George W. Bush nominates Lieutenant General Douglas Lute to become "war czar," tasked with coordinating the wars in Iraq and Afghanistan.

JUNE 15 In Washington, D.C., the Department of Defense announces that the 28,500-man "surge" to Iraq is complete, with American troop strength at 160,000 men and women.

SEPTEMBER 11 In Washington, D.C., Lieutenant General David H. Petraeus testifies before Congress that the military "surge" has greatly reduced violence levels in Iraq.

NOVEMBER 6 The recent loss of six Americans makes 2007 the deadliest year of fighting in Iraq; the total number of dead is 852.

NOVEMBER 24 In Diyala Province, Iraq, a brigade of 5,000 American soldiers returns home, reducing overall troop strength at 157,000.

DECEMBER 10 In Hilmand Province, Afghanistan, Army, NATO, and Afghan forces capture the Taliban stronghold of Musa Qala, one of the main poppy-growing regions and a major income source for terrorists.

DECEMBER 29 In Iraq, Lieutenant General David H. Petraeus reports that terrorist attacks are down by 60 percent since the start of the military "surge" in June 2007. Petraeus still considers al-Qaeda the greatest threat to Iraqi stability and reconciliation.

DECEMBER 31 The Associated Press reports that 100 American soldiers have died in Afghanistan this year, the highest number since OPERATION ENDURING FREEDOM began in October 2001. An estimated 4,500 militants and 925 Afghan police have also been killed.

2008

JANUARY 8 In Diyala Province, Iraq, Army and Iraqi security forces conduct OPERATION IRON HARVEST to eliminate final pockets of al-Qaeda operatives.

MARCH 23 In Baghdad, Iraq, a roadside bomb kills four Army soldiers; the total number of war-related fatalities is now 4,000.

APRIL 6 In the Shok Valley, Afghanistan, Captain Kyle Walton and his team from the 3rd Battalion, 3rd Special Force Group, engages 200 dug-in Taliban; 10 Silver Stars are awarded to Walton and his men.

APRIL 8–9 In Washington, D.C., General David H. Petraeus testifies before Congress that violence continues to decline in Iraq, but success remains fragile. He recommends that once troop strength drops to 140,000 men, future withdrawals should be suspended for 45 days.

JUNE 10 In Afghanistan, U.S. forces engage in a fight with Taliban militants just astride the Pakistani border. An air strike follows, which the Pakistani government claims kills 11 of its paramilitary soldiers.

JULY 13 In southeast Afghanistan, a remote Army outpost is attacked by an estimated 200 Taliban fighters; nine Americans die in the fighting.

AUGUST 22 In northern Iraq, an Army UH–60 Black Hawk helicopter crashes and kills all 14 soldiers on board; mechanical failure is blamed.

SEPTEMBER 1 Control of Anbar Province, Iraq, is turned over to the Iraqi military by the U.S. Army. The so-called "Sunni awakening" induces many tribes and former insurgents to take up arms against al-Qaeda foreign terrorists.

SEPTEMBER 16 In Iraq, General Raymond T. Odierno succeeds Lieutenant General David H. Petraeus as head of the Multi-National Force-Iraq.

OCTOBER 5 In Mosul, Iraq, American troops act on a tip from the locals and kill Abu Qaswarah, a Moroccan who was the number-two al-Qaeda leader; four other militants die with him.

OCTOBER 31 In Tampa, Florida, Lieutenant General David H. Petraeus receives his fourth star and assumes control of the U.S. Central Command

(CENTCOM). He will direct military actions in Iraq, Afghanistan, and the Middle East from this locale.

NOVEMBER 14 In Washington, D.C., Major General Ann E. Dunwoody receives her fourth star and becomes the first American woman promoted to full general.

DECEMBER 20 The Associated Press reports that, since OPERATION IRAQI FREEDOM began in March 2003, 4,209 members of the U.S. military have died in combat.

Bibliography

Adams, George R. *General William S. Harney: Prince of Dragoons*. Lincoln: University of Nebraska Press, 2006.

Adams, Kevin. *Class and Race in the Frontier Army: Military Life in the West, 1870–1890*. Norman: University of Oklahoma Press, 2009.

Adams, Thomas K. *The Army After Next: The First Postindustrial Army*. Stanford, Calif.: Stanford Security Studies, 2008.

Agnew, Jeremy. *Life of a Soldier on the Western Frontier*. Missoula, Mont.: Mountain Press Pub. Co., 2008.

Alexander, Larry. *Shadows in the Jungle: The Alamo Scouts Behind Japanese Lines in World War II*. New York: NAL Caliber, 2009.

Anderson, Charles R. *Days of Lightning, Years of Scorn: Walter C. Short and the Attack on Pearl Harbor*. Annapolis, Md.: Naval Institute Press, 2005.

Anderson, Christopher J. *The War in Korea: The U.S. Army in Korea, 1950–1953*. Mechanicsburg, Pa.: Stackpole Books, 2001.

Arnold, James R. *Jeff Davis's Own: Cavalry, Comanches, and the Battle for the Texas Frontier*. Edison, N.J.: Castle Books, 2007.

———. *Jungle of Snakes: A Century of Counterinsurgency Warfare from the Philippines to Iraq*. New York: Bloomsbury Press, 2009.

Axelrod, Alan. *Patton: A Biography*. New York: Palgrave Macmillan, 2006.

———. *Bradley*. New York: Palgrave Macmillan, 2008.

Bacevich, Andrew J., and Efraim Inbar, eds. *The Gulf War of 1991 Reconsidered*. Portland, Ore.: Frank Cass, 2003.

Bahmanyar, Mir. *Shadow Warriors: A History of the U.S. Army Rangers*. Westminster, Md.: Osprey Direct, 2006.

Baker, Horace L. *Argonne Days in World War I*. Columbia: University of Missouri Press, 2007.

Barnett, Louise K. *Touched by Fire: The Life, Death, and Mythic Afterlife of George Armstrong Custer*. Lincoln: University of Nebraska Press, 2006.

Barry, John W. *The Midwest Goes to War: The 32nd Division in the Great War*. Lanham, Md.: Scarecrow Press, 2007.

Bates, Thomas M. *The Prairie Wars, 1840–1890*. Bloomington, Ind.: AuthorHouse, 2006.

Black, Robert W. *Ghost, Thunderbolt, and Wizard: Mosby, Morgan, and Forrest in the Civil War*. Mechanicsburg, Pa.: Stackpole Books, 2008.

Blake, Michael. *Indian Yell: The Heart of an American Insurgency*. Flagstaff, Ariz.: Northland Pub., 2006.

Blumenson, Martin, and Kevin Hymel. *Patton: Legendary Commander*. Washington, D.C.: Potomac Books, 2008.

Bonekemper, Edward H. *Grant and Lee: Victorious and Vanquished Virginia*. Westport, Conn.: Praeger Publishers, 2008.

Bonk, David, and Peter Denis. *Chateau-Thierry & Belleau Wood, 1918: America's Baptism of Fire on the Marne*. New York: Oxford Pub., 2007.

Boose, Donald W. *Over the Beach: U.S. Army Amphibious Operations in the Korean War*. Fort Leavenworth, Kan.: Combat Studies Institute Press, 2008.

Borden, Arthur M. *A Better Country: Why America Was Right to Confront Iraq*. Lanham, Md.: Hamilton Books, 2008.

Borneman, Walter R. *1812: The War that Forged a Nation*. New York: HarperCollins Publishers, 2004.

Bourque, Stephen A. *Jayhawk! The VII Corps in the Persian Gulf War*. Washington, D.C.: Department of the Army, 2002.

Brands, H.W. *Andrew Jackson, His Life and Times*. New York: Doubleday, 2005.

Braun, Robert A. *Bloody Lake: The Battle of Pecatonica, June 16, 1832, A Battle of the Black Hawk War*. Janesville, Wis.: Phalanx Press, 2005.

Broadwater, Robert P. *American Generals of the Revolutionary War: A Biographical Dictionary*. Jefferson, N.C.: McFarland, 2007.

———. *Civil War Medal of Honor Recipients: A Complete Illustrated Record*. Jefferson, N.C.: McFarland, 2007.

Buhite, Russell D. *Douglas MacArthur: Statecraft and Stagecraft in America's East Asian Policy*. Lanham, Md.: Rowman and Littlefield, 2008.

Bussey, Charles M. *Firefight at Yechon: Courage and Racism in the Korean War*. Lincoln: University of Nebraska Press, 2002.

Byerly, Carol R. *Fever of War: The Influenza Epidemic in the U. S. Army during World War I*. New York: New York University Press, 2005.

Cameron, Robert S. *Mobility, Shock, and Firepower: The Emergence of the U.S. Army's Armor Branch, 1917–1945*. Washington, D.C.: Center of Military History, United States Army, 2008.

Campbell, James. *The Ghost Mountain Boys: Their Epic March and the Terrifying Battle for New Guinea*. New York: Crown Publishers, 2007.

Carafano, James. *GI Ingenuity: Improvisation, Technology, and Winning World War II*. Westport, Conn.: Praeger Security International, 2006.

Carbone, Gerald M. *Nathanael Greene: A Biography of the American Revolution*. New York: Palgrave Macmillan, 2008.

Carlisle, Rodney P. *Persian Gulf War*. New York: Facts on File, 2003.

Carney, John T., and Benjamin F. Schemmer. *No Room for Error: The Covert Operations of America's Special Tactics Units from Iran to Afghanistan*. New York: Ballantine Books, 2002.

Carney, Stephen A. *Gateway South: The Campaign for Monterrey*. Washington, D.C.: U.S. Army Center of Military History, 2005.

———. *Guns Along the Rio Grande: Palo Alto and Resaca de la Palma*. Washington, D.C.: U.S. Army Center of Military History, 2005.

———. *The Occupation of Mexico, May 1846–July 1848*. Washington, D.C.: U.S. Army Center of Military History, 2006.

Carroll, John M., and Colin F. Baxter. *The American Military Tradition: From Colonial Times to the Present*. Lanham, Md.: Rowman & Littlefield, 2007.

Cate, Alan C. *Founding Fighters: The Battlefield Leaders Who Made American Independence*. Westport, Conn.: Praeger Security International, 2006.

Chadwick, Bruce. *The First American Army: The Untold Story of George Washington and the Men Behind America's First Fight for Freedom*. Naperville, Ill.: Sourcebooks, 2007.

Chambers, Larry. *Recondo: LRRPs in the 101st*. New York: Random House Pub., 2004.

Chartrand, Rene, and William Youngblood. *Santa Anna's Army, 1821–48*. Oxford, U.K.: Osprey, 2004.

Clary, David A. *Adopted Son: Washington, Lafayette, and the Friendship that Saved the Revolution*. New York: Bantam Books, 2007.

Clodfelter, Micheal. *The Lost Battalion and the Meuse-Argonne, 1918: America's Deadliest Battle*. Jefferson, N.C.: McFarland, 2007.

Coats, Stephen D. *Gathering at the Golden Gate: Mobilizing for War in the Philippines, 1898*. Fort Leavenworth, Kan.: Combat Studies Institute Press, 2006.

Coffman, Edward M. *The Regulars: The American Army, 1898–1941*. Cambridge, Mass.: Belknap Press, 2007.

Colley, David. *Decision at Strasbourg: Ike's Strategic Mistake to Halt the Sixth Army Group at the Rhine in 1944*. Annapolis, Md.: Naval Institute Press, 2008.

Cosmas, Graham A. *MACV: The Joint Command in the Years of Escalation, 1962–1967*. Washington, D.C.: Center of Military History, U.S. Army, 2006.

———. *MACV: The Joint Command in the Years of Withdrawal, 1968–1973*. Washington, D.C.: Center of Military History, U.S. Army, 2007.

Cozzens, Peter. *The Army and the Indian*. Mechanicsburg, Pa.: Stackpole Book, 2005.

Cunningham, John T. *The Uncertain Revolution: Washington and the Continental Army at Morristown*. West Creek, N.J.: Down the Shore Pub., 2007.

Cusick, James G. *The Other War of 1812: The Patriot War and the American Invasion of Spanish East Florida*. Athens: University of Georgia Press, 2007.

Dalessandro, Robert J., and Michael G. Knapp. *Organization and Insignia of the American*

Expeditionary Force, 1917–1923. Atglen, Pa.: Schiffer Pub., 2008.

Danby, Jeff. *Day of the Panzer: A Story of American Heroism and Sacrifice in Southern France.* Havertown, Pa.: Casemate, 2007.

Davis, Don. *Stonewall Jackson.* New York: Palgrave Macmillan, 2007.

Davis, Robert T. *The Change of Adaptation: The U.S. Army in the Aftermath of Conflict, 1953–2000.* Fort Leavenworth, Kan.: Combat Studies Institute Press, 2008.

Davison, Eddy W. *Nathan Bedford Forrest: In Search of the Enigma.* Gretna, La.: Pelican Pub. Co., 2007.

DeFelice, James. *Rangers at Dieppe: The First Combat Action of U.S. Army Rangers in World War II.* New York: Berkeley Caliber, 2008.

Delay, Brian E. *War of a Thousands Deserts: Indian Raids and the U.S.-Mexican War.* New Haven, Conn.: Yale University Press, 2008.

De Quesada, A. M. *The Spanish-American War and Philippine Insurrection, 1898–1902.* New York: Osprey Pub., 2007.

Donlish, Gerald A. *General Winfield Scott: The Development and Application of Political/Civil-Military Concepts during the Mexican War.* Carlisle Barracks, Pa.: U.S. Army War College, 2002.

Donovan, Jim. *A Terrible Glory: Custer and Little Bighorn—The Last Great Battle of the American West.* New York: Little, Brown, 2008.

Doran, Robert E. *Horsemanship at Little Big Horn: A Study of U.S. Army Tactics.* West Conshohocken, Pa.: Infinity Pub., 2007.

Dougherty, Kevin. *Civil War Leadership and Mexican War Experience.* Jackson: University Press of Mississippi, 2007.

Dugard, Martin. *The Training Ground: Grant, Lee, Sherman, and Davis in the Mexican War, 1846–1848.* New York: Little, Brown, 2008.

Dunstan, Simon. *1st Air Cavalry in Vietnam: The "First Team."* Havertown, Pa.: Casemate Pub., 2004.

Durant, Michael J. *The Night Stalkers: Top Secret Missions of the U.S. Army's Special Operations Aviation Regiment.* New York: G.P. Putnam's Sons, 2007.

Durham, Roger S. *Guardian of Savannah: Fort McAllister, Georgia, in the Civil War and Beyond.* Columbia, S.C.: University of South Carolina, 2008.

Edgerton, Robert B. *"Remember the Maine—To Hell with Spain": America's 1898 Adventure in Imperialism.* Lewiston, N.Y.: Edwin Mellen Press, 2005.

Edwards, Paul M. *The Korean War.* Westport, Conn.: Greenwood Press, 2006.

———. *The Hill Wars of the Korean Conflict: A Dictionary of Hills, Outposts, and Other Sites of Military Action.* Jefferson, N.C.: McFarland, 2006.

———. *Korean War Almanac.* New York: Facts on File, 2006.

Eisenhower, John S. D. *Zachary Taylor.* New York: Times Books, 2008.

Evans, Anthony A. *Gulf War: Desert Shield and Desert Storm, 1990–1991.* London: Greenhill Books, 2003.

Ferling, John E. *Almost a Miracle: The American Victory in the War of Independence.* New York: Oxford University Press, 2007.

Ferrell, Robert H. *Five Days in October: The Lost Battalion of World War I.* Columbia: University of Missouri Press, 2005.

———. *America's Deadliest Battle: Meuse-Argonne, 1918.* Lawrence: University Press of Kansas, 2007.

———. *The Question of MacArthur's Reputation: Cote de Chatillon, October 14–16, 1918.* Columbia: University of Missouri Press, 2008.

Fleming, Thomas J. *The Perils of Peace: America's Struggle for Survival after Yorktown.* New York: Smithsonian Books/Collins, 2007.

Field, Ron. *Buffalo Soldiers, 1892–1918.* Oxford, U.K.: Osprey, 2005.

———. *U.S. Infantry in the Indian Wars, 1865–1891.* New York: Osprey Pub., 2007.

Frank, Richard B. *MacArthur.* New York: Palgrave Macmillan, 2007.

Fredriksen, John C. *The United States Army in the War of 1812: Concise Biographies of Commanders, Operational Histories of Regiments, with Bibliographies of Published and Primary Sources.* Jefferson, N.C.: McFarland and Co., 2009.

Gaff, Alan D. *Blood in the Argonne: The "Lost Battalion" of World War I.* Norman: University of Oklahoma Press, 2005.

Gaines, James R. *For Liberty and Glory: Washington, Lafayette, and Their Revolutions.* New York: W.W. Norton, 2007.

Gillon, Steven M. *Ten Days that Unexpectedly Changed America: Shays' Rebellion—America's First Civil War.* New York: Three Rivers Press, 2006.

Glasrud, Bruce A. *Buffalo Soldiers in the West: A Black Soldier's Anthology*. College Station: Texas A&M University Press, 2007.

Glatthaar, Joseph T. *General Lee's Army: From Victory to Collapse*. New York: Free Press, 2008.

Graham, Kent, ed. *Battle: The Nature and Consequences of Civil War Combat*. Tuscaloosa: University of Alabama Press, 2008.

Grant, Rebecca. *The First 600 Days of Combat*. Washington, D.C.: IRIS Press, 2004.

Greene, Jerome A. *Washita: The U.S. Army and the Southern Cheyennes, 1867–1869*. Norman: University of Oklahoma Press, 2004.

———. *Yellowstone Command: Colonel Nelson A. Miles and the Great Sioux War, 1876–1877*. Norman: University of Oklahoma Press, 2006.

———. *Indian War Veterans: Memories of Army Life and Campaigns in the West, 1864–1898*. New York: Savas Beatie, 2007.

Greene, A. Wilson. *Civil War Petersburg: Confederate City in the Crucible of War*. Charlottesville: University of Virginia Press, 2006.

Grenier, John. S. *The First Way of War: American War Making on the Frontier, 1607–1814*. New York: Cambridge University Press, 2005.

Griswold, Terry. *Delta: America's Elite Counterterrorist Force*. St. Paul, Minn.: Zenith Press, 2005.

Groom, Winston. *Patriotic Freedom: Andrew Jackson and Jean Laffite at the Battle of New Orleans*. New York: Alfred A. Knopf, 2006.

Grotelueschen, Mark E. *The AEF Way of War: The American Army and Combat in World War I*. New York: Cambridge University Press, 2007.

Hacker, Barton C. *American Military Technology: The Life Story of a Technology*. Westport, Conn.: Greenwood Press, 2006.

Haines, Aubrey L. *Battle of Big Hole: The Story of the Landmark Battle of the 1877 Nez Perce War*. Guilford, Conn.: TwoDot, 2007.

Hamilton, Richard F. *President McKinley, War, and Empire*. New Brunswick, N.J.: Transaction Publishers, 2006.

Haney, Eric L. *Inside Delta Force: The Story of America's Elite Counterterrorist Unit*. New York: Delta Trade Paperbacks, 2005.

Harris, Stephen L. *Duty, Honor, Privilege: New York's Silk Stocking Regiment and the Breaking of the Hindenburg Line*. Dulles, Va.: Potomac Books, 2006.

———. *Harlem's Hell Fighters: The African American 369th Infantry in World War I*. Dulles, Va.: Brassey's, 2005.

Hatch, Alden. *General George Patton: Old Blood and Guts*. New York: Sterling, 2006.

Hatch, Thom. *Black Kettle: The Cheyenne Chief Who Sought Peace but Found War*. Hoboken, N.J.: John Wiley & Sons, 2004.

Hawkins, Walter L. *Black Military Leaders: A Biographical Dictionary*. Jefferson, N.C.: McFarland, 2007.

Heidler, David S., and Jeanne T. Heidler. *Old Hickory's War: Andrew Jackson and the Quest for Empire*. Baton Rouge: Louisiana State University Press, 2003.

———. *The Mexican War*. Westport, Conn.: Greenwood Press, 2006.

Hendrickson, Kenneth E. *The Spanish-American War*. Westport, Conn.: Greenwood Press, 2003.

Hickey, Donald R. *Don't Give Up the Ship! Myths of the War of 1812*. Urbana: University of Illinois Press, 2006.

Hicks, Anne. *The Last Fighting General: The Biography of Robert Tryon Frederick*. Atglen, Pa.: Schiffer, 2006.

Hoff, Thomas A. *U.S. Doughboy, 1916–19*. Oxford, U.K.: Osprey, 2005.

Hogan, David W. *The Story of the Noncommissioned Officer Corps: The Backbone of the Army*. Washington, D.C.: Center of Military History, United States Army, 2007.

Hogeland, William. *The Whiskey Rebellion: George Washington, Alexander Hamilton, and the Frontier Rebels Who Challenged America's Newfound Sovereignty*. New York: Scribner, 2006.

Holzimmer, Kevin C. *General Walter Krueger: Unsung Hero of the Pacific War*. Lawrence: University Press of Kansas, 2007.

Hunt, Geoffrey. *Colorado's Volunteer Infantry in the Philippine Wars, 1898–1899*. Albuquerque: University of New Mexico Press, 2006.

Hurst, James W. *Pancho Villa and Black Jack Pershing: The Punitive Expedition in Mexico*. Westport, Conn.: Praeger Publishers, 2007.

Ives, Christopher K. *U.S. Special Forces and Counterinsurgency in Vietnam: Military Innovation and Institutional Failure, 1961–63*. New York: Routledge, 2007.

Jeffers, H. Paul. *Onward We Charge: The Heroic Story of Darby's Ranger's in World War II*. New York: NAL Caliber, 2007.

———. *Command of Honor: General Lucien Truscott's Path to Victory in World War II*. New York: NAL Caliber, 2008.

Jefferson, Robert F. *Fighting for Hope: African American Troops of the 93rd Infantry Division in World War II and Postwar America*. Baltimore: Johns Hopkins University Press, 2008.

Johnson, Timothy D. *A Gallant Little Army: The Mexico City Campaign*. Lawrence: University Press of Kansas, 2007.

Jones, Seth G. *Counterinsurgency in Afghanistan*. Santa Monica, Calif.: RAND National Defense Research Institute, 2008.

Jones, Timothy A. *Military Proconsuls: The Army in its Role in Military Governance*. Carlisle Barracks, Pa.: U.S. Army War College, 2007.

Jung, Patrick J. *The Black Hawk War of 1832*. Norman: University of Oklahoma Press, 2007.

Kaminski, John P. *Lafayette: Boy General*. Madison, Wis.: Parallel Press, 2007.

Klokner, James B. *The Officer Corps of Custer's Seventh Cavalry, 1866–1876*. Atglen, Pa.: Schiffer Pub., 2007.

Knights, Michael. *Cradle of Conflict: Iraq and the Birth of Modern U.S. Military Power*. Annapolis, Md.: Naval Institute Press, 2005.

Kolb, Richard K., ed. *Battles of the Korean War: American Engage in Deadly Combat, 1950–1953*. Kansas City, Mo.: Veterans of Foreign Wars of the United States, 2003.

Korda, Michael. *Ike: An American Hero*. New York: HarperCollins, 2007.

Krass, Peter. *Portrait of War: The U. S. Army's First Combat Artists and the Doughboy's Experience in World War I*. Hoboken, N.J.: J. Wiley, 2007.

La Bree, Clifton. *New Hampshire's General John Stark: Live Free or Die; Death Is Not the Worst of Evils*. Portsmouth, N.H.: Peter E,. Randall, 2007.

Lacey, Jim. *Pershing*. New York: Palgrave Macmillan, 2008.

Lagguth, A. J. *Union 1812: The Americans Who Fought the Second War of Independence*. New York: Simon and Schuster, 2006.

Lanning, Michael L. *American Revolution 100: The Battles, People, and Events of the American War for Independence*. Naperville, Ill.: Sourcebooks, 2008.

Latimer, Jon. *1812: War with America*. Cambridge, Mass.: Belknap Press of Harvard University Press, 2007.

Laver, Harry S., and Jeffrey J. Matthews. *The Art of Command: Military Leadership from George Washington to Colin Powell*. Lexington: University Press of Kentucky, 2008.

Leepson, Marc. *Desperate Engagement: How a Little-known Civil War Battle Saved Washington, D.C., and Changed American History*. New York: Thomas Dunne Books, 2008.

Lefkowitz, Arthur S. *Benedict Arnold's Army: The 1775 American Invasion during the Revolutionary War*. New York: Savas Beatie, 2008.

Lengel, Edward G. *General George Washington: A Military Life*. New York: Random House, 2007.

———, ed. *The Glorious Struggle: George Washington's Revolutionary War Letters*. New York: Smithsonian Books/Collins, 2007.

———. *To Conquer Hell: The Meuse-Argonne, 1918*. New York: Henry Holt, 2008.

Lewis, Adrian R. *The American Culture of War: The History of U. S. Military Force from World War II to Operation Iraqi Freedom*. New York: Routledge, 2006.

Lind, Michael. *The American Way of Strategy*. New York: Oxford University Press, 2006.

Linn, Brian M. *Echo of Battle: The Army's Way of War*. Cambridge, Mass.: Harvard University Press, 2007.

Lockhart, Paul D. *The Drillmaster of Valley Forge: The Baron de Steuben and the Making of the American Army*. New York: Smithsonian Books, 2008.

Lyman, Robert. *The Generals: From Defeat to Victory, Leadership in Asia, 1941–1945*. London: Constable, 2008.

Lytle, Richard M. *The Soldiers of America's First Army, 1791*. Lanham, Md.: Scarecrow Press, 2004.

———. *The Old Guard in 1898: A Short History of the Third United States Infantry Regiment*. Lanham, Md.: Scarecrow Press, 2007.

Mahnken, Thomas G. *Technology and the American Way of War since 1945*. New York: Columbia University Press, 2008.

Malcomson, Robert. *Capital in Flames: The American Attack on York, 1813*. Montreal: Robin Brass Studio, 2008.

Mansoor, Peter R. *Baghdad at Sunrise: A Brigade Commander's War in Iraq*. New Haven, Conn.: Yale University Press, 2008.

Marshall, Joseph. *The Day the World Ended at Little Bighorn*. New York: Viking, 2006.

Marvel, William. *Lincoln's Darkest Year: The War in 1862*. Boston: Houghton Mifflin, 2008.

Matthews, Matt. *The U.S. Army on the Mexican Border: A Historical Perspective*. Fort Leavenworth, Kan.: Combat Studies Institute Press, 2007.

McCallum, Jack E. *Leonard Wood: Rough Rider, Surgeon, Architect of American Imperialism.* New York: New York University Press, 2006.

McChristian, Douglas C. *Uniforms, Arms, and Equipment: The U.S. Army on the Western Frontier, 1880–1892.* Norman: University of Oklahoma Press, 2007.

———. *Fort Laramie: Military Bastion of the High Plains.* Norman, Ok.: Arthur H. Clark Co., 2009.

McKenney, Janice E. *The Organizational History of Field Artillery, 1775–2003.* Washington, D.C.: Center of Military History, United States Army, 2007.

McKinney, Mike. *Chariots of the Damned: Helicopter Special Operations from Vietnam to Kosovo.* New York: Thomas Dunne/St. Martin's Press, 2002.

McManus, John C. *Alamo in the Ardennes: The Untold Story of the American Soldiers Who Made the Defense of Bastogne Possible.* Hoboken, N.J.: Wiley, 2007.

Miller, Edward G. *Nothing Less than Full Victory: Americans at War in Europe, 1944–1945.* Annapolis, Md.: Naval Institute Press, 2007.

Miller, Susan A. *Coacoochee's Bones: A Seminole Saga.* Lawrence: University Press of Kansas, 2003.

Missall, John. *The Seminole Wars: America's Longest Indian Conflict.* Gainesville: University Press of Florida, 2004.

Mockaitis, Thomas R. *Iraq and the Challenge of Counterinsurgency.* Westport, Conn.: Praeger Security International, 2008.

Moore, Robin. *Hunting Down Saddam: The Inside Story of the Search and Capture.* New York: St. Martin's Press, 2004.

Murphy, Edward F. *Dak To: America's Sky Soldiers in South Vietnam's Central Highlands.* New York: Ballantine Books, 2007.

Nagy, John A. *Rebellion in the Ranks: Mutinies of the American Revolution.* Yardley, Pa.: Westholme Publishing, 2007.

Neimeyer, Charles P. *The Revolutionary War.* Westport, Conn.: Greenwood Press, 2007.

Nester, William R. *The Arikara War: The First Plains Indian War.* Missoula, Mont.: Mountain Press, 2001.

Nolan, Keith W. *House to House: Playing the Enemy's Game in Saigon, May 1968.* St. Paul, Minn.: Zenith Press, 2006.

Nunnally, Michael L. *American Indian Wars: A Chronology of Confrontation between Native Peoples and Settlers and the United States Military, 1500s–1901.* Jefferson, N.C.: McFarland, 2007.

Odom, William O. *After the Trenches: The Transformation of the U.S. Army, 1918–1939.* College Station: Texas A&M University Press, 2008.

O'Sullivan, Christopher D. *Colin Powell, American Power, and Intervention from Vietnam to Iraq.* Lanham, Md.: Rowan & Littlefield, 2009.

Patterson, Benton R. *The Generals: Andrew Jackson, Sir Edward Pakenham, and the Road to the Battle of New Orleans.* New York: New York University Press, 2005.

Pegler, Martin. *Sniper: A History of the U.S. Marksmen.* Oxford, U.K.: Osprey, 2009.

Perry, Mark. *Partners in Command: George Marshall and Dwight Eisenhower in War and Peace.* New York: Penguin Group USA, 2008.

Petrie, Stewart J. *Bloody Path to the Shenandoah: Fighting with the Union VI Corps in the American Civil War.* Shippensburg, Pa.: Burd Street Press, 2004.

Phelps, M. William. *Nathan Hale: The Life and Death of America's First Spy.* New York: Thomas Dunne Books, 2008.

Phillips, R. Cody. *Operation Joint Guardian: The U.S. Army in Kosovo.* Washington, D.C.: Center of Military History, U.S. Army, 2007.

Piecuch, Jim, and John M. Beakes. *Cool Deliberate Courage: John Eager Howard in the American Revolution.* Charleston, S.C.: Nautical and Aviation Pub Co. of America, 2008.

Pinheiro, John C. *Manifest Ambition: James K. Polk and Civil-Military Relations during the Mexican War.* Westport, Conn.: Praeger Security International, 2007.

Prados, John. *Vietnam: The History of an Unwinnable War, 1945–1975.* Lawrence: University Press of Kansas, 2009.

Puls, Mark. *Henry Knox: Visionary General of the American Revolution.* New York: Palgrave Macmillan, 2008.

Pushies, Fred J. *82nd Airborne.* Minneapolis, Minn.: MBI Pub. Co., 2008.

Rafuse, Ethan S. *Robert E. Lee and the Fall of the Confederacy, 1863–1865.* Lanham, Md.: Rowman and Littlefield, 2008.

Randolph, Stephen P. *Powerful and Brutal Weapons: Nixon, Kissinger, and the Eastern Offensive.* Cambridge, Mass.: Harvard University Press, 2007.

Rearman, Mark J., and Jeffrey Charlton. *From Transformation to Combat: The First Stryker*

Brigade at War. Washington, D.C., Center of Military History, U.S. Army, 2007.

Reid, Brian H., and Joseph G. Dawson. *The Vistas of American Military History, 1800–1898.* London: Routledge, 2007.

———. *America's Civil War: The Operational Battlefield.* Amherst, N.Y.: Prometheus Books, 2008.

Remini, Robert V. *Andrew Jackson.* New York: Palgrave Macmillan, 2008.

Reno, Linda D. *The Maryland 400 in the Battle of Long Island.* Jefferson, N.C.: McFarland, 2008.

Richards, Leonard L. *Shays' Rebellion: The American Revolution's Final Battle.* Philadelphia: University of Pennsylvania Press, 2002.

Ricks, Thomas E. *The Gamble: General David Petraeus and the American Military Adventure in Iraq, 2006–2008.* New York: Penguin Press, 2009.

Robins, James S. *Last in Their Class: Custer, Pickett, and the Goats of West Point.* New York: Encounter Books, 2006.

Rooney, David. *Stilwell the Patriot: Vinegar Joe, the Brits, and Chiang Kai-shek.* Mechanicsburg, Pa.: Stackpole Books, 2005.

Rose, Alexander. *Washington's Spies: The Story of America's First Spy Ring.* New York: Bantam Books, 2007.

Rosenau, William. *Special Operation Forces and Elusive Enemy Ground Targets: Lessons from Vietnam and the Persian Gulf War.* Santa Monica, Calif.: RAND, 2001.

Rowe, Mary E. *Bulwark of the Republic: The American Militia in the Antebellum West.* Westport, Conn.: Praeger, 2003.

Ruggero, Ed. *The First Men In: U.S. Paratroopers and the Fight to Save D-Day.* New York: HarperCollins, 2006.

Ruiz, Fernando S. *MacArthur of the Philippines.* New York: Vantage Press, 2005.

Salecker, Gene E. *Rolling Thunder Against the Rising Sun: The Combat History of U.S. Army Tank Battalions in the Pacific in World War II.* Mechanicsburg, Pa.: Stackpole Books, 2008.

Sapolsky, Harvey M. *U.S. Military Innovation since the Cold War: Creation with Destruction.* New York: Routledge, 2009.

Sarkesian, Sam C. *The U.S. Military Profession in the Twenty-First Century: War, Peace, and Politics.* New York: Routlege, 2006.

Schumacher, Gerald. *To Be a U.S. Army Green Beret.* St. Paul, Minn.: Zenith Press, 2005.

Schwab, Orrin. *The Gulf Wars and the United States: Shaping the Twenty-First Century.* Westport, Conn.: Praeger Security International, 2008.

Schweikart, Larry. *America's Victories: Why the U. S. Wins Wars and Will Win the War on Terror.* New York: Sentinel, 2006.

Sharpe, Mike. *101st Airborne Division in Vietnam: The Screaming Eagles.* Havertown, Pa.: Casemate Pub., 2005.

Shay, Michael E. *The Yankee Division in the First World War: In the Highest Tradition.* College Station: Texas A&M University Press, 2008.

Showalter, Dennis E. *Patton and Rommel: Men of War in the Twentieth Century.* New York: Berkley Caliber, 2005.

Silbey, David. *A War of Frontier and Empire: The Philippine-American War, 1899–1902.* New York: Hill and Wang, 2008.

Simon, Jay W. *Crisis of Command in the Army of the Potomac: Sheridan's Search for an Effective General.* Jefferson, N.C.: McFarland, 2008.

Slotkin, Richard. *Lost Battalions: The Great War and the Crisis of American Nationality.* New York: Henry Holt, 2005.

Smith, David, and Graham Turner. *New York, 1776: The Continentals' First Battle.* Oxford, U.K.: Osprey, 2008.

Smith, Michael. *Killer Elite: The Inside Story of America's Most Secret Special Operations Team.* New York: St. Martin's Press, 2008.

Stanton, Shelby L. *Vietnam Order of Battle.* Mechanicsburg, Pa.: Stackpole Books, 2003.

———. *U.S. Army Uniforms of the Cold War: 1948–1973.* Mechanicsburg, Pa.: Stackpole Books, 1994.

Stephenson, Michael. *Patriot Battles: How the War of Independence Was Fought.* New York: HarperCollins, 2007.

Sterner, C. Douglas. *Go for Broke: The Nisei Warriors of World War II Who Conquered Germany, Japan, and American Bigotry.* Clearfield, Utah: American Legacy Historical Press, 2008.

Stoffey, Robert E. *Fighting to Leave: The Final Years of America's War in Vietnam, 1972–1973.* Minneapolis, Minn.: MBI Pub., 2008.

Stone, David J. *Wars of the Cold War: Campaigns and Conflicts, 1945–1990.* Havertown, Pa.: Casemate, 2004.

Swisher, James K. *The American Revolution in the Southern Backcountry.* Gretna, La.: Pelican Pub. Co., 2008.

Tate, Michael L. *The American Army in Transition, 1865–1898*. Westport, Conn.: Greenwood Press, 2007.

Taylor, Adam. *The Divided Ground: Indians, Settlers, and the Northern Borderland of the American Revolution*. New York: Vintage Books, 2007.

Taylor, Lonn. *The Star-Spangled Banner: The Making of an American Icon*. New York: Smithsonian Books, 2008.

Thomason, John W., and George B. Clark. *The United States Second Division Northwest of Chateau Thierry in World War I*. Jefferson, N.C.: McFarland, 2006.

Tomes, U. S. *Defense Strategy from Vietnam to Operation Iraqi Freedom: Military Innovation and the New American Way of War, 1973–2003*. New York: Routledge, 2006.

Toomey, Charles L. *XVIII Airborne Corps in Desert Storm: From Planning to Victory*. Central Point, Ore.: Hellgate Press, 2004.

Trask, Kerry A. *Black Hawk: The Battle for the Heart of America*. New York: Henry Holt, 2006.

Trauschweitzer, Ingo. *The Cold War U.S. Army: Building Deterrence for Limited War*. Lawrence: University Press of Kansas, 2008.

Troiani, Don, and James Kochan. *Don Troiani's Soldiers of the American Revolution*. Mechanicsburg, Pa.: Stackpole Books, 2007.

Ucko, David H. *The New Counterinsurgency Era: Transforming the U.S. Military for Modern Wars*. Washington, D.C.: Georgetown University Press, 2009.

Utley, Robert M. *The Last Days of the Sioux Nation*. New Haven, Conn.: Yale University Press, 2004.

Vandervort, Bruce. *Indian Wars of Mexico, Canada, and the United States, 1812–1900*. New York: Routledge, 2006.

Venzon, Anne C. *America's War with Spain: A Selected Bibliography*. Lanham, Md.: Scarecrow Press, 2003.

Viola, Herman J. *Trail to Wounded Knee: The Last Stand of the Plains Indians, 1860–1890*. Washington, D.C.: National Geographic, 2004.

Votaw, John F., and Duncan Anderson. *The American Expeditionary Forces in World War I*. Oxford, U.K.: Osprey, 2005.

Ward, Harry M. *George Washington's Enforcers: Policing the Continental Army*. Carbondale: Southern Illinois University Press, 2006.

Waselkov, Gregory A. *A Conquering Spirit: Fort Mims and the Redstick War of 1813–1814*. Tuscaloosa: University of Alabama Press, 2006.

Weinberger, Caspar W. *Home of the Brave: Honoring the Unsung Heroes in the War on Terror*. New York: Forge, 2006.

Weintraub, Stanley. *Iron Tears: America's Battle for Freedom, Britain's Quagmire, 1775–1783*. New York: Free Press, 2005.

———. *15 Stars: Eisenhower, MacArthur, Marshall; Three Generals Who Saved the American Century*. New York: NAL Caliber, 2007.

Welsome, Eileen. *The General and the Jaguar: Pershing's Hunt for Pancho Villa: A True Story of Revolution and Revenge*. Lincoln: University of Nebraska Press, 2007.

Werner, Bret. *Uniforms, Equipment, and Weapons of the American Expeditionary Forces in World War I*. Atglen, Pa.: Schiffer Military History, 2006.

Wert, Jeffry D. *Cavalryman of the Lost Cause: A Biography of J. E. B. Stuart*. New York: Simon and Schuster, 2008.

Wheeler, James S. *The Big Red One: America's Legendary 1st Infantry Division from World War I to Desert Storm*. Lawrence: University Press of Kansas, 2007.

Williams, Glenn F. *Year of the Hangman: George Washington's Campaign against the Iroquois*. Yardley, Pa.: Westholme, 2005.

Wilson, Joe. *The 784th Tank Battalion in World War II: History of an African American Armored Unit in Europe*. Jefferson, N.C.: McFarland, 2007.

Winton, Harold R. *Corps Commanders of the Bulge: Six American Generals and Victory in the Ardennes*. Lawrence: University Press of Kansas, 2007.

Wishnevsky, Stephen T. *Courtney Hicks Hodges: From Private to Four-Star General in the United States Army*. Jefferson, N.C.: McFarland, 2006.

Wood, Edward W. *Worshiping the Myths of World War II: Reflections on America's Dedication to War*. Washington, D.C.: Potomac Books, 2006.

Woodworth, Steven E. *Decision in the Heartland: The Civil War in the West*. Westport, Conn.: Praeger, 2008.

———. *Sherman*. New York: Palgrave Macmillan, 2008.

Worley, D. Robert. *Shaping U.S. Military Forces: Revolution or Relevance in a Post-Cold War*

World. Westport, Conn.: Praeger Security International, 2006.

Wright, Donald P. *The United States Army in Operation Iraqi Freedom, May 2003–January 2005*. Fort Leavenworth, Kan.: Combat Studies Institute, 2008.

Wright, Robert K. *Airborne Forces at War: From Parachute Test Platoon to the 21st Century*. Annapolis, Md.: Naval Institute Press, 2007.

Wright, Stephen L. *The Last Drop: Operation Varsity, March 24–25, 1945*. Mechanicsburg, Pa.: Stackpole Books, 2008.

Wukovits, John F. *Eisenhower*. New York: Palgrave Macmillan, 2006.

Yates, Lawrence A. *The U.S. Military Intervention in Panama: Origins, Planning, and Crisis Management, June 1987–December 1989*. Washington, D.C.: Center of Military History, United States Army, 2008.

Yeide, Harry. *Steeds of Steel: A History of American Mechanized Cavalry in World War II*. St. Paul, Minn.: Zenith Press, 2008.

Yenne, Bill. *Rising Sons: The Japanese American GIs Who Fought for the United States in World War II*. New York: Thomas Dunne Books, 2007.

———. *Indian Wars: The Campaign for the American West*. Yardley, Pa.: Westholme Publishing, 2006.

Zaloga, Steve. *U.S. Airborne Divisions in the ETO, 1944–45*. New York: Osprey Pub., 2007.

———. *Armored Thunderbolt: The Sherman Tank in World War II*. Mechanicsburg, Pa.: Stackpole Books, 2008.

Zimmerman, Dwight J., and John D. Gresham. *Beyond Hell and Back: How America's Special Operations Forces Became the World's Greatest Fighting Unit*. New York: St. Martin's Press, 2007.

Index

Note: Page numbers followed by *f* refer to entries found in photo captions.

About the Author

JOHN C. FREDRIKSEN is an independent historian and the author of 20 reference books on various subjects. He received his doctorate in military history from Providence College.